Lecture Notes in Computer Science 15715

Founding Editors

Gerhard Goos
Juris Hartmanis

AF820947

The series Lecture Notes in Computer Science (LNCS), including its subseries Lecture Notes in Artificial Intelligence (LNAI) and Lecture Notes in Bioinformatics (LNBI), has established itself as a medium for the publication of new developments in computer science and information technology research, teaching, and education.

LNCS enjoys close cooperation with the computer science R & D community, the series counts many renowned academics among its volume editors and paper authors, and collaborates with prestigious societies. Its mission is to serve this international community by providing an invaluable service, mainly focused on the publication of conference and workshop proceedings and postproceedings. LNCS commenced publication in 1973.

Adrián Pastor López-Monroy ·
Alejandro Rosales-Pérez ·
Jesús Ariel Carrasco-Ochoa ·
José Francisco Martínez-Trinidad ·
José Arturo Olvera-López
Editors

Pattern Recognition

17th Mexican Conference, MCPR 2025
Guanajuato, Mexico, June 25–28, 2025
Proceedings

Springer

Editors
Adrián Pastor López-Monroy
Centro de Investigación en Matemáticas (CIMAT)
Guanajuato, Mexico

Alejandro Rosales-Pérez
Centro de Investigación en Matemáticas (CIMAT)
Guanajuato, Mexico

Jesús Ariel Carrasco-Ochoa
Instituto Nacional de Astrofísica, Óptica y Electrónica (INAOE)
Puebla, Mexico

José Francisco Martínez-Trinidad
Instituto Nacional de Astrofísica, Óptica y Electrónica (INAOE)
Puebla, Mexico

José Arturo Olvera-López
Benemérita Universidad Autónoma de Puebla (BUAP)
Puebla, Mexico

ISSN 0302-9743 ISSN 1611-3349 (electronic)
Lecture Notes in Computer Science
ISBN 978-3-031-96254-7 ISBN 978-3-031-96255-4 (eBook)
https://doi.org/10.1007/978-3-031-96255-4

This Springer imprint is published by the registered company Springer Nature Switzerland AG
The registered company address is: Gewerbestrasse 11, 6330 Cham, Switzerland

Preface

The Mexican Conference on Pattern Recognition 2025 (MCPR 2025) was the 17th event in the series, this time organized by the Department of Computer Science of the Mathematics Research Center (CIMAT), and the Department of Computer Science of the Instituto Nacional de Astrofísica, Óptica y Electrónica (INAOE) of Mexico. The conference was hosted by the Mexican Association for Computer Vision, Neurocomputing, and Robotics (MACVNR), a member society of the International Association for Pattern Recognition (IAPR). MCPR 2025 took place in Guanajuato, Guanajuato, Mexico, between June 25–28, 2025.

MCPR aims to provide a forum for the exchange of scientific results, practice, and new knowledge, and to promote collaboration between research groups in pattern recognition and related areas in Mexico and the world.

In this edition, as in previous years, MCPR 2025 attracted Mexican researchers and participation from all over the world. We received 70 manuscripts from authors in 11 countries: Argentina, Brazil, Colombia, Cuba, France, Mexico, Norway, Paraguay, South Africa, Spain, and the USA. Each paper was strictly peer reviewed by at least two members of the Program Committee. All members of the Program Committee are experts in many fields of pattern recognition. As a result of a single-blind peer review, 36 papers were accepted for presentation at the conference and included in these conference proceedings.

We were very honored to have as invited speakers such internationally recognized researchers as

- Steven Bethard, College of Information Science, University of Arizona, USA.
- Mariano Rivera, Department of Computer Science, Mathematics Research Center (CIMAT), Mexico.
- Daniel Pimentel, Wisconsin Institute for Discovery, University of Wis-consin-Madison, USA.

The editors thank everyone who devoted much time and effort to running MCPR 2025 successfully. In particular, we thank all the authors who contributed to the conference. In addition, we give special thanks to the invited speakers who shared their keynote addresses on various pattern recognition topics during the conference. We are also very grateful for the efforts and the quality of the reviews of all members of the Program Committee and additional reviewers. Their work allowed us to maintain the high quality of the contributions to the conference and provided a conference program of a high standard.

Finally, but not less important, we thank the Department of Computer Science of the Mathematics Research Center (CIMAT) for supporting this event.

We are sure that MCPR 2025 provided a fruitful forum for Mexican pattern recognition researchers and the broader international pattern recognition community.

June 2025

Adrián Pastor López-Monroy
Alejandro Rosales-Pérez
Jesús Ariel Carrasco-Ochoa
José Francisco Martínez-Trinidad
José Arturo Olvera-López

Organization

General Conference Co-chairs

Adrián Pastor López-Monroy	CIMAT, Mexico
Alejandro Rosales-Pérez	CIMAT, Mexico
Jesús Ariel Carrasco-Ochoa	INAOE, Mexico
José Francisco Martínez-Trinidad	INAOE, Mexico
José Arturo Olvera-López	BUAP, Mexico

Local Arrangement Committee

Batard, Thomas	CIMAT, Mexico
Becerra, Hector M.	CIMAT, Mexico
Cervantes Cuahuey, Brenda Alicia	INAOE, Mexico
Dalmau, Oscar	CIMAT, Mexico
Hayet, Jean-Bernard	CIMAT, Mexico
Hernández Leandro, Norberto A.	CIMAT, Mexico
Moreno Galván, Diego Aarón	CIMAT, Mexico
Sánchez Vega, Fernando	CIMAT, Mexico
Tavarez Rodríguez, Judith	CIMAT, Mexico
Van Horebeek, Johan	CIMAT, Mexico

Program Committee

Antunes, F	University of Coimbra, Portugal
Araujo, A.	Universidade Federal de Minas Gerais, Brazil
Biasotti, S.	IMATI-CNR, Italy
Borges, D. L.	Universidade de Brasília, Brazil
Bruneau, P.	Luxembourg Institute of Science and Technology, Luxembourg
Cabrera, S.	University of Texas at El Paso, USA
Cimmino, L.	University of Salerno, Italy
Couto, P.	CITAB-UTAD, Portugal
Escalante-Balderas, H. J.	INAOE, Mexico
Fabregas, E.	National University of Distance Education of Spain, Spain

Facon, J.	Pontifícia Universidade Católica do Paraná, Brazil
Figueroa, K.	UMSNH, Mexico
Fumera, G.	University of Cagliari, Italy
Godoy, D.	UNICEN, Argentina
Grau, A.	Universitat Politècnica de Catalunya, Spain
Heutte, L.	Université de Rouen, France
Hurtado-Ramos, J. B.	CICATA-IPN, Mexico
Ibn-Khedher, M.	IRT-SystemX, France
Jiang, X.	University of Münster, Germany
Kampel, M.	Vienna Univerity of Technology, Austria
Kim, S. W.	Myongji University, South Korea
Lazo-Cortés, M. S.	ITTLA, TecNM, Mexico
Levano, M. A.	Universidad Católica de Temuco, Chile
Mandal, B.	Uppsala University, Sweden
Milián-Núñez, V.	Universidad de las Ciencias Informáticas, Cuba
Mitrea, D.	Technical University of Cluj-Napoca, Romania
Moctezuma, M.	UNAM, Mexico
Molina, J. M.	Universidad Carlos III de Madrid, Spain
Montes-Y-Gomez, M.	INAOE, Mexico
Morales, E.	INAOE, Mexico
Moreno-Cañadas, A.	National University of Colombia, Colombia
Nalepa, J.	Silesian University of Technology, Poland
Nida, N.	University of Engineering and Technology Taxila, Pakistan
Oliveira, J. L.	University of Aveiro, Portugal
Palagyi, K.	University of Szeged, Hungary
Pedrini, H.	University of Campinas, Brazil
Perez-Suay, A.	Universitat de València, Spain
Realpe, M.	ESPOL, Ecuador
Roman-Rangel, E.	ITAM, Mexico
Rudrusamy, B.	Heriot-Watt University Malaysia, Malaysia
Salas, J.	IPN, Mexico
Sanchez, J. A.	Universitat Politècnica de València
Sanchez-Cortes, D.	Groupe Mutuel Holding SA, Switzerland
Sansone, C.	Università di Napoli, Italy
Shrestha, R.	Oslo Metropolitan University, Norway
Silva, C.	University of Coimbra, Portugal
Sossa-Azuela, J. H.	CIC-IPN, Mexico
Subbarayappa, S.	M. S. Ramaiah University of Applied Sciences, India
Sánchez-Salmerón, A. J.	Universitat Politècnica de València, Spain
Tuama, A.	Northern Technical University, Iraq

Valle, M. E.	Universidade Estadual de Campinas, Brazil
Wang, Q.	Southeast University, China

Additional Reviewers

Altamirano-Robles, L.	INAOE, Mexico
Carbajal-Hernández, J. J.	CIC-IPN, Mexico
Casavantes, M.	INAOE, Mexico
García-Borroto, M.	Universidad de La Habana, Cuba
García-Hernández, R. A.	UAEM, Mexico
González-Blancas, L.	INAOE, Mexico
Lakouari, N.	INAOE, Mexico
Morales-Reyes, A.	INAOE, Mexico
Pérez-Espinosa, H.	INAOE, Mexico
Pérez-Sansalvador, J.	INAOE, Mexico
Sánchez-Díaz, G.	UASLP, Mexico
Valdovinos, R. M.	UAEM, Mexico
Vergara-Villegas, O. O.	UACJ, Mexico
Villatoro-Tello, E.	IDIAP, Switzerland

Sponsoring Institutions

Department of Computer Science of the Mathematics Research Center (CIMAT)
Instituto Nacional de Astrofísica, Óptica y Electrónica (INAOE)
Mexican Association for Computer Vision, Neurocomputing and Robotics (MACVNR)
Secretaría de Ciencias, Humanidades, Tecnología e Innovación (SECIHTI)

Contents

Computer Vision

Medical Applications of Pattern Recognition

Pattern Recognition and Machine Learning Techniques

Detection of Concept Drift in Bayesian Networks

Miranda Naian Ramírez-Cruz[1(✉)], Luis Enrique Sucar[1], Eduardo F. Morales[1], and Jesús Joel Rivas[2]

[1] Instituto Nacional de Astrofísica, Óptica y Electrónica, San AndrÃl's Cholula, Mexico
mir.ramirezc@gmail.com

[2] Universidad Tecnológica de Tecamachalco, Tecamachalco, Mexico

Abstract. Concept drift, a phenomenon where statistical properties of variables change over time, poses significant challenges to predictive models by reducing their performance in dynamic environments. This work presents a framework for detecting concept drift in Bayesian Networks by leveraging probabilistic inference and dynamic updates of Conditional Probability Tables (CPTs). Drift detection is achieved using sliding windows to monitor deviations in probabilistic inference, while CPT updates are guided by adaptive retraining to realign to the evolving data distribution. The proposed approach is quantitatively evaluated using a symmetric divergence metric, ensuring robust tracking of changes across data segments and adaptability to diverse drift scenarios. It was evaluated on synthetic datasets with induced drift, showing excellent performance in drift detection and parameters' update.

Keywords: Concept drift · Bayesian Networks · Drift detection · Drift adaptation

1 Introduction

Concept drift refers to the phenomenon in predictive modelling where the statistical properties of a target variable change over time [1]. These shifts, which can occur suddenly or gradually, can significantly impact predictive models' performance. Formally, concept drift is observed when the joint probability distribution $P(x)$ evolves over time, such that:

$$P_t(\mathbf{x}) \neq P_{t+1}(\mathbf{x}) \tag{1}$$

where $\mathbf{x}$ represents the set of variables and t denotes time. This evolution stems from changes in the joint probability distribution $P(\mathbf{x})$. As the environment evolves, models trained on specific conditions may gradually lose their accuracy, since they rely on outdated assumptions. This problem often arises in real-world scenarios, such as stock market predictions, medical diagnoses, and environmental monitoring, where underlying patterns evolve due to external factors.

A. P. López-Monroy et al. (Eds.): MCPR 2025, LNCS 15715, pp. 3–12, 2025.
https://doi.org/10.1007/978-3-031-96255-4_1

Drift detection has been studied in various domains, particularly for adapting models to non-stationary environments. Bach and Maloof [2] introduced a Bayesian model comparison approach for virtual concept drift detection, focusing on probabilistic reasoning to identify changes in conditional distribution. Cabañas et al. [3] introduced an approach based on Conditional Linear Gaussian Bayesian Networks with latent variables for handling discrete streaming data, enabling drift detection in mixed discrete and continuous domains. Later, Alsuwat et al. [4] proposed a method using discrete Bayesian networks with latent variables to detect both posterior and uncertainty drifts, demonstrating sensitivity to changes in data distributions over time. Additionally, in a survey presented by Hinder et al. [5], different statistical methods for drift detection in general probabilistic models are explored.

While the existing methods have achieved significant progress, they primarily focus on drift detection without providing mechanisms for further adaptation, and often fall short in working efficiently with subtle changes or limited data volumes. Furthermore, the reliance on specific structures, data distributions and prior knowledge, limits their flexibility and applicability to diverse scenarios.

This work proposes a framework to identify the presence of concept drift in the context of Bayesian Networks (BN) by monitoring probabilistic inference and the mitigation of its effects by updating the network's Conditional Probability Tables (CPTs). Unlike prior methods, limited to specific Bayesian structures or distribution assumptions, our approach applies to general Bayesian models and operates independently of latent variables, simplifying the modelling process and reducing computational overhead, enabling rapid adaptation using few samples.

2 Methodology

2.1 Drift Detection

The proposed approach for drift detection is based on probabilistic inference over temporal windows. A sample is drawn from the dataset, with a subset of its variables randomly selected as observed to infer the states of the remaining non-sampled variables. The inference process combines the observed data and the network's structure to estimate the values of unobserved nodes [6]. The goal is to reconstruct the complete sample by determining the states of the missing variables and compared them with the actual values. The drift detection process is as follows:

1. **Observed and missing data:** The partial sample is represented as a vector $x = [x_1, x_2, ..., x_n]$ where each x_i is either observed or missing. Observed values are directly assigned to their corresponding nodes according to the variable's probability distribution using logic sampling [7].
2. **Topological processing:** Nodes are processed in topological order, ensuring that parents nodes are assigned values before their children.
3. **Probabilistic estimation:** The state of each unobserved node is determined by forward sampling using observed nodes as evidence.

4. **Completion of the sample:** After all nodes are processed, the complete sample is reconstructed as $x' = [x'_1, x'_2, ..., x'_n]$, where all missing values are replaced by their inferred states.
5. **Coincidence computation:** The inferred sample is compared with the original sample taken from the dataset, obtaining a coincidence percentage.
6. **Batch resampling:** This process is repeated for n iterations, each time randomly selecting a new subset of observed nodes; finally, the mean coincidence percentage across all iterations is obtained.
7. **Drift detection:** The inference procedure is conducted using a sliding window, calculating the mean coincidence percentage for the collection of samples within each window. A drift in the underlying data distribution is signalled when the average coincidence percentage across a defined number of consecutive windows drops below a predetermined threshold.
8. **Sliding window aggregation:** To mitigate potential inaccuracies caused by small sample sizes, as long as no new negative drift is detected, data from multiple consecutive windows are aggregated to form a composite subset of windows, providing more reliable estimates. The aggregation of multiple sliding windows ensures that the detection process is not solely reliant on individual windows, benefitting from a broader historical context. This adaptive approach further improves the model's reliability, reducing the risk of overfitting to short-term fluctuations in the data.

2.2 Drift Adaptation

Upon detecting drift, the Bayesian network's CPTs are dynamically updated to better align with the evolving data distribution. This is accomplished by recalibrating the CPTs using the Beta Distribution, as described by Eq. 2 [7]:

$$P(b_i) = \frac{k + a + 1}{n + a + b + 2} \tag{2}$$

where $a/(a + b)$ represents the prior CPTs estimate, k/n denotes the empirical probability derived from the data, where k is the frequency of occurrence of a given event b_i in n samples.

Initially, a higher weight is assigned to the empirical data, which is more reflective of the most recent observations after drift detection. This adaptation mechanism allows the model to prioritize data-derived estimates when the prior knowledge is likely to be outdated due to drift. As more data is processed and incorporated, the prior knowledge is gradually refined, allowing an increase in the confidence (weight) assigned to it. This iterative refinement ensures a balanced integration of historical knowledge and new incoming data, resulting in more accurate and context-sensitive updates over time.

2.3 Performance Evaluation

One of the challenges in evaluating drift adaptation relying solely on inference accuracy arises when the probabilities within the CPTs get closer to a uniform distribution across all possible states of a variable. Under these conditions, inference accuracy decreases because the nodes probabilities lack sufficient differentiation between states. However, this does not necessarily indicate a failure in the learning or adaptation processes. The CPTs may still accurately represent the true uniform distributions and faithfully capture the underlying data structures. The inability to enhance inference accuracy in such scenarios is a natural consequence of the uniform probabilities where the intrinsic uncertainty of high-entropy distributions causes that no state is probabilistically favoured.

To address this phenomenon, the Jensen-Shannon (JS) divergence (Eq. 3), a symmetric and bounded measure that captures the divergence between two probability distributions, is employed to evaluate the similarity between the learned and ground truth CPTs [8]. Unlike inference accuracy, which reflects only prediction reliability, the JS divergence measures how well the learned CPTs represent the true probabilistic structure of the data, even in high-entropy scenarios.

$$JS(P \parallel Q) = \frac{1}{2}(KL(P \parallel M) + KL(Q \parallel M)) \tag{3}$$

where P and Q are the probability distributions being compared, $M = \frac{1}{2}(P + Q)$ represents the midpoint distribution, and KL denotes the Kullback-Leibler divergence.

The JS divergence is bounded between 0 (identical distributions) and 1 (maximum divergence). For interpretability, it is converted into a percentage similarity metric:

$$CPTsimilatity = (1 - JS(P \parallel Q)) \times 100 \tag{4}$$

Inference accuracy assesses the reliability of predictions but may not accurately reflect CPT quality under high-entropy conditions, while CPT similarity measures how well the framework learns to reflect the true data distribution, independently of the accuracy of predictions.

3 Experimental Setting

Composed by subsets (segments) with different CPT values, a synthetic dataset was constructed to control and evaluate drift detection effectively, using:

- **Initial segment** based on the original distribution of the test network.
- **Perturbations** of the existing probabilities for subsequent CPTs, bounded by a change parameter (Δp), ensuring diverse distributions between segments.

3.1 Logic Sampling

Logic sampling, a stochastic simulation algorithm, was implemented to generate samples [7]. Nodes are processed in topological order, ensuring parent nodes are sampled before their children. For each node, a random value $r \sim U(0,1)$ determines its state (we assume binary variables):

$$X_i = \begin{cases} 1 & \text{if } r < P(X_i = 1 \mid Pa(X_i)), \\ 0 & \text{otherwise.} \end{cases} \tag{5}$$

3.2 Drift Induction

By systematically altering CPTs within the network to induce drift, a ground truth is established to evaluate the detection and adaptation mechanisms, assessing the frameworks' ability to respond to changes in the underlying data distribution. To simulate real-world scenarios with evolving distributions:

1. **Segment sampling:** The total dataset is divided into segments, each generated using a different set of CPTs.
2. **Change points:** Change times are selected randomly, ensuring diverse transitions across the dataset.

The following expression describes the probability perturbation for the CPTs of the different segments:

$$P'(X_i = 1|Pa(X_i)) = \min(1, \max(0, P(X_i = 1)) + \Delta p)), \tag{6}$$

where Δp is a random value sampled uniformly: $\Delta p \sim U(-C_p, C_p)$.

The **magnitude of probability perturbation** (C_p) when transitioning between different segments, controls how much CPTs can vary when generating new ones, ensuring the evolution is gradual and constrained, simulating realistic parameter drift. Small C_p values result in fewer variations, making the CPTs for consecutive segments more similar, while large C_p values allow greater variations, simulating abrupt changes. The updated probabilities are clamped to ensure they remain valid within the range $[0, 1]$.

Being n the total number of samples, and k the number of segments, let $c_1, c_2, ..., c_k$ be the change points. From this, a dataset containing the samples and segment labels, and the CPTs for each segment, is constructed.

3.3 Empirical Testing

To validate the proposed framework, the Chest Clinic network [9] (also referred to as Asia or Lung Cancer) and the Cat Hide network were used (Fig. 1), as they are well-established benchmarks in BNs research.

4 Results

This section evaluates the performance of the proposed algorithm under diverse experimental conditions. Table 1 summarizes the key parameters used to simulate various drift scenarios, from gradual to abrupt changes. These parameters correspond to the experiments presented in the section; however, additional experiments with alternative parameter settings were also conducted to further assess the robustness of the algorithm. The analysis focuses on the algorithm's sensitivity to drift and ability to adapt.

Our methodology and evaluation approach distinguishes itself from previous work through direct observation of inference performance and CPTs for the entire

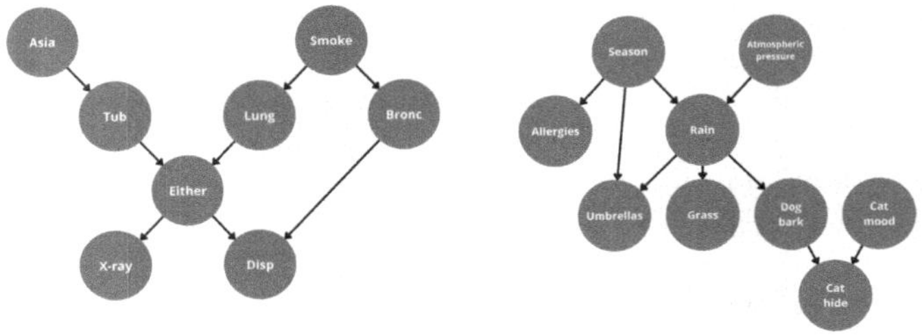

(a) Chest clinic network (b) Cat hide network

Fig. 1. Bayesian networks used in the experiments.

Table 1. Experiment parameters

Parameter	Value
Experiments	100
Sample range	[5,000, 15,000]
C_p range	[0.05. 0.35]
Segments range	[2,6]
Observed nodes	2
Window size	50
Overlap step size	12
Drift threshold	80%

model, allowing an iterative learning process during experimentation, rather than only detecting partial static model snapshots through latent variables. Although a direct comparison of the final results would be valuable, the closed nature of the detection approach, lack of adaptation to the upcoming distributions, and datasets used in related works present a limitation. Implementing local versions of these comparative approaches is beyond the scope of this study.

4.1 Chest Clinic

First, we will discuss the results from the experiments using the Chest Clinic network. Figure 2 provides a detailed view of the CPT adaptation process in response to drift from a single experiment, using the similarity measure based on the JS divergence. As shown by the marks, the changes in similarity correspond to the segment transitions, effectively demonstrating the system's capability of detecting and adapting to drift. Next, we will discuss the results obtained from the complete set of experiments (Fig. 3).

Figure 3a illustrates the mean CPT similarity of approximately 96.33% with a standard deviation of ±2.8%. The histogram reveals a clear right-skewed distribution, indicating that most similarity values are concentrated near the upper

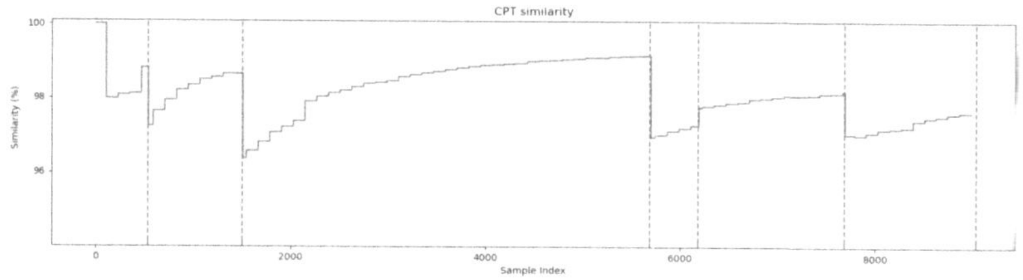

Fig. 2. Drift detection and CPT adaptation process. Each drop in similarity marks the detection of drift, indicating a shift in the underlying data distribution. Upon detecting drift, the system initiates the adaptation phase, progressively adjusting the prior CPTs to better align with the new distribution. Vertical dotted lines denote the samples indices where drift was introduced.

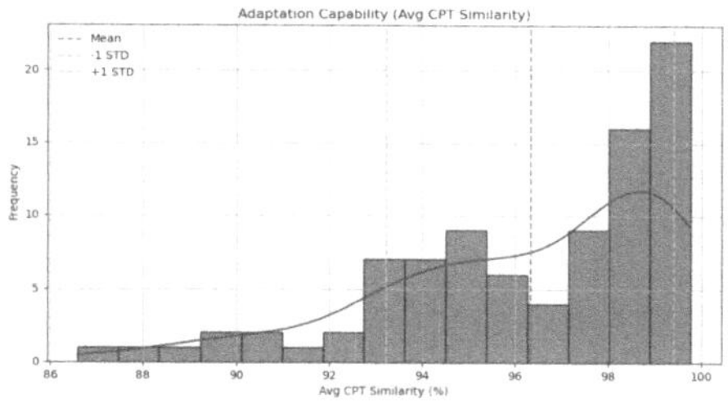

(a) Adaptation capability (CPTs)

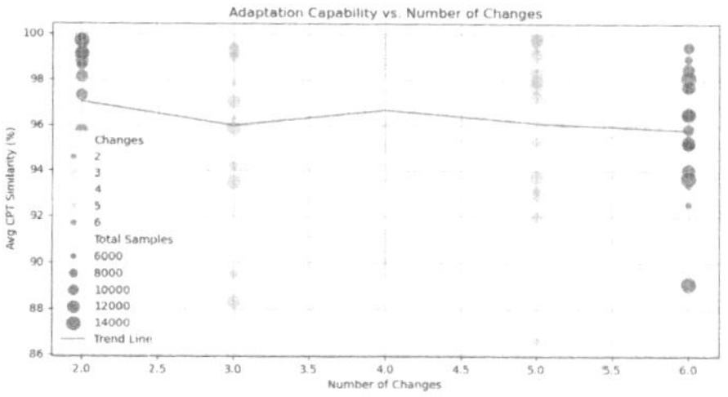

(b) CPTs similarity vs. Number of changes

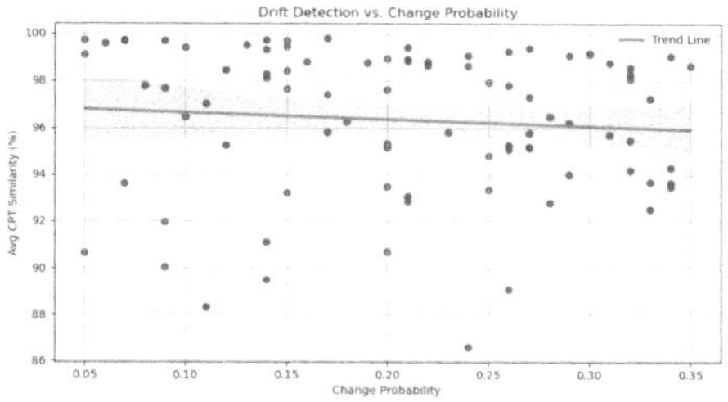

(c) CPTs similarity vs. Change probability

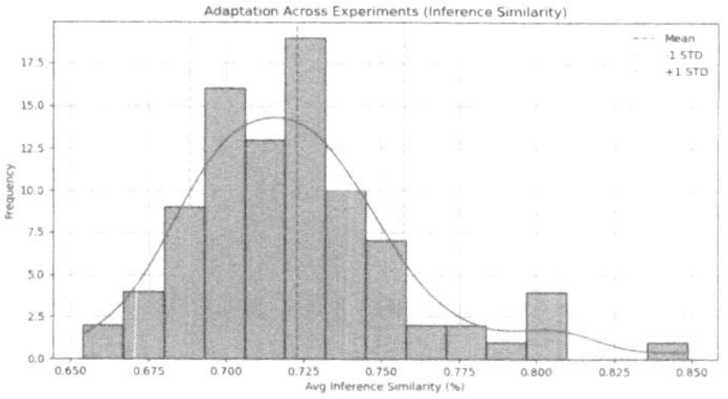

(d) Adaptation capability (inference)

Fig. 3. Performance overview across various drift scenarios. (a) Average CPT similarity across experiments, highlighting the mean and standard deviations. (b) Adaptation capability as a function of the number of changes and total number of samples. (c) Drift detection in relation to drift severity. (d) Distribution of average inference similarity across experiments, highlighting the mean and standard deviation.

end of the range. This skewness implies that negative deviations from the mean are less frequent than positive deviations, suggesting that the algorithm consistently performs near or above the mean level of similarity in most cases.

Figure 3b illustrates the relationship between the number of changes and the average CPT similarity, with the markers being the experiments and their sizes indicating the total number of samples. The red line exhibits a very slight negative correlation, suggesting that as the number of changes increases, the average CPT similarity remains largely stable, with only minor variations. The distribution of points shows high consistency in similarity scores across different number of changes, particularly for scenarios with fewer changes. Larger number of changes exhibit slightly more dispersion but still maintain a high similarity score overall, reflecting the algorithm's robustness. Notably, the size of the markers does not seem to significantly influence the average CPT similarity, suggesting that the algorithm performs consistently irrespective of data size.

Figure 3c illustrates a slight negative correlation between C_p (magnitude of perturbations) and average CPT similarity, as indicated by the weak downward trend in the regression line. This trend suggests that the algorithm's ability to adapt and maintain high similarity scores is only marginally affected by increasing levels of drift severity. The slight slope of the trend line, combined with the consistently high similarity values across all levels of change probability and the narrow confidence interval surrounding the trend line, underscores the algorithm's robustness in handling diverse drift scenarios.

Figure 3d illustrates the distribution of average inference similarity across experiments, with a mean value of approximately 72.5% and a standard deviation of ±2.5%. The histogram reveals a near-normal distribution, with most experiments clustered around the mean, reflecting consistent inference performance across varying experimental conditions. Even when the inference similarity averages are relatively lower, the average CPT similarity (as seen in previous graphs) remains consistently higher. This suggest that the algorithm is particularly robust in maintaining structural adaptation of the CPTs, even when the inferred probabilities deviate from the expected values.

4.2 Cat Hide

Next, we will discuss the results from the experiments using the Cat Hide network. Similarly to the findings in Sect. 4.1, Fig. 4a shows that the average CPT similarity remains high (96.48% ± 2.6%), with little degradation even under conditions of frequent or abrupt drift, following the same trend of near or above average behaviour. In Fig. 4b the stability observed in the trend line indicates that the algorithm scales well in both the number of drift occurrences and dimensions of the dataset. The results from Fig. 4c reveal a slight negative trend, as observed with the Chest Clinic network experiments, further suggesting that the algorithm is only barely affected by levels of drift severity. Finally, Fig. 4d, while showing slightly lower averages (70.95% ± 2.8%), most likely due to the increased complexity of the network, supports the framework's ability to ensure that the CPTs remain well aligned with the true data distribution.

4.3 Discussion

The results demonstrate the algorithm's ability to address drift across diverse scenarios. By effectively balancing sensitivity to drift with adaptability, the framework ensures timely detection of changes while maintaining alignment with

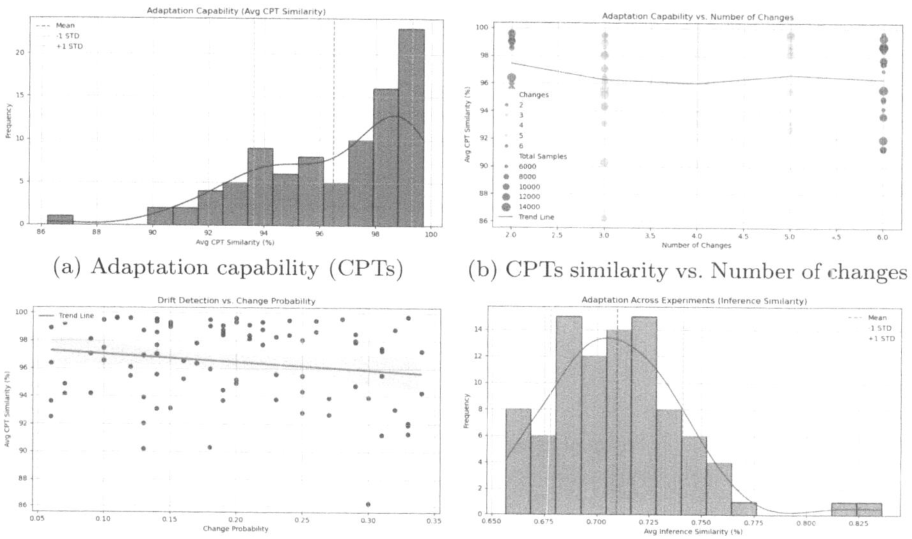

(a) Adaptation capability (CPTs)

(b) CPTs similarity vs. Number of changes

(c) CPTs similarity vs. Change probability

(d) Adaptation capability (inference)

Fig. 4. Cat hide network analysis. Performance overview across various drift scenarios. (a) Average CPT similarity across experiments, highlighting the mean and standard deviations. (b) Adaptation capability as a function of the number of changes and total number of samples. (c) Drift detection in relation to drift severity. (d) Distribution of average inference similarity across experiments, highlighting the mean and standard deviation.

evolving data distributions. The observed stability across varying magnitudes of drift, numbers of changes and sample sizes reflects the algorithm's adaptability in handling both gradual and abrupt shifts in data.

The framework showcases the capacity to balance the trade-off between inference and CPT similarity, ensuring that while the inference accuracy might be affected by high-entropy conditions, the underlying model remains well-adapted. Although the experiments were done with binary variables, this is not an intrinsic limitation of the method; it can handle multivalued discrete variables.

Our framework demonstrates high sensitivity in detecting both gradual and abrupt concept drift while also efficiently adapting to evolving data, ensuring reliable model performance over time. While most recent methods, such as Hinder et al. [5] and Alsuwat et al. [4], effectively detect drift, they lack adaptation mechanisms, limiting their ability to maintain long-term model reliability. In contrast, our approach not only detects drift with comparable accuracy but also ensures continued alignment with changing data distributions.

5 Conclusions

We have developed framework for detecting concept drift in Bayesian Networks, and updating the model parameters in response to these changes. The experimental results validate the framework's approach to drift detection and adaptation, making it a reliable solution for dynamic and evolving datasets.

As future work we aim to extent our framework to larger networks, to assess its scalability. Additionally, we plan to expand it to detect drift caused by changes in the network's structure; to address not only parameter changes but also shifts in the network's topology, further broadening its applicability.

References

1. Tsymbal, A.: The problem of concept drift: Definitions and related work, Technical Report, 2004. https://publications.scss.tcd.ie/tech-reports/reports.04/TCD-CS-2004-15.pdf
2. Bach, S.H., Maloof, M.A.: A bayesian approach to concept drift. Adv. Neural Inf. Process. Syst. (NIPS) **10**, 1–9 (2010)
3. Cabañas, R., Cano, A., Gómez-Olmedo, M., Masegosa, A.R., Moral, S.: Concept drift detection in discrete streaming data using probabilistic graphical models. Proc. BNAIC **2017**, 1–12 (2017)
4. Alsuwat, H., Alsuwat, E., Valtorta, M., Rose, J., Farkas, C.: Modeling concept drift in the context of discrete bayesian networks. In: Proceedings of the 11th International Joint Conference on Knowledge Discovery, Knowledge Engineering and Knowledge Management (IC3K 2019), pp. 214– 224, 2019. https://doi.org/10.5220/0008384702140224
5. Hinder, F., Vaquet, V., Hammer, B.: One or two things we know about concept drift–a survey on monitoring in evolving environments. part a: Detecting concept drift. Front. Artif. Intell. **6** (2023). https://doi.org/10.3389/frai.2024.1330257
6. Henrion, M.: Propagating uncertainty in bayesian networks by probabilistic logic sampling. In: Lemmer, J.F., Kanal, L.N. (eds.) Uncertainty in Artificial Intelligence, ser. Machine Intelligence and Pattern Recognition, vol. 5, North-Holland, pp. 149–163, 1988. https://doi.org/10.1016/B978-0-444-70396-5.50019-4
7. Sucar, L.E.: Probabilistic Graphical Models: Principles and Applications, 2nd. Springer Nature, Cham, Switzerland (2021). https://doi.org/10.1007/978-3-030-61943-5
8. Lin, J.: Divergence measures based on the shannon entropy. IEEE Trans. Inf. Theory **37**(1), 145–151 (1991). https://doi.org/10.1109/18.61115
9. Lauritzen, S.L., Spiegelhalter, D.J.: Local computations with probabilities on graphical structures and their application to expert systems. J. R. Stat. Soc. Ser. B (Methodological) **50**(2), 157–224 (1988)

Hausdorff Distance Optimization in Low-Density Point Clouds

Misael A. Rivas-Juarez[1], Osvaldo A. Tapia-Dueñas[2], and Hermilo Sánchez-Cruz[1](✉)

[1] Departamento de Ciencias de la Computación, Universidad Autónoma de Aguascalientes, Aguascalientes 20100, Mexico
herssan@gmail.com

[2] Department of Mathematics, Computer Science, and Data Science, John Carroll University, University Heights, OH, USA

Abstract. A new procedure is presented for point cloud optimization based on the reduction of the Hausdorff distance (error metric) between a point cloud and the 3D object it represents. This approach is crucial for accurately representing a 3D object while using a minimal number of points. This is achieved by utilizing two point clouds of the same 3D object but with different point densities: a high-density point cloud (original) and a low-density point cloud (simplified). The high-density cloud guides the reordering of points in the simplified cloud, ensuring alignment with the original positions. The methodology of this work is as follows. Each simplified point cloud is scaled to match the range of the original cloud. Both clouds are then aligned in the same spatial domain to establish neighborhoods of points in the original cloud that correspond to one or more points in the simplified cloud. Finally, the points in the simplified cloud are reordered based on their respective neighborhoods in the original cloud. Our procedure proves to be effective in reducing the Hausdorff distance presented in the simplified point clouds while the resulting point clouds appear more similar to the original.

Keywords: Point clouds · Hausdorff distance · Machine learning · Hierarchical clustering · 3D Shape

1 Introduction

The growing area of computer vision makes point clouds an increasingly useful resource for the representation of three-dimensional (3D) objects. This is because efficient storage, processing and transmission of 3D objects are necessary in virtual environments that process large amounts of data in the form of 3D objects, which must also be processed on the various devices that can view and even interact with them; and, as mentioned in [1], using unstructured 3D data, such as point clouds, can lead to an efficient workflow without the need for lengthy optimization processes. We can even see that point clouds have had applications in the fields of animation [2], video [3–5], CAD systems [6–8] and virtual reality environments [1,9].

A. P. López-Monroy et al. (Eds.): MCPR 2025, LNCS 15715, pp. 13–25, 2025.
https://doi.org/10.1007/978-3-031-96255-4_2

The representation of a 3D object with point clouds consists of using ordered points so that the contour of the same 3D object can be replicated by the ordered points. Obviously, this task can be complicated when deciding the density of points that a point cloud should have to represent a 3D object. Since, with a higher density of points, there will be a more faithful representation of the object in question preserving most of its characteristics; although there will also be a greater demand on the storage and processing of the represented object. For the above, numerous contributions can be found in the literature that present ways to reduce the density in a point cloud that represents a 3D object while maintaining the shape of the object and, as far as possible, its main characteristics so that both the point clouds and the objects they represent are as similar as possible. [10–12].

The Hausdorff distance is a parameter that helps to know how far away the representation of a point cloud can be from the 3D object it represents, in other words, it is a way to visualize how much the representation error is in the point cloud. In this way, by reducing the Hausdorff distance, it is possible to increase the similarity between the point cloud and the object it represents, although in the literature it is possible to find other approaches to achieve the increase in this similarity. As in the case of [13] that seeks to reconstruct and preserve characteristic curves in point clouds to faithfully represent shape models. That kind of works make a specific analysis in the represented object to extract its main characteristics and after applying them in the point clouds. This work will not follow this approach; we will reorder points considering the positions that every point could get to preserve the original characteristics in the 3D represented object.

The Hausdorff distance between point clouds C_1 and C_2 can be defined as follows:

$$Hau(C_1, C_2) = \max\left\{\max_{p_1 \in C_1}\left\{\min_{p_2 \in C_2}\{\|p_1, p_2\|\}\right\}, \max_{p_1 \in C_2}\left\{\min_{p_2 \in C_1}\{\|p_1, p_2\|\}\right\}\right\}, \tag{1}$$

where $\|p_1, p_2\|$ is the euclidean distance between points p_1 and p_2.

This work is based on the reduction of the Hausdorff distance between an original point cloud (high point density) and a simplified point cloud (low point density) of the same 3D object. Both are superimposed in the same space to reorder the points in the simplified cloud considering the points of the original cloud, with the aim of reducing the error found in the simplified point cloud with respect to the 3D object it represents. It is important to mention that the hierarchical clustering method will be used to achieve this goal. In the literature, we can find contributions that apply this machine learning method on high-density point clouds to unite them and even segment them [14,15]. In this work, such machine learning method will be applied to segment small numbers of points.

The methodology for minimizing the Hausdorff distance begins with the simplified point clouds generated using the method described in [12] and proceeds through scaling the simplified point cloud by getting the axes range in the original point cloud, followed by obtaining point neighborhoods in the original cloud by superimposing the original and simplified clouds to form them, and. finally reassigning the points in the simplified cloud by choosing whether use all the points in the simplified cloud or using only one point per original cloud neighborhood. In Fig. 1 the methodology is illustrated highlighting the key sub-steps within each step.

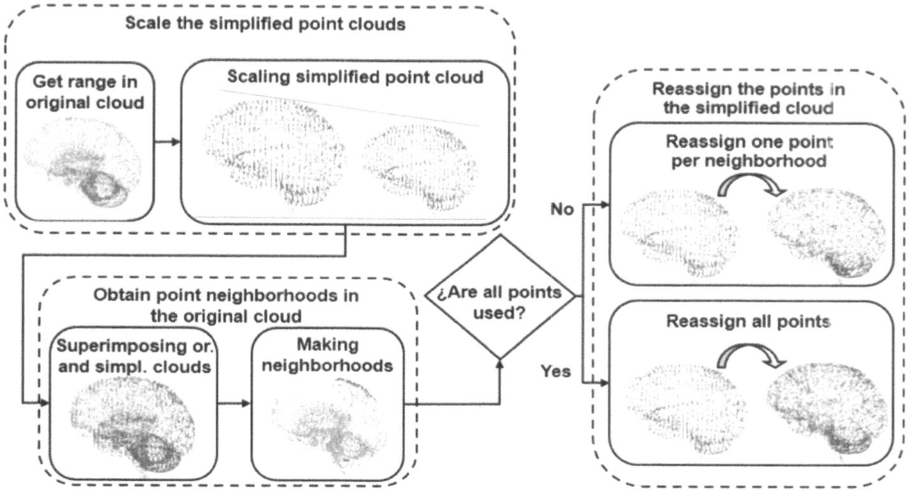

Fig. 1. Methodology steps diagram.

2 Scale the Simplified Point Clouds

As can be seen in the procedure applied in [12], the simplified point clouds obtained are in ranges discretized by the voxelization on the 3D objects that it seeks to represent with a low density of points. This makes the range in which the simplified clouds are located quite distant from the range in which an original point cloud of a 3D object can be found. For this reason, an adjustment is made in the scale of the simplified point clouds so that each one is in the same respective range in which each of the original point clouds is found. In Fig. 2 a comparison can be seen between an original and a simplified point cloud in the original range of each one.

Now, considering that it is only necessary to adjust the range in which the simplified point clouds are without affecting their shape, it is decided to use the min-max scaling, given by the following formula for each of the coordinates at the points of the simplified point cloud:

$$V_{scaled} = \left[\left(\frac{V - V_{min}}{V_{max} - V_{min}} \right) (max - min) \right] + min, \tag{2}$$

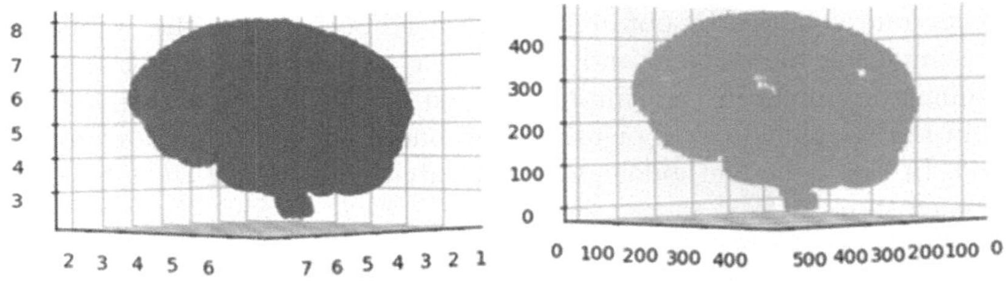

(a) Original point cloud (b) Simplified point cloud

Fig. 2. Point clouds in their original range.

where:

- V_{scaled} is the result of the scaling.
- V is the original value to escale.
- V_{max} and V_{min} are the minimum and maximum values in the original data (on each axis).
- max and min are the limits of the desired range for the final scale, they will be taken from the range in which each original point cloud is.

Applying this scaling yields as outcome the simplified point cloud in the original point cloud scale. After scaling the simplified point clouds, they are aligned within the same space as the original point cloud. This alignment is essential for calculating the Hausdorff distance and for proceeding with the subsequent steps of the methodology.

3 Obtain Point Neighborhoods in the Original Cloud

To achieve the greatest reduction in Hausdorff distance, each point in the simplified cloud must be brought as close as possible to the points in the original cloud. This requires determining with points in the original cloud should be taken into account when reassigning each point in the simplified cloud. First, the coordinates of a point in the original cloud will be taken, a radius (r) will be added to each of its axes, and the points in the simplified cloud that are within the range obtained for each of the axes will be selected. With them, the Euclidean distance of each of the resulting points will be calculated, so only those whose distance from the point in the simplified cloud is less than or equal to the radius will be worked with. The value of r will be equal to one-tenth of the length of the axis with the greatest displacement in the original point cloud and, if no nearby points are found in the simplified point cloud, it will be increased by its same value until points are found. Then, the smallest distance from the original cloud point to the detected points of the simplified cloud will be selected, and the original point will become part of the neighborhood of the simplified cloud point with such smallest distance. In this way, by going through all the points of the original cloud and applying this procedure to each one of them, all the points in the original cloud are segmented into neighborhoods where, up to now, they correspond to a single point of the simplified cloud. Figure 3 presents a two-dimensional (2D) example of these steps, where circles represent the original point cloud and triangles represent the simplified point cloud.

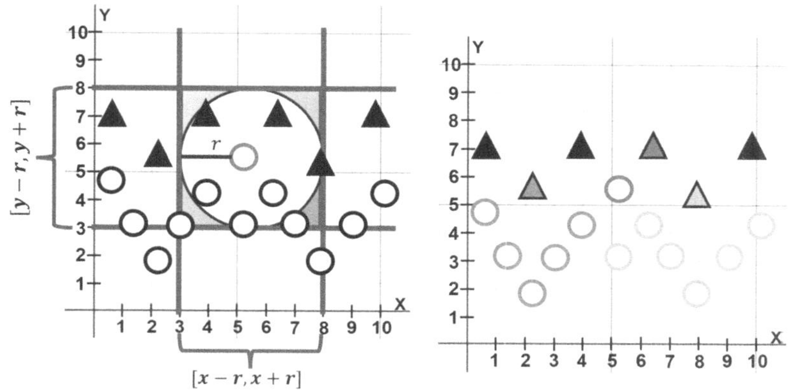

(a) Point detection with detection radius

(b) Neighborhoods linked to their nearest simplified cloud point

Fig. 3. 2D example of initial neighborhoods detection in original point cloud.

The decision was made to compare the results obtained by using all the points in the simplified cloud versus using only one point per neighborhood. Therefore, in order to obtain the results when using all the points in the simplified cloud, each of the points that were left without an assigned neighborhood in the previous step is traversed and a detection radius is applied to identify the nearby neighborhoods in the original point cloud and decide which one they will be matched with. It must be considered that, in order to use all the points in the simplified cloud, the neighborhoods in the original cloud cannot be less than the number of assigned points in the simplified cloud; therefore, if an unassigned point in the simplified cloud had a closest neighborhood in the original cloud with the same number of points assigned in the simplified cloud, the unassigned point will be assigned to the next closest neighborhood which has more points than their assigned in the simplified cloud.

4 Reassign the Points in the Simplified Cloud

By analyzing the neighborhoods formed in the original point cloud and the number of points in the simplified cloud that correspond to each of them, different scenarios are found in which the Hausdorff distance can be reduced by reassigning each point in the simplified cloud as close as possible to all the points in its corresponding neighborhood in the original cloud. Firstly, there are scenarios in which a single point in the simplified cloud corresponds to a neighborhood formed in the original cloud. Therefore, the following cases can arise:

a. If the neighborhood has only one point, the simplified cloud point will take its place.
b. If the neighborhood has two points, the simplified cloud point will be located exactly halfway between those two points.
c. If the neighborhood has n points, where $n > 2$, the two furthest points in the neighborhood are first identified to obtain the midpoint between them; if, when calculating the distance from that location to the neighborhood points, it is observed that the distance to the two furthest points in the neighborhood is the greatest, then that location is selected to position the simplified cloud point. If not, then the optimal position is searched on each axis that allows the smallest possible distance to all the neighborhood points.

Figure 4 shows a 2D example of the results in each of these scenarios, where the circles represent points of the original cloud, the triangles represent points of the simplified cloud, and the stars represent the location where the Hausdorff distance can be most reduced in each context.

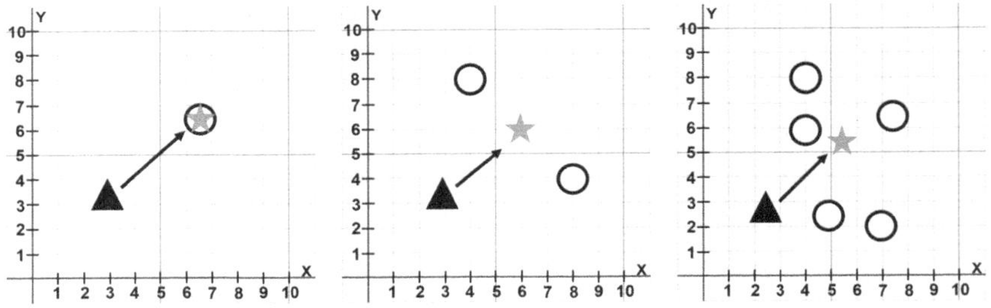

(a) Scenario one to one (b) Scenario one to two (c) Scenario one to n

Fig. 4. Scenarios for each neighborhood with one point of the simplified cloud.

There are also scenarios in which several points in the simplified cloud correspond to a neighborhood formed in the original. Therefore, the following cases can arise:

a. If a neighborhood of n points in the original cloud corresponds to n points in the simplified cloud, each point in the simplified cloud is assigned to the closest point in the original cloud.
b. If a neighborhood of n points in the original cloud corresponds to $n-1$ points in the simplified cloud, each point in the simplified cloud is first assigned to the closest point in the original cloud. Then, the point in the original cloud that is closest to the point in the same original cloud that was not assigned is placed to place the point in the simplified cloud in an intermediate location between them.

c. If a neighborhood of n points in the original cloud corresponds to m points in the simplified cloud, where $n - 2 \leq m$: first, hierarchical clustering is used to segment the neighborhood into m clusters; then it is decided which cluster is closest to each point in the simplified cloud; Finally, each point in the simplified cloud is assigned to its closest cluster depending on the number of points in the cluster, scenarios are repeated where a single point in the simplified cloud corresponds to a neighborhood of the original cloud.

Figure 5 shows a 2D example of the results in each of these scenarios, where the circles, triangles and stars represent the same concept as in Fig 4. It can be seen that in the n to m scenario the circles that are the same color belong to the same cluster after applying hierarchical clustering.

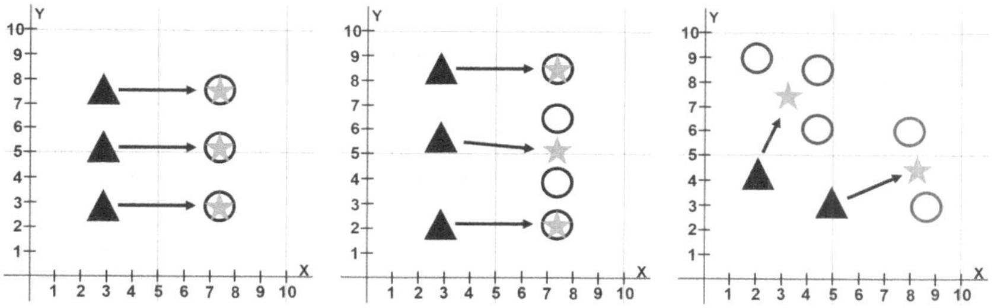

(a) Scenario n to n (b) Scenario $n-1$ to n (c) Scenario m to n

Fig. 5. Scenarios for each neighborhood with several points of the simplified cloud.

5 Results

For this work, the original and simplified point clouds of five figures were used: Bunny, Brain, Cow, Dragon, and Happy Buddha. Table 1 presents a comparison of the number of points in the original cloud and in the simplified cloud from [12], along with the Hausdorff distance between the original point cloud (C_O) and the simplified point cloud (C_S).

After applying the previously explained procedure on these objects, optimized point clouds (C_{OP}) were obtained with the results observed in Table 2 taking into account that percentage reduction in points column considers the number of points in the original cloud and that the percentage reduction in $Hau(C_O, C_S)$ column considers the values shown in Table 1.

As can be seen in Table 2, whether it is decided to use only one point of the simplified cloud per neighborhood of the original cloud or if it is decided to use all points, a considerable reduction in the Hausdorff distance can be obtained. This represents optimization both in the number of points used and in the error ($Hau(C_O, C_S)$) presented by the simplified clouds of [12] in a short amount of

Table 1. Comparison between original point cloud and simplified point cloud.

Object	No. of points in original cloud	No. of points in simplified cloud[a]	% of reduct. points	$Hau(C_O, C_S)$
Bunny	35,947	12,406	65	0.0085
Brain	18,844	6,488	66	1.0625
Cow	2,903	1,007	65	0.8112
Dragon	22,998	8,017	65	0.0103
Happy Buddha	7,108	2,072	71	0.0362

[a] Ref. [12] does not share this data, the simplified point clouds were obtained directly from the authors.

time. Although it can also be seen that in most cases if it is decided to use all the points of the simplified clouds, a greater reduction in the Hausdorff distance is obtained at the cost of sacrificing the reduction that could be obtained in the number of points and preserving the same percentage of reduction in points shown in Table 1 than if only one point per neighborhood were used.

Table 2. Optimization results on simplified point clouds.

Object	Method (points used)	No. of points obtained	% of reduct. points	$Hau(C_O, C_{OP})$	% of reduct. in $Hau(C_O, C_S)$	Time (sec)
Bunny	All points	12,406	65	0.0042	51	784.0623
	1 per neigh.	10,510	71	0.0042	51	150.9606
Brain	All points	6,488	66	0.5496	48	113.8293
	1 per neigh.	4,449	76	0.5912	44	54.4065
Cow	All points	1,007	65	0.417	49	8.5730
	1 per neigh.	799	72	0.4313	47	4.2653
Dragon	All points	8,017	65	0.0055	47	210.6668
	1 per neigh.	7,229	69	0.0058	44	105.1385
Happy Buddha	All points	2,072	71	0.0124	66	33.6237
	1 per neigh.	1,106	84	0.0130	64	14.4578

Now, in order to compare the present work with other contributions that we can find in the literature, specifically in [10,11], we proceeded to calculate the maximum error distance, which is also referred as the Hausdorff distance, between the original point clouds and the simplified point clouds of [12] and the clouds optimized by our method. The maximum error distance is calculated as follows:

$$\Delta_{max}(C_1, C_2) = \max_{p_1 \in C_1} \left\{ \min_{p_2 \in C_2} \{\|p_1, p_2\|\} \right\}, \tag{3}$$

where $\|p_1, p_2\|$ is the euclidean distance between points p_1 and p_2.

As can be seen in Table 3, our method, both when using all points of the simplified cloud and when using only one point per neighborhood of the original cloud, managed to obtain better results in terms of the maximum error distance while maintaining a relatively low number of points.

Table 3. Comparison of results between methods.

Object	No. of points in original cloud	Method	No. of points obtained	$\Delta_{max}(C_O, C_n)$
Bunny	35,947	Ref [10]	16,476	0.005151
		Ref [11]	**1,797**	0.006019
		Ref [12]	12,406	0.0064[a]
		Our method (all points)	12,406	**0.0042**
		Our method (1 per neigh.)	10,510	**0.0042**
Dragon	437,645	Ref [10]	33,960	0.44323
	22,998	Ref [12]	8,017	0.0103[a]
		Our method (all points)	8,017	**0.0055**
		Our method (1 per neigh.)	**7,229**	0.0058

[a] Ref [12] does not share this data, it was calculated during the development of this work.

Furthermore, the results of applying this procedure on the simplified point clouds obtained by [12] also lead to an improvement in the visual aspect. In the example shown in Fig. 6, the characteristics of the original object Fig. 6(a) that were modified in the procedure of [12] to obtain the simplified clouds Fig. 6(b) can be seen, such as the holes between the bunny's legs and some curvatures in the legs; not to mention that the simplified cloud has its points formed in such a way that layers are distinguished, which makes them not appear homogeneously distributed. In this way, by applying the procedure explained in this work and choosing to use only one point of the simplified point cloud per original cloud neighborhood, the characteristics of the original object were obtained again while the optimized point cloud Fig. 6(c) shows a more homogeneous distribution so that empty spaces are not perceived as conspicuous between the points.

The other objects used in this work (Brain, Cow, Dragon and Happy Buddha) also showed visual improvements after applying the procedure explained. All of them recover features of the original object while the points that make them up are seen to be distributed in a more homogeneous way. This can be seen in Figs. 7, 8, 9 and 10.

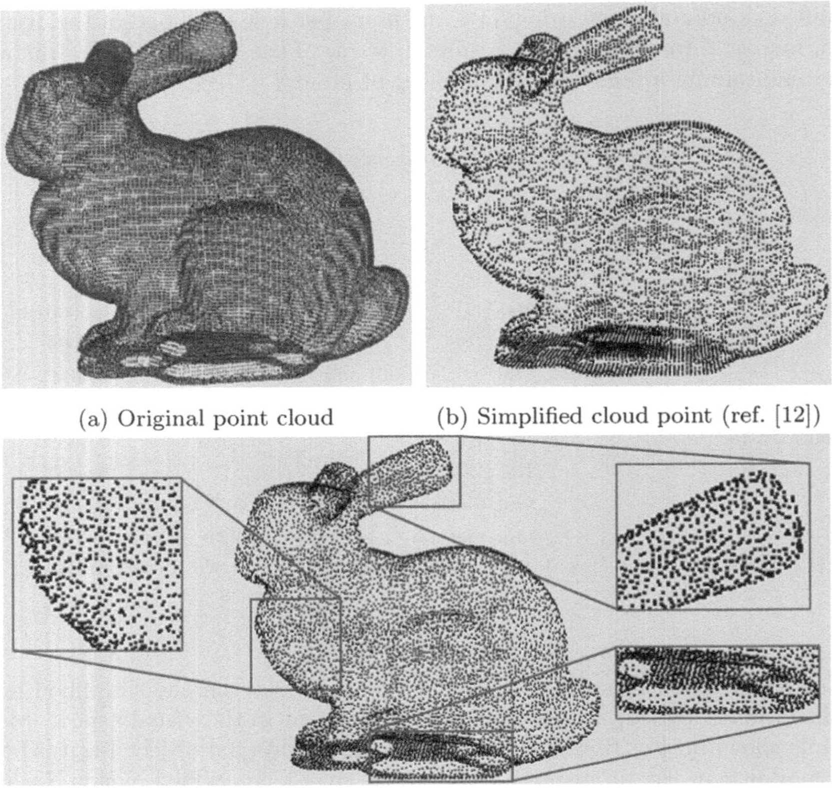

(a) Original point cloud (b) Simplified cloud point (ref. [12])

(c) Optimized point cloud (1 point per neighborhood)

Fig. 6. Comparison between point clouds of the same object 3D (Bunny).

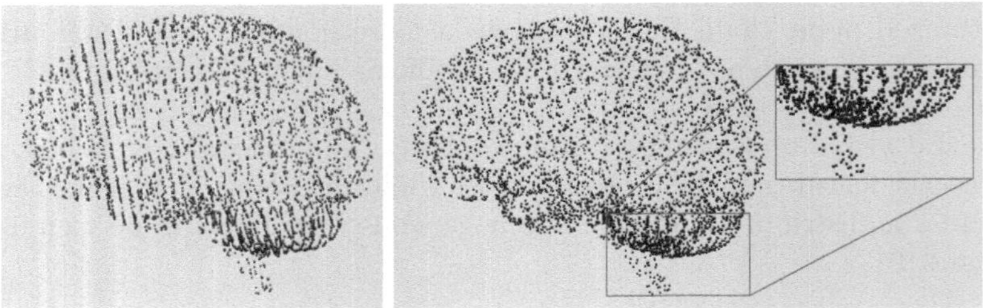

(a) Simplified cloud point (ref. [12]) (b) Optimized point cloud (1 point per neighborhood)

Fig. 7. Comparison between point clouds (Brain).

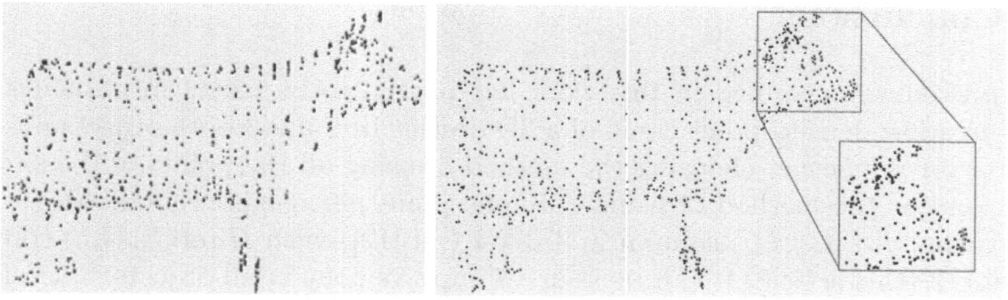

(a) Simplified cloud point (ref. [12])

(b) Optimized point cloud (1 point per neighborhood)

Fig. 8. Comparison between point clouds (Cow).

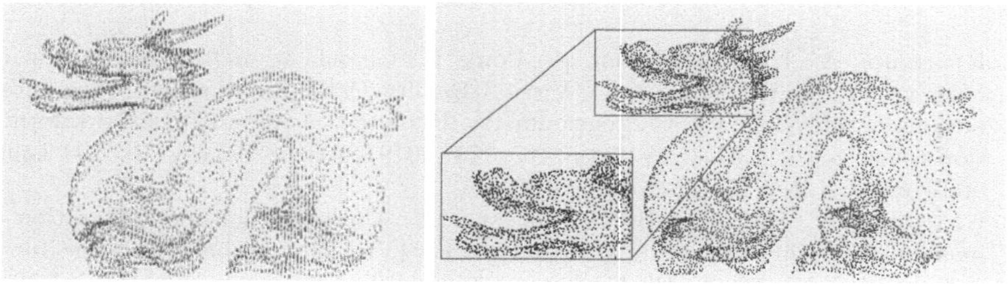

(a) Simplified cloud point (ref. [12])

(b) Optimized point cloud (1 point per neighborhood)

Fig. 9. Comparison between point clouds (Dragon).

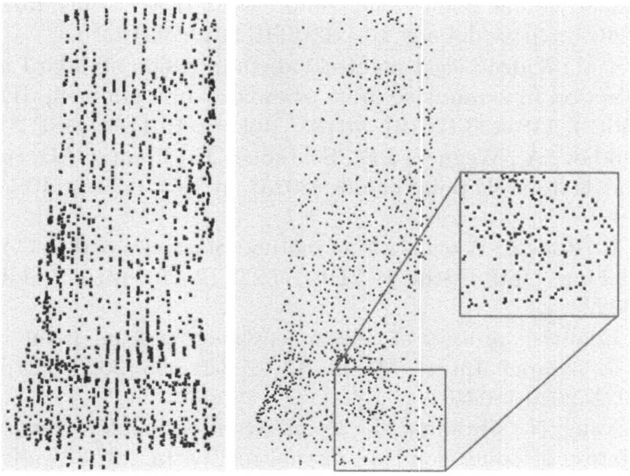

(a) Simplified cloud point (ref. [12])

(b) Optimized point cloud (1 point per neighborhood)

Fig. 10. Comparison between point clouds (Happy Buddha).

6 Conclusions

The procedure explained in this work has proven to be useful in reducing the error in a low-density point cloud of a 3D object. In Table 3 both objects present a lower error whether choosing the method of using all the points of the simplified cloud or the method of using only one point per neighborhood. Also when comparing $Hau(C_o, C_s)$ column in Table 1 (ref [12]) with $Hau(C_o, C_{op})$ column in Table 2 (this article) it can be seen an improvement in all objects. Therefore, it can be concluded that an improvement in the error is achieved while some characteristics of the 3D object that could have been lost in the simplification procedure by [12] are recovered.

References

1. Kharroubi, A., Hajji, R., Billen, R., Poux, F.: Classification And Integration Of Massive 3d Points Clouds In A Virtual Reality (VR) Environment, The International Archives of the Photogrammetry, Remote Sensing and Spatial Information Sciences, vol. XLII-2/W17, pp. 165–171 (2019). https://doi.org/10.5194/isprs-archives-XLII-2-W17-165-2019
2. Kharroubi, A., Hajji, R., Billen, R., Poux, F.: Classification and integration of massive 3d points clouds in a virtual reality (VR) environment. In: The International Archives of the Photogrammetry, Remote Sensing and Spatial Information Sciences, vol. XLII-2/W17, pp. 165–171 (2019). https://doi.org/10.5194/isprs-archives-XLII-2-W17-165-2019
3. Liu, Z., et al.: Point cloud video streaming: challenges and solutions. IEEE Netw. **35**(5), 202–209 (2021). https://doi.org/10.1109/MNET.101.2000364
4. Li, L., Li, Z., Zakharchenko, V., Chen, J., Li, H.: Advanced 3D motion prediction for video-based dynamic point cloud compression. IEEE Trans. Image Process. **29**, 289–302 (2020). https://doi.org/10.1109/TIP.2019.2931621
5. Jang, E.S., et al.: Video-based point-cloud-compression standard in MPEG: from evidence collection to committee draft [standards in a nutshell]. IEEE Signal Process. Mag. **36**(3), 118–123 (2019). https://doi.org/10.1109/MSP.2019.2900721
6. Liu, Y., Obukhov, A., Wegner, J.D., Schindler, K.: Point2CAD: reverse engineering CAD models from 3D point clouds (2023). https://doi.org/10.1109/cvpr52733.2024.00361
7. Fan, J., Ma, L., Zou, Z.: A registration method of point cloud to CAD model based on edge matching. Optik (Stuttg) **219**, 165223 (2020). https://doi.org/10.1016/j.ijleo.2020.165223
8. Liu, J.: An adaptive process of reverse engineering from point clouds to CAD models. Int. J. Comput. Integr. Manuf. **33**(9), 840–858 (2020). https://doi.org/10.1080/0951192X.2020.1803501
9. Alexiou, E., Yang, N., Ebrahimi, T.: PointXR: a toolbox for visualization and subjective evaluation of point clouds in virtual reality. In: 2020 Twelfth International Conference on Quality of Multimedia Experience (QoMEX), pp. 1–6. IEEE (2020). https://doi.org/10.1109/QoMEX48832.2020.9123121
10. El Sayed, A.R., El Chakik, A., Alabboud, H., Yassine, A.: An efficient simplification method for point cloud based on salient regions detection. RAIRO - Oper. Res. **53**(2), 487–504 (2019). https://doi.org/10.1051/ro/2018082

11. Leal, E., Sanchez-Torres, G., Branch-Bedoya, J.W., Abad, F., Leal, N.: A saliency-based sparse representation method for point cloud simplification. Sensors **21**(13), 4279 (2021). https://doi.org/10.3390/s21134279
12. Tapia-Dueñas, O.A., Sánchez-Cruz, H., López, H.H.: 3D object simplification using chain code-based point clouds. Multimedia Tools Appl. **82**(6), 9491–9515 (2023). https://doi.org/10.1007/s11042-022-13588-3
13. Fugacci, U., Romanengo, C., Falcidieno, B., Biasotti, S.: Reconstruction and preservation of feature curves in 3D point cloud processing. Comput. Aided Des. **167**, 103649 (2024). https://doi.org/10.1016/j.cad.2023.103649
14. Feng, C., Taguchi, Y., Kamat, V.R.: Fast plane extraction in organized point clouds using agglomerative hierarchical clustering. In: 2014 IEEE International Conference on Robotics and Automation (ICRA), pp. 6218–6225. IEEE (2014). https://doi.org/10.1109/ICRA.2014.6907776
15. Xu, Y., Yao, W., Tuttas, S., Hoegner, L., Stilla, U.: Unsupervised segmentation of point clouds from buildings using hierarchical clustering based on gestalt principles. IEEE J. Sel. Top. Appl. Earth Obs. Remote Sens. **11**(11), 4270–4286 (2018). https://doi.org/10.1109/JSTARS.2018.2817227

Extremal Topologies for the Merrifield-Simmon Index on Dendrimers in Drug Delivery

Guillermo De Ita, Michelle Guerra, Juan Pintor(✉), and Cybele Moutinho

Fac. Cs. de la Computación, Benemérita Universidad Autónoma de Puebla, Edif. CCO1, 14 Sur y San Claudio, C.U., Puebla, Mexico
juan.pintor@correo.buap.mx

Abstract. This study presents a computational framework for identifying extreme dendrimer topologies. This study also considers how to form extreme dendrimer topologies when new components are added. This is a relevant task in the area of pattern recognition for structural molecular modeling. Using graph-theoretic techniques, we show how to compute the Merrifield-Simmons (M-S) index, which measures independent vertex sets in the molecular graph to analyze dendrimer branching, stability, and encapsulation. An efficient algorithm, based on post-order traversal and Fibonacci recurrence, computes the M-S index for polyphenylene dendrimers, ensuring scalability for complex structures.

Keywords: Merrifield-Simmons index · Dendrimers · Polyphenylene Composes · Recognizing extreme topologies · Efficient algorithms

1 Introduction

Since their initial successful studies in the 1980s, dendrimers have attracted significant attention, particularly in the 1990s. Research on dendrimers spans a wide range of applications, including gene therapy, imaging, diagnostics, nanomedicine, and drug delivery systems. The development of dendrimer-based capsules is key in advancing therapeutic compounds for disease treatment and prevention. However, the process from discovery to a market-ready drug is often lengthy and expensive, sometimes taking up to 15 years due to factors like high R&D costs, regulatory challenges, and the complexity of biological systems.

Dendrimers have become a prominent area of research, generating around 20,000 publications to date. While they consist of repeating units similar to polymers, dendrimers differ from classical polymers in two main characteristics: (i) they are synthesized step-by-step, ensuring a precisely defined and reproducible structure, and (ii) they possess a highly branched 3D architecture, achieved through the use of branching units as building blocks in their synthesis. The term "dendrimer" was coined by D.A. Tomalia, derived from the Greek words

A. P. López-Monroy et al. (Eds.): MCPR 2025, LNCS 15715, pp. 26–35, 2025.
https://doi.org/10.1007/978-3-031-96255-4_3

(dendron), meaning "tree," and (meros), meaning "part" [2]. Dendrimers are typically constructed layer-by-layer from a central core, with each new layer defining a new "generation" (denoted G) through the repetition of two consecutive reactions.

The unique structure of dendrimers has led to numerous applications, especially in catalysis and materials science, and a particular focus on their biomedical properties, especially in the field of vnanomedicine," which bridges nanotechnology and medicine [9,12]. Many dendrimers are comparable in size and shape to biomacromolecules such as proteins and enzymes, and they are generally non-immunogenic [17]. A significant part of their biological properties involves drug delivery, which is a central focus of this review [16,18].

The Merrifield-Simmon (M-S) index shows strong correlations with drug delivery efficiency, supporting a hybrid approach that integrates topological indices with simulations to optimize nanocarriers. This methodology enhances nanomedicine by enabling the personalized design of molecular systems tailored to specific therapeutic needs.

Computational modeling has become an essential tool in almost every stage of drug discovery. In special, pattern recognition tools have been developed to recognize extreme topologies into the area of molecular modeling, for example, for recognizing the topologies when dendrimers can improve the solubility and bioavailability of drugs. A key feature of dendrimers in drug delivery is their ability to control the transport of anticancer drugs and nucleic acids, making them promising candidates for cancer therapy. Furthermore, nano therapy combined with computational simulations offers molecular-level insights into key parameters such as drug and carrier selection, drug loading, biological response, and the rate of cellular uptake and release, which would otherwise require significant manual effort to assess [15].

2 Related Work

The use of computational modeling to design nanocarriers has seen remarkable advancements in recent decades. This approach facilitates the exploration of complex molecular structures and predicts their physicochemical properties prior to experimental synthesis. Dendrimers, which are branched macromolecules with a central core and successive layers of monomers, have emerged as ideal systems for drug delivery due to their structural versatility and high loading capacity. Numerous studies highlight the role of dendrimers in improving the bioavailability of hydrophobic drugs and reducing systemic toxicity [20]. Furthermore, computational models have proven instrumental in optimizing the interaction properties between dendrimers and bioactive molecules, enabling simulations that save time and resources in experimental development [13].

The M-S index, a metric that describes the connectivity and topology of molecular graphs, has become a pivotal tool for characterizing dendrimer structures. This index allows for the evaluation of critical aspects such as branching density and accessibility of functional sites, which are determining factors in their medical applications [19]. Recent research has integrated efficient algorithms for computing the M-S index in dendrimers, facilitating the correlation between their molecular architecture and functional properties [1]. These advancements not only enhance the predictive capacity of computational models but also pave the way for tailored dendrimer designs to meet specific needs in drug delivery.

In the realm of medical applications, dendrimers have proven effective in targeted drug delivery, gene therapies, and imaging diagnostics [8,11]. Their ability to modulate size, surface charge, and chemical functionalization makes them versatile platforms for biomedical applications. The integration of the M-S index into these systems optimizes dendrimer design to maximize drug delivery efficiency, reducing adverse effects and improving therapeutic specificity [10,14]. Thus, the development of algorithms for efficient M-S index computation not only drives research in nanocarrier design but also contributes to the advancement of safer and more effective therapies in modern medicine.

3 Using Computational Modeling to Design Nanocarriers

Computational modeling is a very useful and efficient way of simulating and optimizing nanocarriers in an easy, reliable, and cost-effective manner for design, drug loading, and release mechanisms. With molecular dynamics and quantum mechanics simulations, the researchers can anticipate drug interactions with dendrimer structures, enhancing their therapeutic potential for targeted drug delivery applications. The models propose an opportunity to change nearby surfaces and structure, improving dendrimers bioavailability, reducing side effects, and facilitating cellular uptake. Furthermore, computational approaches greatly reduce experimental burdens and focus attention and resources on promising dendrimer candidates to provide a faster drug development pipeline and increase the potential of personalized medicine use.

The M-S index is a well-studied topological index. However, its application in Quantitative Structure-Activity Relationship (QSAR) and Quantitative Structure-Property Relationship (QSPR) studies remains underexplored. The M-S index of a molecular graph G is defined as the number of independent vertex sets in G, including the empty set. This index provides valuable insights into molecular stability and the structural properties of polymers and dendrimers.

The calculation of topological indices, such as the M-S index, has been advanced by specialized algorithms that predict molecular properties without the need for direct experimentation. These indices rely on graph traversal algorithms and the connectivity between nodes (atoms) in a molecular structure. Furthermore, hybrid computational approaches that combine graph theory with artificial intelligence and deep learning techniques [5] are becoming increasingly essential for analyzing large molecular databases, a crucial step in the discovery of new pharmacological compounds and materials.

Dendrimers have become valuable in cancer therapy, diagnostic imaging, and vaccine development due to their precise nanoscale structure, which supports applications in supramolecular chemistry, host-guest interactions, and self-assembly. Cancer treatment and imaging efficiently deliver therapeutic agents to targeted cells. In vaccines, dendrimers act as both antigen carriers and immune-stimulating adjuvants, enhancing immune response and efficacy [3]. This study calculates the Merrifield-Simmons index for polyphenylene dendrimers. By quantifying vertex set independence, this index helps reveal node "disconnectedness," indicating, for example, a high capacity for drug encapsulation and controlled release due to the separation of active regions.

4 Computing the Merrifield-Simmons Index on Polyphenylene Dendrimers

In this work, let $G = (V, E)$ denote a connected, undirected, simple graph, where V represents the set of vertices and E the set of edges. Two vertices $v, w \in V$ are *adjacent* if $\{v, w\} \in E$, commonly denoted as vw.

The *neighborhood* of a vertex $x \in V$, $N(x)$, is defined as $N(x) = \{y \in V : \{x, y\} \in E\}$, while its *closed neighborhood* includes x itself: $N[x] = N(x) \cup \{x\}$. The degree of x, $\delta(x)$, equals the cardinality of $N(x)$, and the maximum degree of the graph is given by $\Delta(G) = \max\{\delta(x) : x \in V\}$. A vertex v is *pendant* if $\delta(v) = 1$, and an edge $e = \{x, y\}$ is pendant if one of its endpoints is a pendant vertex.

A **path** P_n in G is a sequence of edges $v_0v_1, v_1v_2, \ldots, v_{n-1}v_n$, with all vertices distinct except possibly $v_0 = v_n$ in the case of a **cycle**. A **tree** is defined as a connected, acyclic graph, ensuring a unique path between any two vertices. The notations P_{n-1}, C_n, and T_n are used to denote a path, cycle, and tree containing n vertices, respectively.

An *independent set* $S \subseteq V$ satisfies $uv \notin E$ for all $u, v \in S$. The set of all independent sets in G is denoted $I(G)$. For a given vertex $v \in V$, the subsets $I_v(G)$ and $I_{-v}(G)$ represent independent sets that include or exclude v, respectively. Computing the total number of independent sets $i(G)$ is known to be a $\#P$-complete problem for graphs where $\Delta(G) \geq 3$ [6].

4.1 Application in Dendrimer Topologies

Graph-theoretic tools, particularly topological indices, are invaluable in chemical research. For a graph $G = (V, E)$, the "charge" of a vertex v, represented by $(\alpha_v, \beta_v)_G$, is defined as $\alpha_v = |I_{-v}(G)|$, the number of independent sets excluding v, and $\beta_v = |I_v(G)|$, the number including v.

Consider the path graph P_n with vertices $V = \{1, 2, \ldots, n+1\}$, where consecutive vertices $i, i+1$ are connected by edges $e_i = \{i, i+1\}$. For subgraphs $G_i = (V_i, E_i)$, comprising the first i vertices, each vertex $v_i \in V(G_i)$ is assigned charges $(\alpha_i, \beta_i)_{G_i}$, corresponding to the independent sets excluding and including v_i. The total independent sets in G_i are given by $\alpha_i + \beta_i$.

For the initial subgraph G_1, the charges are $(\alpha_1, \beta_1) = (1, 1)$, since $I(G_1) = \{\emptyset, \{v_1\}\}$. The recurrence relations:

$$\alpha_{i+1} = \alpha_i + \beta_i, \quad \beta_{i+1} = \alpha_i$$

generate the Fibonacci sequence for P_n, such that $i(P_n) = F_{n+2}$, where F_{n+2} denotes the $(n+2)$-th Fibonacci number.

4.2 Charge Computation for Trees

Given a rooted tree $T = (V, E)$ with a root $v_r \in V$, leaf vertices are those with degree one, while internal nodes have degrees exceeding one. Using a post-order traversal, subgraphs $T_i = (V_i, E_i)$ are constructed, where each vertex $v_i \in V$ is assigned charges (α_i, β_i). Here, $\alpha_i = |I_{-v_i}(T_i)|$, $\beta_i = |I_{v_i}(T_i)|$, and $i(T_i) = \alpha_i + \beta_i$.

For a leaf v, the charges are $(\alpha_v, \beta_v) = (1, 1)$. For internal nodes, the Fibonacci recurrence applies:

$$\alpha_{i+1} = \alpha_i + \beta_i, \quad \beta_{i+1} = \alpha_i.$$

For nodes with multiple children, the Hadamard product is used:

$$(\alpha_1, \beta_1) \cdot (\alpha_2, \beta_2) = (\alpha_1 \cdot \alpha_2, \beta_1 \cdot \beta_2).$$

The algorithm processes nodes in $O(n+m)$, where n and m denote the counts of vertices and edges, respectively.

4.3 Charge Computation for Cycles

Let $C_n = (V, E)$ represent a cycle with n vertices. Each vertex has degree two. Decomposing C_n as $P_{n-1} \cup \{c_m\}$, where P_{n-1} is a path and $c_m = \{v_n, v_1\}$ is the frond edge, the count of independent sets corresponds to the n-th Lucas number:

$$i(C_n) = L_n = F_{n+1} + F_{n-1}.$$

5 Maximizing M-S Index of a Dendrimer When a New Phenylene is Inserted

A polyphenylene dendrimer is characterized by a tree-like structure where vertices are replaced by hexagonal cycles, with each vertex representing a phenylene unit. The dendrimer has a central core from which phenylene units extend in a hexagonal arrangement, affecting its symmetry and spatial distribution. As the generation increases, the structure becomes more complex, enhancing surface area and interaction potential. Connectivity is ensured by covalent bonds, providing stability. The hexagonal symmetry plays a key role in the uniform distribution of phenylene units, influencing reactivity and molecular interactions. Topological indices, such as the Merrifield-Simmons (M-S) index, describe branching and connectivity, enabling comparisons of dendritic structures. This configuration also supports self-assembly into organized structures, crucial for applications in nanotechnology, nanomedicine, and chemical sensing [7].

The algorithm to compute the M-S index involves a post-order traversal, visiting each child phenylene, computing its charge, and transferring it to the parent phenylene vertex, as shown in Algorithm 1.

A post-order traversal on a tree, where child nodes are processed before their parent node, serves as the foundational framework for this algorithm. In the first step, the charge of each leaf phenylene is calculated, and it is assigned as $(13, 5)$. This charge is then propagated upward via the connectivity edge linking the leaf phenylene h_i to its parent phenylene h_p. Specifically, the transfer occurs through an edge $\{v_x, v_p\} \in E$, where $v_x \in V(h_i)$ is adjacent to $v_p \in V(h_p)$. The propagation mechanism applies a Fibonacci-type recurrence, ensuring the systematic incorporation of connectivity edge properties into the charge transfer process.

Algorithm 1. Computation of the Charge for Each Vertex in the Dendrimer

Input: Dendrimer structure as a rooted tree with hexagonal units.
Output: Merrifield-Simmons Index (M-S Index).

Post-order traversal: Start from the leaves.
for each leaf v_x **do** $(\alpha_{v_x}, \beta_{v_x}) \leftarrow (13, 5)$
    for each parent v_p of v_x **do**
        Update charges:

$$\alpha_{v_p} \leftarrow \alpha_{v_p} + \beta_{v_x}, \quad \beta_{v_p} \leftarrow \alpha_{v_x}$$

    end for
end for
Clockwise traversal: For internal vertices v_x in the phenylene structure:
for each v_x **do**
    Update parent charges:

$$\alpha_{v_p} \leftarrow \alpha_{v_p} + \beta_{v_x}, \quad \beta_{v_p} \leftarrow \alpha_{v_x}$$

end for
Root vertex: At v_r, compute:

$$\text{M-S Index} = \alpha_r + \beta_r$$

For instance, consider an internal hexagon h_i within the dendrimer structure, connected to its k child phenylenes $h_1, \ldots, h_k$ and a single parent hexagon h_p, as illustrated in Fig. 1. The connectivity edge between h_i and h_p is represented by $\{v_i, v_p\} \in E$, where $v_i \in V(h_i)$ and $v_p \in V(h_p)$. The objective is to integrate a new phenylene unit P_x into the dendrimer by selecting the optimal connection vertex v_i within h_i. This selection aims to maximize the Merrifield-Simmons (M-S) index of the resulting dendrimer structure. The M-S index, defined as the total number of independent sets in the graph, serves as a measure of branching and connectivity efficiency.

By systematically evaluating the charges for all potential connection vertices $v_i \in V(h_i)$, the vertex that yields the maximum M-S index for the updated dendrimer structure is selected as the optimal connection point for P_x. This approach ensures that the addition of P_x enhances the structural and functional properties of the dendrimer by optimizing its topological index. Figure 1 schematically represents how the charge for the vertices of an internal phenylene of the dendrimer is computed.

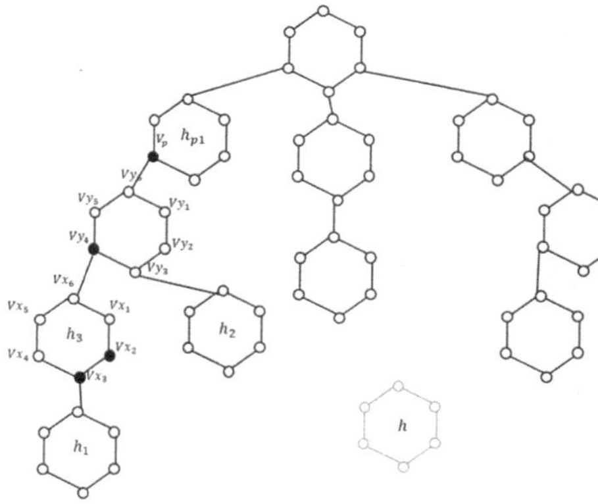

Fig. 1. Computing the charge for an internal phenylene of a dendrimer.

During step 2 in Algorithm 1, after the transfer of charges from each child phenylene to vertices within h_i, a clockwise traversal of vertices and edges in h_i initiates. This traversal begins from the first vertex following $v_x \in V(h_i)$, designated as $v_{x_i} \in V(h_i)$, and initiates two computational threads, denoted by L_p[1] and L_s[2], as it can be seen in Table 1. If v_{x_i} does not have an initial charge, then its charge is initialized as $(1, 1)$ in L_p and $(0, 1)$ in L_s. But if v_{x_i} has already an associated charge $(\alpha_{x_i}, \beta_{x_i})$, this charge is retained in L_p. Meanwhile, L_s is initialized with the charge $(0, \beta_{x_i})$.

The clockwise traversal continues from v_{x_i} until reaching the vertex $v_x \in V(h_i)$, visiting all edges of the current hexagon and applying the Fibonacci rule for each new edge that is visited. Meanwhile, the product rule is applied if the current vertex has a previous charge. When the last edge $\{v_x, v_{x_i}\} \in E(h_i)$ is visited, it is considered as a frond edge, and then the subtracted rule is applied on the charges from the threads L_p and L_s. For example, considering the charges $(\alpha_{xp}, \beta_{xp})$ in L_p and $(\alpha_{xs}, \beta_{xs})$ in L_s, then the subtracted rule yields as final charge for v_x: $(\alpha_{xp}, \beta_{xp} - \beta_{xs})$. This computed charge is subsequently transferred to vertex $v_p \in V(h_p)$ via the connectivity edge $\{v_x, v_p\} \in E$ and applying a Fibonacci rule. Figure 1 schematically represents how the charge for the vertices of an internal phenylene of the dendrimer is computed. The post-order search continues until it reaches the root phenylene, denoted as h_r, which has no further connections to parent phenylene.

[1] L_p: Principal computing threads.
[2] L_s: Secondary computing threads.

Given a new phenylene h and a dendrimer D (see Fig. 1), the question is: where h must be connected to D, in order to maximize (minimize) the M-S index of $(D \cup H)$?. We have found a hierarchy for the values of $i(D \cup h)$. The first case that maximize $(D \cup h)$, is when h is disconnected from D since it has a maximum independence between h and D and then $i(D \cup h) = i(D) \cdot i(h)$. However, if h would be part of D, then we must find in which phenylene from D, h is connected.

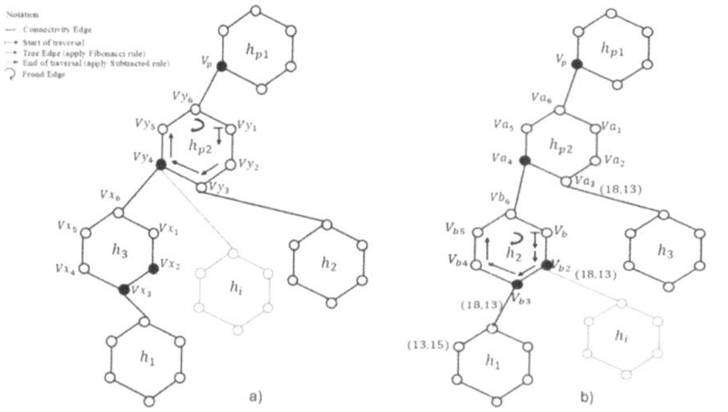

Fig. 2. Phenylene Dendrimer.

Table 1. Computing the charges for the vertices of the dendrimer case a

Connections	$h_1 \rightarrow$ v_{x3}	$h_2 \rightarrow$ v_{y3}	$h_i \rightarrow$ v_{y4}	$v_{x6} \rightarrow$ v_{y4}
Charges	$(13, 5) \rightarrow (18, 13)$	$(13, 5) \rightarrow (18, 13)$	$(13, 5) \rightarrow (18, 13)$	$(214, 85) \rightarrow (299, 85)$

	v_{x1}	v_{x2}	v_{x3}	v_{x4}	v_{x5}
L_p	$(1, 1)$	$\rightarrow(2, 1)$	$\rightarrow(3, 2) \cdot (18, 13) = (54, 26) \rightarrow$	$(80, 54) \rightarrow$	$(134, 80)$
L_s	$(0, 1)$	$\rightarrow(1, 0)$	$\rightarrow(1, 1) \cdot (18, 13) = (18, 13) \rightarrow$	$(31, 18) \rightarrow$	$(49, 31)$

	v_{b_6}	v_{a_4}
L_p	$(214, 85)$	$(299, 85)$
L_s	$(80, 49)$	

Subtracted rule on $\{v_{x6}, v_{x_i}\}$
$(214, 134 - 49) = (214, 85)$

	v_{y1}	v_{y2}	v_{y3}	v_{y4}
L_p	$(1, 1)$	$\rightarrow(2, 1)$	$\rightarrow(3, 2) \cdot (18, 13) = (54, 26) \rightarrow$	$(299, 85)(18, 13)[80, 54] = (968760, 59670)$
L_s	$(0, 1)$	$\rightarrow(1, 0)$	$\rightarrow(1, 1) \cdot (18, 13) = (18, 13) \rightarrow$	$(299, 85)(18, 13)(31, 18) = (166842, 19890)$

	v_{y5}	v_{y6}	V_p
L_p	$\rightarrow (1028430, 968760) \rightarrow$	$(1997190, 1028430)$	$(2838888, 1997190)$
L_s	$\rightarrow (186732, 166842)$	$\rightarrow (353574, 186732)$	

Subtracted rule on $\{v_{x6}, v_{x_i}\}$
$(199719, 1028430 - 186732)$
$= (199719, 841698)$

Based on the results of [4], it is recognized that in an array of phenylenes A, to connect a new phenylene h in the second position of the array A, maximize the value $i(A \cup_2 h)$. The previous result justifies the values in Table 1, where the configuration $(D \cup_2 h)$, i.e., h must be inserted in the second phenylene of the largest arm of the dendrimer in order to maximize $i(D \cup_2 h)$, as it is illustrated in Fig. 2b, and in the last row in Table 1.

Table 2. Computing the charges for the vertices of the dendrimer case b

Connections	$h_1 \rightarrow$ v_{b3}	$h_i \rightarrow$ v_{b2}	$h_3 \rightarrow$ v_{a3}
Charges	$(13, 5) \rightarrow (18, 13)$	$(13, 5) \rightarrow (18, 13)$	$(13, 5) \rightarrow (18, 13)$

	v_b	v_{b_2}	v_{b_3}	v_{b_4}	v_{b_5}
L_p	$(1, 1) \rightarrow (18, 13) \cdot$	$(2, 1) = (36, 13) \rightarrow$	$(49, 36) \cdot (18, 13) = (882, 468) \rightarrow$	$(1350, 882) \rightarrow$	$(2232, 1350)$
L_s	$(0, 1) \rightarrow (18, 13) \cdot$	$(1, 0) = (18, 0) \rightarrow$	$(18, 18) \cdot (18, 13) = (324, 234) \rightarrow$	$(558, 324) \rightarrow$	$(882, 558)$

	v_{x_6}	v_{y_4}
L_p	$(3582, 2232)$	$(4932, 3582)$
L_s	$(1440, 882)$	

Subtracted rule on $\{v_{x6}, v_{x_i}\}$
$(3582, 2232 - 882) = (3582, 1350)$

	v_{y1}	v_{y_2}	v_{y_3}	v_{y_4}
L_p	$(1, 1) \rightarrow$	$(2, 1) \rightarrow$	$(3, 2) \cdot (18, 13) = (54, 26) \rightarrow$	$(4932, 3582)(80, 54) = (394560, 193428)$
L_s	$(0, 1) \rightarrow$	$(1, 0) \rightarrow$	$(1, 1) \cdot (18, 13) = (18, 13) \rightarrow$	$(4932, 3582)(31, 18) = (152892, 64476)$

	v_{a_5}	v_{a_6}	V_p
L_p	$\rightarrow (587988, 394560) \rightarrow$	$(982548, 587988)$	$(1353168, 982548)$
L_s	$\rightarrow (217368, 152892) \rightarrow$	$(370260, 217368)$	

Subtracted rule on $\{v_{a6}, v_{x_i}\}$
$(982548, 587988 - 217368)$
$= (982548, 370620)$

Furthermore, in [4], it is shown that inserting a new phenylene h in any extremal phenylene of the array, minimizes the M-S index of $i(D \cup h)$. For example, the results in Table 2 show a non maximum nor minimum topological configuration.

6 Conclusion

The Merrifield-Simmons (M-S) index is a crucial tool for analyzing dendrimer structure and properties, offering insights into stability, connectivity, and optimization potential for applications in pharmacology, nanomedicine, and materials science. Quantifying independent vertex sets in molecular graphs provides a measure of structural stability and suitability for drug delivery.

Our study introduces a computational framework with linear complexity for efficiently calculating the M-S index in dendrimers using Fibonacci-based recurrence relations. Our method allows us to recognize extreme configurations, facilitating the analysis of complex structures, an essential task in molecular design and optimization, particularly for drug encapsulation and controlled release.

Beyond drug delivery, the M-S index also enhances understanding of dendrimer topologies, aiding in the design of nanoscale structures for applications in sensing, environmental monitoring, and energy technologies. This research advances interdisciplinary innovation by integrating topological insights into molecular behavior and design.

References

1. Banerjee, A., Roy, A.: Cosine similarity-based algorithms for optimized drug delivery design in dendrimers. Comput. Struct. Biotechnol. J. **20**, 465–479 (2022). https://doi.org/10.1016/j.csbj.2022.01.015

2. Caminade, A.M., Turrin, C.O., Laurent, R., Ouali, A., Delavaux-Nicot, B.: Dendrimers: Towards Catalytic, Material and Biomedical Uses. John Wiley & Sons, Hoboken (2011)
3. Chowdhury, S., Toth, I., Stephenson, R.J.: Dendrimers in vaccine delivery: recent progress and advances. Biomaterials **280**, 121303 (2022)
4. De Ita Luna, G., López, P.B., Contreras González, M., Marcial Romero, J.R.: Extremal graphs for the number of independent sets on polygonal chains joined by cutting edges. Int. J. Comb. Optim. Prob. Inf. **15**(2) (2024)
5. Estrada, E.: Uriarte: recent advances on the role of topological indices in drug discovery research. Curr. Med. Chem. **8**(13), 1573–1588 (2001). https://doi.org/10.2174/0929867013371923
6. Greenhill, C.: The complexity of counting colourings and independent sets in sparse graphs and hypergraphs. Comput. Complex. **9**, 52–72 (2000)
7. Hammer, B.A., Müllen, K.: Expanding the limits of synthetic macromolecular chemistry through polyphenylene dendrimers. J. Nanopart. Res. **20**(10), 262 (2018)
8. Johnson, C., et al.: Impact of core modifications on dendrimer-based drug delivery efficiency. Chem. Rev. **121**, 7451–7498 (2021). https://doi.org/10.1021/acs.chemrev.0c00949
9. Klajnert, B., Peng, L., Cena, V. (eds.): Dendrimers in Biomedical Applications. RSC Publishing, Cambridge (2013)
10. Lee, D.: Graph-based approaches in drug delivery optimization for dendrimers. J. Chem. Phys. **150**, 094102 (2019). https://doi.org/10.1063/1.5085508
11. Liu, J., Cheng, Q.: Dendrimers as gene delivery agents for cancer therapy. Mol. Pharm. **17**(8), 2536–2550 (2020). https://doi.org/10.1021/acs.molpharmaceut.0c00483
12. Menjoge, A.R., Kannan, R.M., Tomalia, D.A.: Dendrimer-based drug and imaging conjugates: design considerations for nanomedical applications. Drug Disc. Today **15**(5–6), 171–185 (2010). https://doi.org/10.1016/j.drudis.2010.01.009
13. Mukherjee, S.: Graph theoretical indices for biological modeling and molecular docking studies of dendrimer drug delivery systems. J. Chem. Inf. Model. **61**(3), 987–1001 (2021). https://doi.org/10.1021/acs.jcim.0c01153
14. Patel, H.: Mathematical indices for nanostructure performance prediction in medicine. Math. Rev. **28**, 200–220 (2021). https://doi.org/10.1016/j.matrev.2020.09.003
15. Smith, J., Doe, J.: Application of merrifield-simmons index in phenylene dendrimers for drug delivery. J. Drug Delivery Syst. **45**(3), 234–240 (2023). https://doi.org/10.1016/j.jdds.2023.02.001
16. Ashwini, T., Narayan, R., Shenoy, P., Nayak, U.: Computational modeling for the design and development of nano based drug delivery systems. J. Molec. Liq. **368**, 120596 (2022). https://doi.org/10.1016/j.molliq.2022.120596
17. Tomalia, D.A., et al.: A new class of polymers: starburst-dendritic macromolecules. Polym. J. **17**(1), 117–132 (1985). https://doi.org/10.1295/polymj.17
18. Xiao, S., Hu, L., Zhang, J., Zheng, Q.: Safety challenges and application strategies for the use of dendrimers in medicine. Pharmaceutics **14**(6), 1292 (2022)
19. Yamamoto, T.: Dendrimers for theranostics: molecular design, properties, and applications in drug delivery and bioimaging. Adv. Drug Deliv. Rev. **156**, 41–65 (2020). https://doi.org/10.1016/j.addr.2019.12.002
20. Zhu, J., Shi, X.: Dendrimer-based nanodevices for targeted drug delivery applications. J. Mater. Chem. B **1**, 4199–4211 (2013). https://doi.org/10.1039/C3TB20724B

Tailoring Bounded Instances for the Job Shop Scheduling Problem Through Unified Particle Swarm Optimization

Alonso Vela Morales[1], José Carlos Ortiz-Bayliss[1], Jorge M. Cruz-Duarte[2], and Ivan Amaya[1](✉)

[1] Tecnologico de Monterrey, School of Engineering and Sciences, 64700 Monterrey, Mexico
{a00815751,jcobayliss,iamaya2}@tec.mx

[2] Université de Lille, CNRS, Inria, Centrale Lille, UMR 9189 CRIStAL, 59000 Lille, France
jorge.cruz-duarte@univ-lille.fr

Abstract. This work proposes bounded instances for the Job Shop Scheduling Problem that we tailored using Unified Particle Swarm Optimization. We developed and evaluated 2000 specialized instances across five sizes to evaluate heuristic performance under controlled, unbiased conditions. Our primary objective is to mitigate the inherent biases of random instances that favor specific heuristics. Our three-phase methodology begins by determining a suitable delta value, generating instances, and analyzing their features. The results indicate compliance with the delta values and balanced heuristic performance. This framework enhances the fairness of algorithm benchmarking and provides a basis for research in solver selection, metaheuristics, and adaptive learning in combinatorial optimization.

Keywords: Combinatorial Optimization · Job Shop Scheduling · Particle Swarm Optimization · Instance Generation

1 Introduction

Optimization problems are crucial in modern research, with applications in various real-world scenarios [1]. The Job Shop Scheduling Problem (JSSP) is particularly challenging due to its NP-hard nature [11]. JSSP involves task allocation across machines to minimize the makespan [12].

Since exact methods are unfeasible for large instances, research has turned to approximated ones. Heuristics offer practical solutions despite lacking optimality guarantees [6]. Algorithm portfolios and selection hyper-heuristics further improve solver performance by choosing the best-fit approach per instance [4].

This work was supported by the research group from the strategic initiative in artificial intelligence at Tecnologico de Monterrey, NUA A00815751.

A. P. López-Monroy et al. (Eds.): MCPR 2025, LNCS 15715, pp. 36–45, 2025.
https://doi.org/10.1007/978-3-031-96255-4_4

However, JSSP remains challenging due to its sensitivity to instance characteristics, which affect heuristic performance [10]. Traditional heuristics, such as Largest Processing Time (LPT) and Shortest Processing Time (SPT) exhibit biases, making it difficult to develop robust algorithms. To address this, we expand on our previous work on JSSP instance generation [13] by using Unified Particle Swarm Optimization (UPSO). This time, we focus on bounded instances with standardized performance gaps across heuristics. We aim to reduce heuristic bias and ensure fair evaluation by creating five instance sets. The remainder of this manuscript is structured as follows: Sect. 2 outlines key concepts. Section 3 details our methodology. Section 4 presents our findings. Finally, Sect. 5 summarizes key insights.

2 Fundamentals

2.1 Job Shop Scheduling Problem

The Job Shop Scheduling Problem (JSSP) is fundamental in operations research, encompassing variations like Flexible, Open, and Flow Shop [14]. This work focuses on the traditional JSSP, where each job follows a sequence of operations assigned to specific machines, aiming to minimize the makespan while considering metrics like tardiness, flow time, and idle time. There are diverse approaches for solving a JSSP instance, including dispatching rules [7], Evolutionary Algorithms [2], and other metaheuristics [5]. We can characterize a JSSP instance using different features, as reviewed by Mirshekarian and Sormaz [8]. There are diverse benchmarks for the JSSP, including those from Taillard and the JSPLIB[1]. However, such instances are oftentimes based on random sampling, which differs from the real nature of instances. So, tailoring instances to solvers is emerging as an alternative that enables customized benchmarks for more robust evaluations [13].

2.2 Instance Generator

In previous research, we proposed a generator to tailor JSSP instances to low-level heuristics [13]. Our approach uses a metaheuristic to solve the inverse problem of identifying the problem instance that satisfies a given behavior. This is achieved by iterating over the search domain, which is defined by each operation's the processing time and target machine of each operation. So, a problem instance with N_j jobs and N_o operations is linked to $2 \times N_j \times N_o$ variables. The solution space is infinite since the processing time can be a real value. However, this also allows one to tailor instances to specific needs. Vectorizing all the design variables encodes an instance to a search agent within the optimizer. Conversely, the value found by a search agent can be reshaped into values for each variable.

[1] https://github.com/tamy0612/JSPLIB.

2.3 Specialized Instances

In the context of this work, a specialized instance is one that has been tailored to a specific heuristic based on an objective function. Since space restrictions forbid us from elaborating on the definitions, it shall suffice to say that an unbounded instance is a specialized instance for which we do not impose any restrictions on the performance of standalone heuristics. In other words, an unbounded instance is generated by minimizing either Eq. (1) or Eq. (2). In the first case, the unbounded instance favors heuristic h_1. In the second case, it hinders it. Here, $c_{\max}(s|h_i)$ is the makespan of the schedule yielded by heuristic h_i.

$$\mathfrak{F}_1 = c_{\max}(s|h_1) - \inf\{\forall h_i \in \mathcal{H}\backslash h_1 : c_{\max}(s|h_i)\} \tag{1}$$

$$\mathfrak{F}_2 = \sup\{\forall h_i \in \mathcal{H}\backslash h_1 : c_{\max}(s|h_i)\} - c_{\max}(s|h_1) \tag{2}$$

Since we have no control over the performance gaps that can be achieved, we can define a target makespan difference ($\Delta \in \mathbb{R}_+$). This leads to Eq. (3) and (4), where the global minimum (zero) represents an instance with the desired performance gap. More details are provided by Vela et al. [13].

$$\mathfrak{F}_3 = (\mathfrak{F}_1 - \Delta)^2 \tag{3}$$

$$\mathfrak{F}_4 = (\mathfrak{F}_2 - \Delta)^2 \tag{4}$$

2.4 Unified Particle Swarm Optimization (UPSO)

UPSO appeared in 2004 as an extension of the original proposal from Eberhart and Kennedy [9]. The extension defines neighborhoods of search agents (particles) that act as small swarms and integrates information with a balancing equation. So, the position of an agent, $\boldsymbol{x}_a^{t+1}$, is updated via Eq. (5), where $\boldsymbol{v}_a^{t+1}$ represents its updated velocity. In turn, the updated velocity depends on the local and global components of the agent $\boldsymbol{l}_a$ and $\boldsymbol{g}_a$, respectively, and the unification factor u, as shown in Eq. (6).

$$\boldsymbol{x}_a^{t+1} = \boldsymbol{x}_a^t + \boldsymbol{v}_a^{t+1} \tag{5}$$

$$\boldsymbol{v}_a^{t+1} = (1-u)\boldsymbol{l}_a + u\boldsymbol{g}_a \tag{6}$$

Nonetheless, both components are velocity measurements of the particle, as indicated in Eq. (7) and (8). Here, ϕ_1 and ϕ_2 are coefficients, and $\boldsymbol{r}_i \in \mathbb{R}^{N_d}$ are random vectors between zero and one. Additionally, $\odot$ is the Hadamard product and χ is the constriction factor [3]. Finally, $\boldsymbol{x}_{a,*}$, $\boldsymbol{x}_{n,*}$, and $\boldsymbol{x}_*$ are the best position for each particle, neighborhood, and the swarm, respectively.

$$\boldsymbol{g}_a = \chi\left(\boldsymbol{v}_a^t + \phi_1\boldsymbol{r}_1 \odot (\boldsymbol{x}_{a,*} - \boldsymbol{x}_a^t) + \phi_2\boldsymbol{r}_2 \odot (\boldsymbol{x}_* - \boldsymbol{x}_a^t)\right) \tag{7}$$

$$\boldsymbol{l}_a = \chi\left(\boldsymbol{v}_a^t + \phi_1\boldsymbol{r}_3 \odot (\boldsymbol{x}_{a,*} - \boldsymbol{x}_a^t) + \phi_2\boldsymbol{r}_4 \odot (\boldsymbol{x}_{n,*} - \boldsymbol{x}_a^t)\right) \tag{8}$$

2.5 Heuristics

We explore the performance of four heuristics for the Job Shop Scheduling Problem (JSSP). Each heuristic selects feasible tasks, *i.e.* they choose from the set of permissible operations for each job. We include two heuristics based on the activity processing times: one that schedules the operation with the Longest Processing Time (LPT) and one that selects the operation with the Shortest Processing Time (SPT). We also incorporate two heuristics to determine the number of pending operations within jobs. Thus, MPA follows a breadth-first approach, scheduling the job with the Most Pending Activities. In contrast, LPA employs a depth-first strategy, scheduling the job with the Least Pending Activities. In the case of ties, the heuristics schedule the job with the lowest ID.

2.6 Features

We incorporated five features from those identified by Mirshekarian *et al.* [8]. Since the names are too complex, we followed the naming convention proposed by Vela *et al.* [13]. We refer to them as *Mirsh222*, *Mirsh15*, *Mirsh29*, *Mirsh282*, and *Mirsh95*. Such features are related to the dynamics of the problem instead of heuristic performance. This supports our goal of evaluating heuristics on a leveled playing field, free from predispositions embedded within the feature set.

3 Methodology

Our main objective is to tailor sets of instances with different sizes for the selected heuristics. For this, we followed a three-phase methodology. First, we identify an adequate Δ for each set of instances, seeking a balanced performance. In the second phase, we tailor 2000 instances based on the selected delta values. The final phase analyzes the tailored instances to determine whether they meet the intended performance criteria across all heuristics. All experiments consider the following UPSO parameters: $N_a = 10$, $\phi_1 = 2.5$, $\phi_2 = 2.5$, and $u = 0.9$.

3.1 Fixed Delta

Since we aim to equalize performance across heuristics, we must identify a delta value that works for all of them. This means that the performance gap associated with all instances of the same size must be equivalent. So, we first tailor 120 unbounded instances for each heuristic, considering five jobs, five machines, five operations, and time ranges between 1 and 100 units. Then, we assess the performance of each heuristic for its respective set, using Eq. (1). We repeat this process for the remaining sizes. We finally choose the largest delta value for each instance set that is achievable by all heuristics.

3.2 Bounded Tailoring

In this phase, we tailor 100 instances for each heuristic and consider five different instances sizes. This leads to 2000 specialized bounded instances. To accomplish this, we generate a large pool of potential instances to account for variability. We evaluate each instance using Eq. (3) and preserve those within an error margin of 5%.

3.3 Analysis and Inspection

Our analysis begins by solving each instance with all the heuristics to verify the uniformity and fairness of the instance distribution. Following, we examine how feature values evolve within some of the instances. This involves comparing pre- and post-solution feature states to understand the impact of heuristic operations on the instances. This sheds light on the dynamics of instance features with different heuristics and can help pinpoint areas for further refinement in instance or heuristic design.

4 Results

We now present the most relevant data associated with our work. We preserve the same structure from Sect. 3 for clarity. Note that all instances are freely available at https://github.com/iamaya2/BaseInstances/tree/master/JobShopScheduling/files/mat/Instances/Tailored.

4.1 Fixed Delta

Figure 1 shows the performance for four sets of 120 specialized instances and with a size of five jobs and five machines (*J5M5*). Each set favors a given heuristic, as the texts above the shaded regions indicate. When the LPT heuristic (LPTvsAll) is favored, the performance gap ranges from 100 to 300 units. However, when favoring the SPT heuristic (SPTvsAll), the range broadens and goes up to 400 units. Still, the largest delta is achieved when favoring the MPA heuristic (MPAvsAll), as it takes values between 300 and 600 units. This significant discrepancy highlights the ability of the MPA heuristic to outperform other alternatives. Finally, instances favoring the LPA heuristic (LPAvsAll) do not exhibit a noteworthy trend, yielding the smallest performance gaps. A delta of 150 units can be consistently achieved across different sets, providing a standardized baseline.

Figure 2 shows the performance of unbounded instances for the remaining sizes. Remarkably, MPA consistently outperformed the other heuristics, with performance gaps ranging from 100 to 1000 units. This highlights the robustness of MPA. In contrast, LPA often established the lowest performance boundary. This trend hints that it might be difficult to generate instances where MPA underperforms or significantly favors LPA. Moreover, this pattern could indicate inherent heuristic strengths and weaknesses, highlighting the need for a

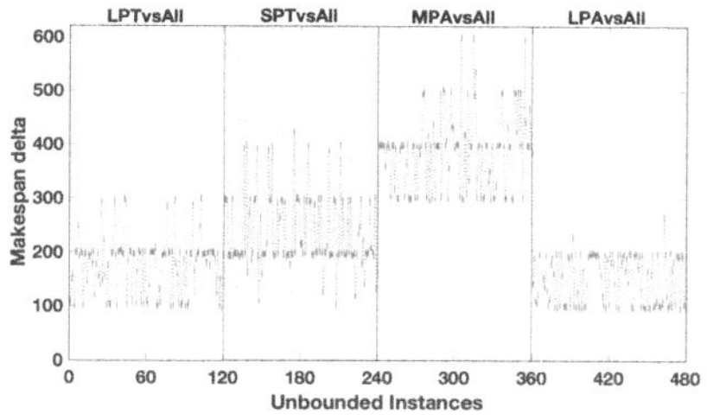

Fig. 1. Performance gap for unbounded JSLI1 instances favoring heuristics.

deeper analysis of how specific job and machine configurations affect heuristic performance. It also points to the potential limitations of LPA in complex scheduling environments, suggesting areas for further heuristic refinement or the development of new strategies, such as hyper-heuristics, that could complement or enhance the existing methods. After analyzing the data, we selected the Δ values shown in Table 1. Note that the values are related to the size of the instances, particularly the number of machines. As the instance becomes more complex, so does Δ, suggesting that larger configurations pose greater flexibility in maintaining performance equity among heuristics.

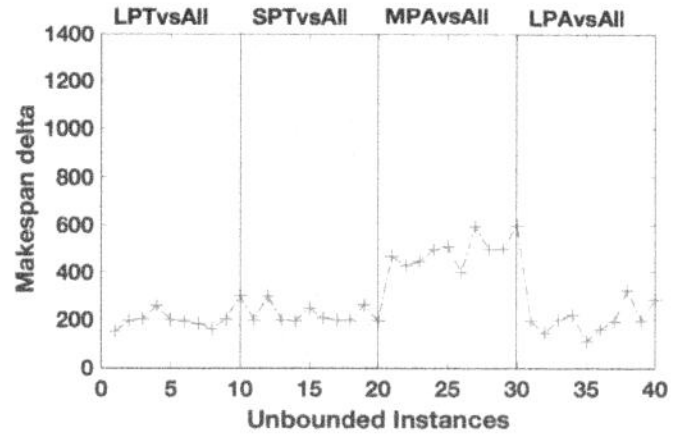

(a) JSLI2

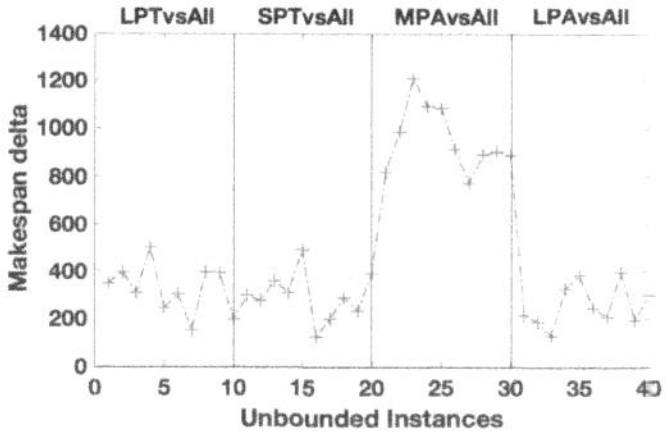

(b) JSLI3

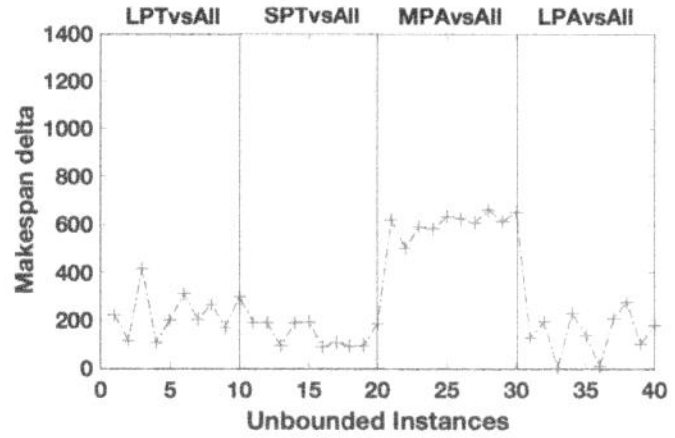

(c) JSLI4

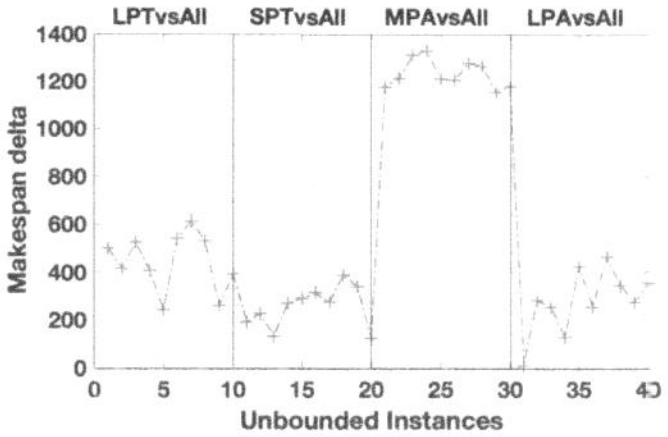

(d) JSLI5

Fig. 2. Performance gap for different sets of unbounded instances.

Table 1. Sets of instances tailored in this work, their size, and relevant data.

Instance Set	Jobs	Machines	Operations	Time Ranges	Δ	Reps
JSLI1	5	5	5	1–100	150	980
JSLI2	10	5	5	1–100	200	700
JSLI3	10	10	10	1–100	300	1070
JSLI4	20	5	5	1–100	200	1070
JSLI5	20	10	10	1–100	300	1120

4.2 Bounded Tailoring

When we set out to tailor 400 instances for each set and with the given Δ, we noticed that not all instances met the expectation, leading to additional tailoring. In Table 1, the column *Reps* indicates the total number of instances tailored for a given size to meet the quota. Note that larger instances and higher Δs need more repetitions since the problem is more complex.

Figure 3 shows a heatmap with normalized makespan values (per column) for 800 instances (those from JSLI1 and JSLI5). Each row provides the makespan achieved by each heuristic. In contrast, each column provides the makespan yielded by each heuristic for a given instance. A value of zero (blue sections) indicates the smallest makespan, *i.e.* the solution that a synthetic oracle would provide. Note the "blue ladder" pattern, which demonstrates the varying dominance of each heuristic across different segments of both sets of instances. As requested, this confirms the generator's ability to achieve balanced heuristic performance.

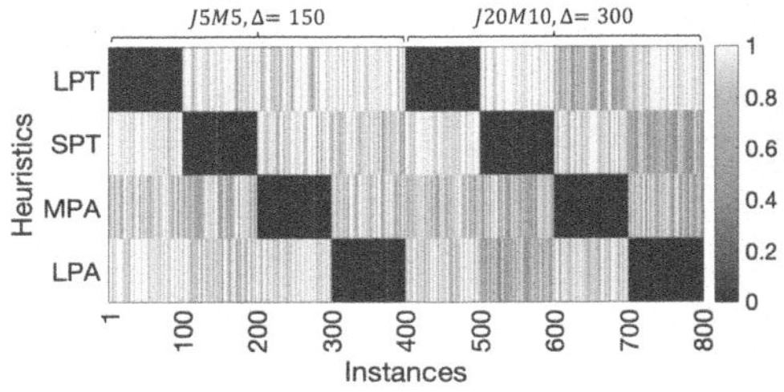

Fig. 3. Normalized makespan (per column) for two sets of bounded instances.

4.3 Analysis and Inspection

Figure 4 shows the performance of each heuristic and a synthetic oracle for each instance set. Data are mostly equally distributed, supporting that performance is balanced across all sets and heuristics. The gap between heuristics and the oracle means that these heuristics are not good enough to solve the generated sets by themselves. The oracle offers an improved solution that ranges between 5% and 18%. This hints at the need for a higher-level approach for solving each specific group of instances, *e.g.* a hyper-heuristic.

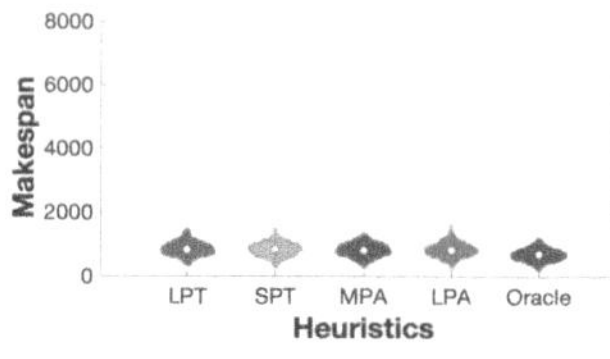

(a) JSLI1, $\Delta = 200$

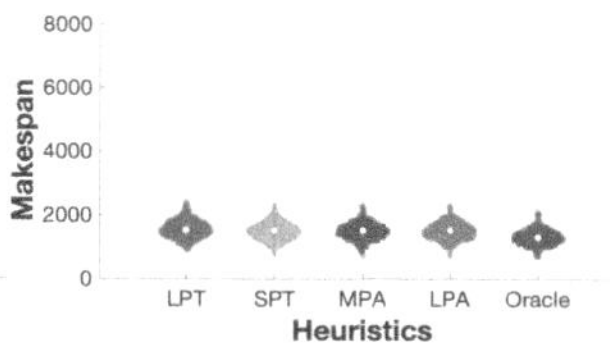

(b) JSLI2, $\Delta = 200$

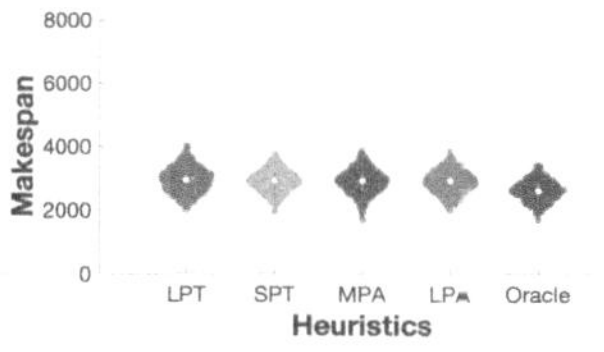

(c) JSLI3, $\Delta = 300$

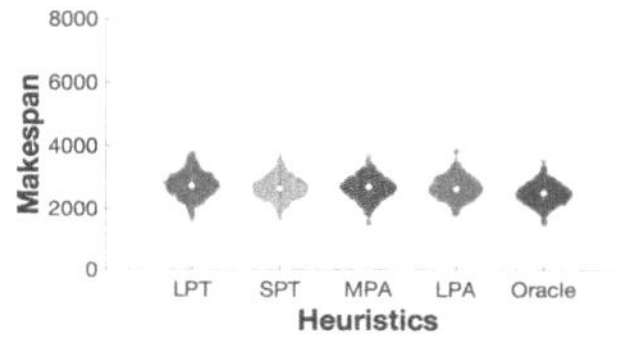

(d) JSLI4, $\Delta = 200$

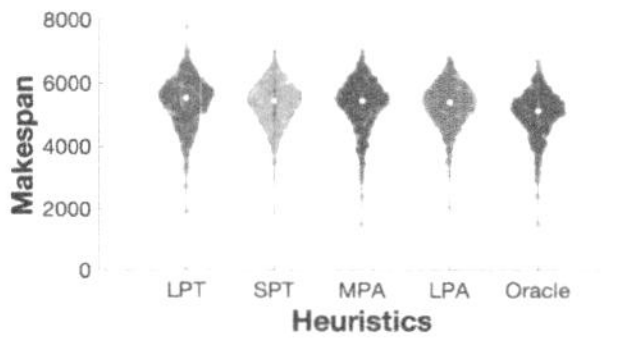

(e) JSLI5, $\Delta = 300$

Fig. 4. Performance distribution for each set of bounded instances.

Figure 5 presents two scatter plots, each illustrating the distribution of 200 instances from the JSLI1 set and for a subset of features (*Mirsh29* and *Mirsh282*). Both visualizations reveal distinct clusters, which suggests that there are inherent differences in the characteristics of instances. Such insights are crucial for developing targeted optimization strategies that leverage the strengths of different heuristics.

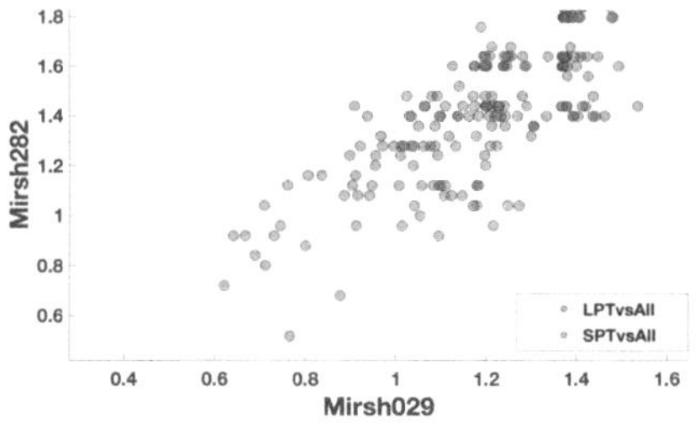

(a) LPTvsAll — SPTvsAll

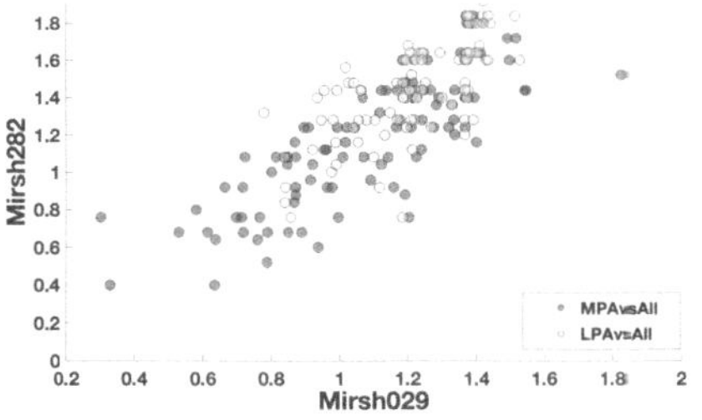

(b) MPAvsAll — LPAvsAll

Fig. 5. Feature distribution for subsets of bounded JSLI1 instances.

Figure 6 shows the evolution of the selected features when solving a JSLI1 instance that favors the LPT heuristic. Although the overall feature evolution is somewhat consistent across heuristics, some differences are evident. Features *Mirsh15*, *Mirsh29*, and *Mirsh282* exhibit an increasing trend, whereas *Mirsh222* and *Mirsh95* show a decreasing one. Figure 6b shows that *Mirsh15* displays a more independent trail for the LPT heuristic. Similarly, Fig. 6a and 6b demonstrate a pronounced divergence in the final values for the MPA heuristic, while early-stage feature divergences are visible in Fig. 6d and 6e. Also, Fig. 6c shows a broader range of responses across heuristics. These observations emphasize the relevance of feature dynamics in developing problem-solving strategies that rely on heuristic characterization.

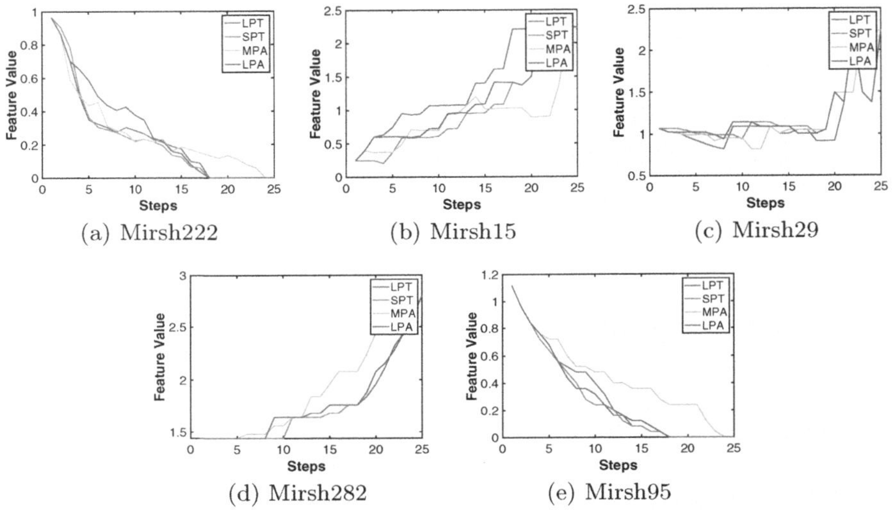

Fig. 6. Feature evolution for a single JSLI1 instance and different solvers.

5 Conclusions

Our work tailored instances for heuristics of the Job Shop Scheduling Problem (JSSP). We successfully generated and analyzed 2000 instances for five different sizes through a three-phase methodology.

Our findings reveal that the selected delta values ensured that no single heuristic consistently outperformed others, enabling an equitable assessment of heuristic performance while neutralizing the inherent biases typically observed with randomly generated sets.

In conclusion, this work sets a foundation for fairer testing of algorithms in scheduling problems and paves the way for research on solver generalization and adaptive learning strategies.

Future research could focus on exploring more sophisticated methods of instance tailoring. Potential avenues include exploring different problem environments, applying machine learning techniques to predict heuristic performance based on instance features, or developing adaptive instance generators that dynamically adjust based on heuristic feedback.

References

1. Ben-Tal, A., Den Hertog, D., De Waegenaere, A., Melenberg, B., Rennen, G.: Robust solutions of optimization problems affected by uncertain probabilities. Manag. Sci. **59**(2), 341–357 (2013)
2. Cheng, T.C., Peng, B., Lü, Z.: A hybrid evolutionary algorithm to solve the job shop scheduling problem. Ann. Oper. Res. **242**(2), 223–237 (2016)
3. Clerc, M., Kennedy, J.: The particle swarm - explosion, stability, and convergence in a multidimensional complex space. IEEE Trans. Evol. Comput. **6**(1), 58–73 (2002)
4. Drake, J.H., Kheiri, A., Özcan, E., Burke, E.K.: Recent advances in selection hyper-heuristics. Eur. J. Oper. Res. **285**(2), 405–428 (2020)
5. Gao, L., Li, X., Wen, X., Lu, C., Wen, F.: A hybrid algorithm based on a new neighborhood structure evaluation method for job shop scheduling problem. Comput. Ind. Eng. **88**, 417–429 (2015)
6. Lara-Cárdenas, E., Silva-Gálvez, A., Ortiz-Bayliss, J.C., Amaya, I., Cruz-Duarte, J.M., Terashima-Marín, H.: Exploring reward-based hyper-heuristics for the job-shop scheduling problem. In: 2020 IEEE Symposium Series on Computational Intelligence (SSCI), pp. 1–8 (2020)
7. Mencía, C., Sierra, M.R., Varela, R.: Depth-first heuristic search for the job shop scheduling problem. Ann. Oper. Res. **206**(1), 265–296 (2013)
8. Mirshekarian, S., Šormaz, D.N.: Correlation of job-shop scheduling problem features with scheduling efficiency. Expert Syst. Appl. **62**, 131–147 (2016)
9. Parsopoulos, K., Vrahatis, M.: UPSO: a unified particle swarm optimization scheme. In: International Conference of Computational Methods in Sciences and Engineering 2004 (ICCMSE 2004) (January), pp. 868–873 (2019)
10. Pinedo, M.L.: Scheduling: Theory, Algorithms, and Systems, 4th edn. Springer, New York (2016)
11. Sanchez, M., Cruz-Duarte, J.M., Ortiz-Bayliss, J.C., Ceballos, H., Terashima-Marin, H., Amaya, I.: A systematic review of hyper-heuristics on combinatorial optimization problems. IEEE Access **8**, 128068–128095 (2020)
12. Taha, H.A.: Operations Research: An Introduction, 10th edn. Pearson, New York (2017)
13. Vela, A., Cruz-Duarte, J.M., Ortiz-Bayliss, J.C., Amaya, I.: Tailoring job shop scheduling problem instances through unified particle swarm optimization. IEEE Access **9**, 66891–66914 (2021)
14. Vela, A., Valencia-Rivera, G.H., Cruz-Duarte, J.M., Ortiz-Bayliss, J.C., Amaya, I.: Hyper-heuristics and scheduling problems: strategies, application areas, and performance metrics. IEEE Access **13**, 14983–14997 (2025)

Empirical Comparison of Density-Based Clustering Algorithms for Large Datasets

Adrián J. Ramírez-Díaz(✉), José Fco. Martínez-Trinidad, and J. Ariel Carrasco-Ochoa

Instituto Nacional de Astrofísica, Óptica y Electrónica, Luis Enrique Erro # 1, Tonantzintla, 72840 Puebla, Mexico
{aramirez,fmartine,ariel}@inaoep.mx

Abstract. Density-based clustering is a technique that can build clusters with arbitrary shapes while filtering noise, making it useful in diverse applications. The increasing volume of data generated by modern systems has driven the development of density-based clustering algorithms capable of handling large datasets. These algorithms employ methods that reduce object comparisons, reducing runtime without compromising clustering quality. Achieving a good balance between quality and runtime is crucial, as it determines the algorithm's applicability to real-world problems where both accuracy and runtime are critical. However, to our knowledge, there is no comparison of recent clustering algorithms under the same framework. This work presents an empirical comparison of five density-based clustering algorithms. The comparison framework ensures a fair evaluation by implementing all algorithms with the same data structures and methods. Public standard datasets are used to assess clustering quality and runtime performance. Our results report the algorithm that achieves the best runtime, the highest clustering quality, and a good trade-off between these two factors, providing valuable insights for selecting the most suitable method for large-scale data processing.

Keywords: Clustering · Large datasets · Density-Based Clustering

1 Introduction

The clustering technique divides datasets into clusters, where objects within the same cluster are similar to each other and distinct from those in other clusters [10,13]. Due to its broad applicability, clustering is widely used, leading to the development of various algorithms capable of handling different types of data, including large datasets [6]. These algorithms have been classified into partitioning, hierarchical and density-based algorithms [3].

Density-based clustering identifies clusters as high-density regions separated by lower-density areas, which allows, filtering noise and detecting clusters with arbitrary shapes [5]. In recent years, several algorithms have been developed to implement density-based clustering by integrating techniques for efficiently handling large-scale data. Among these algorithms are S-DBSCAN [16], Improved

A. P. López-Monroy et al. (Eds.): MCPR 2025, LNCS 15715, pp. 46–55, 2025.
https://doi.org/10.1007/978-3-031-96255-4_5

KMEANS [15], K-DBSCAN [9], KNN-BLOCK DBSCAN [8], and RS-DBSCAN [7], all of which are density-based clustering algorithms designed for large datasets.

The strategies employed by the aforementioned algorithms to process large datasets are different, as do the techniques they use to build clusters. Therefore, the purpose of this research is to conduct an empirical evaluation of these algorithms in order to assess their performance in terms of quality and runtime, under the same framework.

The remainder of this paper is structured as follows. Section 2 describes the density-based clustering algorithms for large datasets used in our study. Section 3 details the experimental design. The results of the experiments are presented and discussed in Sect. 4. Finally, Sect. 5 discusses the conclusions and future work.

2 Clustering Algorithms Under Study

This section describes some of the most recent density-based algorithms for large datasets included in this study: S-DBSCAN, Improved KMEANS, K-DBSCAN, KNN-BLOCK DBSCAN, and RS-DBSCAN. First, the DBSCAN algorithm is described, as it provides the foundation and key concepts the analyzed algorithms employ.

DBSCAN is one of the most widely used density-based clustering algorithms; however, it is unsuitable for large datasets due to the number of object-to-object comparisons required. Nevertheless, DBSCAN defines many of the concepts utilized by recent algorithms. Like other clustering algorithms, DBSCAN compares two objects using a function that measures their dissimilarity, typically employing metrics such as the Euclidean distance. To define the density of a region, DBSCAN uses two parameters: epsilon (ϵ), which sets the maximum dissimilarity between two objects to be considered neighbors, and $minPts$, which defines the minimum number of objects required for a region to be classified as dense. DBSCAN classifies each object as core, border, or noise to build clusters. It then combines core and border objects using their neighborhoods to create clusters.

S-DBSCAN [16] was proposed to adapt DBSCAN to large datasets. SDBSCAN uses three phases: Partitioning, Processing, and Combining to do this. The Partitioning phase divides the dataset into P parts, each created randomly, ensuring all parts have similar sizes. In the second phase, each part is clustered with DBSCAN, using the same parameters ϵ and $minPts$ for all partitions. The resulting clusters are called partial clusters. The third phase merges the partial clusters. The distance between each pair of clusters within the same partition is calculated, and the minimum distance d_{min} for each partition is obtained. Next, the global minimum distance D_{min} is determined from the list of partial d_{min} distances. Finally, clusters whose centroid distance is less than D_{min} are merged.

Improved K-Means [15] combines partition-based and density-based algorithms in a hybrid approach to processing large datasets, enabling it to build clusters with arbitrary shapes. Improved K-Means processes large datasets by randomly selecting a small, representative sample of the dataset, with the sample size defined by the user. For each object in the sample, its neighborhood is determined using the parameter ϵ. Objects having more than $minPts$ neighbors (a dense neighborhood), become the initial clusters. These clusters are merged based on the distances between their centroids and the farthest objects within each cluster. Then, the algorithm groups the remaining objects outside the sample. Each object is either classified into one of the existing clusters or used to create a new cluster. The process continues until all objects are clustered.

K-DBSCAN [9], proposed by its authors in 2021, combines the KMeans++ [1] and DBSCAN algorithms to cluster large datasets. The algorithm consists of three phases; in the first phase, the dataset is partitioned using KMeans++, an algorithm that iteratively refines clusters by selecting centroids based on object distribution. Unlike standard KMeans++, K-DBSCAN does not require full convergence before proceeding. In the second phase, K-DBSCAN processes the partitions using DBSCAN with the same ϵ and $minPts$ values for all partitions. Finally, in the last phase, the resulting clusters from each partition are combined. Their distances are evaluated using their centroids and farthest objects to determine whether two clusters can be merged. If the clusters meet the criteria for merging, DBSCAN is applied again to analyze and refine the clusters.

KNN-BLOCK DBSCAN [8], proposed in 2021, enhances DBSCAN by improving clustering quality and accelerating the processing of large datasets. First, it partitions the dataset using a modified K-nearest neighbors algorithm, FLANN [17]. This method groups objects into units called blocks, based on the parameter ϵ. After partitioning, each block is classified into one of three categories: core-blocks, non-core-blocks, or noise-blocks. This classification is determined using the parameter $minPts$ and the block density. In the final stage, the classified blocks are combined to build clusters. Core-blocks connected through shared objects are merged into the same cluster. Objects in non-core-blocks are then assigned to the closest cluster, and objects that do not fit into any cluster are discarded as noise. Finally, objects in noise-blocks are marked as noise. KNN-BLOCK DBSCAN builds the clusters by identifying density peaks, based on the idea that the cluster centers should have a higher density.

The RS-DBSCAN algorithm [7], introduced in 2024, builds on earlier approaches by combining sampling and partitioning strategies to handle large datasets. First, the algorithm extracts P random samples of size s. Each sample is an independent subset. Each sample is processed using the RNN-DBSCAN algorithm [4]. Unlike DBSCAN, RNN-DBSCAN does not require specifying ϵ and $minPts$; instead, it relies solely on the parameter k, representing the number of nearest neighbors. After processing the samples, a representative object is build for each cluster, with its centroid and the mean, minimum, and maximum objects-to-centroid distances. The representative objects are then grouped using RNN-DBSCAN, producing a set of global clusters. The final step assigns each object in the dataset to a representative object and, consequently, to the cluster associated with that object.

3 Experimental Design

This section describes the design of the experiments to evaluate the performance of density-based clustering algorithms regarding quality and runtime.

3.1 Metrics

External metrics (which rely on ground-truth labels) are commonly used to evaluate the quality of density-based clustering algorithms. In our experiments, two of the most used external metrics in the literature were employed: Adjusted Rand Index (ARI) [11] and Adjusted Mutual Information (AMI) [18]. In the runtime experiments, only processing times were measured, excluding reading and writing operations.

3.2 Datasets

Our experiment evaluates clustering quality using ten synthetic datasets, widely used in the literature for assessing density-based clustering algorithms, sourced from Tomas Barton's repository [2]. Additionally, we employed ten larger datasets from the UCI Machine Learning repository [14], which exhibit diversity in dimensions and object counts, to assess runtime performance.

Table 1 describes the datasets used in the quality and runtime experiments. This table includes the dataset name, the number of objects, the dimensionality of each object, the experiments in which the dataset is used, and the parameters ($\epsilon, minPts$) that, according to the literature, have reported good results assessing density-based algorithms such as DBSCAN [9,12,19].

3.3 Parameter Tuning

S-DBSCAN uses three parameters: ϵ, $minPts$, and P. The parameters ϵ and $minPts$ are the same as in DBSCAN, while P defines the number of partitions. Improved K-Means also uses ϵ and $minPts$ but introduces an additional parameter, S, to specify the sample size. K-DBSCAN employs the same three parameters as S-DBSCAN. KNN-BLOCK DBSCAN requires only ϵ and $minPts$, using these to partition the dataset. RS-DBSCAN differs as it does not rely on ϵ or $minPts$. Instead, it uses P (the number of partitions) and two parameters for the nearest neighbors, k_1 and k_2, where k_1 is used to analyze the partitions and k_2 to combine them. The authors suggest that k values can be set similarly to $minPts$.

Table 1 shows the recommended ϵ and $minPts$ values for each dataset based on prior studies, as these datasets are commonly used to evaluate density-based clustering algorithms. The quality experiments were conducted using these values. In partition-based algorithms (S-DBSCAN, K-DBSCAN, and RS-DBSCAN), two partitions were created for each dataset ($P = 2$) since larger values often result in excessive noise labeling. Sample-based algorithms used a 50%

Table 1. Datasets and parameter settings used to evaluate density-based clustering algorithms.

Dataset	Objects	Dimensions	Usage	Epsilon(ϵ)	$MinPts$
Flame	240	2	Quality	6	1.0
Pathbased	300	2	Quality	4	1.0
Jain	373	2	Quality	3	2.9
Compound	399	2	Quality	5	1.0
R15	600	2	Quality	3	0.3
Aggregation	788	2	Quality	6	1.21
2G_unbalance	1050	2	Quality	7	0.1
Complex8	2551	2	Quality	4	14.89
Complex9	3031	2	Quality	5	12.1
Cluto-t4-8k	8000	2	Quality	10	9.5
Abalone	4177	8	Runtime	4	0.035
Dry_beam	13611	16	Runtime	4	0.16
Gas-drift	13910	128	Runtime	5	0.4
Letter	20000	16	Runtime	4	0.35
Nomao	34465	118	Runtime	5	1.98
Statlog (Shuttle)	58000	9	Runtime	5	0.02
Accelerometer	153000	4	Runtime	4	0.065
Skin Segmentation	245057	3	Runtime	4	0.01
3D Road Network	434874	4	Runtime	4	0.01
Poker-hand	1000000	10	Runtime	8	0.25

sample size, corresponding to analyzing a single partition from two. For nearest-neighbor parameters in RS-DBSCAN, k_1 and k_2 were set equal to $minPts$, as recommended by its authors.

The recommended ϵ and $minPts$ values for runtime experiments were also used for each dataset; however, the number of partitions was fixed based on the dataset size. The number of partitions was set to $P \approx \sqrt{n}$, where n is the dataset size. This partitioning approach is used in [9] for this type of evaluation. Samples were also adjusted according to dataset size, selecting 10% of the data. For nearest-neighbor parameters in RS-DBSCAN, k_1 and k_2 were again set equal to $minPts$, following the authors' recommendations.

4 Experiments and Results

This section presents the results of empirically comparing the density-based clustering algorithms for large datasets included in our study, as explained in the previous section. For a fair comparison between the analyzed algorithms, we implemented each of them in Python. The experiments were performed on a computer with two Intel Xeon E5-2620 processors at 2.40GHz, 256 GB of RAM, and Linux Ubuntu 22.

4.1 Clustering Quality Results

For each algorithm, tests were conducted using the parameters described in the previous section. The resulting clusters from each test were evaluated using the ARI and AMI metrics. Table 2 displays the results obtained from assessing the clustering produced by each algorithm across different datasets. The algorithm with the highest score in each metric is highlighted for each dataset. The table also includes each algorithm's mean and standard deviation across the datasets.

Table 2. Clustering Quality results using ARI and AMI metrics.

DATASET	IKMEANS		RSDBSCAN		KDBSCAN		SDBSCAN		KNNBLOCK	
	ARI	AMI	ARI	AMI	ARI	AMI	ARI	AMI	ARI	AMI
2Gunbalance	−0.010	0.036	−0.058	0.028	**0.857**	**0.837**	0.726	0.702	0.752	0.729
aggregation	0.224	0.442	0.692	0.826	0.752	0.827	0.681	0.737	**0.954**	**0.941**
cluto-t4-8k	0.135	0.334	0.574	0.652	0.017	0.085	0.565	0.690	**0.865**	**0.871**
complex8	0.056	0.241	0.138	0.590	**0.988**	**0.982**	0.560	0.726	0.945	0.943
complex9	0.149	0.372	0.161	0.630	**0.946**	**0.950**	0.266	0.638	0.923	0.957
compound	0.220	0.389	0.467	0.692	0.628	0.629	0.426	0.646	**0.877**	**0.867**
Flame	0.098	0.294	0.394	0.499	0.019	0.028	0.155	0.290	**0.796**	**0.732**
Jain	0.069	0.176	0.099	0.360	0.010	0.007	**0.692**	**0.529**	0.234	0.429
pathbased	0.108	0.223	0.281	0.442	0.352	0.397	0.096	0.312	**0.388**	**0.495**
R15	0.062	0.341	**0.919**	**0.959**	0.313	0.648	0.791	0.857	0.808	0.875
Mean	0.111	0.285	0.367	0.568	0.488	0.539	0.496	0.613	**0.754**	**0.784**
Std. Dev.	**0.074**	**0.119**	0.302	0.258	0.395	0.384	0.248	0.184	0.245	0.188

According the results shown in Table 2, KNN-BLOCK-DBSCAN achieved the highest scores in five datasets, outperforming the other algorithms. K-DBSCAN ranked second, obtaining the best results in three datasets. RS-DBSCAN and S-DBSCAN each achieved the highest score in one dataset. Lastly, Improved K-Means had the lowest ARI and AMI scores across all datasets. KNN-BLOCK-DBSCAN obtained the highest mean scores, followed by S-DBSCAN, K-DBSCAN, RS-DBSCAN, and finally, Improved K-Means. KNN-BLOCK-DBSCAN obtained a low standard deviation similar to S-DBSCAN's, but the latter had worse quality results. K-DBSCAN got a higher standard deviation, indicating a greater dispersion in the results. While RS-DBSCAN had a lower standard deviation than K-DBSCAN, it was higher than KNN-BLOCK-DBSCAN. Improve KMeans had the lowest standard deviation; however, its quality results are the worst.

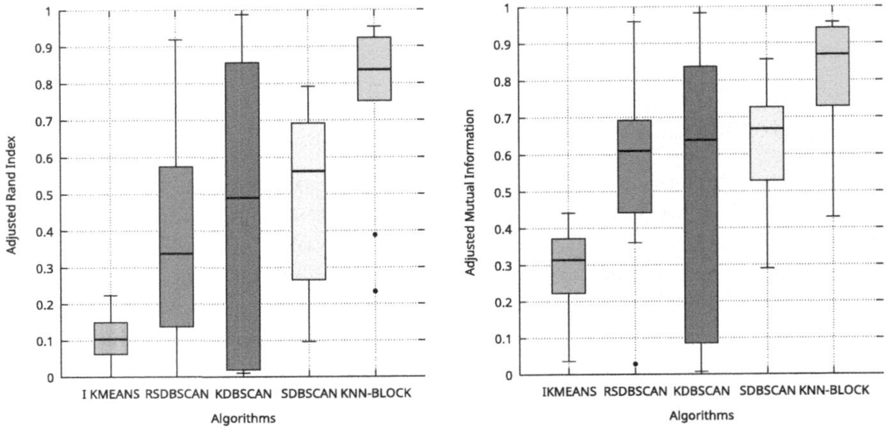

(a) Adjusted Rand Index (b) Adjusted Mutual Information

Fig. 1. Distribution of quality using ARI and AMI metrics.

Figure 1 shows the box plot with the results obtained when evaluating the clustering produced by the algorithms across the datasets using ARI and AMI metrics. Figure 1a presents the distribution of the values obtained using the ARI metric, while Fig. 1b shows the distribution obtained with AMI. Each figure contains five boxplots, one for each algorithm. The boxes represent the interquartile range (IQR), from the first (Q1) to the third quartile (Q3). The whiskers show the data range, from the minimum to the maximum score. The thick line indicates the median, and points outside the whiskers are outliers.

These figures show that KNN-BLOCK-DBSCAN achieves the highest mean with low deviation, consistently outperforming the other algorithms in both metrics. S-DBSCAN ranks second, surpassing K-DBSCAN. Although K-DBSCAN reaches sometimes highest values, S-DBSCAN has a more compact distribution in both metrics and a higher mean. K-DBSCAN and RS-DBSCAN exhibit broader distributions, indicating that they do not consistently perform well across all datasets. Finally, Improved K-Means remains the algorithm with the lowest clustering quality. If we only focus on quality, the experiment results show that the best option is KNN-BLOCK-DBSCAN. However, since these algorithms are designed for process large datasets, runtime is also important when selecting an algorithm.

4.2 Runtime Experiments

Runtime experiments were conducted using large datasets, as they have a larger number of objects and greater variability in dimensions. A 24-h runtime limit was set, and missing results corresponds to algorithms that exceeded this time limit. While reported runtime could improve on faster architectures, the focus of these experiments aimed to ensure a fair comparison by controlling the data structures and methods used in all algorithm implementations. The runtime results are presented in Fig. 2, showing the runtime in seconds of all algorithms across the tested datasets. The times are displayed on an logarithmic scale.

In the previous experiment, KNN-BLOCK-DBSCAN achieved the highest quality; however, Fig. 2 reveals that it also has the highest runtime, making it unable to process the largest datasets. In contrast, the Improve Kmeans algorithm, which had the lowest quality, is the fastest one. RS-DBSCAN and K-DBSCAN exhibit similar behaviors, and although K-DBSCAN is slower, neither could process the largest dataset within the established time limit. S-DBSCAN ranks as the second-best in quality and is the second-fastest algorithm; consequently, S-DBSCAN is the best density-based clustering algorithm for large datasets of all the evaluated algorithms.

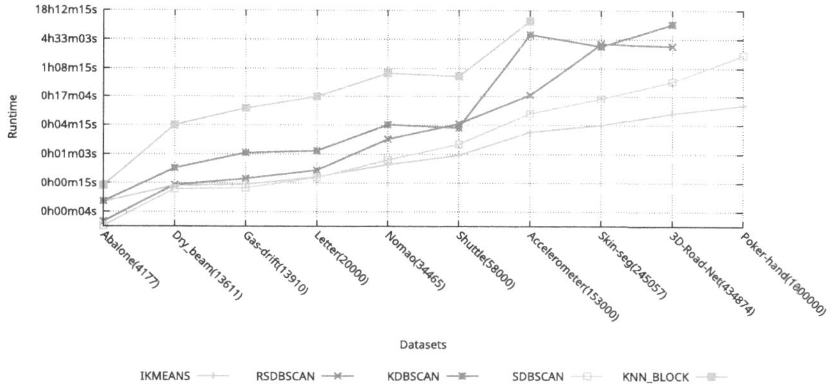

Fig. 2. Runtime of the Evaluated Clustering Algorithms on Datasets of Different Sizes.

When comparing runtime results with those from the quality experiments, it becomes evident that algorithms with better runtime performance tend to exhibit lower clustering quality. Conversely, higher quality often comes at the cost of higher runtime. Striking a balance between runtime and quality is crucial when working with large datasets, as some techniques may yield superior clustering quality results but require a significantly higher runtime, making them impractical for specific datasets. The quality and runtime experiments show that S-DBSCAN achieves the best balance between these two objectives. It processes all datasets within a reasonable runtime while maintaining good clustering quality.

5 Conclusion and Future Work

This study empirically compared five density-based clustering algorithms designed for large datasets. The analyzed algorithms employ common strategies for handling large-scale data, such as partitioning and sample extraction.

The experimental framework was carefully designed to ensure fair evaluation, encompassing the standardization of algorithm implementations, dataset selection, widely accepted density-based clustering metrics, and parameter tuning ranges informed by prior studies.

The results show that algorithms that obtained better clustering quality rely on dataset partitioning. This approach divides the dataset into smaller segments while leveraging all objects during clustering, resulting in higher-quality clusters. On the other hand, when runtime is the priority, algorithms that use sample extraction are more efficient. By analyzing a smaller, representative subset of a large dataset, these methods significantly reduce processing time; however, their clustering quality depends heavily on how well the selected sample is representative of the whole dataset.

The results also show that the choice of an algorithm will depend on the problem's requirements. If the priority is the highest quality and sufficient computational resources and time are available, KNN-BLOCK-DBSCAN is the best option. Conversely, in environments where a fast clustering is crucial, Improve Kmeans is preferable, as it offers a shorter runtime but it sacrifices quality. If a balance between quality and runtime is required, S-DBSCAN is the best choice, as it offers fast runtime without overly compromising clustering quality.

Future research could investigate the impact of parallel processing techniques on the runtime and scalability of density-based clustering algorithms. Additionally, exploring methods to achieve a better balance between clustering quality and runtime, such as developing more efficient sampling strategies or hybrid approaches, is also a research line for future work.

Acknowledgments. This research was financially supported by the Secretaría de Ciencia, Humanidades, Tecnología e Innovación (SECIHTI) through the scholarship grant 778974.

References

1. Arthur, D., Vassilvitskii, S.: K-means++: the advantages of careful seeding. In: Proceedings of the Eighteenth Annual ACM-SIAM Symposium on Discrete Algorithms, SODA '07, pp. 1027–1035. Society for Industrial and Applied Mathematics (2007)
2. Barton, T.: Clustering-benchmark (2019). https://github.com/deric/clustering-benchmark. https://github.com/deric/clustering-benchmark
3. Bhattacharjee, P., Mitra, P.: A survey of density based clustering algorithms. Front. Comp. Sci. **15**(1), 151308 (2020). https://doi.org/10.1007/s11704-019-9059-3
4. Bryant, A., Cios, K.: Rnn-dbscan: a density-based clustering algorithm using reverse nearest neighbor density estimates. IEEE Trans. Knowl. Data Eng. **30**(6), 1109–1121 (2018). https://doi.org/10.1109/TKDE.2017.2787640
5. Campello, R.J., Kröger, P., Sander, J., Zimek, A.: Density-based clustering. Wiley Interdisc. Rev. Data Min. Knowl. Disc. **10**(2), e1343 (2020)
6. Chen, L., Pan, Z., Yuan, L.: Study on clustering computing methods of big data. In: Proceedings of the 2nd International Conference on Information Technologies

and Electrical Engineering. ICITEE-2019. Association for Computing Machinery, New York (2020)
7. Chen, Y., Yang, Y., Pei, S., Chen, Y., Du, J.: A simple rapid sample-based clustering for large-scale data. Eng. Appl. Artif. Intell. **133**, 108551 (2024). https://doi.org/10.1016/j.engappai.2024.108551
8. Chen, Y., et al.: Knn-block dbscan: fast clustering for large-scale data. IEEE Trans. Syst. Man Cybern. Syst. **51**, 3939–3953 (2021)
9. Gholizadeh, N., Saadatfar, H., Hanafi, N.: K-dbscan: an improved dbscan algorithm for big data. J. Supercomput. **77**(6), 6214–6235 (2021)
10. Giordani, P., Ferraro, M.B., Martella, F.: Introduction to clustering. In: An Introduction to Clustering with R, pp. 3–5. Springer, Heidelberg (2020)
11. Halkidi, M., Batistakis, Y., Vazirgiannis, M.: Cluster validity methods: part i. ACM SIGMOD Rec. **31**(2), 40–45 (2002)
12. Hanafi, N., Saadatfar, H.: A fast dbscan algorithm for big data based on efficient density calculation. Expert Syst. Appl. **203**, 117501 (2022)
13. Jain, A.K.: Data clustering: 50 years beyond k-means. Pattern Recogn. Lett. **31**(8), 651–666 (2010)
14. Kelly, M., Longjohn, R., Nottingham, K.: The uci machine learning repository (2023). https://archive.ics.uci.edu
15. Lu, W.: Improved k-means clustering algorithm for big data mining under hadoop parallel framework. J. Grid Comput. **18**(2), 239–250 (2020)
16. Luo, G., Luo, X., Gooch, T.F., Tian, L., Qin, K.: A parallel dbscan algorithm based on spark. In: 2016 IEEE International Conferences on Big Data and Cloud Computing (BDCloud), Social Computing and Networking (SocialCom), Sustainable Computing and Communications (SustainCom) (BDCloud-SocialCom-SustainCom), pp. 548–553 (2016). https://doi.org/10.1109/BDCloud-SocialCom-SustainCom.2016.85
17. Muja, M., Lowe, D.G.: Scalable nearest neighbor algorithms for high dimensional data. IEEE Trans. Pattern Anal. Mach. Intell. **36**(11), 2227–2240 (2014)
18. Romano, S., Vinh, N.X., Bailey, J., Verspoor, K.: Adjusting for chance clustering comparison measures. J. Mach. Learn. Res. **17**(134), 1–32 (2016)
19. Wang, Y., Wang, D., Zhou, Y., Zhang, X., Quek, C.: VDPC: variational density peak clustering algorithm. Inf. Sci. **621**, 627–651 (2023). https://doi.org/10.1016/j.ins.2022.11.091. https://www.sciencedirect.com/science/article/pii/S0020025522013822

Exact Versus Approximate Patterns in Dissimilarity-Based Graph Embedding for Supervised Classification

Daybelis Jaramillo-Olivares(✉), J. Ariel Carrasco-Ochoa, and José Fco. Martínez-Trinidad

Instituto Nacional de Astrofísica, Óptica y Electrónica, Luis Enrique Erro # 1, Tonantzintla, 72840 Puebla, Mexico
{daybelis,ariel,fmartine}@inaoep.mx

Abstract. Dissimilarity-based graph embedding transforms a graph into a vector representation, using a dissimilarity measure to capture relevant information between graphs. Dissimilarity-based graph embedding has been widely applied to supervised classification in social network analysis, bioinformatics, and biomedicine. Moreover, graph patterns have been used for dissimilarity-based graph embedding, since they represent regularities within the data. Mining graph patterns follows two main approaches: exact and approximate. In this paper, we compare the performance for supervised classification of dissimilarity-based graph embeddings built from exact versus approximate graph patterns. Our evaluation was conducted on four benchmark graph collections using different supervised classifiers, with accuracy and F1-score as performance metrics. The study reported in this paper allowed us to determine which kind of graph patterns, exact or approximate, allows building the dissimilarity-based graph embedding that achieves the highest supervised classification performance.

Keywords: Graph patterns · Dissimilarity-based Graph Embedding · Supervised classification

1 Introduction

Graph structures have become widely employed for their flexibility and versatility in representing relationships between objects [1], enabling them to capture complex relationships within the data. Some domains where graph structures are used are bioinformatics [2], social network analysis [3], cheminformatics [4], and biomedicine [5], among others.

Graph pattern mining discovers graph patterns within a single graph or a graph collection. These graph patterns are frequent subgraphs based on a user-specified threshold [6–8]. Graph patterns can be categorized into exact patterns, which match subgraphs with one-to-one correspondence (isomorphism), and approximate patterns, which allow flexibility in the structure or labels of

A. P. López-Monroy et al. (Eds.): MCPR 2025, LNCS 15715, pp. 56–67, 2025.
https://doi.org/10.1007/978-3-031-96255-4_6

the subgraphs. This last one is useful when data is noisy or the goal is to identify relationships that exact patterns cannot capture.

In the literature, exact frequent subgraph miners, such as gSpan [9] and FSG [10], have been reported. Exact graph patterns have been used to construct a vector representation called Graph Embedding [11]. Graph Embedding employs the exact patterns mined in a dataset to build a vector for each graph, which in each entry contains the dissimilarity between each mined pattern and the graph.

On the other hand, algorithms that mine approximate patterns from graph collections have also been reported, such as SUBDUE [12], gApprox [13], AGrAP [14], APGM [15], VEAM [16], and REAFUM [17], among others, which also have been used for graph embedding. Dissimilarity-based Graph Embedding has been used for classification [18,19]; however, no study has compared the usefulness of approximate versus exact graph patterns mined from a graph collection for supervised classification through dissimilarity-based graph embedding. Therefore, this paper compares Dissimilarity-based Graph Embedding using Exact versus Approximate Patterns for Supervised Classification.

The remainder of this paper is organized as follows: Sect. 2 provides some basic concepts. Section 3 describes the methodology employed to evaluate the usefulness of exact and approximate graph patterns, mined from graph collections, to build the Dissimilarity-based Graph Embedding for supervised classification. Section 4 presents the experiments carried out across real world graph collections and discusses the results. Finally, Sect. 5 presents the conclusions and future work.

2 Basic Concepts

First, the concept of a graph will be defined, as the main structure used in this study. A graph is a structure used to represent relationships between objects. It consists of a set of vertices V, and a set of edges E, connecting pairs of vertices. Depending on the nature of the relationships, graphs can be directed, where edges have a specific direction, or undirected, where edges represent bidirectional relationships. Additionally, graphs may include labels or weights on vertices and edges to include additional information, such as the type of objects represented by vertices or the nature of relationships represented by edges. In this paper, we are interested in labeled graphs with labeled vertices and edges.

Definition 1 (Labeled graph). *A labeled graph* $G = (V, E, L_V, L_E, \ell_V, \ell_E)$, *is a graph that has labels assigned to vertices and edges, where* L_V *and* L_E *are the sets of possible vertices and edges labels, respectively, and* $\ell_V : V \rightarrow L_V$ *assigns labels to vertices and* $\ell_E : E \rightarrow L_E$ *assigns labels to edges.*

On the other hand, a subgraph is a graph contained within another graph.

Definition 2 (Subgraph). *A labeled graph* $g = (V', E', L'_V, L'_E, \ell'_V, \ell'_E)$ *is a subgraph of* $G = (V, E, L_V, L_E, \ell_V, \ell_E)$, *denoted* $g \subseteq G$,*if the vertices and edges of* g *are subsets of the vertices and edges in* G, $L'_V \subseteq L_V$, $L'_E \subseteq L_E$, *and* $\ell'_V = \ell_V|V'$, $\ell'_E = \ell_E|E'$.

Graph pattern mining aims to identify patterns within a given single graph or a graph collection. In this paper, we are interested in frequent graph patterns mined from graph collections.

Definition 3 (Graph collection). *A graph collection, represented as* $\mathcal{D} = \{G_1, G_2, \ldots, G_n\}$*, consists on a set of graphs. The graphs in the collection are grouped by shared properties.*

Frequent graph patterns can be mined exactly or approximately. Exact patterns are mined using graph isomorphism, which aims to identify subgraphs that perfectly match. Formally, this is defined as follows:

Definition 4 (Frequent exact pattern). *A frequent exact pattern is a subgraph* g_p*, for which there exists an isomorphic match in at least* σ *graphs in a graph collection* $\mathcal{D}$*, where* σ *is a predefined minimum support threshold.*

A subgraph g_p *has an isomorphic match in a graph* $G_i \in \mathcal{D}$*, if there exists a subgraph* $g_i \subseteq G_i$ *such that* g_i *is isomorphic to* g_p*. Also, the labels on vertices and edges have to match exactly.*

In contrast, approximate or inexact patterns allow some tolerance or flexibility; in this way, a pattern is said to be similar to another, even if its structure or labels differ less than a predefined dissimilarity threshold. This dissimilarity is measured with metrics such as the graph edit distance, which evaluates the minimum number of operations needed to transform one graph into another.

Definition 5 (Frequent approximate pattern). *A frequent approximate pattern is a subgraph* g_p*, such that there exists a similar subgraph in at least* σ *graphs in a graph collection* $\mathcal{D}$*, where* σ *is a predefined minimum support threshold.*

A subgraph g_p *is similar to a subgraph* $g_i \subseteq G_i \in \mathcal{D}$*, if* $d(g_p, g_i) \leq \delta$*, where* δ *denotes a predefined dissimilarity threshold and* d *is a graph dissimilarity function (commonly based on the graph edit distance). If* $\delta = 0$*,* g_p *is a frequent exact pattern.*

Dissimilarity-based graph embedding transforms graphs into a numerical representation as a point in a vector space [20]. This vector can be formed by computing dissimilarities between a graph and each graph pattern in a graph collection. In our study, we used the dissimilarity function defined below, which is based on the graph edit distance (GED). It considers all the operations required to transform a graph into another [21]. The more operations required, the greater the dissimilarity between the graphs. Since GED is an NP-hard problem that computes the minimum cost of these operations, requiring significant computational resources, we use instead a heuristic approach that accumulates cost values as patterns appear.

Definition 6 (Dissimilarity function). *Given two graphs* G_1 *and* G_2*, the dissimilarity function, represented as* $d(G_1, G_2)$*, is defined as:*

$$d(G_1, G_2) = \sum_{i=1}^{k} c(V_i) + \sum_{j=1}^{m} c(E_j)$$

where $c(V_i)$ and $c(E_j)$ are respectively the costs of the k modifications on vertices and the m modifications on edges (k or m could be zero), required to transform G1 into G2. The modifications include: insertion, deletion, and label substitution.

3 Experimental Methodology

We employed a five-fold cross-validation to evaluate the graph embedding using graph patterns for supervised classification. Each graph collection was randomly split into five parts. In each iteration, a fold was used as testing set and the remaining four were used for training. The following process was carried out for each fold:

1. **Mining Graph Patterns for each class:** For each class in the training set, graph patterns (exact and approximate) were mined separately using a graph miner.
2. **Joining the mined patterns from all classes:** After mining the patterns (exact and approximate) for each class, the patterns were joined across all classes, resulting in a unique set of mined patterns for the training set, denoted as $\mathcal{P}$.
3. **Dissimilarity-based Graph Embedding using Patterns:** Dissimilarity-based Graph Embedding refers to build a vector from a graph based on the dissimilarity between graphs [18]. In this paper, we built the Dissimilarity-based Graph Embedding using graph patterns (exact and approximate) and a dissimilarity function based on the graph edit distance. In this way, a graph G and the mined patterns $\mathcal{P}$ are used to build a vector $z = [d_{min}(G, g_{p_1}), \ldots, d_{min}(G, g_{p_{|\mathcal{P}|}})]$. For each pattern $g_{p_j} \in \mathcal{P}$, we compute the dissimilarity function $d(g_i, g_{p_j})$ (see Definition 6) for all occurrences g_i of g_{p_j} in G and select the minimum dissimilarity value $d_{min}(g_i, g_{p_j})$.
   In this way, given a graph collection $\mathcal{D}$ separated in training and testing sets, each graph $G \in \mathcal{D}$ is embedded using the patterns mined in the training set. Thus, transforming the graph collection $\mathcal{D} = \{G_1, G_2, \ldots, G_n\}$, into a vector set $\mathcal{Z} = \{z_1, z_2, \ldots, z_n\}$. Then, conventional supervised classifiers developed for vectors can be applied.
4. **Evaluation:** To assess the dissimilarity-based graph embedding employing patterns (exact or approximate) different supervised classifiers were evaluated using two metrics: accuracy and F1-score.

Since the only thing that changes is the dissimilarity embedding built with exact or approximate patterns in step 3, it allows us to compare both embeddings.

4 Experiments

In this section, we present the results of the experiments conducted to evaluate the usefulness for supervised classification of the dissimilarity-based graph embedding built from exact and approximate graph patterns. The experiments were performed on computer running Linux Ubuntu 22, equipped with two Intel Xeon E5-2620 processors at 2.40GHz and 256 GB RAM.

For our experiments the *PTC* graph collections were used. These graph collections were obtained from the Network Repository [22] and contain compounds labeled according to carcinogenicity (positive or negative) in female mice (FM), female rats (FR), male mice (MM) and male rats (MR). They were selected because they are labeled graph collections.

Table 1 summarizes the characteristics of the *PTC* graph collections. It includes the graph collection size $|\mathcal{D}|$, the number of labels for vertices and edges, denoted by $|LV|$ and $|LE|$ and the number of graphs per class, denoted by $|C_1|$ and $|C_2|$.

Table 1. Description of the PTC graph collections.

Graph Collection	$\|\mathcal{D}\|$	$\|LN\|$	$\|LE\|$	$\|C_1\|$	$\|C_2\|$
PTC-FM	349	18	4	206	143
PTC-FR	351	19	4	230	121
PTC-MM	336	18	4	207	129
PTC-MR	344	20	4	192	152

In the literature, some algorithms mine exact graph patterns, such as gSpan [9] and FSG [10], while others focus on mining approximate graph patterns such as, SUBDUE [12], gApprox [13], AGrAP [14], VEAM [16]. However, to the best of our knowledge, just one algorithm, REAFUM [17], can mine approximate patterns allowing label and structural variations in vertices and edges in a graph collection given a dissimilarity threshold and a support threshold. In REAFUM, if the dissimilarity threshold is set to zero, it can also mine exact graph patterns. Thus, we use this miner for our experiments.

REAFUM was executed varying the dissimilarity threshold δ, which defines how much dissimilar the pattern occurrences could be, from zero (exact patterns) to two, with increments of 1; while the support threshold σ, which determines how frequently the pattern must appear within the graph collection, was set to 40% and 50% for exact patterns and 80% and 90% for approximate patterns. These support thresholds were used to allow mining enough exact graph patterns since high support values tend to mine very few or even no patterns, making it impossible to build the dissimilarity-based graph embeddings. Given that approximate patterns are more flexible regarding dissimilarity, this allowed us to use higher support values.

Table 2 presents the mean number of patterns mined in the training set of the 5-fold cross-validation. It shows that varying the dissimilarity threshold δ impacts the number of patterns mined. Allowing more tolerance by increasing the dissimilarity threshold tends to result in a higher number of patterns mined. Additionally, varying the support threshold σ also affects the number of patterns mined, as decreasing the support means that a pattern is considered frequent if it is present in fewer graphs within the graph collection, obtaining more patterns.

Table 2. Mean of the number of patterns mined of 5-fold cross-validation for the graph collections of Table 1.

Graph Collection	Dissimilarity δ/ Support σ					
	$\delta = 0$		$\delta = 1$		$\delta = 2$	
	$\sigma = 40\%$	$\sigma = 50\%$	$\sigma = 80\%$	$\sigma = 90\%$	$\sigma = 80\%$	$\sigma = 90\%$
PTC-FM	12.4	9.8	18	10	66.2	41.8
PTC-FR	13.4	9.6	14.4	10.6	55.2	35.6
PTC-MM	13.8	8.8	15	10	56.6	32.6
PTC-MR	16.6	9.8	16.2	10.6	61	37.2

Table 3 and Table 4 present the mean metric value results from the 5-fold cross-validation of six different classifiers (k-Nearest Neighbors (KNN), Linear Support Vector Machines (SVM), Decision Tree, Gradient Boosting Machines (GBM), Random Forest, and Neural Networks using the Multi-Layer Perceptron Classifier) evaluated across four graph collections. These classifiers were taken from the scikit-learn library in Python, using their default parameters, and were selected to represent different classification strategies. The best result for each classifier on the graph collections is highlighted in bold. Table 3 shows the mean accuracy results, while Table 4 shows the mean F1-score results. Different dissimilarity δ and support σ thresholds are considered to observe how they impact the classifiers' performance.

From Table 3, it is observed that an increase in the dissimilarity threshold leads to better performance, the dissimilarity threshold $\delta = 2$ being the most accurate in most cases. The best results were obtained for frequent approximate patterns with a dissimilarity threshold $\delta = 2$ and a support threshold $\sigma = 80\%$. The worst results were obtained for the exact patterns with a dissimilarity threshold $\delta = 0$. It suggests that approximate patterns tend to achieve better accuracy than exact patterns for these graph collections.

Table 3. Mean accuracy of 5-fold cross-validation.

Classifier/Graph Collection	Dissimilarity δ/ Support σ					
	$\delta = 0$		$\delta = 1$		$\delta = 2$	
	$\sigma = 40\%$	$\sigma = 50\%$	$\sigma = 80\%$	$\sigma = 90\%$	$\sigma = 80\%$	$\sigma = 90\%$
Decision Tree						
PTC-FM	0.6139	0.6432	0.7095	0.6461	**0.7349**	0.7266
PTC-FR	0.6443	0.6466	0.6922	0.6499	0.7206	**0.7246**
PTC-MM	0.6607	0.6363	0.6704	**0.7420**	0.7162	0.6950
PTC-MR	0.6215	0.5916	0.6745	0.6038	0.6574	**0.6886**
GBM						
PTC-FM	0.6428	0.6638	0.6796	0.6241	**0.7210**	0.7072
PTC-FR	0.6324	0.6322	**0.7011**	0.6808	0.6993	0.6751
PTC-MM	0.6686	0.6196	0.6520	0.6988	**0.7411**	0.7040
PTC-MR	0.6403	0.6035	0.6446	0.5717	0.6680	**0.6929**
KNN						
PTC-FM	0.4792	0.4312	0.6455	0.5247	**0.6766**	0.6498
PTC-FR	0.3820	0.3682	0.6311	0.5552	**0.6896**	0.6632
PTC-MM	0.5270	0.4129	0.5647	0.5307	0.5851	**0.6265**
PTC-MR	0.5687	0.4542	**0.5975**	0.5509	0.5468	0.5945
Linear SVM						
PTC-FM	0.6532	0.6532	0.6455	0.6297	**0.7041**	0.6395
PTC-FR	0.6363	0.6548	0.6682	0.6682	**0.6866**	0.6541
PTC-MM	0.6616	0.5785	0.6180	0.6627	0.6088	**0.6681**
PTC-MR	0.5958	0.5890	0.5534	0.5946	0.6173	**0.6273**
Neural Networks						
PTC-FM	0.6115	0.6192	0.6346	0.6336	**0.6827**	0.6541
PTC-FR	0.6140	0.6116	0.6746	0.6490	0.6617	**0.6689**
PTC-MM	0.6638	0.6217	0.6361	0.6551	**0.6673**	0.6507
PTC-MR	0.5941	0.5931	0.5812	0.6125	0.6300	**0.6458**
Random Forest						
PTC-FM	0.6290	0.6592	0.7161	0.6153	**0.7301**	0.7196
PTC-FR	0.6315	0.6217	0.7087	0.6464	**0.7603**	0.7497
PTC-MM	0.6531	0.6319	0.6726	0.7048	**0.7593**	0.7214
PTC-MR	0.6122	0.5951	0.6973	0.5971	**0.7030**	0.7011

Table 4 presents the results of the evaluation using the F1-score metric, where it is observed that the classifiers perform better in most cases with a higher dissimilarity threshold obtaining the best results with a dissimilarity threshold of $\delta = 2$ with a support threshold $\sigma = 80\%$. The worst results were obtained

Table 4. Mean F1-score of 5-fold cross-validation.

Classifier/Graph Collection	Dissimilarity δ/ Support σ					
	$\delta = 0$		$\delta = 1$		$\delta = 2$	
	$\sigma = 40\%$	$\sigma = 50\%$	$\sigma = 80\%$	$\sigma = 90\%$	$\sigma = 80\%$	$\sigma = 90\%$
Decision Tree						
PTC-FM	0.4156	0.4235	**0.6311**	0.5051	0.6711	0.6451
PTC-FR	0.2813	0.1439	0.5172	0.4298	**0.5774**	0.5635
PTC-MM	0.4819	0.3917	0.5541	0.6172	**0.6338**	0.5771
PTC-MR	0.5399	0.4154	0.6065	0.5299	0.5986	**0.6381**
GBM						
PTC-FM	0.4732	0.4901	0.5629	0.4341	**0.6179**	0.6015
PTC-FR	0.1684	0.0967	0.4444	0.3300	**0.4801**	0.4352
PTC-MM	0.5015	0.3971	0.5037	0.5447	**0.6406**	0.5690
PTC-MR	0.5743	0.4697	0.5779	0.4823	0.6214	**0.6304**
KNN						
PTC-FM	0.5683	0.5609	**0.6200**	0.6012	0.5977	0.6041
PTC-FR	0.3818	0.4575	**0.4952**	0.4802	0.4766	0.4812
PTC-MM	0.5106	0.5240	0.4888	**0.5723**	0.4499	0.5184
PTC-MR	**0.6434**	0.6031	0.6046	0.6206	0.5074	0.5600
Linear SVM						
PTC-FM	0.5156	0.5156	0.4306	0.4467	**0.5952**	0.4738
PTC-FR	0.0286	0.0000	0.0959	0.0959	**0.4934**	0.1824
PTC-MM	**0.5087**	0.2074	0.3802	0.5035	0.4538	0.5003
PTC-MR	0.4768	0.4694	0.3502	0.4225	**0.5143**	0.4998
Neural Network						
PTC-FM	0.4824	0.3701	0.4155	0.4160	**0.5618**	0.4882
PTC-FR	0.2930	0.1401	0.2304	0.1498	**0.3676**	0.2996
PTC-MM	**0.5239**	0.4174	0.3649	0.4362	0.4921	0.4541
PTC-MR	0.5097	0.4068	0.4244	0.4515	**0.5313**	0.4939
Random Forest						
PTC-FM	0.4634	0.4856	**0.6464**	0.4880	0.6436	0.6378
PTC-FR	0.2663	0.1673	0.5436	0.4350	**0.6027**	0.5805
PTC-MM	0.5127	0.4115	0.5611	0.5869	**0.6685**	0.6158
PTC-MR	0.5581	0.4701	**0.6514**	0.5297	0.6483	0.6500

with a dissimilarity threshold $\delta = 0$, corresponding to exact patterns, as they only outperformed approximate patterns in three out of the 24 tests.

Figure 1 and Fig. 2 present box plots summarizing the distribution of the metric values obtained from the classifiers. Figure 1 presents the distribution of the accuracy, while Fig. 2 presents the distribution of F1-score. In these plots, each box corresponds to a different combination of dissimilarity and support thresholds, which allows us to compare how the thresholds variations influence the classifiers performance.

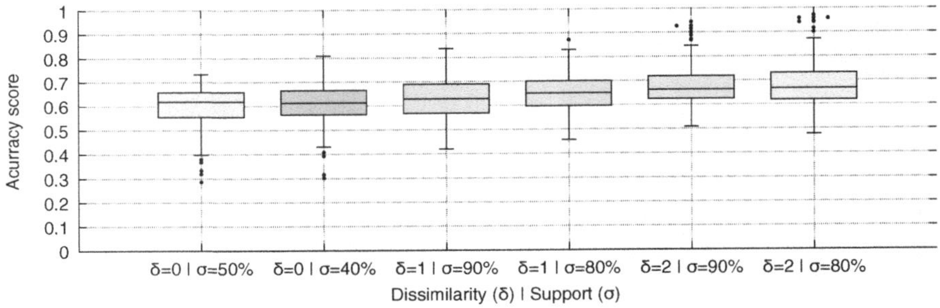

Fig. 1. Box plot comparing the distribution of the accuracy across the multiple classifiers varying the dissimilarity δ and support σ thresholds.

Figure 1 shows the dissimilarity-based graph embeddings built with approximate patterns consistently obtained higher accuracy values, being the dissimilarity threshold $\delta = 2$ with support threshold $\sigma = 80\%$, the one that achieves the highest accuracy compared to the other combinations. It is also observed that the worst results are those with a dissimilarity threshold $\delta = 0$, which correspond to the exact graph patterns. Even though the number of patterns mined when $\delta = 0$ (exact graph patterns) are similar to the number of patterns mined with $\delta = 1$, the classifiers performed better with approximate graph patterns.

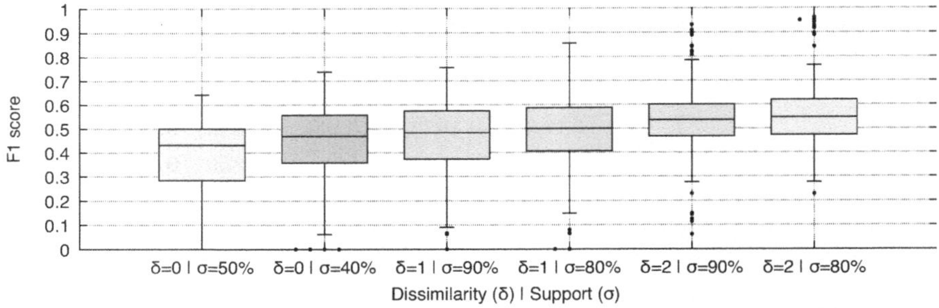

Fig. 2. Box plot comparing the distribution of the F1-score across the multiple classifiers varying the dissimilarity δ and support σ thresholds.

In Fig. 2, the results obtained using the F1-score metric have the same behavior as the results reported with the accuracy metric, being the dissimilarity threshold $\delta = 2$ with support threshold $\sigma = 80\%$ the one with the highest F1-score values. The worst results were also obtained with exact patterns. Additionally, the dispersion of the F1-score metric values is greater than the dispersion of the accuracy metric values.

The higher accuracy and F1-score values obtained by the dissimilarity-based graph embeddings built with approximate graph patterns, compared to exact patterns, led us to conclude that allowing variations in the patterns (approximate graph patterns) improves the performance of dissimilarity-based graph embeddings for supervised classification.

5 Conclusion and Future Work

This paper compares dissimilarity-based graph embedding using exact versus approximate graph patterns for supervised classification. Dissimilarity-based graph embedding using graph patterns aims to transform a graph into a vector representation where each entry captures the dissimilarity between each mined graph pattern and the graph. Exact and approximate graph patterns were mined using REAFUM [17], which allows mining both types of patterns from graph collections. We assessed the effectiveness of dissimilarity-based graph embeddings, built using exact and approximate patterns, in supervised classification on four benchmark graph collections. For this evaluation, we employed six supervised classifiers including k-Nearest Neighbors (KNN), Linear Support Vector Machines (SVM), Decision Tree, Gradient Boosting Classifier (GBM), Random Forest, and Neural Networks. The performance was evaluated with accuracy and F1-score metrics.

From our experiments, we can conclude that allowing variations in mining graph patterns captures better information for building dissimilarity-based graph embeddings for supervised classification, as they outperformed the dissimilarity-based graph embeddings built with exact graph patterns in both accuracy and F1-score. This finding in our experiments highlights the advantage of using approximate graph patterns for dissimilarity-based graph embedding in supervised classification. It also highlights the importance of developing more algorithms for mining approximate graph patterns allowing differences in labels and structure in graph collections, since, as we already mentioned, we only found one algorithm able to mine this kind of patterns.

In the future, we will explore the performance of dissimilarity-based graph embedding built using approximate graph patterns for other tasks, such as clustering.

Acknowledgments. This research was financially supported by the Secretaría de Ciencia, Humanidades, Tecnología e Innovación (SECIHTI) through the scholarship grant 778343.

References

1. Aggarwal, C.: Managing and Mining Graph Data. Springer, New York (2010)
2. Liu, Y., et al.: EpiGraphDB: a database and data mining platform for health data science. Bioinformatics **37**(9), 1304–1311 (2020). https://doi.org/10.1093/bioinformatics/btaa961
3. Li, L., Ding, P., Chen, H., Wu, X.: Frequent pattern mining in big social graphs. IEEE Trans. Emerg. Topics Comput. Intell. **6**(3), 638–648 (2022). https://doi.org/10.1109/TETCI.2021.3067017
4. Cerruela-García, G., Cuevas-Muñoz, J.M., García-Pedrajas, N.: Graph-based feature selection approach for molecular activity prediction. J. Chem. Inf. Model. **62**(7), 1618–1632 (2022). https://doi.org/10.1021/acs.jcim.1c01578
5. Li, M.M., Huang, K., Zitnik, M.: Graph representation learning in biomedicine and healthcare. Nat. Biomed. Eng. **6**(12), 1353–1369 (2022). https://doi.org/10.1038/s41551-022-00942-x
6. Jiang, C., Coenen, F., Zito, M.: A survey of frequent subgraph mining algorithms. Knowl. Eng. Rev. **28**(1), 75–105 (2013). https://doi.org/10.1017/S0269888912000331
7. Ramraj, T., Prabhakar, R.: Frequent subgraph mining algorithms - a survey. Procedia Comput. Sci. **47**, 197–204 (2015). https://doi.org/10.1016/j.procs.2015.03.198
8. Mrzic, A., Meysman, P., Bittremieux, W., Moris, P., Cule, B., Goethals, B., Laukens, K.: Grasping frequent subgraph mining for bioinformatics applications. BioData mining **11**(1), 1–24 (2018)
9. Yan, X., Han, J.: gspan: graph-based substructure pattern mining. In: 2002 IEEE International Conference on Data Mining. Proceedings, pp. 721–724 (2002). DOI: https://doi.org/10.1109/ICDM.2002.1184038
10. Kuramochi, M., Karypis, G.: Frequent subgraph discovery. In: Proceedings 2001 IEEE International Conference on Data Mining, pp. 313–320. IEEE (2001)
11. Alam, M.T., Ahmed, C.F., Samiullah, M., Leung, C.K.: Discriminating frequent pattern based supervised graph embedding for classification. In: Karlapalem, K., et al. (eds.) PAKDD 2021. LNCS (LNAI), vol. 12713, pp. 16–28. Springer, Cham (2021). https://doi.org/10.1007/978-3-030-75765-6_2
12. Holder, L.B., Cook, D.J., Djoko, S.: Substructure discovery in the subdue system. In: Proceedings of the 3rd International Conference on Knowledge Discovery and Data Mining, AAAIWS'94, pp. 169–180. AAAI Press (1994)
13. Chen, C., Yan, X., Zhu, F., Han, J.: gapprox: mining frequent approximate patterns from a massive network. In: Seventh IEEE International Conference on Data Mining (ICDM 2007), pp. 445–450 (2007). https://doi.org/10.1109/ICDM.2007.36
14. Flores-Garrido, M., Carrasco-Ochoa, J.-A., Martínez-Trinidad, J.F.: AGraP: an algorithm for mining frequent patterns in a single graph using inexact matching. Knowl. Inf. Syst. **44**(2), 385–406 (2014). https://doi.org/10.1007/s10115-014-0747-x
15. Jia, Y., Zhang, J., Huan, J.: An efficient graph-mining method for complicated and noisy data with real-world applications. Knowl. Inf. Syst. **28**(2), 423–447 (2011). https://doi.org/10.1007/s10115-010-0376-y
16. Acosta-Mendoza, N., Gago-Alonso, A., Pagola, J.: Frequent approximate subgraphs as features for graph-based image classification. Knowl.-Based Syst. **17**, 381–392 (2012). https://doi.org/10.1016/j.knosys.2011.12.002

17. Li, R., Wang, W.: REAFUM: Representative Approximate Frequent Subgraph Mining, pp. 757–765 (2015). https://doi.org/10.1137/1.9781611974010.85
18. Bunke, H., Riesen, K.: Graph classification based on dissimilarity space embedding. In: da Vitoria Lobo, N., Kasparis, T., Roli, F., Kwok, J.T., Georgiopoulos, M., Anagnostopoulos, G.C., Loog, M. (eds.) SSPR /SPR 2008. LNCS, vol. 5342, pp. 996–1007. Springer, Heidelberg (2008). https://doi.org/10.1007/978-3-540-89689-0_103
19. Fuchs, M., Riesen, K.: Graph embedding in vector spaces using matching-graphs. In: Reyes, N., et al. (eds.) SISAP 2021. LNCS, vol. 13058, pp. 352–363. Springer, Cham (2021). https://doi.org/10.1007/978-3-030-89657-7_26
20. Bunke, H., Riesen, K.: Improving vector space embedding of graphs through feature selection algorithms. Pattern Recogn. **44**(9), 1928–1940 (2011). https://doi.org/10.1016/j.patcog.2010.05.016. https://www.sciencedirect.com/science/article/pii/S0031320310002360
21. Sanfeliu, A., Fu, K.-S.: A distance measure between attributed relational graphs for pattern recognition. IEEE Trans. Syst. Man Cybern. SMC **13**(3), 353–362 (1983). https://doi.org/10.1109/TSMC.1983.6313167
22. Rossi, R.A., Ahmed, N.K.: The network data repository with interactive graph analytics and visualization. In: AAAI (2015). https://networkrepository.com

Optimized Early Detection of Bark Beetles Through Automated Segmentation and Machine Learning Classification

Marco Esaú Martínez García[1], Alejandra Cruz-Bernal[2](✉), and Carlos Alberto Ugalde-Caballero[2]

[1] Computer Systems Engineering, Universidad Autónoma de Ciudad Juárez, Chihuahua, Mexico
al203780@alumnos.uacj.mx

[2] Departamento de Robótica, Universidad Politécnica de Guanajuato, Cortazar, Guanajuato, Mexico
{acruz,cugalde}@upgto.edu.mx

Abstract. Bark beetles have become an escalating concern in Mexico's forests, as extreme and highly variable climate conditions have turned these insects into a significant infestation threat. Currently, rangers manually count beetles after they are trapped, capturing images with their cellphones and sending them to specialized teams. These teams count and classify the beetles to point establishment strategies under the Mexican Official Norm *NOM-019-SEMARNAT-2006*. Nevertheless, the delay between image acquisition and expert analysis can extend to over a couple of weeks, enough time for beetle populations to grow into an infestation if the actions are not taken in time. To address this delay, we proposed a segmentation and classification pipeline designed to provide a preliminary assessment of the captured images, flagging those with concerning beetle counts. Segmentation was achieved using Connected Component Labeling, while classification was performed through a Convolutional Neural Network, both showing a favorable performance.

Keywords: Connected Component Labeling · Bark Beetles Segmentation · Convolutional Neural Network · ResNet50

1 Introduction

The bark beetles of the genus Dendroctonus are among the most significant pests in coniferous forests worldwide. Their presence at epidemic levels leads to the death of millions of trees, causing substantial ecological and economic damage according to [1] and [2]. Mexico, with its extensive coniferous forests, is not spared from the devastation caused by these insects, affecting various states across the country. The National Forestry Commission (CONAFOR) shares the status of the situation monthly via the Bark Removing Insects report [3].

A. P. López-Monroy et al. (Eds.): MCPR 2025, LNCS 15715, pp. 68–77, 2025.
https://doi.org/10.1007/978-3-031-96255-4_7

According to the most recent report for June 2024, the states at very high risk of bark beetle attacks all states cross the Sierra Madre Occidental, medium-risk states of the Sierra Madre Oriental, as well as the Trans-Mexican Volcanic Belt, which corresponds to the mountainous areas in Mexico. Moreover, the impact and effects due to the climatic change have been severe since 2013, this is, 12% of pine forests in Mexico experienced infestations [3] and these were destroyed.

Currently in Mexico, the procedure to acquire and process the information referent to pest control in the forests is carried out manually in its entirety. The forest ranger periodically checks the traps placed in the trees and sends them to the relevant authorities for identification and analysis. The following measures are performed depending on the guidelines listed in the Mexican Official Norm *NOM-019-SEMARNAT-2006* [4]. However, the delay from capture to official identification is a critical problem spanning from a couple of weeks to an entire month or more.

On the other hand, popular techniques developed for the detection of pests, such as acoustic detection described in [5,6] might be cheaper and faster to implement; but, it is necessary to quantify them as well, which leads to this increased difficulty. To mitigate this problem, significant optimization can be achieved by using advanced computer vision techniques and image processing to perform segmentation and classification of captured insects [7]; thus, several proposals have been suggested to accurately identify bark beetles, as presented in [7–11]. In the case of Mexico, the traps are implemented as a preventive mechanism using a Lindgren funnel trap as explained in [12] and [13].

The present proposal involves the first scheme to develop an automatic process for the detection, segmentation, and counting of bark beetles. This process should provide early and timely detection, consisting of a classification process through Machine Learning (ML) and a segmentation process through heuristics and image processing such as Connected Component Labeling (CCL), both of which shall be evaluated and fine-tuned to achieve the best performance, providing a preliminary and quick overview when it comes to studying these pests.

2 Methodology

Figure 1 presents a schematic diagram corresponding to the proposal. The first step is the *segmentation process*, which extracts the insects from the whole image. The effectiveness of this phase relies on choosing a segmentation technique that fits the image's environment; thus, the proposal includes testing some representative methods, such as Sliding Window or Connected-Component Labeling.

It should be noted that the acquisition process, even if significantly important, is not determinant for the training models according to Rustia *et al.* in [24]. Nevertheless, for the segmentation process, a pair of limitations are presented in our proposal including the expected image environment inside the Lindgren trap as illustrated in Fig. 2, where the distribution of bark beetles is not uniform and the background is not consistent.

Factors such as the illumination or the distance between the insects and the vision sensor may vary minimally, thus slight changes can distort the size of

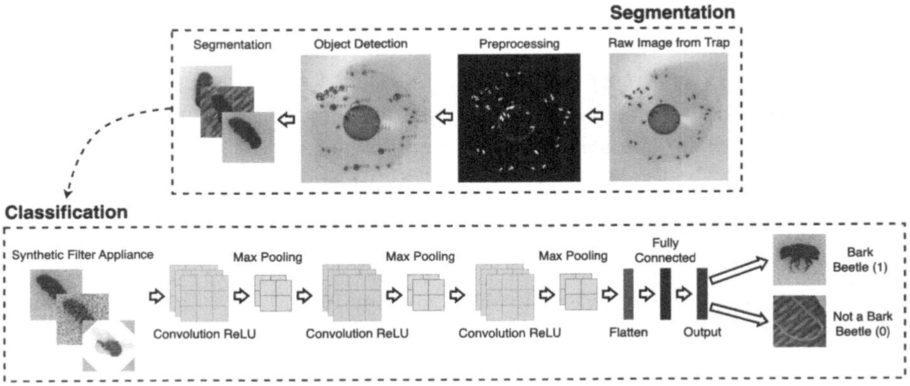

Fig. 1. Schematic description.

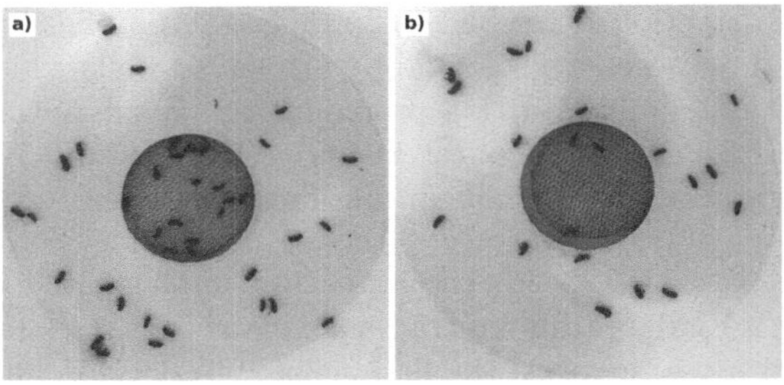

Fig. 2. a) Example image with brown cloth; b) Example image with red cloth. (Color figure online)

the insects. In this sense, the sliding window technique contemplates that insect sizes are relatively uniform and hence an average window size (100 × 100 pixels) was selected to realize the segmentation process. Considering that, the acquired image resolution 4032 × 3042 pixels, the full length of a bark beetle is close to 5 mm; in this case, with a scale of approx. 20 pixels to 1 mm.

The Connected-Component Labeling method was carried out by identifying groups of adjacent foreground pixels. These connected components ideally hold the coordinates to segment each insect individually, allowing for subsequent classification of each one of the components. Therefore, with this new proposal, we still had to address the varying distance between the insects and the vision device. To manage this, we labeled the components with different colors based on their area, as shown in Fig. 1 in the picture corresponding to object detection. While all components will be input into the classification pipeline regardless of their area, this labeling helps the segmentation process assess the accuracy after preprocessing.

For the *classification process* manual cropping was performed from the original dataset to obtain a dataset of individual insects to perform data augmen-

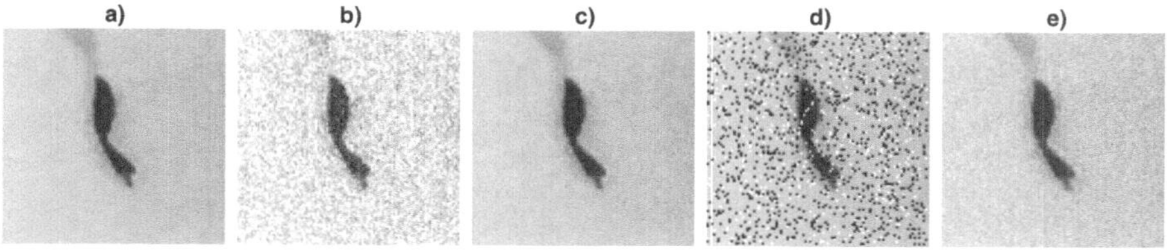

Fig. 3. a) Original Image; b) Gauss Filter; c) Poisson Filter; d) Salt & Pepper Filter; e) Speckle Filter.

tation to have robust training for the proposed model. The generation of synthetic images is carried out as a result of applying noise filters (see, Fig. 3) to enrich the training of the model as done in [15], improving the model's ability to handle noisy data and simulate varying conditions of lighting, texture, and distortion. Filters parameters are given in the range: Poisson noise, scaling factors of $[1.0, 20.0]$; Salt-and-Pepper noise, combinations of noise ratios $[0.02, 0.8]$. Gaussian noise $[(0, 25), (0, 60)]$; Speckle noise $[0.05, 0.4]$.

The ideal model to perform classification is through a Convolutional Neural Network (CNN) due to its ability to preserve spatial information and all of the background work supporting it, such as [14,16]. However, other non-spatial models might result in effective if the model's complexity is not very demanding, for example *Support Vector Machine* [17–19] and ANN (Artificial Neural Networks) [20]. In this current proposal, we aim to detect the highest amount of features as well as the most significant, striving for both quantity and quality.

The core information in an image is the intensity per pixel in each color channel and the spatial arrangement of these pixels. CNNs leverage this data format to extract the maximum number of features from each image in the dataset. While a CNN was the first suggestion for our proposal, classification was also tested through other linear models, including ANN, K-Nearest Neighbors (KNN), Naïve Bayes (NB), and Kernel Support Vector Machines (SVM).

The selection of the CNN architecture concerning the proposed initial design was inspired by *VGGNet*. It consists of a series of small 3×3 convolutional layers, each followed by a max-pooling layer, culminating in a fully connected layer as explained in [25]. Given the dataset's complexity, the architecture started with only three convolutional layers. To ensure proper performance, the chosen optimizer was *AdamW* with *cosine decay* and a starting learning rate 1×10^{-3} to improve generalization and prevent large gradient updates, both contributing to avoid overfitting.

Due to the sigmoid nature of classification and the dataset's size of 3,276 images from both classes, this architecture is enough for a significant performance.

Even with this in mind, variation of the CNN was also tested through the use of ResNet50 as the base model to leverage transfer learning (see, Fig. 4). As argued in [21], competitive performance can be achieved using pretrained models, which have been trained on large datasets and can be adapted to specific tasks via transfer learning techniques. ResNet50 was selected out from a broad variety of base models due to its residual connections, which help train networks by mitigating issues like gradient vanishing.

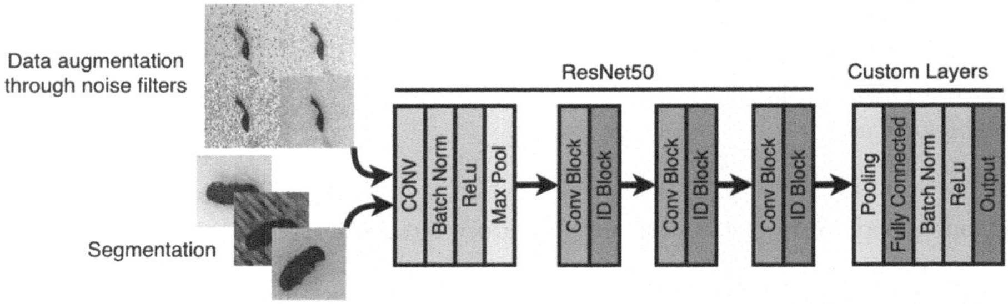

Fig. 4. ResNet50 as base model.

On top of the base model, custom layers were added to be trained on the dataset specific to this study. These include a flattened layer, a dense layer with ReLU activation, and a dropout layer to reduce overfitting risk. Initially, all pretrained model layers remain frozen, so only the custom layers are trained. Later, in a second fine-tuning phase, the last layers of the base architecture (10 for the presented results) are unfrozen, allowing their weights to be adjusted to fit the current training without compromising previously learned knowledge. During this phase, a reduced learning rate of 1×10^{-5} prevents abrupt changes in optimized weights.

Concerning the metrics for segmentation, the accuracy consisted of evaluating the average ratio between the detected number of insects in the image and the real number of insects, as well as the *Intersection over Union* ($IoU = \frac{A \bigcup B}{A \bigcap B}$) metric, which compares the overlap between the automatic segmentation and a manually generated reference segmentation, as specified in [22]. This metric will allow a more comprehensive evaluation of the system's performance, both in terms of correct detection and the minimization of false positives and negatives [23].

3 Results

From the perspective of a first approximation, it is important to note that the acquisition process can be performed through a simple vision system (vision sensor iPhone 12 cellular or cellular with similar characteristics, for example) and that it is conducted in a semi-controlled environment inside the Lindgren funnel trap. Near 100 images were acquired with a similar methodology proposed by Sun *et al.* in [14].

The CCL technique was compared to the sliding window method, with the latter presenting an accuracy below 0.6. In contrast, CCL demonstrated good performance with an accuracy of 0.925 over the expected bark beetles to count per image. Around 60 images were tested for the segmentation process, with Fig. 5 as an example of the result of highlighting detected bark beetles.

This imbalance, as listed in Table 1, is primarily attributed to residual noise remaining after preprocessing. Despite this, the evaluation of aspect ratio, saturation, and shape of the resultant components after preprocessing allowed to discard the remaining segments of cloth after preprocessing, to only target the beetles.

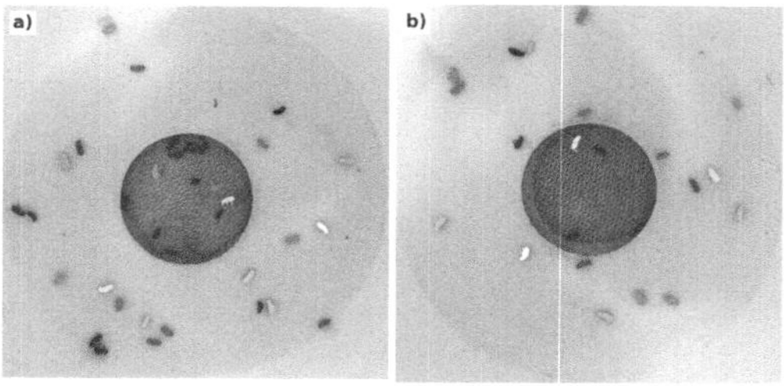

Fig. 5. Segmented insects highlighted by colors under different backgrounds.

Table 1. Average performance metrics for IoU and its derivatives

Metric	Score
Average IoU	28.69%
Average Precision	33.79%
Average Recall	69.76%
Average Accuracy	97.86%

Image preprocessing involved converting the colored images into gray-scale, and the original test set performed well, achieving an accuracy of 96%. However, after adding the Salt & Pepper, Poisson, Gaussian, and Speckle filters all together, they yielded the best performance as seen in Table 2.

Table 2. CNN's accuracy variation through noise filters

Kernel	Accuracy	Loss
Without	96%	13.14%
Gauss	100%	2.7%
Salt & Pepper	100%	2.7%
Poisson	100%	4.43%
Speckle	93.04%	24.15%
All 3	98.61%	15.91%

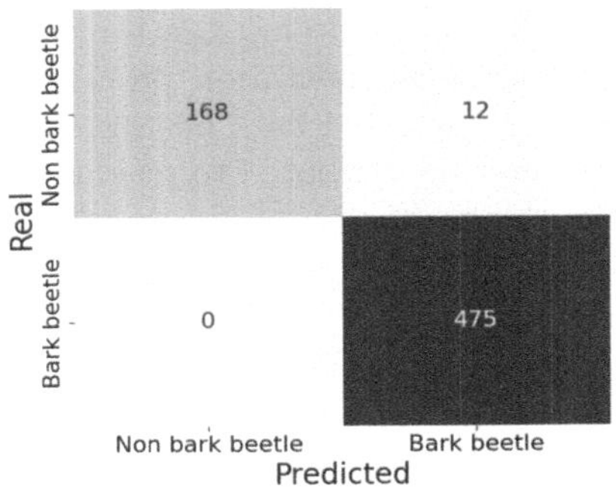

(a) VGGNet CNN.

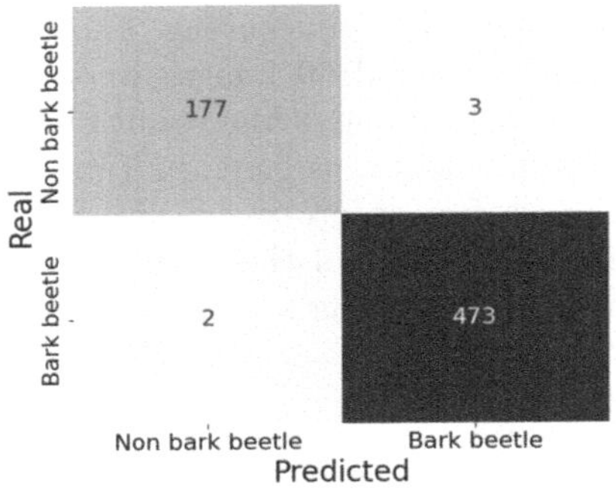

(b) ResNet50 CNN.

Fig. 6. Classification's confusion matrices.

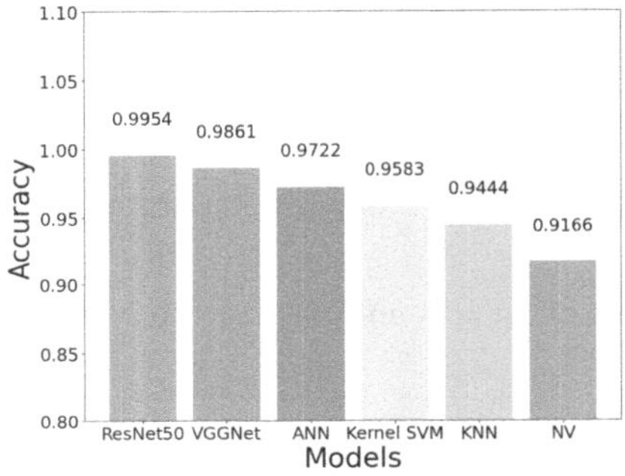

(a) Accuracy classification model.

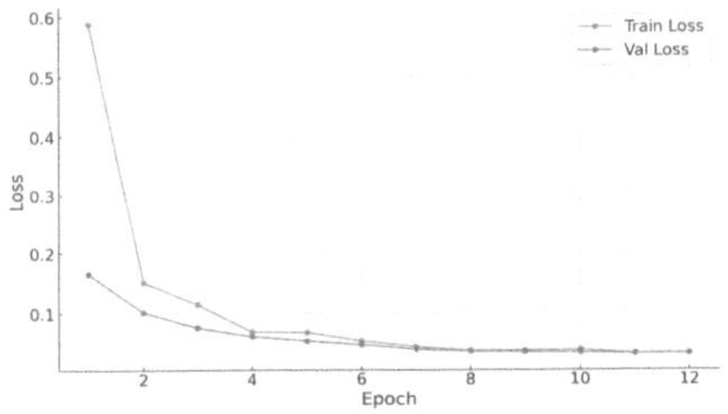

(b) Loss function's evolution on base model's training for ResNet50.

Fig. 7. Performance evaluation of several training models.

4 Discussion

The ResNet50 CNN achieved the highest accuracy it is shown in the confusion matrix in Fig. 6b. However, it is noteworthy that the other models also performed remarkably well, as shown in Fig. 7a. This outcome is understandable given the current dataset, considering the data augmentation and the use of a transfer learning technique for a small dataset. Given the almost perfect score of the ResNet50, it may be assumed that this is a deficient model, but the steady and progressive evolution of the loss functions shown in Fig. 7b demonstrates that this is a reliable model. It is possible to expect performance to change as we incorporate more insect species and introduce greater complexity to the setup. Additionally, the high accuracy observed can be partly attributed to the inclusion of the resultant images after applying the various noise filters discussed earlier as part of the training set.

In contrast to the existing literature on insect detection, where segmentation typically involves precisely tuned and complex models using techniques such as ANNs or applying models to different regions of an image, our approach demonstrates that introducing CCL after proper preprocessing has yielded significant results. This success is attributed to the high contrast between the insects and their background. It is worth mentioning that [26] proves that the sliding window does not offer good performance when it comes to segmentation, supporting its lacking performance. However, this method may prove insufficient when dealing with insects that do not exhibit such pronounced contrast, a common challenge in the field.

5 Conclusion

CCL proved to be a sufficient and optimal solution for detecting insects inside the Lindgren trap. Its precision is satisfactory for alerting the relevant authorities about the presence and concentration of insects in specific regions. This is further supported by the impressive time efficiency between inputting an image and classifying each of its detected subjects, which brings a substantial improvement to the current process, which is completely manual, reducing a period that may take up to a couple of weeks down to a couple of minutes. The CNN performed exceptionally well, though this is expected to change as the dataset becomes more complex. The high accuracy of the secondary classification models in this study serves as a clear example that minimally complex cases can also rely on non-spatial models, which contrasts with the common opinion in the field of image processing and analysis. These results encourage building this into a more robust and complex solution, which might not only be in the scope of bark beetles in Mexico but many kinds of insects in diverse environments.

Disclosure of Interests. The authors have no competing interests to declare that are relevant to the content of this article.

References

1. Raffa, K.F., Grégoire, J.C., Lindgren, B.S.: Natural history and ecology of bark beetles. In: Vega, F.E., Hofstetter, R.W. Bark Beetles (eds.) Academic Press, vol. 1, pp. 1–40 (2015). https://doi.org/10.1016/B978-0-12-417156-5.00001-0
2. Sáenz-Romero, C., et al.: Abundance of *Dendroctonus frontalis* and *D. mexicanus* (Coleoptera: Scolytinae) along altitudinal transects in Mexico: implications of climatic change for forest conservation. PLoS One **18**(7) (2023). https://doi.org/10.1371/journal.pone.0288067
3. Comisión Nacional Forestal.: Descortezadores, enemigos de los bosques templados. (2024). https://www.gob.mx/conafor/articulos/descortezadores-enemigos-de-los-bosques-templados. Accessed 17 Sept 2024
4. Secretaría de Medio Ambiente y Recursos Naturales.: NORMA Oficial Mexicana NOM-019-SEMARNAT-2006. In: Diario Oficial de la Federación (2008). https://dof.gob.mx. Accessed 17 Sept 2024

5. Phung, Q.V., Ahmad, I., Habibi, D., Hinckley, S.: Automated insect detection using acoustic features based on sound generated from insect activities. Acoust. Aust. **45**(2), 445–451 (2017). https://doi.org/10.1007/s40857-017-0095-6
6. Banga, K.S., Kotwaliwale, N., Mohapatra, D., Giri, S.K.: Techniques for insect detection in stored food grains: an overview. Food Control **94**, 167–176 (2018). https://doi.org/10.1016/j.foodcont.2018.07.008
7. Mamdouh, N., Khattab, A.: YOLO-based deep learning framework for olive fruit fly detection and counting. IEEE Access **9**, 84252–84262 (2021). https://doi.org/10.1109/ACCESS.2021.3088075
8. Amarathunga, D.C., Grundy, J., Parry, H., Dorin, A.: Methods of insect image capture and classification: a systematic literature review. Smart Agric. Technol. (2021). https://doi.org/10.1016/j.atech.2021.100023
9. Nagar, H., Sharma, R.S.: A comprehensive survey on pest detection techniques using image processing. In: 2020 4th International Conference on Intelligent Computing and Control Systems (ICICCS) (2020). https://doi.org/10.1109/iciccs48265.2020.9120889
10. Gao, Y., et al.: Application of machine learning in automatic image identification of insects - a review. Ecol. Inf. **80** (2024). ISSN 1574-9541. https://doi.org/10.1016/j.ecoinf.2024.102539. https://www.sciencedirect.com/science/article/pii/S1574954124000815. Accessed 1 Sept 2024
11. De Cesaro Júnior, T. and Rieder, R.: Automatic identification of insects from digital images: a survey. Comput. Electron. Agric. **178** (2020). ISSN 0168-1699. https://doi.org/10.1016/j.compag.2020.105784. https://www.sciencedirect.com/science/article/pii/S0168169920311224. Accessed 1 Sept 2024
12. Lindgren, B.S., Gries, G., Pierce, H.D., et al.: Dendroctonus pseudotsugae hopkins (Coleoptera: Scolytidae): production of and response to enantiomers of 1-methylcyclohex-2-en-1-ol. Chem, J. **18**, 1201–1208 (1992). https://doi.org/10.1007/BF00980074
13. Stevens, M.M., Warren, G.N., Mo, J., Schlipalius, D.I.: Maintaining DNA quality in stored-grain beetles caught in Lindgren funnel traps. J. Stored Prod. Res. **47**(2), 69–75 (2011). https://doi.org/10.1016/j.jspr.2010.10.002
14. Sun, Y., Liu, X., Yuan, M., Ren, L., Wang, J., Chen, Z.: Automatic in-trap pest detection using deep learning for pheromone-based Dendroctonus valens monitoring. Biosyst. Eng. **176**, 140–150 (2018). https://doi.org/10.1016/j.biosystemseng.2018.10.012
15. Kasinathan, T., Singaraju, D., Uyyala, S.R.: Insect classification and detection in field crops using modern machine learning techniques. Inf. Process. Agric. **8**, 446–457 (2018). https://doi.org/10.1016/j.inpa.2020.09.006
16. De Cesaro Júnior, Rieder, T.R., Di Domênico, J.R., Lau, D.: InsectCV: a system for insect detection in the lab from trap images. Ecol. Inf. **67** (2022). ISSN 1574-954. https://doi.org/10.1016/j.ecoinf.2021.101516. https://www.sciencedirect.com/science/article/pii/S1574954121003071. Accessed 17 Sept 2024
17. Deng, L., Wang, Y., Han, Z., Yu, R.: Research on insect pest image detection and recognition based on bio-inspired methods. Biosyst. Eng. **169**, 139–148 (2018). https://doi.org/10.1016/j.biosystemseng.2018.02.008
18. Ebrahimi, M.A., Khoshtaghaza, M.H., Minaei, S., Jamshidi, B.: Vision-based pest detection based on the SVM classification method. Comput. Electron. Agric. **137**, 52–58 (2017). https://doi.org/10.1016/j.compag.2017.03.016

19. Yao, Q., et al.: An insect imaging system to automate rice light-trap pest identification. J. Integr. Agric. **11**(6), 978–985 (2012). https://doi.org/10.1016/s2095-3119(12)60089-6
20. Espinoza, K., Valera, D.L., Torres, J.A., López, A., Molina-Aiz, F.D.: Combination of image processing and artificial neural networks as a novel approach for the identification of Bemisia tabaci and Frankliniella occidentalis on sticky traps in greenhouse agriculture. Comput. Electron. Agric. **127**, 495–505 (2016). https://doi.org/10.1016/j.compag.2016.07.008
21. Sanmorino, A., Kesuma, H.: Fine-tuning a pre-trained ResNet50 model to detect distributed denial of service attack. Bull. Electr. Eng. Inf. **13**(2), 1362–1370 (2024). https://doi.org/10.11591/eei.v13i2.7014
22. Taha, A.A., Hanbury, A.: Metrics for evaluating 3D medical image segmentation: analysis, selection, and tool. BMC Med. Imaging **15**(1), 29 (2015). https://doi.org/10.1186/s12880-015-0068-x
23. Radecic, D.: Top 10 Machine Learning Evaluation Metrics for Classification - Implemented in R. Appsilon. (2024). https://www.appsilon.com/post/machine-learning-evaluation-metrics-classification. Accessed 17 Sept 2024
24. Rustia, D., Erh Lin, C., Chung, J.-Y., Zhuang, Y.-J., Hsu, J.-C., Lin, T.-T.: Application of an image and environmental sensor network for automated greenhouse insect pest monitoring. J. Asia-Pac. Entomol. (2019). https://doi.org/10.1016/j.aspen.2019.11.006
25. Bangar, S.: VGG-Net Architecture Explained (2022). https://medium.com/@siddheshb008/vgg-net-architecture-explained-71179310050f. Accessed 17 Sept 2024
26. Nam, N.T., Hung, P.D.: Pest detection on traps using deep convolutional neural networks. In: Proceedings of the 2018 International Conference on Control and Computer Vision (ICCCV) (2018). https://doi.org/10.1145/3232651.3232661

Handling Constraints in Clustering via Multi-Objective Evolutionary Algorithms

Alejandro Rosales-Pérez, Norberto A. Hernández-Leandro(✉), and Erika-Tatiana Rueda-Santos

Centro de Investigación en Matemáticas, Avenida Alianza Centro 502, Parque de Investigación e Innovación Tecnológica, Apodaca, Nuevo León, Mexico
{alejandro.rosales,norberto.hernandez,erika.rueda}@cimat.mx

Abstract. This work proposes a multi-objective evolutionary constrained clustering (MOECC) approach that leverages the strengths of multi-objective evolutionary algorithms (MOEAs) to efficiently explore trade-offs between clustering quality and constraint adherence. Using MOEA/D, our method decomposes the problem into multiple subproblems, optimizing them simultaneously while maintaining diversity across the solution space. We evaluated MOECC on 31 benchmark datasets and compared its performance with state-of-the-art constrained clustering techniques. The results demonstrate that our approach consistently achieves superior clustering quality while minimizing constraint violations, particularly in scenarios with limited prior information. These findings highlight the effectiveness of MOECC in generating diverse, high-quality clustering solutions that adapt to different constraint levels and data characteristics.

Keywords: Constrained clustering · Multi-objective optimization · Evolutionary algorithms · MOEA/D

1 Introduction

Traditional clustering is an unsupervised learning task that aims to identify groups of objects, known as clusters, such that objects placed in the same group are more similar to each other than to those in other groups. Although clustering has proven to be a powerful analysis technique in several domains, incorporating background information may help find more accurate partitions. Constrained clustering (CC) offers an alternative to traditional clustering methods by incorporating prior knowledge. That information can be represented as instance-level, cluster-level, features-level, or distance-level constraints. The intuitive and easily interpretable nature of instance-level constraints, which define relationships between data points to facilitate grouping, has led to their widespread adoption [2]. Such constraints can stem from expert knowledge, textual co-occurrence, or user-provided similarity assessments.

A. P. López-Monroy et al. (Eds.): MCPR 2025, LNCS 15715, pp. 78–89, 2025.
https://doi.org/10.1007/978-3-031-96255-4_8

While pairwise constraints offer advantages, their effective use in clustering is a significant hurdle. Strict enforcement of constraints may compromise cluster quality, resulting in less compact and well-separated groups. Trying to achieve both high-quality clusters and strong constraint satisfaction inherently leads to a multi-objective optimization problem. The goal is to create well-formed clusters (by traditional clustering standards), but this must be done subject to the given pairwise constraints.

This paper introduces MOECC, a multi-objective approach to constrained clustering, to resolve this inherent conflict. This multi-objective approach optimizes two aspects of cluster quality, while satisfying constraints via the epsilon-constraint method. The primary contributions of this paper are the following: i) we introduce a novel multi-objective optimization framework for pairwise constrained clustering, ii) we propose a cluster-based crossover as an evolutionary operator, iii) we introduce a post-processing technique to handle with the resulting Pareto front to build a final clustering, and iv) we empirically demonstrate the effectiveness of our approach on an extensive number of dataset.

The remainder of this paper is organized as follows: Sect. 2 presents the main concepts related to constrained clustering and multi-objective optimization. Section 3 describes the proposed MOECC. Section 4 presents the datasets and the experimental configuration used to assess MOECC and Sect. 5 shows the reported results. Finally, Sect. 6 shows the main conclusions.

2 Preliminaries

2.1 Constrained Clustering

Constrained Clustering (CC) enhances traditional clustering by integrating partial prior knowledge through constraints, guiding data grouping beyond inherent similarities. These constraints, derived from expert input or feedback, fall into four categories: i) **instance-level** with must-link/cannot-link pairs enforce similarity/dissimilarity between data points; ii) **cluster-level** restrictions on cluster size, balance, or variance; iii) **feature-level** with attribute relationships or prioritization (e.g., weighting specific features); and **distance-based** that requires a minimum separation (γ-constraints) or proximity requirements (ε-constraints).

Pairwise constraints (must-link/cannot-link) are popular for embedding relational knowledge into clustering, aligning groups with domain insights. Constrained clustering combines the flexibility of unsupervised methods with expert guidance, making it useful for applications such as personalized recommendations, biomedical analysis, and market segmentation. By incorporating these constraints, the approach reduces the ambiguity inherent in similarity-based methods and ensures clusters reflect both data patterns and contextual knowledge.

2.2 Multi-Objective Optimization

Multi-Objective Optimization Problems (MOPs) involve optimizing conflicting objectives simultaneously. A solution is Pareto optimal if no objective improves without worsening another; all such solutions form the Pareto Frontier.

Multi-Objective Evolutionary Algorithms (MOEAs), like MOEA/D [12], decompose MOPs into scalar subproblems via weighted aggregations, enabling simultaneous exploration of multiple directions. This yields diverse, high-quality solutions. In clustering, MOEA/D balances criteria (e.g., compactness vs. connectivity) and manages constraint violations, critical for robust outcomes. By integrating decomposition and evolutionary search, MOEA/D addresses complex trade-offs, outperforming traditional methods in scenarios with competing priorities.

3 MOECC: Multi-Objective Evolutionary Constrained Clustering

This section introduces our proposed Multi-Objective Evolutionary Constrained Clustering (MOECC) method. MOECC uses the MOEA/D algorithm and the ε-constraint method to handle clustering problems with pairwise constraints.

3.1 Representation and Evolutionary Operators

The encoding used in an EA is crucial for its effectiveness. In evolutionary clustering, three main representations are used: label-based, cluster-based, and graph-based [4]. We use a label-based encoding because it straightforwardly describes the clusters with any shape. In this representation, an individual is encoded as an n-dimensional vector, where each position corresponds to a dataset instance. For a solution with k clusters, each position takes a value $c_i \in \{1, \ldots, k\}$ indicating the cluster to which that instance belongs.

The MOECC generates the initial population randomly. For the ith individual, a random integer $k_i \in \{2, \ldots, 20\}$ is chosen, and each variable is assigned a random integer value in $[1, k_i]$. This method ensures diverse clustering structures by varying the number of clusters among individuals. Although initial solutions are limited to 20 clusters, evolutionary operators allow exploration of a broader range.

The MOECC algorithm tackles clustering problems using a specialized crossover and mutation strategy designed for cluster-based solutions. Algorithm 1 presents the cluster-based crossover method used in MOECC. Initially, the cluster partitions C_{p^a} and C_{p^b} of parents p^a and p^b are retrieved (lines 1 and 2). A random selection of groups from C_{p^a} is then transferred to the child solution $C_{p^{child}}$ (lines 4–8) to preserve information from one parent. Next, a subset $C'_{p^b} \subset C_{p^b}$ is formed by excluding instances already in $C_{p^{child}}$ (line 9). This partial clustering is processed in one of two ways: either by incorporating the groups from C'_{p^b} directly into $C_{p^{child}}$ (line 11) or by assigning each instance in C'_{p^b} to the nearest centroid in $C_{p^{child}}$ (line 14). Notably, this crossover enables exploration of solutions with varying numbers of clusters.

Algorithm 1. Cluster-based crossover used in MOECC

1: Let p^a and p^b two parent individuals.
2: Let C_{p^a} and C_{p^b} the cluster partitions given by p^a and p^b, respectively.
3: $C_{p^{child}} \leftarrow \emptyset$.
4: **for** each group $c^i_{p^a} \in C_{p^a}$ **do**
5:     **if** rand < 0.5 **then**
6:         $C_{p^{child}} \leftarrow C_{p^{child}} \cup c^i_{p^a}$
7:     **end if**
8: **end for**
9: $C'_{p^b} \leftarrow C_{p^b} \setminus C_{p^{child}}$.
10: **if** rand < 0.5 **then**
11:     $C_{p^{child}} \leftarrow C_{p^{child}} \cup C'_{p^b}$
12: **else**
13:     **for** each group $c^i_{p^b} \in C'_{p^b}$ **do**
14:         Add each instance in $c^i_{p^b}$ to the cluster with the nearest centroid in $C_{p^{child}}$.
15:     **end for**
16: **end if**
17: Let p^{child} the corresponding encoding of $C_{p^{child}}$.

Algorithm 2 describes the neighborhood-based mutation [7]. This operator randomly selects some instances based on a mutation probability. A randomly chosen instance is randomly assigned to one of its k nearest neighbors (lines 4-5). This approach groups similar objects within the neighborhood. Note that although the mutation operator computes k-nearest neighbors, pre-computing and storing them can mitigate the computational cost.

Algorithm 2. neighborhood-based mutation used in MOECC

1: Let p^c and individual and p_m the mutation rate.
2: **for** each instance $\mathbf{x}_i \in \mathbf{X}$ **do**
3:     **if** rand $< p_m$ **then**
4:         Find the k-nearest neighbors of $\mathbf{x}_i \in \mathbf{X} \setminus \{\mathbf{x}_i\}$.
5:         Move $\mathbf{x}_i$ to the group of one of its k-nearest neighbors randomly selected.
6:     **end if**
7: **end for**

3.2 Fitness Function and Constraint Handling

The goal of clustering is to create groups that exhibit high similarity among their instances and minimize the dispersion within each group. To achieve this goal, the MOECC focuses on optimizing two criteria: clustering compactness and connectedness. Compactness, or within-cluster variance, measures the proximity of data points within a cluster to its center. This objective function is calculated by summing the squared differences between the instance and its centroid, i.e.,

$$C_o\left(p^i\right) = \sum_{c_j \in C_{p^i}} \sum_{\mathbf{x}_k \in c_j} \left(\mathbf{x}_k - \mu_j\right)^2, \tag{1}$$

where C_{p^i} is the partition given by the individual p^i and μ_j is the centroid of the cluster c_j.

Connectedness is estimated through the connectivity score [7]. Connectivity measures the extent to which similar instances are grouped in different clusters. That means, a well-connected cluster puts each instance and its l-nearest neighbors in the same cluster. Connectivity is computed as follows:

$$C_n\left(p^i\right) = \frac{1}{n} \sum_{j=1}^{n} \left(\sum_{h=1}^{l} \delta\left(\mathbf{x}_j, \mathbf{x}_{nn_h}\right) \right), \tag{2}$$

where n is the dataset size and $\delta\left(\mathbf{x}_j, \mathbf{x}_{nn_h}\right)$ is a function that takes the value of $\frac{1}{h}$ if the instance $\mathbf{x}_j$ and 0 otherwise.

MOECC operates within the MOEA/D framework. After evaluating the values in the objective function of a solutions, they are aggregated into a single score using the Tchebycheff technique. Once the solution quality is estimated, its feasibility is assessed using the ε-constraint handling method. Solutions are compared in lexicographic order–first by constraint violations and then by the Tchebycheff score–thereby prioritizing feasible solutions over infeasible ones. The ε-constraint criteria indicate that the solution p^a is preferable to p^b if one of the following rules is met:

$$\left(g\left(p^a \mid \lambda, \mathbf{z}^*\right), \phi\left(p^a\right)\right) <_\epsilon \left(g\left(p^b \mid \lambda, \mathbf{z}^*\right), \phi\left(p^b\right)\right) \iff$$
$$\begin{cases} g\left(p^a \mid \lambda_i, \mathbf{z}^*\right) < g\left(p^b \mid \lambda_i, \mathbf{z}^*\right) & \text{if } \phi\left(p^a\right), \phi\left(p^b\right) \leq \varepsilon; \\ g\left(p^a \mid \lambda_i, \mathbf{z}^*\right) < g\left(p^b \mid \lambda_i, \mathbf{z}^*\right) & \text{if } \phi\left(p^a\right) = \phi\left(p^b\right); \\ \phi\left(p^a\right) < \phi\left(p^b\right) & \text{otherwise.} \end{cases}$$

where $\phi\left(\cdot\right)$ is the amount of violated contraints and ε is the relaxation constraint threshold and is defined dynamically during the search. The value of ε gradually decreases during the T generations, as explained in [11].

3.3 Post-processing

A MOP generates a set of Pareto-optimal solutions that balance compactness and connectivity. Although these solutions are equivalent from an optimization standpoint, final selection still requires domain expertise. Rather than choosing a single solution, we aggregate the entire Pareto front by constructing a co-occurrence matrix [5], which records the frequency with which instance pairs are clustered together across all solutions. Consensus clustering is then performed in two phases: first, instances that consistently appear together form stable groups; second, the remaining instances are assigned through a weighted majority vote based on their co-occurrence frequencies and guided by prior knowledge. This method leverages the full Pareto set, ensuring robustness and adherence to domain constraints without expert intervention.

4 Experimental Settings

In this section, we outline our experimental setup. Section 4.1 details the benchmark datasets, and Sect. 4.2 describes the evaluation metrics and tests used to assess performance.

4.1 Datasets

We evaluated MOECC on 31 benchmark datasets. Table 1 details each dataset samples, features, classes, and majority-to-minority ratio, enabling an assessment across diverse problem characteristics.

The class label to generate the set of constraints. The number of constraints for each dataset under different degrees of partial information is determined as follows:

$$|\mathcal{C}| = \frac{1}{2}\left(\lfloor r \cdot n \rfloor\right)\left(\lfloor r \cdot n \rfloor - 1\right), \tag{3}$$

where $r \in [0, 1]$ is the ratio of samples and n is the number of samples.

MOECC is compared with **Linear Constrained Vector Quantization Error (LCVQE)** [10], **Relational Diritchlet Process Means (RDPM)** [9], **SHADE$_{CC}$**, and **ME-MOEAD$_{CC}$** [6]. LCVQE, SHADE$_{CC}$, and ME-MOEAD$_{CC}$ require specify the number of clusters. To ensure a fair comparison, the number of clusters in each dataset is optimized using the bootstrap method [1]. This method generates B replications, which are grouped into k clusters. Then, the cluster stability is estimated by computing the Hartigan clustering index [8] for each replication. The process is repeated for different values of k, and the value with the most stable index is selected. Then the interquartile range for each k value is determined, such that the smaller the interquartile, the greater the stability.

4.2 Performance Metrics and Analysis Tools

We adopted a set of metrics to assess the performance of each clustering technique. The set of metrics includes the **Adjusted Rand Index (ARI)**, **V-measure (V)**, and **Constraints violations ratio (CVR)**. It measures the rate of violated constraints.

Table 1. Description of datasets based on the number of samples, number of features, number of classes, the ratio between majority class (n_M) and minority class (n_m) and the number of constraints under different degrees of partial information.

Dataset	Samples	Features	Classes	n_M/n_m	10%	15%	20%	25%	30%
accent_voice	329	12	6	5.6897	496	1176	2080	3321	4753
appendicitis	106	7	2	4.0476	45	105	210	325	465
balance	625	4	3	5.8776	1891	4278	7750	12090	17391
bands	365	19	2	1.7037	630	1431	2628	4095	5886
bank_note	1372	4	2	1.2492	9316	20910	37401	58653	84255
bench	208	60	2	1.1443	190	465	820	1326	1891
breast_cancer	569	30	2	1.6840	1540	3570	6328	10011	14365
bupa	345	6	2	1.3793	561	1275	2346	3655	5253
cafeina_consumption	1885	12	7	138.5000	17578	39621	70876	110685	159330
cleveland	297	13	5	12.3077	406	946	1711	2701	3916
diabetes	768	8	2	1.8657	2850	6555	11628	18336	26335
digits	1797	63	10	1.0517	15931	36046	64261	100576	144991
divorce	170	54	2	1.0238	136	300	561	861	1275
glass	214	9	6	8.4444	210	496	861	1378	2016
heart_failure	299	12	2	2.1146	406	946	1711	2701	3916
ionosphere	351	32	2	1.7857	595	1326	2415	3741	5460
iris	150	4	3	1.0000	105	231	435	666	990
led7digit	500	7	10	1.5405	1225	2775	4950	7750	11175
libras_movement	360	90	15	1.0000	630	1431	2556	4005	5778
mammographic	830	5	2	1.0596	3403	7626	13695	21321	30876
monk-2	432	6	2	1.1176	903	2016	3655	5778	8256
plants	1600	128	100	1.0000	12720	28680	51040	79800	114960
qsar_biodeg	1055	41	2	1.9635	5460	12403	22155	34453	49770
sonar	208	60	2	1.1443	190	465	820	1326	1891
spectfheart	267	44	2	3.8545	325	780	1378	2145	3160
steel_plates_fault	1941	33	2	1.8841	18721	42195	75078	117370	169071
tae	151	5	3	1.0612	105	231	435	666	990
vehicle	846	18	4	1.0955	3486	7875	14196	22155	31878
wdbc	569	30	2	1.6840	1540	3570	6328	10011	14365
wine	178	13	3	1.4792	136	325	595	946	1378
zoo	101	16	7	10.2500	45	105	190	300	435

We employed the hierarchical Bayesian test [3] to compare MOECC with reference methods. This approach estimates posterior probabilities to determine if one algorithm outperforms the other or if their performance is practically equivalent, regardless of the number of datasets. It also provides more detailed insights than the null hypothesis significance test, even when the latter fails to reject the null hypothesis. In this study, we consider two methods equivalent if their difference is below 0.01.

5 Experimental Results

In this section, we evaluated our method on 31 benchmark datasets with diverse characteristics and varying constraint levels. Using metrics like ARI, V-measure, and CVR, our approach outperformed state-of-the-art techniques by effectively balancing intra-cluster similarity and connectivity. Notably, it achieved high clustering quality with fewer constraint violations, even with limited external guidance.

5.1 Comparing the Clustering Quality

This experimental aims to assess the performance of MOECC under different levels of constraints, and comparing the performance to those reported by reference methods.

The results for the hierarchical Bayesian analysis is shown in Fig. 1 for the all considered constraints levels. The results are graphically depicted through the barycenter plots, where the left region represents the probability that MOECC outperforms the reference method, the right side the probability that reference method outperforms MOECC, and the top side the probability that both methods have a practical equivalent performance.

Based on Table 2 and Fig. 1, the following observations can be made. Regardless of the amount of partial information provided by the constraints, MOECC consistently achieved the highest ARI and V measure compared to the reference methods. Furthermore, RDPM, SHADE_{CC}, and MOECC improved as the number of constraints increased, enhancing the quality of the partition, while LCVQE and MEMOEA/D_{CC} maintained nearly constant overall performance concerning the constraint count. On the `cafeina_consumption` dataset, MOECC was outperformed by RDPM at all constraint levels, likely due to the dataset's high group imbalance; however, the performance gap remained below 2%. In datasets with many clusters–such as `libras_movement` (15 groups) and `plants` (100 groups)–MOECC outperformed RDPM and other methods, with its advantage growing alongside the number of clusters. Even with a relatively small fraction of constraints, MOECC significantly outperformed the reference methods, reaching an overall performance above 0.90 at 20% constraint levels. Notably, despite neither MOECC nor RDPM having prior knowledge of the true number of clusters, both outperformed LCVQE, SHADE_{CC}, and MEMOEA/D_{CC}. In terms of constraint satisfaction, MOECC exhibited the lowest violation rate among the evaluated methods.

Bayesian analysis strongly favored MOECC, as the center of mass consistently fell within the MOECC region at constraint levels of 10%, 15%, and 20%, indicating a 1.0 probability of outperforming the other methods. Finally,

Table 2. Summary of Mean Performance Results for Different Constraint Levels

Constraint Level	LCVQE	RDPM	MEMOEA/DCC	SHADECC	MOECC
ARI					
10%	0.2226	0.3949	0.2189	0.0310	0.7363
15%	0.2236	0.5643	0.2402	0.0530	0.8854
20%	0.2233	0.6933	0.2465	0.0835	0.9418
25%	0.2224	0.7700	0.2459	0.1087	0.9733
V-measure					
10%	0.2656	0.4270	0.2534	0.0370	0.7193
15%	0.2658	0.5834	0.2690	0.0524	0.8689
20%	0.2655	0.7057	0.2755	0.0787	0.9274
25%	0.2649	0.7816	0.2740	0.1043	0.9597
CVR					
10%	0.3425	0.1967	0.3231	0.3278	0.0106
15%	0.3427	0.1379	0.3146	0.3537	0.0079
20%	0.3430	0.1011	0.3165	0.3628	0.0053
25%	0.3434	0.0822	0.3205	0.3635	0.0043

Bayesian testing revealed nearly equivalent performance for 25% and 30% of the constraints, with the center of mass situated within the region of practical equivalence. It is noteworthy that at 30% constraints, the performance variability exceeded 0.15, suggesting a high degree of variability among replicas, particularly for RDPM.

Generally, MOECC exploited the information given through the constraints, and showed superior performance in most problems. Although, for problems with 25% and 30% of constraints, RDPM and MOECC had a practical performance, the behavior of MOECC over different sets of constraints was more stable than that obtained by RDPM.

5.2 Analyzing the Number of Clusters

In this section, we analyzed the number of clusters found by RDPM and MOECC. The aim is to assess how efective is MOECC to find the true number of clusters. LCVQE, MEMOEAD$_{CC}$, and SHADE$_{CC}$ were not considered for comparison as those methods require the number of clusters as a hyper-parameter, which was set equal to the expected number of clusters.

Table 3 compares the number of clusters obtained by RDPM and MOECC. It also shows the expected number of clusters for each dataset. The reported results are the median value over 30 replications for each dataset.

From Table 3, both methods automatically determine the number of clusters, and their accuracy improves with more constraints. With 10% constraints, RDPM correctly identified the cluster count in 8 out of 31 datasets and MOECC

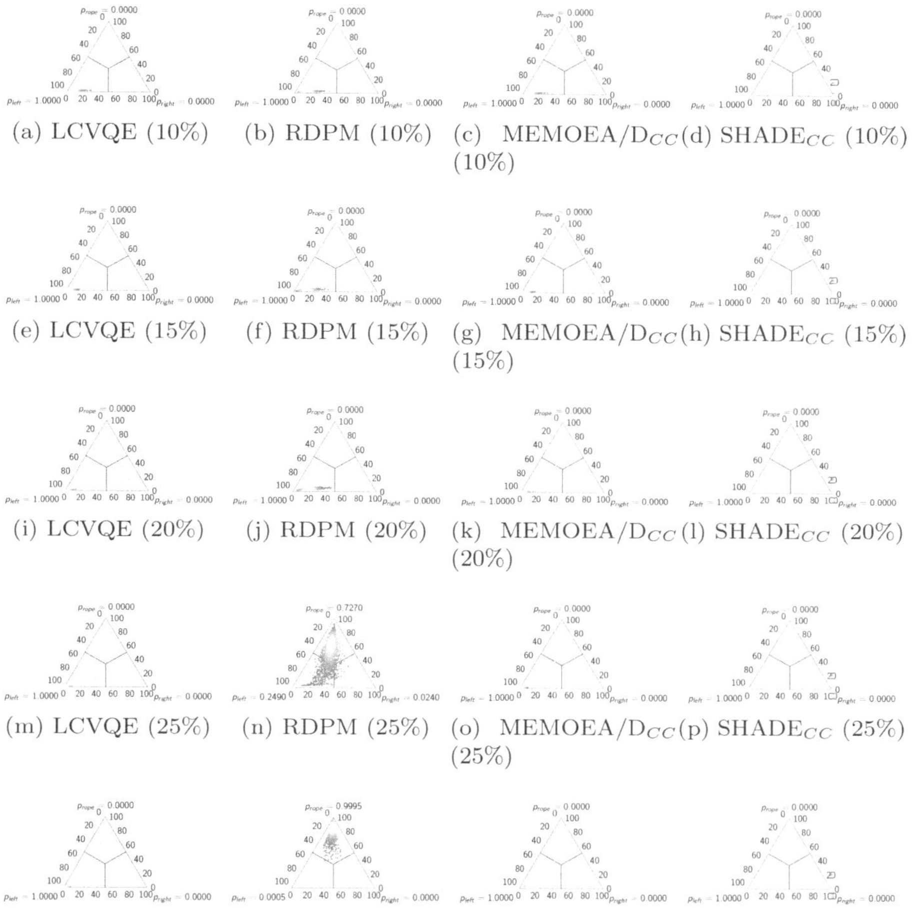

(a) LCVQE (10%) (b) RDPM (10%) (c) MEMOEA/D$_{CC}$ (10%) (d) SHADE$_{CC}$ (10%)

(e) LCVQE (15%) (f) RDPM (15%) (g) MEMOEA/D$_{CC}$ (15%) (h) SHADE$_{CC}$ (15%)

(i) LCVQE (20%) (j) RDPM (20%) (k) MEMOEA/D$_{CC}$ (20%) (l) SHADE$_{CC}$ (20%)

(m) LCVQE (25%) (n) RDPM (25%) (o) MEMOEA/D$_{CC}$ (25%) (p) SHADE$_{CC}$ (25%)

(q) LCVQE (30%) (r) RDPM (30%) (s) MEMOEA/D$_{CC}$ (30%) (t) SHADE$_{CC}$ (30%)

Fig. 1. Posterior distribution for ARI score when comparing MOECC with the reference methods for at the 10%, 15%, 20%, 25%, and 30% of constraints. The region of the bottom-left (p_{left}) represents MOECC, the region at the top (p_{rope}) is for practical eqivalence, and the region in the bottom-right (p_{right}) represents the reference method.

in 11 out of 35. At 15% constraints, RDPM succeeded in 10 out of 31 datasets versus MOECC's 21 out of 31; at 20%, the results were 12 out of 31 for RDPM and 21 out of 31 for MOECC. For 25% and 30% constraints, RDPM achieved 17 out of 31 while MOECC reached 26 out of 31, with the 30% solutions yielding cluster counts closer to the true values.

Table 3. Number of cluster found by RDPM and MOECC. The reported values are the median over the 30 replications of each dataset. For each case, we show in boldface when matching with the expected number of clusters.

Dataset	Real	10%		15%		20%		25%		30%	
		RDPM	MOECC	RDPM	MOECC	RDPM	MOECC	RDPM	MOECC	RDPM	MOECC
accent_voice	6	3	13	3	14	3	8	**6**	**6**	**6**	**6**
appendicitis	2	3	3	3	4	3	3	3	**2**	3	**2**
balance	3	8	4	8	**3**	8	**3**	7	**3**	7	**3**
bands	2	3	3	3	**2**	3	**2**	3	**2**	3	**2**
bank_note	2	**2**	**2**	**2**	**2**	**2**	**2**	**2**	**2**	**2**	**2**
bench	2	4	4	4	**2**	4	**2**	**2**	**2**	**2**	**2**
breast_cancer	2	3	**2**	**2**	**2**	**2**	**2**	**2**	**2**	**2**	**2**
bupa	2	**2**	4	**2**	**2**	**2**	**2**	**2**	**2**	**2**	**2**
cafeina_consumption	7	9	14	10	20	10	26	11	29	10	33
cleveland	5	4	12	**5**	12	6	9	6	7	7	6
diabetes	2	3	**2**	3	**2**	**2**	**2**	**2**	**2**	**2**	**2**
digits	10	14	11	16	**10**	11	**10**	**10**	**10**	**10**	**10**
divorce	2	3	**2**	3	**2**	3	**2**	3	**2**	3	**2**
glass	6	4	7	5	9	5	8	7	7	7	7
heart_failure	2	3	4	3	**2**	**2**	**2**	**2**	**2**	**2**	**2**
ionosphere	2	16	3	9	**2**	3	**2**	**2**	**2**	**2**	**2**
iris	3	**3**	**3**	**3**	**3**	**3**	**3**	**3**	**3**	**3**	**3**
led7digit	10	8	25	**10**	22	12	12	13	**10**	13	**10**
libras_movement	15	12	26	12	29	14	30	16	25	18	16
mammographic	2	**2**	**2**	**2**	**2**	**2**	**2**	**2**	**2**	**2**	**2**
monk	2	9	**2**	9	**2**	**2**	**2**	**2**	**2**	**2**	**2**
plants	100	19	121	24	162	31	236	40	180	50	104
qsar_biodeg	2	3	**2**	**2**	**2**	**2**	**2**	**2**	**2**	**2**	**2**
sonar	2	5	5	5	**2**	5	**2**	3	**2**	**2**	**2**
spectfheart	2	3	3	3	**2**	**2**	**2**	**2**	**2**	**2**	**2**
steel_plates_fault	2	3	**2**	**2**	**2**	**2**	**2**	**2**	**2**	**2**	**2**
tae	3	2	6	**3**	8	4	6	**3**	**3**	4	**3**
vehicle	4	2	9	2	**4**	2	**4**	2	**4**	2	**4**
wdbc	2	3	**2**	3	**2**	**2**	**2**	**2**	**2**	**2**	**2**
wine	3	7	**3**	6	**3**	6	**3**	5	**3**	4	**3**
zoo	7	8	5	8	6	8	6	8	**7**	8	**7**

6 Conclusions

In this paper, we addressed clustering with constrained pairwise constraints. We proposed MOECC, a multi-objective approach that optimizes the connectivity and compactness of clusters while handling constraints via the epsilon-constraint method.

Through rigorous experimentation with 31 datasets, we empirically demonstrated the effectiveness of our proposed approach compared to state-of-the-art methods. MOECC was also able to find the right number of clusters for most datasets, outperforming reference methods.

As future work, exploring other multi-objective optimization algorithms could further enhance the efficiency and effectiveness of our approach, as well as investigating alternative types of constraints and their integration within MOECC. Finally, interactive visualization and exploration of the Pareto front could empower users to effectively navigate and select the most suitable constrained clustering solution for their specific needs.

Acknowledgements. We acknowledge funding from SECIHTI under research project numbers CBF2023-2024-2797 and CBF2023-2024-3976.

References

1. Jain, A.K., Moreau, J.V.: Bootstrap technique in cluster analysis. Pattern Recogn. **20**(5), 547–568 (1987). https://doi.org/10.1016/0031-3203(87)90081-1
2. Basu, S., Banerjee, A., Mooney, R.J.: Semi-supervised clustering by seeding. In: Proceedings of the Nineteenth International Conference on Machine Learning, ICML '02, pp. 27–34. Morgan Kaufmann Publishers Inc., San Francisco (2002)
3. Benavoli, A., Corani, G., Demšar, J., Zaffalon, M.: Time for a change: a tutorial for comparing multiple classifiers through bayesian analysis. J. Mach. Learn. Res. **18**(1), 2653–2688 (2017)
4. Figueiredo, E., Macedo, M., Siqueira, H.V., Santana, C.J., Gokhale, A., Bastos-Filho, C.J.: Swarm intelligence for clustering—a systematic review with new perspectives on data mining. Eng. Appl. Artif. Intell. **82**, 313–329 (2019). https://doi.org/10.1016/j.engappai.2019.04.007
5. Fred, A.L., Jain, A.K.: Combining multiple clusterings using evidence accumulation. IEEE Trans. Pattern Anal. Mach. Intell. **27**(6), 835–850 (2005). https://doi.org/10.1109/TPAMI.2005.113
6. González-Almagro, G., Rosales-Pérez, A., Luengo, J., Cano, J.R., García, S.: ME-MEOA/D$_{CC}$: multiobjective constrained clustering through decomposition-based memetic elitism. Swarm Evol. Comput. **66**, 100939 (2021). https://doi.org/10.1016/j.swevo.2021.100939
7. Handl, J., Knowles, J.: An evolutionary approach to multiobjective clustering. IEEE Trans. Evol. Comput. **11**(1), 56–76 (2007). https://doi.org/10.1109/TEVC.2006.877146
8. Hartigan, J.A.: Clustering. Ann. Rev. Biophys. Bioeng. **2**(1), 81–102 (1973)
9. Khashabi, D., Wieting, J., Liu, J.Y., Liang, F.: Clustering with side information: from a probabilistic model to a deterministic algorithm. arXiv preprint arXiv:1508.06235 (2015)
10. Pelleg, D., Baras, D.: K-means with large and noisy constraint sets. In: Kok, J.N., Koronacki, J., Mantaras, R.L., Matwin, S., Mladenič, D., Skowron, A. (eds.) ECML 2007. LNCS (LNAI), vol. 4701, pp. 674–682. Springer, Heidelberg (2007). https://doi.org/10.1007/978-3-540-74958-5_67
11. Takahama, T., Sakai, S.: Constrained optimization by the ε constrained differential evolution with gradient-based mutation and feasible elites. In: 2006 IEEE International Conference on Evolutionary Computation, pp. 1–8 (2006). https://doi.org/10.1109/CEC.2006.1688283
12. Zhang, Q., Li, H.: MOEA/D: a multiobjective evolutionary algorithm based on decomposition. IEEE Trans. Evol. Comput. **11**(6), 712–731 (2007). https://doi.org/10.1109/TEVC.2007.892759

Analysis of Children's Emotions in Sketches Using Classical and Deep Learning Approaches

Ricardo Ramos-Aguilar[1(✉)], Daniel Sánchez-Ruiz[1], Liliana Estela Rubí-Sánchez[2], Eric Ramos-Aguilar[1], Karla Rivera-Lima[1], and Gerardo Suarez-Gonzalez[1]

[1] Unidad Interdisciplinaria de Ingeniería Campus Tlaxcala Instituto Politécnico Nacional, Guillermo Valle 11, Centro, 90000 Tlaxcala de Xicohténcatl, Tlax, Mexico
{rramosa,dsanchezro,eramosa,gsuarezg}@ipn.mx, kriveral2100@alumno.ipn.mx

[2] Universidad de la Salud Calle Vasco de Quiroga 1401, Colonia Santa Fe, Alcaldía Álvaro Obregón, C.P. 01210 Ciudad de México, Mexico
liliana.rubis@unisa.cdmx.gob.mx

Abstract. Emotion recognition in children's drawings provides valuable insights into their psychological and emotional states. This study compares two computational approaches for classifying positive and negative emotions in sketches drawn by children aged four to eight. The first approach employs classical machine learning techniques, where shape and intensity features are extracted from grayscale and binary images. These feature vectors are then evaluated using Support Vector Machines (SVM), Multilayer Perceptron (MLP), and Random Forest classifiers, with the best accuracy reaching 80% using SVM with a linear kernel.

The second approach applies a pre-trained Vision Transformer (ViT) model, exploring the effects of data augmentation and fine-tuning on the classification performance. The ViT model achieved 76.5% accuracy with transfer learning.

The results highlight the effectiveness of SVM and ViTs for analyzing children's drawings, demonstrating that classical methods can perform competitively in small datasets. Meanwhile, deep learning models show promise but require more extensive datasets for optimal performance.

Keywords: Emotion Recognition · children · family sketches · machine learning

1 Introduction

Emotions are natural human reactions that provide valuable information about behavior and the surrounding environment. Childhood is a critical period for acquiring essential social skills, shaping interactions, and fostering emotional development [20]. From infancy to adolescence, emotional growth influences

A. P. López-Monroy et al. (Eds.): MCPR 2025, LNCS 15715, pp. 90–100, 2025.
https://doi.org/10.1007/978-3-031-96255-4_9

social relationships, academic performance, and overall well-being. Understanding emotions is key to self-awareness and interpersonal behavior, as poor emotional knowledge in early years is linked to social difficulties, attention problems, and low academic achievement [9]. It has been shown that poor emotional knowledge in childhood and adolescence is associated with a variety of problematic outcomes, such as difficulties in social interaction, attention problems at school, low academic performance, and both internalizing and externalizing symptoms [16].

Child abuse and neglect are major global concerns, affecting children's psychological well-being and social adjustment. Abuse involves harmful acts, while neglect refers to failures in providing basic needs like medical care, education, or protection. Neglected children often struggle to express emotions and recognize others' facial expressions, interpreting them differently based on their experiences [12].

Traditional methods for assessing emotions, such as questionnaires and psychometric tests, have limitations, especially for young children with underdeveloped communication skills. Drawings offer an alternative, as they reflect personality and emotional states. The Family Drawing (FD) test is widely used in clinical settings to evaluate children's perceptions of relationships and attachment. While not a comprehensive assessment, it provides a non-invasive way for children to express emotions [19].

Identifying emotions is a process that involves a wide variety of instruments, such as questionnaires, psychometric tests, qualitative techniques, among others. Each of these tools serves different purposes aimed at understanding the processes of emotional identification, comprehension, categorization, and regulation. Emotions in children represent a complex phenomenon, as their emergence is accompanied by various changes, such as heart rate, electrodermal response, activation of neural networks, discourse analysis records, self-reporting, maternal assessment, and changes in facial expressions [5,21].

It is of clinical interest to analyze children's drawings and detect their psychological meanings in mental health centers. However, this task is complex, time-consuming, and costly for both specialists and parents. Additionally, the procedure includes several steps before and after the drawing analysis stage, such as psychologists formulating specific questions for parents and manually analyzing their responses [1].

Given the complexity of manual emotional analysis in children's drawings, computational approaches offer promising solutions. Although studies on emotion recognition in drawings are limited, machine learning techniques have demonstrated effectiveness in this field. It is important to analyze and understand the emotional behavior of children to guide its application for specialists, parents, teachers, and others. Therefore, this study proposes two approaches to classify positive and negative emotions in drawings made by children aged four to eight years.

This study contributes a novel perspective by comparing classical and deep learning approaches on a newly collected dataset composed of spontaneous children's family sketches. Unlike prior work relying on controlled, guided tasks, our data was collected in natural settings with no instructions, enhancing ecological validity. This real-world setup offers new insights into emotion recognition techniques under unconstrained, authentic conditions. The motivation behind this study is to explore children's emotions in a non-invasive manner, and one possible approach is through the analysis of their drawings. The proposed ML and DL methods aim to recognize the environment depicted in the drawings using basic image classification techniques [4,18]. While the primary objective is not a direct comparison between methods, the goal is to evaluate their performance in addressing this problem.

The structure of this paper is as follows: the next section describes related works; subsequently, the proposed methodology is presented; then, the results are shown; and finally, the conclusions are discussed.

2 Related Works

The intersection of artificial intelligence and emotional analysis in visual arts has gained significant attention in recent years. Researchers have explored various machine learning and deep learning techniques to understand how visual elements–such as colors, shapes, and textures–contribute to emotional perception. This section reviews key studies that have applied computational models to classify emotions in artworks, highlighting the strengths and limitations of each approach.

Brinkman [6] explored the use of machine learning to classify emotions evoked by abstract expressionist paintings. It investigated the relationship between visual elements (e.g., shapes, colors, textures) in these paintings and the emotional responses they elicit in human observers. The results showed that the algorithms achieved accuracy of 73. 33% (MAE 0.16) for arousal, 46.67% (MAE 0.28) for dominance, and 73.33% (MAE 0.28) for valence. Arousal was the most predictable dimension, with edge features and color intensity diversity being key predictors. Dominance proved difficult to predict, raising questions about its relevance as an emotional measure. Valence predictions suggested that the absence of small horizontal lines might correlate with less pleasant observations, though further research is needed.

Weng et al. [22] investigated the use of machine learning to predict emotional responses to abstract expressionist paintings. They analyzed how visual elements like shapes, colors, and textures influence emotions, focusing on three dimensions: arousal, dominance, and valence. Machine learning algorithms achieved 73.33% accuracy for arousal, 46.67% for dominance, and 73.33% for valence. Arousal was the most predictable, with edge features and color intensity diversity as key predictors. Dominance proved unreliable, while valence suggested a link between the absence of small horizontal lines and less pleasant observations.

Ahmad Khan et al. [14] identified emotional states through cues such as facial expressions, voice tones, and behavior. This study used handwriting and drawing as behavioral metrics, leveraging their integration of motor and cognitive processes. An attention-based transformer model was proposed to analyze the samples, embedding stroke points into a high-dimensional space, and using self-attention to predict emotions. The model captured long-range correlations, outperforming traditional recurrent neural networks (RNNs). It achieved 92. 64% accuracy in the EMOTHAW dataset, demonstrating its effectiveness in detecting emotions from handwriting and drawing.

Chirosca et al. [8] employed three machine learning algorithms to identify the most likely artist for a sketch or its contour, achieving promising results with around 92% confidence. The models used were faster R-CNN architectures, reinforcement learning, and vector extraction tools. The proposed tool serves as a foundation for future advancements, aiming to assist artwork evaluators in accurately attributing and analyzing sketches.

Zhang et al. [24] presented a small emotional vision language model (SEVLM) to understand visual art, identify emotion categories, and generate explanations. SEVLM combines emotion modeling and input-output alignment to overcome the limitations of small models. It used valence-arousal-dominance (VAD) knowledge and a contrastive head to align emotional features and improve the precision of the explanation. The model was tested on affective datasets, where SEVLM outperformed baseline models and rivals larger models like LLaVA 7B and GPT-4(V) after fine-tuning. It achieved strong performance.

He et al. [13] explored emotion analysis through hand-drawn paintings, addressing issues such as subjectivity and inefficiency in existing methods by proposing a CNN-based approach. The method was tested in a Chinese university, achieving a 72.1% accuracy in emotion classification. Although increasing training data improves CNN performance, data collection and labeling was costly.

Despite these advancements, limitations remain. The subjectivity of emotional perception poses challenges for consistency in model predictions. Additionally, data collection and labeling remain costly and time-consuming. While CNN models improve performance with more training data, scalability issues persist. These findings highlight the need for further refinement in both model architectures and dataset quality to enhance the accuracy and applicability of emotion classification.

Although numerous studies have explored emotion classification in art and handwriting using either classical or deep learning techniques, few have performed a structured comparison within a spontaneous children's sketch dataset. Our work seeks to fill this gap by analyzing both approaches under the same experimental conditions and dataset.

3 Methods and Materials

In this study, two methodologies for emotion evaluation are proposed: the first is based on classical machine learning approaches with a feature extraction method, and the second follows a deep learning approach. The objective of this study is to conduct an empirical comparison of classical and deep learning methods for binary emotion recognition in children's drawings. The goal is to evaluate which technique is more effective under real-world constraints, particularly when data availability is limited.

For the first approach, shape and intensity features were extracted from grayscale and binary images, generating feature vectors that were evaluated using machine learning techniques such as support vector machines, multilayer perceptron, and random forests. In the second approach, a pre-trained Vision Transformer model was applied, based on the one defined in the work of Dosovitskiy et al. [11]. For this approach, data augmentation was explored, as well as the effect of fine-tuning the pre-trained model with the augmented dataset.

3.1 Dataset

The dataset used in this study was built through a manual collection process involving 100 children aged four to eight years, an age range considered ideal for evaluation [10]. During the data collection process, the children were provided with a dedicated space within their classrooms, along with the necessary materials and time to freely draw their families. This activity was conducted without direct intervention, interviews, or specific instructions, allowing the children an average of 18 min to complete their drawings.

Subsequently, the drawings were analyzed by a psychologist specializing in drawing analysis, who labeled them into groups of positive and negative emotions. The dataset resulted in 58 drawings classified as expressing positive emotions and 42 as negative, with an imbalance ratio of 0.276, which is considered a moderate imbalance. The image dimensions are 1696×2192 pixels. Figure 1 presents two sample images from the dataset: (a) represents a positive emotion according to expert evaluation, while (b) represents a negative emotion. This study considers only these two emotion categories.

(a) (b)

Fig. 1. Sample family sketches from dataset (a) Positive emotion (b) Negative emotion

3.2 Classical Machine Learning Approach

Feature Extraction. The classical machine learning approach is illustrated in Fig. 2, which consists of four stages. The process begins with the dataset of 100 labeled images. Next, the feature extraction stage is applied. Since some of the drawings were created using colors, all images were converted to grayscale. The images were then divided into four sections to extract local features. This division was determined based on the general size of individual objects in the drawings and the space utilized within the sheets.

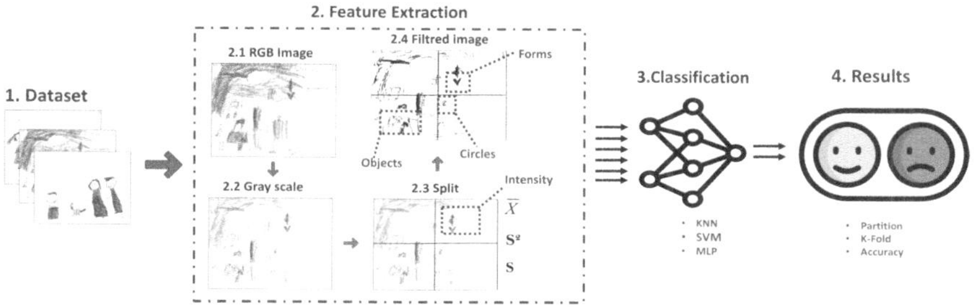

Fig. 2. Methodology based on feature engineering

According to Ancona [?], a psychodiagnostic analysis of emotions in drawings is based on stroke intensity, object size, shading, orientation, and the structure of the body and face. Given the presence of multiple indicators and variations in drawing styles, a generalization of the suggested analysis was proposed. Statistical features of intensity–such as sum, mean, standard deviation, and variance–were extracted for both the segmented regions and the complete image. Additionally, Gaussian filters, Canny edge detection, and binarization techniques were applied to detect contours, count circles, and identify objects of different shapes.

3.3 Deep Learning Approach

Visual Transformers (ViTs) have emerged as a groundbreaking advancement in the field of computer vision, revolutionizing the way images are classified and understood. Unlike traditional convolutional neural networks (CNNs), which rely on localized filters to process visual data, Visual Transformers leverage the power of self-attention mechanisms to capture global relationships within an image [11]. This allows them to efficiently model long-range dependencies and intricate patterns, leading to superior performance in image classification tasks.

Studies utilizing fine-tuned ViTs have shown promising results in emotion classification, as these models can analyze subtle visual cues, including color distribution, texture variations, and shape patterns. Compared to traditional CNNs, fine-tuned ViTs often achieve higher accuracy due to their ability to process global image context [23]. Fine-tuning ViTs involves adapting pre-trained transformer models to new datasets through transfer learning techniques. This process enables models to retain knowledge from large-scale image corpora while learning task-specific features more effectively [23].

By fine-tuning pre-trained ViT models on domain-specific datasets, researchers aim to improve their adaptability and performance in specialized applications, such as emotion classification in artistic and hand-drawn representations. In this work, a pre-trained visual transformer model was used, and subsequently, the same model was employed by performing fine-tuning with all the data from the dataset. Figure 3 illustrates the methodology followed by this approach.

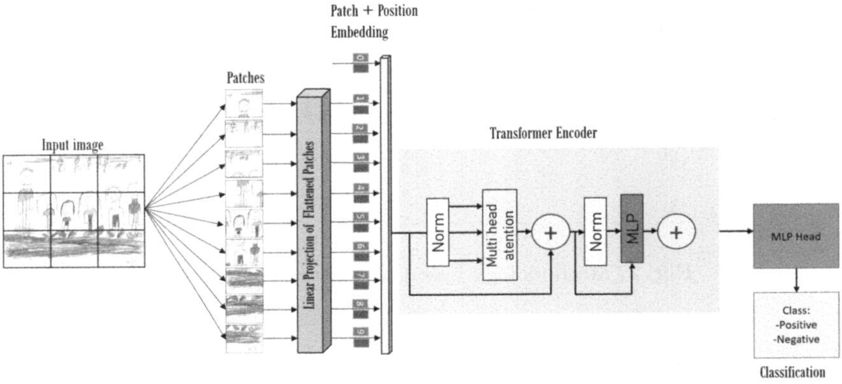

Fig. 3. Methodology based on deep learning techniques

4 Results

In this section are presented the results that were obtained during the experimentation phase. For the design of the experiments, the Python programming language, the PyTorch library, and the cloud-based development tool Google Colab were used. The results of the proposed methods described in Sects. 3.2 and 3.3 are summarized in Table 1. In the experiments for both approaches, a binary classification of negative and positive emotions is proposed, as these can be grouped in this manner. However, this does not imply that they are opposites; it is merely a grouping criterion [2,7]. The dataset exhibited an imbalance ratio of 0.276, with more positive drawings than negative. Data augmentation techniques were employed to reduce this imbalance. While augmentation improved the general performance of the ViT model, the minority class still experienced slightly lower precision, underscoring the persistent impact of imbalance on model learning.

For all classical machine learning experiments (first seven rows), K-Nearest Neighbors (KNN), Support Vector Machine (SVM), Multilayer Perceptron

(MLP), and Random Forest were used. The feature input remained the same for all models. The first experiment corresponds to the first four rows, where an 80/20 stratified split was used for training and testing, respectively. A combinatorial parameter search was conducted, yielding the highest result with SVM at 75.

Following this result, a grid search was applied to SVM using extreme and intermediate parameter values: C = 0.1, 1, 10, 100, gamma = 0.001, 0.01, 0.1, 1, and three different kernels. For this evaluation, a cross-validation metric was employed to determine the optimal parameters. Additionally, a segment of the dataset was reserved for testing. Consequently, rows 5, 6, and 7 in Table 1 present accuracy results (fourth column) as the average of 5K-fold cross-validation using the best parameters (shown in the third column), along with the accuracy obtained on the test set. The highest results were achieved with 70% accuracy in 5K-fold cross-validation and 80% accuracy on the test set.

Table 1. Binary classification accuracy on dataset.

Methods	Evaluation	Parameters	Accuracy
KNN	80-20 stratified	K = 3 and Minkowski distance	60%
SVM	80-20 stratified	Linear, C = 1 y gamma = 0.001	**75%**
MLP	80-20 stratified	one hidden layer with 22 units	60%
Random forest	80-20 stratified	10 trees	
SVM	5K-Fold and test	Linear, C = 1, gamma = 0.001	**70%/80%**
SVM	5K-Fold and test	RBF. C = 1, gamma = 0.001	60%/60%
SVM	5K-Fold and test	Poly, C = 1, gamma = 0.001	60%/70%
Vision Transformer	5K-Fold	lr = 0.001, optimizer = AdamW	**76.5%**
Vision Transformer	5K-Fold & Fine-Tuning	lr = 0.001, optimizer = AdamW	71.5%

For the deep learning-based approach, the Vision Transformer (ViT) model pre-trained on ImageNet-21k (14 million images, 21,843 classes) at a resolution of 224 × 224, and fine-tuned on ImageNet 2012 (1 million images, 1,000 classes) at a resolution of 224 × 224, was used as the initial configuration [11]. In all experiments, a learning rate of 0.001, an AdamW optimizer, and a CrossEntropy loss criterion were defined.

Since deep learning approaches require more data to achieve better results, data augmentation was performed on the original dataset. This augmentation doubled the size of the original dataset. To augment each image, a transformation was randomly selected from the following options:

- Random Horizontal Flip
- Random Rotation in the interval of $-10°$ to $10°$
- Randomly adjusting the brightness, contrast, saturation, and hue of an image by a factor of 0.2%

The results shown in the Table 1 display the performance obtained using cross-validation with 5 folds. The first result for the Visual Transformer method shows the accuracy achieved with the pre-trained model and data augmentation, while the second reported result includes fine-tuning. In both experiments, the test and validation sets are stratified. Interestingly, the results indicate that fine-tuning yielded worse performance, which could be attributed to the small size of the dataset, potentially causing the model to overfit and generalize poorly to unseen data.

Fine-tuning the Vision Transformer model on the limited dataset led to a reduction in accuracy (from 76.5% to 71.5%). This likely resulted from overfitting, as the model's large parameter space was not fully supported by the available training samples. Regularization strategies or freezing partial layers may be explored in future experiments.

As observed in Table 1, the results obtained are considerably high. Currently, there are no related studies directly comparable to the work developed in this study. The closest research includes the work of Likforman, who achieved an accuracy of 63.8% for three emotions in text-annotated images [17], and He, who used a dataset of drawings and questionnaires, obtaining an accuracy of 72.1% for six emotions [13]. The dataset consists of 100 instances, which is still relatively small. However, these are preliminary tests aimed at understanding the dataset's behavior and how its features perform with different classifiers. Although there is a class imbalance of 0.276, the experiments are stratified, and the AUC ranges from 0.84 to 0.9, indicating a good capacity to distinguish between the two classes. This study relies on an indirect evaluation approach, based solely on the assessment of children's drawings. This presents challenges due to the variability in drawing styles, artistic abilities, and representational approaches [15].

5 Conclusions and Future Work

This study demonstrates the potential of computational approaches for emotion recognition in children's drawings, comparing classical machine learning methods with deep learning models. The SVM classifier with a linear kernel achieved the highest accuracy (80%), showing that traditional methods can be effective, especially when working with small datasets. On the other hand, Vision Transformers (ViTs) achieved 76.5% accuracy, but fine-tuning the model led to a performance drop (71.5%), likely due to overfitting caused by the dataset's limited size.

The significance of this research lies in its contribution to non-invasive emotional assessment methods for children, which could be beneficial for psychologists, educators, and caregivers. By automating emotion classification from drawings, this approach may provide a valuable tool for early detection of emotional distress, facilitating interventions when needed.

Although the computational models employed are established, the novelty of this work lies in its comparative focus within a unique and freely produced dataset. The absence of scripted drawing tasks provides an original context to examine how models perform when applied to unstructured, real-life emotional expressions in children's artwork.

This study opens new avenues for future research in affective computing and child psychology. A promising direction would be expanding the dataset to improve generalization, ensuring that deep learning models like ViTs can leverage their full potential.

An interesting direction for future research is the development of hybrid models that combine handcrafted features, such as stroke intensity and spatial structure, with deep learning embeddings from models like ViT. Such hybridization may boost performance by leveraging both interpretability and high-level representations. Finally, integrating multimodal data, such as speech or handwriting analysis, may lead to a more comprehensive understanding of children's emotional states.

References

1. Alshahrani, A., Almatrafi, M.M., Mustafa, J.I., Albaqami, L.S., Aljabri, R.A.: A children's psychological and mental health detection model by drawing analysis based on computer vision and deep learning. Eng. Technol. Appl. Sci. Res. **14**(4), 15533–15540 (2024). https://doi.org/10.48084/etasr.7812. https://etasr.com/index.php/ETASR/article/view/7812
2. An, S., Ji, L.J., Marks, M., Zhang, Z.: Two sides of emotion: exploring positivity and negativity in six basic emotions across cultures. Front. Psychol. **8** (2017). https://doi.org/10.3389/fpsyg.2017.00610. https://www.frontiersin.org/journals/psychology/articles/10.3389/fpsyg.2017.00610
3. Ancona, F., Ancona, M., Gómez-Maqueo, E.: Psicodiagnóstico clínico del niño. Editorial El Manual Moderno (2016). https://books.google.com.mx/books?id=fwF8DQAAQBAJ
4. Bhardwaj, A., Di, W., Wei, J.: Deep Learning Essentials: Your hands-on guide to the fundamentals of deep learning and neural network modeling. Packt Publishing Ltd. (2018)
5. Bisquerra Alzina, R., LOPEZ CASSA, E.: La evaluación en la educación emocional: Instrumentos y recursos. Aula Abierta **50**(4), 757–766 (2021). https://doi.org/10.17811/rifie.50.4.2021.757-766. https://reunido.uniovi.es/index.php/AA/article/view/16685
6. Brinkman, E.: Recognition of the emotion in abstract expressionistic paintings using a machine learning approach. Master's thesis, University of Twente (2008)
7. Bulagang, A.F., Weng, N.G., Mountstephens, J., Teo, J.: A review of recent approaches for emotion classification using electrocardiography and electrodermography signals. Inf. Med. Unlocked **20**, 100363 (2020). https://doi.org/10.1016/j.imu.2020.100363
8. Chirosca, G., Rădvan, R., Muscommaat, S., Pop, M., Chirosca, A.: Machine learning models for artist classification of cultural heritage sketches. Appl. Sci. **15**(1), 212 (2024)
9. Conte, E., Ornaghi, V., Grazzani, I., Pepe, A., Cavioni, V. Emotion knowledge, theory of mind, and language in young children: testing a comprehensive conceptual model. Front. Psychol. **10** (2019).https://doi.org/10.3389/fpsyg.2019.02144. https://www.frontiersin.org/journals/psychology/articles/10.3389/fpsyg.2019.02144

10. Corman, L.: Le test du dessin de famille. Presses universitaires de France (1982)
11. Dosovitskiy, A., et al.: An image is worth 16x16 words: transformers for image recognition at scale (2021). arxiv:2010.11929
12. Gonzalez, D., McCall, J., et al.: Child abuse and neglect (2017)
13. He, T., Li, C., Wang, J., Wang, M., Wang, Z., Jiao, C.: An emotion analysis in learning environment based on theme-specified drawing by convolutional neural network. Front. Public Health **10**, 958870 (2022)
14. Khan, Z.A., et al.: Emotion detection from handwriting and drawing samples using an attention-based transformer model. PeerJ Comput. Sci. **10**, e1887 (2024)
15. Koizumi, M., Takagishi, H.: The relationship between child maltreatment and emotion recognition. PloS one **9**, e86093 (2014). https://doi.org/10.1371/journal.pone.0086093
16. Kujawa, A., et al.: Emotion recognition in preschool children: associations with maternal depression and early parenting. Dev. Psychopathol. **26**(1), 159–170 (2014). https://doi.org/10.1017/S0954579413000928
17. Likforman-Sulem, L., Esposito, A., Faundez-Zanuy, M., Clemencon, S., Cordasco, G.: Emothaw: a novel database for emotional state recognition from handwriting and drawing. IEEE Trans. Hum.-Mach. Syst. **47**(2), 273–284 (2017). https://doi.org/10.1109/thms.2016.2635441
18. Loussaief, S., Abdelkrim, A.: Machine learning framework for image classification. In: 2016 7th International Conference on Sciences of Electronics, Technologies of Information and Telecommunications (SETIT), pp. 58–61. IEEE (2016)
19. Pace, C.S., Muzi, S., Vizzino, F.: Family drawing for assessing attachment in children: weaknesses and strengths. Front. Psychol. **13** (2022). https://doi.org/10.3389/fpsyg.2022.980129. https://www.frontiersin.org/journals/psychology/articles/10.3389/fpsyg.2022.980129
20. Sanchis-Sanchis, A., Grau, M.D., Moliner, A.R., Morales-Murillo, C.P.: Effects of age and gender in emotion regulation of children and adolescents. Front. Psychol. **11** (2020). https://doi.org/10.3389/fpsyg.2020.00946. https://www.frontiersin.org/journals/psychology/articles/10.3389/fpsyg.2020.00946
21. Camila Becerra, P.C.T.: cómo se estudian las emociones en los niños? técnicas conductuales y fisiológicas para evaluar las respuestas emocionales durante la infancia. Cuadernos de Neuropsicología / Panamerican J. Neuropsychol. (2017). https://www.redalyc.org/articulo.oa?id=439656187014
22. Weng, H.C., et al.: Drawing as a window to emotion with insights from tech-transformed participant images. Sci. Rep. **14**(1), 11571 (2024)
23. Xie, H., et al.: Emovit: revolutionizing emotion insights with visual instruction tuning (2024). arxiv:2404.16670
24. Zhang, J., Zheng, L., Wang, M., Guo, D.: Training a small emotional vision language model for visual art comprehension. In: European Conference on Computer Vision, pp. 397–413. Springer, Heidelberg (2024). https://doi.org/10.1007/978-3-031-72855-6_23

Heuristic-Based Optimization Using Elementary Cellular Automata: A Preliminary Study on the Knapsack Problem

José Eduardo Zárate-Aranda and José C. Ortiz-Bayliss(✉)

School of Engineering and Sciences, Tecnologico de Monterrey,
64849 Monterrey, Mexico
{A01630299,jcobayliss}@tec.mx

Abstract. This study introduces two heuristic-based solvers inspired by Wolfram's Elementary Cellular Automaton. The solvers use the automaton rules to solve combinatorial optimization problems using two relatively different strategies. The first solver uses the rules to combine solutions produced by individual heuristics. In contrast, the second uses the rules to combine heuristics and later uses such heuristics to solve the problem. As we can observe, the second solver addresses the solving process indirectly. These solvers were tested on 400 synthetic Knapsack Problem instances and compared against two fundamental heuristics: MAXPW and MINW. Results indicate that while our approach demonstrates some adaptability and generates competitive solutions, it keeps plenty of opportunities for improvement.

Keywords: Elementary Cellular Automaton · Heuristics · Hyper-heuristics · Knapsack Problem

1 Introduction

Heuristics are algorithms designed to find suitable solutions to optimization problems within reasonable time constraints, mainly when classical methods are impractical or ineffective [20]. Heuristic methods are particularly useful for solving complex Combinatorial Optimization Problems (COPs), including NP-hard problems. Although heuristics have successfully been used in various problem domains, hyper-heuristics is a new trend that extends how individual heuristics operate. Hyper-heuristics (HHs) operate as high-level frameworks that guide the selection and implementation of lower-level heuristics to address complex optimization problems. The concept was first introduced in the early 2000s to refer to "heuristics to choose heuristics" within the context of optimization [7,9]. Hyper-heuristics are characterized by the ability to adaptively choose the most suitable heuristic according to the current state of the search process, thereby

A. P. López-Monroy et al. (Eds.): MCPR 2025, LNCS 15715, pp. 101–109, 2025.
https://doi.org/10.1007/978-3-031-96255-4_10

improving both efficiency and problem-solving performance [6,10]. Unlike conventional heuristics, hyper-heuristics do not explore the solution space directly but function at a higher level, coordinating the application of different heuristics to better align with the specific attributes of the problem at hand [6,19].

This study focuses on the Knapsack Problem (KP), a well-studied combinatorial optimization problem with numerous variations and real-world applications [3]. The KP involves selecting items to maximize total value while ensuring the total weight does not exceed a given limit. The KP has applications in cryptography, applied mathematics, investment selection, and asset-backed securitization [23]. This study focuses on developing solvers for the KP using ideas inspired by the Elementary Cellular Automaton (ECA) proposed by Wolfram [26]. We propose two innovative ideas for solving the KP using an ECA. The ECA is a discrete computational model comprising a grid of cells where each cell exists in a finite set of states. The state of each cell is updated simultaneously according to predefined local rules that consider the states of neighboring cells. The generated patterns serve as guidelines for selection heuristics, aiding in the decision-making process throughout the optimization [6,19].

The remainder of this work is structured as follows. Section 2 provides relevant definitions and an overview of related works. Section 3 details the proposed hyper-heuristic model. Section 5 presents the experimental setup, performance evaluation, and comparative analysis against conventional heuristics. Finally, Sect. 6 discusses the key findings, limitations, and potential directions for future research.

2 Background and Related Work

2.1 The Knapsack Problem

The knapsack problem (KP) involves selecting a subset of items, each with a weight and profit, to maximize total profit without exceeding capacity. The KP has been widely studied as a fundamental combinatorial optimization problem [1, 13,25], with solutions categorized as exact or approximation methods. Although we can find many different versions of this problem in the literature, this work will focus on its simplest version, the 0/1 knapsack problem. We cannot fraction the items in this version, so they are either packed or not packed within the knapsack.

Exact methods, such as linear programming [4,17], branch-and-bound [15, 29], and dynamic programming [5,11], guarantee optimal solutions but are computationally infeasible for large instances due to exponential complexity [2]. Approximation methods, such as heuristics, metaheuristics, and hyper-heuristics, offer scalable alternatives. Heuristics provide fast, domain-specific solutions, while metaheuristics generalize across problems [30]. Hyper-heuristics further abstract the process by selecting or generating low-level heuristics for efficient optimization [18,21,24].

2.2 The Elementary Cellular Automaton

The Elementary Cellular Automaton (ECA) is a type of cellular automaton extensively studied by Stephen Wolfram in his research on complex The Elementary Cellular Automaton (ECA) is a type of cellular automaton extensively studied by Wolfram in his research on complex systems [26]. This automaton consists of a grid of cells that update simultaneously based on local rules considering neighboring states. Despite their simplicity, these rules can produce intricate global behaviors, as seen in Conway's Game of Life, a two-dimensional automaton illustrating how basic rules generate complex patterns over time [12].

Cellular automata have diverse applications across various fields. In biotechnology, they model cellular growth and metabolism, aiding metabolic flux analysis [16]. In environmental science, they simulate ecological processes like wildfire spread and ecosystem dynamics [8]. They also have applications in cryptography for pseudorandom sequence generation and image processing for encryption tasks [14,27].

3 Solution Approach

Our solution leverages an ECA that generates patterns that allow us to solve the KP. These patterns represent two distinct strategies.

- In the first strategy, ECA-H, the patterns represent a solution to the problem instance, which allows for solving the problem directly by working on the solution space.
- With the second strategy, ECA-HH, we produce a hyper-heuristic. The patterns represent a sequence of heuristics later used to solve the problem instance. Thus, we solve the problem indirectly, using the patterns to decide which heuristics to use.

Unlike conventional methods that rely on instance-specific features like profit, weight, or correlation [19,28], our model requires no problem characterization through any of these features. Instead, we use fixed ECA rules to guide decision-making and how we solve the problems. This structured yet dynamic approach removes dependencies on specific instance characteristics, enhancing generalizability.

Before detailing how these two strategies work, we introduce the key elements of our model.

3.1 The Heuristics

In heuristic-based KP solvers, items are selected iteratively based on predefined rules provided by the heuristics. Our model employs only two straightforward heuristics, ensuring a structured yet adaptable selection process driven by the ECA rules. These two heuristics work as follows:

- **MINW:** Prioritizes the lightest items that fit within capacity. MINW attempts to pack the item that leaves the maximum space available for future items.
- **MAXPW:** Calculates the profit-to-weight ratio of each item and prefers the one with the largest ratio.

Other heuristics are available in the literature, but we wanted to use the binary representation from the ECA for this preliminary study. Future work will be devoted to extending our approach to incorporate more heuristics.

3.2 The KP Instances

We evaluated the solvers using 400 synthetic KP instances, each containing 100 items and a maximum capacity of 64 weight units. Item weights and profits range from 1 to 64 and 1 to 32, respectively. Each heuristic performs best in 25% of instances, leading to further subdivision into four subsets—SDEF, SMAXP, SMAXPW, and SMINW—where the best-performing heuristics are DEF, MAXP, MAXPW, and MINW, respectively. This structured distribution ensures a balanced evaluation of hyper-heuristic performance. We generated these instances using the algorithm proposed by Plata et al. [22], and are publicly available at https://bit.ly/3wvxPly. While our instance set size may seem limited initially, it ensures that no single heuristic consistently dominates the rest. Besides, we acknowledge the preliminary nature of our investigation and the need for further experimentation.

3.3 Performance Metrics

As with other studies focused on the KP, the solution's profit is the primary measure of quality–the higher the profit, within the constraints of the knapsack's capacity, the better the solution.

4 Solution Model

This model utilizes a one-dimensional ECA. Each problem instance is represented as an $n \times n$ ECA grid. For this study, grids are fixed at 100×100, meaning each generation consists of 100 cells (corresponding to the number of items), which evolve for a maximum of 100 generations. The ECA-HH model works as follows.

4.1 Using the Elementary Cellular Automaton to Solve the Knapsack Problem

In ECA-HH, each cell's state represents the selection of a low-level heuristic for constructing a solution. The model evolves through generations, with the final (100th) generation defining the pattern generated by the ECA rules. This pattern will decide which heuristic to use whenever an item is selected. In other words, ECA-HH is how we use an ECA to produce a straightforward hyper-heuristic. We used MAXPW to generate an initial solution where the items, in the order provided by the instance, are marked as 1 to indicate if MAXPW chose to pack the item and 0 otherwise. This produces a valid initial state to start constructing the pattern. While ECA states indicate heuristic selections, the initial state reflects item inclusion/exclusion based on MAXPW. Once inserted into the CA, this state drives heuristic selection for solution construction.

Each of the 256 rules independently explores the search space, producing different heuristic sequences. The performance of each rule is assessed based on the summed profit across all KP instances. Finally, the best-performing rule—yielding the highest total profit—is selected as the optimal HH rule set. By following this undirected evolutionary approach, ECA-HH enables the emergence of diverse heuristic strategies, expanding the solution space and offering an alternative method for combinatorial optimization.

The first model, ECA-HH, relies on simple heuristics, while its variant, ECA-H, introduces a hybrid approach to solving the instances. ECA-H does not make real-time heuristic selections. Instead, it pre-generates solutions using the two heuristics, MAXPW and MINW. Then, it uses the 256 rules to evolve the solutions directly. Thus, the pattern obtained at the last generation represents a solution to the instance.

5 Experimental Results

ECA-HH operates without a training set, as the ECA rules predefine its heuristic selection strategy. This eliminates dependence on instance-specific properties, allowing the ECA to generate heuristic choices step by step based on internal rules. We tested ECA-HH on the test set described in Sect. 3.2 to assess its effectiveness. This evaluation ensures its performance under real-world conditions by directly applying rule-based decision-making to test instances.

To analyze the methods' performance, we analyze the profit obtained, where higher values indicate better performance. The profit reflects how well the solvers deal with the distinct problem instances, demonstrating the adaptability of ECA-H and ECA-HH in exploring diverse solution spaces.

Figure 1 presents the distribution of the profits for heuristics and the proposed models on the test set.

Results indicate that MAXPW achieves the best profit with minimal variability. ECA-HH follows closely, though with greater fluctuation, while ECA-H mirrors MAXPW's performance, suggesting it effectively generalizes from it. ECA-H emulates MAXPW as the top-performing method. Meanwhile, despite a slightly lower but competitive median profit, ECA-HH exhibits larger variability due to its dynamic heuristic selection.

To validate our results, we conducted Wilcoxon signed-rank tests to compare the performance of MAXPW, MINW, ECA-HH, and ECA-H, assessing whether ECA-HH and ECA-H differ significantly from MAXPW and MINW.

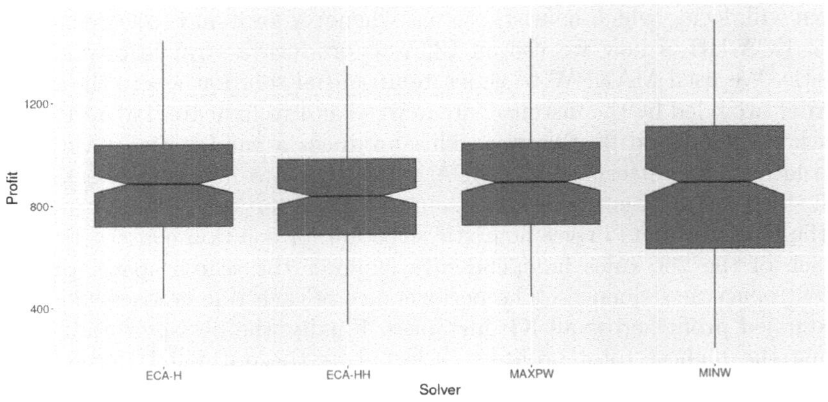

Fig. 1. Profit of ECA-H, ECA-HH, and the two individual heuristics in the test set.

The hypotheses are as follows. The two-sided null hypothesis, H_0, states that there is no difference in median performance between models, while the two-sided alternative hypothesis, H_1, suggests a difference exists. We constructed a table where we present the results of the Wilcoxon tests between each pair of methods.

Table 1. p-values of the Wilcoxon test between every pair of methods.

	MINW	MAXPW	ECA-HH	ECA-H
MINW	–	0.480	0.216	0.480
MAXPW	0.480	–	**0.010**	1.000
ECA-HH	0.216	**0.010**	–	**0.010**
ECA-H	0.480	1.000	**0.010**	–

As we can observe from Table 1, there is no statistical difference between MAXPW and ECA-H (p-value = 1.0), meaning that ECA-H replicates the performance of MAXPW. Regarding ECA-H and MAXPW, the p-value resulting from the corresponding test is 0.010, which suggests that the two methods have different medians, with a 5% significance level.

6 Conclusion and Future Work

Given the preliminary nature of this work, we recognize various research paths that might be worth exploring in the future. First, we see an opportunity regarding the ECA rules. For example, investigating more complex transition rules beyond Wolfram's elementary rules (extending beyond binary rules) might improve the balance between exploration and exploitation and refine heuristic selection for complex instances. Finally, we are also aware that we must test our approaches on larger instances to assess computational efficiency and broader applicability. Besides, we must compare our approaches against other methods from the literature to validate our proposal's actual contribution. Addressing these areas of opportunity could make ECA-H and ECA-HH more robust and adaptable, further establishing ECA-based methods as viable alternatives for solving combinatorial optimization problems like the KP.

References

1. Adamuthe, A.C., Sale, V.N., Mane, S.U.: Solving single and multi-objective 01 knapsack problem using harmony search algorithm. J. Sci. Res. **64**, 160–167 (2020). https://doi.org/10.37398/JSR.2020.640136
2. Agung, C., Christine, N.: Performance analysis of optimization methods for solving traveling salesman problem. Innov. Technol. Sci. Solut. Industr. 69–75 (2021). https://doi.org/10.30837/ITSSI.2021.15.069
3. Assi, M., Haraty, R.A.: A survey of the knapsack problem. In: 2018 International Arab Conference on Information Technology (ACIT), pp. 1–6. IEEE (2018). https://doi.org/10.1109/ACIT.2018.8672677
4. Best, M.J., Ritter, K.: Linear Programming Active Set Analysis and Computer Programs. Prentice Hall, Englewood Cliffs (1985)
5. Bhargava, A.Y.: Dynamic Programming, vol. 1, chap. 9, 1 edn. Manning Publications (2016)
6. Bian, Y., Li, Z., Guo, J., Zhao, R.: Concrete hyperheuristic framework for test case prioritization. J. Softw.: Evol. Process **30** (2018). https://doi.org/10.1002/smr.1992
7. Burke, E., Gendreau, M., Hyde, M., Kendall, G., Ochoa, G., Özcan, E., Qu, R.: Hyper-heuristics: a survey of the state of the art. J. Oper. Res. Soc. **64**, 1695–1724 (2013). https://doi.org/10.1057/jors.2013.71
8. i Casas, P.F., Casanovas, J., Figueras, J., Guasch, A.: Formalizing geographical models using specification and description language: the wildfire example. In: 2013 Winter Simulations Conference (WSC), pp. 1961–1972. IEEE (2013). https://doi.org/10.1109/WSC.2013.6721575
9. Cowling, P., Kendall, G., Soubeiga, E.: Hyperheuristics: a tool for rapid prototyping in scheduling and optimisation. In: Cagnoni, S., Gottlieb, J., Hart, E., Middendorf, M., Raidl, G.R. (eds.) EvoWorkshops 2002. LNCS, vol. 2279, pp. 1–10. Springer, Heidelberg (2002). https://doi.org/10.1007/3-540-46004-7_1
10. Drake, J.H., Özcan, E., Burke, E.K.: Modified choice function heuristic selection for the multidimensional knapsack problem. In: Sun, H., Yang, C.-Y., Lin, C.-W., Pan, J.-S., Snasel, V., Abraham, A. (eds.) Genetic and Evolutionary Computing. AISC, vol. 329, pp. 225–234. Springer, Cham (2015). https://doi.org/10.1007/978-3-319-12286-1_23
11. Eddy, S.R.: What is dynamic programming? Nat. Biotechnol. **22**, 909–910 (2004). https://doi.org/10.1038/nbt0704-909

12. Fridenfalk, M.: The introduction of a quantum mirror in the game of life cellular automaton. In: 2015 IEEE Games Entertainment Media Conference (GEM), pp. 1–2. IEEE (2015). https://doi.org/10.1109/GEM.2015.7377243
13. Huang, Y., Wang, P., Li, J., Chen, X., Li, T.: A binary multi-scale quantum harmonic oscillator algorithm for 0–1 knapsack problem with genetic operator. IEEE Access **7**, 137251–137265 (2019). https://doi.org/10.1109/ACCESS.2019.2942340
14. Karmakar, S., Mukhopadhyay, D., Roy Chowdhury, D.: *d*-monomial tests of non-linear cellular automata for cryptographic design. In: Bandini, S., Manzoni, S., Umeo, H., Vizzari, G. (eds.) ACRI 2010. LNCS, vol. 6350, pp. 261–270. Springer, Heidelberg (2010). https://doi.org/10.1007/978-3-642-15979-4_28
15. Kellerer, H., Pferschy, U., Pisinger, D.: Basic Algorithm Concepts, 1 edn., pp. 27–29. Springer, Heidelberg (2004). https://doi.org/10.1007/978-3-540-24777-7
16. Meadows, A.L., Roy, S., Clark, D.S., Blanch, H.W.: Optimal design of metabolic flux analysis experiments for anchorage-dependent mammalian cells using a cellular automaton model. Biotechnol. Bioeng. **98**, 221–229 (2007). https://doi.org/10.1002/bit.21414
17. Mougouei, D., Powers, D., Moeini, A.: An integer linear programming model for binary knapsack problem with dependent item values. In: Peng, W., Alahakoon, D., Li, X. (eds.) AI 2017. LNCS (LNAI), vol. 10400, pp. 144–154. Springer, Cham (2017). https://doi.org/10.1007/978-3-319-63004-5_12
18. Olivas, F., Amaya, I., Ortiz-Bayliss, J.C., Conant-Pablos, S.E., Terashima-Marin, H.: A fuzzy hyper-heuristic approach for the 0-1 knapsack problem. In: 2020 IEEE Congress on Evolutionary Computation (CEC), pp. 1–8. IEEE (2020). https://doi.org/10.1109/CEC48606.2020.9185710
19. Olivas, F., Amaya, I., Ortiz-Bayliss, J.C., Conant-Pablos, S.E., Terashima-Marín, H.: Enhancing hyperheuristics for the knapsack problem through fuzzy logic. Comput. Intell. Neurosci. **2021**, 1–17 (2021). https://doi.org/10.1155/2021/8834324
20. PhD, H.L.: Heuristics, pp. 625–654. Apress (2022). https://doi.org/10.1007/978-1-4842-6797-4_11
21. Pillay, N., Beckedahl, D.: EvoHyp - a java toolkit for evolutionary algorithm hyper-heuristics. In: 2017 IEEE Congress on Evolutionary Computation, pp. 2706–2713. IEEE (2017). https://doi.org/10.1109/CEC.2017.7969636
22. Plata-González, L.F., Amaya, I., Ortiz-Bayliss, J.C., Conant-Pablos, S.E., Terashima-Marín, H., Coello, C.A.C.: Evolutionary-based tailoring of synthetic instances for the knapsack problem. Soft Comput. **23**, 12711–12728 (2019). https://doi.org/10.1007/s00500-019-03822-w
23. Pushpa, S.K., Mrunal, T.V., Suhas, C.: A study of performance analysis on knapsack problem. In: National Conference on "Recent Trends in Information Technology". International Journal of Computer Applications (2016)
24. Sánchez-Díaz, X., Ortiz-Bayliss, J.C., Amaya, I., Cruz-Duarte, J.M., Conant-Pablos, S.E., Terashima-Marín, H.: A feature-independent hyper-heuristic approach for solving the knapsack problem. Appl. Sci. **11**, 10209 (2021). https://doi.org/10.3390/app112110209
25. Santoso, K.A., Kurniawan, M.B., Kamsyakawuni, A., Riski, A.: Hybrid cat-particle swarm optimization algorithm on bounded knapsack problem with multiple constraints. In: Proceedings of the International Conference on Mathematics, Geometry, Statistics, and Computation (IC-MaGeStiC 2021), pp. 244–248. Atlantis Press (2022). https://doi.org/10.2991/acsr.k.220202.045
26. Wolfram, S.: A New Kind of Science. Wolfram Media (2002)

27. Wu, S.T.W.S.T.: An application of keystream using cellular automata for image encryption in IoT. J. Internet Technol. **24**, 149–162 (2023). https://doi.org/10.53106/160792642023012401014
28. Zárate-Aranda, J.E., Ortiz-Bayliss, J.C.: An exploratory study on machine-learning-based hyper-heuristics for the knapsack problem. In: Mezura-Montes, E., Acosta-Mesa, H.G., Carrasco-Ochoa, J.A., Martínez-Trinidad, J.F., Olvera-López, J.A. (eds.) Pattern Recognition, pp. 119–128. Springer, Cham (2024)
29. Zeng, Z., et al.: Information-driven path planning for hybrid aerial underwater vehicles (2022)
30. Zerovnik, J.: Heuristics for NP-hard optimization problems - simpler is better!? Logist. Sustain. Transp. **6**, 1–10 (2015). https://doi.org/10.1515/jlst-2015-0006

Language Processing and Recognition

Dynamic Strategy for Recognizing the Mexican Sign Language Alphabet: Bridging Static and Dynamic Signs

Jesús Antonio Navarrete-López(✉), Jesús Javier Gortarez-Pelayo, and Irvin Hussein Lopez-Nava(✉)

Centro de Investigación Científica y de Educación Superior de Ensenada (CICESE), 22860 Ensenada, Baja California, Mexico
{jnavarrete,jgortarez,hussein}@cicese.edu.mx

Abstract. Sign language recognition is a crucial element in the development of accessible communication technologies, particularly for addressing communication barriers between hearing and non-hearing individuals. This study presents a unified approach for recognizing the complete Mexican Sign Language (LSM) alphabet, which includes 21 static and 6 dynamic signs. The methodology involves extracting keypoints from video frames captured from 20 subjects, considering different frame lengths. Machine learning models were trained and evaluated on both static and dynamic signs, assessing performance for each letter individually and by groups. The model using the starting and middle frames achieved the best performance (efficacy and efficiency), with an F1-score of 0.97. The unified framework aims to support continuous and real-time recognition, enhancing tools for inclusion and reducing communication gaps with the Deaf community.

Keywords: Sign language recognition · Dynamic sign recognition · Mexican sign language · Lengua de señas mexicana

1 Introduction

Mexican Sign Language (LSM) is a vital component of the Deaf community in Mexico, serving as a primary means of communication, cultural expression, and identity. However, the barriers faced by LSM users often result in significant communication challenges, limiting their access to education, healthcare, and employment opportunities, as well as their integration into broader society [8]. Research has highlighted the unique grammatical, morphological, and syntactic structures of sign languages, emphasizing their complexity and richness as natural languages.

Sign languages encompass both static signs–those involving fixed handshapes–and dynamic signs, which are characterized by movement, facial expressions, and temporal patterns [2]. At the most basic level, signs represent

A. P. López-Monroy et al. (Eds.): MCPR 2025, LNCS 15715, pp. 113–122, 2025.
https://doi.org/10.1007/978-3-031-96255-4_11

letters of the alphabet to spell out words that may not have specific signs. As one progresses, individual signs can represent entire words, where each sign corresponds to a concept or object, such as "mom" or "eat". As communication advances, these words combine into phrases and sentences, governed by unique rules for sentence structure, word order, and grammatical markers, which allow nuanced expression. This structure enables users to convey thoughts, emotions, and concepts with precision, similar to spoken language.

The study of the alphabet in sign languages primarily focuses on hand postures, known as fingerspelling. In the structure of a hand sign, three key elements can be distinguished: (i) the hand configuration, known as `queirem`, which includes hand shapes such as open, closed, or retracted fingers; (ii) the place of articulation, called `toponem`, which refers to the location where the sign is made, such as in front of the body or forehead; and (iii) the hand movement, or `kinema`, which encompasses straight, circular, or angular motions. While `toponem` is consistent for both static and dynamic signs, with the hand positioned in front of the body, static signs only require the identification of the `queirem`.

Existing Sign Language Recognition (SLR) approaches have predominantly centered on static signs of the LSM alphabet, leveraging computer vision and machine learning (ML) techniques to identify hand configurations or `queirems`. For instance, [1] and [9] introduced deep learning-based systems utilizing the Inception V3 model and convolutional neural networks, achieving classification accuracies of 91% and 83%, respectively, for the 21 static signs. In contrast, [7] employed traditional ML techniques, including k-NN, Random Forest, and support vector machines (SVM), coupled with 21 hand keypoints extracted using MediaPipe, which achieved an average F1-score exceeding 0.98 for recognizing all static signs. These systems excel at recognizing isolated and static signs, highlighting the need for solutions that include both static and dynamic signs to fully capture the temporal and spatial aspects essential for real-world applications.

Recent advancements in deep learning have led to the creation of SLR systems capable of recognizing both static and dynamic LSM signs. [5] presents a system utilizing an OAK-D camera and recurrent neural network architectures, including LSTM and GRU. A dataset of 3,000 samples including 4 static (A, B, C, D) and 4 dynamic (J, K, Q, X) signs was created, with 3D keypoints of the hands using MediaPipe. The LSTM model delivered the best results, achieving 97% accuracy on clean data and 90% on noisy data. The same dataset was utilized in [6] where the authors proposed a SLR system based on spatiotemporal attention mechanisms combined with a general neural network architecture. Using 67 3D keypoints from the face, body, and hands extracted with MediaPipe, the model achieved 99% accuracy in recognizing 30 LSM signs. Computational efficiency is optimized by selecting only eight frames per sign. Finally, in [4] a hybrid system for recognizing the extended LSM alphabet and dynamic signs was introduced. Using MediaPipe, 3D hand keypoints were extracted, with preprocessing to remove irrelevant variations. The system uses a fully connected neural network for the 21 static signs and specialized algorithms for the 6 dynamic gestures, while also accounting for the letters LL and RR. It achieved an average accuracy of 91% and facilitates recognition in uncontrolled environments.

This proposed study aims to combine hand keypoints extracted from 2D-videos as feature vectors for training SVM-based classification models to simultaneously recognize the 21 static signs and 6 dynamic signs of the LSM alphabet. Furthermore, static data will be adapted to dynamic settings to investigate how the number of frames affects classification performance.

2 LSM Alphabet

The LSM alphabet comprises 27 signs, excluding double signs like LL and RR. Most of these are static, with a subset of six dynamic signs: J, K, Ñ, Q, X, and Z (see Fig. 1). As mentioned earlier, static signs primarily rely on the execution of the `queirem`, with the `toponem` influencing meaning in other contexts. The `kinema` is present but varies minimally and typically ignored in alphabet usage.

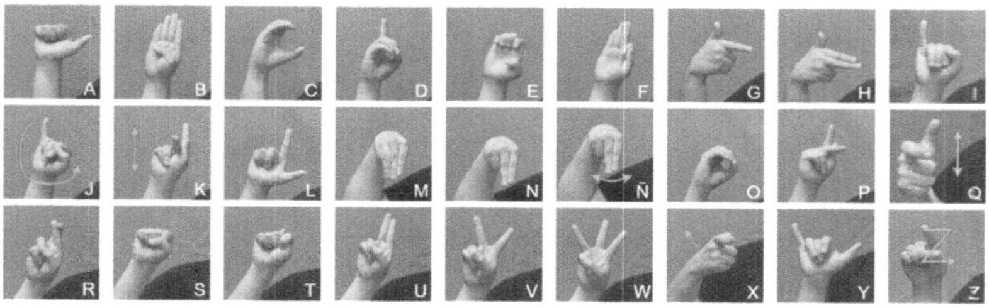

Fig. 1. LSM alphabet. Arrows indicate movement (`kinema`) in dynamic signs.

Dynamic signs are characterized by the prominence of `kinema` in their execution, which consists of three main phases: (i) the initiation, where `queirem` and `toponem` are similar to those in static signs, (ii) the midpoint, where the `kinema` occurs and induce changes in the `toponem`, and (iii) the final, where the `toponem` typically returns to its initial state, except for J and Z. In all cases, the `queirem` remains unchanged.

Figure 2 illustrates examples of these elements. First, three `queirems` ('A', 'Y', 'C') share the same `toponem`. When the `toponem` of the sign 'A' changes, its meaning shifts to "hoy" (*today*) or "ayer" (*yesterday*) in LSM. Additionally, when the `kinema` of the sign for 'I' changes to a concave upward movement, it transforms into the letter 'J'.

3 Methods

To classify static and dynamic signs within the same model, all signs must be converted into a dynamic approach, where a sequence of frames captures the

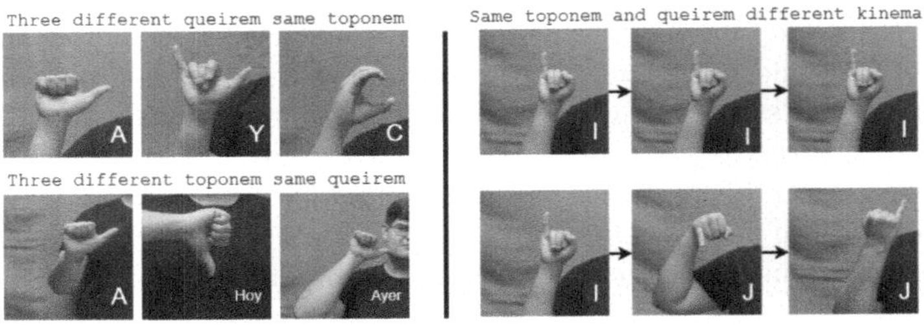

Fig. 2. Examples of `queirem`, `toponem`, and `kinema` in LSM.

movement of the sign. Figure 3 presents the proposed methodology. It begins with constructing a corpus of LSM alphabet signs from data collected from individuals. The 2D videos are then transformed into hand keypoints and processed. Two dimensionality reduction techniques are applied. Finally, classification models are trained and evaluated. These steps are described in detail below.

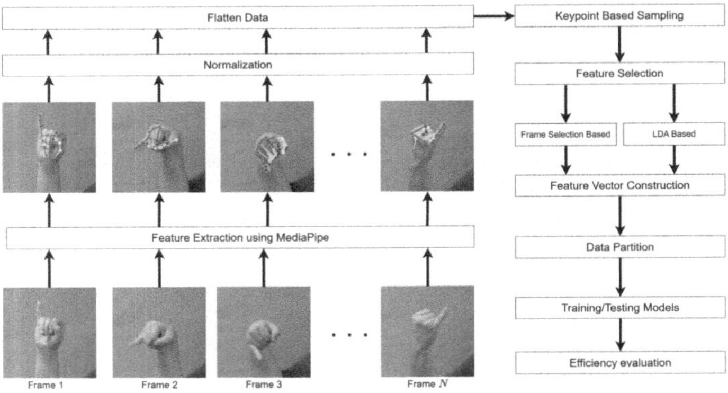

Fig. 3. Proposed methodology for classifying complete LSM alphabet.

3.1 Data Capturing

The static sign dataset of LSM[1] comprising images of 21 static letters collected from 20 subjects and divided into three subsets based on variability levels–from minimal to high–was used. The subset with the least variability (denoted as subset A) was selected, containing 92,703 images with a resolution of 360 × 360 pixels. To transition to a dynamic approach, videos were reconstructed by combining the images of each letter per subject, thereby adding the dynamic effect to the signs, resulting in 20 videos per letter.

[1] Ricardo Morfín. (2023). Mexican Sign Language Alphabet (static signs only). Zenodo. https://doi.org/10.5281/zenodo.10067509.

In addition, data for dynamic signs were collected in an environment similar to that used for the static sign dataset, with a uniform green background and optimal lighting to aid in hand keypoint extraction. 2D videos were recorded from 20 subjects, each repeating every letter 5 times. The data was captured using a Nikon D5500 camera at a resolution of 1280×720 pixels and a frame rate of 30 frames per second. This new dataset is available for use in other research.[2]

3.2 Feature Extraction and Data Preprocessing

The complete dataset, which includes the 27 signs shown in Fig. 1, was processed using the Mediapipe tool with the Hands model[3]. This model extracts 21 hand keypoints for each frame: four keypoints from each finger corresponding to their joints, along with a reference keypoint (origin) from the wrist. Each keypoint consists of x and y coordinates indicating its position within the image.

To account for variations in hand positioning across videos, it is essential to normalize the keypoint coordinates. A 2D feature vector $V = (v_1, v_2, \ldots, v_n) \in \mathbb{N}^{2n}$ is used, where each element $v_i = (v_i^x, v_i^y)$ represents a hand keypoint. Two vectors are calculated as follows: $V_x = (v_1^x, v_2^x, \ldots, v_n^x)$ and $V_y = (v_1^y, v_2^y, \ldots, v_n^y)$. The x coordinate vector is then normalized as follows: $V_x^* = \frac{V_x - \overline{V_x}}{\sigma(V_x)}$, where $\overline{V_x}$ is the mean of the vector V_x and $\sigma(V_x)$ is its standard deviation. The same procedure is applied to the y coordinate vector, resulting in the final feature vector $V^* = [V_x^*, V_y^*] \in \mathbb{N}^{2n}$.

To increase the number of samples for training the models, the *Frame Skip Sampling* method described in [3] was employed. Let $S = (f_1, f_2, \ldots, f_l)$ be a sequence of frames, where l is the total length of the video. A fixed number of frames $n = 30$ is selected, and the average spacing between frames is computed as $z = \left\lfloor \frac{l}{n-1} \right\rfloor$. The indices for the baseline sequence are determined by $Y = (y, y+z, y+2z, \ldots, y+(n-1)z) \in \mathbb{N}^n$, where $y = \left\lfloor \frac{l-z(n-1)}{2} \right\rfloor$. To generate additional samples, a random sequence of integers $R = (r_1, r_2, \ldots, r_n) \in [1, z]^n$ is created. This sequence is added to the baseline sequence as $Y_{\text{new}} = (Y_1 + R_1, Y_2 + R_2, \ldots, Y_n + R_n)$, resulting in a new sample of fixed size with 30 frames.

The method applied in this study requires the factor $z > 1$, which ensures $n < l$ to avoid duplicate samples generated by the random sequence R. As a result, videos with $l < 30$ were discarded (only one video was excluded from the dataset). Videos with $30 \leq l < 60$ were reduced to 30 frames by selecting indices from the baseline sequence, excluding the random factor. For videos with $l > 60$ the *Frame Skip Sampling* method was employed. For dynamic signs, 50 new instances were generated per video, while for static signs, 250 new instances were created per video, resulting in a total of 130,459 instances used to train the

[2] Navarrete López, J. A., & Lopez-Nava, I. H. (2025). Mexican Sign Language Alphabet (dynamic signs only). Zenodo. https://doi.org/10.5281/zenodo.14689869.

[3] MediaPipe Hands. https://github.com/google-ai-edge/mediapipe/blob/master/docs/ solutions/hands.md.

classification models, ensuring that the final dataset is balanced across classes. This approach ensured that the final dataset was balanced across all classes.

3.3 Feature Selection

All instances of the signs had a duration of 30 frames (*baseline*), adhering to the video capture standard. However, not all frames are strictly necessary to characterize signs in the LSM alphabet. Thus, new instances were generated with fewer frames, ensuring the sequential integrity of the sign. The frame selection was defined as $\delta = \frac{l-1}{n-1}$, and for $i = 0, 1, \ldots, n-1$, the i-th index was computed as $k_i = round(i\delta) + 1$. The selected frames correspond to the set $S = \{k_0, k_1, \ldots, k_{n-1}\}$, with indices in the range $[1, l]$. Using this approach, subsets with frame counts of $\{20, 15, 10, 5, 4, 3\}$ were created. For the 3-frame subset, the indices represent the Begin, Middle, and End (B-M-E) of the sequences. Additional subsets were generated with 2 and 1 frames: Begin-End (B-E), Begin-Middle (B-M), Middle-End (M-E), Begin (B), Middle (M), End (E). In Fig. 4, a representative image of some of the subsets can be observed.

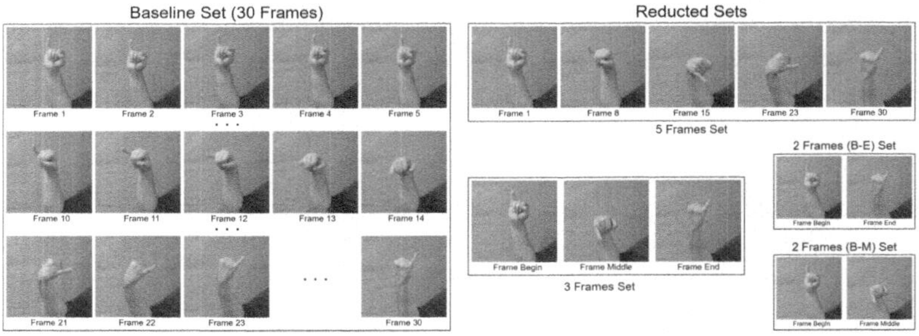

Fig. 4. Examples of different subsets with sign J.

Additionally, the dimensionality reduction algorithm Linear Discriminant Analysis (LDA) was applied using our *baseline* as input. This technique transforms the original representation of the keypoints, which also results in the loss of sequence temporality. Tests were conducted with up to 26 components, with 22 components being identified as optimal for achieving the best results.

3.4 Classification

The classification models were trained using Support Vector Machines (SVM), implemented through the `SVC` function from the *scikit-learn* library. The Radial Basis Function (RBF) kernel was selected for its ability to capture nonlinear relationships within the data. Hyperparameters were set to `C = 1` and `gamma = scale`, based on configurations recommended in a prior study. The `C` parameter regulates the penalty for classification errors, while the `gamma` parameter automatically adjusts the influence range of each sample by scaling it according to the data dimensions. This adjustment promotes convergence and stability during the training process.

A Leave-One-Out Cross-Validation approach was employed. In each iteration, two subjects were removed for the testing phase, one from each dataset with the same identifier, while the remaining subjects were used for the training phase.

4 Results

The models were trained and evaluated using feature vectors (subsets) comprising 130,459 instances. The number of features varied from 30 (frames) * 42 (2:x,y * 21:keypoints) to three subsets considering only 1 (frame) * 42. The classification results, evaluated using the F1-score metric, are presented in the boxplots in Fig. 5. Overall, the classifiers exhibited good performance, though in 4 of them, at least 2 letters showed poor results (B-E, B, M, E).

When analyzing the classification averages, it is evident that classifiers utilizing more frames tend to have slightly better performance. This confirms that not all information is necessarily required to recognize manual configurations of the LSM alphabet.

It is also noteworthy that some models, which consider 3 or fewer frames, do not contain outliers (B-M, M-E). This may suggest that, when faced with redundant information, there is an increased risk of confusion between classes.

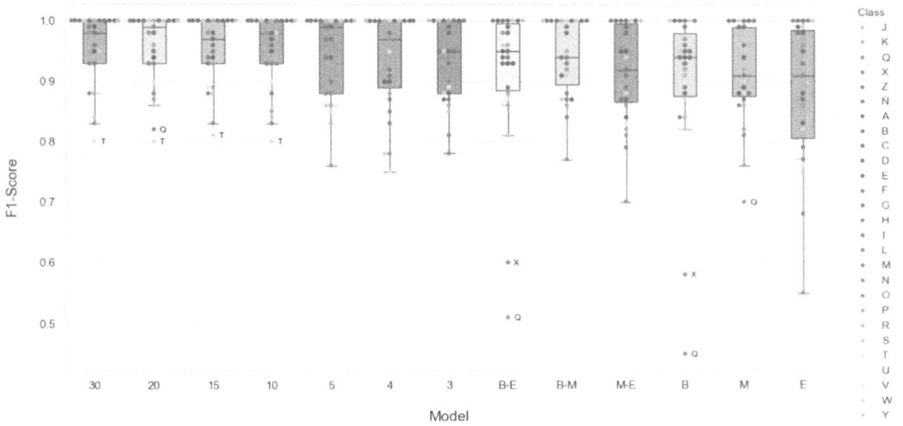

Fig. 5. Classification results per model.

Figure 6 presents the model performance by class or letter, with the six dynamic signs displayed at the top. To the left, the `Baseline` is shown, achieving an F1-Macro value of 0.95. Notably, the 10-frame model achieves the same performance but with three times fewer data and is referred to as the `Medium` model. Another notable model is one that considers only 2 frames: B-M, whose results were close to the baseline, and is labeled the `Lite` model. As expected, models considering two or fewer frames exhibit the lowest performance, particularly when only considering the begin (B) or end frame (E) and the dynamic signs.

It is important to note that the worst performance metrics correspond to the letters Q and X, followed by S and T. This suggests that the sequences must have enough variety to be distinguishable from other classes. On the other hand, some static letters, such as H, I, L, W, and Y, demonstrate excellent performance across all models.

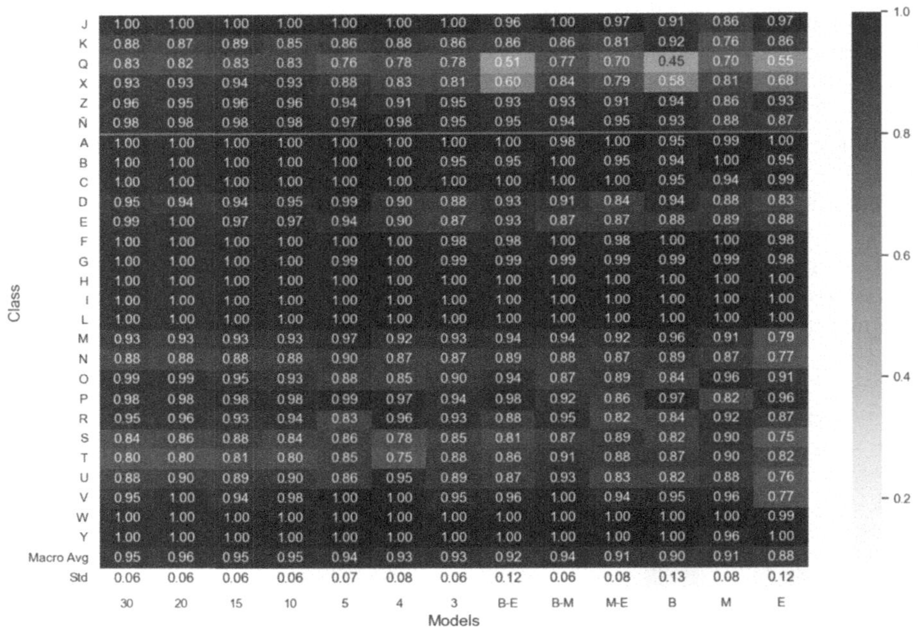

Fig. 6. Classification results per class.

To analyze in detail the classification confusions between letters, Fig. 7 presents examples from 3 frames (B-M-E) for the letters with the lowest performance. For the letters Q and X, it is observed that the `queirem` is the same; however, the difference in `kinema` could not be captured to differentiate them. The other case involves the letters S and T. Despite lacking significant `kinema` like the dynamic letters, the `queirem` is very similar, with only a slight variation in the pose of the index finger.

If the classification model will be part of a real-time SLR system, it is essential to conduct efficiency tests to better understand its response time, particularly focusing on the importance of an appropriate feature selection technique. Factors such as representation, speed, and explainability play a crucial role.

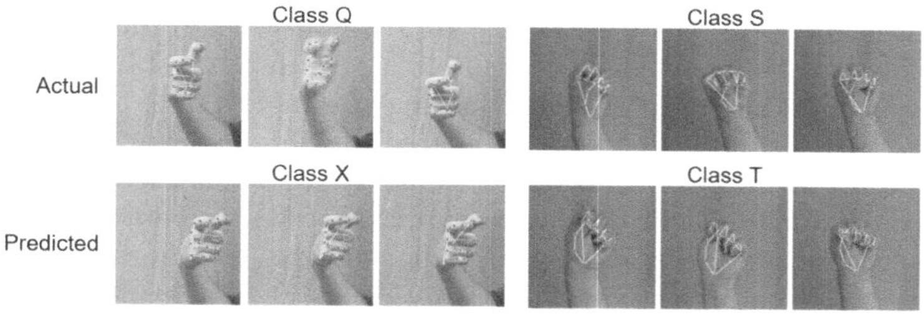

Fig. 7. Examples of confusion in models.

Table 1 presents three of the best models that use 30, 10, and 2 frames as input, as well as the LDA technique, which shows a slight improvement in F1-score. However, the time required to transform the data representation is significant, contrasting with the relatively lower training time. This is compounded by the lack of explainability in LDA components.

The *Lite* model, despite having a feature vector almost four times larger compared to LDA, demonstrates clear advantages in feature extraction time, training, and inference. Furthermore, it achieves results comparable to the *baseline* model while offering greater explainability. This is because the critical information for classifying a dynamic manual sign intuitively lies in the beginning and the midpoint of the performed sign.

Table 1. Efficiency results of the best models, with time reported in seconds.

Model	Input	Time Feat Extraction	Time Feat Selection	# Feat	Time Train	Time Inference	F1-score
Baseline	30 frames	1.33±0.06	N/A	1260	86.72	0.0050 ± 0.0003	0.97
Medium	10 frames	0.47±0.02	N/A	420	30.11	0.0020 ± 0.0002	0.95
Lite	2 frames	0.12±0.01	N/A	84	7.49	0.0010 ± 0.0001	0.97
LDA	30 frames	1.33±0.06	26.93	22	2.14	0.0003 ± 0.0004	0.99

5 Conclusions

This study presented a comprehensive method for classifying the complete alphabet of LSM. Various strategies were explored to improve the models performance, such as the use of subsets with varying frame counts. The results demonstrate that robust classification can be achieved without the need for deep learning techniques, highlighting the efficiency and suitability of simpler models for this task. The best balance between effectiveness and efficiency for real-time applications was the model that considers only a couple of video frames.

On the other hand, the limited availability of annotated datasets tailored for LSM compounds the challenge, as most datasets focus on static signs or lack sufficient diversity to train robust models. This shortcoming hinders the scalability and generalizability of existing SLR systems. In this study, the dynamic signs of the LSM alphabet were collected and integrated into the static sign dataset, and these resources are now available to the community.

This research is motivated by its potential to offer a comprehensive solution to SLR for LSM. By addressing both static and dynamic signs, it seeks to improve the accessibility and usability of LSM recognition systems, promoting inclusivity for deaf and hard-of-hearing individuals. The next step is to evaluate the system under real-world conditions, testing with diverse users, environments, and signer variability to ensure generalizability.

Acknowledgments. We thank R. Morfín and M.A. Peñaloza, and the volunteers who assisted with data capture and contributed as subjects. We also acknowledge SECIHTI for the Master's degree grants 1294009 (JANL) and 1351117 (JJGP).

References

1. Alejandro, S.M., Antonio, N.C.J.: A real-time deep learning system for the translation of Mexican signal language into text. In: 2021 Mexican International Conference on Computer Science (ENC), pp. 1–7. IEEE (2021)
2. Cruz Aldrete, M.: Gramática de la Lengua de Señas Mexicana. Ph.D. thesis, El Colegio de México (2008)
3. Ko, S.K., Kim, C.J., Jung, H., Cho, C.: Neural sign language translation based on human keypoint estimation. Appl. Sci. **9**(13), 2683 (2019)
4. Lara-Cázares, A., Moreno-Armendáriz, M.A., Calvo, H.: Advanced hybrid neural networks for accurate recognition of the extended alphabet and dynamic signs in Mexican sign language (MSL). Appl. Sci. **14**(22), 10186 (2024)
5. Mejía-Peréz, K., Córdova-Esparza, D.M., Terven, J.: Automatic recognition of Mexican sign language using a depth camera and recurrent neural networks. Appl. Sci. (Switz.) **12**(11) (2022)
6. Miah, A., Hasan, M., Okuyama, Y., Tomioka, Y., Shin, J.: Spatial-temporal attention with graph and general neural network-based sign language recognition. Pattern Anal. Appl. **27**(2), 37 (2024)
7. Morfín-Chávez, R.F., Gortarez-Pelayo, J.J., Lopez-Nava, I.H.: Fingerspelling recognition in Mexican sign language (LSM) using machine learning. In: Mexican International Conference on Artificial Intelligence, pp. 110–120. Springer (2023)
8. Pfister, A.E.: Forbidden signs: deafness and language socialization in Mexico City. Ethos **45**(1), 139–161 (2017). https://doi.org/10.1111/etho.12151
9. Sánchez-Vicinaiz, T.J., Camacho-Pérez, E., Castillo-Atoche, A.A., Cruz-Fernandez, M., García-Martínez, J.R., Rodríguez-Reséndiz, J.: Mediapipe frame and convolutional neural networks-based fingerspelling detection in mexican sign language. Technologies **12**(8), 124 (2024)

Classification of Suicidal Texts Based on Emotional Change Detection Using LSTM

María del Carmen García-Galindo[1](✉), Ángel Hernández-Castañeda[1,2], René Arnulfo García-Hernández[1], and Yulia Ledeneva[1]

[1] Autonomous University of the State of Mexico, Instituto Literario 100, Col. Centro. C.P., 50000 Toluca, Mexico, Mexico
marycarmeng142@gmail.com, angelhc2305@gmail.com, renearnulfo@hotmail.com, yledeneva@yahoo.com

[2] Cátedras SECIHTI, 03940 Mexico City, Mexico

Abstract. Suicide remains a critical public health concern, often stemming from the profound emotional distress caused by mental health disorders. In today's digital age, social media platforms have become common spaces for individuals to express suicidal thoughts, largely due to the sense of anonymity they provide. Detecting suicidal ideation on these platforms is crucial for early intervention and for preventing this ongoing mental health crisis. This study introduces a computational approach for identifying suicidal thoughts by analyzing the emotional tone of text at the sentence level. Our method leverages a Long Short-Term Memory (LSTM) model to process emotional data and track fluctuations in emotion throughout the text. The results demonstrate that our approach can effectively detect subtle emotional shifts, even in the absence of explicit death-related language.

Keywords: Suicide detection · Emotional content · LSTM · Sentiment analysis

1 Introduction

Suicidal ideation refers to recurring and intentional thoughts about ending one's own life [6]. It is widely regarded as one of the primary warning signs of an individual's intent to attempt suicide [12]. Suicide is recognized as one of the most pressing public health challenges [2,6]. In 2021, it was identified as the third leading cause of death among individuals aged 15 to 29 years globally [21].

The causes of suicide are complex and multifaceted [1,16]. Key psychological factors that have been identified include personality traits, emotional distress, mood fluctuations, mental pain, and cognitive distortions [10,18,20].

Mental pain, also referred to as psychache [16], is a profound and intolerable form of emotional suffering. It is often linked to a range of distressing emotions, such as shame, guilt, humiliation, loneliness, fear, anguish, affectlessness, helplessness, and terror [16,17].

A. P. López-Monroy et al. (Eds.): MCPR 2025, LNCS 15715, pp. 123–132, 2025.
https://doi.org/10.1007/978-3-031-96255-4_12

Matthews [10] reports that 56% of individuals who have died by suicide cited psychological pain as their primary motive. Other studies also suggest that suicide is unlikely to occur without the presence of mental pain [17]. In this context, Zhang et al. [23] highlight that emotional information is crucial for diagnosing mental health disorders.

People express their suicidal thoughts, feelings, and emotions through various textual resources [7,23]. These resources include interviews, suicide notes, clinical notes, and social media posts [5,12,22,23]. As a result, there has been growing research interest in detecting mental illness by analyzing textual content [23].

In this study, we develop a system to automatically identify the presence of 15 distinct emotions at the sentence level within the analyzed documents. We then employ a Long Short-Term Memory (LSTM) network to capture the dependencies in emotional changes throughout the document. This approach enables our method to classify documents as suicidal or non-suicidal, while also providing valuable insights into the emotion-based factors underlying suicide.

The rest of the paper is organized as follows: Sect. 2 provides background and a review of related work. Section 3 describes our proposed method. The experimental setup and results are presented in Sect. 4. Finally, Sect. 5 presents the conclusions.

2 Related Works

Suicide has been studied across various fields using diverse techniques. Traditional methods for detecting suicide risk primarily rely on clinical approaches, such as personal interviews and assessment scales [11]. However, due to the stigma surrounding mental illness, 80% of patients do not receive effective diagnosis or treatment [13,23].

Since suicide can be attributed to a manifestation of mental pain linked to various emotions [10], several studies in recent years have explored the role of emotional information in the automatic detection of mental illnesses.

Deep learning-based approaches, such as Convolutional Neural Networks (CNN) and Recurrent Neural Networks (RNN), have shown superior performance over traditional machine learning methods in suicide detection tasks [23].

In this regard, the study by Sawhney et al. [13] focused on identifying emotional patterns linked to suicide risk, using an approach based on emotional phases and temporality. To detect emotions in tweets, the authors employed a BERT model fine-tuned with Plutchik's wheel of emotions, an LSTM to capture the temporal progression of the user's emotions, and phase-adaptive convolutions (PAC) to identify the most relevant emotions based on the user's emotional state at a given time, considering both past and recent emotional phases. However, Plutchik's wheel presents emotions as opposites, which limits classification by failing to capture complex emotional transitions. Furthermore, PHASE relies on the user's tweet history, meaning that if this history is insufficient or ambiguous, the resulting emotional representation may be compromised.

Sawhney et al. [14] propose STATENet, a transformer-based model designed for suicide risk detection on social media. This model integrates both linguistic and emotional features from tweets, leveraging Plutchik's wheel of emotions and a time-aware approach to incorporate the user's historical emotional context. The results show that STATENet significantly outperforms competing methods, achieving an F1 score of 0.7990, demonstrating the effectiveness of emotional and temporal cues in suicide risk assessment. However, the study has limitations, such as its reliance on the user's previous tweet history, which may impact accuracy if the history is insufficient or ambiguous.

As mentioned earlier, some models heavily rely on the user's previous tweet history to construct an emotional representation. If this history is insufficient, ambiguous, or of low quality, the models may struggle to accurately detect suicide risk. Additionally, Plutchik's wheel categorizes emotions as opposites, which may limit the models' ability to capture the complexity of emotional transitions within an individual. Another drawback is that these models tend to analyze emotions at a global level, either assigning a predominant emotion or considering them within a large-scale historical context. This approach may fail to adequately capture the nuanced and complex emotions present within a single text.

In this study, we propose a model for identifying suicidal texts focuses on sentence-level analysis to learn dependency through emotional changes within a note. We use a model that determines the degree of presence of each emotion in text and a LSTM neural network to learn relationships and dependencies through emotions changes. Our study is characterized by the exploration of several types of suicide notes such as texts related to consummated suicide (where it is known that the person died by suicide), texts of suicidal intentions (where it is unknown whether the person actually died), and texts on general topics.

3 Proposed Architecture

The present study examines the impact of emotional changes as a key factor in detecting suicidal texts. Figure 1 provides a general overview of our proposed method, which is described as follows.

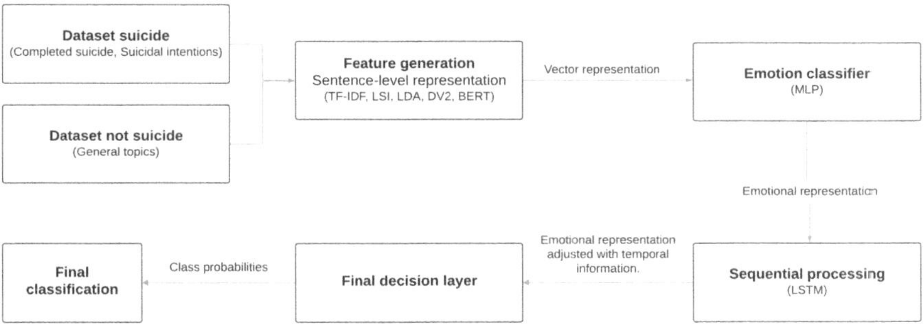

Fig. 1. General scheme of the proposed method.

In the first step, each document is segmented into sentences, and feature extraction is performed using TF-IDF, LDA, LSI, Doc2Vec, and the BERT model. Overall feature generation methods, with the exception of TF-IDF and BERT, were trained using the Wikipedia dataset. The vector representation of each sentence is then input into a Multilayer Perceptron (MLP) to assess the degree of emotional presence within the sentences. Since documents consist of a sequence of sentences, an LSTM network is employed to capture relationships and emotional patterns across the sentences in the document. Finally, the output from the LSTM is passed through a fully connected layer to perform the final binary classification (suicide notes vs. non-suicide notes).

3.1 Datasets

In this study, three types of datasets–consummated suicide, suicide ideation, and general domain–were used to validate our proposed approach. A description of each dataset is provided below (Table 1).

Table 1. Description of the corpus used

Class	# Documents	Avg. words	Avg. sentences
Completed suicide	309	50	5
Suicidal intentions	309	143	10
General topics	255	110	6

- **Notes of consummated suicide:** this corpus contains a total of 309 notes written by individuals who died by suicide. The texts were collected from news articles, online publications, books, and previous studies [4,9,15]. Although not validated by mental health professionals, their authenticity is supported by the fact that all correspond to confirmed suicide cases. These notes offer the advantage of providing verified content directly associated with consummated suicide, in contrast to Reddit notes, which do not necessarily guarantee authenticity
- **Notes of suicidal intentions:** this dataset consists of 309 notes expressing suicidal thoughts, collected from the *r/SuicideWatch* and *r/Depression* subreddits on the social media platform Reddit. The notes were manually curated based on specific keywords and phrases related to suicide.
- **Notes on general topics:** this collection consists of 255 public notes covering general topics such as culture, economy, politics, music, food, and sports. The texts were gathered from six different subreddits on Reddit: *r/culture*, *r/economy*, *r/politics*, *r/music*, *r/food*, and *r/sports*.
- **CEASE** [3]**:** this collection contains 499 sentences, each labeled with one of 15 emotions.

In the preprocessing stage, we removed URLs and user mentions.

3.2 Identification of Suicide Notes

The goal of the present study is to identify suicide risk by preprocessing texts and obtaining an emotional representation of each sentence in the analyzed documents.

First, each document is separated into sentences, and each sentence is converted into numerical vectors by applying various methods such as TF-IDF, Latent Dirichlet Allocation (LDA), Latent Semantic Indexing (LSI), Doc2Vec, and BERT. Next, we employ a feedforward neural network, trained on the CEASE dataset, to determine the emotional distribution of each text. This model was configured with a hidden layer containing 50 units, a sigmoid activation function, and an output layer with 15 dimensions (corresponding to the 15 emotions in the CEASE dataset). This step generates a vector representing the emotional distribution, where each feature corresponds to the probability of a particular emotion.

We hypothesize that the author's emotional state and its fluctuations throughout the document are crucial indicators for identifying suicidal ideation. Therefore, we selected an LSTM neural network due to its ability to process sequential data and capture dependencies between emotional variations across the text. The LSTM receives a sequence of 15-dimensional vectors representing the emotional distribution of each sentence. The hidden state of the LSTM is then passed to a final decision layer, where a softmax function is used to provide class probabilities for binary classification (suicidal vs. non-suicidal).

4 Experiments and Results

Our analysis proceeds in three main steps. First, we examine the datasets, identifying and comparing the most frequent features and words in each. Next, we analyze and compare the emotional changes detected across the documents. Finally, we assess the performance of the proposed model in classifying suicidal texts across different contexts.

To determine the emotional distribution of each document, we trained an MLP using the CEASE dataset. The dataset was partitioned into training (70%), validation (20%), and test (10%) subsets. We evaluated the performance of the emotion classifier using precision, recall, and F-score as evaluation metrics.

The results reported in Table 2 indicate a heterogeneous performance of the emotion classifier across the evaluated categories. Despite the observed performance limitations in classifying some emotions, the obtained emotion-based features remain valuable for identifying suicidal texts. However, a more robust training dataset could improve performance in emotion classification and, consequently, in suicide classification as well.

Figure 2 illustrates a comparison of emotional distributions across different types of documents. It shows the sentence-level emotion distribution for one document from each dataset. The graphs plot emotions on the horizontal axis and their corresponding probabilities on the vertical axis. It can be observed that several emotions are more intense in both the general domain texts (Fig. 2(a))

Table 2. Performance of the emotion classifier (per class)

Class	Precision	Recall	F-score
Abuse	0.2100	0.8000	0.3300
Anger	1.0000	0.5000	0.6700
Blame	1.0000	0.3300	0.5000
Fear	1.0000	0.7500	0.8600
Forgiveness	0.6700	0.6700	0.6700
Guilt	0.6000	0.5000	0.5500
Peacefulness	0.3300	0.3300	0.3300
Hopefulness	0.0000	0.0000	0.0000
Hopelessness	0.2000	0.2500	0.2200
Information	0.5000	0.4000	0.4400
Instruction	0.3300	1.0000	0.5000
Love	0.5000	0.3300	0.4000
Pride	0.0000	0.0000	0.0000
Sorrow	1.0000	0.6000	0.7500
Thankfulness	0.5000	0.4000	0.4400

and the suicidal ideation texts (Fig. 2(b)). For instance, the activation of multiple emotions may serve as a cue for suicide ideation detection. In contrast, in the case of consummated suicide (Fig. 2(c)), the emotional distribution of the note indicates that the author focused on specific emotions. This pattern may suggest that the individual was experiencing a stage of emotional dysregulation.

A five-fold cross-validation was implemented to evaluate the performance of the proposed method, in addition the standard deviation (SD) is also reported. Table 3 presents the results of classifying completed suicide notes and general topic notes. As shown, traditional representation-based methods such as TF-IDF, LSI, LDA, and Doc2Vec exhibit similar performance, with F-scores ranging from 0.7235 ($\pm$0.0300) to 0.7385 ($\pm$0.0230). While all models exhibited low variability (SD $<$ 0.05), BERT demonstrated superior performance–exceeding traditional methods by more than 12%.

In the second experiment, we classified notes expressing suicidal intentions and general topic notes. The results, presented in Table 4, indicate that TF-IDF and LDA achieve intermediate performance, while LSI and Doc2Vec yielded the lowest averages and higher variability, reflecting limitations in predictive capability and stability. As observed in the first experiment, BERT outperforms all other methods, achieving the highest and most consistent scores across all metrics, with notably low standard deviation (SD) values, indicating both superior performance and high stability in its results.

Table 5 shows the classification results between notes of completed suicide and notes of suicidal intentions.

Table 3. Completed suicide vs General topics

Method	Precision (mean ± SD)	Recall (mean ± SD)	F-score (mean ± SD)
TF-IDF	0.7522 (±0.0260)	0.7305 (±0.0375)	0.7244 (±0.0398)
LSI	0.7432 (±0.0208)	0.7305 (±0.0250)	0.7289 (±0.0300)
LDA	0.7481 (±0.0265)	0.7376 (±0.0217)	0.7385 (±0.0230)
Doc2Vec	0.7328 (±0.0332)	0.7233 (±0.0302)	0.7235 (±0.0300)
BERT	0.8695 (±0.0445)	0.8635 (±0.0440)	**0.8637** (±0.0463)

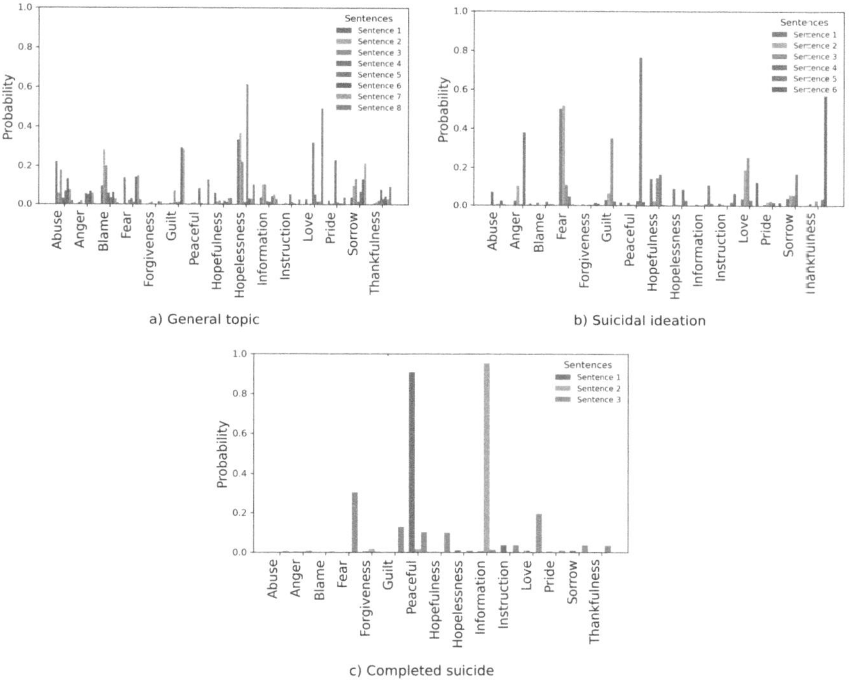

Fig. 2. Emotional changes in texts on general topics, suicidal ideation, and completed suicide.

Table 4. Suicidal intentions vs General topics

Method	Precision (mean ± SD)	Recall (mean ± SD)	F-score (mean ± SD)
TF-IDF	0.6865 (±0.0559)	0.6683 (±0.0592)	0.6633 (±0.0642)
LSI	0.5099 (±0.1271)	0.5496 (±0.0348)	0.5095 (±0.0894)
LDA	0.6480 (±0.0637)	0.5797 (±0.0566)	0.5647 (±0.0703)
Doc2Vec	0.5023 (±0.1577)	0.5196 (±0.0629)	0.4658 (±0.1169)
BERT	0.8528 (±0.0442)	0.8473 (±0.0411)	**0.8475** (±0.0431)

The classification of suicidal ideation and completed suicide generally yields higher performance compared to the classification between suicidal ideation and general topics. This improvement may be due to differences in language usage: texts expressing suicidal ideation often contain more explicit terms related to suicide, while completed suicide notes typically feature more universally recognized emotional expressions. These distinct emotional cues make it easier to differentiate between suicidal ideation and completed suicide.

Table 5. Completed suicide vs Suicidal intentions

Method	Precision (mean ± SD)	Recall (mean ± SD)	F-score (mean ± SD)
TF-IDF	0.7524 (±0.0511)	0.7362 (±0.0468)	0.7341 (±0.0458)
LSI	0.7344 (±0.0355)	0.7249 (±0.0383)	0.7210 (±0.0381)
LDA	0.7714 (±0.0353)	0.7508 (±0.0430)	0.7454 (±0.0448)
Doc2Vec	0.7429 (±0.0295)	0.7298 (±0.0320)	0.7271 (±0.0369)
BERT	0.8316 (±0.0292)	0.8269 (±0.0255)	**0.8270** (±0.0273)

The overall results indicate that BERT outperforms other methods in emotion identification, making it particularly effective for detecting suicide notes when combined with LSTMs.

Our results indicate that the system is capable of identifying expressions of suicidal ideation, even in the absence of explicit terms related to suicide. For instance (examples were paraphrased to ensure the privacy of the original data), correct classified notes such as *I can't find a reason to keep going anymore. All I ever wanted was to be loved. I gave you everything I had* and *All I wish for now is to fall asleep and never wake up again* do not contain explicit words about suicide.

To the best of the authors' knowledge, there is no publicly available collection that allows for a direct comparison between suicide detection-related studies. However, this work presents a partial comparison of the proposed methods for suicide detection, as shown in Table 6. Each study uses a different dataset, mostly collected from social media platforms such as Reddit and Twitter.

Table 6. Partial comparison of the proposed approach with respect to other studies

Author	Dataset	Description	F-score
This study	Notes of consummated suicide	Emotional features + LSTM	0.8637
This study	Reddit posts (SuicideWatch)	Emotional features + LSTM	0.8475
Sawhney et al. [13]	Twitter posts	Phase-aware LSTM	0.8050
Sawhney et al. [14]	Twitter posts	Transformer-based approach	0.7990
Kodati et al. [8]	Reddit posts (SuicideWatch)	Transformer-based models	0.8980
Wang et al. [19]	Twitter posts	SVM, BiLSTM, CNN, GRU	0.8430

5 Conclusions

In this paper, we employ an emotion classifier and an LSTM network to capture emotional shifts within documents, enabling the accurate differentiation of texts across various domains. This approach not only facilitates the identification of key emotions but also allows for the analysis of their intensity and progression throughout the text.

Our dataset analysis reveals that texts expressing suicidal ideation often contain explicit suicide-related terms, though the occurrence of the act remains uncertain. In contrast, completed suicide texts tend to express intense emotions more subtly, frequently without direct references to suicide, despite the act being known to have occurred.

The results from our experiments demonstrate that emotion-based patterns enable effective classification of notes related to suicidal ideation, completed suicide, and general topics.

Additionally, the experiments highlight the effectiveness of BERT as a feature generation method. Its advanced semantic representations provide a deeper understanding of emotional content, significantly enhancing the model's ability to accurately identify suicide notes.

Acknowledgements. We would like to thank the Autonomous University of the State of Mexico and the Secretaría de Ciencia, Humanidades, Tecnología e Innovación (SECI-HTI) for their support.

References

1. Abdulsalam, A., Alhothali, A.: Suicidal ideation detection on social media: a review of machine learning methods. Soc. Netw. Anal. Min. **14**(1), 1–16 (2024)
2. Coppersmith, G., Leary, R., Whyne, E., Wood, T.: Quantifying suicidal ideation via language usage on social media. In: Joint Statistics Meetings Proceedings, Statistical Computing Section, JSM, vol. 110 (2015)
3. Ghosh, S., Ekbal, A., Bhattacharyya, P.: Cease, a corpus of emotion annotated suicide notes in English. In: Proceedings of the Twelfth Language Resources and Evaluation Conference, pp. 1618–1626 (2020)
4. Gunn, J.F., Lester, D.: Twitter postings and suicide: an analysis of the postings of a fatal suicide in the 24 hours prior to death. Suicidologi **17**(3) (2012)
5. Guo, X., Sun, Y., Vosoughi, S.: Emotion-based modeling of mental disorders on social media. In: IEEE/WIC/ACM International Conference on Web Intelligence and Intelligent Agent Technology, pp. 8–16 (2021)
6. Haque, R., Islam, N., Islam, M., Ahsan, M.M.: A comparative analysis on suicidal ideation detection using NLP, machine, and deep learning. Technologies **10**(3), 57 (2022)
7. Ji, S., Pan, S., Li, X., Cambria, E., Long, G., Huang, Z.: Suicidal ideation detection: a review of machine learning methods and applications. IEEE Trans. Comput. Soc. Syst. **8**(1), 214–226 (2020)
8. Kodati, D., Tene, R.: Identifying suicidal emotions on social media through transformer-based deep learning. Appl. Intell. **53**(10), 11885–11917 (2023)

9. Malini, N., Tan, V.: Forensic linguistics analysis of Virginia Woolf's suicide notes. Int. J. Educ. **9**(1), 53–58 (2016)
10. Matthews, J.D.: Cognitive behavioral therapy approach for suicidal thinking and behaviors in depression. Ment. Disord.-Theor. Empir. Perspect. 24–43 (2013)
11. Ortega, M.G.: Comportamiento suicida. Qartuppi, S. de RL de CV, Sonora (2018)
12. Ralarala, M.K., Kaschula, R.H., Heydon, G.: Language and the Law: Global Perspectives in Forensic Linguistics from Africa and Beyond, vol. 3. African Sun Media (2022)
13. Sawhney, R., Joshi, H., Flek, L., Shah, R.: Phase: learning emotional phase-aware representations for suicide ideation detection on social media. In: Proceedings of the 16th Conference of the European Chapter of the Association for Computational Linguistics: Main Volume, pp. 2415–2428 (2021)
14. Sawhney, R., Joshi, H., Gandhi, S., Shah, R.: A time-aware transformer based model for suicide ideation detection on social media. In: Proceedings of the 2020 Conference on Empirical Methods in Natural Language Processing (EMNLP), pp. 7685–7697 (2020)
15. Schoene, A.M., Dethlefs, N.: Unsupervised suicide note classification. In: Workshop on Issues of Sentiment Discovery and Opinion Mining at Knowledge Discovery and Data Mining (KDD), pp. 1–9 (2018)
16. Shneidman, E.S.: Commentary: suicide as psychache. J. Nerv. Ment. Dis. **181**(3), 145–147 (1993)
17. Tossani, E.: The concept of mental pain. Psychother. Psychosom. **82**(2), 67–73 (2013)
18. Verrocchio, M.C., Carrozzino, D., Marchetti, D., Andreasson, K., Fulcheri, M., Bech, P.: Mental pain and suicide: a systematic review of the literature. Front. Psych. **7**, 108 (2016)
19. Wang, N., et al.: Learning models for suicide prediction from social media posts. arXiv preprint arXiv:2105.03315 (2021)
20. Weishaar, M.E., Beck, A.T.: Hopelessness and suicide. Int. Rev. Psychiatry **4**(2), 177–184 (1992)
21. World Health Organization: WHO: (2025). https://www.who.int/news-room/fact-sheets/detail/suicide
22. Zhang, T., Schoene, A.M., Ji, S., Ananiadou, S.: Natural language processing applied to mental illness detection: a narrative review. NPJ Digit. Med. **5**(1), 1–13 (2022)
23. Zhang, T., Yang, K., Ji, S., Ananiadou, S.: Emotion fusion for mental illness detection from social media: a survey. Inf. Fusion **92**, 231–246 (2023)

Synthetic Corpus of Emotions for Detection of Depression in Social Networks

Erick Barrios González, Mireya Tovar Vidal(✉), and María Teresa Torrijos Muñoz

Faculty of Computer Science, Benemerita Universidad Autonoma de Puebla, 14 sur y Av, San Claudio, C.U., Puebla, Mexico
erick.barrios@viep.com.mx, {mireya.tovar,teresa.torrijos}@correo.buap.mx

Abstract. The detection of mental disorders through Natural Language Processing (NLP) has gained significant attention, particularly in the field of depression detection. Despite the availability of various corpora for English, Spanish-language resources remain limited. To address this gap, this study presents a synthetic corpus based on Plutchik's emotion model, designed to enhance depression detection in Spanish-language social media messages. This work compares three different corpora: the Twitter Sentiment analysis corpus, the LiSSS corpus, and the created synthetic corpus. Each dataset is used to train emotion-detection models, which then generate emotion vectors as input for a multilayer perceptron neural network to classify users as depressed or non-depressed. The results demonstrate the effectiveness of emotion-based features for depression detection and highlight the potential of synthetic corpora. The comparison shows that the synthetic corpus is statistically similar to a corpus generated and labeled by humans. Moreover, the results of the model based on the synthetic corpus perform as well as or better than other corpora labeled by humans.

Keywords: Depression · Plutchik · Spanish corpus · NLP

1 Introduction

The detection of mental disorders, particularly depression, has gained relevance in natural language processing (NLP). Labeled corpora are essential for training and evaluating models that identify linguistic patterns linked to these conditions. Spanish corpora are limited compared to English corpora, posing a significant challenge for progress in this field. Existing Spanish corpora for depression detection mainly consist of data collected from social media platforms like Twitter, now called X. These corpora typically include messages or posts from users labeled according to symptoms of depression. However, access to authentic data faces ethical and privacy barriers, leading to the development of synthetic corpora. The emergence of text-generating models has enabled the creation of

A. P. López-Monroy et al. (Eds.): MCPR 2025, LNCS 15715, pp. 133–143, 2025.
https://doi.org/10.1007/978-3-031-96255-4_13

datasets designed to specialize models for specific tasks. This work presents a synthetic corpus for emotion detection in Spanish messages, used for depression detection on social media. It includes related work (Sect. 2), corpus creation methodology (Sect. 3), model training (Sect. 3.4), and a comparative analysis of results with other labeled corpora (Sect. 4).

2 Related Work

Depression detection on social media has emerged as a key research area, driven by the personal nature of user-generated content. This has encouraged the use of natural language processing (NLP) and machine learning to analyze such data and identify signs of mental disorders. In particular, some studies have explored emotion detection in Spanish to support this task. For example, [12] built a new corpus with 16 emotions, emphasizing negative emotions, and evaluated various transformer-based models (both encoder-only and encoder-decoder). Other studies focus on predicting emotions in different contexts, such as [4], which examines Twitter users' emotional reactions after reading Spanish news articles. Additionally, some studies focus on English-language datasets for detecting depression using emotions, such as [1] and [2], which implement a representation called Bag of Sub-Emotions (BoSE). This approach assumes that emotions can be represented more accurately at a detailed level rather than broad categories like "joy" or "sadness". There are motion-labeled corpora are not publicly available, requiring researchers to request access or participate in competitions, as in the case of the EmoEvalEs 2021 dataset [13]. Therefore, this study selects freely accessible corpora available online, such as [9] and [11]. A key aspect of this work is the creation of a synthetic corpus based on Plutchik's emotion model [8]. This widely used psychological model organizes emotions in a wheel structure, categorizing eight primary emotions: joy, sadness, fear, anger, surprise, anticipation, trust, and disgust. These emotions have direct opposites (e.g., joy vs. sadness) and can combine to form more complex emotional states. Finally, this study addresses the classification of depressive and non-depressive users based on the MentalRiskES 2023 task introduced at IberLEF 2023, which targets the early detection of mental disorders in Spanish-language messages from Telegram users. The focus is specifically on Subtask 2a, which involves binary classification for identifying signs of depression. Teams that used emotion-based features include UMUTeam [7] and SINAI [5]. UMUTeam proposed two fine-tuned BETO-based models, one of which incorporated emotional features via joint learning. SINAI focused on filtering neutral messages and summarizing texts, training one model exclusively on the EmoEvent dataset and another on a Depressive User Dataset, later fine-tuned with EmoEvent [14].

3 Methodology

This section describes the corpus selection, the creation of the Plutchik emotion corpus, and the implementation of emotion corpora (*Plutchik*, *LISSS* and *Twitter Sentiment Analysis corpus*) for detecting depression symptoms.

3.1 Dataset

In this work, three Spanish-language corpora oriented toward emotion classification were used. The first is the *Twitter Sentiment Analysis corpus* from Kaggle [11], consisting of 2,591 records. It is organized into 20 distinct emotions and grouped into five general sentiment categories: *joyful* (350 texts), *mad* (530), *peaceful* (660), *powerful* (420), and *sad* (360). The corpus was created using Twitter Scraper and built by mapping words to corresponding sentiments.

Emotion-wise, the distribution includes: *Confident* (140), *Daring* (110), *Distant* (130), *Embarrassed* (130), *Frustrated* (120), *Irritated* (140), *Isolated* (120), *Jealous* (140), *Loving* (130), *Optimistic* (110), *Overwhelmed* (140), *Playful* (130), *Relaxed* (130), *Secure* (140), *Responsive* (110), *Sleepy* (150), *Thankful* (150), *Successful* (140), *Stupid* (90), and *Surprised* (140).

The second corpus used is the *LiSSS* [9] corpus, which contains five different emotions. In this corpus, a text may include more than one emotion. For example, the sentence *"The only thing that hurts me about dying is that it is not out of love."* would be classified under both *love* and *pain*. This corpus is composed of literary texts and has been annotated by human annotators. There are two versions of this corpus: one labeled by a single annotator and another labeled by multiple annotators. The version annotated by multiple annotators was used in this study. In this version, two voting strategies—democratic and majority—were applied to determine the final label of each sentence. The distribution of texts by emotion in the *LiSSS* corpus is as follows: 1,378 texts express anger, 1,813 express love, 1,784 convey fear, 1,678 reflect happiness, and 2,378 correspond to sadness or pain.

The third corpus is a synthetic dataset created based on *Plutchik's wheel of emotions*. This model proposes eight basic emotions and introduces complementary emotions. For example, *sadness* has *joy* as its complementary counterpart. Following this approach, the corpus includes three types of examples per emotion: one where the emotion is clearly expressed, one where the emotion is ambiguous (with respect to its complementary emotion), and one where no emotion is expressed. For instance, the sentence *"Today has been a surprising day because many things have happened"* is ambiguous between *joy* and *sadness*, while *"Today is Thursday"* is neutral. The corpus was generated using the mini version of ChatGPT 4.0, which enabled the creation of blocks of 200 texts [10]. A total of 400 texts were generated for each emotion, along with 400 ambiguous and 400 neutral texts for each emotion. The maximum text length was limited to 200 words per text. In total, 400 texts were created for each of the eight emotions, resulting in 3,200 explicit emotional texts, 3,200 ambiguous texts, and 400 neutral examples, making a final collection of 6,800 texts. All generated texts were reviewed with a custom script to detect length violations, duplicates, and mismatches with the intended description. Final verification was done manually to ensure correctness. Although no issues arose within a single query using the same prompt, continuous validation was required when multiple prompts were used to adjust the content of a text set.

Two examples of indications used are the following: *"Crea 200 oraciones en las que se perciba la tristeza de forma ambigua, considerando la definición de tristeza según Plutchik."* and *"Crea 200 oraciones adicionales como si fueran escritas por una persona"*.

3.2 MentalRiskES 2023 Corpus

Subtask 2a of MentalRiskES 2023 consists of a **binary classification**, meaning it detects whether a Telegram user suffers from depression or not. For this, two labels are used: **0** for "*control*", indicating that the user does not suffer from depression, and **1** for "*suffers*", indicating that the user is experiencing this disorder. The corpus is divided into *trial corpus*, *training corpus*, and *evaluation corpus*. In total, there are records for 335 users, of which 167 are *control* users and 168 have depression. The corpus distribution is addressed in Sect. 3.6.

3.3 Input Information

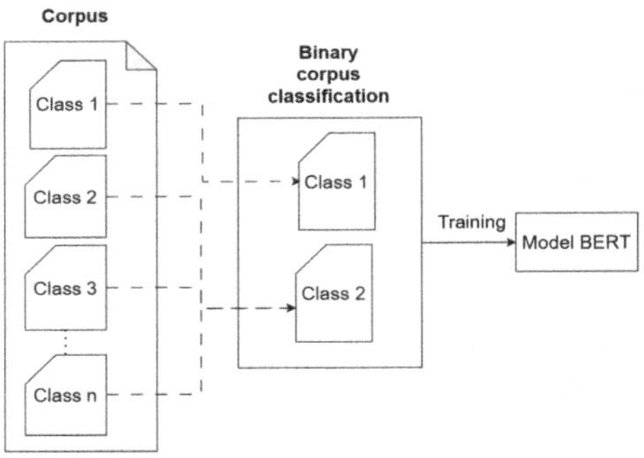

Fig. 1. Architecture implemented in proposal 1, for multiclass classification, a One-vs-All (OvA) strategy was adopted, training a separate binary classifier for each emotion category against all others.

To perform the final classification, each user is represented by a vector indicating the frequency of detected emotions in their messages. For example, User 1: [1, 17, 2, 1, 1, 4, 5] reflects one joyful text, 17 surprising, two angry, etc. To prevent anomalies during learning, the values were normalized by subtracting the minimum and dividing by the range (maximum minus minimum). To detect emotions in texts, two training approaches were developed.

Proposal 1 uses the *Twitter Sentiment Analysis corpus* [11] and the *LiSSS* corpus, employing a **One-vs-All** strategy: a separate binary classifier is trained for each emotion, treating it as the positive class and all others as negative (see Fig. 1).

Proposal 2 applies to the *synthetic Plutchik corpus*, enabling **three-class classification**—explicit emotional messages, neutral messages, and ambiguous messages.

3.4 Training of Emotion-Specialized Models

To train the emotion classification models, the **BERT-base-spanish-wwm-cased** model [3] was used, with an additional dense layer for **multi-emotion classification**. This model was chosen due to its specific training for the Spanish language and its superior performance compared to Multilingual BERT [3].

Each corpus was divided into **80% for training** and **20% for evaluation**, and a distinct set of hyperparameters was applied per dataset, with minimal variation. Models were trained between 10 and 21 epochs depending on performance, saving the best version whenever the weighted F_1 score improved on the validation set to prevent overfitting. The weighted F_1 score was selected due to the class imbalance present in the datasets.

Configuration 1 (*Twitter Sentiment Analysis corpus*). *Maximum text length* = 200, *Batch size* = 16, *Number of classes* = 2, *Learning rate* = 2e−5.

Configuration 2 ("LISSS"). *Maximum text length* = 200, *Batch size* = 77, *Number of classes* = 2, *Learning rate* = 3e−5.

Configuration 3 ("Corpus Plutchik ChatGPT"). *Maximum text length* = 200, *Batch size* = 16, *Number of classes* = 3, *Learning rate* = 2e−5.

3.5 Training of the Final Classification Model

For the final classification between users with depression and those without, a **multilayer perceptron neural network** was chosen. To feed this model, an emotion prediction model was implemented to determine which emotions are present in the evaluated texts. These texts correspond to messages from users who will be classified as depressed or not. As mentioned in Subsect. 3.3, the input for the neural network is a data vector containing the count of each emotion per user. This information does not include the temporal order of the messages from different users. These three hyperparameter configurations were used for the final classification models, one for each corpus. Since each model has a different number of input features, each configuration was tuned using a grid search algorithm to find the values that achieved optimal performance.

3.6 Classification and Evaluation

The overall process is illustrated in Fig. 2, which summarizes how predictions are generated, transformed into vectors, and fed into the final model.

The training and test corpus were used for model training. For cross-validation, the training corpus was divided into two subsets. Figure 3 illustrates the number of instances in the test set and each created subset.

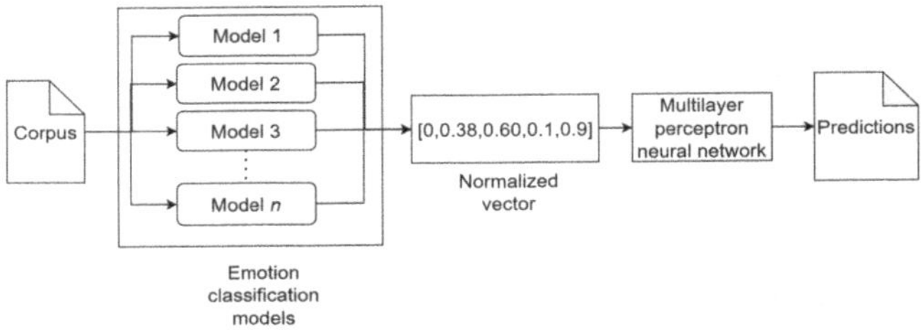

Fig. 2. General process for the depression detection model.

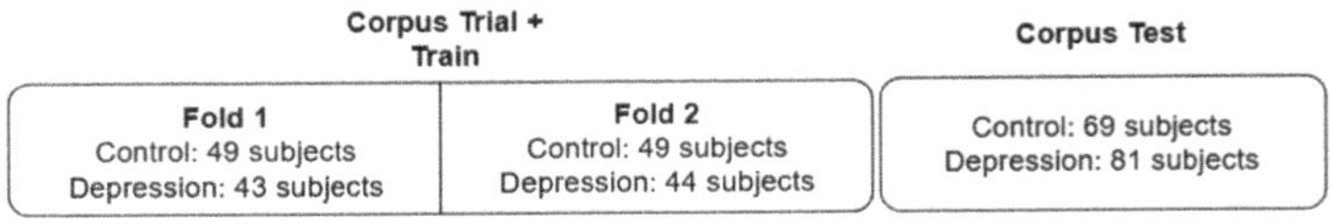

Fig. 3. Folds set 1, set 2, and test set for depression detection.

4 Results

This section presents the analysis of the included corpora, the results obtained by the models for emotion classification, and, finally, the overall outcomes of the implementations for depression detection.

4.1 Corpus Analysis

Lexical variety can be measured with the Type-Token Ratio (TTR), which refers to the proportion of unique (different) words in relation to the total number of words in a text [6]. It is calculated by dividing the number of unique words by the total number of words. A high value indicates a varied vocabulary, while a low value suggests word repetition. To calculate lexical variety, words were converted to lowercase, and punctuation marks were filtered.

Figure 4 shows the respective graphs of lexical variety in each corpus. The *LISSS corpus* contains texts with a lexical variety lower than 0.7. On the other hand, the *Twitter Sentiment Analysis corpus* [11] has a lexical variety higher than 0.6. Finally, although it may seem that the *Plutchik corpus* has less lexical variety due to the scale of the figures, the synthetic corpus has a lexical variety greater than 0.8, with a higher frequency of texts compared to the other corpora.

Figure 4 shows the respective graphs for text length distribution in the used corpora. The three corpora have a majority concentration of 45 words per text. Additionally, both the *Plutchik synthetic corpus* and the *Twitter Sentiment Analysis corpus* [11] have less diversity in the length of their texts. Although there are differences in distribution, they do not appear to indicate any significant variation.

Figure 5 shows four word clouds corresponding to the *Twitter Sentiment Analysis corpus* [11] and the *ChatGPT Plutchik* corpus, as these are the corpora

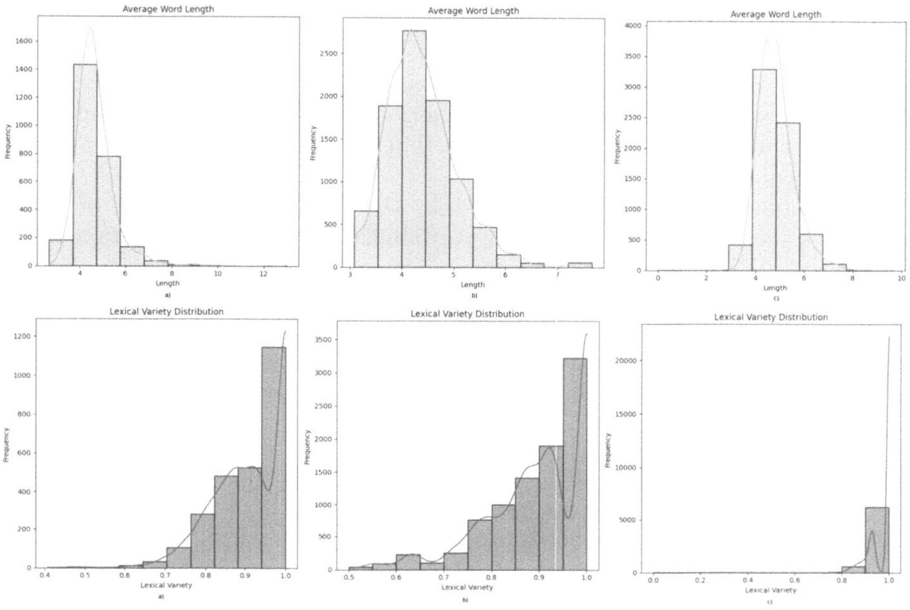

Fig. 4. Lexical variety for corpora and text length for each corpus (Length 1 = 10):: a) *Twitter Sentiment Analysis corpus*, b) *LISSS*, c) *ChatGPT Plutchik*

Fig. 5. Word cloud of the most important TF-IDF terms by emotion: a) Surprise in the *Twitter Sentiment Analysis corpus*, b) Surprise in the *ChatGPT Plutchik* corpus, c) Confident in the *Twitter Sentiment Analysis corpus*, d) Confident in the *ChatGPT Plutchik* corpus.

that have shown the best performance. To generate these word clouds, both corpora were labeled using spaCy's `es_core_news_sm` model, which enabled the removal of stopwords by filtering out words with the following part-of-speech tags: [PRON, SYM, ADP, NUM, PUNCT, DET, ADV, PART, CCONJ, CONJ, SCONJ, AUX]. These clouds correspond to the only two emotions shared by both corpora. The words were obtained by applying the TF-IDF algorithm, allowing the visualization of the semantic similarity between the two datasets.

4.2 Results of Emotion Classification

The evaluation of the proposed binary classification model was carried out using the *weighted* F_1*-score* metric, as the task involves detecting specific emotions across different texts. The F_1-*score* is a harmonic mean of precision and recall, and the weighted version takes into account the imbalance of class distributions by assigning different weights to each class. This makes it particularly suited for imbalanced classification tasks, like emotion detection, where some emotions may appear more frequently than others. This was achieved using the $\mathtt{F_1}$*_score* function from scikit-learn.

The training of models specialized in the *Sentiment Analysis in Spanish Tweets* corpus showed significant variability based on the emotion being detected. An F_1-score above 0.958 was achieved for detecting the emotions of confidence, daring, embarrassment, irritation, frustration, and isolation. However, for the remaining emotions, the F_1-score was lower than 0.462. This may indicate that these emotions are more complex to identify, or that a more suitable dataset is required to capture their characteristics more effectively. Regardless, there is no clear pattern between the number of texts per emotion and the performance of the respective models.

Regarding the training of specialized models using the *LISSS* corpus, the F_1-scores were consistently below 0.518, despite containing ten times more texts than the *Sentiment Analysis in Spanish Tweets* corpus. This is likely due to the greater diversity in writing styles, as the texts are literary in nature.

Finally, when training specialized models using the *Plutchik ChatGPT* corpus, most models achieved an F_1-score above 0.99.

4.3 Results in Depression Detection

This section presents the results obtained with both emotion corpora, compared to other competitors in "MentalRiskES 2023". To fine-tune the "perceptron" neural network, the obtained macro-F_1 scores in folds 1 and 2 were balanced by performing a "grid search" with different parameters for the neural network. Folds 1 and 2 consist of the training and trial sets combined. To obtain the result corresponding to the test set, the entire training corpus was used.

Configuration 1 (*Twitter Sentiment Analysis corpus*). Multilayer perceptron neural network configuration: *learning_rate_init* = 0.005, *activation* = 'logistic', *hidden_layer_sizes* = (44,46), *max_iter* = 50.

Configuration 2 ("LISSS"). Multilayer perceptron neural network configuration: *learning_rate_init* = 0.002, *activation* = 'logistic', *hidden_layer_sizes* = (8,8), *max_iter* = 63.

Configuration 3 ("Corpus Plutchik ChatGPT"). Multilayer perceptron neural network configuration: *learning_rate_init* = 0.003, *activation* = 'logistic', *hidden_layer_sizes* = (30,40), *max_iter* = 128.

Table 1 presents the classification models based on those trained with the *synthetic Plutchik corpus*, the *LISSS corpus*, and the *Sentiment Analysis on the Spanish Tweets Corpus*. The results show that the model utilizing features derived from the *synthetic Plutchik corpus* achieved the best performance. The models based on the *LISSS corpus* and the *Sentiment Analysis on the Spanish*

Table 1. Macro F_1 and standard deviation obtained in different folds for each corpus and Macro F_1 for the test set.

Corpus	Fold 1	Fold 2	Std	Test
Twitter Sentiment Analysis	0.4999	0.4832	0.0083	0.3133
LISSS	0.4492	0.4362	0.0065	0.3521
Plutchik ChatGPT	0.5948	0.5946	0.0003	0.5709

Tweets Corpus demonstrated lower-than-expected performance on the test set, likely due to their limited ability to detect neutral emotions or a general lack of capacity to generalize, as these corpora were not specifically designed to identify such emotions in textual messages.

The superior results of the synthetic corpus model may be attributed to the flexibility offered by creating a tailored labeled dataset aligned with the methodology's requirements such as labeling focused on detecting specific emotions in text and filtering out ambiguous messages. However, upon closer examination, there is no way to guarantee that the classifications made by the model trained on the *synthetic Plutchik corpus* achieve the same weighted F_1 score consistently. This can only be determined accurately if the message corpus is formally annotated based on the emotions represented in Plutchik's wheel of emotions. Until then, it can be stated that the labeling used is an approximation of such a formal annotation.

The proposed approach based on the *Plutchik*-derived corpus achieved a Macro-F_1 score of 0.5709, outperforming the *Twitter Sentiment Analysis* corpus (0.3133) and the *LISSS* corpus (0.3521). This demonstrates that emotion-based features derived from the *Plutchik* model, provide valuable information for depression detection in social media messages, achieving competitive performance in comparison to other approaches.

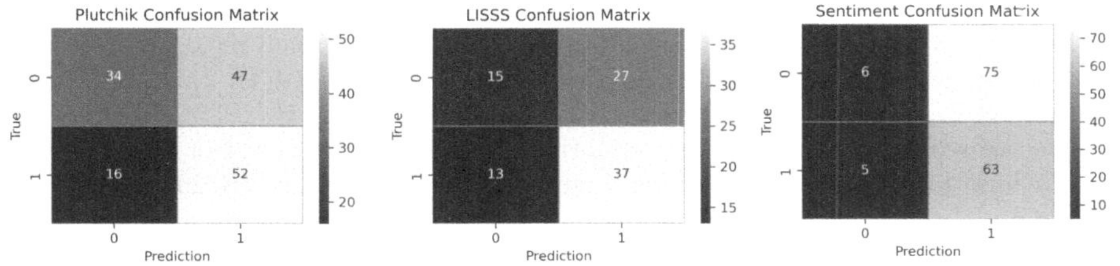

Fig. 6. Confusion matrix for the 3 proposed models, based on the corpus used

Figure 6 shows the matrix of the models based on the *LISSS* and *Plutchik* corpora show that they have relatively balanced model performance, but still make considerable errors in both classes. With the model based on the corpus *Twitter Sentiment Analysis* it has been surprising how the matrix reflects good performance in class 1, however, it seriously fails to correctly identify class 0.

5 Conclusions

This study demonstrates the potential of using synthetic corpora for detecting depression in Spanish-language social media messages. The creation of a synthetic corpus based on Plutchik's emotion model proved to be a valuable resource, approximating emotion detection as it would be with a human-labeled dataset. By training individual emotion classification models and incorporating their outputs into a final user-level classification model, the proposed approach, although it does not compete with the best state-of-the-art proposals, shows that emotion-based features provide valuable information for depression detection on social media. Additionally, the use of deep learning architectures, particularly transformer-based models and multilayer perceptrons, contributed to the effectiveness of the approach. Future work should focus on expanding the synthetic corpus, improving the corpus creation methodology to ensure it captures a wider range of expressions that may be useful for detecting emotions, as well as exploring the creation of synthetic corpora with different types of labeling, testing additional architectures for depression classification, and integrating temporal information from user messages to improve classification performance. The findings emphasize the importance of creating synthetic corpora for mental health detection in NLP applications and contribute to the development of better resources for Spanish-language mental health analysis.

References

1. Aragón, M.E., López-Monroy, A.P., González-Gurrola, L.C., Montes-y Gómez, M.: Detecting depression in social media using fine-grained emotions. In: Burstein, J., Doran, C., Solorio, T. (eds.) Proceedings of the Conference of the North American Chapter of the Association for Computational Linguistics: Human Language Technologies, Minneapolis, Minnesota, vol. 1, pp. 1481–1486 (2019). https://aclanthology.org/N19-1151
2. Aragón, M.E., López-Monroy, A.P., González-Gurrola, L.C., Montes-y Gómez, M.: Detecting mental disorders in social media through emotional patterns - the case of anorexia and depression. IEEE Trans. Affect. Comput. **14**(1), 211–222 (2023)
3. Cañete, J., Chaperon, G., Fuentes, R., Ho, J.-H., Kang, H., Pérez, J.: Spanish pre-trained BERT model and evaluation data. In: Proceedings of the Practical Machine Learning for Developing Countries Workshop at ICLR 2020, pp. 1–10. arXiv, Ithaca (2020)
4. Gambino, O.J., Calvo, H.: Predicting emotional reactions to news articles in social networks. Comput. Speech Lang. **58**, 280–303 (2019). https://doi.org/10.1016/j.csl.2019.03.004
5. González-Silot, S., Martínez-Cámara, E., Ureña López, L.A.: SINAI at MentalRisk: using emotions for detecting depression. In: Montes-y-Gómez, M., et al. (eds.) Proceedings of the Iberian Languages Evaluation Forum (IberLEF 2023) co-located with the Conference of the Spanish Society for Natural Language Processing (SEPLN 2023), CEUR Workshop Proceedings, vol. 3496. CEUR-WS.org (2023). https://ceur-ws.org/Vol-3496/mentalriskes-paper10.pdf

6. L. Jockers, M., Thalken, R.: Measures of lexical variety. In: Text Analysis with R. QMHSS, pp. 81–91. Springer, Cham (2020). https://doi.org/10.1007/978-3-030-39643-5_7
7. Pan, R., García-Díaz, J.A., Valencia-García, R.: UMUTeam at MentalRiskES2023@IberLEF: transformer and ensemble learning models for early detection of eating disorders and depression. In: Montes-y-Gómez, M., et al. (eds.) Proceedings of the Iberian Languages Evaluation Forum (IberLEF 2023), CEUR Workshop Proceedings, vol. 3496. CEUR-WS.org (2023). https://ceur-ws.org/Vol-3496/mentalriskes-paper9.pdf
8. Plutchik, R.: Emotions: a general psychoevolutionary theory. In: Approaches to Emotion, vol. 197, pp. 197–219. Psychology Press (2014)
9. Moreno-Jiménez, L.-G., Torres-Moreno, J.-M.: LISSS: a corpus of literary Spanish sentimental sentences for emotions detection. In: CILCC, pp. 63–68. CILCC, Colombia (2020)
10. OpenAI: ChatGPT: Assistant de IA basado en lenguaje natural. https://www.openai.com/chatgpt. Accessed 13 Feb 2025
11. PhilipSanM: Twitter Sentiment Analysis in Spanish Tweets (v1). https://www.kaggle.com/datasets/philipsanm/sentiment-analysis-in-spanish-tweets. Accessed 25 Oct 2023
12. Salmerón-Ríos, A., García-Díaz, J.A., Pan, R., Valencia-García, R.: Fine grain emotion analysis in Spanish using linguistic features and transformers. PeerJ Comput. Sci. **10**, e1992 (2024). https://doi.org/10.7717/PEERJ-CS.1992
13. Plaza-del-Arco, F.M., Jiménez-Zafra, S.M., Montejo-Ráez, A., Molina-González, M.D., Ureña-López, L.A., Martín-Valdivia, M.T.: Overview of the EmoEvalEs task on emotion detection for Spanish at IberLEF 2021. In: Proceedings of IberLEF 2021, pp. 1–2. CEUR Workshop Proceedings (2021)
14. Plaza del Arco, F.M., Strapparava, C., Urena Lopez, L.A., Martin, M.: EmoEvent: a multilingual emotion corpus based on different events. In: Calzolari, N., et al. (eds.) Proceedings of the Twelfth Language Resources and Evaluation Conference, pp. 1492–1498. European Language Resources Association, Marseille (2020). https://aclanthology.org/2020.lrec-1.186/

Deep Neural Networks and Log-Mel Spectrogram for Emotion Recognition Through Spanish Speech

Juan A. Ramirez-Quintana[1(✉)], Ricardo S. Ang-Foster[1], Mario I. Chacon-Muguia[1], Abimael Guzman-Pando[2], and Alma D. Corral-Saenz[1]

[1] PVR Lab, Tecnologico Nacional de Mexico/I.T. Chihuahua, 31200 Chihuahua, Chih, Mexico
{juan.rq,m24060167,mario.cm,alma.cs}@chihuahua.tecnm.mx

[2] Facultad de Medicina y Ciencias Biomedicas, Universidad Autonoma de Chihuahua, 31125 Chihuahua, Chih, Mexico
aguzmanp@uach.mx

Abstract. Speech emotion recognition is a paramount topic due to its applications in affective computing, marketing, and mental health. Although extensive research has been conducted on SER for languages such as English and Chinese, studies in Spanish remain scarce despite Spanish being one of the most spoken languages in the world. In particular, there is a lack of research on deep learning techniques for SER in Spanish. This paper proposes a method based on the logarithmic mel spectrogram along with a deep neural network for emotion recognition from Spanish speech. The selection of the neural network is based on evaluating the performance and computational cost of models commonly used in emotion recognition, including ResNet-50, MobileNet-V2, EfficientNet-B0, VGG-16, Inception-V3, and Long Short-Term Memory networks (LSTMs). The experiments were conducted using the EmoMatchSpanishDB dataset, which consists of 2,005 Spanish speech signals classified into seven emotion categories. The results indicate that the proposed method performs best with EfficientNet-B0 and outperforms other methods tested on the EmoMatchSpanishDB dataset.

Keywords: Deep Neural Networks · Deep Learning · Speech Emotion Recognition · Spanish Language Analysis

1 Introduction

Speech Emotion Recognition (SER) is an important research field in signal processing and Artificial Intelligence (AI) due to its applications in affective computing, mental health support, customer service monitoring, and education. By analyzing acoustic and linguistic properties, SER models can identify the emotional states expressed in a speaker's voice. This capability allows computers to interpret emotional cues and respond more effectively.

A. P. López-Monroy et al. (Eds.): MCPR 2025, LNCS 15715, pp. 144–153, 2025.
https://doi.org/10.1007/978-3-031-96255-4_14

Deep learning and AI models have demonstrated their effectiveness in SER development [1,2]. For example, Convolutional Neural Network (CNN) architectures such as ResNet, MobileNet, EfficientNet, VGG, and Inception are commonly used to classify audio signals through spectrogram-based techniques [1,3,4]. Additionally, Long Short-Term Memory (LSTM) networks have proven to be effective in capturing the temporal dependencies present in audio sequences [2,5].

However, efforts in developing SER systems with deep learning and other AI models have primarily concentrated on English and Chinese [6,7]. Thus, the research challenge is to adapt SER for various languages, as emotions are expressed differently through speech in different cultures and languages. Intonation, prosody, paralinguistic, and phonetic variations can differ between languages, so it is necessary to use specific processing methodologies and adjustments to model different speech approaches [2,8]. Therefore, expanding SER and AI research to include additional languages not only enhances the applicability of these systems but also helps to mitigate linguistic biases in artificial intelligence models [9].

In particular, research on SER in Spanish is minimal compared to other languages. The scarcity of public datasets and the lack of comparative studies of deep learning models applied to this language represent a significant challenge, especially considering that Spanish is the fourth most spoken language worldwide [9,10]. Given the increasing adoption of voice-based technologies in Spanish-speaking countries, addressing this gap is crucial to improving human-machine interaction in Spanish-speaking contexts [10]. This paper proposes a method for speech emotion recognition in Spanish using a logarithmic mel spectrogram (LM-Spectrogram) in conjunction with a deep neural network (DNN). The LM-Spectrogram is employed to extract the essential features required for accurate classification by the DNN. Various models commonly used in emotion recognition were evaluated to select the most effective DNN in the proposed method. These models include ResNet-50, MobileNet-V2, EfficientNet-B0, VGG-16, Inception-V3, and Long Short-Term Memory (LSTM) networks. The experiments were conducted using the EmoMatchSpanishDB (EmoMatch) dataset, which was developed through a protocol designed to evoke seven different emotions in Spanish-speaking participants who are not professional actors.

The rest of the paper is organized as follows: Sect. 2 details the materials and methods, while Sect. 3 presents the proposed method. Section 4 reports the results, and Sect. 5 summarizes the conclusions.

2 Materials and Methods

This section describes the EmoMatch dataset and the DNNs used to determine the best model for SER in Spanish.

2.1 Dataset

EmoMatch was released in 2023 [9] and consists of 4,200 audio files recorded in .wav format and produced by 50 speakers. Each participant produced 12 Spanish sentences, which were repeated seven times to correspond to seven evoked emotions. These emotions include the six basic identified by Ekman (Anger, Disgust, Fear, Joy, Sadness, and Surprise) and Neutral. Emotions were labeled through a crowdsourcing process involving 194 native Spanish speakers who evaluated the samples using a perception test based on majority voting and a binomial hypothesis test. As a result, 2,020 files were consistently labeled according to the induced emotion. The dataset can be downloaded after signing an agreement and emailing it. In response, 2,005 audio files from the 2,020 files are shared, and these files are labeled as Table 1 shows.

Table 1. Labeling of the 2,005 provided audio files.

Anger	Disgust	Fear	Joy	Sadness	Surprise	Neutral
316	128	262	256	274	297	472

The EmoMatch dataset was selected for this work because its methodology for generating the labels is better designed and documented than other SER datasets. Similarly to SER datasets, emotions in EmoMatch are elicited rather than spontaneous, which is useful for benchmarking and comparative evaluation of SER architectures [6,7].

2.2 Deep Neural Networks

The DNNs chosen for this paper are the most widely reported in various state-of-the-art emotion recognition methods [1,6,7]. These networks are ResNet-50, MobileNet-V2, EfficientNet-B0, VGG-16, Inception-V3, and a LSTM.

ResNet-50. This CNN employs convolutional layers that preserve the original data while incorporating skip connections to reuse the activation maps from previous layers. These connections simplify the training process by reducing the depth. This architecture is highly effective in SER because it can extract intricate features from audio signals, thereby enhancing the accuracy of emotional state identification [11].

MobileNet-V2. It is an optimized CNN designed for efficient performance on mobile devices. Its design uses lightweight and depthwise convolutions to filter features and introduce nonlinearities. This network has been adapted to process spectral features of audio signals, such as mel spectrograms, allowing the extraction of emotional patterns with reduced computational burden. This efficiency facilitates the implementation of SER systems on resource-constrained devices [12].

EfficientNet-B0. This network has an architecture that combines depthwise convolutions and inverted bottleneck layers to optimize feature extraction. This architecture has been applied to SER due to its accuracy and balance of computational efficiency. Additionally, this network analyzes spectral features of audio signals, allowing the extraction of emotional patterns with a moderate computational load [13].

VGG-16. The architecture of this CNN has 16 layers arranged in a sequential architecture that allows hierarchical feature extraction. This network has proven effective in SER because it processes spectral features of audio signals, allowing the extraction of complex emotional patterns. This adaptation is based on VGG16's ability to capture fine details in the input data, improving the accuracy of classifying emotional states [14].

Inception-V3. This model extracts hierarchical and high-level features using various receptive field sizes. This network analyzes audio signals using spectrograms to identify abstract features for SER purposes. Based on the Inception module, its design allows the network to capture relevant patterns across different frequencies and time scales, making it more effective than simpler models. [15].

LSTM. It is a recurrent neural network designed to model data sequences. They address the issue of gradient vanishing through control gates, which enables them to capture long-term dependencies. These networks are fundamental in SER for their ability to capture long-term temporal dependencies in data sequences, allowing the modeling of emotional dynamics present in voice signals [16].

3 Proposed Method

The proposed method consists of four main blocks, as Fig. 1 illustrates. The first block is the input, which comprises an audio file with the raw data. The second block is a feature selection based on the LM-Spectrogram and Mel Frequency Cepstral Coefficients (MFCC). The third block utilizes a Deep Neural Network (DNN) to extract deep abstract features. Finally, the fourth block is the classification, a set of Fully Connected Layers (FCL) that determines the emotion in the audio file. The following subsections describe each block of the proposed method.

3.1 Input

The input consists of a 2.43-s audio file in .wav format, which contains a Spanish sentence represented by raw data denoted as $A(n)$, where $n = 0, \ldots, N-1$, $N = 116,640$. The sampling frequency of the audio is 48 kHz. Figure 2 illustrates an example of $A(n)$ corresponding to a Spanish sentence.

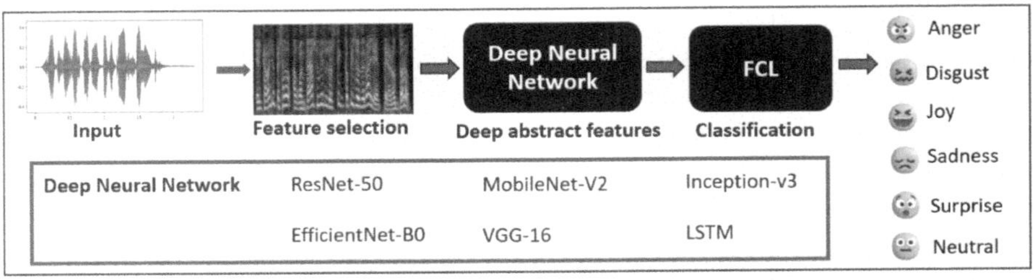

Fig. 1. Architecture of the proposed method.

3.2 Feature Selection

Feature selection is an important step in SER that identifies the most relevant representations of the audio signal for classification. After conducting extensive experiments with various audio representations, we found that the LM-Spectrogram performed best with CNNs, while MFCCs were more effective with LSTMs. The LM-Spectrogram and MFCCs are a collection of time-frequency features that encode various speech phonetic, prosodic, and paralinguistic properties. These properties include intonation, energy, pauses, rhythm, duration, and timbre. Hence, LM-Spectrogram and MFCC reduce dimensionality while preserving the interclass variance necessary for emotion classification, and they have been extensively utilized in several recent deep-learning methods for SER [6,7]. Then, the output of this layer is the response of LM-Spectrogram or MFCC, $B(k,n)$, where k is the frequency index and n is the time index.

The DNNs used in this experiment must have the same input size, so $B(k,n)$ was resized with linear interpolation to a size of $224 \times 224 \times 3$. Figure 2 presents an example of the LM-Spectrogram and MFCCs of $A(n)$ with a Spanish sentence.

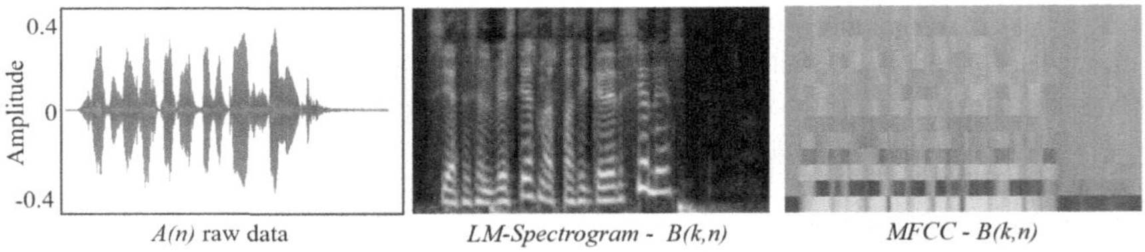

Fig. 2. LM-Spectrogram and MFCC features of *01-Alegria-05.png* file.

3.3 Deep Abstract Feature Layers

The deep abstract features are high-level representations learned by DNNs during the training. The proposed method employs either the LSTM architecture or a baseline CNN model to identify these features. The baseline CNN model consists of convolutional layers that generate abstract features, but it does not include any classification layers. The baseline models examined in this paper are derived from the ResNet-50, MobileNet-V2, EfficientNet-B0, VGG-16, and Inception-V3 architectures.

3.4 Classification Layers

This block categorizes the Spanish sentence into Anger, Disgust, Fear, Joy, Sadness, Surprise, or Neutral. Figure 3 illustrates the classification block developed based on the classifiers of [4,17].

The input of this block is the deep abstract features derived from either the baseline CNN models or the LSTM network. The first layer of the classification is a two-dimensional Global Average Pooling to reduce the dimensionality of the input. The following layer is an FCL with 128 neurons and ReLU activation, which learns complex combinations of the extracted features. An L2 regularization is added to improve generalization, penalize excessive values, and mitigate overfitting. A Batch Normalization layer is included to stabilize the training and normalize the previous layer's activations, accelerating convergence and reducing sensitivity to changes in the learning rate. Subsequently, a Dropout layer is applied to randomly deactivate 40% of the neurons in each iteration, preventing the model from depending excessively on specific units and improving its generalization capacity. Finally, an FCL with softmax with seven neurons–one for each emotion class– is added for the categorization.

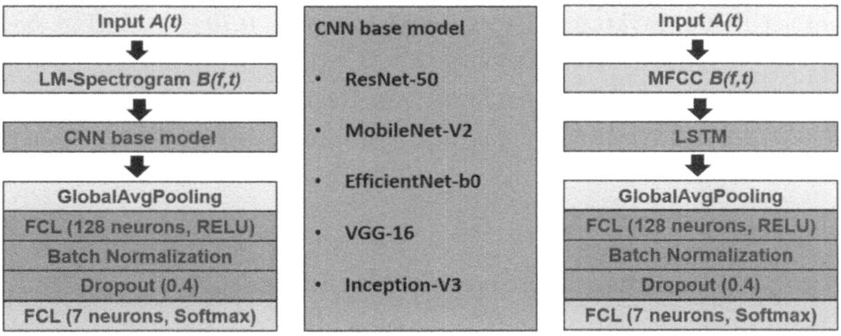

Fig. 3. DNN and classification blocks.

4 Results

The training and testing experiments were conducted using a Dell workstation with an Intel Xeon CPU running at 2.40 GHz, 12 GB of RAM, and an RTX graphics card. The training process used the ADAM optimizer, a learning rate of 0.0001, 50 epochs, and a batch size of 32.

4.1 Evaluation of DNNs Models

The evaluation of the DNNs was carried out in terms of performance and computational cost. The metrics used to measure performance are Accuracy (Acc), F score (F1), Precision (P), and Recall (R) [18]. Regarding computational cost, the metrics used are the number of parameters (Par), floating point operations (FLOPS), memory footprint (RAM), and frames per second (FPS) [19].

Table 2 presents the evaluation results of the proposed method, utilizing the networks described in Sect. 2.2. The network with the best performance is EfficientNet-B0, which achieved the highest score in Acc, F1, R, and the second-best P. VGG-16 ranked second, obtaining the highest P and the second position in Acc, F1, and R. ResNet-50 exhibited a performance similar to VGG-16 but ranked third overall. Inception-V3 and MobileNet-V2 produced regular results, whereas LSTM yielded the lowest performance.

Regarding computational cost, LSTM achieved the best results. MobileNet-V2 and EfficientNet-B0 ranked second and third, respectively. Inception-V3 and ResNet-50 followed in fourth and fifth place with regular results. Finally, VGG-16 reported the highest computational cost.

Table 2. ML and DNN comparison.

Method	Acc ↑	F1 ↑	P ↑	R ↑	Par ↓	FLOPS ↓ Gflops	RAM ↓ MB	FPS ↑
ResNet-50	64.68%	0.636	0.648	0.632	23,851,399	7.72	90.9	364.84
MobileNet-V2	51.12%	0.4881	0.513	0.511	2,426,367	0.599	9.2	518.81
EfficientNet-B0	**69.84%**	**0.697**	0.698	**0.698**	4,214,954	0.79	16.1	584.04
VGG-16	65.34%	0.639	**0.726**	0.653	14,781,767	30.71	56.4	324.94
Inception-V3	56.61%	0.569	0.612	0.566	22,066,471	5.68	84.2	537.87
LSTM	46.13%	0.443	0.445	0.461	**550,983**	**0.155**	**2.1**	**611.98**

4.2 Other Approaches Reported in the Literature

Table 3 displays the results of various methods that used the dataset described in Sect. 2.1. In [9], the authors of the EmoMatch dataset applied an SVM classifier in combination with MFCC, eGeMAPS, and COMPARE algorithms for feature extraction, achieving an accuracy of 65%. The methods proposed in [8] utilized eGeMAPS and Discrete Wavelet Transform (DWT) for feature extraction alongside an SVM classifier with a radial basis function kernel, reporting a recall of 56.9%. In [20], two methods were evaluated. The first method employed a Multi-Layer Perceptron (MLP), which achieved an Unweighted Average Recall of 69% using the COMPARE algorithm. The second method involved a hybrid CNN-LSTM model using Mel-Spectrograms, which also achieved an accuracy of 65%. Finally, the methods outlined in [2] and [21] employed Transformer and CNN architectures but did not produce satisfactory results.

Table 3. ML and DNN comparison.

Method	Feature	Model	Metric	Results
[9]	MFCC	SVM	Acc ↑	64.3%
[9]	eGeMAPS	SVM	Acc ↑	65.4%
[9]	COMPARE	SVM	Acc ↑	65%
[8]	eGeMAPS	SVM	Recall ↑	54.4%
[8]	DWT	SVM	Recall ↑	56.9%
[20]	eGeMAPS	MLP	Recall ↑	65%
[20]	COMPARE	MLP	Recall ↑	69%
[20]	Mel-Spectrogram	CNN-LSTM	Acc ↑	65%
[2]	Large Speech Model	Transformer	F1 ↑	36.1%
[21]	Spectrograms	CNN	Acc ↑	41%

4.3 Discussion

It can be observed that MobileNet-V2, Inception-V3, and LSTM yield lower results than most of the methods listed in Table 3. In contrast, the performance of VGG-16 and ResNet-50 is comparable to those presented in the same table. EfficientNet-B0 performs better than the methods reported in both Table 2 and Table 3. Additionally, EfficientNet-B0 has a significantly lower computational cost than Inception-V3, ResNet-50, and VGG-16.

EfficientNet-B0 outperformed the Spanish emotion recognition task using LM-Spectrograms. Its optimized architecture enables the efficient extraction of discriminative patterns in spectrotemporal representations of speech in Spanish, which exhibits considerable prosodic variability from different accents and dialectics. Furthermore, the low number of parameters allows for learning relevant features and adequate generalization with a few samples.

5 Conclussions

This paper proposes a method for emotion recognition with a speech in Spanish based on a logarithmic mel spectrogram and a deep neural network. The network was chosen based on an evaluation of performance and computational cost, where the evaluated networks include ResNet-50, MobileNet-V2, EfficientNet-B0, VGG-16, Inception-V3, and LSTM. The experiments were carried out using the EmoMatch dataset.

Regarding the experimental results, LSTM and MobileNet-V2 reported the lowest computational cost, but they also exhibited lower performance than the other DNNs and the methods tested in the EmoMatch dataset. Inception-V3 achieved regular results concerning performance and computational cost. VGG-16 and ResNet-50 produced performance results comparable to the methods tested in the EmoMatch dataset. However, their computational cost was significantly high. In contrast, EfficientNet-B0 outperformed both DNNs and methods tested with EmoMatch while maintaining the third-lowest computational cost. Nevertheless, the computational cost of EfficientNet-B0 is slightly higher than that of LSTM and MobileNet-V2 but significantly lower than that of VGG-16 and ResNet-50.

Consequently, EfficientNet-B0 was the best-performing network in terms of both computational cost and accuracy. Its architecture effectively facilitates the extraction of discriminative features in a spectro-temporal representation, helping to prevent overfitting and improving generalization in a language with high prosodic variability, such as Spanish. In future work, more profound research on the architecture of EfficientNet-B0 using Explainable Artificial Intelligence (XAI) methods will be developed to generate a better SER in the Spanish language with enhanced performance.

Acknowledgments. This research was funded by Tecnologico Nacional de Mexico grants 19182.24-P and CHIH-PYR-2025-21864.

Disclosure of Interests. The authors declare that they have no conflicts of interest.

References

1. Bhangale, K.B., Kothandaraman, M.: Survey of deep learning paradigms for speech processing. Wireless Pers. Commun. **125**, 1913–1949 (2022)
2. D'Asaro, F., Márquez-Villacís, J., Rizzo G., Bottino, A.: Using large speech models for feature extraction in cross-lingual speech emotion recognition. In: CLiC-it 2024: Tenth Italian Conference on Computational Linguistics, Pisa, pp. 1–8 (2024)
3. Piczak, K.J.: Environmental sound classification with convolutional neural networks. In: 25th International Workshop on Machine Learning for Signal Processing (MLSP), Boston, pp. 1–6 (2015)
4. Presannakumar, K., Mohamed, A.: Fusion spectrogram for sound classification using 2D convolutional neural network. In: Gabbouj, M., Pandey, S.S., Garg, H.K., Hazra, R. (eds.) E2A 2022. LNEE, vol. 1088, pp. 637–650. Springer, Singapore (2024). https://doi.org/10.1007/978-981-99-6855-8_49
5. Andayani, F., Theng, L.B., Tsun, M.T., Chua, C.: Recognition of emotion in speech-related audio files with LSTM-transformer. In: International Conference on Computing and Informatics (ICCI), New Cairo, Cairo, Egypt, pp. 087–091 (2022)
6. Smith, K.K., Victoria, B.V., Esmaeil, S.N., Rajendra Acharya, U.: Emotion recognition and artificial intelligence: a systematic review (2014–2023) and research recommendations. Inf. Fusion **102**, 102019 (2024)
7. Al-Dujaili, M.J., Ebrahimi-Moghadam, A.: Speech emotion recognition: a comprehensive survey. Wireless Pers. Commun. **129**, 2525–2561 (2023)
8. Mallol-Ragolta, A., Spiesberger, A., Barba, A.S., Schuller B.: Prototypical networks for speech emotion recognition in Spanish. In: IberSPEECH 2024, Aveiro, pp. 221–225 (2024)
9. Garcia-Cuesta, E., Salvador, A.B., Pãez, D.G.: EmoMatchSpanishDB: study of speech emotion recognition machine learning models in a new Spanish elicited database. Multimed. Tools Appl. **83**, 13093–13112 (2024)

10. Pana, R., García-Díaza, J.A., Rodríguez-García, M.A., Valencia-García, R.: Spanish MEACorpus 2023: a multimodal speech–text corpus for emotion analysis in Spanish from natural environments. Comput. Stand. Interfaces **90**, 103856 (2024)
11. Lee, M., Lee, M.: Performance improvement of speech emotion recognition using ResNet model with data augmentation-saturation. Appl. Sci. **15**(4), 1–17 (2025)
12. Akinpelu, S., Viririm, S., Adegun, A.: Lightweight deep learning framework for speech emotion recognition. IEEE Access **11**, 77086–77098 (2023)
13. Asritha, A., Dusyanth, C., Sianyengele, O., Suprith, B.V., Srinivas, P.V.V.S., Kumar, M.L.: Efficient speech emotion recognition for resource-constrained devices. In: 2nd International Conference on Augmented Intelligence and Sustainable Systems (ICAISS), Trichy, pp. 765–772 (2023)
14. Hason Rudd, D., Huo, H., Xu, G.: An extended variational mode decomposition algorithm developed speech emotion recognition performance. In: Kashima, H., Ide, T., Peng, W.C. (eds.) PAKDD 2023. LNCS, vol. 13937, pp. 219–231. Springer, Cham (2023). https://doi.org/10.1007/978-3-031-33380-4_17
15. Dal-Ri, F.A., Cifariello-Ciardi, F., Conci, N.: Speech emotion recognition and deep learning: an extensive validation using convolutional neural networks. IEEE Access **11**, 116638–116649 (2023)
16. Kumar, C.S.A., Maharana, A.D., Krishnan, S.M., Hanuma, S.S.S., Lal, G.J., Ravi, V.: Speech emotion recognition using CNN-LSTM and vision transformer. In: Abraham, A., Bajaj, A., Gandhi, N., Madureira, A.M., Kahraman, C. (eds) IBICA 2022. LNNS, vol. 649, pp. 86–97. Springer, Cham (2023). https://doi.org/10.1007/978-3-031-27499-2_8
17. Amparan-Ortega, N.C., Ramírez-Quintana, J.A., Chacón-Murguia, M.I., Corral-Saenz, A.D.: Deep neural network evaluation for emotion recognition through facial expressions analysis. In: 21st International Conference on Electrical Engineering, Computing Science and Automatic Control (CCE), pp 1–6. IEEE, Mexico City (2024)
18. Mustapha, M., et al.: A hybrid machine learning approach for imbalanced irrigation water quality classification. Desalin. Water Treat. **321**, 100910 (2025)
19. Desislavov, R., Martínez-Plumed, F., Hernández-Orallo, J.: Trends in AI inference energy consumption: Beyond the performance-vs-parameter laws of deep learning. Sustain. Comput.: Inform. Syst. **38**, 100857 (2023)
20. Cabrera-Rodríguez, D.: Sistema de Identificación de Emociones a partir de Audios en Español Basado en Redes Neuronales Multiobjetivo. Universidad Politecnica de Madrid (2024)
21. González-Almansa Laredo, A.: Sistema de Identificación de Emociones Independiente del Hablante Basado en Redes Neuronales Convolucionales. Universidad Politecnica de Madrid (2023)

Phonetic Spectral Image Representation for Yuhmu Language Analysis

Eric Ramos-Aguilar[1,2](✉), J. Arturo Olvera-López[1], and Ivan Olmos-Pineda[1]

[1] Facultad de Ciencias de la Computación, Benemérita Universidad Autónoma de Puebla, Puebla, Mexico
eric.ramosag@alumno.buap.mx, {jose.olvera,ivan.olmos}@correo.buap.mx
[2] Instituto Politécnico Nacional, UPIIT, Tlaxcala, Mexico

Abstract. This paper focuses on the analysis of spectral phonetic image representations for the Yuhmu language of Ixtenco, Tlaxcala, a tonal language with limited resources, using Implicit Phonetic Segmentation (IPS). The main objective is to develop tools for automatic phoneme segmentation and pronunciation analysis, supporting the study and preservation of this indigenous language. Natural Language Processing (NLP) techniques are employed to analyze the phonetic features of Yuhmu. A total of 66,559 phonetic representations were generated from words in a base dictionary, revealing variability in the representation of phonemes. The obtained results indicated a significant Segment Error Rate (SER) with improvements in segmentation performance through specific parameter combinations, leading to a substantial reduction in SER. In some cases, SER reached optimal levels. Additionally, the average values for MSE, SAM, and SCC demonstrated strong consistency in the analyzed data.

Keywords: Audio Processing · Spectral Phonetic Analysis · Low-Resource Languages

1 Introduction

Natural Language Processing (NLP) is an interdisciplinary field that combines Artificial Intelligence, and linguistics to study how computers interact with human language, using data representations such as audio, text, video, or images. Nowadays, these data are crucial for training models that address tasks like translation, text or speech generation, and speech recognition.

Language analysis, particularly pronunciation, requires a large amount of data to train Machine Learning models, as linguistic behavior varies across instances, and aspects such as tone, intonation, affixes, and semantic relationships must be considered. To train these models, approximately 8,000 balanced instances are required to ensure an acceptable representation of the data and improve results [5].

A. P. López-Monroy et al. (Eds.): MCPR 2025, LNCS 15715, pp. 154–164, 2025.
https://doi.org/10.1007/978-3-031-96255-4_15

However, when studying low-resource languages, the challenge lies in the lack of digital data, which suggests the use of algorithms such as transfer learning or fine-tuning to generate results from pre-existing models. Languages with limited resources face difficulties due to the decay of some languages and the lack of representation in both documents and recordings.

The lack of digital corpora for Indigenous Languages of Mexico (ILMs) plays a significant role in their analysis. Currently, the Yuhmu language lacks a digital phoneme database for training Machine Learning approaches. Therefore, this work proposes a methodology to analyze Mel-spectrograms of Yuhmu language phonemes, which will aid in voice analysis and the recognition of phoneme error rates in words.

The paper is organized as follows: Sect. 2 describes related work on the analysis topic. Section 3 presents the database used in this analysis. Section 4 explains in detail the proposed method for the analysis of segmental phonemes and its results. Finally, the conclusions are presented in Sect. 5.

2 Related Work

Pronunciation is essential in communication and learning a second language, and errors in articulation causes difficulties for oral communication. Therefore, automatic speech recognition (ASR) systems that evaluate pronunciation are highlighted, where it is crucial that both the speaker produces phonemes correctly and the model is well-trained for accurate assessment [10].

Currently, ILMs have not been included in ASR studies due to the lack of digital corpora for model training. Most works on ILMs have been conducted manually, focusing on syntactic analyses to identify semantic elements. For example, [9] performs a manual copla analysis of Mixtec, while [15,16] describe intonational features and voiced sound production in Otomi from Tultepec. Similarly, [13] analyzes Nahuatl in terms of sentence or word start times. These studies use a reduced number of speakers: [9] considers six Mixtec speakers, [16] includes eight Otomi speakers from Tultepec, and [13] involves thirty Nahuatl speakers from Puebla.

The use of robust corpora evaluated in other languages to train neural networks and subsequently assess them in low-resource languages is common when information about a target language is limited. For example, [12] utilized the LibriSpeech corpus to create an automatic speech recognition (ASR) system for Tamil, while [2] explored the use of the VoxForge corpus to train neural networks for African languages. Additionally, PHOIBLE, a corpus containing phonetic data from over 2,000 languages, has supported the development of Allosaurus, a tool recognizing phonemes in multiple languages, including low-resource ones [5], and the Common Voice Corpus 8.0 has been applied for Uzbek, with recordings in various dialects [6].

Different Machine Learning approaches are used, such as transfer learning, which is applied in [2] to train a Convolutional Neural Network (CNN) on a corpus containing 7 Indo-European languages, improving African language identification by 10% when using 22 h of the Lwazi corpus. In the case of Uzbek, an End-To-End Deep Neural Network model with a Hidden Markov Model is applied in ASR, achieving a Word Error Rate (WER) of 16.4% and 17.6% on different datasets [6].

Some authors, due to the lack of data in low-resource languages, have created their own databases. For example, [14] presents a Tamil and Malay corpus with 7,582 expressions, while [17] describes the creation of a corpus for Tibetan speech recognition, composed of 28,000 expressions from native speakers. Additionally, [7] reports a corpus with 900 expressions for the Pashto dialect.

Acoustic features used for the analysis of low-resource languages include Mel-Frequency Cepstral Coefficients (MFCC) [5–7,12] and Perceptual Linear Prediction (PLP) [2], which represent the smoothed short-term spectrum, similar to human hearing.

3 Yuhmu Language Dataset

The Yuhmu language is a variant of Otomi (a macro-language of the Otomangue linguistic group spoken by an ethnic and cultural group distributed in the central-southern region of Mexico), located in the municipality of Ixtenco, Tlaxcala, Mexico. Yuhmu consists of 32 phonemes classified according to the International Phonetic Alphabet (IPA), including 12 vowels (V) that can be oral or nasal. It also includes 20 consonants (C) categorized based on the location of the articulatory organs in the vocal tract. Unlike vowels, consonants can be voiced or voiceless.

Considering the presence of phonetic sounds in Yuhmu words, a database of 300 digital audio recordings (as the base dictionary) was created, representing words spoken in the language. These recordings incorporate all phonetic sounds with the aim of having a representative sample of the phonemes. The word selection is based on the analysis developed in [1], which describes the phonemes in the language and is subjectively analyzed. Dictionary-based words consider 3 repetitions per word, following patterns such as C-V, C-C-V, C-C-C-V, and C-V-V-V, which can appear at the beginning, middle, or end of the word, sometimes forming a single word.

Digital recordings are preprocessed with noise reduction, amplification, and trimming. These recordings include phonetic transcriptions that represent the pronunciation rather than following a conventional writing system. The dataset is not publicly available due to confidentiality restrictions; however, it may be accessible upon e-mail request for academic or research purposes.

4 Proposed Method

This section describes the proposed method for the analysis of the digital audio database and the generation of phonetic spectral images through implicit phonetic segmentation (IPS). In the first phase, Mel-scaled spectrograms are generated, a threshold is applied, and a SER evaluation is performed to identify the phonetic segments. In the second phase, the spectral image is segmented into smaller images representing phonemes, and in the third phase, a statistical analysis of the phonetic image similarity is conducted for each word. The proposed method is detailed in the following sections (see Fig. 1).

4.1 Implicit Phonetic Segmentation

Implicit phonetic segmentation (IPS) is based on the premise that the voice characteristics within the phonetic segment exhibit stability. It identifies patterns through distributions or changes in properties to infer whether divisions should be made independently of labeled text, without the use of data or text alignment for analysis [3].

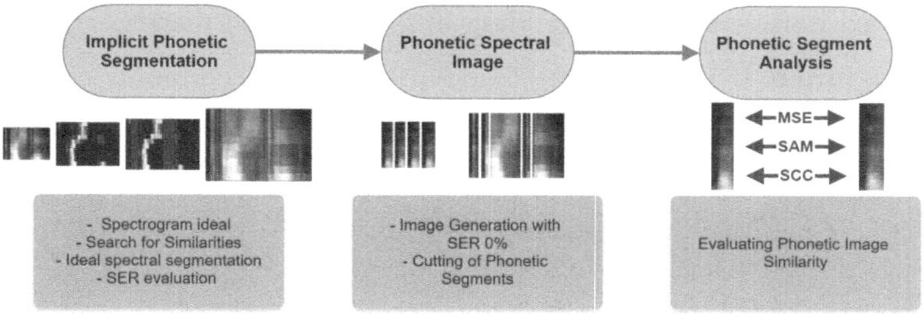

Fig. 1. Phases of the methodology for generating the Yuhmu phonetic database.

IPS is fundamental process that encompasses several key tasks to achieve optimal results. The results help to identify the optimal spectrogram, which can be manipulated using similarity and thresholding techniques to achieve precise segmentation. This process involves multiple steps that, when correctly implemented, ensure high-quality phonetic segmentation, improving the reliability of the obtained results.

Mel-scale Spectrum. The Mel scale (Eq. 1) is a nonlinear transformation of frequency in Hertz (Hz) to a logarithmic scale that is perceptually closer to how humans perceive sounds. The conversion is carried out using:

$$F_{Mel} = 2595 Log_{10}(1 + \frac{F}{1000}) \tag{1}$$

where F is the frequency in Hertz [8]. A Mel-scaled spectrogram represents a digital signal in terms of time, amplitude, and frequency. The process of extracting Mel spectrograms involves dividing the signal into uniformly sized windows, computing the discrete Fourier transform (DFT) for each window, obtaining the periodogram that represents the energy by frequency, filtering frequencies and energies using a Mel filter bank, and finally calculating the logarithm of the energy for each filter.

To obtain an optimal spectral representation, a parameter search is performed using the Grid Search method, which evaluates all possible combinations of parameters to find the one that provides the best performance [4]. The process involves dividing the audio signal into short or overlapping segments, capturing both the temporal and frequency information. Each window undergoes a Fourier analysis, transforming it from the time domain to the frequency domain, visualizing the signal's energy across different frequencies during the time segment [8].

For optimizing the analysis, it is recommended to use a Hanning window with a size between 20 and 40 ms, with 5 ms increments, and an overlap of 25%, 50%, or 75%. Although the literature suggests using between 15 and 20 Mel bands, a range of 15 to 45 Mels is proposed to capture more information in the spectrogram and its resulting matrix. A larger number of Mels will allow for a more detailed representation of the data in the generated matrix.

Cosine Distance. It is a measure of similarity (Eq. 2), commonly used to compare the orientation of vectors in a multidimensional space [11]. The formula for cosine distance between two vectors **x** and **y** is defined as:

$$Cos_D(x,y) = \frac{\sum_{i=1}^{n}(x_i)^2 \cdot \sum_{i=1}^{n}(y_i)^2}{\sqrt{\sum_{i=1}^{n}(x_i)^2} \cdot \sqrt{\sum_{i=1}^{n}(y_i)^2} \cdot \sum_{i=1}^{n}(x_i \cdot y_i)} \tag{2}$$

where:

- x_i and y_i are the components of the vectors **x** and **y**, respectively.
- n is the length of the vectors (the number of components).
- The dot product $(x_i \cdot y_i)$ is the sum of the products of the corresponding components of the two vectors.
- The denominator contains the magnitudes (norms) of the vectors **x** and **y**.

This metric is applied to the Mel-scale spectral matrix to identify similarities between columns, considering that phonetic information is represented over time (x-axis of the spectral matrix). Therefore, it is necessary to generate a similarity between columns that provide contrast in information and/or similarity, differentiating groups of phonetic features. This is because the spectral matrix shows the energies of the digital signal, which are the unions of the phonemes without a phonetic segmentation that can be analyzed computationally.

After calculating the cosine distance between the columns of the spectral matrix, a min-max normalization of the information displayed in the matrix is performed. Information close to zero, which introduces noise into the segment search, is identified and removed. Four thresholds (0.1, 0.2, 0.3, 0.4) are applied, as the information representing the phonemes is generally above 0.4 (analyzed through histograms). The purpose is to filter the relevant phoneme information by placing zeros at points under the threshold values, obtaining a visual representation of the regions where phonetic segments were found, separating the data in the matrix, and converting it into an image to visualize the information segmentation (see Fig. 2a and b).

SER Evaluation. In the spectral segmentation process, after applying the threshold to the resulting matrix, the columns of zeros located at the center of each automatically detected data set are highlighted. This allows for counting the segments, excluding the initial and final zero columns. Subsequently, the segments are overlapped with the spectrogram, which facilitates the delimitation of the spectral information and the extraction of the phonetic representation of each word (see Fig. 2a, and b).

The visual representation in phonetic segmentation is crucial, as generating IPS for the Yuhmu language allows for the visualization of segmented representations. IPS provides both statistical results for the phonemes and a visual representation of the spectrogram, facilitating the comparison between the image and the digital representation of the audio for subsequent sound segmentation.

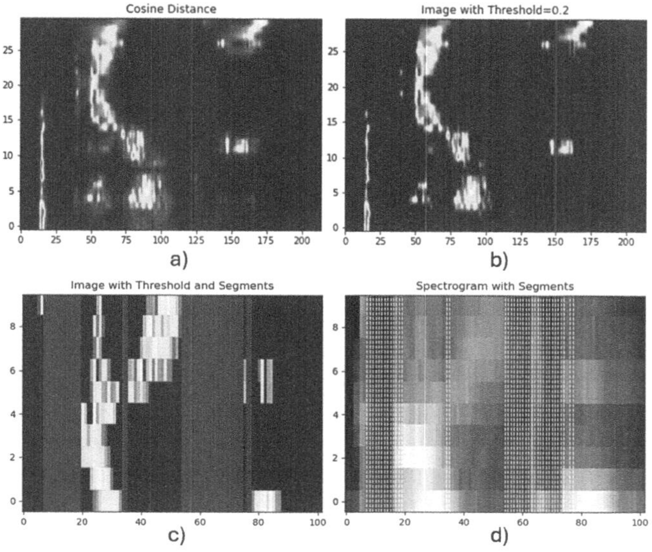

Fig. 2. a) Sample of the resulting matrix after applying cosine distance to the Mel-scale spectral matrix. b) Representation of the threshold application on the resulting Cosine Distance matrix (Fig. 2a). c) Representation of segments highlighting the zero columns. d) Overlap of segments represented by dashed lines found in the matrix with threshold on the Mel-scale spectrogram. Navy blue tones represent null information, red tones represent high information, and light blue tones represent low information. (Color figure online)

In the implicit analysis, an automatic search for segments is performed by comparing the number of segments found with the number of phonemes each word contains. This comparison is evaluated using Eq. 3, which is the Segmentation Error Rate (SER), defined as:

$$SER = \frac{\#error\_segments}{\#reference\_segments} \tag{3}$$

where $\#error\_segments$ is the absolute value of the total number of segments minus the number of segments found, and $\#reference\_segments$ is the total number of segments that each word contains.

4.2 Phonetic Spectral Image Representation

When performing the statistical analysis of the IPS, results have been found where, through dynamic parameters in the spectrogram and the application of the threshold, a SER of 0% is achieved. This finding is present in 18,271 parameter combinations, with occurrences of all the words in these combinations (See Table 1).

Table 1. Example of dynamic parameters with 0% SER for the word "abeja" spoken in Yuhmu.

Audio spoken word	Number of filters	Overlap %	Threshold	SER %
Bee	15	50	0.1	0
Bee	20	75	0.4	0
Bee	30	25	0.2	0
Bee	40	25	0.2	0

Upon obtaining the combinations of dynamic parameters, images of the resulting spectrograms are generated with lines of phonetic segmentation (the central lines of the detected sets are considered for segmentation), allowing for a spectral separation of the phonemes (Fig. 3). All generated images have a size 969 × 770 pixels, offering a balance between visual quality and file size, preserving details and approaching a panoramic image (aspect ratio 4:3), which can result in an acceptable spectral representation.

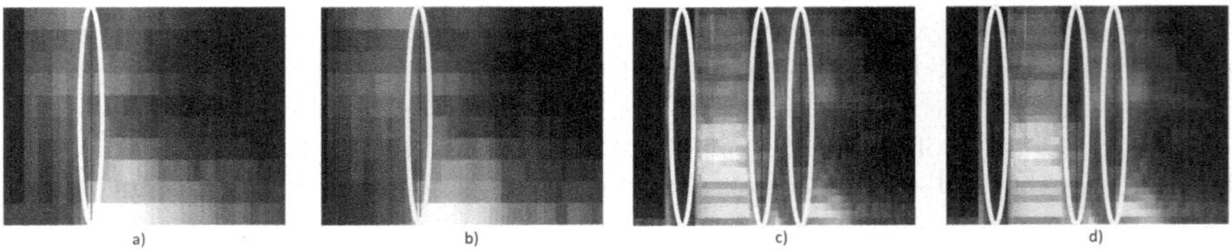

Fig. 3. Images a) and b) are spectrograms of the word "abuela" spoken in Yuhmu with two different dynamic parameters and the representation enclosed in the oval. Images c) and d) are spectrograms of the word "aguamiel" spoken in Yuhmu with two different dynamic parameters and the representation enclosed in the oval.

Subsequently, the segments are cropped and grouped into folders according to their phoneme and word, considering this image separation, and labeling is done based on the phonemes represented by each segment. This allows for the generation of groupings of the phonetic representations of each word, and even further segmentation of the word into phonetic parts (see Fig. 4).

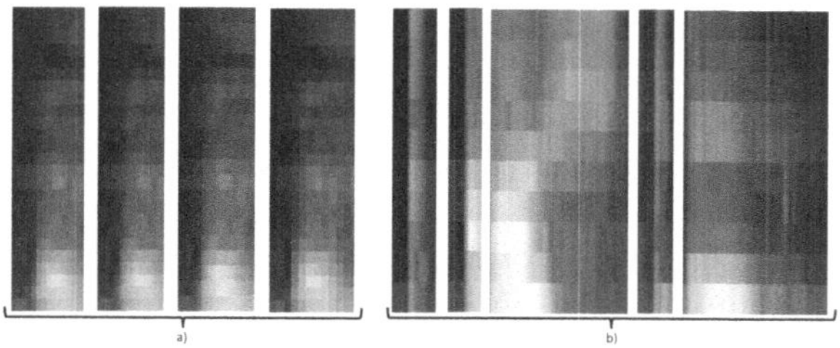

Fig. 4. a) Representation of cropped segments from the phoneme "á", which has an upward intonation. b) Separate images of the word "amarillo" spoken in Yuhmu, which considers five segments and six phonemes.

4.3 Phonetic Segment Analysis

The segments integrated into the labeled folders mentioned in the previous section are analyzed subjectively, finding a match between them. On the other hand, an image similarity analysis is performed for each folder containing the phonetic segments. Three measures are considered: Mean Squared Error (MSE), Spectral Angle Mapping (SAM), and Spatial Correlation Coefficient (SCC).

The MSE, SAM, and SCC are complementary metrics that allow for an exhaustive image analysis. MSE measures the intensity differences between pixels, with a range of $[0, \infty)$, where 0 indicates an identical image and higher values indicate greater differences. SAM evaluates spectral similarity by comparing the angle between the spectral vectors of the pixels, with a range of $[0°, 90°]$, where $0°$ indicates perfect spectral similarity and $90°$ represents the maximum dissimilarity. Meanwhile, SCC analyzes spatial correlation, observing how the structures and patterns in the images align, with a range of $[-1, 1]$, where 1 indicates perfect correlation, -1 indicates perfect negative correlation, and 0 indicates no spatial correlation. Together, these metrics provide a comprehensive evaluation encompassing intensity differences, spectral similarity, and spatial organization, facilitating detailed analysis in image processing [18].

5 Complementary Results

The methodology presented considers three relevant stages: (1) IPS, (2) phonetic spectral imaging, and (3) phonetic segment analysis, in which a thorough analysis is carried out, obtaining 0% SER in IPS. This results in 95,040 spectral images ideal for performing segmentation, which represents approximately 19% of the total results.

The analysis of the phonetic and spectral representations of the words in the studied set provides an interesting view of the distribution and variability of the data. There is a total of 66,559 phonetic representations distributed across the proposed database. Some words have more phonemes, which leads to more phonetic representations, while others may have fewer. This behavior reflects the phonetic diversity that can exist among the analyzed words.

The average number of phonetic representations per word is approximately 222, suggesting that, in general, each word contributes a moderate number of phonetic representations to the total set. However, since it is mentioned that words have different numbers of phonemes, the distribution of these representations per word is not uniform, meaning that some words contribute more representations than others.

Additionally, the number of spectral representations per phoneme is approximately 2,893, which gives an idea of the amount of information contained in each word. The MSE analysis shows that, in general, errors are low, although some representations have higher errors. The SAM indicates a moderate angular discrepancy between the representations, while the SCC reveals a strong correlation between them, suggesting that the representations are mostly consistent and coherent. These results are presented in Table 2, providing a clear view of how the spectral representations behave in terms of error, angular discrepancy, and correlation.

Table 2. Evaluation results for the total phonetic segments of words with MSE, SAM, and SCC metrics.

Statistic	Average MSE	Average SAM	Average SCC
Minimum	0.007282995	0.09941566	0.506736492
Maximum	0.097597743	0.5048923	0.944077851
Standard deviation	0.023841557	0.068048942	0.231423758

By counting the total phonetic representations, it is possible to estimate the number of phonemes involved in the words of the database, providing a clearer view of the relationship between phonemes and spectral representations. In terms of variability, the fact that words have different numbers of phonemes suggests that there is a large dispersion in the number of phonetic representations per word.

6 Conclusions

This research proposes a phonetic analysis represented in spectral images, which is highly useful in applications for learning and teaching indigenous languages, as it allows speakers and researchers to detect phonetic variations and adjust their pedagogical methods according to the linguistic reality of the language in question.

The development of a spectral phonetic database will not only facilitate the automatic segmentation of phonemes but also enable pronunciation analysis, distinguishing between correct and incorrect pronunciations.

Moreover, working with low-resource languages like Yuhmu provides a pathway for the development of new NLP technologies that can be applied not only to this specific language but also to many other indigenous languages in Mexico and other regions. In this context, the necessary data has been gathered to work on a model from scratch, without relying on Machine Learning techniques, transfer learning, or fine-tuning, as has been done in other works. This allows for the development of models specifically designed for Yuhmu from Ixtenco.

In terms of revaluation, our proposal is useful as a powerful tool for strengthening the cultural and linguistic identity of indigenous peoples, promoting a space for indigenous languages to be heard, documented, and taught.

Acknowledgments. This research is supported by CONAHCYT scholarship number 1169943, VIEP-BUAP 594, and UPIIT-IPN 20242590 research projects.

References

1. Esperanza, M.I.Y.G., Alarcón Montero, R.: Manual para la escritura de los sonidos del Yuhmu. Secretaría de Cultura, Instituto Nacional de Antropología e Historia, 1 edn. (2024)
2. Feng, K., Chaspari, T.: Low-resource language identification from speech using transfer learning. In: 2019 IEEE 29th International Workshop on Machine Learning for Signal Processing (MLSP), pp. 1–6. IEEE (2019)
3. Javed, M., Baig, M., Qazi, S.A.: Unsupervised phonetic segmentation of classical Arabic speech using forward and inverse characteristics of the vocal tract. Arab. J. Sci. Eng. **45**, 1581–1597 (2020)
4. Kim, J.: Iterated grid search algorithm on unimodal criteria. Virginia Polytechnic Institute and State University (1997)
5. Li, X., et al.: Universal phone recognition with a multilingual allophone system. In: ICASSP 2020-2020 IEEE International Conference on Acoustics, Speech and Signal Processing (ICASSP), pp. 8249–8253. IEEE (2020)
6. Mukhamadiyev, A., Khujayarov, I., Djuraev, O., Cho, J.: Automatic speech recognition method based on deep learning approaches for Uzbek language. Sensors **22**(10), 3683 (2022)
7. Nisar, S., Tariq, M.: Dialect recognition for low resource language using an adaptive filter bank. Int. J. Wavelets Multiresolut. Inf. Process. **16**(04), 1850031 (2018)
8. Pangaonkar, S., Panat, A.: A review of various techniques related to feature extraction and classification for speech signal analysis. In: ICDSMLA 2019: Proceedings of the 1st International Conference on Data Science, Machine Learning and Applications, pp. 534–549. Springer, Singapore (2020)
9. Penner, K.L.: Prosodic structure in Ixtayutla Mixtec: evidence for the foot. Ph.D. thesis, University of Alberta (2019)

10. Qiu, X.P., Sun, T.X., Xu, Y.G., Shao, Y.F., Dai, N., Huang, X.J.: Pre-trained models for natural language processing: a survey. SCI. CHINA Technol. Sci. **63**(10), 1872–1897 (2020). https://doi.org/10.1007/s11431-020-1647-3
11. Rahutomo, F., Kitasuka, T., Aritsugi, M., et al.: Semantic cosine similarity. In: The 7th International Student Conference on Advanced Science and Technology ICAST, vol. 4, p. 1. University of Seoul South Korea (2012)
12. Rajendran, S., et al.: Language dialect based speech emotion recognition through deep learning techniques. Int. J. Speech Technol. **24**(3), 625–635 (2021). https://doi.org/10.1007/s10772-021-09838-8
13. Sahagun, A.S.: Spanish VOT production by L1 Nahuat speakers. Ph.D. thesis, University of Saskatchewan (2021)
14. Shi, K., et al.: Computer-assisted language learning system: automatic speech evaluation for children learning Malay and Tamil. In: Proceedings of the Interspeech 2020, pp. 1019–1020 (2020)
15. Turnbull, R.: The phonetics and phonology of lexical prosody in san jerónimo acazulco otomi. J. Int. Phon. Assoc. **47**(3), 251–282 (2017)
16. Velásquez Upegui, E.P.: Entonación del español en contacto con el otomí de san ildefonso tultepec: enunciados declarativos e interrogativos absolutos. Anuario de letras. Lingüística y filología **8**(2), 143–168 (2020)
17. Wang, W., Yang, X., Yang, H.: End-to-end low-resource speech recognition with a deep CNN-LSTM encoder. In: 2020 IEEE 3rd International Conference on Information Communication and Signal Processing (ICICSP), pp. 158–162. IEEE (2020)
18. Zhu, Y., Zhang, X., Jiang, B., Su, C., Wang, M., Zhang, K.: Comparison of performance of fusion methods for sentinel-2 and GF-2 satellite images and the potential in land use classification: a case study from reservoirs in hainan island, china. In: 2024 12th International Conference on Agro-Geoinformatics (Agro-Geoinformatics), pp. 1–6 (2024)

Multi-label Classification of Texts on Harassment and Discrimination with Neural Networks

Ana Laura Lezama-Sánchez[1] and Mireya Tovar Vidal[2](✉)

[1] Facultad de Artes Plásticas y Audiovisuales, Benemerita Universidad Autonoma de Puebla, 72570 Puebla, Mexico
analaura.lezama@correo.buap.mx

[2] Faculty of Computer Science, Benemerita Universidad Autonoma de Puebla, 72570 Puebla, Mexico
mireya.tovar@correo.buap.mx

Abstract. This paper uses neural networks to classify texts related to harassment and discrimination in various contexts, such as workplace harassment, school bullying, and sexism. In this research, it is proposed to address harassment in different environments through an approach based on Long Short-Term Memory (LSTM) models. The main objective is to develop a model capable of identifying patterns of harassment in texts, improving detection accuracy, and reducing biases present in traditional methods. By using LSTM networks, the model can process text sequences and associate multiple relevant labels, improving the detection of subtle and complex forms of harassment. This work contributes to efforts to combat harassment by providing a solution that can help better understand and address these issues in texts derived from real-world experiences. The results obtained show a precision of 0.8212, a recall of 0.6883, an F_1 of 0.7489, and an accuracy of 0.7782, confirming strong performance in classifying texts related to harassment and discrimination.

Keywords: workplace harassment · school bullying · social harassment · generative adversarial networks · artificial intelligence · detection · machine learning

1 Introduction

In recent years, harassment and discrimination in various social and professional settings have gained increasing relevance, generating strong interest both in society and academia to find effective ways to identify and address these issues. Digital platforms and social media have allowed people to share their experiences of harassment and discrimination, facilitating the collection of large volumes of textual data that can be analyzed to detect patterns and discriminatory behaviors. However, the classification and analysis of these texts remain challenging due to the complex and often subtle nature of harassment [9].

A. P. López-Monroy et al. (Eds.): MCPR 2025, LNCS 15715, pp. 165–174, 2025.
https://doi.org/10.1007/978-3-031-96255-4_16

The goal in this work is to understand how people experience harassment and discrimination in different contexts, such as workplace harassment, school bullying, and sexism, through the analysis of real-life accounts shared on the *Everyday Sexism* Project website (everydaysexism.com). Specifically, it aims to identify recurring themes and patterns in these harassment stories to improve the ability to detect and classify discriminatory behaviors. For this purpose, a corpus extracted from the website, consisting of 95,746 stories, is used, providing a broad and diverse basis of experiences related to harassment and discrimination [10].

In this context, neural networks, specifically Long Short-Term Memory (LSTM) models, are employed to process and analyze text sequences, assigning multiple labels to each document. This allows for more precise and detailed classification of the texts, identifying various forms of harassment in a single account. By addressing this problem with a multi-label classification approach, the model enhances its ability to detect complex patterns that may be overlooked by traditional methods [11].

This work contributes to efforts to combat harassment and discrimination by offering an innovative technological solution for the automatic analysis of texts. In doing so, it provides a better understanding of how these issues manifest in shared experiences and helps address them more effectively in different contexts. Although the texts are in English, the model plays an essential role in detecting harassment in texts from diverse environments.

The article is structured as follows: Sect. 2 presents the related works in this paper. Section 3 provides a review of previous works in the literature related to the topic. Section 4 describes the proposed model for text classification. Section 5 presents the results obtained. Finally, Sect. 6 presents the Conclusions and the References consulted during the development of this work.

2 Related Works

In this section, several key concepts relevant to the development of an effective cyberbullying detection method are presented.

Bullying or harassment, regardless of context or age, is a repetitive and abusive behavior directed at a person with the intention of causing physical, emotional, or psychological harm. This phenomenon can manifest in various settings, such as in the school environment, where harassment among students of any age is a form of violence expressed through physical aggression, verbal abuse, or social exclusion. Similarly, in the streets, it takes the form of street harassment, which involves inappropriate or intimidating behavior towards individuals, especially women, in public spaces. In the workplace, harassment translates into hostile or discriminatory behaviors towards an employee, creating a toxic work environment. Although these types of harassment occur in different contexts, they all share the characteristic of causing suffering to the victim, highlighting the urgent need to eradicate these behaviors and promote more respectful and safe environments for everyone [12].

To effectively study multi-label classification in texts, advanced technologies in Natural Language Processing (NLP) and deep learning are currently used. NLP enables computers to process human language, facilitating the analysis of large volumes of textual data generated on digital platforms from various types of activities. By applying NLP techniques, valuable insights can be extracted and relevant patterns can be detected in texts, which is crucial for label classification [13].

Based on NLP, machine learning algorithms are employed. These algorithms involve training models to recognize patterns and make predictions from data. In this context, models are trained to identify labels associated with each text, automating the classification process and improving its efficiency [14].

However, to achieve greater precision, deep learning techniques are used, a specialized subset of machine learning that aims to emulate the functioning of the human brain. Advanced deep neural network architectures allow models to be trained with greater accuracy compared to traditional classifiers. The complex structure of these models facilitates the capture of more intricate patterns and nuances in the data, significantly improving classification performance [15].

Within deep learning models, LSTM (Long Short-Term Memory) neural networks are employed, which process textual data by analyzing sequences both forward and backward. This provides a deeper understanding of the context and meaning of the text, improving the detection of subtle and context-dependent signs. Thus, NLP, machine learning, deep learning, and LSTM neural networks form an integrated framework to detect and mitigate cyberbullying. The integration of these technologies enables the creation of more effective tools to improve safety and well-being in various digital environments [15].

3 State of the Art

In this section, we review previous research related to the topic of text classification and discrimination detection. Understanding the current state of the field is crucial for identifying existing gaps and positioning the proposed model within the broader academic discourse. This review highlights the main approaches, methodologies, and findings in the literature, providing a foundation for the subsequent discussion of the proposed model.

Alrawashdeh et al. (2024) [1] present a study on workplace cyberbullying among academic staff at Jordanian universities, analyzing its relationship with social capital and self-esteem. The dataset were collected through an anonymous online survey. The results indicate that cyberbullying decreases with higher social capital, but no significant relationship was found with self-esteem. The authors suggest that policymakers in higher education in Jordan should promote social capital among academics due to its benefits for self-esteem and stress prevention. Finally, they recommend conducting further research to understand the causes of low self-esteem among academics, as well as to clarify the relationship between self-esteem and workplace cyberbullying.

Rejeb et al. (2025) [2] propose a comprehensive review of cyberbullying across various platforms, employing a combined methodological approach of keywords analysis and main path analysis (MPA) on 5,183 documents. Key topics include digital literacy, the dual role of social media, and the use of technology to detect and mitigate cyberbullying. The authors suggest future work and practical applications, thereby providing a detailed and dynamic view of cyberbullying, which constitutes a valuable contribution to both academic knowledge and practical approaches to address it.

Cirillo et al. (2025) [3] present an evaluation of the effectiveness of 20 generative Large Language Models (LLMs) in detecting cyberbullying in social media posts. The authors used a new machine learning approach based on prompts and evaluated the LLMs on binary and multiclass classification tasks using posts from platforms such as X, Facebook, and Reddit. They then compared the performance of these LLMs with 24 traditional machine learning and natural language processing models, focusing on their ability to identify harmful content. The results showed that the LLMs, especially models such as Claude 3.0 and Mistral, performed well in detecting various types of cyberbullying. Additionally, expert evaluations of the models' explanations revealed that the Claude and Mistral models provided clearer, more coherent, and relevant explanations compared to others.

Kumar et al. (2025) [4] present a study focused on analyzing and classifying cases of cyberbullying using a Kaggle dataset with labeled texts on various bullying behaviors. The methodological approach includes data preprocessing, which involves the removal of punctuation, conversion to lowercase, elimination of stop words, and the application of techniques such as stemming and lemmatization. For feature extraction, they applied the Term Frequency-Inverse Document Frequency (TF-IDF) method, highlighting terms indicative of bullying behaviors. The results showed that the dataset is a valuable resource for developing machine learning models capable of detecting sexist and racist content in tweets. The authors note that this study advances the understanding of cyberbullying detection by facilitating analysis through binary classification, enabling compati- bility with binary classification models and laying the groundwork for future advancements in cyberbullying detection.

Li et al. (2025) [5] present a study addressing the issue of cyberbullying on social media platforms, which can lead to severe consequences such as depression, self-harm, and suicide. The authors focus on a two-stage cyberbullying detection framework that uses multi-view features and decision fusion strategies. The first stage focuses on identifying cyberbullying texts, while the second stage categorizes the specific forms of bullying present in those texts. Additionally, they extracted features from various views, such as Content, Profanity, and User views, to capture bullying behaviors. To enhance detection effectiveness, they applied a decision fusion strategy that combines features from both single and multiple views. The results demonstrated the effectiveness of the proposed framework, achieving an $F_1$of 89.66% and an AUC of 95.98% in Stage I, and an F_1 of 74.25% and an Accuracy of 79.01% in Stage II. The authors conducted an interpretability analysis, highlighting the importance of multi-view features, particularly those from the Content view, as essential for effective cyberbullying detection.

Research continues with Mali et al. (2025) [6], who propose a deep learning model to detect aggressive activities such as cyberbullying. To achieve this, they extracted data from platforms like Formspring, Instagram, and MySpace with the goal of identifying cyberbullying behaviors. The data was then processed using preprocessing techniques that included removing stop words, whitespace, and converting comments to lowercase. The authors applied the Lexical Density (LD) Metric and Feature Density (FD) to calculate the language complexity in the datasets. Subsequently, they performed a feature selection process using the Binary Chimpanzee Optimization (BCO) technique to select the appropriate subset of features to improve classification performance. The selected features were used to detect cyberbullying behaviors. To identify cyberbullying-related textual content, they employed a bidirectional gated unit with attention (SBi-GRU), along with the BERT model as a base classifier to recognize and categorize aggressive behaviors in the textual content. The experiment was carried out using Matlab software, yielding performance with precision values of 99.12%, 94.73% in accuracy, 97.45% in recall, and F_1 of 93.91%.

On the other hand, MohammedJany et al. (2025) [7] present a study focused on cyberbullying detection. They propose a multimodal cyberbullying detection model (MCB) capable of identifying bullying in both images and text. The approach used a pretrained VGG16 model to detect bullying in images and an XLM-RoBERTa model with BiGRU to detect bullying in text. The integration of these models, along with attention mechanisms and other techniques such as CLIP and CentralNet, allowed the authors to detect cyberbullying in memes combining text and images. The developed model achieved an accuracy of 74%, indicating its effectiveness in identifying most cyberbullying activities.

On the other hand, Zhu et al. (2025) [8] propose a study that used the Light Gradient Boosting Machine (LightGBM) to identify and classify the importance of various risk and protective factors in cyber-aggression. Additionally, they employed the SHAP (SHapley Additive exPlanations) technique to estimate the predictive effects of each variable, and two-dimensional partial dependence (PD) plots to examine interactions between predictors. They used a corpus from a Chinese university population on social media. Out of 30 potential factors, the most important ones they identified were attitudes toward violence, revenge motivation, anti-bullying attitudes, moral disengagement, and anger.

In this research, a multi-label classification model will be developed using natural language processing and deep learning techniques. A sequential neural network will be designed, employing embedding and LSTM layers to predict multiple labels. The model will be trained and evaluated using performance metrics such as precision, recall, and F_1.

4 Methodology

In this section presents the methodology for developing and evaluating a deep learning-based model for multi-label text classification related to harassment and discrimination. We describe the data preprocessing pipeline, the rationale behind our model design choices, and the evaluation process.

Our approach comprises the following stages:

1. Data Loading and Preprocessing: We loaded the dataset, stored in CSV format, which includes a column named *content* with the text entries and a column *tags* with the corresponding labels. We replaced missing values (NaN) in the label column with empty strings. Then, we converted each label string into a list of tags to enable multi-label processing for each instance.
2. Text Tokenization: To prepare the textual data for input into the neural network, we tokenized the content using a vocabulary limited to the 10,000 most frequent words. Allowed us to strike a balance between vocabulary coverage and computational efficiency. We converted each document into a sequence of integers and then padded each sequence to a fixed length of 100 tokens. We chose this sequence length based on the dataset's average length of the texts, which we determined through empirical analysis. Although this value proved adequate for our current experiments, we consider it a tunable parameter for future improvements.
3. Label Binarization: We used the *MultiLabelBinarizer* from the *scikit-learn* library to convert the list of labels for each document into a binary vector. Each position in the vector corresponds to a specific label, with a value of 1 indicating its presence. This format is well-suited for multi-label classification tasks.
4. Data Splitting: We randomly split the dataset into a training set (70%) and a test set (30%) to evaluate the model's performance on unseen data. This approach helps us assess the model's generalization ability to new examples.
5. Neural Network Architecture: We implemented a deep learning model using the Keras library with a sequential architecture. The model consists of the following layers:
   (a) Embedding Layer: We used an embedding layer to transform input word indices into dense vectors of 128 dimensions. We configured this layer to be trainable so that the model could learn semantic representations specific to the context of harassment and discrimination. By training the embeddings from scratch, we allowed the model to adapt the word representations to the particular vocabulary of our dataset rather than relying on pre-trained embeddings. This decision enabled us to directly evaluate the effectiveness of learning domain-specific features from the data.
   (b) LSTM Layer: We added a Long-Short-Term Memory (LSTM) layer to capture long-term dependencies in the text since this recurrent neural network effectively models sequential data. LSTMs are particularly effective at preserving information across long contexts and processing variable-length input, essential for natural language understanding. Given the importance of word order and contextual relationships in text classification tasks, we chose this architecture to enhance the model's ability to learn nuanced patterns in language related to harassment and discrimination.

(c) Dense Layer: We added a fully connected layer to reduce the dimensionality of the LSTM output and to facilitate better abstraction of learned features.
(d) Output Layer: The output layer contains one neuron per label and uses the sigmoid activation function to predict each label's presence independently. This configuration is appropriate for multi-label classification, where labels are not mutually exclusive.

6. Training and Evaluation: We trained the model for 10 epochs and configured it with the Adam optimizer and the binary cross-entropy loss function, relying on their proven robustness and effectiveness in multi-label classification tasks. We selected the number of epochs based on preliminary experiments that indicated stable learning within this range. We aimed to focus the evaluation on the model architecture and the dataset's characteristics using well-established training configurations. We used accuracy, precision, recall, and F_1 for evaluation, as these metrics provide a comprehensive view of the model's performance across multiple labels.
Throughout the development process, we deliberately chose a basic LSTM-based architecture with a trainable embedding layer to explore how well a foundational sequential model could handle the complexities of multi-label classification in harassment and discrimination contexts. While more advanced alternatives exist, such as pre-trained language models, we prioritized establishing a strong baseline on this underexplored dataset.

5 Results

In this section, we present the results obtained from the developed model. The dataset used for the evaluation of the model is described below.

5.1 Dataset

The dataset used in this study consists of a total of 95,746 stories extracted from the website *everydaysexism.com*. These stories cover various experiences related to harassment and discrimination, providing a broad and diverse foundation for analysis. We used a dataset derived from the Everyday Sexism Project, which contains thousands of first-person reports of sexist incidents. This dataset has previously been used for topic modeling to uncover latent themes and semantic structures within the narratives [16]. In Fig. 1 are the key characteristics of the dataset:

5.2 Model Evaluation

After preprocessing the data and training the model, the following performance results were obtained by evaluating the model on the test set using the metrics of

Table 1. Summary of the dataset used

Description	Value
Corpus source	Extracted from *everydaysexism.com*
Number of stories	95,746 stories
Purpose of corpus	Provide a broad and diverse base of experiences related to harassment and discrimination
Classes	workplace harassment, Harassment, Discrimination, Sexism, Other

precision, accuracy, recall, and F_1 (see Table 2) to assess its performance in multilabel classification. In addition to evaluating the performance of the proposed model, two additional models were implemented for comparison purposes.

The LSTM_2 model is based on the same architecture as the proposed model (LSTM_1), but with different hyperparameters. Specifically, while both models share the same network structure, the LSTM_2 model uses a different set of parameters, such as dropout rate and batch size, compared to the proposed model.

The second model used is Logistic Regression, a linear classification algorithm, combined with the OneVsRest strategy (one vs. all). We included this traditional machine learning model as a baseline to provide a point of reference for evaluating the performance of the more complex deep learning approaches. Logistic Regression is commonly used in text classification tasks due to its simplicity and surprisingly competitive performance in high-dimensional spaces like text data.

The LSTM_1 model demonstrates balanced performance compared to the other two models. It particularly excels in recall (0.6883) and F_1 (0.7489), where it outperforms LSTM_2. Although it is slightly inferior to the logistic regression model in some metrics, it remains a solid option. On the other hand, the logistic regression model shows the best precision (0.8590) and F_1 (0.7588), making it the most robust model in terms of balancing precision (0.8590) and recall (0.6795), although its recall is slightly lower than that of the LSTM_1 model. The LSTM_2 model performed the worst across all metrics, suggesting that it is not an ideal option for this work.

This analysis suggests that the LSTM_1 model may be preferable in applications where detecting positives is key, while the Logistic Regression model could be a stronger choice if precision is the main objective.

These results indicate a performance in the original model in predicting multiple labels, with the highest precision value of 0.8212, while recall shows a slightly lower value of 0.6883. The F_1 of 0.7489 reflects a balance between precision and recall, and the overall accuracy of 0.7782 suggests that the model performs well across all classes. To further illustrate the model's performance, we provide a sample of the results obtained during testing. Table 3 presents a comparison between the original text, the original label assigned to each text, and the pre-

Table 2. Model performance evaluation metrics

Metric	LSTM_1	LSTM_2	Logistic regression
Precision	0.8212	0.7257	0.8590
Recall	0.6883	0.6382	0.6795
F_1	0.7489	0.6792	0.7588
Accuracy	0.7782	0.7257	0.7641

dicted label produced by the model. This example highlights the model's ability to accurately predict multiple labels in a multi-label classification context.

Table 3. Example of the obtained results

Original text	Original label	Predicted label
Out in a club with my cousin, both...	Sexism	Sexism
On one of our recent secret shopper...	Sexism	Sexism
2 incidences in one night at a nightclub...	Harassment	Harassment
My mom (a teacher) participated in an ...	Other	Discrimination
Does school bus count for public...	Public harassment	Public harassment

6 Conclusions

In this study, we developed and evaluated a deep learning-based multilabel classification model to predict multiple labels in text data. The results indicate that the model performs well, with precision, recall, and F_1 values demonstrating its ability to predict labels with a good balance between precision and recall. Specifically, the model achieved a precision of 0.8212, recall of 0.6883, F_1 of 0.7489, and accuracy of 0.7782.

The findings highlight the effectiveness of the model in multilabel classification tasks, where multiple labels can be assigned to each text. However, the recall value suggests that there is still room for improvement in capturing all relevant labels in some cases. This may be attributed to the fact that the text is labeled by individuals who narrated their experiences, meaning the labels could be somewhat incorrect or inconsistent. Such inconsistencies could influence the model's ability to predict all relevant labels correctly, as manual labeling may contain ambiguities or human errors.

As future work, it is proposed to improve the model's ability to detect less frequent labels and achieve better recall results. Additionally, exploring different deep learning architectures or integrating external features could further enhance the model's performance. Moreover, applying the model to other datasets would help assess its generalization ability and robustness across different domains.

References

1. Alrawashdeh, M.N., Alsawalqa, R.O., Alnajdawi, A., Aljboor, R., AlTwahya, F., Ibrahim, A.M.: Workplace cyberbullying and social capital among Jordanian university academic staff: a cross-sectional study. Humanit. Soc. Sci. Commun. **11**(1), 1–12 (2024)
2. Rejeb, A., Rejeb, K., Zrell, I., Süle, E.: Tracing knowledge diffusion trajectories in the research field of cyberbullying. Heliyon **11**(1), 1–21 (2025)
3. Cirillo, S., Desiato, D., Polese, G., Solimando, G., Sugumaran, V., Sundaramurthy, S.: Exploring the ability of emerging large language models to detect cyberbullying in social posts through new prompt-based classification approaches. Inf. Process. Manag. **62**(3), 1–29 (2025)
4. Kumar, A., Kumar, R., Prasad, A.: Analysis of cyberbullying behaviors using machine learning: a study on text classification. LatIA **13**(3), 1–7 (2025)
5. Li, T., Zeng, Z., Sun, S.: A two-stage cyberbullying detection based on multi-view features and decision fusion strategy. Appl. Intell. **55**(4), 1–21 (2025)
6. Mali, M.K., et al.: Automatic detection of cyberbullying behaviour on social media using Stacked Bi-GRU attention with BERT model. Expert Syst. Appl. **262**, 125641 (2025)
7. MohammedJany, S., Killi, C., Rafi, S., Rizwana, S.: Detecting multimodal cyberbullying behaviour in social-media using deep learning techniques. J. Supercomput. **81**(1), 1–26 (2025)
8. Zhu, W., et al.: Dissecting the predictors of cyber-aggression through an explainable machine learning model. Aggress. Behav. **51**(1), e70013 (2025)
9. Rospenda, K.M., Richman, J.A.: Harassment and discrimination. In: Handbook of Work Stress, pp. 149–188 (2005)
10. Fnais, N., et al.: Harassment and discrimination in medical training: a systematic review and meta-analysis. Acad. Med. **89**(5), 817–827 (2014)
11. De Obesso, M., Rivero, C., Márquez, O.C.: Artificial intelligence to manage workplace bullying. J. Bus. Res. **160**, 113813 (2023)
12. Waseem, M., Nickerson, A.B.: Identifying and addressing bullying. Weill Cornell Medicine New York and New York Medical College; University at Buffalo, SUNY (2023)
13. Joshi, H.: Natural language processing of electronic health records for predicting Alzheimer's disease. In: Deep Generative Models for Integrative Analysis of Alzheimer's Biomarkers, pp. 141–174. IGI Global (2025)
14. Kiouri, D.P., Batsis, G.C., Chasapis, C.T.: Structure-based approaches for protein-protein interaction prediction using machine learning and deep learning. Biomolecules **15**(1), 141 (2025)
15. Basha, S., et al.: Exploring deep learning methods for audio speech emotion detection: an ensemble MFCCs. CNNs and LSTM. Appl. Math. **19**(1), 75–85 (2025)
16. Melville, S., Eccles, K., Yasseri, T.: Semantic Map of Sexism: Topic Modelling of Everyday Sexism Project Entries. CoRR abs/1711.08930 (2017)

Exploring a Multimodal Language Model for Auto-Captioning and Visual Question Answering in Histopathology Images

Johan Sánchez and Angel Cruz-Roa(✉)

GITECX & AdaLab, Universidad de los Llanos, Villavicencio, Colombia
{johan.sanchez,aacruz}@unillanos.edu.co

Abstract. This study explores implementation and evaluation a multimodal (visual & text) language model for auto-captioning and visual question answering (VQA) tasks in histopathology images. The selected architecture integrates CLIP-prefix with GPT-2 models, combining the image understanding capabilities of vision models with the text generation abilities of language models. This approach demonstrates the potential of multimodal models to serve as supportive tools in medical image interpretation, assisting tasks such as auto-captioning and visual question answering (VQA), while maintaining manageable computational requirements. For auto-captioning, experiments were conducted using the ARCH dataset, which includes histopathology images and textual descriptions from scientific sources (books and journal papers). The best-performing model achieved an accuracy of 82%, a BLEU score of 71%, and a CIDER score of 4.9 metrics commonly used to assess the quality of generated textual descriptions. Qualitative analysis of test images suggests a strong alignment between predicted and actual descriptions. For VQA, a model was optimized using the PathVQA dataset, which contains diverse pathological images paired with questions and answers. The optimized model achieved an accuracy of 84%, a BLEU score of 67%, and a CIDER score of 1.9, reflecting strong alignment between generated answers and reference responses. Qualitative evaluations revealed a high consistency between predicted answers and corresponding visual content. These preliminary findings suggest that multimodal models can serve as intelligent assistants ("co-pathologists") to support pathology workflows. By automating and improving the accuracy of image-based textual descriptions, these models could enhance diagnostic precision, reduce errors in pathology reports, and optimize clinical decision-making, especially in critical cases like cancer diagnosis.

Keywords: Computational Pathology · Deep learning · Digital pathology · Language models · Multimodal Analysis · Natural language processing

A. P. López-Monroy et al. (Eds.): MCPR 2025, LNCS 15715, pp. 175–188, 2025.
https://doi.org/10.1007/978-3-031-96255-4_17

1 Introduction

Pathology reporting is essential to clinical practice, as it directly impacts diagnostic accuracy and patient treatment. However, it faces challenges due to human errors stemming from fatigue, distractions, and insufficient training. These factors can compromise both the transcription of notes and the interpretation of histopathology slides, potentially leading to misdiagnoses and inadequate treatments [1,2].

Digital pathology (DP) is a subfield of pathology that focuses on managing and analyzing information generated from digitized specimen slides thanks to slide pathology scanners which allow to obtain the whole-slide images (WSIs). Through computer-based technology and virtual microscopy, it allows viewing, managing, sharing, and analyzing digital slides on computer monitors. This field has applications in diagnostic medicine and aims to achieve more efficient and cost-effective diagnoses, prognoses, and disease predictions through advances in technology [3]. Recently, DP has revolutionized the field of pathology and cancer research by incorporating novel computational image analysis techniques and artificial intelligence into the growing area of computational pathology. Computational Pathology (CPath) refers to the 'omics' or 'big-data' approach by integrating diverse sources of patient information including pathology images and metadata to discover patterns and extract high-level features. Machine learning (ML) and AI techniques are often used to process WSIs and related data, enabling advanced image interpretation at scale [4].

In the past decade, there have been significant advancements in artificial intelligence (AI) and machine learning (ML) techniques, particularly in deep learning (DL) and Transformer architectures, for both image and text analysis [5]. Techniques such as convolutional neural networks (CNNs) and vision transformers (ViTs) have demonstrated high performance across a variety of vision tasks, including natural images, medical imaging, and histopathology [6]. Similarly, recurrent neural networks (RNNs), including methods such as long short-term memory (LSTM) and gated recurrent units (GRUs), as well as large language model (LLM) Transformer architectures like bidirectional encoder representations from transformers (BERT), generative pre-trained transformers (GPTs), and LLaMA, have been successfully applied to natural language processing (NLP) tasks in multiple fields, these applications range from general-purpose text analysis to specialized domains such as medical and pathology-related language processing [7,8].

Given the increasing workload and complexity in histopathological diagnostics, there is a growing need for intelligent tools that can support specialists in interpreting large volumes of image data with consistency and precision. In this study, propose a multimodal language model that combines visual and textual analysis for histopathology image understanding. This approach integrates CLIP-prefix and GPT-2 architectures to automatically generate image captions and answer visual questions, facilitating the interpretation of pathology slides. This hybrid model acts as a decision-support tool by assisting pathologists with relevant textual insights derived directly from visual data.

The proposed model was trained and evaluated on two datasets: ARCH for auto-captioning and PathVQA for visual question answering. It achieved strong results, including up to 82% accuracy and a BLEU score of 71% in captioning, and 84% accuracy with a BLEU score of 67% in VQA. These findings highlight the potential of multimodal models as co-pilot assistants in digital pathology, enhancing diagnostic precision, reducing transcription errors, and improving clinical decision-making, especially in critical scenarios such as cancer diagnosis. The rest of the paper is organized as follows: Sect. 2 presents the related work, the Sect. 3 presents the methodology with the architectures used based on CLIP-prefix and GPT-2, the dataset descriptions, the performance measures and the experimental design. Section 4 depicts the quantitative and qualitative results of auto-captioning and VQA experiments. Finally, Sect. 5 concludes the main findings of this study and envision future work.

2 Related Work

Recent advances in multimodal learning have shown significant promise in bridging the gap between visual and textual representations for medical image analysis. One notable example is PathChat, a large multimodal language model developed collaboratively by researchers at Harvard Medical School and the MIT Computer Science and Artificial Intelligence Laboratory (CSAIL) [16]. PathChat builds upon foundational models such as GPT-4 and integrates them with domain-specific visual encoders to interpret histopathology whole-slide images (WSIs) and interact with users through natural language prompts. It represents a clinically aligned tool capable of performing tasks such as slide description, region-of-interest highlighting, and question answering in pathology workflows, setting a benchmark for real-world AI assistance in clinical diagnostics.

In parallel, CLIP (Contrastive Language-Image Pre-training) [17] and its variants have demonstrated strong capabilities in aligning visual and textual representations, enabling zero-shot and few-shot learning across various domains. In the medical field, adaptations of CLIP have been explored to bridge the semantic gap between medical images and their corresponding textual annotations. For instance, MedCLIP [18] and BioViL [19] adapt the CLIP architecture using domain-specific datasets, yielding improved performance in radiology report generation, disease classification, and retrieval tasks.

Within the field of histopathology, several studies have begun exploring CLIP-based methods to interpret microscopic tissue images. Lu et al. [20] proposed a framework for zero-shot transfer learning in histopathology using visual-language contrastive pretraining, achieving an average accuracy of 70.2% in cancer subtype classification tasks. Similarly, Lai et al. [21] introduced CLIPath, a technique that fine-tunes CLIP using visual feature fusion to improve pathology image classification, addressing domain-shift challenges between natural and medical images.

Despite these advances, most previous studies have focused on classification or retrieval tasks and often rely on radiology or dermatology datasets. The integration of CLIP with causal language models such as GPT-2 for generative tasks (e.g., automatic captioning and visual question answering in histopathology) remains underexplored. This study aims to address this gap by adapting a CLIP-prefix architecture to generate structured outputs in a pathology context, and evaluating its performance on real-world datasets such as ARCH and PathVQA.

3 Methodology

3.1 Multimodal Architecture

As a result of the review of previous work, the multimodal (visual and textual) language model architecture based on transformers and deep learning used by [9] was selected (Fig. 1). This architecture integrates the capabilities of vision models to interpret medical images with the ability of language models to understand and generate coherent textual output. Specifically, it leverages the pre-trained CLIP (Contrastive Language-Image Pretraining) visual encoder to extract a meaningful latent representation from the input pathology image (I), capturing low-level features and high-level semantic content. This image embedding is then transformed through a learnable mapping network—often implemented as an MLP or Transformer—into a prefix vector that can be fed into the GPT-2 decoder model. The purpose of this prefix is to guide the language generation process based on visual content without retraining the entire GPT-2 model. Simultaneously, a natural language question (Q) is provided, which is tokenized and embedded using the GPT-2 tokenizer. To help the model understand the task context and enforce alignment between visual and textual modalities, the input sequence is formatted using structured prompt engineering. The prompt follows a consistent format with delimiters such as "question:", "context:", and "answer:", which not only improves the model's focus but also allows it to better distinguish between the input modalities and task expectations.

3.2 Vision Encoder

The CLIP-Prefix (Contrastive Language-Image Pretraining) model [10], based on transformers, was successfully utilized for image captioning in natural, medical and pathological images. It was adapted to extract relevant visual features, enhancing the understanding of visual content. This model takes an image as input and generates a detailed description of its content. Hence, this model was used as a starting point for visual representation and textual description associated.

3.3 Language Model

The language model used in this architecture is a causal autoregressive model, such as GPT, which generates text sequentially from left to right. It is called causal because each generated word depends only on the previous words in the

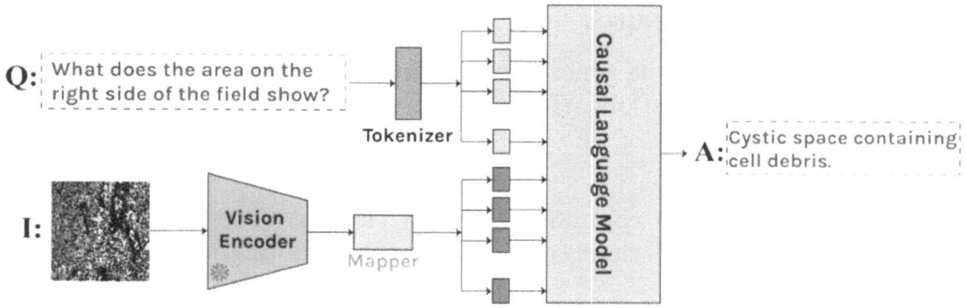

Fig. 1. Open-Ended VQA Architecture [9].

sequence, with no access to future words. This is achieved by masked attention mechanisms that prevent the model from seeing subsequent tokens during prediction. Thus, the model can construct coherent and contextually accurate responses based on previously processed information, such as the tokenized question and the visual representation of the image [9].

3.4 Pathology Datasets

ARCH Dataset. Training the auto-captioning model requires a dataset containing a diverse array of images along with their corresponding descriptions. For this purpose, the ARCH dataset [11] was selected. This dataset comprises histopathology images paired with textual descriptions. Examples of this dataset are shown in Sect. 3, Figs. 2 and 3. The image and description data are sourced from two categories:

- **Scientific Articles:** A total of 3,309 images were extracted, each accompanied by detailed descriptions.
- **Specialized Books:** A collection of 4,270 images was gathered, along with their respective descriptive texts.

PathVQA Dataset. The VQA model requires a dataset that includes images, questions, and corresponding answers. For this purpose, the PathVQA dataset was selected [12]. This dataset consists of 4,998 images covering a range of pathological variations and a total of 32,799 question-answer pairs. Among these, 16,334 (49.8%) are Yes/No questions, while 16,465 (50.2%) are open-ended questions, including categories such as 'What' (13,402; 40.9%), 'Where' (1,268; 4.0%), 'How' (1,014; 3.0%), 'How much/How many' (294; 0.9%), 'When' (285 0.9%), and 'Whose' (202; 0.6%). Examples from this dataset are presented in Sect. 3, Figs. 4 and 5.

3.5 Performance Measures

To evaluate the quality of the generated descriptions and the ability of the model to answer open-ended questions, three metrics were used, Accuracy, BLEU and CIDEr.

Accuracy. Accuracy is a common metric in classification that measures the percentage of correct predictions compared to the total predictions made [13].

$$\text{Accuracy} = \frac{TP + TN}{TP + TN + FP + FN}$$

where TP are the True Positives, TN are the True Negatives, FP are the False Positives, and FN are the False Negatives.

Bilingual Evaluation Understudy (BLEU). BLEU quantifies the correspondence between the generated candidate descriptions by comparing them with human description references, measuring matches in n-grams [14]. It is a weighted geometric mean of all the modified n-gram precisions, multiplied by the brevity penalty as follows:

$$BLEU_w(\hat{S}; S) := BP(\hat{S}; S) \cdot \exp\left(\sum_{n=1}^{\infty} w_n \ln p_n(\hat{S}; S)\right)$$

where $BP(\hat{S}; S)$ is the brevity penalty among the list of reference and candidate descriptions $(\hat{S}; S)$ and the weighting vector w is a probability distribution.

Consensus-Based Image Description Evaluation (CIDEr). This metric utilizes the Term Frequency-Inverse Document Frequency (TF-IDF) calculation, assigning greater weight to specific and relevant words [15]. It is defined as follows:

$$\text{TF-IDF}(t, d) = \frac{f_{t,d}}{\sum_{t' \in d} f_{t',d}} \times \log\left(\frac{N}{1 + n_t}\right)$$

where

$f_{t,d}$: Frequency of term t in document d.

N: Total number of documents in the corpus.

n_t: Number of documents containing the term t.

The similarity between generated descriptions and references was measured using cosine similarity as follows:

$$\text{Cosine similarity } (A, B) = \frac{A \cdot B}{\|A\| \|B\|} = \frac{\sum_{i=1}^{n} A_i B_i}{\sqrt{\sum_{i=1}^{n} A_i^2} \sqrt{\sum_{i=1}^{n} B_i^2}}$$

where A and B are vectors representing documents, phrases or words in a vector space. $A \cdot B$ is the dot product between the vectors A and B, and $\|\cdot\|$ corresponds to the Euclidean norm definition.

3.6 Experimental Design

Two separate experiments were conducted to assess the capabilities of the multimodal language model. The first experiment focused on the auto-captioning task using books and articles separately, while the second evaluated its performance in visual question answering.

For the auto-captioning experiment, the ARCH dataset was randomly split into three subsets: 80% for training, 20% of the training set for validation, and 20% of the entire original dataset for testing. The training and validation subsets were used to optimize model parameters and select the best configuration based on performance metrics.

For the visual question answering experiment, the PathVQA dataset also has three subsets from the original data source: train with 2,599 images and 19,654 questions with answers, validation with 832 images and 6,259 questions and their answers, and test with 858 images and 6,719 questions and their answers.

During the training process for both experiments, three relevant parameters according to previous works were defined and adjusted to optimize the performance of models. The experiments were conducted within the following parameter ranges:

- learning rate: $[1e-3, 1e-4, 1e-5]$
- warm-up step: $[400, 600, 800, 1000]$
- prefix-length: $[5, 8, 10, 15]$

Both experiments were performed with the training and validation datasets for parameter exploration. After finding the best parameter combination, the models were trained with those values of the best parameter configuration by combining the training and validation sets. Finally, these models were evaluated in the testing dataset for quantitative and qualitative analysis.

For auto-captioning experiments, a NVIDIA GeForce®RTX 2080 Ti (12 GB VRAM) was used to train each parameter's combination of the model, while for VQA experiments, NVIDIA GeForce®RTX 4090 (24 GB VRAM) was used.

4 Results

Auto-Captioning. The auto-captioning model achieved the best performance with the parameter values of learning rate: 1e-4, warm-up step: 800, and prefix length: 5, in both subsets, the one trained with images from specialized books (*Books*) and the one trained with images from scientific articles (*Art*). Table 1 shows some of the different experiments performed varying the parameter values of learning rate (lr), warm-up steps (ws) and prefix length (k), and their performance measures evaluated in validation with histopathology images and descriptions from scientific articles.

Table 2 shows some of the different experiments performed varying the parameter values and their performance measures evaluated in validation with histopathology images and descriptions specialized books.

Table 1. Performance measures of different experiments varying parameter values of the multimodal language model for auto-captioning using scientific articles using ARCH dataset. The experiment with the best performance is highlighted in green.

Experiment	learning rate	warm-up steps	prefix length	Accuracy	BLEU	CIDEr
Artsws600lr1e-3k5	1,00E-03	600	5	0.16	0.17	0.77
Artsws600lr1e-3k10	1,00E-03	600	10	0.16	0.16	0.83
Artsws600lr1e-3k15	1,00E-03	600	15	0.15	0.22	0.97
Artsws600lr5e-3k10	5,00E-03	600	10	0.15	0.15	0.13
Artsws800lr1e-3k10	1,00E-03	800	10	0.18	0.16	0.96
Artsws600lr1e-4k10	1,00E-04	600	10	0.79	0.77	5.79
Artsws600lr1e-5k10	1,00E-05	600	10	0.87	0.83	3.15
Artsws600lr1e-4k15	1,00E-04	600	15	0.42	0.41	4.54
Artsws600lr1e-4k5	1,00E-04	600	5	0.91	0.90	7.05
Artsws400lr1e-4k5	1,00E-04	400	5	0.60	0.59	5.16
Artsws800lr1e-4k5	1,00E-04	800	5	0.93	0.92	7.72
Artsws800lr1e-4k8	1,00E-04	800	8	0.90	0.89	6.87
Artsws600lr1e-4k8	1,00E-04	600	8	0.67	0.65	4.84
Artsws800lr1e-4k10	1,00E-04	800	10	0.78	0.77	5.79
Artsws1000lr1e-4k5	1,00E-04	1000	5	0.37	0.35	3.93

Table 2. Performance measures of different experiments varying parameter values of the multimodal language model for auto-captioning using specialized books using ARCH dataset. The experiment with the best performance is highlighted in green.

Experiment	learning rate	warm-up steps	prefix length	Accuracy	BLEU	CIDEr
Booksws800lr1e-3k10	1,00E-03	800	10	0.20	0.18	0.86
Booksws600lr1e-4k10	1,00E-04	600	10	0.95	0.95	7.23
Booksws600lr1e-5k10	1,00E-05	600	10	0.96	0.90	7.50
Booksws600lr1e-5k5	1,00E-05	600	5	0.96	0.94	5.02
Booksws600lr1e-4k5	1,00E-04	600	5	0.95	0.95	7.37
Booksws800lr1e-4k5	1,00E-04	800	5	0.96	0.95	7.32
Booksws800lr1e-4k8	1,00E-04	800	8	0.92	0.92	5.41
Booksws600lr1e-4k8	1,00E-04	600	8	0.93	0.93	6.14
Booksws600lr1e-4k7	1,00E-04	600	15	0.89	0.80	1.07
Booksws700lr1e-4k5	1,00E-04	1000	5	0.89	0.80	1.07

The performance measures quantitatively evaluate the precision and relevance of the descriptions generated by the models concerning the reference descriptions. In addition, the models were qualitatively compared and visually evaluated with histopathology image samples from the test dataset, as shown in Figs. 2 and 3.

Table 3. Performance measures of different experiments varying parameter values of the multimodal language model for visual question answering using PathVQA dataset. The experiment with the best performance is highlighted in green.

Experiment	learning rate	warmup steps	prefix length	Accuracy	BLEU	CIDEr
Pathws600lr1e-3k5	1,00E-03	600	5	0.32	0.26	0.91
Pathws800lr1e-3k10	1,00E-03	800	10	0.85	0.39	1.90
Pathws600lr1e-5k10	1,00E-05	600	10	0.79	0.09	1.00
Pathws600lr1e-4k5	1,00E-04	600	5	0.97	0.48	2.16
Pathws800lr1e-4k5	1,00E-04	800	5	0.84	0.66	1.89
Pathws800lr1e-4k8	1,00E-04	800	8	0.85	0.66	1.91
Pathws600lr1e-4k8	1,00E-04	600	8	0.85	0.34	1.73
Pathws400lr1e-4k8	1,00E-04	600	15	0.87	0.38	2.16
Pathws800lr1e-4k10	1,00E-04	800	10	0.83	0.63	1.81

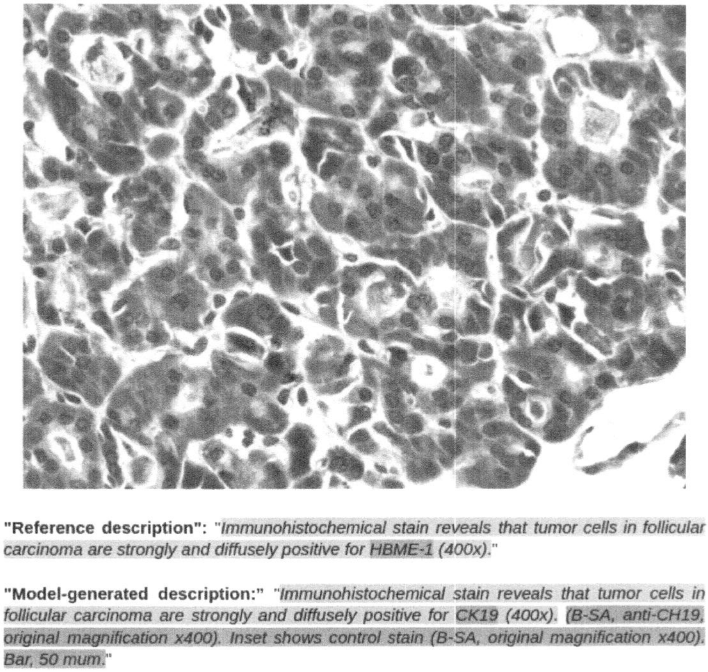

Fig. 2. Histopathology image sample from the test dataset with the corresponding reference description (actual) and model-generated description (predicted) using the trained model with scientific articles. Accurate prediction (green), error prediction (red) and different additional prediction (purple). (Color figure online)

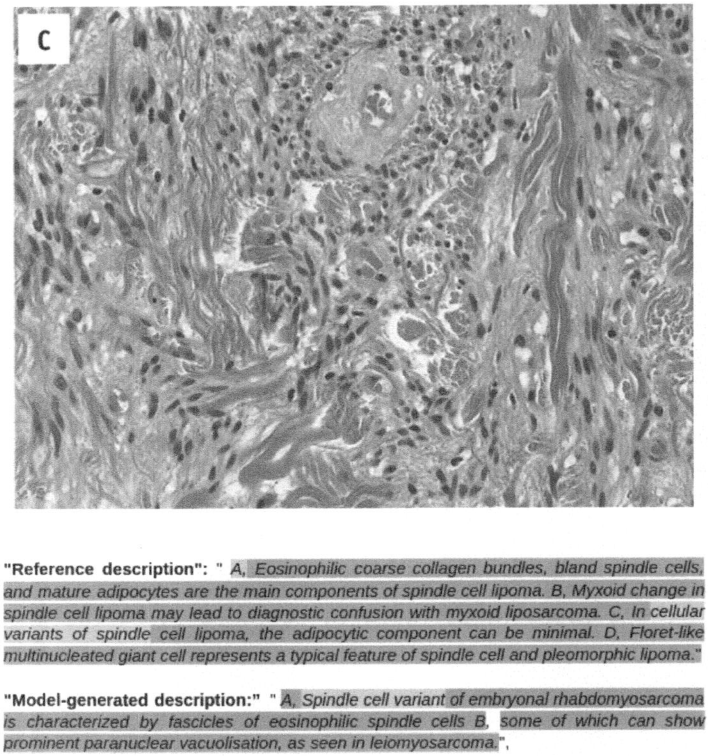

Fig. 3. Histopathology image sample from the test dataset with the corresponding reference description (actual) and model-generated description (predicted) using the trained model with specialized books. Accurate prediction (green), error prediction (red) and different additional prediction (purple). (Color figure online)

Visual Question Answering. The VQA model was trained using the pre-trained weights of the best auto-captioning model as a basis. The best performance was achieved with the following parameter values of learning rate: 1e-4, warm-up step: 800 and prefix length: 8. Table 3 shows the different experiments performed varying the parameter values and their performance measures evaluated in validation using both training and validation subsets from PathVQA dataset (*Path*).

The performance measures quantitatively evaluate the precision of the answers generated from histopathology images and questions by the best VQA model concerning the real answer. In addition, the VQA model was qualitatively compared and visually evaluated with histopathology image samples from the test dataset, with their corresponding questions and answers as shown in Figs. 4 and 5.

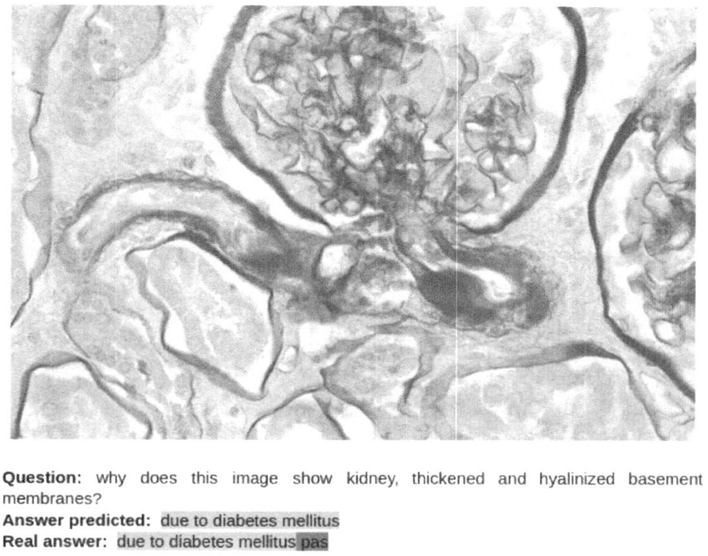

Fig. 4. Predicted answer to an open-ended histopathology image question. Correct (green) and additional prediction (purple) (Color figure online)

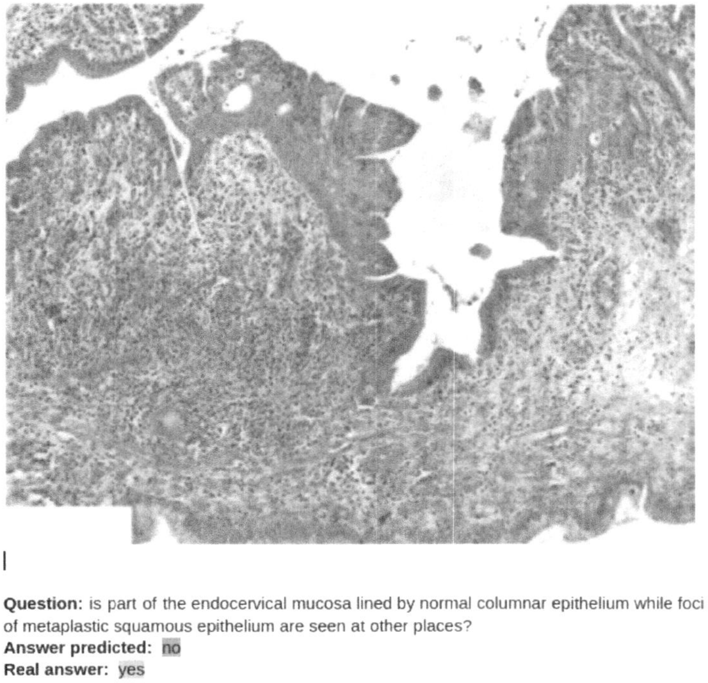

Fig. 5. Predicted answer to a yes/no histopathology image question. Correct (green) and error (red). (Color figure online)

The scripts for the training of the models and the data with their respective subsets division are available in the repository: https://gitlab.com/epi7210337/pathvqa.git.

5 Conclusions

Two multimodal language models were explored and evaluated for histopathology images. The first one is for auto-captioning task of describing the visual content inside a histopathology image, and the second one is for the visual question answering task of answering yes/no or open-ended questions about the visual content of histopathology images (light microscopy, hematoxylin-eosin, immunohistochemistry and special stains), with a high generalization capability.

Experimental results and adaptation on the selected pathology datasets from ARCH and PathVQA confirmed that the implemented CLIP-prefix-based architecture effectively integrates visual and textual information with reduced computational overhead. This capability enables the training and generation of a multimodal generative model using a diverse set of data, achieving an accuracy rate exceeding 80%.

The two explored models, auto-captioning and VQA, have the potential to support the pathology workflow by assisting pathologists in reviewing images and answering specific questions. This could enhance the accuracy and efficiency of describing visual content in specific regions of digital histopathology slides. Additionally, these models may help reduce errors in pathology reports that could impact patient diagnosis and treatment, particularly in critical cases such as cancer.

Future works include obtaining more histopathology datasets for those tasks because are very limited in this task and domain, and the exploration of large multimodal models or using foundational models as starting points to distilled models to increase the performance and generalization capabilities.

Acknowledgments. The authors thank GITECX and AdaLab for computational workstations and GPUs resources provided for experimentation. This study was partially supported by projects BPIN 2019000100060 "Implementation of a Network 357 for Research, Technological Development and Innovation in Digital Pathology (Red-Pat) supported by Industry 4.0 technologies" from FCTeI of SGR resources, approved by OCAD of FCTeI, and project 110192092345 "Program for the Early Detection of Premalignant Lesions and Gastric Cancer in urban, rural and dispersed areas in the Department of *Nariño*" of call No. 920 of 2022 of MinCiencias.

References

1. Poller, D.N., Bongiovanni, M., Cochand-Priollet, B., Johnson, S.J., Perez-Machado, M.: A human factor event-based learning assessment tool for assessment of errors and diagnostic accuracy in histopathology and cytopathology. J. Clin. Pathol. **73**(10), 681–685 (2020). https://doi.org/10.1136/JCLINPATH-2020-206538
2. Badrick, T., Shane Brown, A.S.A.: Identifying human factors as a source of error in laboratory quality control. J. Lab. Precis. Med. **8** (2023). https://doi.org/10.21037/JLPM-23-7/COIF
3. Jahn, S.W., Plass, M., Moinfar, F.: Digital pathology: advantages, limitations and emerging perspectives. J. Clin. Med. **9**(11), 3697 (2020). https://doi.org/10.3390/JCM9113697
4. Fuchs, T.J., Wild, P.J., Moch, H., Buhmann, J.M.: Computational pathology analysis of tissue microarrays predicts survival of renal clear cell carcinoma patients. In: Metaxas, D., Axel, L., Fichtinger, G., Székely, G. (eds.) MICCAI 2008. LNCS, vol. 5242, pp. 1–8. Springer, Heidelberg (2008). https://doi.org/10.1007/978-3-540-85990-1_1
5. de la Torre, J.: Transformadores: Fundamentos teoricos y Aplicaciones (2023). https://arxiv.org/abs/2302.09327v1
6. Henry, E.U., Emebob, O., Omonhinmin, C.A.: Vision Transformers in Medical Imaging: A Review (2022). https://arxiv.org/abs/2211.10043v1
7. Segura-Bedmar, I., Camino-Perdones, D., Guerrero-Aspizua, S.: Exploring deep learning methods for recognizing rare diseases and their clinical manifestations from texts. BMC Bioinform. **23**(1) (2021). https://doi.org/10.1186/s12859-022-04810-y
8. Xie, Q., et al.: Me LLaMA: Foundation Large Language Models for Medical Applications (2024). https://arxiv.org/abs/2402.12749v5
9. van Sonsbeek, T., Derakhshani, M.M., Najdenkoska, I., Snoek, C.G.M., Worring, M.: Open-ended medical visual question answering through prefix tuning of language models. Lecture Notes in Computer Science (Including Subseries Lecture Notes in Artificial Intelligence and Lecture Notes in Bioinformatics). LNCS, vol. 14224, pp. 726–736 (2023). https://doi.org/10.1007/978-3-031-43904-9_70
10. Mokady, R., Hertz, A., Bermano, A.H.: Clipcap: Clip prefix for image captioning (2021). https://doi.org/10.48550/arXiv.2111.09734
11. Gamper, J., Rajpoot, N.: Multiple Instance Captioning: Learning Representations from Histopathology Textbooks and Articles (2021). https://doi.org/10.48550/arXiv.2103.05121
12. He, X., Zhang, Y., Mou, L., Xing, E., Xie, P.: PATHVQA: 30000+ Questions for Medical Visual Question Answering (2020)
13. James, G., Witten, D., Hastie, T., Tibshirani, R.: An Introduction to Statistical Learning (2021). https://doi.org/10.1007/978-1-0716-1418-1
14. Papineni, K., Roukos, S., Ward, T., Zhu, W.-J.: Bleu: a method for automatic evaluation of machine translation. In: Proceedings of the 40th Annual Meeting of the Association for Computational Linguistics, Philadelphia, Pennsylvania, USA. Association for Computational Linguistics (2002). https://aclanthology.org/P02-1040
15. Vedantam, R., Lawrence Zitnick, C., Parikh, D.: CIDEr: Consensus-based Image Description Evaluation (2015). https://arxiv.org/abs/1411.5726
16. Wang, Z., Huang, J., et al.: PathChat: Interactive Visual Dialogue System for Whole Slide Image Interpretation (2023). https://arxiv.org/abs/2309.05600

17. Radford, A., Kim, J.W., et al.: Learning transferable visual models from natural language supervision. In: Proceedings of the 38th International Conference on Machine Learning (2021). https://arxiv.org/abs/2103.00020
18. Zhang, Y., et al.: Contrastive Vision–Language Pre-Training for Radiology: MedCLIP (2022). https://arxiv.org/abs/2212.12494
19. Boecking, B., et al.: BioViL: Self-Supervised Vision-Language Pretraining Without Parallel Images and Text (2022). https://arxiv.org/abs/2201.01278
20. Lu, M.Y., et al.: Visual Language Pretrained Multiple Instance Zero-Shot Transfer for Histopathology Images (2023). https://arxiv.org/abs/2306.07831
21. Lai, Y., et al.: CLIPath: fine-tune CLIP with visual feature fusion for pathology image classification. In: Proceedings of the IEEECVF International Conference on Computer Vision Workshops (ICCVW), pp. 1234–1243 (2023)

Computer Vision

Automatic Counting System in a Region of Interest from Videos Taken by Drones

Guillermo A. Jiménez-Frías[1], Francisco J. Hernandez-Lopez[2], Thomas Batard[1](✉), Silvana Forti-Sosa[3], and Eduardo Pérez-Pech[3]

[1] Centro de Investigación en Matemáticas A.C., Guanajuato, Mexico
{guillermo.jimenez,thomas.batard}@cimat.mx
[2] SECIHTI - Centro de Investigación en Matemáticas A.C., CIMAT Unidad Mérida, Merida, Mexico
fcoj23@cimat.mx
[3] Universidad Modelo, Merida, Mexico
silvana.forti@gmail.com,eduardo.perez.pech@gmail.com

Abstract. Implementing road infrastructure projects to improve connectivity and communication in developing countries begins with traffic flow statistics for better planning. This article presents an automatic counting system in videos taken by drones from a segment of interest and a dataset explicitly designed for this task. The input to the system consists of the video and the segment given by the user; the output is a table with the count of eight classes of relevant objects in the Yucatan area: car, truck, bus, combi, motorcycle, bike, mototaxi and pedestrian. The counting system has sequentially integrated modules that perform the tasks of detection, tracking, and counting, respectively. First, the detection module uses a fine-tuned and trained YOLOv4 model. Then, the tracking module uses the Intersection over Union method. Finally, the counting module selects those that have crossed the segment of interest from the tracked objects for the first time. The system reports a weighted average accuracy of 80.38%.

Keywords: Computer Vision · Object Detection · Object Tracking · Automatic Counting · Deep Learning

1 Introduction

A fundamental characteristic of economic growth in any nation is the development of transportation systems adapted and planned according to the needs of people and spatial information. In Mexico, between 2010 and 2022, the number of registered motor vehicles in circulation grew by almost 74.4%, going from nearly 31.5 million to almost 55.2 million [1]. To control traffic and reduce its consequences, such as congestion, increased travel time, fuel consumption, and driver stress, it is necessary to improve the design and consider the possible creation of roads considering traffic control and management strategies.

A. P. López-Monroy et al. (Eds.): MCPR 2025, LNCS 15715, pp. 191–200, 2025.
https://doi.org/10.1007/978-3-031-96255-4_18

Traffic monitoring has become a key technique for collecting information on traffic conditions due to faster and more accurate video analysis. In turn, unmanned aerial vehicles (drones) offer advantages over traditional sensors, such as video surveillance cameras, by obtaining minimal occlusion between objects, reducing shadows, and having a better vision [2]. Furthermore, drones are versatile as they can be used in various fixed and non-fixed, complex or dangerous scenarios and avoid the expense of installing infrastructure. With this, the drone can provide efficient data acquisition for traffic analysis.

On the other hand, deep learning has become the state of the art for solving problems due to the increasing computing capacity, the creation of more extensive and more specific databases, and the application to various fields. In this context, different automatic detection and tracking models have been tested to generate traffic monitoring systems in particular situations and have proven to be accurate and efficient for real-time applications [3–5].

Therefore, this work proposes an algorithm that automatically counts vehicles and pedestrians in videos taken by drones, where the counting is done over areas of interest. The areas of interest will be segments, and these will be generated by the user interactively or by reading a file with the coordinates of the segments in the reference frame of the first image of the video.

Another contribution of this work is generating a labeled dataset as a reference point for measuring automatic counting systems under the traffic conditions stated above. Such a data set was used to measure the performance of the proposed system. It consists of a family of videos marked with segments, the respective coordinates of segments, three manual counts performed on each segment by a group of assistants, and the execution times of the system in each test[1].

This article is organized as follows: Sect. 2 summarizes related work on automatic counting; Sect. 3 presents our proposal; Sect. 4 presents the experiments and results; Finally, in Sect. 5, we discuss our conclusions.

2 Related Work

In this section we include work related to automatic counting. Here, we will mention some systems that are part of the state of the art for particular counting cases and from which this work was inspired.

In [3], a vehicle counting system is developed using a combination of optical flow and block matching to estimate motion patterns. The counting is done using input and output rectangles relative to the vehicles in the image. Once a vehicle enters the street intersection, the *SubME* [11] motion estimation algorithm is executed as a tracking tool. Then, the Taylor series approximation is used to refine the search and the direction of the vehicle relative to the input box is obtained. The system does not use a vehicle detector in advance. Its counting results are relative to the routes generated by the entry and exit rectangles.

[1] The dataset is available at: https://github.com/MemoJmz/YucaMex-MOCS.

They show accuracies between 14.29% and 100%. The main error arises from the synchronized movement of some vehicles and motorcycles, which the system misinterprets as one single vehicle.

In [4], a method is proposed that achieves 90% accuracy for vehicle counting in videos with a static background and 85% accuracy in videos with a moving background acquired from a camera installed on a drone. For the case of moving background, they calculate *SURF* [12] features for image registration and camera motion estimation, detecting vehicles in the same reference frame. The system requires a virtual line to determine the area where moving objects will be counted. They use the background subtraction method *ViBe* [13] to detect moving objects and the kernelized correlation filter algorithm to track such objects.

In [5], a three-stage system is proposed. First, object detection is based on *YOLOv2* [9] running every N frames. Second, features are extracted and analyzed on all N frames using *K-means* clustering and the *Kanade-Lucas-Tomasi* [10] tracking method. Finally, the obtained points are assigned an identifier, meaning it is a detected vehicle. These points are again tracked, updated, refined, and clustered on each frame. The method achieves an average detection accuracy of 91.1% in the analyzed videos.

3 Methodology

The proposed method introduces an algorithm based on a pre-trained neural network to detect vehicles and pedestrians, classifies the detected vehicles into seven categories (car, truck, bus, combi, motorcycle, bike, and mototaxi), tracks the movement of each vehicle, and counts the classified vehicles that cross the counting segment.

In short, the video is captured by a drone over a road intersection and then stored. The first frame of the video is retrieved and a segment is drawn to cross the traffic route where the object count is to be performed; this is referred to as the *segment of interest*. Its coordinates are stored along with the video. So, the area of interest is the area around the segment of interest. Once the video and the segment are available, the pre-trained deep-learning model detects and classifies the objects. Then, the intersection over union method is used to track the vehicles that appear in each frame. When the object crosses the segment for the first time, it is recorded by a counter. The step-by-step explanation of the method is shown in Fig. 1.

3.1 Detection Module: YOLOv4

This section describes the object detection model used in this work. The work draws on the detection results obtained in [8], where several detection models were used, with the YOLOv4 method [6] being the most prominent for this task.

The trained network is fed with frames of 3840×2160 pixels, which resizes to 896×896 and normalizes each color channel automatically for training and deployment. Using transfer learning-based fine-tuning, the model was trained

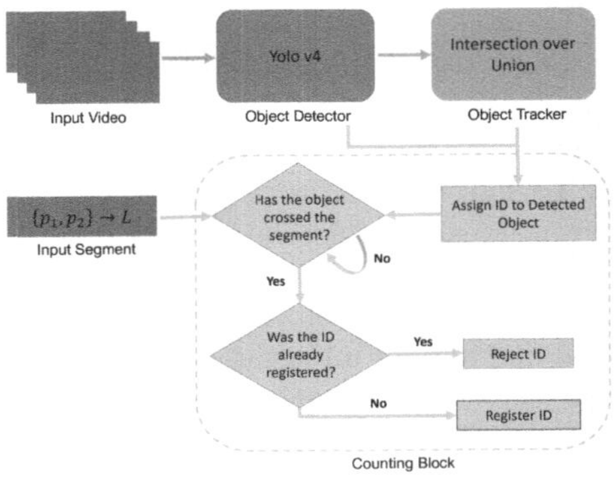

Fig. 1. Counting Diagram. The flow and processing of frames through the modules of the automatic counting system are illustrated.

on the dataset reported in [8]. The output of this module is a list of detected objects defined by bounding boxes, confidences, and respective classes.

Fine-Tuning Based on Transfer Learning. The YOLOv4 model is pre-trained with the *COCO* [7] image set. The transfer learning process used consisted of initializing the weights with that dataset and training the entire network with the dataset reported in [8].

The model was trained using an Intel(R) Core (TM) i9-9920×3.5GHz CPU, Ubuntu 20.04 (64 bit), 16 hyper-threading cores, 48 GB of RAM and a Nvidia Quadro RTX 8000 GPU rated 7.5 and 48 GB of RAM. Some of the hyperparameters of the YOLOv4 model were modified with the following values:

- Model input size 896×896 pixels.
- Number of lots (batch): 64, with 32 subdivisions.
- Number of channels (colors): 3.
- Number of classes: 8.
- Anchor boxes: $[(11, 19), (20, 20), (12, 40), (30, 30), (24, 82), (52, 43), (58, 60), (33, 113), (78, 93)]$. The boxes were obtained using the method of *KMeans++*.

The set of classes of interest correspond to *car, truck, bus, combi, motorcycle, bike, mototaxi* and *pedestrian*, see Fig. 2. It is worth mentioning that there are three particular classes: cars correspond to sedan or hatchback type vehicles; *mototaxi* are vehicles from the Yucatan region, Mexico; and trucks represent the class with the most varied vehicles, as they include vans with open cabins, with closed cabins or cargo boxes, tortons, and trailers.

3.2 Tracking Module

After processing each frame of an input video and obtaining the segments of interest, it is necessary to track these objects to assign them an identifier *ID*.

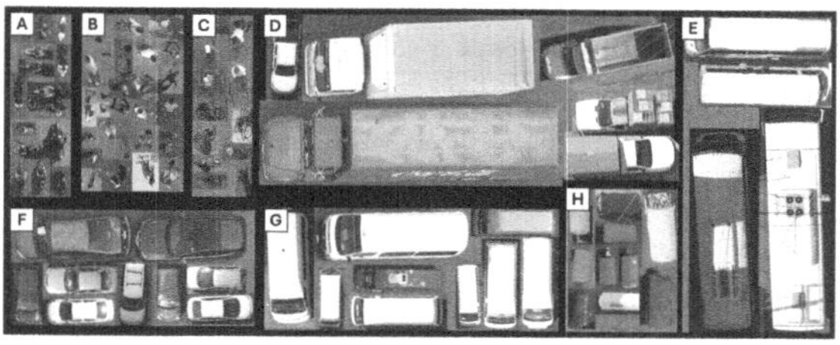

Fig. 2. Sample of objects grouped by class. (A) Motorcycle, (B) Pedestrian, (C) Bike, (D) Truck, (E) Bus, (F) Car, (G) Combi, (H) Mototaxi.

This ID is used to differentiate them from objects that appear in the scene and have not been tracked and to determine when they cross the segment of interest.

Intersection over Union. Video capture using drones provides overhead images that allow viewing of objects with minimal overlap and occlusion between them. Because of this, the intersection over union (IoU) metric is an intuitive and straightforward solution to integrate as a tracking algorithm.

In each frame t, we have two lists of bounding boxes, B_{MV} and B_t, representing the objects tracked in the previous frames and objects detected in the current frame. We want to determine whether an object appearing in the current frame already has an identifier, that is, it is already being tracked. We can identify three subsets of bounding boxes: $B_{MV} \cap B_t$ are the objects that were tracked from the precious to the current frame; $B_{MV} \setminus B_t$ are objects that were no longer tracked in actual frame, possibly having disappeared from the scene; and $B_t \setminus B_{MV}$ correspond to new objects in the scene.

Multiple Vehicle and Pedestrian Tracking. Algorithm 1 describes the steps of the tracking module based on IoU. This algorithm is executed from the second frame, where the tracked objects B_{MV} are updated. The values $\tau_v = 0.07$ and $\tau_p = 0.01$ are considered motion thresholds for vehicles and pedestrians, respectively. The δ_{IoU} value was set to 0.15 empirically when testing on the dataset.

Multiple Object Counting from a Segment. The next step after obtaining the object identifiers is to consider a criterion when crossing the segment. The procedure is shown in the Algorithm 2. The region of interest R will be generated by thickening the given segment $l = \{p_1, p_2\}$ based on its inclination. The counter then increments the respective class when an object intersects R. $\tau = 2$ is considered the slope threshold and $2 * d$ is the width of the region R, with $d = 1$.

Algorithm 1: Multiple Vehicle and Pedestrian Tracking

Input: B_{MV}: bounding boxes of tracked objects throughout the video; B_t: bounding boxes of detected objects in the current frame t

Output: Updated B_{MV}

$B_{aux} \leftarrow \emptyset$;

foreach $b \in B_{MV}$ **do**

  Find $c^\star$ that solves:

$$\max_{c \in B_t} \quad \text{IoU}(c, b) \quad \text{subject to} \quad \text{IoU}(c, b) > \delta_{IoU}$$

  if $c^\star$ *is found* **then**

    $B_{aux} \leftarrow B_{aux} \cup \{c^\star\}$ and $B_t \leftarrow B_t \setminus \{c^\star\}$;

    if *distance(b, c) exceeds* τ_v *or* τ_p **then**

      Mark the object as moving and assign a tracking ID ;

$B_{MV} \leftarrow B_{aux} \cup B_t$;

return B_{MV} ;

4 Experiments and Results

To implement the method and conduct our experiments, we first captured videos with a drone positioned between 30 and 70 m high to capture road intersections in several cities in Yucatan, Mexico. We consider a sample of nine videos; see Fig. 3. Each video has a definition of 3840×2160 pixels with a duration of 6:49 min (**0027**), 5:27 min (**0089**), 5:27 min (**0362**), 3:10 min (**0597**), 4:50 min (**0614**), 9:41 min (**0674**), 4:16 min (**0861**), 4:50 min (**0883**), and 5:28 min (**4040**). The videos are recorded at 30 frames per second. Then, up to three segments (called $\mathbf{S_1}, \mathbf{S_2}$ and $\mathbf{S_3}$) were considered per video, depending on the traffic flow, and with them, each test performed consists of running the counting system on one of these segments. On the other hand, six people participated in the manual counting of each test. Three counts were performed per test video, and their average was used as the *ground truth*. Table 1 presents the average of the respective manual counts.

The experiments consisted of executing the automatic counting system on the previous set of videos by varying the number of consecutive frames to be processed, $n = 1, 2, \ldots, 5$. That is, an experiment consists of setting n and then only processing the frames with index $i = k * n$, with $k \in \mathbb{Z}_{\geq 0}$, where the first frame has the index zero.

Metrics. We consider two metrics to report the performance of the automatic counting system: the *precision* and the *weighted precision* per class. First, the accuracy of the automatic counting system for the class i is computed as follows:

$$\overline{P}_i = \frac{1}{K} \sum_{k=1}^{K} P_i^k, \tag{1}$$

Algorithm 2: Definition of Region Interest and Counting Procedure

Input: Two points p_1, p_2 defining a segment; tracked objects B_{MV}
Output: Class counters updated

$\Delta x \leftarrow |p_2.x - p_1.x|$;
$\Delta y \leftarrow |p_2.y - p_1.y|$;
if $\Delta x < \tau$ **then**
  $v \leftarrow [d, 0]$
else if $\Delta y < \tau$ **then**
  $v \leftarrow [0, d]$
else
  $t \leftarrow -\Delta x / \Delta y$;
  $v \leftarrow \left[d/\sqrt{1+t^2}, (t \cdot d)/\sqrt{1+t^2}\right]$
$R \leftarrow$ rectangle with opposite vertices $p_1 + v$ and $p_2 - v$;
foreach $b \in B_{MV}$ **do**
  if $R \cap b \neq \emptyset$ *and b has not been counted* **then**
    Increment class counter for b **and mark** b **as counted** ;

Fig. 3. Videos (first frame). In each video, a different number of segments can be seen, each differentiated by the colors red, green and blue; this is because a different number of tests were performed on each video. (Color figure online)

where

$$P_i^k = \left(1 - \frac{|C_i^k - \mu_i^k|}{\mu_i^k}\right) * 100 \tag{2}$$

is the accuracy for the test video k and class i, C_i^k is the result of automatic counting, μ_i^k is the mean of the manual counts, and K is the number of test videos.

On the other hand, the weighted accuracy for class i is

$$\widehat{P}_i = \sum_{k=1}^{K} \lambda_i^k P_i^k, \tag{3}$$

Table 1. Ground truth table, each value represents the Average of three Manual Counts of the number of objects in each class.

Class	0027			0089	0362			0597			0614			0674	0861		0883	4040	Total
	S_1	S_2	S_3	S_1	S_1	S_2	S_3	S_1	S_2	S_3	S_1	S_2	S_3	S_1	S_1	S_2	S_1	S_2	
Car	36	61	39	5	4	3	7	0	9	15	20	0	16	16	8	0	46	33	318
Truck	4	9	5	4	4	0	5	0	2	3	4	0	9	9	4	0	16	8	86
Bus	2	1	1	0	0	0	0	0	1	0	0	0	1	0	0	0	0	3	9
Combi	1	2	3	0	1	0	1	0	0	2	1	0	1	0	1	0	7	0	20
Motorcycle	10	7	13	2	9	2	12	0	8	6	15	0	7	22	9	0	35	25	182
Bike	3	1	5	1	5	3	3	0	1	1	0	0	1	0	1	0	2	4	31
Mototaxi	6	7	6	1	38	21	61	0	0	1	0	0	0	8	15	0	17	2	183
Pedestrian	8	0	0	6	23	24	14	4	0	0	0	7	3	6	30	20	1	3	149

where $\lambda_i^k = \mu_i^k / T_i$ is the proportion of objects of class i in the test video k, and T_i is the total number of objects in all test videos of class i.

Table 2 shows the average accuracy per class (column) where each row contains the results when varying the number of frames to be processed $n = 1, 2, \ldots, 5$. The last column contains the mean of the average accuracy of all classes for each n. Similarly, the weighted average accuracy is shown in Table 3.

Table 2. Table of average percentages of accuracies, each value represents the average of accuracies over all tests for the respective class and n.

n	Car	Truck	Bus	Combi	Motorcycle	Bike	Mototaxi	Pedestrian	Mean
1	89.20	62.48	86.11	74.21	74.87	51.48	52.89	18.56	63.72
2	88.51	63.87	86.11	74.21	73.72	30.56	53.22	18.60	61.10
3	86.82	59.28	86.11	74.21	74.80	24.35	53.22	18.50	59.66
4	87.19	62.68	86.11	74.21	72.48	41.39	53.22	34.73	64.00
5	88.72	65.18	86.11	74.21	69.07	34.72	52.89	38.85	63.72

We can see from Table 2 that the accuracies for most classes do not show a significant variation depending on the number of frames processed $n = 1, 2, \ldots, 5$. However, the pedestrian and bicycle classes are the exception and show unfavorable results. The reason is that the tracking method incorrectly follows the objects. On the other hand, the car and bus classes are the ones that present a precision greater than 86.82% and 86.11%, respectively, in all executions.

In Table 3, we notice some interesting results due to the number of objects in each class. The truck, mototaxi, and pedestrian classes obtained a weighted precision of 82.56%, 94.86% and 82.01%, respectively, when averaged over the executions n. This improvement, when compared to the ones reported in Table 2,

Table 3. Table of average percentages of weighted accuracies over all test videos for the respective class and n.

n	Car	Truck	Bus	Combi	Motorcycle	Bike	Mototaxi	Pedestrian	Mean
1	92.14	82.56	66.67	80.0	88.46	54.84	94.54	83.22	80.30
2	91.82	82.56	66.67	80.0	86.26	58.06	95.08	82.55	80.38
3	91.55	80.23	66.67	80.0	87.36	41.94	95.08	78.52	77.66
4	91.82	82.56	66.67	80.0	74.73	54.84	95.08	85.23	78.87
5	91.51	84.88	66.67	80.0	57.69	51.61	94.54	80.54	75.93

comes from the fact that these are classes with a high proportion of objects in the tests. The car class obtained, on average, a weighted precision of 91.76%, slightly higher than its precision reported in Table 2 considering that it is the class with the highest number of objects. The combi, motorcycle, and bike classes also had a slightly higher performance, averaging 80.0%, 78.9%, and 52.25%. The bus class obtained, on average, a weighted accuracy of 66.67%, representing an inconsistent performance of the automatic counting system compared to its result in Table 2 and to the other classes. This result is a consequence of the few instances of this class available to train the detection model. The bike class obtained, on average, a weighted accuracy of 52.25%. This is the class with the most detection errors, which is due to two main factors. First, this is a class with a small number of objects, then the shape of the bicycle structure can go unnoticed and, therefore, the object can be confused with a pedestrian.

5 Conclusions

The main contributions of this work include the creation of a specialized dataset for counting vehicles and pedestrians from segments in drone-recorded video and an automatic counting system for such videos. The zenith drone view ensures minimal obstruction of tracked objects, which enables detailed traffic information. The proposed system achieves acceptable weighted precision, offering a solid comparison point for future research.

In future work, we plan to incorporate stabilization methods to compensate for drone instability under certain weather conditions and novel tracking techniques powered by neural networks and the Kalman filter [14]. We plan to use this work as a starting point for a route counting system. Also, conduct exhaustive experiments to determine whether the empirical values set for the rest of the parameters are adequate, including δ_{IoU}, τ_v, τ_p, etc. Despite our results, the approaches used in the detection and tracking modules need to be verified on sets with a more significant number of instances.

References

1. Economía y Sectores Productivos. Parque Vehicular. Vehículos de Motor Registrados en Circulación - Instituto Nacional de Estadística y Geografía. https://www.inegi.org.mx/programas/vehiculosmotor/. Accessed 12 Feb 2024
2. Ebrahimi, S.G., Seifnaraghi, N., Ince, E.A.: Traffic analysis of avenues and intersections based on video surveillance from fixed video cameras. In: 2009 IEEE 17th Signal Processing and Communications Applications Conference, pp. 848–851. IEEE (Institute of Electrical and Electronics Engineers), Antalya, Turkey (2009). https://doi.org/10.1109/SIU.2009.5136529
3. Prommool, P., Auephanwiriyakul, S., Theera-Umpon, N.: Vision-based automatic vehicle counting system using motion estimation with Taylor series approximation. In: 2016 6th IEEE International Conference on Control System, Computing and Engineering (ICCSCE), pp. 485–489. IEEE (Institute of Electrical and Electronics Engineers), Penang, Malaysia (2016). https://doi.org/10.1109/ICCSCE.2016.7893624
4. Xuezhi, X., Mingliang, Z., Ning, L., Abdulmotaleb, E.S.: Vehicle counting based on vehicle detection and tracking from aerial videos. Sensors **18**(8), 2560–2577 (2018)
5. Gomaa, A., Minematsu, T., Abdelwahab, M.M., Abo-Zahhad, M., Taniguchi, R.: Faster CNN-based vehicle detection and counting strategy for fixed camera scenes. Multimedia Tools Appl. 1–29 (2022). https://doi.org/10.1007/s11042-022-12370-9
6. Bochkovskiy, A., Chien-Yao, W., Hong-Yuan, M.: YOLOv4: Optimal Speed and Accuracy of Object Detection arXiv preprint arXiv:2004.10934 (2020)
7. Tsung-Yi, L., et al.: Microsoft COCO: Common Objects in Context arXiv preprint arXiv:1405.0312 (2014)
8. Salcedo, J.: Master's thesis: Conteo Automático de Vehículos en Movimiento a Partir de Videos Tomados por Drones. Centro de Investigación en Matemáticas, A.C. (2024)
9. Redmon, J., Farhadi, A.: YOLO9000: better, faster, stronger. In: IEEE Conference on Computer Vision and Pattern Recognition (CVPR), pp. 6517–6525 (2017)
10. Sheorey, S., Keshavamurthy, S., Yu, H., Nguyen, H.: Uncertainty estimation for KLT tracking. In: Asian Conference on Computer Vision, pp. 475–487. Springer (2014)
11. Chan, S., Vo, D., Nguyen, T.: Subpixel motion estimation without interpolation. In: IEEE International Conference on Acoustics, Speech and Signal Processing 2010, Dallas, Texas, pp. 722–725 (2010)
12. Bay, H., Ess, A., Tuytelaars, T., Gool, L.: Speeded-up robust features (SURF). Comput. Vis. Image Understand **110**, 346–359 (2008)
13. Barnich, O., Droogenbroeck, M.: ViBe: a universal background subtraction algorithm for video sequences. IEEE Trans. Image Process. **10**, 1709–17 (2011)
14. Wojke, N., Bewley, A., Paulus, D.: Simple online and realtime tracking with a deep association metric. In: IEEE International Conference on Image Processing (ICIP), pp. 3645–3649 (2017)

Real-Time Image Analysis Using a Depth Camera for UAV Applications

Arturo Javier Aceves Ramírez(✉) and Leopoldo Altamirano-Robles

National Institute of Astrophysics, Optics, and Electronics, Luis Enrique Erro 1, Puebla, Mexico
arturo.aceves@inaoe.mx, robles@inaoep.mx

Abstract. Depth cameras have demonstrated their ability to provide accurate distance measurements of the surrounding environment in multiple application areas. Similarly, UAVs are increasingly being deployed in various real-world scenarios. However, these platforms often operate under constraints such as limited computational power and strict weight restrictions. Therefore, some UAVs use a depth camera to have depth data. As raw depth data often contain significant noise or inaccurate measurements at different scales as distance changes, image correction techniques are essential for unplanned obstacle avoidance. We examine multiple steps to enhance image data for UAV obstacle avoidance, including the calibration process, the selection of a hole-filling filtering method to improve depth image quality by reducing the number of invalid pixels. We also propose an image processing algorithm based on exponential decay that mitigates the root mean square error of the distance measurements within 3,000 mm, 5,000 mm, and 7,000 mm by 0.64%, 4.42%, and 6.53% respectively relative to ground truth measurements. Finally, the algorithm was deployed on an NVIDIA Jetson Nano board, achieving 27 FPS on a 30 FPS configuration. The results obtained in this study enhance the quality of image data from this type of sensor, contributing to improved performance in UAV image analysis in challenging environments.

Keywords: Depth Image · Image Processing · UAV vision · Adaptive Correction

1 Introduction

Depth cameras have become widely used sensors in recent years. Their applications range from geographic map reconstruction [1], vision systems for welding robots [2] to the estimation of human anthropometric parameters [3]. This widespread adoption is mainly due to their ability to capture depth information at a relatively low cost. Like LiDAR sensors, depth cameras can reconstruct a scene within a specific field of view, enabling the extraction of spatial information as if it were observed directly by a human.

A. P. López-Monroy et al. (Eds.): MCPR 2025, LNCS 15715, pp. 201–212, 2025.
https://doi.org/10.1007/978-3-031-96255-4_19

Autonomous vehicle systems heavily rely on distance estimation to avoid collisions with surrounding objects, and unmanned aerial vehicles are no exception. UAVs have gained significant importance in commercial delivery [4] and military applications [5] due to their versatility and mobility. Integrating depth sensors with UAVs represents a natural progression for implementing object detection and collision avoidance systems. However, achieving a good performance requires the development of robust algorithms, proper sensor calibration, and data correction techniques to enhance the accuracy of depth information. This situation is critical, as multiple studies [6–8] have already utilized depth images as a foundation for obstacle avoidance.

In this work, we analyze the capabilities of depth cameras and propose several steps to refine depth image data. Our objective is to improve the quality of depth information for future autonomous path correction applications.

2 Related Works

Depth image correction can be achieved through various approaches. For instance, Vasudevan et al. [9] and Park et al. [10] propose different methods to reduce the number of invalid pixels and erroneous data caused by flying pixels, utilizing RGB data and neighboring pixel information for correction. Similarly, Xin et al. [11] apply multiple pixel-level operations to eliminate flying pixels, enhancing depth image segmentation. In these works, the number of invalid pixels in the image is reduced, resulting in more defined object borders. However, they do not analyze the error in distance measurement compared to the actual distance.

Several studies have explored multiple stereo camera fusion techniques (devices with more than one depth sensor) to improve depth image quality. Merrell et al. [12] proposed two algorithms to fuse multiple-depth images, enhancing the reconstruction of 3D models and real-world buildings. Xie et al. [13] introduced a three-camera fusion method to reduce the overall root mean square error (RMSE) in-depth measurements. In contrast, He et al. [14] proposed a multi-camera weighted correction approach to improve accuracy on flat and spherical surfaces at a distance of 1.5 m. In these works, the main goal was to enhance image reconstruction and depth data accuracy using multiple images or cameras.

This analysis leaves us with two approaches: one focuses on improving object definition without comparing it to real-world distances, while the other enhances depth measurement accuracy through multiple cameras. Therefore, improving the depth of the image using only a single camera in real time remains an open problem.

3 Depth Camera Selection and Calibration

First, we define the system constraints: the computing and image acquisition modules will operate on a relatively large UAV (655 mm) in outdoor environments, requiring optimized processing on embedded devices and reliable long-range depth sensing. While Time-of-Flight (ToF) and laser-based systems are commonly used, stereo vision sensors—based on dual-camera setups instead of emitter-receiver configurations—have gained traction due to their lower cost and reliability in dynamic conditions. Several manufacturers, such as Orbbec, ZED, and Oak-D, offer stereo cameras with diverse features; however, Intel's RealSense series is widely adopted in research for its accessibility, comprehensive software libraries, and tools for handling environmental variability. For this study, we selected the Intel RealSense D455 model from the D450 series—known for offering the most extensive working range among its peers—as a baseline for our initial implementation [15].

This camera offers an ideal depth sensing range from 0.5 to 6 m, with an absolute error of 2% for distances under 4 m and 4% beyond that. It features a depth field of view (FOV) of 87° × 58°, and can detect objects as close as 320 mm. The distance between its depth sensors is 95 mm, while the distance from the sensor to the protective glass is 4.55 mm. It also allows adjustment of frame rate and resolution, each involving specific trade-offs. Higher resolutions generate more depth data but reduce the maximum achievable frame rate, which is a critical factor for real-time applications on embedded platforms such as the Jetson Nano. To maintain stable performance and reduce computational load, we selected a resolution of 640 × 480 pixels, which provides 307,200 depth values per frame. This setting is approximately 32% lighter than the 848 × 480 resolution (407,040 values) and allows for a consistent frame rate of 30 fps, which is sufficient for our application.

One of the strengths of the RealSense system is its simplified calibration procedure, enabled by the Depth Quality Tool. In our case, the Tare Calibration was applied, as our objective is not precise 3D reconstruction but rather ensuring reliable depth estimations for obstacle avoidance. This method uses a calibration target with four reference points forming a rectangle and known distance from the camera to establish a ground truth. The target also includes a Gaussian blur to enhance texture detection during the process.

Additionally, a notable feature is that the calibration is stored internally within the camera controller. This on-chip calibration ensures that the parameters remain consistent across systems and are independent of the external computer used for the process.

To assess depth quality, the manufacturer provides a reference table for comparing calibration results against recommended thresholds. The calibration process yields an absolute health value, where lower values indicate better performance. Values below 0.25 are considered optimal (see Fig. 1 for calibration procedure and results).

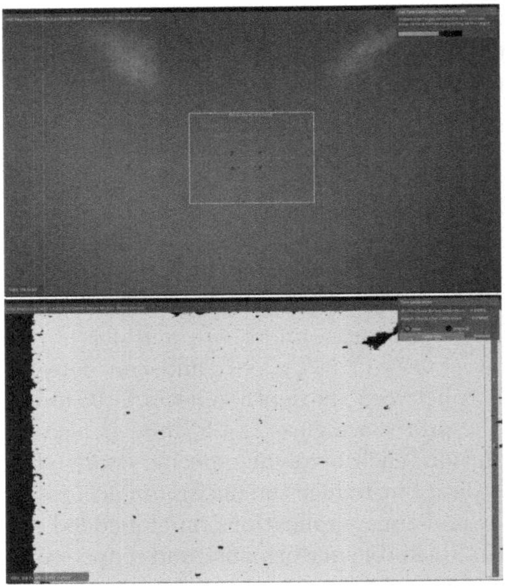

Fig. 1. Calibration view of the depth camera. The calibration process resulted in a −0.0370% health check, compared with the 0.2125% from the last calibration. This represents a 5.74-fold improvement in depth data quality. Source: Own work.

4 Image Acquisition and Filters

We utilize the Python Realsense SDK to obtain the depth data and identify the optimal configuration for this work.

A notable challenge in depth imaging is disparity, which often results in invalid pixels or shadow-like artifacts near object edges—especially at close range and along image borders. In the D455 model, these effects, most prominent on the left side, can be partially corrected through calibration. To further address these artifacts, the SDK already includes post-processing filters that reduce invalid pixels and smooth depth variations. While each filter introduces specific trade-offs, such as increased noise or error, maximizing obstacle information takes precedence over absolute accuracy in UAV navigation contexts.

Four filters are available to enhance image quality and reduce disparity; decimation, edge-preserving, temporal, and hole-hilling.

For this study, minimizing image disparity is the primary objective. It is important to note that the SDK does not classify border disparities as invalid pixels (and thus, not counted on invalid percentages), meaning they remain visible in controlled environments.

Among the evaluated methods, the fole-filling filter performs best (see Fig. 2) in reducing disparity while preserving depth continuity. Consequently, this filter is selected for depth image processing in this study. It is essential to mention that this filter adds at least 3% more error and noise to the measurements, as mentioned by the manufacturer on [15].

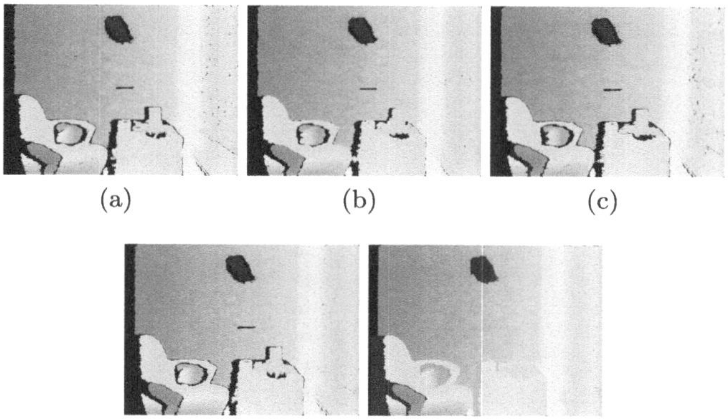

Fig. 2. Post-processed depth images using Jet scaling, resulting in varying percentages of valid pixels. (a) No filter - 96.7%, (b) Decimation filter - 97.23%, (c) Spatial filter - 96.9%, (d) Temporal filter - 97.23%, (e) Hole filling filter - 100%. Source: Own work.

5 Depth Camera Characterization and Corrections

We previously mentioned that the amount of information is more critical than accuracy. However, the latter can be improved once the initial filter has been selected. As a starting point, the manufacturer provides an Eq. (1) to estimate the root mean square (RMS) error associated with their products:

$$DeepthRMS = 2 \times tan(\frac{HFOV}{2}) \times \frac{D^2 \times Subpixel}{ResX \times Baseline} \tag{1}$$

Here, $HFOV$ is the horizontal field of view (in degrees), D is the measured distance (mm), $Subpixel$ represents disparity sensitivity influenced by surface and lighting conditions, $ResX$ is the horizontal resolution (pixels), and $Baseline$ is the separation between the depth sensors (mm). This expression assumes raw, unprocessed depth data.

To evaluate measurement quality, distances of 1,000 mm, 3,000 mm, 5,000 mm, and 7,000 mm were acquired from the image center over 20-second intervals. A second-degree polynomial regression was then fitted to the data using QR decomposition to model the trend (see Fig. 3).

Furthermore, we computed the residuals between the ground truth and the regression model to evaluate their discrepancies. Table 1 shows those results (see Fig. 4 for a comparison of the different RMS).

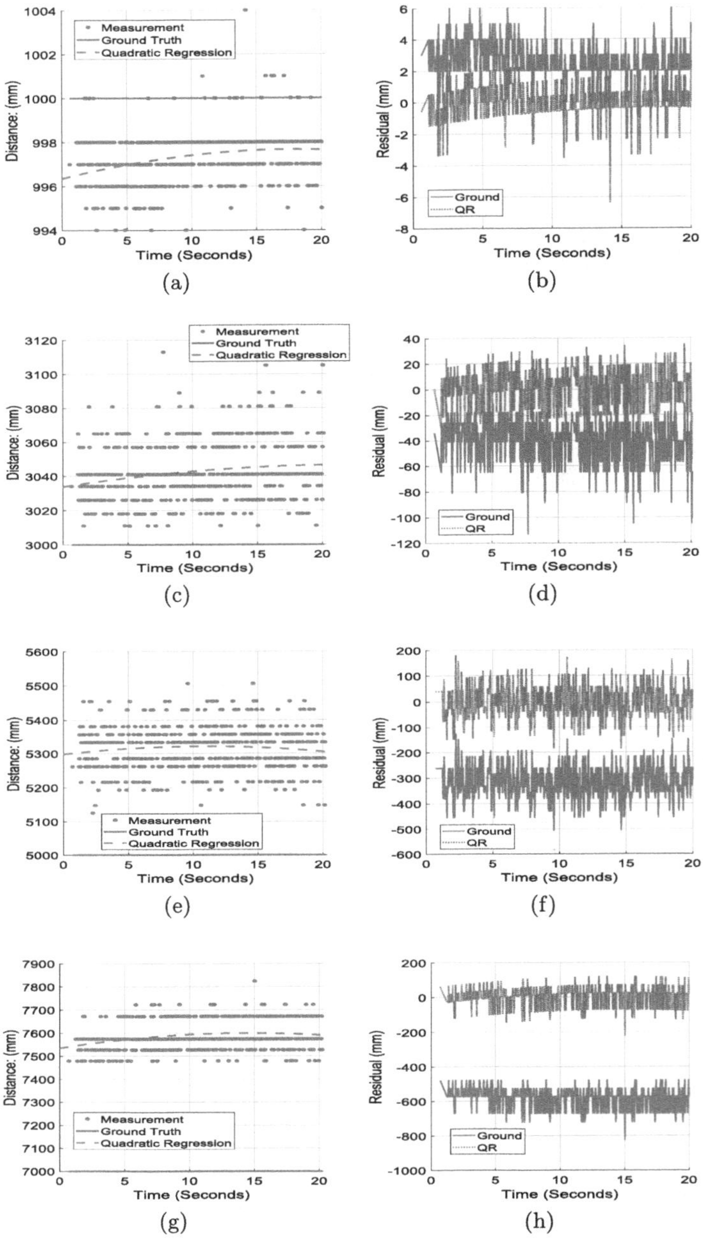

Fig. 3. Measurement results of the camera at multiple distances. From top to bottom, each row corresponds to measurements at 1, 3, 5, and 7 m. The left column shows the camera measurements compared to the ground truth and the quadratic regression. The right column displays the residuals between the ground truth and the regression. A noticeable offset in the residuals increases with distance. Source: Own work.

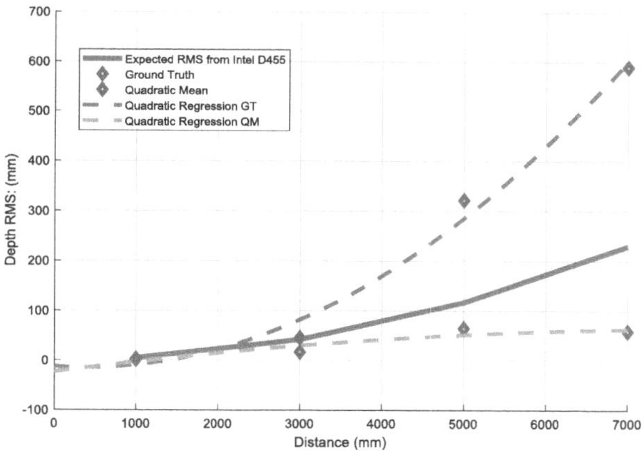

Fig. 4. Comparison between the expected RMS error, the RMS error with respect to ground truth data at each measurement point, and the RMS error obtained from the quadratic regression applied to the raw data at each measurement point (referred to as "Quadratic Mean" in the figure). Additionally, the quadratic regression was computed using the last two data sets to provide an overview of the RMS error trend. Source: Own work.

Table 1. Comparison of RMS errors between the ground truth, regression model, mean measurement, and subpixel estimation.

Ground Truth (mm)	RMS GT (mm)	RMS QR (mm)	Mean (mm)	Subpixel
1000	2.9179 (0.29%)	1.1125 (0.11%)	997.3252	0.0935
3000	45.5641 (1.52%)	16.7685 (0.56%)	3042	0.1622
5000	321.8589 (6.44%)	64.7113 (1.29%)	5315	0.4124
7000	589.0141 (8.41%)	58.4627 (0.84%)	7585	0.3851

As the distance increases, the RMS error also grows, particularly in the ground truth data, where subpixel estimations indicate a decline in measurement quality. The quadratic regression follows a similar trend but with an offset that becomes more noticeable at longer distances, although it remains close to the average of the measured values. To correct this behavior within the 1,000 to 7,000 mm operating range, we propose an empirical approach that mirrors the regression curve while eliminating the offset. This correction is based on an exponential decay function, which introduces minimal adjustments at short distances and gradually increases the correction factor as distance grows:

A pixel operation in the form of Eq. (2), which progressively reduces the pixel depth value as it increases, can enhance the camera's measurement accuracy—and, to a lesser extent, its precision—within the specified range (1,000 mm to 7,000 mm).

$$D_m(d) = d \times e^{-d \times k} \tag{2}$$

where D_m represents the modified distance, d is the measured distance, and k is a scaling factor.

To evaluate its practical behavior, the proposed formula was applied to the measured data using different values of k. The RMS error was then computed and compared against the expected values derived from the camera model on a graphic (see Fig. 5).

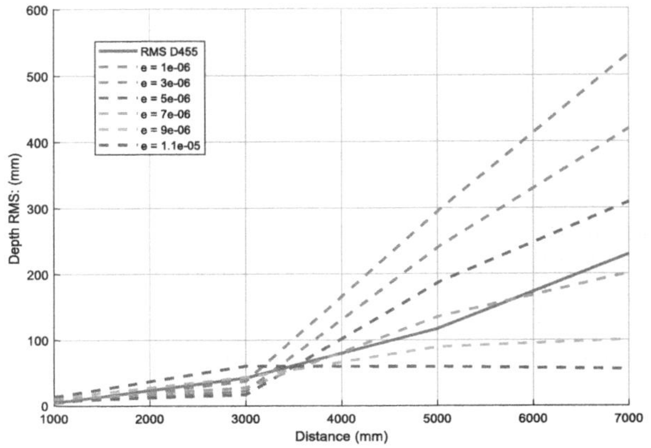

Fig. 5. Comparison of the RMS error (with ground truth) for different k values and the expected behavior. Source: Own work.

The results show that some of the tested values of k significantly reduce the RMS error. The best performance at long distances is observed with $k = 1\times10^{-5}$, although this choice results in a higher RMS error within the 1,000-3,000 mm range. For this shorter range, the optimal value is $k = 5 \times 10^{-6}$. Table 2 presents the exact RMS values for each case on columns 2 and 3.

For our application, we select the first value, as it yields lower overall error (0.79% vs. 4.41%) at greater distances.

To validate the effectiveness of this correction, we implemented this operation in our acquisition program on python (using the element-wise multiplication of NumPy) and repeated the measurements at the same ratios (see Fig. 6). Table 2 also gives the results of the pixel operation on column 4.

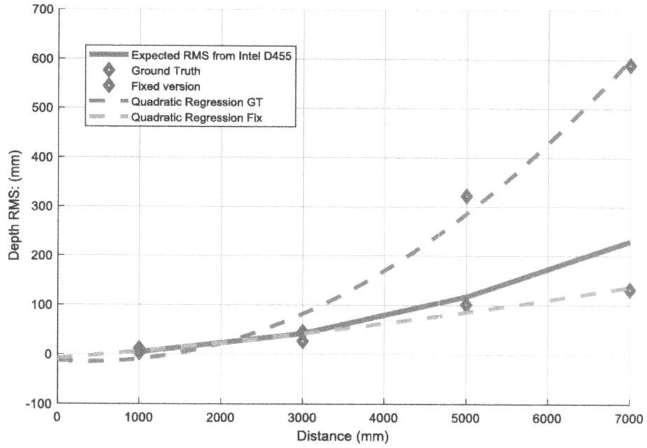

Fig. 6. Comparison between RMS (with ground truth) of original measurements, processed measurements and expected behavior. Source: Own work.

Table 2. RMS values for the theorical best performers values of k, and the real RMS of measurements with the pixel operation applied.

G.T. (mm)	$k = 5 \times 10^{-6}$ (mm)	$k = 1 \times 10^{-5}$ (mm)	Operation RMS (mm)
1000	7.7225 (0.77%)	13.6042 (1.36%)	11.6517 (1.16%)
3000	16.9894 (0.57%)	60.0564 (2%)	26.7950 (0.89%)
5000	186.2837 (3.73%)	59.1834 (1.18%)	100.7718 (2.02%)
7000	308.6697 (4.41%)	55.3351 (0.79%)	131.5612 (1.88%)

6 Embedded Device Implementation and Frame Rate Analysis

As this approach is intended for implementation on a UAV, it is crucial to ensure that the proposed operation modifies the image at a frequency that allows the vehicle to make corrections without requiring it to stop every time an obstacle is detected. Additionally, given that the UAV is expected to operate with a high degree of autonomy, the device responsible for image acquisition and correction must be on the vehicle. Thus, it must be as lightweight as possible.

An NVIDIA Jetson Nano (4 GB RAM) was used due to its low weight and compatibility with the Intel SDK. A minimal support structure was also designed to mount the camera and embedded device (Fig. 7).

The algorithm described previously was deployed on the embedded device, executing the image acquisition process 30 times. Frame processing time and total execution time were recorded, with the SDK frame rate fixed at 30 FPS as stated in Sect. 3. Table 3 summarizes the results.

(a) (b) (c)

Fig. 7. Experimental setup for the camera. (a) Environment with the support that holds the embedded device and the camera, (b) RGB image taken with the camera, (c) Depth image of (b).

Table 3. Image acquisition performance on the Jetson Nano. The bottom section presents the RMS related to the 30 FPS defined in the SDK, the mean FPS across all measurements, and the FPS calculated based on the total elapsed time.

Frame	Time (s)	FPS	Elapsed time (s)
1	0.0398	25.1484	0.0398
5	0.0366	27.3047	0.1889
10	0.0394	25.3737	0.3796
15	0.0364	27.4401	0.5670
20	0.0357	27.9930	0.7523
25	0.0330	30.2598	0.9235
30	0.0357	28.0244	1.0971
	RMS (FPS)	**Mean**	**Total FPS**
	3.0312	27.4753	27.3449

7 Results and Discussion

In the article's third section, we present a camera calibration procedure that improves the camera's absolute health check 5.74-fold compared to the factory configuration.

In the article's fourth section, we determined that the Realsense SDK hole-filling filter was the most effective in eliminating invalid pixels, achieving 100% reliability, excluding the disparity pixels on the left border. However, this filter performs worse than other proposed methods in object reconstruction, as it may lose finer details addressing flying pixels. RGB fusion methods are preferable for more accurate reconstruction, but it is necessary to implement this kind of algorithm (as Vasudevan et al. [9] and Park et al. [10]) and see the computing impact on small devices, like the Jetson Nano proposed here. This is proposed as a future research line, as this could also improve the RMS error we faced on this work.

In the article's fifth section, we proposed an exponential decay operation with a scaling factor of $k = 1 \times 10^{-5}$ to enhance accuracy in the 5,000-7,000 mm range. For this value, our pixel operation resulted in a positive difference of 0.64%, 4.42%, and 6.53% at 3,000 mm, 5,000 mm, and 7,000 mm, respectively. Conversely, a negative difference of 0.7% was observed on the 1,000 mm measurement. This result indicates that our operation improves measurements at long distances but introduces noise at closer ranges.

In the article's sixth section, the algorithm was deployed on a Jetson Nano, achieving 27.4753 FPS with an RMS deviation of 3.0312 FPS from the target 30 FPS, confirming its suitability for real-time embedded applications. Further study of alternative enhancement algorithms is recommended, especially considering the computational constraints of UAV systems.

It is important to consider that, despite the tools and features provided by depth cameras, challenges such as direct light sources, object reflectivity, and transparency remain difficult to fully address using stereo cameras and other light-based sensing technologies. These phenomena can lead to erroneous depth measurements and contribute to RMS errors. These limitations underline the relevance of exploring sensor fusion algorithms and physical optical filters as a promising avenue for improving measurement quality. Further research in this area is suggested as a potential direction for future work.

8 Conclusion

As stereo technologies become more affordable, a wider range of devices can incorporate them to enhance the measurements required for various projects. Furthermore, unmanned aerial vehicles (UAVs) increasingly demand more sophisticated sensors to capture environmental conditions better. Assessing the reliability of these technologies and improving their performance, whether through pixel-level operations or sensor fusion, is crucial, particularly for projects operating in complex environments, such as the Dragonfly rotorcraft or the Ingenuity helicopter.

In this context, we explored the capabilities of edge technology stereo cameras and carried out the necessary steps for image acquisition. By analyzing the error behavior, we developed and proposed an algorithm to reduce it, thereby enhancing the accuracy of the acquired data and contributing to the refinement of vision-based sensing for UAV applications.

Acknowledgments. We sincerely appreciate the support of Secihti for providing its financial support through a master's scholarship for the first author.

Data Availibility Statement. The code and data will be publicly available on GitHub following the presentation and publication of the associated first author's master's degree "Real-Time Quadrotor Trajectory Update Based on Area Analysis for Adaptive Evasion of Undetected Obstacles" thesis work.

Disclosure of Interests. The authors declare that the findings of this study may be used in future research related to image processing and obstacle avoidance. However, there are no competing interests affecting the results presented in this paper

References

1. Masiero, A., Sofia, G., Tarolli, P.: Quick 3D with UAV and TOF camera for geomorphometric assessment. Int. Arch. Photogram. Remote Sens. Spatial Inf. Sci. XLIII-B1-2020, 259–264 (2020)
2. Li, M., Huang, J., Xue, L., et al.: A guidance system for robotic welding based on an improved YOLOv5 algorithm with a RealSense depth camera. Sci. Rep. **13**, 21299 (2023). https://doi.org/10.1038/s41598-023-48318-8
3. Krzeszowski, T., Dziadek, B., França, C., Martins, F., Gouveia, É.R., Przednowek, K.: System for estimation of human anthropometric parameters based on data from kinect v2 depth camera. Sensors (2023)
4. Holt, K.: Amazon plans to start drone deliveries in the UK and Italy next year. Engadget (2023). https://www.engadget.com/amazon-plans-to-start-drone-deliveries-in-the-uk-and-italy-next-year-185027120.html
5. Parrot: Parrot selected by the U.S. defense innovation unit as a major drone supplier (2020). https://www.parrot.com/en/newsroom/parrot-diu-blue-suas
6. Haque, A.U., Nejadpak, A.: Obstacle Avoidance Using Stereo Camera. arXiv (2017). https://doi.org/10.48550/arXiv.1705.04114
7. Kalidas, A.P., Joshua, C.J., Md, A.Q., Basheer, S., Mohan, S., Sakri, S.: Deep reinforcement learning for vision-based navigation of UAVs in avoiding stationary and mobile obstacles. Drones **7**(4), 245 (2023). https://doi.org/10.3390/drones7040245
8. Park, J., Choi, A.J.: Vision-based in-flight collision avoidance control based on background subtraction using embedded system. Sensors **23** (2023)
9. Vasudevan, E., Sridhara, S.N., Pavez, E., Ortega, A., Singh, R., Kalluri, S.: Color-guided flying pixel correction in depth images. In: 2024 IEEE 26th International Workshop on Multimedia Signal Processing (MMSP), pp. 1–6 (2024)
10. Park, H.J., Kim, K.B.: Depth image correction for intel realsense depth camera. Indones. J. Electr. Eng. Comput. Sci. (2020)
11. Qiao, X., Ge, C., Yao, H., Deng, P., Zhou, Y.: Valid depth data extraction and correction for time-of-flight camera. In: Proceedings of SPIE 11433, Twelfth International Conference on Machine Vision, 114332K (2020). https://doi.org/10.1117/12.2557533
12. Merrell, P., et al.: Real-time visibility-based fusion of depth maps. In: Proceedings of the IEEE International Conference on Computer Vision, pp. 1–8 (2007). https://doi.org/10.1109/ICCV.2007.4408984
13. Xie, Z., Zhao, M., He, Y.: Research on depth information acquisition of array camera based on depth map fusion. In: 2023 5th International Conference on Frontiers Technology of Information and Computer (ICFTIC), pp. 759–762 (2023)
14. He, Y., Chen, S.: Error correction of depth images for multiview time-of-flight vision sensors. Int. J. Adv. Rob. Syst. (2020). https://doi.org/10.1177/1729881420942379
15. Intel. Intel RealSense Product Family D400 Series. Rev. 19, p. 90 (2024). https://www.intelrealsense.com/wp-content/uploads/2024/10/Intel-RealSense-D400-Series-Datasheet-October-2024.pdf?_ga=2.233788766.1534421282.1738190205-1484730474.1738021416

Extending Reference-Based Texture Transformers for Image Dehazing

Esteban Reyes-Saldaña and Mariano Rivera(✉)

Centro de Investigacion en Matematicas A.C., 36120 Guanajuato, Mexico
{esteban.reyes,mrivera}@cimat.mx

Abstract. Image dehazing is a specific image restoration task that aims to recover the quality and clarity of a haze image caused by ambient phenomena. In this paper, we present a novel transformer-based approach for image restoration and texture enhancement. Our model adopts novel Reference Super-Resolution (RefSR) deep models capable of transferring high-resolution texture information from a reference image to a blurred image, and we named it TTDN. Our approach employs a VGG19-based network for deep feature extraction and then unfolds these features into patches. Then, we incorporate textures at multiple scales, enhanced by gradient density information, into a cohesive reconstruction through a simple residual network. Experimental results demonstrate that our approach achieves competitive state-of-the-art performance for both peak signal-to-noise ratio (PSNR) and structure similarity index (SSIM) metrics. Moreover, our approach offers a significant contribution to the field by adapting the RefSR paradigm and improving the computational feasibility of patch-based texture transfer. Experimental results in the test RESIDE-indoor data set show competitive metric results that other SOTA methods while improving efficiency in large-scale images by using larger patches with larger strides. Our results suggest that the proposed transfer strategy can be applied to other image restoration tasks, offering a promising avenue for future research.

Keywords: Image Dehazing · Texture Transformers · Texture Transference

1 Introduction

The paradigm of image restoration aims to recover accurate visual patterns for tasks such as image deraining, dehazing, and super-resolution. Image dehazing specifically targets recovering clarity and reducing distortions caused by environmental factors, manifesting as changes in contrast and color intensity [19]. Several theoretical approaches have been developed to model this physical phenomenon [3,6,20]. Since the emergence of convolutional neural networks (CNNs) in image processing [12], substantial advances have been made specifically in image dehazing [21,29]. However, standard CNN methods often struggle to capture long-range dependencies due to their local assumptions. To address

A. P. López-Monroy et al. (Eds.): MCPR 2025, LNCS 15715, pp. 213–223, 2025.
https://doi.org/10.1007/978-3-031-96255-4_20

this limitation, U-Net-based approaches [21] have been proposed, demonstrating improved performance, as exemplified in [13]. More recently, transformer architectures [24], originally successful in natural language processing (NLP) due to their self-attention mechanisms, have been adapted to image tasks. For example, Vision Transformers (ViT) [4] utilize self-attention by splitting images into flat patches to effectively identify correlations. Methods such as [7,16,25] incorporate attention mechanisms into U-Net architectures for image dehazing, achieving state-of-the-art (SoTA) results employing channel attention to overcome computational issues associated with spatial self-attention.

The concept of texture transfer from high-fidelity reference images has been successfully applied to image dehazing [5], particularly by quantifying fog in dynamic scenes. Such reference-based image enhancement strategies have also found success in other image restoration domains, notably super-resolution [31]. The approach involves providing a high-quality reference along with a degraded image and transferring vital information to improve reconstruction. Certain data sets [31] offer custom-made paired reference images specifically for Reference Super-Resolution (RefSR). However, in the absence of explicitly paired references, alternative approaches include selecting random images from the same data set or using self-referential strategies.

Image Super-Resolution, as image hazing, is another problem related to image restoration. Image Super-Resolution operates under two primary paradigms: Single Image Super-Resolution (SISR) and Reference-Based Super-Resolution (RefSR). Similarly to image dehazing, SISR aims to restore critical texture, color, and structural information. RefSR differs by explicitly utilizing texture transfer from a reference image exhibiting certain similarities. Recent advancements leveraging Vision Transformers have significantly improved RefSR outcomes. For example, TTSR [28] employs attention mechanisms, effectively transferring textures from a reference image by computing attention matrices Q, K, V through a learnable feature extractor and using cross-attention to enhance SR reconstruction. Other contributions [15] introduced novel backbone architectures capable of better feature extraction and refinement. Additional works [26,27] highlight the need for improved texture searches to yield clearer images, using multiple references for enhanced accuracy. Methods such as [9,18] implement a two-stage texture filtering process: initial operation of a coarse block search followed by a dense, refined search, optimizing memory usage by conducting correlations at lower resolutions. These approaches incorporate final corrections through contrast or gradient adjustments.

While reference-based texture transfer is beneficial for both super-resolution and image dehazing, existing methods exhibit limitations: specifically, inaccuracies in matching patches between degraded and high-quality images, and inefficient memory usage. To mitigate these issues, we propose a more efficient patch-based search strategy. Unlike previous methods such as [28], our approach partitions images into 6×6 patches with a stride of $s = 2$, thereby reducing memory consumption and allowing the processing of large-scale images during dense correlation searches. We use *TopK* patch matches between low-quality and high-quality images to improve restoration results.

Our methodology uses a VGG19-based network for deep feature extraction and then unfolds these features into patches. An optimized search algorithm identifies *TopK* patch correspondences using larger kernel sizes and strides, significantly improving memory efficiency compared to [18,28]. Finally, we incorporate textures at multiple scales, enhanced by gradient density information, into a cohesive reconstruction through a simple residual network.

The main contributions of this paper are as follows.

1. Adapting a RefSR Transformer-based method to the image dehazing task, leveraging reference-based texture transfer.
2. Introducing an efficient texture matching strategy that employs larger kernel and stride sizes, optimizes memory usage, and maintains high PSNR/SSIM performance.
3. Proposing a Gradient Density-Enhancing Module (GDE) that merges textures from multiple feature scales by a straightforward recurrent network.
4. Conducting comprehensive experiments on established datasets, demonstrating the effectiveness of our texture transfer methodology across various image restoration tasks.

The code is available at https://github.com/esteban-rs/TTDN-dehaze.

2 Method

Our proposal, the Texture Transformer Dehaze Network (TTDN), consists of four modules: Feature Encoder (FE), Search and Transfer Module (ST), Cross-Scale Feature Integration (CSFI) and Gradient Density Enhancing Module (GDE). The main scheme is shown in Fig. 1. First, FE encodes the haze image (x_h). Then, the relevant textures of the reference are selected and merged into the haze features by the CSFI module. Finally, gradient information, from the image reference, is incorporated in the reconstruction by the GDE module, not illustrated.

The model produces a texture-enhanced dehaze image. It inputs (x_h, y_h, y). x_h represents the input haze image, y_h is the haze version of the reference image, and y is a clear reference image without haze. Using the FE, we produce Q, K, V feature maps and find the correlation matrix (R) using Q, K normalized inner product between patches. Then we filtered the best patches based on the correlation matrix R and then we took the matches *TopK* for each patch. We integrate the features obtained on three different scales using a Cross Scale Feature Integration [28] and finally, we add the gradient density of the image x_h to improve structural information and create the clear dehaze image. The following subsections present the details of the modules mentioned above.

2.1 Feature Encoder

We transform the data into a new representation with more evident complex characteristics at different resolutions. For this purpose, we used the output in

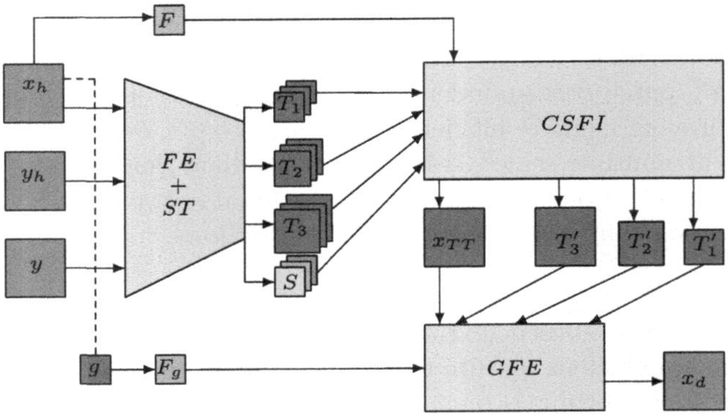

Fig. 1. Texture transformer for dehazing network architecture.

different blocks (resolutions) of the VGG19 [22] backbone previously trained with ImageNet [1]. Let (x_h, y_h, y) be the input to our feature encoder. The output can be formulated as

$$\left[\mathbf{Q}^l\right]_{l=1,2,3} = FE(x_h) \tag{1}$$

$$\left[\mathbf{K}^l\right]_{l=1,2,3} = FE(y_h) \tag{2}$$

$$\left[\mathbf{V}^l\right]_{l=1,2,3} = FE(y) \tag{3}$$

where l denotes the depth of FE. Similarly to [28], we take three depths of features from VGG19. This reduces the highness and width of the tensor by a factor of 2 from the level l to the next level $l + 1$. In addition, the number of channels of the three feature tensors is 64, 128, and 256; respectively (Fig. 2).

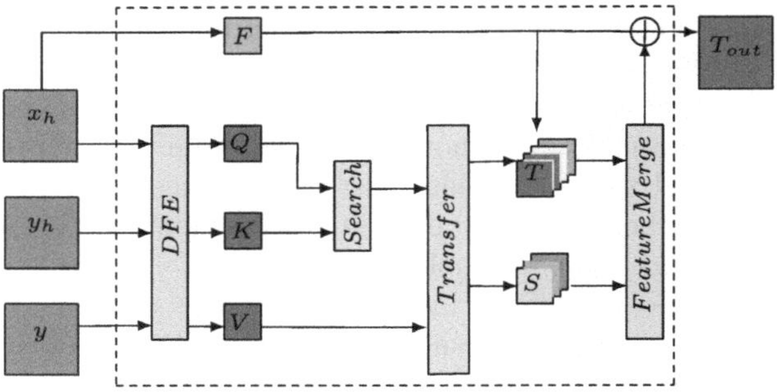

Fig. 2. The feature encoder computes the texture features of the input (x_h, y_h, y). For each texture pixel in the hazed image, we transfer *TopK* texture pixels from the reference; see text.

2.2 Search and Transfer Module

We infer correlations between x_h and y_h using attention through $\mathbf{Q}^l$ and $\mathbf{K}^l$. First, we divide $\mathbf{Q}^l, \mathbf{K}^l$ into overlapping patches $q_i^l : i \in [1, 2, \ldots, H_{LR} \times W_{LR}]$ and $k_j^l : j \in [1, 2, \ldots, H_{Ref} \times W_{Ref}]$, respectively. The correlation matrix is computed as the normalized inner product

$$c_{i,j}^l = \left\langle \frac{q_i^l}{||q_i^l||}, \frac{k_j^l}{||k_j^l||} \right\rangle. \tag{4}$$

For each q_i^l, we keep the $TopK(\cdot)$ score-indices of the key patches $\{k_j^l\}_{j=1}^{H_{Ref} \times W_{Ref}}$. Different from the original transformer TTSR [28] that use only the arg max and max score for each patch and other recent methods [9,18] that perform a double search, we introduce more feature information by obtaining several index and score mappings $H^l = \{H_1^l, H_2^l, \ldots, H_K^l\}$ and $S^l = \{S_1^l, S_2^l, \ldots, S_K^l\}$ where

$$H^l, S^l = TopK(C^l) \tag{5}$$

Using these index mappings, we select the best textures from V^l using the Hard Attention Matrices (H^l) matrices as index

$$T_n^l = S_n^l \cdot \mathbf{V}_{H_n^l}^l. \tag{6}$$

where $n \in \{1, 2, \ldots, K\}$. In experiments, we only use $l = 3$ for matrix correlation calculation and interpolate it to select textures at the highest levels.

2.3 Cross-Scale Feature Integration

Inspired by SoTA methods for style/texture transferring [8,30], We integrate the previous attention results at different scales following [28]; this can be modeled as

$$x_{TT}, T_1, T_2, T_3 = CCFI(\{T^l\}_{l=1,2,3});$$

where x_{TT} is the merged texture using the same Cross Scale configuration that [28] and T_1, T_2, T_3 are the synthesized textures at the three scale levels.

2.4 Gradient Enhancing Density Module

To provide more information about the structure of the haze image, some work has been done [17,23]. We incorporate a Gradient Enhancement module to add structural and edge information to the partial output of the $CSFI(\cdot)$. First, we extract the Gradient Density for each of the RGB image channels and convolve the image with 3×3 Sobel filter kernels [11] from x and y derivative directions; K_x and K_y, respectively. and calculate Gradient Density as

$$GD(I) = \sqrt{(K_x * I)^2 + (K_y * I)^2}.$$

Now, we pass the density of the image gradient g through a residual feature extractor: $F_g = GFE(g)$. Finally, using the output from $CSFI(\cdot)$: x_{TT}, T_1, T_2, T_3, the final image is formulate as

$$\begin{aligned} x_{1g} &= RB_1(Conv(Concat(F_g, T_3))) \\ x_{2g} &= RB_2(Conv(Concat(x_{1g}\uparrow, T_2))) \\ x_{3g} &= RB_3(Conv(Concat(x_{3g}\uparrow, T_3))) \\ x_d &= Conv(Concat(x_{3g}, x_{TT})) \end{aligned}$$

where $RB(\cdot)$ represents a residual scheme and $\uparrow$ is $2\times$ bicubic upsampling.

2.5 Loss Function

The overall loss is

$$\mathcal{L}_{total} = (chw)^{-1}||x - x_h||_1, \tag{7}$$

with c, h, w the channel, height, weight of x_h and x the image to dehaze.

2.6 Implementation Details

The window size for extracting patches is set to $k = 6$ with padding $s = 2$ for both training and testing. For both x_h and for the extraction of shallow gradient features, we use residual blocks 16. The architecture of the residual blocks in the model $CSFI$ is [16, 8, 4] and [9, 9, 9] for GDE for each level. To find the correlation matrix, we use only the deepest feature extractor level to perform matrix multiplication and up-sample it to higher levels. We use data augmentation for training by randomly flipping up and left-right followed by a random rotation of $90°, 180°, 270°$ with a batch fixed to 1. An Adam optimizer with $lr = 1e^{-4}$, $\beta_1 = 0.9$, $\beta_2 = 0.999$ and default $\epsilon = 1e^{-8}$. All experiments were performed in a single GPU NVIDIA GeForce RTX 3090 using PyTorch. The average time per epoch was 1.96 hours for a total of 13990 augmented pair images and a total of 400 epochs. The capability of the purpose model to be tested in a single GPU (24Gb) is an important advantage when considering the image resolutions in the correlation matrix calculation.

3 Experiments and Results

3.1 Metrics and Datasets

Following the recent work, we use two metrics to evaluate our results: Peak signal-to-noise ratio (PSNR) and structure similarity index (SSIM) [10]. The PSNR is defined as

$$PSNR(f, g) = 10 \log_{10}(255/\text{mse}(f, g))$$

where mse is the Mean Square Error. SSIM is defined as

$$SSIM(f, g) = l(f, g)c(f, g)s(f, g)$$

Table 1. Quantitative metric results of the generated images using PSNR/SSIM.

Method	PSNR	SSIM
U-Former [25]	31.91	0.971
DM2F [2]	34.29	0.984
CL2S [20]	35.36	0.981
GridDehazeNet [16]	32.16	0.984
U2-Former [7]	**36.42**	0.988
TTDN (ours)	35.43	**0.989**

with $l(f,g) = (2\mu_f\mu_g + k_1)/(\mu_f^2 + \mu_g^2 + k_1)$, $c(f,g) = (2\sigma_f\sigma_g + k_2)/(\sigma_f^2 + \sigma_g^2 + k_2)$, $s(f,g) = (2\sigma_{fg} + k_3)/(\sigma_f\sigma_g + k_3)$, $\{c_k\}_{k=1,2,3}$ are parameters (constants) of the metrics, $\{\mu_z\}_{z=f,g}$ and $\{\sigma_z^2\}_{z=f,g,fg}$ are the mean values and (co)variances, respectively. The first term compares the luminescence, the second term compares the contrast, and the third term compares the structure.

3.2 Datasets

To prove the effectiveness of the proposed transformer for the image transfer feature in the dehazing task, we use the RESIDE-indoor data set [14]. It contains 13,990 indoor haze images with a certain haze grade. Since there are no direct reference pairs, we choose a random image from the dataset. We used 500 synthetic haze test images to evaluate them and also used a random image from the test set as a reference. All dehaze results are evaluated for PSRN and SSIM on the Y channel of the YCbCr space.

3.3 Results

To evaluate our method, we performed experiments on the RESIDE-Indoor dataset. Table 1 summarizes the main results (PSNR and SSIM metrics) of our proposal and SotA methods. Our model shows competitive metric results and is computationally efficient when processing large-scale images. Figure 3 shows some visual results with other novel models and Fig. 4 compares the results using different haze gradients.

We also compared different configurations of our model with kernel, padding, and stride sizes. Table 2 shows that the use of larger kernels with larger strides is efficient in calculating the correlation matrix in 4. This allows us to manage larger images (up to 1024px in the testing phase).

3.4 Ablation Study

We study different configurations for our model. Table 3 shows the importance of different modules in our model. The results show the importance of adding the Gradient Density Enhanced module and also using more textures in the Eq. 5. All models were trained in a single GPU using the RESIDE Indoor TestSet.

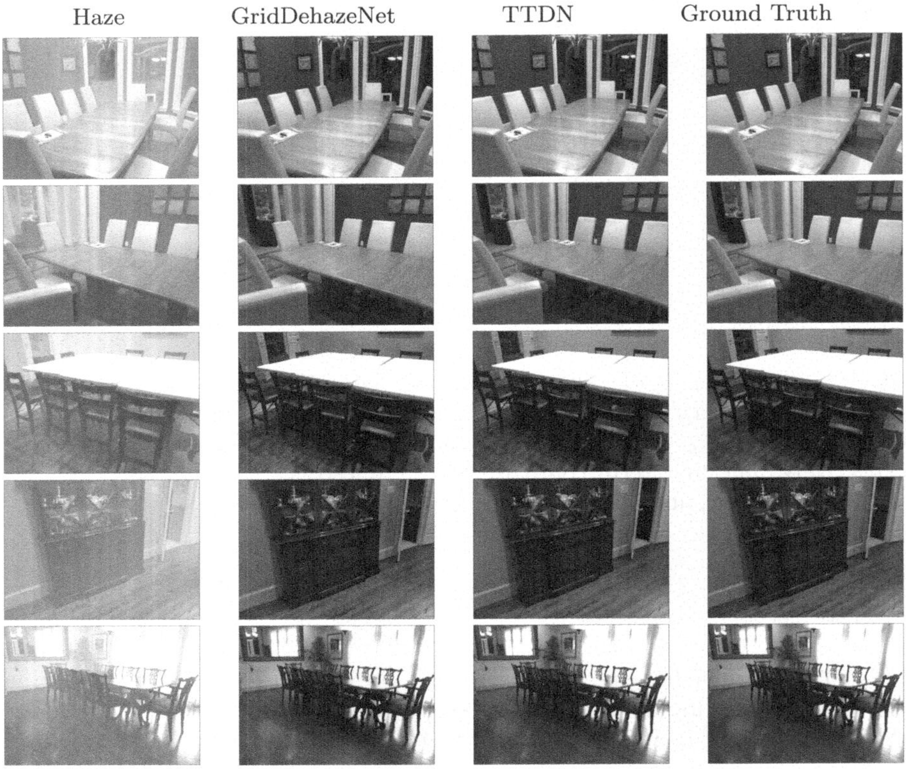

Fig. 3. Experimental visual results: we compare our model with available testing models online using Reside Indoor Test Set.

Table 2. Method hyperparameters for calculating the correlation matrix between input and reference image.

Kernel Size	padding	stride	Correlation shape for input $(1024, 1024, 3)$
3×3	1	1	$(256 \times 256, 3 \times 3 \times 256)$
6×6	2	2	$(128 \times 128, 6 \times 6 \times 256)$
12×12	4	4	$(64 \times 64, 12 \times 12 \times 256)$

Table 3. Proposed model performance for different configuration: PSNR and SSIM metrics.

Config	PSNR/SSIM	Params(M)
TTDN (no GDE)	36.38/.987	9.92
TTDN (top-1)	36.28/.983	10.25
TTDN (top-2)	36.35/.987	10.65
TTDN (top-3)	**36.42/.989**	10.91

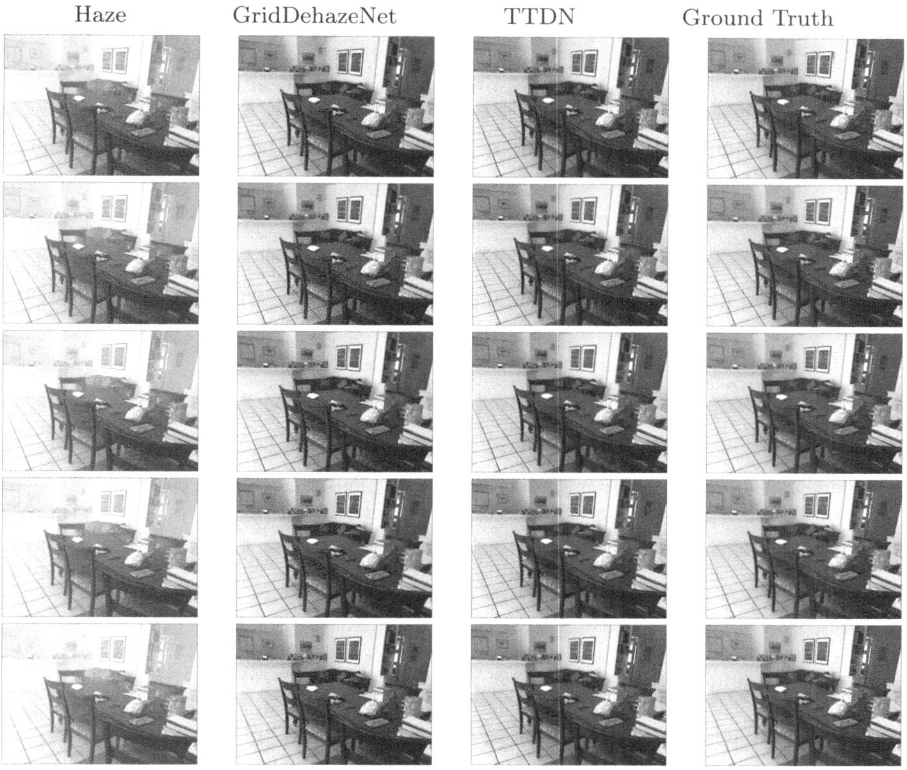

Fig. 4. We compared our results with different haze degrees from five to ten sampling an image for the RESIDE-INDOOR dataset.

4 Conclusions

We presented a novel transformer-based method for image dehazing, leveraging Reference Super-Resolution (RefSR) strategies. Our proposed TTDN approach effectively restores hazy images by transferring detailed texture information from a high-resolution reference image to the degraded input, substantially enhancing visual clarity and quality. We addressed critical issues such as memory inefficiency and inaccuracies in texture matching by introducing an optimized patch-splitting strategy that significantly improves computational scalability without compromising performance. Additionally, our Gradient Density Enhancing Module effectively incorporates structural and edge information, further refining the restoration quality.

Experimental evaluations confirmed that TTDN achieves state-of-the-art performance, as demonstrated by competitive PSNR and SSIM metrics, thereby validating its effectiveness in image-dehazing applications. By successfully adapting the RefSR paradigm to the dehazing domain and enhancing computational efficiency in texture transfer processes, our method contributes significantly to both theoretical and practical aspects of image restoration research. The promising results indicate that our proposed texture transfer approach can be extended to other image restoration scenarios, providing a solid foundation for future exploration. Ultimately, our work underscores the substantial potential of transformer-based architectures to address persistent challenges in image restoration, and we anticipate it will inspire continued advancements in this field.

Acknowledgments. This work was supported in part by SECIHTI, Mexico: PhD scholarship (ER-S) and research grant CB-A1-43858 (MR).

References

1. Deng, J., Dong, W., Socher, R., Li, L., Li, K., Fei-Fei, L.: Imagenet: a large-scale hierarchical image database. In: Proceedings of IEEE CVPR, pp. 248–255. IEEE (2009)
2. Deng, Z., et al.: Deep multi-model fusion for single-image dehazing. In: Proceedings of IEEE/CVF ICCV, pp. 2453–2462 (2019)
3. Dong, J., Pan, J.: Physics-based feature dehazing networks. In: Vedaldi, A., Bischof, H., Brox, T., Frahm, J.-M. (eds.) ECCV 2020. LNCS, vol. 12375, pp. 188–204. Springer, Cham (2020). https://doi.org/10.1007/978-3-030-58577-8_12
4. Dosovitskiy, A., et al.: An image is worth 16x16 words: transformers for image recognition at scale. In: Proceedings of ICLR (2021)
5. El Khoury, J., Thomas, J.B., Mansouri, A.: A database with reference for image dehazing evaluation. J. Imaging Sci. Technol. **62**(1), 10503–1 (2018)
6. Fattal, R.: Dehazing using color-lines. ACM Trans. Graph. (TOG) **34**(1), 1–14 (2014)
7. Feng, X., Ji, H., Pei, W., Li, J., Lu, G., Zhang, D.: U^2-former: nested U-shaped transformer for image restoration via multi-view contrastive learning. IEEE Trans. Circuits Syst. Video Technol. **34**(1), 168–181 (2023)
8. Gatys, L., Ecker, A., Bethge, M.: A neural algorithm of artistic style. J. Vis. **16**(12), 326 (2016)
9. Guo, K., Chen, L., Zhu, X., Kui, X., Zhang, J., Shi, H.: Double-layer search and adaptive pooling fusion for reference-based image super-resolution. ACM Trans. Multimed. Comput. Commun. Appl. **20**(1), 1–23 (2023)
10. Horé, A., Ziou, D.: Image quality metrics: PSNR vs. SSIM. In: Proceedings of ICPR, pp. 2366–2369 (2010)
11. Kanopoulos, N., Vasanthavada, N., Baker, R.: Design of an image edge detection filter using the sobel operator. IEEE J. Solid-State Circ. **23**(2), 358–367 (1988)
12. Krizhevsky, A., Sutskever, I., Hinton, G.E.: Imagenet classification with deep convolutional neural networks. Commun. ACM **60**(6), 84–90 (2017)
13. Lee, Y.W., Wong, L.K., See, J.: Image dehazing with contextualized attentive U-net. In: Proceedings of IEEE ICIP, pp. 1068–1072. IEEE (2020)
14. Li, B., et al.: Benchmarking single-image dehazing and beyond. IEEE Trans. Image Process. **28**(1), 492–505 (2019)
15. Lin, R., Xiao, N.: Dual projection fusion for reference-based image super-resolution. Sensors **22**(11), 4119 (2022)

16. Liu, X., Ma, Y., Shi, Z., Chen, J.: Griddehazenet: attention-based multi-scale network for image dehazing. In: Proceedings of the IEEE/CVF International Conference on Computer Vision, pp. 7314–7323 (2019)
17. Liu, Z., Feng, R., Wang, L., Zeng, T.: Gradient prior dilated convolution network for remote sensing image super-resolution. IEEE J. Sel. Top. Appl. Earth Obs. Remote Sens. **16**, 3945–3958 (2023)
18. Lu, L., Li, W., Tao, X., Lu, J., Jia, J.: MASA-SR: matching acceleration and spatial adaptation for reference-based image super-resolution. In: Proceedings of the IEEE/CVF Conference on Computer Vision and Pattern Recognition, pp. 6368–6377 (2021)
19. Narasimhan, S.G., Nayar, S.K.: Vision and the atmosphere. Int. J. Comput. Vis. **48**, 233–254 (2002)
20. Rohn, Y.: Rethinking the elementary function fusion for single-image dehazing (2024)
21. Ronneberger, O., Fischer, P., Brox, T.: U-net: convolutional networks for biomedical image segmentation. In: Proceedings of MICCAI, Part III 18, pp. 234–241. Springer (2015)
22. Simonyan, K., Zisserman, A.: Very deep convolutional networks for large-scale image recognition, pp. 1–14. Computational and Biological Learning Society (2015)
23. Sun, J., Xu, Z., Shum, H.Y.: Gradient profile prior and its applications in image super-resolution and enhancement. IEEE Trans. Image Process. **20**, 1529–1542 (2010)
24. Vaswani, A.: Attention is all you need. In: Advances in Neural Information Processing Systems (2017)
25. Wang, Z., Cun, X., Bao, J., Zhou, W., Liu, J., Li, H.: Uformer: a general U-shaped transformer for image restoration. In: Proceedings of the IEEE/CVF Conference on Computer Vision and Pattern Recognition, pp. 17683–17693 (2022)
26. Xie, Y., Xiao, J., Sun, M., Yao, C., Huang, K.: Feature representation matters: end-to-end learning for reference-based image super-resolution. In: Computer Vision – ECCV, pp. 230–245 (2020)
27. Yan, X., Zhao, W., Yuan, K., Zhang, R., Li, Z., Cui, S.: Towards content-independent multi-reference super-resolution: adaptive pattern matching and feature aggregation. In: Computer Vision – ECCV, pp. 52–68. Springer (2020)
28. Yang, F., Yang, H., Fu, J., Lu, H., Guo, B.: Learning texture transformer network for image super-resolution. In: Proceedings of IEEE CVPR, pp. 5791–5800. IEEE (2020)
29. Zamir, S.W., et al.: Learning enriched features for real image restoration and enhancement. In: Vedaldi, A., Bischof, H., Brox, T., Frahm, J.-M. (eds.) ECCV 2020. LNCS, vol. 12370, pp. 492–511. Springer, Cham (2020). https://doi.org/10.1007/978-3-030-58595-2_30
30. Zeng, Y., Fu, J., Chao, H., Guo, B.: Learning pyramid-context encoder network for high-quality image inpainting. In: Proceedings of IEEE CVPR, pp. 1486–1494. IEEE (2019)
31. Zhang, Z., Wang, Z., Lin, Z., Qi, H.: Image super-resolution by neural texture transfer. In: Proceedings of IEEE CVPR, pp. 7982–7991. IEEE (2019)

Vision-Based Formation Control Using Visual Servoing and Virtual Homographies

Edgar I. Chavez-Aparicio(✉), Hector M. Becerra, and Jean-Bernard Hayet

Computer Science Department, Centro de Investigación en Matemáticas (CIMAT), Jalisco S/N, Col. Valenciana, 36023 Guanajuato, GTO, Mexico
{edgar.chavez,hector.becerra,jbhayet}@cimat.mx

Abstract. This paper introduces a novel formation control algorithm for unmanned air vehicles equipped with cameras. It leverages the use of consensus theory to share visual information in a Multiple Agent System. Then, multiple-view geometry is used through the use of synthetic homographies that define a set of reference points to be used by a image-based visual servoing based controller. Our algorithm is distributed and does not require prior information other than the relative states of agents. Also, this approach does not require to know a global reference frame which is appealing for the GPS-denied environments. We present convincing experiments performed under the Gazebo simulator.

Keywords: Formation control · Visual geometry · Visual servoing

1 Introduction

Ranging from construction techniques [7] to fire management [10] or agriculture [5], the applications of coordinated control within swarms of robots have flourished in the last few years. In many areas, casting large, complex problems into a set of smaller coordinated tasks between multiple robots has become particularly attractive because this form of decentralized approaches tends to provide solutions that are, by design, scalable, flexible, robust, and low-cost.

One kind of coordinated tasks involves robot formation control [16], i.e. the design of control laws to drive a set of agents into a geometric pattern of reference, as used for example in entertainment applications [6]. One of the most common approaches for formation control involves using a *distributed* architecture, where the robots do not rely on a centralized control and, instead, communicate between each other to coordinate their actions. We are interested in solving the formation control problem in the case of autonomous air vehicles (AAV) and through computer vision, i.e. by using the *images* taken from the cameras onboard each AAV and by leveraging multiple view geometry.

More specifically, we aim to control and coordinate the movement of a set of N camera-agents using only visual information and a communication network among these agents. Our proposed method is based in a well established type

A. P. López-Monroy et al. (Eds.): MCPR 2025, LNCS 15715, pp. 224–233, 2025.
https://doi.org/10.1007/978-3-031-96255-4_21

of control known as Image-Based Visual Servo (IBVS), coupled with the use of synthetic homographies created from a desired virtual structure, that will lead the agents towards the formation. We recall that a homography is a projective transformation matrix that relates projected planar points between perspectives.

Coupling IBVS and homographies has been used in single camera scenarios. In [8], intermediate homographies between the current and goal states are built using the current state information to specify waypoints the robot should reach. Then the control velocities are calculated directly from the entries of the homographies. This approach switches the control to follow different paths in function of the priority task to be accomplished. This allows to reach the desired position while maintaining an observed target within the camera field of view. In [3], the control is also obtained directly from elements of the homography matrix relating the current and goal state. Since this matrix tends to the identity matrix when reaching the goal state, the controller uses the difference of both matrices.

Synthetic homography matrices are used in [4] to make an aircraft follow a given trajectory. The homographies are created from an interpolation of a series of known images and IBVS is used within the aircraft to follow the path.

The formation problem has also been tackled by combining homography information and visual servo approaches, in a eye-to-hand configuration. In [9], a set of differential robots moving in a plane are controlled through homographies that relate the current and target positions. However, our approach seeks the possibility of not using an external viewer, but rather onboard information.

We introduce a novel formation control algorithm that combines IBVS and consensus theory, leveraging a virtual structure using synthetic homographies. Our algorithm is distributed, does not require training information other than the relative states of agents, in comparison to the classical IBVS. Moreover, our approach is flexible and can reach formations up to translations and rotations.

2 Preliminaries

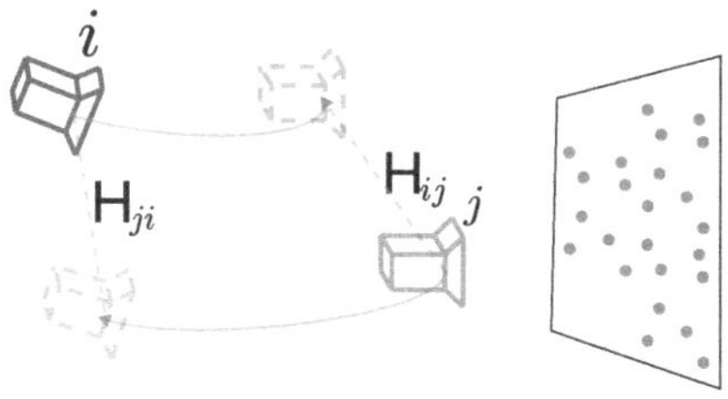

Fig. 1. Desired control performance for two neighboring cameras i, j where virtual positions (dashed) are defined by the homographies $\mathbf{H}_{ij}$. Each camera follows its virtual reference using a classical IBVS approach.

We consider a free-flying camera with state $\mathbf{x} = [\mathbf{t}^T, \boldsymbol{\theta}^T]^T \in \mathbb{R}^6$, where $\mathbf{t} = [x, y, z]^T$ describes the translation and $\boldsymbol{\theta} = [\phi, \theta, \psi]^T$ the roll, pitch and yaw angles in a global frame. The camera kinematics is taken as a single integrator:

$$\dot{\mathbf{x}}(t) = \mathbf{v}, \tag{1}$$

where $\mathbf{v} = [\boldsymbol{v}^T, \boldsymbol{\omega}^T]^T$, with $\boldsymbol{v} = [v_x, v_y, v_z]^T$ the linear velocity and $\boldsymbol{\omega} = [\omega_x, \omega_y, \omega_z]^T$ the angular velocity of the the camera reference frame in global coordinates.

The camera is modeled as a standard pinhole camera able to *track* the image projections of a set of 3D points $\mathbf{P}_k = [X_k, Y_k, Z_k]^T$. In this work we assume that the projected features $\mathbf{s}_k = [\mathrm{x}_k, \mathrm{y}_k]^T$ are normalized (i.e. the camera is assumed to have unitary focal length), which implies $[\mathrm{x}_k, \mathrm{y}_k]^T = [X_k^c/Z_k^c, Y_k^c/Z_k^c]^T$.

2.1 Image-Based Visual Servoing

Image-based visual servoing (IBVS) drives a controlled camera so that a set of K image features $\mathbf{s} \triangleq [\mathbf{s}_1^T, ..., \mathbf{s}_K^T]^T$ match reference cues $\mathbf{s}^* = [\mathbf{s}_1^{*T}, \ldots, \mathbf{s}_K^{*T}]^T$ obtained at the desired state $\mathbf{x}^*$. To do so, the relationship between the derivative of the image features and the camera velocity is as follows [2]:

$$\dot{\mathbf{s}}_k = \mathbf{L}_{\mathbf{s}_k} \mathbf{v}, \tag{2}$$

being $\mathbf{L}_{\mathbf{s}_k} \in \mathbb{R}^{2M \times 6}$ the *interaction matrix* associated to the image points $\mathbf{s}_k$:

$$\mathbf{L}_{\mathbf{s}_k} = \begin{bmatrix} -\frac{1}{Z_k^c} & 0 & \frac{\mathrm{x}_k}{Z_k^c} & \mathrm{x}_k \mathrm{y}_k & -(1+\mathrm{x}_k^2) & \mathrm{y}_k \\ 0 & -\frac{1}{Z_k^c} & \frac{\mathrm{y}_k}{Z_k^c} & 1+\mathrm{y}_k^2 & -\mathrm{x}_k \mathrm{y}_k & -\mathrm{x}_k \end{bmatrix}, \tag{3}$$

where Z_k^c is the *depth* of the k-th feature $\mathbf{s}_k$, often *unknown* in practice.

IBVS defines an error $\mathbf{e} = \mathbf{s} - \mathbf{s}^*$ and uses a control law of the form $\mathbf{v} = -\gamma \hat{\mathbf{L}}_{\mathbf{s}}^+ \mathbf{e}$ with a gain $\gamma > 0$ and an *approximate* interaction matrix $\hat{\mathbf{L}}_{\mathbf{s}}$ since the Z_k^c have to be estimated. The $^+$ operator indicates the Moore-Penrose pseudoinverse matrix. With at least 4 feature points, this control law yields $\mathbf{s} \to \mathbf{s}^*$ [2] and, under ideal conditions, $\mathbf{x} \to \mathbf{x}^*$. Even if $\hat{\mathbf{L}}_{\mathbf{s}}$ is approximate, in practice this control shows local asymptotic stability in a surprisingly large [2] neighborhood at $\mathbf{x}^*$.

Along this work, we make use of the following transformation $\boldsymbol{T} \in \mathbb{R}^{6 \times 6}$ composed by a rotation $\mathbf{R}$ and translation $\mathbf{t}$ to be applied on velocity vectors:

$$\boldsymbol{T} = \begin{bmatrix} \mathbf{R} & [\mathbf{t}]_\times \mathbf{R} \\ \mathbf{0}_{3\times 3} & \mathbf{R} \end{bmatrix}. \tag{4}$$

2.2 Consensus Theory

Within a network of N agents, *attaining a consensus* means reaching an agreement on a quantity that depends on the agents states [13]. Such a network is modeled as a graph $\mathcal{G}$, with a vertex set $\mathcal{V}(\mathcal{G})$ and an edge set $\mathcal{E}(\mathcal{G})$. The set of neighbors of a vertex v_i is denoted by $\mathcal{N}_i(\mathcal{G}) \triangleq \{v_j : \forall v_j | (v_i, v_j) \in \mathcal{E}(\mathcal{G})\}$.

For a system described through state variables $\mathbf{x}_i \in \mathbb{R}^S$ within a vector $\mathbf{x}(t) = [\mathbf{x}_1(t)^T, \ldots, \mathbf{x}_N(t)^T]^T \in \mathbb{R}^{NS}$, a consensus formulation uses a local error

$$\mathbf{e}_i(t) = \sum_{j \in \mathcal{N}_i} a_{ij}(\mathbf{x}_i(t) - \mathbf{x}_j(t)). \tag{5}$$

The joint error vectors is $\mathbf{e} = (\mathcal{L} \otimes \mathbf{I}_N)\mathbf{x}$ with $\otimes$ the Kronecker product, $\mathcal{L}$ the Laplacian of $\mathcal{G}$, and $\mathbf{I}_S$ the $S \times S$ identity matrix. With $\dot{\mathbf{e}} = (\mathcal{L} \otimes \mathbf{I}_N)\dot{\mathbf{x}}$, this system reaches consensus under the feedback control law $\mathbf{u}(t) = -k\mathbf{e}(t)$ for a single integrator dynamics $\dot{\mathbf{x}} = \mathbf{u}$ [12], describing an equivalent system $\dot{\mathbf{x}} = -k(\mathcal{L} \otimes \mathbf{I}_N)\mathbf{x}$. It has been shown that this reaches $\mathrm{Ker}((\mathcal{L} \otimes \mathbf{I}_N)) := \{\mathbf{x} | \mathbf{x}_i = \mathbf{x}_j \forall i, j \in [1, N]\}$ in exponential time as $\mathbf{e} \to \mathbf{0}$ under the condition of $\mathcal{G}$ to be connected. From this, formation control can be solved by using a state definition which implies that a desired shape is approached when $\mathbf{e} \to \mathbf{0}$. The resulting feedback control is distributed as each state only relies on the information of its neighbors.

3 Proposed Approach

Consider a pair of cameras, indexed by i, l, with absolute positions and orientations given by $\mathbf{x}^i = [\mathbf{t}^i, \boldsymbol{\theta}^i]^T$. We aim to drive camera i, with its current relative pose $\mathbf{t}^{il}, \mathbf{R}^{il}$ with respect to camera l to a pose $\mathbf{t}^*, \mathbf{R}^*$ relative to l.

We propose a leader-follower approach where camera l is associated to a set of reference features $\mathbf{s}_k^*$ that define implicitly the relative pose of i. We assume that these features are the projections of *planar* 3D features, hence the desired relative position between i and l can be expressed through a homography ($\mathbf{H}^*$) between the view at pose l and the virtual reference pose. The features viewed by camera l are mapped up to a scale into the reference view for camera i as

$$\mathbf{s}_k^* \propto \mathbf{H}^* \mathbf{s}_k^j, \tag{6}$$

where the * super-index indicates the reference frame for the projected feature.

The homography matrix $\mathbf{H}^*$ represents, up to scale, the relation between two poses viewing the same plane with normal vector $\mathbf{n}$ and can be expressed as:

$$\mathbf{H}^* = \mathbf{R}^* + \mathbf{t}^* \mathbf{n}^T / d. \tag{7}$$

From this, an IBVS approach can be used in way that the camera i reaches the reference relative pose $*$ by defining the image error for feature k as follows:

$$\mathbf{e}_k^i = \mathbf{s}_k^i - \mathbf{s}_k^* = \mathbf{s}_k^i - h(\mathbf{H}^*, \mathbf{s}_k^l), \tag{8}$$

where $h(\mathbf{H}, \mathbf{p})$ is the non-linear mapping of $\mathbf{p} \in \mathbb{R}^2$ through the homography $\mathbf{H}$:

$$h(\mathbf{H}, \mathbf{p}) \triangleq \frac{1}{\mathbf{H}_3[\mathbf{p}^\top, 1]^T} [\mathbf{H}_1[\mathbf{p}^T, 1]^T, \mathbf{H}_2[\mathbf{p}^T, 1]^T]^T, \tag{9}$$

where $\mathbf{H}_1, \mathbf{H}_2, \mathbf{H}_3$ are the rows of $\mathbf{H}$. The complete feature error vector $\mathbf{e}^i \triangleq [\mathbf{e}_1^i, \cdots, \mathbf{e}_K^i]^T$ follows:

$$\dot{\mathbf{e}}^i = \dot{\mathbf{s}}^i - \dot{\mathbf{s}}^* = \mathbf{L}_{\mathbf{s}^i} \mathbf{v}^i - \dot{\mathbf{s}}^*, \tag{10}$$

where $\mathbf{L}_{\mathbf{s}^l}, \mathbf{L}_{\mathbf{s}^i}$ are the *stacked* interaction matrices for each set of features. Focusing on the second term above, the time derivative of the image features positions in the reference view, $\dot{\mathbf{s}}^*$, a consequence of the leader motion. Since the reference features $\mathbf{s}^*$ are subjected to the velocities of the virtual frame as $\dot{\mathbf{s}}^* = \mathbf{L}_{\mathbf{s}^*}\mathbf{v}^*$ and the virtual camera can be seen as a body subjected to a rigid transformation between reference frames, the induced velocities of $\mathbf{s}^*$ are obtained from $\mathbf{v}^l$ through:

$$\dot{\mathbf{s}}^* = \mathbf{L}_{\mathbf{s}^*}\mathbf{v}^* = \mathbf{L}_{\mathbf{s}^*}\boldsymbol{T}_l^*\mathbf{v}^l \tag{11}$$

In this work, we consider two different situations with different control laws, one where the joint motion of several agents is *collaborative* and another where one agent acts as a moving *leader*. For the first case, our control law is a proportional feedback; for the second one, we propose a robust, Super-Twisting (ST) sliding mode control [14], able to deal with unknown dynamics of the error induced by a moving leader.

3.1 Visual Error over a Graph for Neighboring Cameras

In the sequel, we will consider N agents in the form of free-flying cameras to formulate a distributed control to achieve a formation; camera labels will be used instead of leader and followers. Besides, we consider a graph $\mathcal{G}$ modeling the communication connectivity between cameras. For each pair of cameras i, j, a homography $\mathbf{H}_{ij}$ is calculated from Eq. 7. From this, each neighboring cameras can project the features to the virtual cameras. Conversely, each agent computes a control law that minimizes the feature error with the virtual cameras defined by its neighbors. A simple case with two neighboring cameras is depicted in Fig. 1. Let $\mathbf{e}_k^i$ be the error for one of the K image features on the i-th camera:

$$\mathbf{e}_k^i = \sum_{j\in\mathcal{N}_i} \mathbf{s}_k^i - \mathbf{s}_k^{j*} = \sum_{j\in\mathcal{N}_i} \mathbf{s}_k^i - h(\mathbf{H}_{ij}, \mathbf{s}_k^j), \tag{12}$$

where j is a neighboring camera. The joint error for agent i is $\mathbf{e}^i = [(\mathbf{e}_1^i)^T, \cdots, (\mathbf{e}_K^i)^T]^T$. The error derivative of the vector can be computed as

$$\dot{\mathbf{e}}^i = \sum_{j\in\mathcal{N}_i} \dot{\mathbf{s}}^i - \dot{\mathbf{s}}^{j*} = |\mathcal{N}_i|\mathbf{L}_{\mathbf{s}^i}\mathbf{v}^i - \sum_{j\in\mathcal{N}_i} \mathbf{L}_{\mathbf{s}^{j*}}\boldsymbol{T}_{ij}^*\mathbf{v}^j, \tag{13}$$

where $\dot{\mathbf{s}}^i = [(\dot{\mathbf{s}}_1^i)^T, \cdots, (\dot{\mathbf{s}}_K^i)^T]$ and $\dot{\mathbf{s}}^{j*} = [(\dot{\mathbf{s}}_1^{j*})^T, \cdots, (\dot{\mathbf{s}}_K^{j*})^T]$ are the joint feature derivatives. Notice that the velocity between the neighboring camera and its virtual reference is $\mathbf{v}^{*j} = \boldsymbol{T}_{ij}^*\mathbf{v}^j$, which is involved in the second term of Eq. 13.

3.2 Proportional Feedback Control

The first control is designed mainly for static conditions where the goal is to reach the desired formation. This scheme is distributed and does not require a leader. The final conditions are expected to be static. It is considered that the control input are the camera velocities. The proposed proportional control is

$$\mathbf{u}^i = -\lambda\mathbf{L}_{\mathbf{s}^i}^+\mathbf{e}^i. \tag{14}$$

Fig. 2. Feature matching between cameras 2 (left) and 0 (right): At the initial conditions (upper row) and close to the final state (lower row).

with $\lambda > 0$ a control gain. In closed loop, Eq. 13 induces error dynamics satisfying

$$\dot{\mathbf{e}}^i = -\lambda|\mathcal{N}_i|\mathbf{L}_{\mathbf{s}^i}\mathbf{L}_{\mathbf{s}^i}^+\mathbf{e}^i + \lambda\sum_{j\in\mathcal{N}_i}\mathbf{L}_{\mathbf{s}^{j*}}\boldsymbol{T}_{ij}^*\mathbf{L}_{\mathbf{s}^j}^+\mathbf{e}^j. \tag{15}$$

The second term can be seen as a perturbation over agent i due to the motion of its neighboring agents. In the case of a static final formation, this term also vanishes and the proportional feedback is enough to achieve $\mathbf{e}^i \to 0$ as $t \to \infty$.

3.3 Super-Twisting Sliding Mode Control

This second scheme is designed for the leader-following case, where one agent takes on a given path unknown for the followers. This tracking problem implies that for followers, a perturbation due to the unknown motion of the leader is present, and a *robust controller* is needed. The Super-Twisting (ST) sliding mode controller has shown good performance in VS schemes [1]. For our vision-based formation control, we present two possible implementations of the ST approach, one over the local visual error and the other over a reduced error space.

The motion of the neighboring cameras can be treated as a unknown disturbance $f(\mathbf{e}, t)$ to be rejected. The error system dynamics can be seen as:

$$\dot{\mathbf{e}}^i = |\mathcal{N}_i|\mathbf{L}_{\mathbf{s}^i}\mathbf{u}^i + f(\mathbf{e}, t). \tag{16}$$

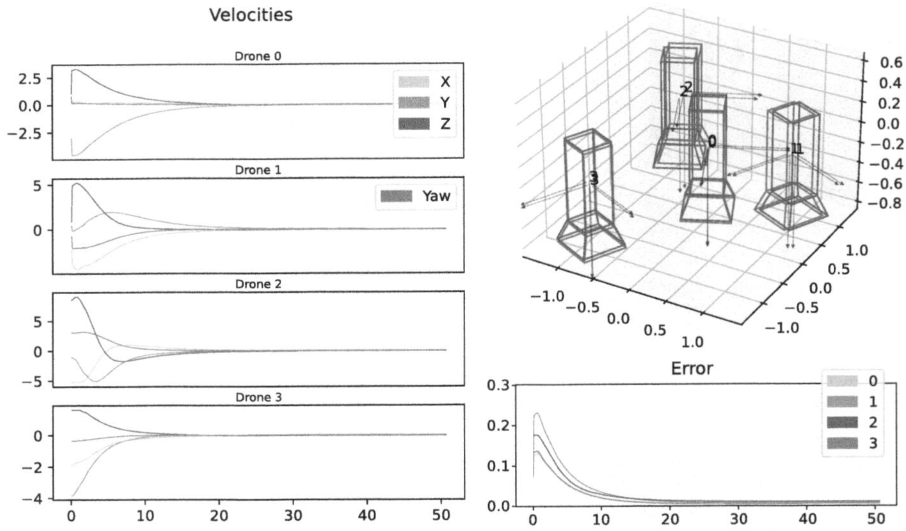

Fig. 3. Proportional control in the static case: Both image errors (bottom right) and velocities (left) tend to zero as the formation is reached. In the upper right, we show that the final formation (red) matches the reference formation (brown). (Color figure online)

In the first variant, we make use of an auxiliary input variable $\boldsymbol{\nu}^i \in \mathbb{R}^{2K}$

$$\mathbf{u}^i = \frac{1}{|\mathcal{N}_i|} \mathbf{L}^+_{\mathbf{s}^i} \boldsymbol{\nu}^i, \tag{17}$$

for which the ST controller is as follows:

$$\boldsymbol{\nu}^i = -k_1 |\mathbf{e}^i|^{1/2} \operatorname{sgn}(\mathbf{e}^i) + \boldsymbol{\mu}^i, \text{ with } \dot{\boldsymbol{\mu}}^i = -k_2 \operatorname{sgn}(\mathbf{e}^i). \tag{18}$$

In the second variant, we rely on a change of variable $\boldsymbol{\xi}^i = \mathbf{L}^+_{\mathbf{s}^i} \mathbf{e}^i / |\mathcal{N}_i|$ where the error space is reduced $\boldsymbol{\xi}^i \in \mathbb{R}^6$. The reduced error dynamics becomes

$$\dot{\boldsymbol{\xi}}^i = \mathbf{L}^+_{\mathbf{s}^i} \mathbf{L}_{\mathbf{s}^i} \mathbf{u}^i + \bar{f}(\mathbf{e}, t), \tag{19}$$

for which the ST controller has the form:

$$\mathbf{u}^i = -k_1 |\boldsymbol{\xi}^i|^{1/2} \operatorname{sgn}(\boldsymbol{\xi}^i) + \boldsymbol{\mu}^i, \text{ with } \dot{\boldsymbol{\mu}}^i = -k_2 \operatorname{sgn}(\boldsymbol{\xi}^i). \tag{20}$$

In both control variants, $k_1 > 0$ and $k_2 > 0$ are control gains that must be set according to the conditions given in [11] in order to satisfy the stability criterion and guarantee convergence of the local visual errors.

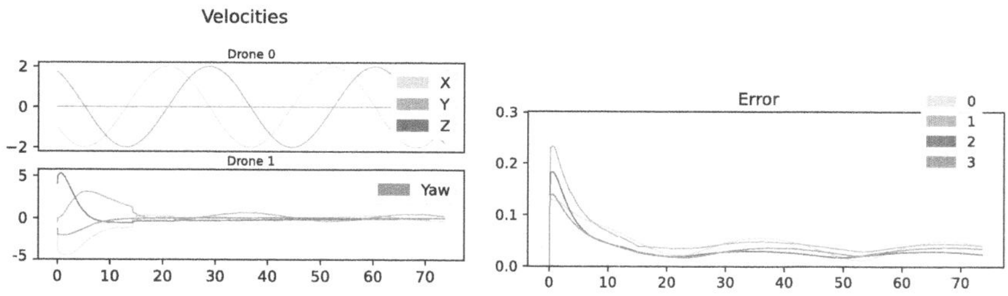

Fig. 4. Proportional control for the tracking case: (left) velocities of cameras 0 and 1, where 0 is the leader; (right) the image errors do not tend to 0.

4 Simulation Results

Our algorithms have been tested within `Gazebo` simulator for quadcopters carrying a camera, in a flat ground scenario (see Fig. 2). Each agent has 4 degrees of freedom (translation and rotation in yaw), hence we only use 4 controls from the 6 computed. Each drone is equipped with a down-facing camera with its optical center at the origin of the drone's reference frame. The features are obtained via ORB detection [15] and tracked via a Lucas-Kanade algorithm [15]. Each agent's features are initially matched to each neighbor's features with the Flann Matcher [15]. Each agent must keep at least 4 features under its field of view. If this does not happen or if it can not find matches with its neighbors, the tracking stops and new features are detected and tracked. The agent height is used as an estimate of features depths. The velocities gains are decoupled in translation and rotation with factors 0.6 and 0.9, respectively. In our simulations, we use a completely connected communication graph $\mathcal{G}$. The initial conditions and reference configurations are the same in all simulations. The desired formation is not planar neither completely aligned as described by $\mathbf{x}^1 = [1.5, 0.5, 1.5, 25°]^T$, $\mathbf{x}^2 = [2, 2, 1, -25°]^T$, $\mathbf{x}^3 = [0.5, 1.5, 1.5, 25°]^T$, $\mathbf{x}^4 = [0, 0, 1, -25°]^T$.

4.1 Proportional Feedback Control

This control makes the image errors tend to zero and is able to replicate the desired formation. This can be seen in Fig. 3, where an aligned representation of the formations is shown to verify the relative positions of the final state of the cameras in contrast to the reference. An example of the change of image features between the initial and final states is presented in Fig. 2, where one can see how the configurations change from being unaligned at the beginning to being aligned, as in the reference configurations. Then, we evaluate the performance in the tracking scenario where camera 0 (leader) has a motion along a flat circle with velocities $\mathbf{v}'^0 = 2[\cos(0.2t), \sin(0.2t), 0, 0]$. In this case, the image error is clearly not compensated for by the control, as seen in Fig. 4. This issue is then solved by using the Super-Twisting robust controller. Visualizations are available in video 1 and video 2 respectively.

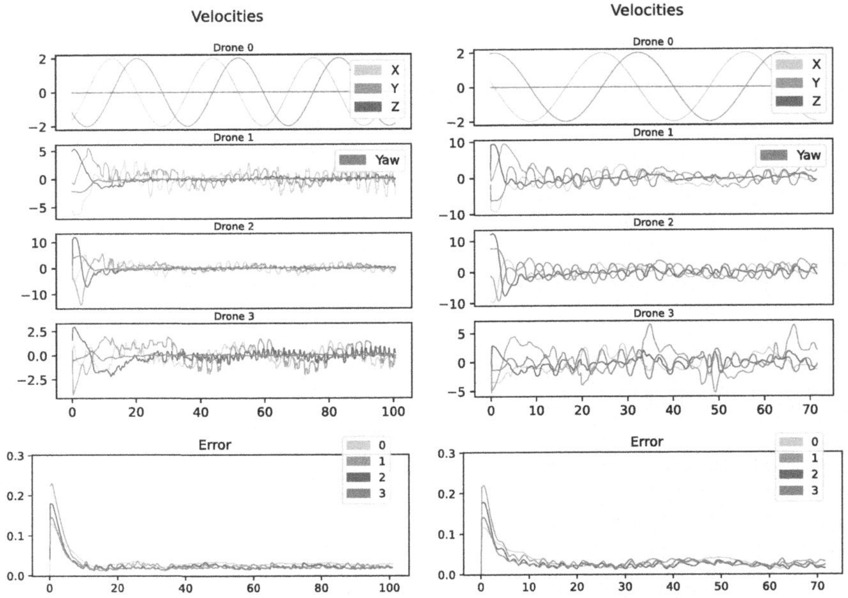

Fig. 5. Super-Twisting control Eq. 18 (left) and Eq. 20 (right) for the tracking case: The velocities (up) remains around zero with some oscillations. The image errors (down) for both cases remain in a lower bound than the proportional case.

4.2 Super-Twisting Sliding Mode Control

Both robust controllers are tested under the same tracking conditions as in the previous simulations. The ST gains have been tuned to $k_1 = 1$, $k_2 = 0.005$ for Eq. 18 (high dimension error space) and $k_1 = 2.5$, $k_2 = 0.005$ for Eq. 20 (reduced error space). In both cases, Fig. 5 shows that the errors are reduced compared to the proportional case. However, the motion has a small oscillatory behavior that does not allow the formation to be fully accurate during the simulation; nevertheless, the formation is tracked better than in the proportional case. Both simulations can be viewed in video 3 and video 4 respectively.

5 Conclusions

A novel distributed formation algorithm has been presented, with convincing experiments under realistic simulations using quadcopters in the Gazebo simulator. Our distributed algorithm relies on well established controllers such as classical IBVS and consensus-based approaches. Our main contribution is the introduction of *virtual homographies* to define a desired formation. We have shown that our approach can be applied to solve the formation reaching and formation tracking problems. Although the proposed approach shows a good performance, a theoretical stability analysis will be done in future work to provide convergence guarantees, even for faster motions of the leader.

References

1. Becerra, H.M., Hayet, J.B., Sagüés, C.: A single visual-servo controller of mobile robots with super-twisting control. Robot. Auton. Syst. **62**(11) (2014)
2. Chaumette, F., Hutchinson, S.: Visual servo control. I. Basic approaches. IEEE Robot. Autom. Mag. **13**(4) (2006)
3. Costanzo, M., Maria, G.D., Natale, C.: Homography-based sampled-data visual servoing. IEEE Control Syst. Lett. **8** (2024)
4. Gonçalves, T., Azinheira, J., Rives, P.: Homography-based visual servoing of an aircraft for automatic approach and landing. In: Proceedings of the IEEE International Conference on Robotics and Automation (2010)
5. Guillet, A., Lenain, R., Thuilot, B., Rousseau, V.: Formation control of agricultural mobile robots: a bidirectional weighted constraints approach. J. Field Robot. **34**(7), 1260–1274 (2017)
6. Huang, J., Tian, G., Zhang, J., Chen, Y.: On unmanned aerial vehicles light show systems: algorithms, software and hardware. Appl. Sci. **11**(16) (2021)
7. Jiménez-Cano, A.E., Sanalitro, D., Tognon, M., Franchi, A., Cortés, J.: Precise cable-suspended pick-and-place with an aerial multi-robot system. J. Intell. Rob. Syst. **105**(3), 68 (2022)
8. López-Nicolás, G., Aranda, M., Mezouar, Y., Sagüés, C.: Visual control for multirobot organized rendezvous. IEEE Trans. Syst. Man Cybern. Part B Cybern. **42**(4) (2012)
9. López-Nicolás, G., Gans, N.R., Bhattacharya, S., Sagüés, C., Guerrero, J.J., Hutchinson, S.: Homography-based control scheme for mobile robots with nonholonomic and field-of-view constraints. IEEE Trans. Syst. Man Cybern. Part B Cybern. **40**(4) (2010)
10. Merino, L., Martínez-de Dios, J.R., Ollero, A.: Cooperative Unmanned Aerial Systems for Fire Detection, Monitoring, and Extinguishing, pp. 2693–2722. Springer (2015)
11. Moreno, J.A., Osorio, M.: Strict Lyapunov functions for the super-twisting algorithm. IEEE Trans. Autom. Control **57**(4), 1035–1040 (2012)
12. Olfati-Saber, R., Fax, J.A., Murray, R.M.: Consensus and cooperation in networked multi-agent systems. Proc. IEEE **95**(1), 215–233 (2007)
13. Ren, W., Beard, R.W.: Distributed consensus in multi-vehicle cooperative control. Springer (2008)
14. Shtessel, Y., Edwards, C., Fridman, L., Levant, A.: Sliding Mode Control and Observation, 1st edn. Birkhäuser Basel (2015)
15. Szeliski, R.: Computer vision: Algorithms and applications, 2nd edn. Texts in Computer Science. Springer (2022)
16. Yu, Z., Zhang, Y., Jiang, B., Fu, J., Jin, Y.: A review on fault-tolerant cooperative control of multiple unmanned aerial vehicles. Chin. J. Aeronautics **35**(1) (2022)

Laser Beam Centroid Detection for Automatic Spatial Filtering: A Comparative Analysis of Machine Vision Algorithms

Gregorio A. Oropeza-Gomez(✉), Onofre Orozco-López, Francisco J. Casillas-Rodríguez, Francisco G. Peña-Lecona, Jesús Muñoz-Maciel, and Miguel Mora-Gonzalez(✉)

Centro Universitario de los Lagos, Universidad de Guadalajara, 47460 Lagos de Moreno, JAL, Mexico
gregorio.oropeza@alumnos.udg.mx, miguel.mora@academicos.udg.mx

Abstract. Achieving optimal beam quality in applications ranging from high-power lasers to interferometric metrology fundamentally relies on precise spatial filtering. While spatial filters effectively remove high-frequency noise and improve beam profiles, their performance is critically dependent on accurate alignment - specifically, the precise centering of the focused laser beam onto the pinhole aperture. Despite decades of research and development in optical filtering, a robust, automated solution for multiple wavelength spatial filter alignment remains an open challenge. This paper focuses on a critical sub-problem within that challenge: the accurate and reliable determination of the diffraction pattern's center, a pre-requisite for any automated alignment system. Was observed that the FBM and CCL are faster that the superpixel methods, but superpixel-based methods were more accurate and precise when its compared to the true centroid, achieving minimum errors of one pixel. An hybrid approach algorithm could be a better solution instead a single one, providing the faster execution time and the consistent accuracy.

Keywords: Superpixels · Centroid · Connected component labeling · Image moment · Optical spatial filtering

1 Introduction

Achieving optimal beam quality in applications ranging from high-power lasers to interferometric metrology fundamentally relies on precise spatial filtering. While spatial filters effectively remove high-frequency noise and improve beam profiles, their performance is critically dependent on accurate alignment - specifically, the precise centering of the focused laser beam onto the pinhole aperture. Despite decades of research and development in optical filtering, a robust, automated solution for multiple wavelength spatial filter alignment remains an open

A. P. López-Monroy et al. (Eds.): MCPR 2025, LNCS 15715, pp. 234–244, 2025.
https://doi.org/10.1007/978-3-031-96255-4_22

challenge. This paper focuses on a critical sub-problem within that challenge: the accurate and reliable determination of the diffraction pattern's center, a prerequisite for any automated alignment system. Traditional methods for spatial filter alignment are often manual, relying on skilled technicians and painstaking adjustments. This approach is not only time-consuming and labor-intensive but also susceptible to human error and inconsistencies, particularly when dealing with the sub-micrometer precision required for many advanced optical systems. While prior work has explored various aspects of spatial filtering, like specialized techniques for specific applications [1–3] a generalized, automated, and high-precision centering method applicable across diverse wavelengths is lacking.

The problem of spatial filter alignment can be effectively reduced to a two-element pointing task: aligning the focused laser spot (element one) with the pinhole (element two). The accuracy of this alignment hinges on the ability to precisely locate the center of the diffraction pattern produced by the focused beam. Existing image processing and machine vision techniques offer potential solutions, but their performance in the context of spatial filter alignment, particularly with respect to noise, wavelength variations, and real-time operation, requires careful evaluation.

We analyze the strengths and weaknesses of each algorithm, considering factors such as computational cost, sensitivity to noise, accuracy, and suitability for real-time implementation in an automated spatial filter alignment system. The goal is to identify the most promising approach for achieving robust, high-precision alignment across a range of operating conditions, ultimately enabling a fully automated, multi-wavelength spatial filtering solution.

2 Theory

2.1 Optical Spatial Filtering

High-precision interferometric measurements rely on illuminating the object under test with a wavefront of uniform intensity. While laser beams are widely used in interferometry, they are susceptible to intensity variations. These variations arise from scattering and diffraction caused by dust particles, imperfections in optical elements, and environmental perturbations. Such non-uniformities in the illuminating wavefront introduce noise into the resulting interference pattern, ultimately limiting the accuracy of the measurement.

To address this, optical spatial filtering provides a robust technique for generating a clean and uniform wavefront. This technique utilizes a converging lens to focus the laser beam onto a precisely positioned pinhole aperture. The pinhole's function is analogous to a low-pass filter in signal processing: it selectively blocks light rays deviating significantly from the optical axis, which typically correspond to high-spatial-frequency noise components. The desired, low-spatial-frequency components of the wavefront, representing the overall beam shape, pass through the pinhole. By ensuring the pinhole is accurately positioned at the focal point and precisely aligned along the X-Y axes, this filtering process effectively mitigates noise, thereby enhancing wavefront uniformity and, consequently, the accuracy of interferometric measurements. The focal plane intensity distribution of a laser beam, after passing through a lens, is described by the Fourier transform of the beam's aperture function.

$$I(f_x, f_y) = |\mathcal{F}[U(x,y)]|^2, \tag{1}$$

where $U(x, y)$ is the aperture function of the incident beam, and f_x, f_y are the spatial frequencies. The spatial filtering is commonly performed by pinhole aperture, that introduces a transfer function $H(f_x, f_y)$, which acts as a low-pass filter:

$$U'(f_x, f_y) = H(f_x, f_y) \cdot U(f_x, f_y), \tag{2}$$

where $H(f_x, f_y)$ is 1 for spatial frequencies within the pinhole cutoff and 0 otherwise. The filtered wavefront is reconstructed by applying the inverse Fourier transform to $U'(f_x, f_y)$:

$$u'(x, y) = \mathcal{F}^{-1}[U'(f_x, f_y)]. \tag{3}$$

This procedure yields a clean and uniform wavefront suitable for high-precision interferometric applications.

Mathematically, this filtering process can be described using Fourier optics:

$$I(x, y) = \mathcal{F}^{-1}\{H(f_x, f_y) \cdot \mathcal{F}\{E(x, y)\}\}, \tag{4}$$

where: $I(x, y)$ is the intensity distribution of the filtered wavefront, $E(x, y)$ is the initial electric field distribution of the laser beam, $H(f_x, f_y)$ is the transfer function of the pinhole aperture, $\mathcal{F}$ and $\mathcal{F}^{-1}$ denote the Fourier transform and its inverse, respectively [4].

2.2 Threshold

Following the optional application of Gaussian blurring, thresholding is employed as a fundamental image segmentation technique. Thresholding transforms a grayscale image into a binary image. This is accomplished by selecting a threshold value, T, and comparing each pixel's intensity to this threshold. Pixels with intensities above T are assigned one intensity value (typically representing white, often 255 in an 8-bit image), while those below T are assigned another (typically representing black, often 0) [5]. This process effectively partitions the image into two distinct regions, often corresponding to foreground objects and background. Adaptive Thresholding (AT) is a sophisticated variant of thresholding designed to address images with varying illumination or significant intensity gradients. Unlike global thresholding, which uses a single, fixed threshold for the entire image, AT calculates a unique threshold for each pixel based on the statistical properties of its local neighborhood. The Otsu method, as implemented in this work, assumes that $M-1$ thresholds, denoted as $[t_1, t_2, t_3, \ldots, t_{M-1}]$ and divide the image into M classes. The resulting threshold operation will be:

$$\{t_1, t_2, \ldots, t_{M-1}\} = arg \max_{0 \leq t \leq L-1} \{\sigma_B^2(t_1, t_2, \ldots, t_{M-1})\} \tag{5}$$

where L are the gray levels and σ_B^2 are the between-class variance [6].

2.3 Morphological Operations

Closing is a morphological operation that combines dilation followed by erosion. Morphological operations are written in terms of the structuring elements "B" and a set "A" of foreground pixels. The inputs/outputs of the morphological operations are binary images, and the set A can be embedded in a complete image I. **Dilation**: With A and B as sets of Z^2 the mathematical dilation of A by B can be defined as:

$$A \oplus B = \{z|(\hat{B})_z \cap A \neq \emptyset\} \tag{6}$$

where $\hat{B}$ are the foreground elements of B.

Erosion: Mathematical erosion can be defined as:

$$A \ominus B = \{z|(B)_z \subseteq A\} \tag{7}$$

And where an image is a rectangular array composed by foreground pixels and background pixels the equation can be defined as:

$$I \ominus B = \{z|(B)_z) \subseteq A and A \subseteq I\} \cup \{A^c|A^c \subseteq I\} \tag{8}$$

where A^c is the set of background pixels.

These operations exhibit a dual relationship, as represented by:

$$(A \ominus B)^c = A^c \oplus \hat{B} \tag{9}$$

and

$$(A \oplus B)^c = A^c \ominus \hat{B} \tag{10}$$

This equations indicates that erosion operation is a complement of the dilation operation [7].

2.4 Border Following

Is an algorithm based in the work [8]. This algorithm systematically scans the binary image to identify and trace the boundaries of connected components (objects). The process proceeds as follows:

1. **Initialization:** The algorithm begins by scanning the image, typically in a raster scan order (from top-left to bottom-right), searching for a pixel that marks the start of an object's outer boundary. This starting pixel is a non-background pixel adjacent to a background pixel.
2. **Iterative Border Following:** Once a starting point is found, the algorithm iteratively follows the connected boundary pixels. It examines the neighborhood of the current pixel (typically using 8-connectivity, considering the eight adjacent pixels) to identify the next pixel belonging to the boundary. The selection of the next pixel is guided by a consistent directionality (clockwise or counter-clockwise) to ensure proper tracing of both outer and inner (hole) boundaries.

3. **Contour Closure:** The border-following process continues until the algorithm returns to the initial starting point, indicating the completion of a single contour.
4. **Exhaustive Search:** The algorithm continues scanning the image for any remaining unvisited object pixels. Upon encountering such a pixel, steps (b) and (c) are repeated to trace the contour of the newly found object. This continues until all object boundaries in the image have been identified.

2.5 Connected-Component Labeling

Connected-component labeling (CCL) is a operation in image processing and computer vision, where the primary objective is to identify and label distinct connected regions within a binary image. The foundation of CCL algorithms lies in the concept of connectivity. In a binary image, two pixels are considered connected if they are adjacent to each other and have the same value (typically 1 for foreground pixels). This notion of connectivity can be further refined into 4-connectivity, where pixels are connected only if they share an edge, and 8-connectivity, where pixels sharing an edge or a corner are considered connected. The goal of CCL is to assign a unique label to each such connected component, effectively distinguishing it from other components. One of the fundamental data structures used in many CCL algorithms is the UNION-FIND data structure, also known as the disjoint-set data structure. This structure efficiently maintains a collection of disjoint sets, each set represents a connected component, and the elements are the pixels. Initially, each pixel is in its own set. As the image is scanned, adjacent pixels with the same value are merged [9].

2.6 Simple Linear Iterative Clustering (SLIC)

The Simple Linear Iterative Clustering (SLIC) algorithm is a centroid-based clustering method used to generate superpixels. It groups pixels based on both color similarity and spatial proximity within the image plane. SLIC operates in a 5-dimensional space, combining the three color channels (l, a, b) and the two spatial coordinates (x, y) of each pixel, denoted as $[l, a, b, x, y]$. Because the color and spatial dimensions have different units and ranges, spatial distances are normalized to ensure accurate distance calculations using the Euclidean norm [10]. The algorithm takes as input the desired number of approximately equally-sized superpixels, K for an image of N pixels. At initialization, K superpixel cluster centers $C_i = [l_i, a_i, b_i, x_i, y_i]^T$ placed on a regular grid, with an initial spacing of S where:

$$S = \sqrt{N/k} \tag{11}$$

This means that the approximate area of each superpixel is S^2. The SLIC algorithm then proceeds iteratively:

1. **Assignment Step:** For each pixel i, the algorithm is associated with the nearest cluster center.

2. **Update Step:** After all pixels have been assigned to a cluster, the new cluster centers are calculated as the mean vector $[l, a, b, x, y]^T$ of all pixels belonging to that cluster.
3. **Error Calculation:** The $L2$ norm of the difference between the new cluster centers and the previous cluster centers is computed

The assignment and update steps are repeated iteratively until the error converges or a maximum number of iterations is reached. In practice, 10 iterations are typically sufficient for convergence.

3 Methodology

This study aims to identify an algorithm suitable for real-time alignment of an optical spatial system. The system requires precise three-dimensional alignment of a laser beam and a pinhole in an optical spatial filter. The primary performance metric for algorithm selection is a combination of computational speed and the accuracy of centroid calculation, compared against a predefined 'true' centroid for each image in the dataset. The alignment process is based on analyzing the diffraction pattern generated when the laser beam passes through the pinhole. Based on the theoretical model of diffraction for circular apertures (the Airy disk), the intensity distribution of this pattern can be approximated as a 3D Gaussian function. The X-Y coordinates of the laser beam's center are assumed to correspond to the centroid of this Gaussian distribution, and the Z-axis alignment is confirmed by the maximum intensity value.

To determine the centroid, the performance of the following algorithms will be evaluated and compared:

1. **Connected-Component Labeling:** Utilizing the scikit-image library in Python, this method identifies and labels connected regions in the image, allowing for centroid calculation of the largest connected component.
2. **Fixed threshold, Border Following and Moments (FBM):** Using the cv2 (OpenCV) library, this approach traces the boundary of the diffraction pattern and calculates its spatial moments. The centroid is derived from these moments.
3. **Superpixel Segmentation with SLIC, Quickshift and Felzenszwalb:** Using Scikit library, this algorithms groups pixels into perceptually meaningful regions (superpixels) based on color and spatial proximity. The centroid is then calculated from the superpixel containing the highest intensity.

These algorithms will be implemented in Python and evaluated using a dataset of images captured from an optical spatial filter. The dataset will include images taken at multiple wavelengths, 635nm, 520, 405nm(corresponding to the Thorlabs PL202, PL201 and PL205). For each algorithm and image, the following metrics will be recorded and analyzed:

1. **Accuracy:** Quantified as the Euclidean distance (in pixels) between the algorithm-calculated centroid and the predefined 'true' centroid position. The

'true' centroid position is established based on the theoretical principles of spatial filtering; it corresponds to the alignment that maximizes the percentage of the laser beam passing through the pinhole.
2. **Computational Time:** Measured as the time taken (in seconds or milliseconds) for the algorithm to process a single image and calculate the centroid.
3. **Robustness to High Exposure Times:** Assessed by evaluating the algorithm's performance (accuracy and computational time) on images with varying exposure levels, particularly focusing on high-exposure scenarios that may introduce saturation or blooming effects.

3.1 Computational Set up

The computational experiments were conducted on a desktop computer running Windows 11, equipped with an AMD Ryzen 5 5600X processor and 64 GB DDR4 RAM at 3200 MT/s. To ensure high reproducibility and a consistent software environment, a Docker container was deployed. This container was based on the official python: 3.10-alpine image from Docker Hub. The use of a container isolates the experimental environment, preventing potential conflicts with system-wide libraries or configurations.

3.2 Dataset

Images for the dataset were acquired using a FLIR Blackfly S BFS-U3-13Y3M-C CCD camera (1280×1024 pixels, 10-bit depth). A bi-convex lens (LB1471-A) with a focal point of 50 mm was positioned between the pinhole and the camera sensor. The pinhole was an Edmund Optics of $10\mu m$ diameter and a Newport M-40X microscope objective was used. Images were taken using motorized linear stages to simultaneously move the pinhole and the CCD camera, effectively moving the laser beam across the pinhole and, consequently, across the CCD camera sensor. The experimental dataset was divided into two subsets: one for evaluating computational time and the other for assessing centroid accuracy. **Subset 1 (Computational Time):** This subset comprised 16,499 images. These images were designed to capture a wide range of laser spot positions across the entire camera sensor, providing a diverse set of inputs for evaluating the algorithms' computational efficiency under varying conditions. The laser spot was systematically moved across the sensor's field of view using a motorized stage. **Subset 2 (Centroid Accuracy):** This subset consisted of 493 images randomly selected from Subset 1, but stratified across 29 distinct base positions of the laser spot on the sensor. These 29 positions were evenly distributed across the sensor area. For each image in this subset, the 'true' centroid position was manually determined and recorded. This 'true' centroid serves as the ground truth for evaluating the accuracy of the algorithm-calculated centroids. The Euclidean distance between the 'true' centroid and the algorithm-calculated centroid was used as the accuracy metric.

4 Results and Discussion

4.1 Time Execution Performance

Figure 1 presents the computational time required for each algorithm on the test subset 1. A significant difference in execution time is observed between the superpixel algorithms and the comparison methods (CCL and FBM). On average, the superpixel algorithms were substantially slower: Approximately 594 times slower than FBM and 29 times slower than CCL. However, this average is heavily influenced by the Quickshift algorithm, which exhibited a significantly higher execution time than the other two superpixel algorithms (SLIC and Felzenszwalb). SLIC demonstrated an 86.52% lower execution time than Quickshift, and Felzenszwalb's execution time was 85.89% lower. To provide a more nuanced comparison, we also considered the average execution time of only SLIC and Felzenszwalb. In this case, CCL was 9 times faster, and FBM remained 192 times faster. Among the superpixel algorithms, SLIC was the most time-efficient, exhibiting a 4.42% faster execution time than Felzenszwalb. However, when considering all methods, FBM demonstrated the fastest execution time, followed by CCL. The execution time results reveal a significant performance difference between the tested algorithms. FBM and CCL consistently outperformed the superpixel methods in terms of speed. Superpixel algorithms, despite their slower processing, offer advantages in representing image structure that are crucial for certain applications. The substantial difference in execution time between Quickshift and the other superpixel algorithms (SLIC and Felzenszwalb) underscores the heterogeneity within this class of algorithms. While SLIC proved to be the fastest superpixel method, it remained considerably slower than both FBM and CCL. This finding positions FBM as a highly competitive option when computational efficiency is a primary concern.

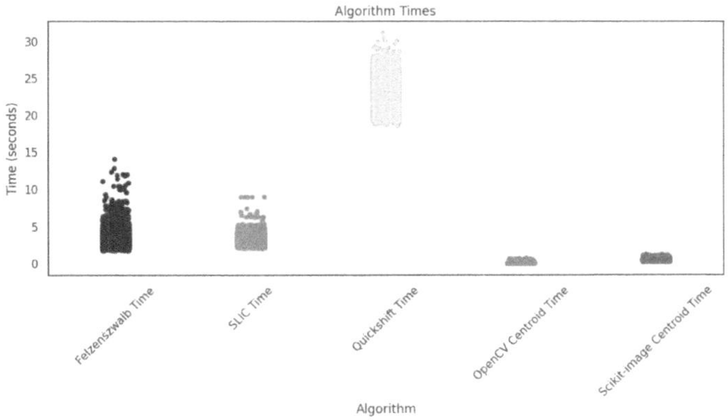

Fig. 1. Execution times for 5 methodologies with 16499 experiments for each algorithm. Each point represents an experiment or image of the subset 1.

4.2 Centroid Accuracy

While the previous section highlighted the superior execution time of the FBM and CCL algorithms compared to superpixel methods, computational speed is not the sole performance metric. Centroid accuracy, which directly impacts the precision of downstream control systems, is critically important. This section analyzes the centroid estimation error of the SLIC, Felzenszwalb, and Quickshift superpixel algorithms in comparison to the FBM and CCL. Figure 2 illustrates the centroid estimation performance when the diffraction pattern is fully contained within the CCD camera sensor's field of view. This analysis utilized a subset of 17 images from a single class within Subset 2 (Subset 2 comprises 493 images from 29 classes, derived from Subset 1). This specific class represents the scenario where the spatial filter is fully aligned. Under these ideal conditions, both FBM and CCL demonstrate superior accuracy. FBM achieved an average Euclidean distance error of 4.47 pixels, and CCL had an average error of 4.74 pixels. In contrast, the superpixel algorithms exhibited significantly higher errors: SLIC (5.01 pixels), Felzenszwalb (61.13 pixels), and Quickshift (84.97 pixels). This demonstrates a clear advantage for FBM and CCL when the entire diffraction pattern is captured. However, the relative performance of the algorithms shifts dramatically when the diffraction pattern is partially occluded, i.e., when the spot is located at the border of the sensor. Figure 3 represents results for 8 of the 29 classes from Subset 2, representing these border-case scenarios. Here, Quickshift and Felzenszwalb show a marked improvement in accuracy, with average centroid errors of 19.69 pixels and 12.74 pixels, respectively. SLIC's performance degrades to an average error of 45.01 pixels, while FBM and CCL exhibit significantly increased errors of 143.84 pixels and 137.82 pixels, respectively. This suggests that Quickshift and Felzenszwalb are more robust to incomplete diffraction patterns, likely because they prioritize finding *some* intensity peak, even if it's not the true, global maximum. FBM and CCL, on the other hand, may be calculating a centroid based on a truncated, and therefore misleading, intensity distribution.

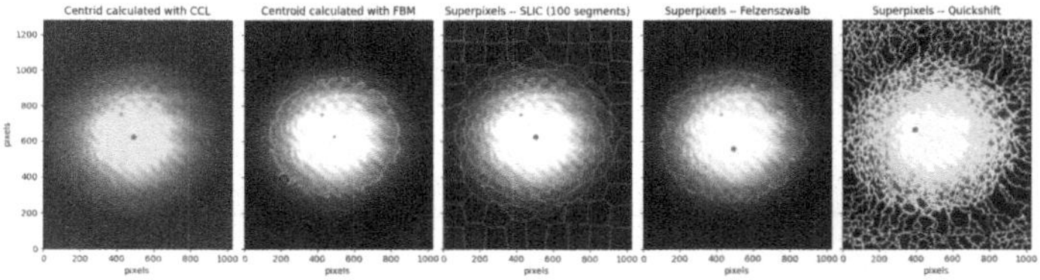

Fig. 2. Representative image for 1 class of the subset 2, where the 5 algorithms are compared. The red dot represents the calculated centroid. (Color figure online)

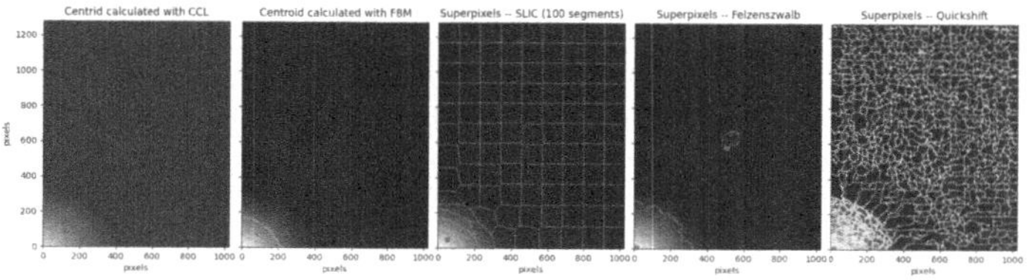

Fig. 3. Representative image for 8 of the 29 classes of subset 2, where this 8 classes are border-case scenarios. The red dot represents the calculated centroid. (Color figure online)

5 Conclusions

This study represents a foundational step towards the development of an auto-aligned spatial filter, designed for enhanced applicability in interferometric metrology and other fields, particularly in non-ideal scenarios. By employing Euclidean distance from the desired centroid and execution time as primary metrics, we have evaluated the performance of several centroid detection machine vision algorithms.

1. **Real-Time Controller Requirements:**
   (a) For real-time control applications, rapid centroid determination is essential. The FBM and CCL demonstrated the shortest execution times, with FBM exhibiting superior speed.
   (b) Superpixel algorithms, such as SLIC and Felzenszwalb, may be suitable for specific systems, although their execution times are generally higher.
   (c) Quickshift was found to be unsuitable due to its excessive processing time.
2. **Centroid Accuracy:**
   (a) The Euclidean distance from the desired centroid served as a measure of accuracy. CCL and FBM exhibited superior accuracy compared to Felzenszwalb and Quickshift.
   (b) Among the superpixel algorithms, SLIC demonstrated the most consistent performance, making it a reliable option when consistency is paramount.

In summary, FBM and CCL offer the fastest execution times, while SLIC provides the most consistent accuracy. Notably, SLIC's relatively low execution time compared to other superpixel algorithms, combined with its ability to estimate cluster size using Eq. (11), enables effective center detection of diffraction patterns. This capability facilitates the approximate determination of diffraction pattern cluster size, thereby enhancing the precision of center detection. As future work will focus on integrating these findings into the design and implementation of an auto-aligned spatial filter, exploring the trade-offs between speed and accuracy in real-world applications.

Acknowledgments. The authors acknowledge financial support from the *Programa de Apoyo a la mejora en las condiciones de producción de los miembros del SNII y SNCA* (PROSNII grants 2023 and 2024). And Mr. Gregorio A. Oropeza-Gomez would also like to acknowledge financial support through a scholarship from CONAHCYT, CVU 1317498.

References

1. Birkbeck, A.L., Zlatanovic, S., Esener, S.C.: Self-aligned spatial filtering using laser optical tweezers. Appl. Opt. **45**(25), 6429–6434 (2006)
2. Weng, J., Zhong, J., Hu, C.: Automatic spatial filtering to obtain the virtual image term in digital holographic microscopy. Appl. Opt. **49**(2), 189–195 (2010)
3. Xiong, H., Zhang, D.: Automatic spatial filtering by combining wavelet-transform modal maxima and mathematical morphology in digital holographic microscopy. Photonics **10**(2) (2023)
4. Goodman, J.W.: Introduction to Fourier optics, 3rd ed. Roberts and Company publishers, Greenwood Village, CO, USA (2005)
5. Lee, S.U., Yoon Chung, S., Park, R.H.: A comparative performance study of several global thresholding techniques for segmentation. Comput. Vision Graph. Image Process. **52**(2), 171–190 (1990)
6. Liu, D., Yu, J.: Otsu method and K-means. In: Proceedings - 2009, 9th International Conference on Hybrid Intelligent Systems, HIS 2009, vol. 1, pp. 344—349. https://doi.org/10.1109/HIS.2009.74
7. Gonzales, R.C., Woods, R.E.: Digital Image Processing, 4th edn. Pearson, New York (2018)
8. Suzuki, S., Be, K.A.: Topological structural analysis of digitized binary images by border following. Comput. Vision Graph. Image Process. **30**(1), 32–46 (1985)
9. Dillencourt, M.B., Samet, H., Tamminen, M.: A general approach to connected-component labeling for arbitrary image representations. J. ACM (JACM) **39**(2), 253–280 (1992)
10. Achanta, R., Shaji, A.: SLIC superpixels compared to state-of-the-art superpixel methods. IEEE Trans. Pattern Anal. Mach. Intell. **34**(11), 2274–2281 (2012)

Towards End-to-End Visual Odometry for Unstructured Agricultural Environments

Víctor Romero-Bautista, Leopoldo Altamirano-Robles(✉), and Raquel Díaz-Hernández

INAOE, Luis Enrique Erro No. 1, 72840 Tonantzintla, Puebla, Mexico
{victor.romero,robles,raqueld}@inaoep.mx

Abstract. Unstructured environments suffer from a lack of helpful visual patterns for ego-motion estimation, such as the agriculture environments, moreover, intrinsic elements of these environments generate conditions that can be considered difficult for most of the state-of-the-art monocular VO/VSLAM systems, which usually fail to estimate the trajectory and generate a map in this type of environments. Deep learning strategies have been studied to improve the performance of VO/VSLAM systems under diverse approaches in structured environments. Nonetheless, scarce investigations have been oriented to the unstructured ones. In this paper, we address the problem of monocular VO in unstructured agricultural environments. A deep learning-based end-to-end monocular VO system is proposed. Firstly, a study of deep learning-based feature extraction models for monocular VO under the conditions of an unstructured agricultural environment is conducted, for this, state-of-the-art CNN models, which use standard convolution, deformable convolution, and convolutional modulation used in ResNet, InternImage, and Conv2Former blocks as the main operators, were evaluated. Second, inspired by DeepVO system, the best feature extractor model identified in our study, and LTC networks, we build an end-to-end monocular VO system. Evaluation results show that the proposed VO system performs better than baseline DeepVO, even in some sequences competitive to state-of-the-art systems.

Keywords: Feature extractor · Unstructured environment · Visual Odometry

1 Introduction

Due to the lack of man-made structures, an agricultural environment can be considered unstructured in which autonomous robots face several obstacles that can be considered difficult for most monocular Visual Odometry (VO) or Visual Simultaneous Localization And Mapping (VSLAM) algorithms in the state of the art. Such obstacles include: texture-less regions, repeatability of patterns

A. P. López-Monroy et al. (Eds.): MCPR 2025, LNCS 15715, pp. 245–256, 2025.
https://doi.org/10.1007/978-3-031-96255-4_23

(visual aliasing), abrupt movements caused by uneven terrain, and non-solid elements that can produce movement in the presence of winds such as plant foliage. As a result, monocular VO/VSLAM systems fail in trajectory estimation and therefore in map generation.

Conventionally, these drawbacks have been addressed by incorporating sensor fusion such as in [4,22], however, this involves several challenges such as the joint calibration of several sensors, as well as the handling of accumulated sensor errors, which requires a more complex system [5].

VO/VSLAM strategies based on deep learning have been used as an exiting alternative to solve problems where classical methods present limitations [3]. These strategies have demonstrated certain robustness under adverse conditions such as illumination drastic changes and dynamic environments [16]. However, when they are assessed under the unstructured environment conditions, such as in agricultural environments, these systems fail in trajectory estimation [19].

In this work, we address the problem of monocular VO in unstructured agricultural environments, we build a deep learning-based monocular VO system employing an end-to-end approach. For this, we inspired in DeepVO [25] system as a framework and in Liquid Time Constant (LTC) networks [11] as the memory unit. To find the correct feature extractor model to employ in our system, we evaluate different state-of-the-art feature extraction models, which are ResNet, InternImage, and Conv2Former, that employs sophisticated operators in their building blocks aiming to expand the receptive field of convolutional neural networks (CNN), such as residual connections with standard convolutions, deformable convolution, and convolutional modulation.

Experiment results show that using the proposed model with the best feature extractor assessed reduces the trajectory estimation error compared to the DeepVO baseline. In addition, some of the trajectory estimation results are competitive compared to state-of-the-art VO/VSLAm systems.

2 Related Work

Several monocular VO/VSLAM algorithms have been proposed in the literature, which have been classified as direct, indirect, deep learning and hybrid [1]. However, few works have focused their development under the conditions of unstructured agricultural environments. Classical and deep learning-based state-of-the-art monocular VO/VSLAM methods fail when are evaluated under the conditions of unstructured agricultural environments as demonstrated in [19].

Few approaches have been proposed to handle the difficulties presented in agricultural environments. In [22], a monocular VO algorithm based on VINS-Mono [18] is proposed, which relies on an IMU sensor to estimate linear motions, while monocular images are employed to compute angular motion; on the other hand, in [28] a stereo-DSO-based [24] VO system is proposed; where one of the main improvements implemented is the key point selection that avoids the drawbacks generated by pattern repeatability, thus generating a consistent map and trajectory. Despite the improvements incorporated, the previously discussed methods still present a high error level during trajectory estimation, which is not feasible for use in real navigation systems. To develop an accurate model for trajectory estimation in agricultural environments, in [4] a system is proposed that fuses different sensor types: GNSS, IMU, and stereo cameras, thus obtaining a VO robust system.

Nevertheless, sensor fusion generates different drawbacks such as sophisticated sensor calibration and computational cost, impacting the autonomous vehicle price, energy consumption, and algorithm complexity. To overcome these drawbacks, in [21] a system combining an OpenVSLAM [23] in a monocular-only approach is proposed, where to solve the scale ambiguity problem, Monodepth2 [9], a depth estimation model based on deep learning, is incorporated, obtaining similar results to its counterparts using stereo cameras. This reveals the incorporation feasibility of deep learning models to decrease the problems presented by conventional VO/VSLAM algorithms in unstructured agricultural environments.

In this work, we believe that a deep learning-based monocular VO system in an end-to-end fashion is reliable for an agricultural environment. To prove this, inspired in DeepVO as a framework, CNN receptive field expansion strategies, and LTC as memory unit, we build an end-to-end monocular VO system for unstructured agricultural environment. This approach does not requires any calibration stage. The results show that the proposed system with the best feature extractor model assessed reduces the trajectory estimation error compared to the baseline DeepVO. In addition, some of the trajectory estimation results are competitive compared to state-of-the-art systems.

3 Methodology

This work is divided into two stages, the first stage consists of identifying a deep learning-based feature extractor model able to extract robust features that allow to estimate of ego-motion from an unstructured agricultural environment; for this, sophisticated deep learning models were employed, which are: ResNet [12], InternImage [26], and Conv2Former [13]. The second stage consists of building and evaluating the proposed system, for which the Rosario [17] dataset was employed. The following subsections describe the DeepVO framework, proposed system, feature extractor models assessed, the dataset, and metrics used

3.1 End-to-End VO System

Given a sequence of monocular rgb images $\mathbf{X}_t$ up to time t, the DeepVO system computes the conditional probability of the poses $\mathbf{Y}_t$, in a probabilistic perspective this can be defined as:

$$\mathrm{P}\left(\mathbf{Y}_t|\mathbf{X}_t\right) = \mathrm{P}\left(\mathbf{y}_1, ..., \mathbf{y}_t|\mathbf{x}_1, ..., \mathbf{x}_t\right) \tag{1}$$

This is done by processing a pair of consecutive images at time $I_{\tau-1}$ and I_τ respectively, where $I_{\tau-1}, I_\tau \in \mathbf{X}_t$, an the output is the 6D relative camera pose in $SE3$.

The DeepVO framework is depicted in Fig. 1, which consist of the feature extractor based on FlowNetS [7] model; a memory unit based on Recurrent Neural Network LSTM [29] model; and finally, the pose estimator based on MLP.

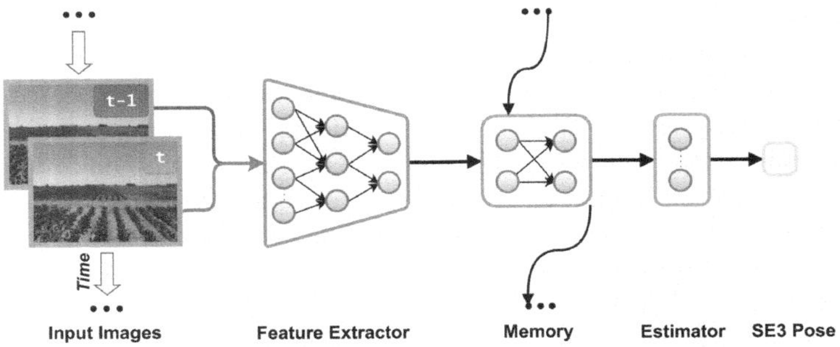

Fig. 1. End-to-end DeepVO framework employed.

To learn the hyper-parameters θ of the DeepVO model, the Euclidean distance between the groundtruth $(\mathbf{p}_\tau, \varphi_\tau)$ at time τ and its estimated one $(\hat{\mathbf{p}}_\tau, \hat{\varphi}_\tau)$ are minimized. The loss function is composed of Mean Squared Error (MSE) of the position $\mathbf{p}$ and orientations φ, which is defined as:

$$\theta^* = \underset{\theta}{argmin} \sum_{i=1}^{N} \sum_{\tau=1}^{t} \|\hat{\mathbf{p}}_\tau - \mathbf{p}_\tau\|_2^2 + \kappa \|\hat{\varphi}_\tau - \varphi_\tau\|_2^2, \tag{2}$$

where θ^* represents the optimal parameters; $\|\cdot\|$ is 2-norm; κ is the scale factor to balance the weights of positions and orientations; and N is the number of samples.

Proposed System. The DeepVO system was developed and tested in the structured environment dataset KITTI [8], where it obtained good results, but when it was trained and assessed in an unstructured agricultural environment, its performance decreased significantly, and the results were not competitive with state-of-the-art systems.

The latter reveals that for a deep learning-based monocular VO system with an end-to-end framework that can perform adequately in an unstructured agriculture environment, sophisticated mechanisms must be employed to enable feature extraction in this type of complex environment.

In this work, we address this problem by building a DeepVO-inspired model, proposing the use of sophisticated feature extraction mechanisms to extract more refined features, and replacing the LSTM memory unit with an LTC model which employs neural circuit policies [15]. We aim to ensure that the proposed system can adequately estimate the trajectory in an unstructured agriculture environment. In the following subsection, the different feature extraction mechanisms investigated are presented.

3.2 Feature Extractor Models

Given the nature of unstructured agricultural environments that lack useful reference landmarks for motion estimation, and following the use of CNN in the base DeepVO system, we conducted a study of receptive field expansion mechanisms in CNN models.

In the state of the art, deep learning based feature extraction models have been proposed in an end-to-end framework used for image classification, recognition or segmentation tasks, such as CNN, ViT [6], and CapsNets [20]. Nevertheless, ViT involves higher computational cost, whereas, CapsNets are still at an early stage of development [14]. So, these models were not considered.

Thus, ResNet, InternImage, and Conv2Former models were employed. A common design property between these models is that they consist of a hierarchical arrangement composed of a stem layer followed by four stages. Each stage is composed of n blocks, which include the residual operation that adds the input information to the output feature map and enables the construction of a deeper model, avoiding gradient vanishing. The stem layer extracts the primary feature maps from the input image, whereas the following stages capture refined features.

We define as the receptive field expansion mechanism to the block designed and its main operator to construct the stages of a model. These models were gradually swapped in the feature extraction model of the proposed system to identify which model performs best. A brief description of these models is presented below.

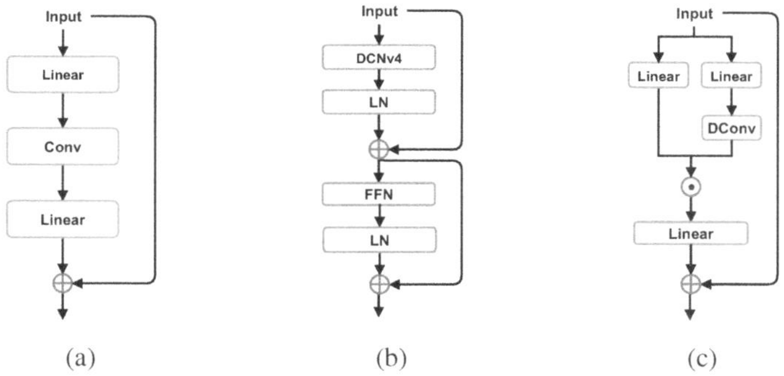

Fig. 2. Blocks employed by the feature extractor models assessed. (a) ResNet; (b) InternImage; (c) Conv2Former; ($\oplus$) means the residual operator, ($\odot$) means the Hadamard product.

ResNet. The stem layer is composed by one convolution operator with kernel size of 7×7, whereas the stages are composed of the block depicted in Fig. 2 (a).

The ResNet block adopts the 3×3 kernel size convolution as the main operator, defined as:

$$\begin{aligned} \mathbf{R} &= \{(-1,-1),(-1,0),...,(0,1),(1,1)\}, \\ y(p_0) &= \sum_{p_n \in \mathbf{R}} x(p_0 + p_n) \cdot w(p_n), \end{aligned} \quad (3)$$

where $\mathbf{R}$ defines the kernel grid; $y(p_0)$ is the output of the neural activation in the current pixel location p_0; x is the input feature map; and $w(p_n)$ is the weight value in the grid location p_n. Different ResNet architectures can be built according to the number of blocks in each stage. We employed the ResNet-18 architecture in our tests.

InternImage. Different from ResNet, the stem layer applies two convolution with 3×3 kernel size to the input image. InternImage block shown in Fig. 2 (b) was designed based on ViTs blocks, which is equipped with more advanced components than ResNet block, such as linear normalization layer (LN), feed-forward networks (FFN), and GELU, furthermore, deformable convolution version 3 (DCNv3) as the main operator. We update this operator by employing the DCNv4 proposed in [27], which is computed as:

$$y(p_0) = \sum_{g \in \mathbf{G}} \sum_{p_n \in \mathbf{R}} x_g(p_0 + p_n + \Delta p_{ng}) \cdot w_g \cdot m_{p_n g}, \quad (4)$$

where, $\mathbf{G}$ denotes the number of aggregation groups; w_g are the projection weights of the group g; m_{gp_n} denotes the modulation scalar of the sampling point p_n in the group g; and Δp_{ng} is the offset corresponding to the location p_n in the group g. In our test, we use the InternImage-Tiny variant.

Conv2Former. This model focuses on replicating ViTs design an thus the performance by replacing the self-attention mechanism with the convolution operator, making a model less computationally expensive than ViTs. Conv2Former block is depicted in Fig. 2 (c), in which the convolutional modulation is performed as the main operator, defined as:

$$\begin{aligned} \mathbf{Z} &= \mathbf{A} \odot \mathbf{V}, \\ \mathbf{A} &= DConv_k(\mathbf{W}_1, \mathbf{X}), \\ \mathbf{V} &= \mathbf{W}_2 \cdot \mathbf{X}, \end{aligned} \quad (5)$$

where, $\mathbf{Z}$ is the output of the convolutional modulation operator; $\mathbf{X}$ is the input token sequence of length N; $\odot$ is the Hadamard product; $\mathbf{W}_1$ and $\mathbf{W}_2$ are the weight matrices of two linear layers, and $DConv_k$ denotes a depthwise convolution with kernel size 11×11. In our test, we use the Conv2Former-T variant.

3.3 Dataset

The Rosario dataset was employed to evaluate the proposed system, it's composed of six sequences captured with an rgb stereo camera, which generates images with size of 670×376; each sequence includes its groundtruth generated using GNSS. The scenes in this dataset are composed of crops, where the camera moves in linear way through the fields until it reaches a return point to rotate and continue with the linear motion, simulating a field robot movements. This scenario is difficulty because there is low texture attributed to at least 50% of the image area corresponding to the sky, and high pattern repeatability attributed to the crops. Figure 3 shown some frames in the Rosario dataset.

(a) (b) (c) (d)

Fig. 3. Frames captured in the Rosario dataset.

3.4 Metric

To evaluate the performance of the proposed system with the different feature extractor models, the Absolute Trajectory Error (ATE) was employed, which is computed as follows:

$$ATE_{trans} = \sqrt{\frac{1}{N}\sum_{i=1}^{N} \left\|T_{gt,i}^{trans} - T_{est,i}^{trans}\right\|^2}, \qquad (6)$$

where $T_{est,i}$ is the estimated trajectory; $T_{gt,i}$ is the groundtruth; N means the total number of poses in a trajectory; and *trans* represents the translation of the variables.

4 Experiments Results

The feature extraction models were assessed separately through the proposed system by replacing the baseline feature extractor based on FlowNetS, thus generating 3 variants of the proposed system, each one using a different feature extractor model (ResNet, InternImage, Conv2Former). These variants were trained with five sequences which are: $\{0, 1, 2, 4, 5\}$; and for test the sequence $\{3\}$ was employed. The input image was resized to 300×150. The learning rate was set to 5×10^{-5}; and 2K epochs. To compute the ATE and trajectory plotting the Evo tool [10] was employed.

In the Table 1, the ATE results obtained by each feature extractor model employed in the proposed system and the vanilla DeepVO model are exposed. ResNet as the feature extractor demonstrated the best performance, reaching an ATE of 5.74 m in the test sequence, whereas in the training sequences reach an ATE of 1.083 m in sequence 2. The worst performance was obtained by the FlowNetS feature extractor model, which is employed in the vanilla DeepVO system.

Table 1. ATE (m) obtained by each feature extractor model variant.

Sequence	FlowNet	ResNet	InternImage	Conv2Former
0	55.088	7.096	6.287	**3.668**
1	18.169	**2.335**	8.069	10.172
2	18.83	**1.083**	3.478	2.552
3	6.451	**5.74**	9.016	28.033
4	30.726	**5.44**	6.474	9.575
5	44.966	**2.144**	9.157	15.958

• Sequences 0,1,2,4,5 were employed for training and sequence 3 for test.

The trajectories generated by each proposed system variants and the vanilla DeepVO are shown in Fig. 4. The dashed line represents the groundtruth and the colored lines represent the trajectories estimated by each system variants. According to the quantitative results exposed in Table 1, trajectories estimated by using ResNet model as feature extractor are more consistent than InternImage, Conv2Former, and FlowNetS.

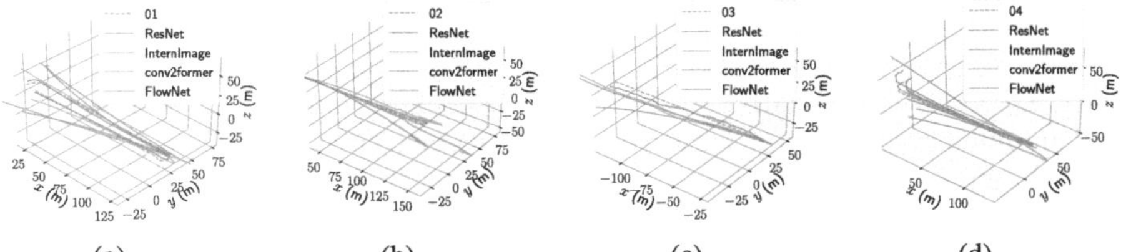

Fig. 4. Qualitative results generated by the variants of the proposed model.

4.1 Comparing Proposed Model Whit State-of-the-Art VO/VSLAM Systems

Once the ResNet model was identified as the best feature extractor model, it was set in the proposed system. Then, using the training approach that consists of using five sequences to train and one to test the model. We trained the proposed model to be tested with the sequence $\{0, 1, 2, 3\}$, therefore, four training stages were carried out.

Table 2 present the ATE results obtained by the proposed system in the tested sequences, and comparing with state-of-the-art models, which are the hybrid system proposed by Shu et al. in [21], MonoViT [30], and ORB-SLAM3 [2] stereo.

Table 2. Comparison of ATE (m) results with state-of-the-art models

Sequence	Proposed	Shu [21]	MonoViT	ORB-SLAM3
1	105.036	12.46	72.17	**6.41**
2	7.923	16.98	**7.3**	10.53
3	**5.74**	14.52	8.08	7.32
4	53.399	13.58	24.70	**7.06**

• MonoViT and ORB-SLAM3 results were taken from [19].

According with the results exposed in the Table 2, the proposed system reaches better performance compared with the others state-of-the-art systems in sequence 3, and in sequence 2 there is a difference of 0.623 m with MonoViT which performs better in this sequence; whereas the worst performance is obtained in sequence 1.

5 Discussion

The feature extraction models assessed using the proposed model based on the DeepVO framework, which are ResNet, InternImage, and Conv2Former, presented better performance than FlowNetS, used in the vanilla DeepVO. This reveals that deeper CNN models can extract more useful features for ego-motion estimation in unstructured agricultural environments.

ResNet presented better performance than InternImage and Conv2Former, suggesting that rigid kernels with a size of 3×3 capture adequate features for ego-motion estimation, in contrast, the use of deformable kernels with a size of 3×3 used in the deformable convolution operator is not optimal, focusing on unsuitable regions of the image, moreover, the use of large rigid kernels used in the convolutional modulation mechanism to emulate the attention mechanism seems to fail to capture adequate features.

In the comparison of the proposed system using ResNet as a feature extractor with state-of-the-art systems, it was identified that in sequences 2 and 3 favorable results are obtained, even superior to the compared systems. However, in sequences 1 and 4, the results were inferior to the rest of the compared systems. These drawbacks are caused by the nature of the dataset, which contains mostly linear motion sequences. That is, sequences $\{0, 1, 4, 5\}$ are composed of approximately 90% linear movements and the rest of rotational and null movements (when the robot gets stuck on the ground), while sequences $\{2, 3\}$ are composed of approximately 100% linear movements. Therefore, the learning process does not contain sufficient examples of rotational movements. Consequently, the performance of the system decreases in sequences with rotational movements.

To overcome this drawback, a data augmentation strategy can be employed; only the rotational motion lapses of each sequence are extracted, aggregating them within the set of learning samples as new sequences. This training approach can improve the results of the proposed system, as shown in Table 3. Here, training was done using sequences $\{0, 2, 3, 4, 5\}$, and the rotational motion lapses of these sequences were added three more times, and sequence $\{1\}$ as the test.

Table 3. Comparison of ATE (m) obtained by employing conventional training and data augmentation methods in sequence 1.

Sequence	Conventional	Data augmentation
1	105.036	99.956

Figure 5 shows the estimated test sequences. Plots (a), (b), and (c), were obtained using the training method described above; plot (d) corresponds to the result obtained using the data augmentation approach of rotational motion sequences. Sequence 1 starts with smooth rotational movements that cause the system turns drastically when is trained conventionally (see Fig. 5 c), whereas with data augmentation the performance improved (see Fig. 5 d), however the estimated trajectory is not well suited. We believe that the appearance difference between sequence 1 (see Fig. 3 b) and the other sequences (see Fig. 3 a,b,c) might influence.

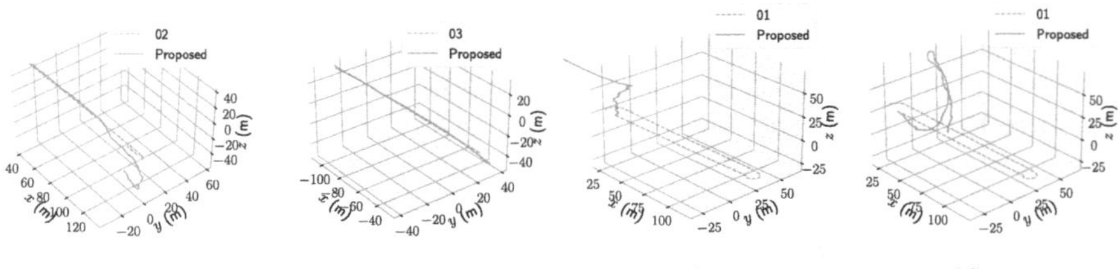

(a) (b) (c) (d)

Fig. 5. Estimated trajectories of the test sequences.

6 Conclusions

Based on the results observed in the experiments, a block architecture based on the residual operator and convolution with rigid kernel using a size of 3×3 is more favorable than employing the DCNv4 and Conv2Former operators for feature extraction in an unstructured agricultural environment. The proposed VO system achieves satisfactory results in the estimation of the test trajectories, where the rotational movements are not extremely pronounced.

As future work, we consider improving the data augmentation method to reduce the susceptibility of the system to rotational movements and appearance difference.

References

1. Barros, A.M., Michel, M., Moline, Y., Corre, G., Carrel, F.: A comprehensive survey of visual slam algorithms. Robotics **11**, 24 (2022)
2. Campos, C., Elvira, R., Rodr'iguez, J., Montiel, J., Tardós, J.D.: Orb-slam3: an accurate open-source library for visual, visual–inertial, and multimap slam. IEEE Trans. Rob. **37**, 1874–1890 (2020)
3. Chen, C., Wang, B., Lu, C.X., Trigoni, A., Markham, A.: A survey on deep learning for localization and mapping: towards the age of spatial machine intelligence. ArXiv arxiv:2006.12567 (2020)
4. Cremona, J., Civera, J., Kofman, E., Pire, T.: Gnss-stereo-inertial slam for arable farming. J. Field Rob. **41**, 2215–2225 (2023)
5. Cremona, J., Comelli, R., Pire, T.: Experimental evaluation of visual-inertial odometry systems for arable farming. J. Field Rob. **39**, 1123–1137 (2022)
6. Dosovitskiy, A., et al.: An image is worth 16×16 words: transformers for image recognition at scale. ArXiv arxiv:2010.11929 (2020)
7. Dosovitskiy, A., et al.: Flownet: learning optical flow with convolutional networks. In: 2015 IEEE International Conference on Computer Vision (ICCV), pp. 2758–2766 (2015)
8. Geiger, A., Lenz, P., Urtasun, R.: Are we ready for autonomous driving? The kitti vision benchmark suite. In: 2012 IEEE Conference on Computer Vision and Pattern Recognition, pp. 3354–3361 (2012)
9. Godard, C., Aodha, O.M., Brostow, G.J.: Digging into self-supervised monocular depth estimation. In: 2019 IEEE/CVF International Conference on Computer Vision (ICCV), pp. 3827–3837 (2018)
10. Grupp, M.: evo: Python package for the evaluation of odometry and slam (2017). https://github.com/MichaelGrupp/evo
11. Hasani, R.M., Lechner, M., Amini, A., Rus, D., Grosu, R.: Liquid time-constant networks. In: AAAI Conference on Artificial Intelligence (2020)
12. He, K., Zhang, X., Ren, S., Sun, J.: Deep residual learning for image recognition. In: 2016 IEEE Conference on Computer Vision and Pattern Recognition (CVPR), pp. 770–778 (2015)
13. Hou, Q., Lu, C., Cheng, M.M., Feng, J.: Conv2former: a simple transformer-style convnet for visual recognition. IEEE Trans. Pattern Anal. Mach. Intell. **46**, 8274–8283 (2022)

14. Kwabena Patrick, M., Felix Adekoya, A., Abra Mighty, A., Edward, B.Y.: Capsule networks – a survey. J. King Saud Univ. - Comput. Inf. Sci. **34**(1), 1295–1310 (2022). https://doi.org/10.1016/j.jksuci.2019.09.014
15. Lechner, M., Hasani, R.M., Amini, A., Henzinger, T.A., Rus, D., Grosu, R.: Neural circuit policies enabling auditable autonomy. Nat. Mach. Intell. **2**, 642–652 (2020)
16. Mokssit, S., Licea, D.B., Guermah, B., Ghogho, M.: Deep learning techniques for visual slam: a survey. IEEE Access **11**, 20026–20050 (2023)
17. Pire, T., Mujica, M., Civera, J., Kofman, E.: The rosario dataset: multisensor data for localization and mapping in agricultural environments. Int. J. Rob. Res. **38**, 633–641 (2018)
18. Qin, T., Li, P., Shen, S.: Vins-mono: a robust and versatile monocular visual-inertial state estimator. IEEE Trans. Rob. **34**, 1004–1020 (2017)
19. Romero-Bautista, V., Altamirano-Robles, L., Díaz-Hernández, R., Zapotecas-Martínez, S., Sanchez-Medel, N.: Evaluation of visual slam algorithms in unstructured planetary-like and agricultural environments. Pattern Recogn. Lett. **186**, 106–112 (2024)
20. Sabour, S., Frosst, N., Hinton, G.E.: Dynamic routing between capsules. Adv. Neural Inf. Process. Syst. **30** (2017)
21. Shu, F., Lesur, P., Xie, Y., Pagani, A., Stricker, D.: Slam in the field: an evaluation of monocular mapping and localization on challenging dynamic agricultural environment. In: 2021 IEEE Winter Conference on Applications of Computer Vision (WACV), pp. 1760–1770 (2020)
22. Song, K., Qiu, R.S., Yang, G., Li, J.: Monocular visual-inertial odometry for agricultural environments. IEEE Access **10**, 103975–103986 (2022)
23. Sumikura, S., Shibuya, M., Sakurada, K.: Openvslam: a versatile visual slam framework. In: Proceedings of the 27th ACM International Conference on Multimedia (2019)
24. Wang, R., Schwörer, M., Cremers, D.: Stereo dso: large-scale direct sparse visual odometry with stereo cameras. In: 2017 IEEE International Conference on Computer Vision (ICCV), pp. 3923–3931 (2017)
25. Wang, S., Clark, R., Wen, H., Trigoni, A.: Deepvo: towards end-to-end visual odometry with deep recurrent convolutional neural networks. In: 2017 IEEE International Conference on Robotics and Automation (ICRA), pp. 2043–2050 (2017)
26. Wang, W., et al.: Internimage: exploring large-scale vision foundation models with deformable convolutions. In: 2023 IEEE/CVF Conference on Computer Vision and Pattern Recognition (CVPR), pp. 14408–14419 (2022)
27. Xiong, Y., et al.: Efficient deformable convnets: rethinking dynamic and sparse operator for vision applications. In: 2024 IEEE/CVF Conference on Computer Vision and Pattern Recognition (CVPR), pp. 5652–5661 (2024)
28. Yu, T., Zhou, J., Wang, L., Xiong, S.: Accurate and robust stereo direct visual odometry for agricultural environment. In: 2021 IEEE International Conference on Robotics and Automation (ICRA), pp. 2480–2486 (2021)
29. Zaremba, W., Sutskever, I.: Learning to execute. ArXiv arxiv:1410.4615 (2014)
30. Zhao, C., et al.: Monovit: self-supervised monocular depth estimation with a vision transformer. In: 2022 International Conference on 3D Vision (3DV), pp. 668–678 (2022)

Medical Applications of Pattern Recognition

Early Detection of Acute Myocardial Infarction (AMI) Risk Using Optimized Machine Learning Models

Vanessa Fontalvo Reniz[1](✉), Carlos Alberto Leones Rivera[1], Yazmina Yolanda Vecino Yepes[1], Jose Escorcia-Gutierrez[2], and Margarita Gamarra[1]

[1] Universidad del Norte, Barranquilla, Colombia
{vreniz,caleones,yazminav,mrgamarra}@uninorte.edu.co
[2] Universidad de la Costa, Barranquilla, Colombia
jescorci56@cuc.edu.co

Abstract. Cardiovascular diseases (CVDs) remain a leading cause of morbidity and mortality worldwide. This study explores the early detection of acute myocardial infarction (AMI) risk through a comparative analysis of eight machine learning models, including Random Forest, Support Vector Machines, and Gradient Boosting, among others. The methodology incorporates an enhanced data preprocessing framework, which involves outlier detection, a combination of nominal and ordinal encoding techniques, and imputation using both K-Nearest Neighbors (KNN) and Random Forest approaches. Feature selection and hyperparameter tuning were performed using Grid Search to optimize model performance. Our results indicate that the Random Forest model with Random Forest imputation achieved the highest accuracy of 68%, demonstrating its effectiveness in predictive tasks. These findings underscore the potential of machine learning models in enhancing clinical decision-making for cardiovascular risk assessment.

Keywords: Acute myocardial infarction · Clinical decision support · Data Mining · Grid Search · Machine learning

1 Introduction

Cardiovascular diseases (CVDs) remain the leading cause of death globally, accounting in 2019 for approximately 32% of all global deaths, claiming an estimated 17.9 million lives [1]. Among these, acute myocardial infarction (AMI), commonly known as a heart attack, is one of the most critical and prevalent conditions, often requiring prompt and accurate diagnosis to mitigate severe outcomes. Traditional diagnostic methods, while widely utilized, are usually limited by their reliance on subjective clinical interpretation and time-consuming procedures, which can delay critical interventions [2].

In this context, machine learning (ML) has emerged as a transformative tool in healthcare, capable of analyzing complex and multidimensional datasets to derive predictive insights. By leveraging ML, healthcare providers can potentially achieve

A. P. López-Monroy et al. (Eds.): MCPR 2025, LNCS 15715, pp. 259–268, 2025.
https://doi.org/10.1007/978-3-031-96255-4_24

faster, more accurate, and objective assessments of AMI risk, thereby supporting timely decision-making in clinical workflows [3].

This work investigates the application of multiple ML models, including Random Forest, Support Vector Machines (SVM), K-Nearest Neighbors (KNN), Naïve Bayes (NV), Decision Tree (DT), Logistic Regression (LR), Gradient Boosting (GB), and AdaBoost (AB), to predict AMI risk using the University of California Irvine (UCI) heart disease dataset. In this context, early detection refers to identifying high-risk patients before the onset of critical symptoms, allowing physicians to intervene in a more timely and informed manner. The study focuses on a comparative analysis of these models, optimizing predictive performance through advanced preprocessing techniques such as K-Nearest Neighbors (KNN) and Random Forest imputation methods to handle missing data. Additionally, hyperparameter tuning via Grid Search is employed to enhance the model's predictive accuracy. A comprehensive evaluation is conducted by comparing key performance metrics, including accuracy, precision, recall, and F1-score, to identify the most effective model for AMI risk prediction.

To support the growing integration of ML in predictive medicine and to provide a robust foundation for future research, this work makes the following key contributions:

- A comparative analysis of eight machine learning models for the early detection of AMI risk.
- The integration of hybrid imputation techniques (KNN and Random Forest) to handle missing data effectively.
- A systematic evaluation based on accuracy, precision, recall, and F1-score to determine the most suitable predictive model.
- The provision of a reproducible workflow for AMI risk prediction to facilitate further research in predictive medicine.

2 Related Work

Several studies have applied machine learning techniques to predict acute myocardial infarction (AMI), focusing on different models, challenges, and advancements. Salet et al. [4] developed and evaluated random forest models for predicting primary care patients' AMI and ischemic heart disease (IHD). The study compared the performance of these models with the traditional SMART algorithm, demonstrating that machine-learning models achieved higher accuracy, sensitivity, and specificity.

Olsson de Capretz et al. [5] analyzed logistic regression and artificial neural networks to predict AMI or 30-day mortality in emergency department chest pain patients. Their study highlighted the effectiveness of using patient demographic data, electrocardiograms (ECGs), and blood tests to improve predictive capabilities, showcasing the potential of ML in enhancing early AMI detection.

Li et al. [6] compared seven machine learning-based models to predict heart failure following AMI. The study identified XGBoost as the best-performing model, emphasizing the importance of optimizing machine learning algorithms for predicting adverse cardiovascular events post-AMI.

Miah et al. [7] conducted a comparative analysis of six ML models, including logistic regression, support vector machines (SVM), decision trees, bagging, XGBoost, and LightGBM. Their findings revealed that XGBoost achieved the highest accuracy, underscoring its potential to improve predictive precision for myocardial infarction.

Despite previous contributions, key gaps remain most studies evaluate models in isolation and overlook the impact of different imputation strategies. Our work addresses these gaps through a unified comparison of eight machine learning models, integrating hybrid imputation techniques and consistent evaluation metrics for early AMI risk detection.

3 Methodology

3.1 Dataset Description

The UCI Heart Disease dataset, sourced from the University of California Irvine Machine Learning Repository [8], contains **920 samples** with **16 features**, including **demographic, clinical, and test data. Age, cholesterol levels, resting blood pressure, and electrocardiographic results** are essential indicators for predicting acute myocardial infarction (AMI). The target variable indicates the presence or absence of AMI.

3.2 Exploratory Data Analysis (EDA)

EDA was performed to analyze data distribution, detect outliers, and handle missing values. Visualizations were employed to identify potential patterns and relationships among features to guide the preprocessing stage.

3.3 Data Preprocessing

The preprocessing step included the following:

1. **Handling Missing Data:** Missing values were found in the **ca** and **thal** variables, which were handled using KNN and Random Forest imputation techniques. KNN was chosen due to its simplicity in handling small datasets, while Random Forest offered better performance in preserving feature relationships, with parameters such as the following:
   - **K-Nearest Neighbors (KNN)** with parameters set to $k = 5$ uniform weighting, auto neighbor search algorithm, and Euclidean distance as the metric.
   - **Random Forest Imputation** with parameters including `n_estimators=100`, `max_depth=None`, `min_samples_split=2`, and `random_state=42`. Hyperparameter tuning was conducted via Grid Search to optimize model performance.

   Hyperparameter tuning was conducted via Grid Search to optimize model performance. Grid Search explored 2 to 4 values per hyperparameter, resulting in 10 to 50 combinations depending on the model.
2. **Categorical Variable Encoding:** A hybrid encoding approach was applied. Nominal encoding was used for variables such as sex, cp (chest pain type), and thal, while ordinal encoding was applied to slope, restecg, and fbs, as these reflect ordered or binary categories.

3. **Outlier Removal:** Outliers were detected using the Z-score method, applied to the variables age, trestbps, chol, thalach, and oldpeak. Values exceeding three standard deviations above or below the mean were considered outliers and removed from the dataset.
4. **Feature Scaling:** Standardization (Z-score normalization) was applied to numerical features to ensure equal weighting across all models.

3.4 Model Selection and Hyperparameter Optimization

Eight machine learning models were implemented, optimized using Grid Search, and evaluated using Cross-Validation (CV). The chosen models and their best parameters were:

1. **Random Forest (RF):**

```
max_depth: None
max_features: 'sqrt'
min_samples_leaf: 2
min_samples_split: 2
n_estimators: 100 (Random Forest Imputation), 200 (KNN Imputation)
```

2. **Support Vector Machine (SVM):**

```
c: 10
gamma: 'scale'
kernel: 'rbf' Radial Basis Function (RBF)
```

3. **K-nearest Neighbors (KNN):**

```
n_neighbors: 7
weights: 'uniform'
algorithm: 'auto'
```

4. **Naïve Bayes (NB):** Gaussian Naive Bayes was used with default parameters.
5. **Decision Tree (DT):**

```
max_depth: 10
max_features: 'sqrt'
min_samples_leaf: 4
min_samples_split: 2
```

6. **Logistic Regression (LR):**

```
c: 0.1 (Random Forest Imputation), 1 (KNN Imputation)
penalty: 'l2'
solver: 'liblinear'
learning_rate: 0.1
max_depth: 3 (KNN Imputation), 5 (Random Forest Imputation)
n_estimators: 50 (KNN Imputation), 200 (Random Forest Imputation)
sub_sample: 1.0 or 0.8
```

7. **AdaBoost (AB):**

```
learning_rate: 0.01
n_estimators: 50 (Random Forest Imputation), 200 (KNN Imputation)
```

Model evaluation was conducted using 5-fold Cross-Validation to ensure generalizability and reduce overfitting. The full implementation, including data preprocessing steps, model training, and evaluation procedures, is publicly available on Kaggle [9] to facilitate reproducibility and further research.

3.5 Evaluation Metrics

Model performance was evaluated using the following standard classification metrics:

1. **Accuracy:** Measures overall model correctness.

$$Accuracy = \frac{TP + TN}{TP + TN + FP + FN} \tag{1}$$

2. **Precision:** Indicates the proportion of correct identifications.

$$Precision = \frac{TP}{TP + FP} \tag{2}$$

3. **Recall:** Measures the proportion of actual positives correctly identified.

$$Recall = \frac{TP}{TP + FN} \tag{3}$$

4. **F1- Score:** The harmonic mean of precision and recall.

$$\mathrm{F1} = 2 \times \frac{Precision \times Recall}{Precision + Recall} \tag{4}$$

3.6 Cross Validation

A 5-fold Cross-Validation approach was used to ensure model generalizability and reduce overfitting. The CV strategy divides the dataset into five equal parts, using four parts for training and one for testing in each iteration, which helps in obtaining unbiased evaluation results.

3.7 Models Comparison

Each model's performance was evaluated using key metrics: accuracy, precision, recall, and F1-score. The results were compared between the two imputation methods, K-Nearest Neighbors (KNN) and Random Forest (RF). The complete workflow of the study is depicted (see Fig. 1).

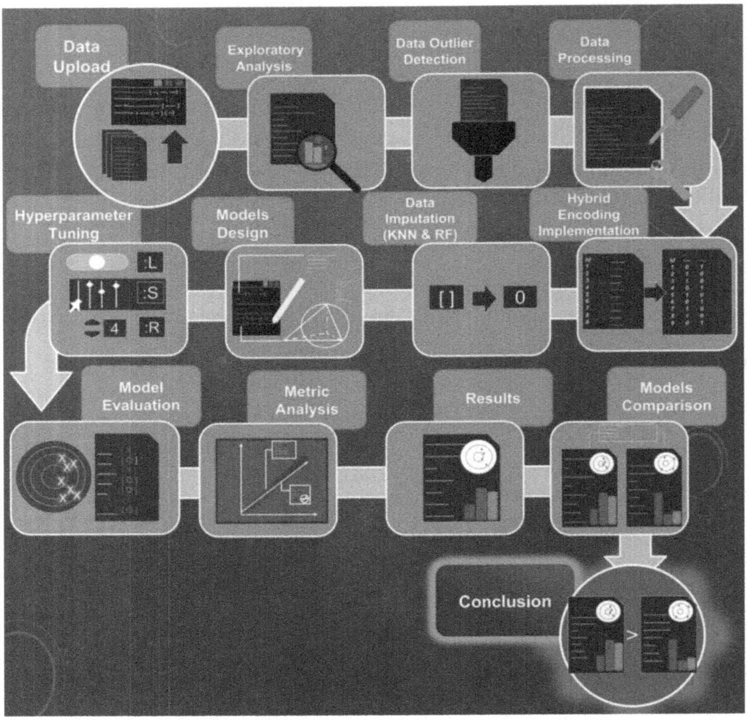

Fig. 1. Machine Learning Workflow Block Diagram.

4 Results and Discussion

4.1 Exploratory Data Analysis (EDA)

The exploratory data analysis (EDA) provided insights into key feature distributions, identified relevant patterns, and addressed data imbalances that could affect model performance. A gender imbalance was observed, with more male than female patients, and most individuals had normal fasting blood sugar levels. The majority were middle-aged, with a flat slope of peak exercise and a considerable presence of exercise-induced angina. Most patients had zero or one major vessel colored by fluoroscopy.

Figure 2 presents distributions for cholesterol levels and maximum heart rate, offering demographic and physiological context. Figure 3 shows resting electrocardiographic results and fasting blood sugar levels, while Fig. 4 includes ST depression and thallium stress test results as key indicators of heart disease presence and severity.

Lastly, the analysis of heart disease presence revealed an imbalanced distribution across different severity levels, with a higher proportion of patients showing no heart disease compared to those with varying degrees of the condition. The target variable distribution showed a higher proportion of patients without AMI compared to those diagnosed, indicating a slight class imbalance in the dataset.

These figures summarize key patterns that guided feature selection and model design. They also underscore the role of preprocessing such as outlier removal, scaling, and imputation in stabilizing data. Notably, ST depression, thallium stress test results, and exercise-induced angina stood out as highly relevant features, reinforcing the clinical value of the predictive models.

a). Cholesterol Level **b). Maximum Heart rate**

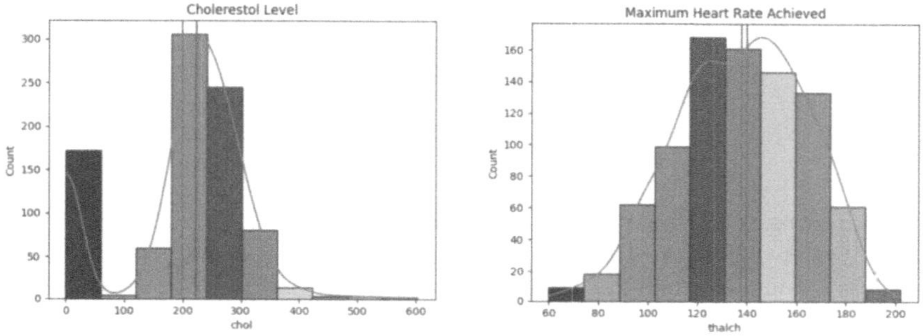

Fig. 2. Demographic and Clinical Feature Distributions.

c). Resting Electrocardiographic **d). Fasting Blood Sugar**

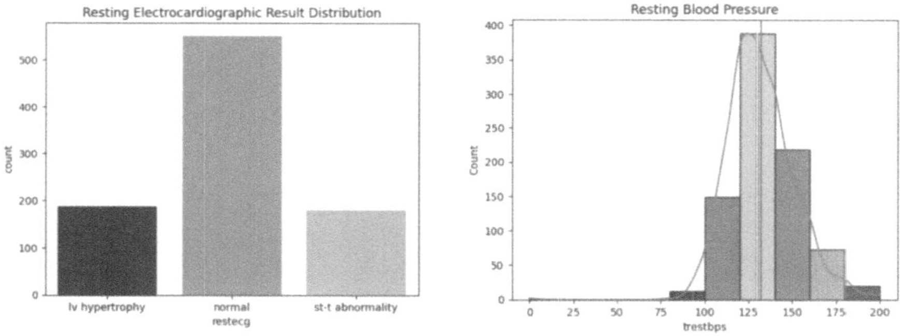

Fig. 3. Exercise and Electrocardiographic Feature Distributions.

The results presented in Table 1 highlight the comparative performance of various machine learning models for the early detection of acute myocardial infarction (AMI) using two distinct imputation techniques: Random Forest and K-Nearest Neighbors (KNN). The table was constructed based on the weighted average values of key performance metrics, including precision, recall, F1-score, and accuracy, to comprehensively assess different class distributions. Random Forest consistently outperforms KNN across all metrics, achieving the highest accuracy (68%), an F1-score of 0.65, a precision of 0.63, and a recall of 0.68 demonstrating its robustness in handling missing data and preserving essential patterns within the dataset. Gradient Boosting follows

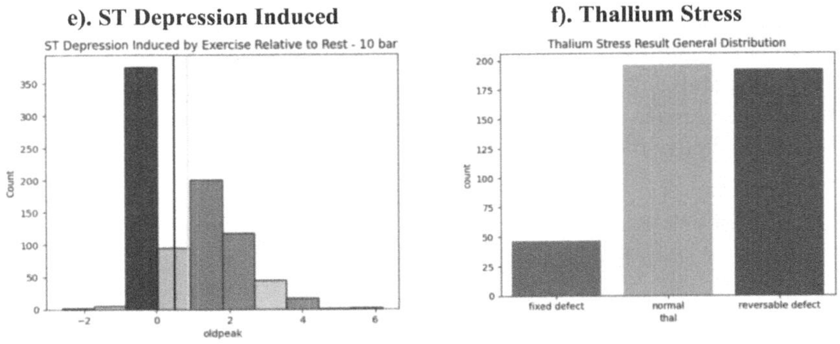

Fig. 4. Cardiac Diagnostic Feature Distributions.

closely, achieving an F1-score of 0.67 and an accuracy of 68%, reinforcing its effectiveness in AMI risk prediction. These results correspond to the test sets generated through 5-fold Cross-Validation, and the consistent performance across folds suggests that no significant overfitting was observed.

Table 1. Test Performance Metrics of Machine Learning Models with Random Forest and KNN Imputation

Model	Imputation	Precision	Recall	F1-Score	Accuracy
Random Forest	Random Forest	0.63	0.68	0.65	0.68
	K-Nearest neighbors	0.64	0.68	0.65	0.68
Support Vector Machine	Random Forest	0.52	0.64	0.57	0.64
	K-Nearest neighbors	0.56	0.64	0.59	0.64
K-Nearest neighbors	Random Forest	0.59	0.66	0.61	0.66
	K-Nearest neighbors	0.59	0.66	0.61	0.66
Naïve Bayes	Random Forest	0.65	0.46	0.53	0.46
	K-Nearest neighbors	0.62	0.46	0.52	0.46
Decision Tree	Random Forest	0.60	0.62	0.61	0.62
	K-Nearest neighbors	0.58	0.57	0.57	0.57
Logistic Regression	Random Forest	0.57	0.65	0.60	0.65
	K-Nearest neighbors	0.55	0.62	0.58	0.62
Gradient Boosting	Random Forest	0.67	0.68	0.67	0.68
	K-Nearest neighbors	0.65	0.67	0.66	0.67
AdaBoost	Random Forest	0.52	0.64	0.57	0.64
	K-Nearest neighbors	0.51	0.62	0.56	0.62

The results show that while Random Forest and Gradient Boosting models demonstrate strong generalization capabilities, other models show varying performance degrees. Specifically, Naïve Bayes exhibits the lowest overall performance, with an accuracy of 0.46, precision of 0.65, and an F1-score of 0.53, indicating its limitations in handling the complexity of the dataset. Support Vector Machines (SVM) and Logistic Regression achieve moderate results.

5 Conclusions

In conclusion, the analysis highlights the crucial role of imputation techniques in AMI prediction performance. Random Forest imputation consistently outperforms K-Nearest Neighbors (KNN) across models, with the Random Forest model achieving the highest accuracy of 68% and better overall metrics. This confirms its effectiveness in handling missing data and enhancing predictive accuracy. Gradient Boosting and Random Forest models showed superior performance, making them strong candidates for clinical application.

This level of performance is consistent with results reported in related studies, where accuracy scores typically range between 65% and 70%, especially for ensemble models like Gradient Boosting and Random Forest. Therefore, our findings are in line with the current state of the art.

Furthermore, the study underscores the importance of carefully selecting preprocessing methods to optimize machine learning outcomes in medical diagnosis. The observed differences in model performance due to imputation techniques highlight the need for tailored data processing strategies that align with the dataset's characteristics. Future work should explore additional preprocessing techniques and feature engineering methods further to improve prediction accuracy and generalizability in real-world healthcare applications.

Disclosure of Interests. The authors have no competing interests to declare relevant to this article's content.

References

1. 'cardiovascular diseases (CVDs)'. https://www.who.int/news-room/fact-sheets/detail/cardiovascular-diseases-(cvds). Accessed 22 Dec 2024
2. Khalil, H.: Traditional and novel diagnostic biomarkers for acute myocardial infarction. Egypt. J. Intern. Med. **34**, 87 (2022). https://doi.org/10.1186/s43162-022-00178-w
3. Nie, S., Zhang, S., Zhao, Y., et al.: Machine learning applications in acute coronary syndrome: diagnosis, outcomes and management. Adv. Ther. (2024).https://doi.org/10.1007/s12325-024-03060-z
4. Salet, N., Gökdemir, A., Preijde, J., van Heck, C.H., Eijkenaar, F.: Using machine learning to predict acute myocardial infarction and ischemic heart disease in primary care cardiovascular patients. PLoS ONE **19**(7), e0307099 (2024)
5. de Capretz, P.O., Björkelund, A., Björk, J., et al.: Machine learning for early prediction of acute myocardial infarction or death in acute chest pain patients using electrocardiogram and blood tests at presentation. BMC Med. Inform. Decis. Mak. **23**, 25 (2023). https://doi.org/10.1186/s12911-023-02119-1

6. Li, X., Shang, C., Xu, C., et al.: Development and comparison of machine learning-based models for predicting heart failure after acute myocardial infarction. BMC Med. Inform. Decis. Mak. **23**, 165 (2023). https://doi.org/10.1186/s12911-023-02240-1
7. Miah, J., Ca, D.M., Sayed, M.A., Lipu, E.R., Mahmud, F., Arafat, S.M.Y.: Improving cardiovascular disease prediction through comparative analysis of machine learning models: a case study on myocardial infarction. In: 15th International Conference on Innovations in Information Technology (IIT) - Track 2: Artificial Intelligence in Data Science (2023). arXiv:2311.00517 [cs.LG]. https://doi.org/10.48550/arXiv.2311.00517
8. Janosi, A., Steinbrunn, W., Pfisterer, M., Detrano, R.: Heart disease. UCI Mach. Learn. Repository (1989). https://doi.org/10.24432/C52P4X
9. Leones, C., Fontalvo, V., Yepes, Y.: ML for Early Detection of Heart Disease. Kaggle (2025). https://www.kaggle.com/code/caleones/ml-for-early-detection-of-heart-disease/input

Deep Learning Approaches for Glaucoma Detection: A Comparative Study of CNN Models on Retinal Fundus Images

Eugenia Arrieta Rodríguez[1,3](✉), José Araque-Gallardo[1,2], Oscar Luis Teheran Forero[3], Emiro De-La-Hoz-Franco[1], and José Escorcia-Gutierrez[1]

[1] Department of Computational Science and Electronic, Universidad de la Costa, CUC, Barranquilla 080020, Colombia

[2] Department of Electronic Engineering, Universidad de Sucre, Sincelejo 700001, Colombia

[3] Universidad del Sinú Elías Bechara Zainúm, Cartagena 130015, Colombia

eugenia.arrieta@unisinu.edu.co

Abstract. Glaucoma is a leading cause of irreversible blindness worldwide. Early detection is crucial to prevent vision loss, but traditional diagnostic methods are subjective and prone to variability. This study compares the performance of three pre-trained convolutional neural network models: ResNet50, VGG16, and InceptionV3 in classifying glaucoma from images of nonglaucoma fundus using the ACRIMA dataset The models were evaluated based on accuracy, recall, precision, F1 score and AUC-ROC metrics. InceptionV3 demonstrated superior performance, achieving perfect classification (100% accuracy and AUC-ROC), while both ResNet50 and VGG16 reached excellent results (97.86% accuracy) with slightly different error patterns. Computational efficiency analysis revealed significant differences, with ResNet50 requiring 74 min for training, InceptionV3 95 min, and VGG16 228 min. These findings indicate that while InceptionV3 offers optimal diagnostic accuracy, ResNet50 provides an excellent balance between performance and computational efficiency, making it potentially more suitable for resource-constrained clinical environments.

Keywords: Glaucoma detection · Retinal image classification · Deep learning · Convolutional neural networks · Medical image analysis

1 Introduction

Glaucoma is a group of eye diseases characterised by an increase in intraocular pressure that causes optic neuropathy and progressive visual field loss. It is one of the leading causes of irreversible blindness in the world and affects millions of people worldwide [17]. Traditional diagnostic methods include evaluation of the optic disc and adjacent retinal nerve fibre layer (RNFL) by a qualified specialist. This assessment is usually performed by ophthalmoscopy or slit-lamp

A. P. López-Monroy et al. (Eds.): MCPR 2025, LNCS 15715, pp. 269–278, 2025.
https://doi.org/10.1007/978-3-031-96255-4_25

bioscopy, often supplemented by perimetry to assess visual field defects. However, these methods are subjective and can lead to inconsistencies and errors due to inter-examiner variability and the subtle nature of early glaucoma changes [11]. Fundus imaging has become a crucial tool in the diagnosis and follow-up of glaucoma. Changes such as a increased optical cup-to-disc ratio, RNFL thinning, and the presence of notches or hemorrhages at the disc margin are critical indicators of glaucoma damage [6]

An example of a cropped fundus image for both a healthy patient and a patient with glaucoma is presented in Fig. 1. In the healthy eye (Fig. 1a), we can observe a normal cup-to-disc ratio with a well-defined neuroretinal rim. The glaucomatous eye (Fig. 1b) displays characteristic pathological changes including an increased cup-to-disc ratio, thinning of the neuroretinal rim, and alterations in the optic disc margin, which are critical indicators of glaucoma damage.

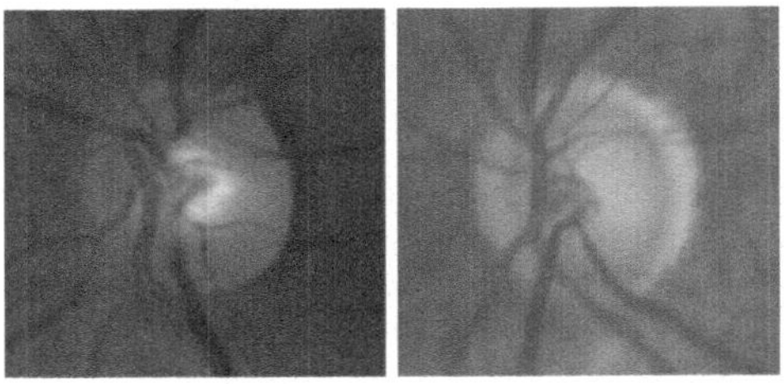

(a) (b)

Fig. 1. ACRIMA dataset samples: (a) Fundus image from a healthy patient; (b) Fundus image from a patient with glaucoma.

The advent of Artificial Intelligence (AI) has significantly impacted ophthalmology, particularly in the diagnosis of glaucoma. AI techniques, especially deep learning models, have shown great promise in automating the detection of glaucoma from fundus images. These methods typically involve pre-processing the images, extracting relevant features, and applying machine learning algorithms to classify the presence or absence of glaucoma. Convolutional Neural Networks (CNNs) are the most widely used architecture for this purpose, given their exceptional performance in image recognition tasks. Among various CNN models, architectures such as VGG19 [14], ResNet50 [7], and InceptionV3 [16] have demonstrated high accuracy and robustness in the detection of glaucoma. These models leverage transfer learning, where pre-trained networks on large datasets (such as ImageNet) are fine-tuned on medical images to improve diagnostic accuracy.

The research by Alayón et al. is a fairly exhaustive comparative study that analyzes 15 different deep learning architectures for glaucoma detection, evaluating them on multiple public datasets. Their main conclusion is that there are no significant differences between traditional CNNs and Vision Transformer-based systems for this specific task, which provides valuable guidance for researchers and developers in this field [12].

The main contributions of this paper can be summarized as follows:

- A comprehensive comparative analysis of three pre-trained CNN architectures (ResNet50, VGG16, and InceptionV3) for glaucoma detection using the ACRIMA fundus imaging dataset.
- Development of a robust transfer learning methodology for ophthalmologic diagnosis, including standardized image pre-processing, hyperparameter optimization, and validation protocols.
- The study demonstrates the feasibility of deep learning approaches for clinical decision support in ophthalmology using only the fundus image.

This paper is organized as follows. Section 2 reviews the related work. Afterwards, Sect. 3 shows the materials and the proposed methodology to address the problem related to glaucoma detection. Thereafter, Sect. 4 exposes the results and the discussion. Finally, Sect. 5 describes the conclusions and future research lines of this study.

2 Related Works

Recent advances in deep learning have achieved state of the art performance in glaucoma detection using fundus images. Key architectures include: The VGG19 architecture was originally introduced by Simonyan and Zisserman in 2014. With its 19 layers, VGG19 has demonstrated excellent performance in ImageNet classification. This architecture has been used to detect tissues with glaucoma by fine-tuning the network on fundus images downloaded from the ACRIMA and ORIGA datasets. The deep architecture of VGG19 captures fine structures and hierarchical patterns in fundus images, enhancing the classification results [14]. In 2015, Szegedy et al. proposed GoogleNet, also known as Inception v1, which introduced inception modules for efficient feature extraction. GoogleNet has been applied to the detection of glaucoma by modifying the last few layers for binary classification. This model has shown promising results when trained and evaluated in the REFUGE dataset, demonstrating its effectiveness in handling fundus images [15]. He et al. (2016) presented ResNet50, a variant of the ResNet architecture with 50 layers, which addresses the vanishing gradient problem in deep networks. ResNet50 has been employed for the prediction of glaucoma by fine-tuning the model on the DRISHT-GS dataset. Its skip connections allow the network to learn residual mappings, making it suitable for extracting features relevant to glaucoma detection [7]. Szegedy et al. (2016) also proposed Inception v3, an extension of GoogleNet with improved inception modules. Inception v3 has been used for the classification of glaucoma by training the model on ACRIMA data. The model's ability to capture spatial hierarchies of features has made it effective in distinguishing between glaucoma and healthy fundus images [16].

Escorcia-Gutierrez et al. have explored various pre-trained convolutional neural network models for the detection of diabetic retinopathy. Their studies emphasize the efficacy of transfer learning in improving diagnostic accuracy for retinal diseases. In a 2022 study, they used ResNet50 and InceptionV3, demonstrating significant improvements in classification performance through transfer learning techniques [3,4]. In 2020, Li et al. proposed AG-CNN, a deep learning model incorporating attention mechanisms for glaucoma detection from fundus images. Trained on the large-scale LAG dataset, which includes attention maps from ophthalmologists, the model achieved 96.2% accuracy and an AUC of 0.975, demonstrating the benefit of attention-guided learning in automated glaucoma screening [10]

In summary, techniques are identified that allow glaucoma classification to be achieved with good results, such as attention mechanisms, new CNN architectures and hybrid models that combine CNNs and RNNs for glaucoma detection.

3 Materials and Methods

3.1 Datasets

The ACRIMA dataset, introduced by Díaz-Pinto et al. (2019), is employed in this study for binary glaucoma classification [2].

This dataset is publicly available and comprises retinal fundus images intended to aid in the development and evaluation of automated glaucoma detection algorithms.The ACRIMA dataset contains a total of 705 images, 309 healthy and 396 with glaucoma. Each image is a full-colour fundus photograph showing the entire posterior segment of the eye, including the optic disc, macula and blood vessels. The images are in TIFF format and have a resolution of 1024×1024 pixels.The ACRIMA dataset was divided using a stratified approach to maintain class distribution: 80% (565 images: 326 glaucoma, 239 non-glaucoma) for training and 20% (140 images: 70 glaucoma, 70 non-glaucoma) for testing. During the training process, we implemented validation in each epoch using a portion of the training data (20% of the training set) to monitor model performance and prevent overfitting.

3.2 Methods

The selection of ResNet50, VGG16, and InceptionV3 for this comparative study was based on multiple factors. First, these architectures have demonstrated superior performance in medical image classification tasks across multiple studies, as reported in [18,19], and [8]. Second, they represent diverse architectural approaches: ResNet50 incorporates residual connections to mitigate vanishing gradients in deep networks; VGG16 offers a straightforward yet effective deep architecture; and InceptionV3 employs parallel convolutions at different scales. Additionally, these models have been widely adopted in ophthalmological applications, providing a relevant benchmark for comparison with existing literature.

While performance reported in previous studies was a consideration, our selection was also motivated by the need to evaluate fundamentally different CNN architectural paradigms within a consistent experimental framework.

ResNet50 was chosen for its deep architecture and residual learning framework, which effectively mitigates the problem of vanishing gradients and enables the training of very deep networks. This model has demonstrated superior performance in various image classification tasks, as reported in [7]. VGG16, with its straightforward yet deep architecture, has been widely utilized in medical image analysis due to its strong performance and generalizability, as evidenced in [14] and further supported by reviews [1,19]. InceptionV3 was selected for its innovative architecture, which employs multiple convolutional filter sizes within the same module to capture various features, thus enhancing its effectiveness in complex image analysis [16]. The capability of this model is corroborated by [8], which supports the use of inception models for retinal image classification tasks.

The images were resized to the required input dimensions for each model (224×224 for ResNet50 and VGG16, 299×299 for InceptionV3), and normalized matching the mean and standard deviation of the ImageNet dataset.

Figure 2 illustrates the comprehensive framework employed in this study for the classification of glaucoma using pre-trained deep learning models. The framework is structured to leverage the strengths of state-of-the-art CNN architectures, specifically ResNet50, VGG19, and InceptionV3, to accurately differentiate between glaucoma and nonglaucoma focus fundus images.

The selection of ResNet50, VGG16, and InceptionV3 for this comparative study was based on multiple factors. First, these architectures have demonstrated superior performance in medical image classification tasks across multiple studies, as reported in [7,14], and [16]. Second, they represent diverse architectural approaches: ResNet50 incorporates residual connections to mitigate vanishing gradients in deep networks; VGG16 offers a straightforward yet effective deep architecture; and InceptionV3 employs parallel convolutions at different scales. Additionally, these models have been widely adopted in ophthalmological applications, providing a relevant benchmark for comparison with existing literature.

In this work, we will employ essential performance metrics for evaluating our machine learning models: Accuracy (measuring the overall proportion of correct predictions), Recall (assessing the model's ability to correctly identify positive cases), Precision (evaluating the accuracy of positive predictions), F1-Score (providing a balanced measure through the harmonic mean of Precision and Recall), and AUC-ROC (measuring the model's discriminative ability across different classification thresholds) [5]. These metrics are calculated using the confusion matrix values: True Positives (TP), True Negatives (TN), False Positives (FP), and False Negatives (FN).

4 Results

In this study, we implemented and compared three pre-trained CNN models: ResNet50, VGG16, and InceptionV3 for the classification of glaucoma using the

ACRIMA dataset. The following flowchart in Fig. 2 summarizes the step-by-step implementation of the algorithm for each model, including data pre-processing, model initialization, training with validation, and testing phases.

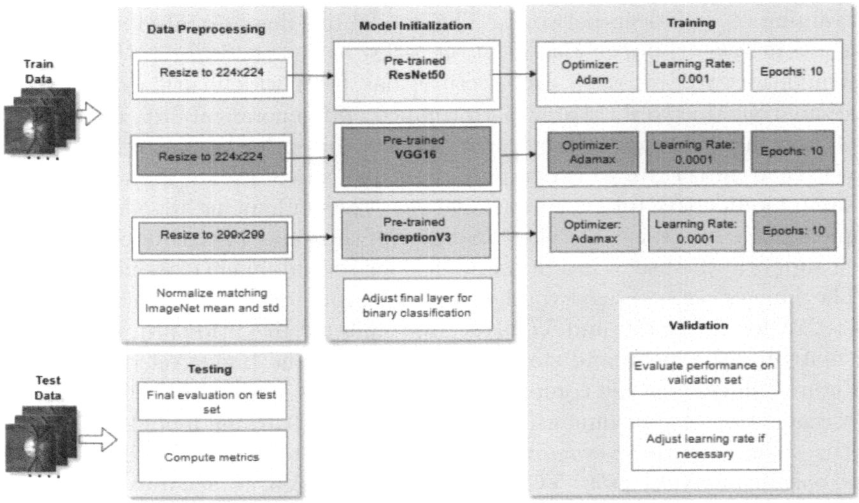

Fig. 2. Flowchart of the implemented algorithm for glaucoma classification using pre-trained models.

The data preprocessing step involved resizing the input images to 224×224 pixels for ResNet50 and VGG16, and to 299×299 pixels for InceptionV3, followed by normalization matching the mean and standard deviation of the ImageNet dataset. Each model was initialized with pre-trained weights and the final layer was adjusted for binary classification.

During training, different optimizers and hyperparameters were used for each model. ResNet50 was trained using the Adam optimizer with a learning rate of 0.001 for 10 epochs. VGG16 was trained using the Adamax optimizer with a learning rate of 0.0001 for 10 epochs, and InceptionV3 was also trained using the Adamax optimizer with a learning rate of 0.0001 for 10 epochs. The validation step involved evaluating the performance on a validation set and adjusting the learning rate if necessary.

The Cross-Entropy Loss function was utilized to measure the discrepancy between the predicted and actual class labels. The training process involved iterating through the training dataset to minimize the loss function, with periodic validation performed after each epoch using a portion of the training data (20%) to monitor overfitting and select the best model weights.

All three CNN models demonstrated excellent performance in classifying glaucoma from non-glaucoma images. As shown in Table 1, InceptionV3 achieved perfect classification with 100% accuracy, recall, precision, F1 score, and AUC-ROC. Both ResNet50 and VGG16 reached the same accuracy of 97.86%, but with different error patterns: ResNet50 misclassified 3 glaucoma cases (achieving 95.71% recall but 100% precision), while VGG16 misclassified 2 glaucoma and 1 non-glaucoma cases (achieving 97.14% recall and 98.57% precision). Among the three models, InceptionV3 emerges as the superior choice for glaucoma classification based on accuracy metrics, while ResNet50 offers advantages in terms of computational efficiency.

These metrics provide a comprehensive evaluation of the ability of the models to classify glaucoma and non-glaucoma in focus fundus images. Performance metrics for each model are summarized in Table 1.

Table 1. Performance metrics of ResNet50, VGG16, and InceptionV3 models on the ACRIMA dataset.

Metrics	ResNet50	VGG16	InceptionV3
Accuracy (%)	97.86	97.86	100.00
Recall (%)	95.71	97.14	100.00
Precision (%)	100.00	98.57	100.00
F1 Score (%)	97.81	97.85	100.00
AUC-ROC (%)	99.86	99.82	100.00
Training Time (min)	74	228	95

The ROC curves for all three models, illustrated in Fig. 3, demonstrate exceptional discriminative capability. InceptionV3 achieved a perfect AUC-ROC of 100%, indicating its ability to completely separate glaucoma from non-glaucoma cases across all possible classification thresholds. ResNet50 and VGG16 also exhibited outstanding performance with AUC-ROC values of 99.86% and 99.82% respectively. These near-perfect ROC curves suggest that all three models, particularly InceptionV3, could serve as highly reliable diagnostic tools for automated glaucoma detection.

Analysis of the training and validation loss curves Fig. 4 reveals distinct convergence patterns for each model. InceptionV3 demonstrated the most rapid convergence, with validation loss dropping sharply within the first two epochs and stabilizing at very low values thereafter. VGG16 showed initial fluctuations in validation loss before achieving stable convergence around epoch 5. ResNet50 exhibited a more gradual decrease in validation loss throughout training. These convergence patterns reflect the architectural differences between the models, with InceptionV3's inception modules facilitating faster learning of discriminative features relevant to glaucoma detection.

The performance of the proposed models was compared with the results reported in other studies, as summarized in Table 2.

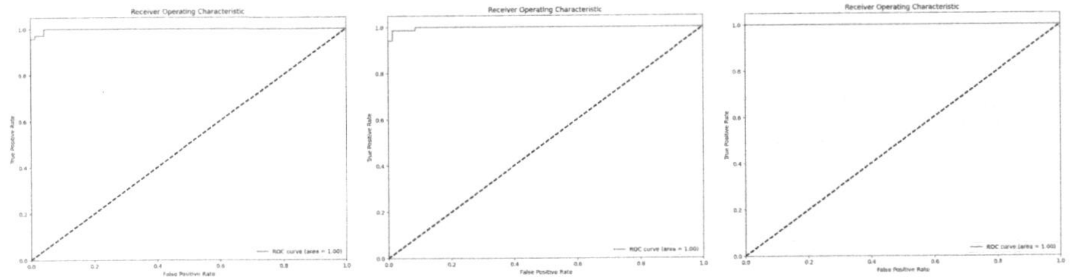

(a) ResNet50 (b) VGG16 (c) InceptionV3

Fig. 3. ROC curves for the evaluated models: (a) ResNet50, (b) VGG16 and (c) InceptionV3.

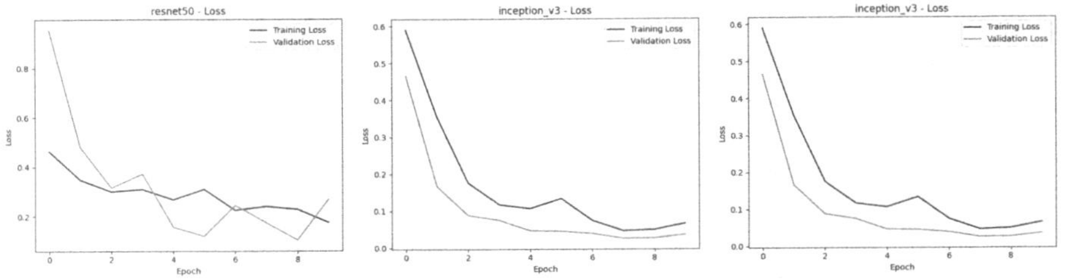

(a) ResNet50 (b) VGG16 (c) InceptionV3

Fig. 4. Training Losses for (a) ResNet50, (b) VGG16, and (c) InceptionV3 over 10 epochs.

Table 2. Comparison of performance metrics of our models with those reported in other studies.

Study	Model	Dataset	Accuracy (%)	AUC-ROC (%)
Prop. method	ResNet50	ACRIMA	97.86 (94.10–99.58)	99.86 (99.10–100.00)
	VGG16	ACRIMA	97.86 (94.10–99.58)	99.82 (99.04–100.00)
	InceptionV3	ACRIMA	100.00 (97.39–100.00)	100.00 (99.72–100.00)
Khan *et al.* [9]	InceptionV3	ORIGA	86.2 (83.8–88.6)	91.3 (89.0–93.6)
Sigut *et al.* [13]	Custom CNN	RIM-ONE	85.6 (83.2–88.0)	90.10 (87.20–92.60)
Khan *et al.* [9]	EfficientDet-D0	REFUGE	89.1 (86.8–91.4)	92.0 (89.7–94.3)

5 Conclusions and Future Research Lines

In this study, we evaluated the performance of three pre-trained convolutional neural network models: ResNet50, VGG16, and InceptionV3 for the classification of glaucoma using the ACRIMA dataset. Our results indicate that InceptionV3 outperforms the other models, achieving perfect accuracy (100

Regarding computational efficiency, significant differences were observed between the three architectures. ResNet50 completed training in approximately

74 min, while InceptionV3 required 95 min, and VGG16 needed substantially more time at 228 min. This represents an important consideration for practical implementation, as ResNet50 offers comparable accuracy to VGG16 while training approximately three times faster.

It is important to clarify that in our study, we employed fine-tuning as a specific application of transfer learning. While transfer learning broadly refers to leveraging knowledge from a pre-trained model for a new task, fine-tuning specifically involves adjusting the pre-trained weights during training on the new dataset. This distinction is crucial as it impacts model performance and training strategy, with fine-tuning generally requiring more computational resources but yielding better adaptation to the target domain.

Future research will focus on further improving the performance of these deep learning models through advanced transfer learning techniques, taking as a reference the work of Escorcia-Gutierrez et al. (2022), which proposes a methodology that applies several pre-processing techniques and the use of transfer learning, combined with the fine-tuning of pre-trained models. Additionally, we plan to evaluate the performance of more recent architectures such as EfficientNet and ConvNeXt on larger and more diverse datasets to assess their generalization capability. Furthermore, we aim to develop a multi-class classification model to assess the severity of glaucoma, which would provide more nuanced information for clinical decision-making.

The methodology and findings of this study serve as a foundation for future research in automated glaucoma detection, potentially leading to more accessible and efficient diagnostic tools for clinical practice. Our comparative analysis provides valuable insights into the strengths and limitations of different CNN architectures for this specific medical imaging task, highlighting the importance of balancing classification performance with computational efficiency.

References

1. Coan, L.J., et al.: Automatic detection of glaucoma via fundus imaging and artificial intelligence: a review. Surv. Ophthalmol. **68**(1), 17–41 (2023)
2. Díaz-Pinto, A., Morales, S., Naranjo, V., Köhler, T., Mossi, J.M., Navea, A.: CNNs for automatic glaucoma assessment using fundus images: an extensive validation. Biomed. Eng. Online **18**(1), 29 (2019). https://doi.org/10.1186/s12938-019-0649-y
3. Escorcia-Gutierrez, J., et al.: Analysis of pre-trained convolutional neural network models in diabetic retinopathy detection through retinal fundus images. In: Lecture Notes in Computer Science, vol. 13293, pp. 202–213 (2022)
4. Escorcia-Gutierrez, J., et al.: Grading diabetic retinopathy using transfer learning-based convolutional neural networks. In: Lecture Notes in Computer Science, vol. 13293, pp. 214–225 (2022)
5. Fawcett, T.: An introduction to ROC analysis. Pattern Recogn. Lett. **27**(8), 861–874 (2006)
6. Girard, M.J., Strouthidis, N.G., Ethier, C.R., Mari, J.M.: Imaging the visual pathway: from the eye to the brain. Ophthalmic Res. **47**(4), 155–160 (2012)

7. He, K., Zhang, X., Ren, S., Sun, J.: Deep residual learning for image recognition. Proceedings of the IEEE Conference on Computer Vision and Pattern Recognition, pp. 770–778 (2016)
8. Ilesanmi, A.E., Ilesanmi, T., Gbotoso, G.A.: A systematic review of retinal fundus image segmentation and classification methods using convolutional neural networks. Healthc. Analyt. **4**, 100261 (2023)
9. Khan, M.A., Cha, J.: An efficient deep learning approach to automatic glaucoma detection using optic disc and optic cup localization. Sensors **22**(2), 434 (2022). https://doi.org/10.3390/s22020434
10. Li, L., et al.: A large-scale database and a CNN model for attention-based glaucoma detection. IEEE Trans. Med. Imaging **39**(2), 413–424 (2020). https://doi.org/10.1109/TMI.2019.2927226
11. Medeiros, F.A., Zangwill, L.M., Bowd, C., Vessani, R.M., Susanna, R., Jr., Weinreb, R.N.: Detection of glaucoma progression with stratus OCT retinal nerve fiber layer, optic nerve head, and macular thickness measurements. Invest. Ophthalmol. Vis. Sci. **52**(1), 105–113 (2011)
12. Raju, M., Shanmugam, K.P., Shyu, C.R.: Application of machine learning predictive models for early detection of glaucoma using real world data. Appl. Sci. **13**(4) (2023). https://doi.org/10.3390/app13042445
13. Sigut, J.F., Díaz-Alemán, T.: Comparison of the performance of convolutional neural networks and vision transformer-based systems for automated glaucoma detection with eye fundus images. Appl. Sci. **13**(23), 12722 (2023). https://doi.org/10.3390/app132312722
14. Simonyan, K., Zisserman, A.: Very deep convolutional networks for large-scale image recognition. arXiv preprint: arXiv:1409.1556 (2014)
15. Szegedy, C., et al.: Going deeper with convolutions. In: Proceedings of the IEEE Conference on Computer Vision and Pattern Recognition, pp. 1–9 (2015)
16. Szegedy, C., Vanhoucke, V., Ioffe, S., Shlens, J., Wojna, Z.: Rethinking the inception architecture for computer vision. In: Proceedings of the IEEE Conference on Computer Vision and Pattern Recognition, pp. 2818–2826 (2016)
17. Tham, Y.C., Li, X., Wong, T.Y., Quigley, H.A., Aung, T., Cheng, C.Y.: Global prevalence of glaucoma and projections of glaucoma burden through 2040: a systematic review and meta-analysis. Ophthalmology **121**(11), 2081–2090 (2014)
18. Zafar, A., Aamir, M., Nawi, N.M., Ali, S., Husnain, M., Samad, A.: A comprehensive convolutional neural network survey to detect glaucoma disease. Mob. Inf. Syst. **2022**(1), 3971516 (2022)
19. Zedan, M.J., Zulkifley, M.A., Ibrahim, A.A., Moubark, A.M., Kamari, N., Abdani, S.R.: Automated glaucoma screening and diagnosis based on retinal fundus images using deep learning approaches: A comprehensive review. Diagnostics **13**(13), 2180 (2023)

Classification of CFD-Generated Aortic Flow Images Using Neural Networks

Edgar Omar Martínez-Jiménez(✉), Leopoldo Altamirano-Robles, Raquel Díaz-Hernández, and Saúl Zapotecas-Martínez

Instituto Nacional de Astrofísica Óptica y Electrónica, Sta. María Tonantzintla, Puebla 72840, Mexico
omar_jim0305@outlook.com

Abstract. Several congenital aortic pathologies, such as Marfan syndrome and aortic coarctation, require imaging for diagnosis, although these methods have limitations in assessing complete blood flow dynamics. Computational fluid dynamics (CFD) offers a noninvasive alternative by creating virtual models from medical images. We propose the combination of convolutional neural networks and CFD as an alternative tool to classify aortic flow images and thus detect these conditions early. No previous study has applied CFD with convolutional neural networks for this purpose. In this study, we used six convolutional neural networks pretrained on 452 images (388 pathological and 64 healthy). MobileNetV2 and ResNet-18 achieved the highest percentages but were more computationally demanding, while the Compact network achieved excellent accuracy with lower computational costs and a faster inference time per image, making it suitable for real-time applications.

Keywords: CFD · Coarctation · Convolutional Neural Networks · Marfan Syndrome

1 Introduction

Computational simulation in fluid dynamics has revolutionized the field of hemodynamics and applied sciences by providing a tool to explore complex flow phenomena that would be impossible to analyze experimentally. Using images generated by computational fluid dynamics (CFD) simulations allows detailed flow analysis, facilitating understanding of phenomena such as turbulence, phase interactions, and fluid behavior in complex geometries. Recently, neural networks have emerged as a crucial ally in classifying and analyzing these patterns, integrating artificial intelligence (AI) with traditional simulation methods [3–9].

CFD has advanced considerably with the development of robust algorithms and high-resolution methods. Modern simulations make it possible to solve complex equations, such as the Navier-Stokes equations, on very fine spatial and temporal scales. Technologies such as the finite element method (FEM), lattice Boltzmann methods (LBM), and large eddy simulation (LES) schemes have

A. P. López-Monroy et al. (Eds.): MCPR 2025, LNCS 15715, pp. 279–289, 2025.
https://doi.org/10.1007/978-3-031-96255-4_26

proven to be essential tools for studying fluid dynamics in complex systems such as human arteries or industrial canals [10,11].

It has been observed that the combination of simulations in hybrid Eulerian-Lagrangian techniques has made it possible to model challenging problems such as coarse particle transport in tubes [3,8]. These advances also generate rich data for AI analysis [6,15].

Hemodynamics has significantly benefited from CFD simulation. Recent simulations have provided insight into phenomena such as flow dynamics in the presence of stenosis or aneurysms and have generated large volumes of data that can be used for the classification of anomalous patterns [5,16,18].

Using neural networks in CFD has opened up new possibilities for automating the classification of flow patterns and reducing the time required to analyze large data sets. In applications such as predicting transitions from laminar to turbulent flow or identifying complex vortices, these tools have proven highly useful. [6,12,13].

For example, the work presented by Xin et al. [6] applied deep learning models to generate approximations of complex three-dimensional flows, achieving a significant reduction in computational costs without compromising accuracy [14]. In addition, these techniques enable predictions based on simulated data, which can guide medical interventions or adjustments in industrial designs [15].

Flow pattern classification has been used in hemodynamics to identify pathological conditions or regions of risk in the arteries and veins. For example, supervised and unsupervised learning models have been used to categorize flows suggestive of elevated blood pressure or turbulence related to inefficient prosthetic designs [7,17].

The combination of CFD simulations with convolutional neural networks represents a significant advance in flow pattern classification, with applications ranging from industrial design to personalized medicine. The importance of simulation lies in its ability to generate detailed and representative data. At the same time, neural networks allow us to analyze and extract useful information from such data in an efficient manner [10,19] (Table 1).

Table 1. Comparison between related works and our proposed methodology.

RELATED WORK	SIMULATION	CLASSIFICATION
Zhao, R., et al. [3]	✓	
Ruijie, Z., et al. [8]	✓	
Francesco, V., et al. [5]	✓	
A. Mariotti, M.N et al. [18]	✓	
Filippos, S., et al. [15]	✓	
Nanda, S., et al. [7]	✓	
Our proposed methodology	✓	✓

In this regard, the present investigation focuses on the accuracy of the models created. Likewise, artificial intelligence is a tool that contributes to simulation and equation-solving to speed up processes and reduce computational costs. It is also confirmed that, as of the date of this article's creation, no research has been found combining the classification of coarctation images and Marfan syndrome pathologies obtained from CFD simulation with pre-trained convolutional neural networks.

2 Theoretical Framework

2.1 Marfan Syndrome

Marfan syndrome is a genetic disorder of autosomal dominant inheritance that affects the elastic fibers of the connective tissue. Its manifestations are observed in those systems and organs where these fibers are in greater concentration, such as the cardiovascular, skeletal, dura mater, eye, skin, integuments, and lung [1].

Cardiovascular alterations are those that mainly condition the prognosis of Marfan syndrome, as they cause the most significant mortality (between 70% and 95% of cases), with aortic dilatation standing out particularly and frequently. The incidence of this dilatation varies according to age, reaching between 40% and 80% in children and between 80% and %100 in adults. Initially, dilatation involves the sinuses of Valsalva and the ascending aorta; its progressive nature affects the aortic root, leading to valvular insufficiency.

2.2 Coarctation of the Aorta

Coarctation of the aorta is classified as a pathology that obstructs the outflow of blood from the left cardiac chambers, increasing left ventricular afterload. If this aortic obstruction is not corrected, the left ventricle will develop hypertrophy as a compensatory mechanism to overcome the resistance caused by aortic narrowing [2].

The increase in left chamber afterload and pressure at the point of obstruction results in an abnormal aortic flow pattern [2]. This, in turn, activates endothelial properties that promote vascular dilatation and remodeling. Likewise, a higher proportion of collagen is observed in the aortic wall proximal to the lesion compared to the distal section [2].

2.3 Physical Properties of Aortic Models

It is important to maintain consistency in terms of the physical units required. It is possible to work in different metric systems, such as the Cegesimal System (CGS), with a variant in millimeters called MGS, and the International System (IS). Therefore, measurable quantities such as length, mass, and time are stated in centimeters (cm), grams (g), and seconds (s), respectively [25].

Other necessary properties are the dynamic viscosity of the blood (μ) measured in $\left(g \cdot cm^{-1} \cdot s^{-1}\right)$, and the blood density (ρ) measured in $\left(g \cdot cm^{-3}\right)$.

The boundary conditions are crucial for obtaining high-quality cardiovascular simulation results. It is essential that the boundary conditions accurately capture the physiology of the vascular networks outside the 3D domain of the model. Several different options are provided for the assignment of boundary conditions on inputs and outputs, as shown in Fig. 1.

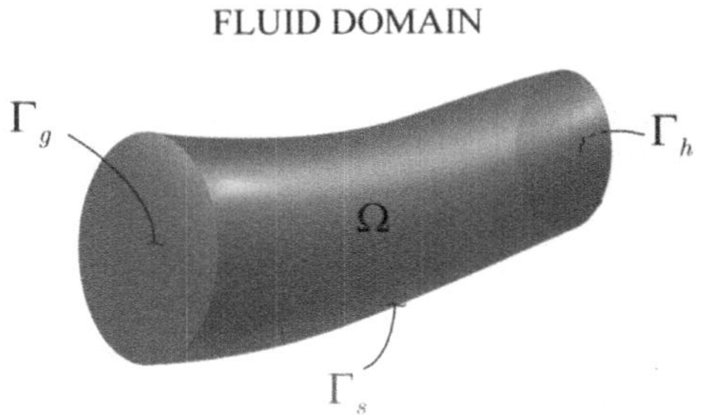

Fig. 1. General representation of a flow domain, where Γ_g is the inflow rate, Γ_h is the outflow rate, Γ_s is the vascular wall, and Ω is the vascular model. Image obtained from [25].

Both the inflow and outflow faces use a prescribed weak pressure to emulate the effects of the descending vasculature, which significantly impacts the results of the numerical simulation. This pressure p is expressed in the form $p = p_0 + RQ$, where R is the resistance parameter of the vasculature, Q is the flow rate passing through the face, and p_0 is a pressure boundary. At the initial face, the pressure boundary has a value of zero, so the prescribed weak pressure will be determined by the resistance and the flow rate [25].

3 CFD Simulation Methodology

3.1 Simulation Process

Using medical images such as computed tomography (CT) scans or magnetic resonance imaging (MRI) and the application of CFD allows for the creation of anatomically accurate three-dimensional models. Additionally, the ability to calculate hemodynamic parameters such as shear stresses on the walls and pressure distributions makes CFD useful for the study of cardiovascular diseases and the design of medical devices [20].

The first step involves segmenting the medical images and identifying the object of interest. A 2D segmentation is used, which is then transformed into solid models, as explained later in this section. Figure 2 describes the process for obtaining a solid model of the object of interest. First, a series of paths along the blood vessels are generated. Then, 2D segmentations are performed along these paths, and subsequently, these segmentations are grouped to create a solid model.

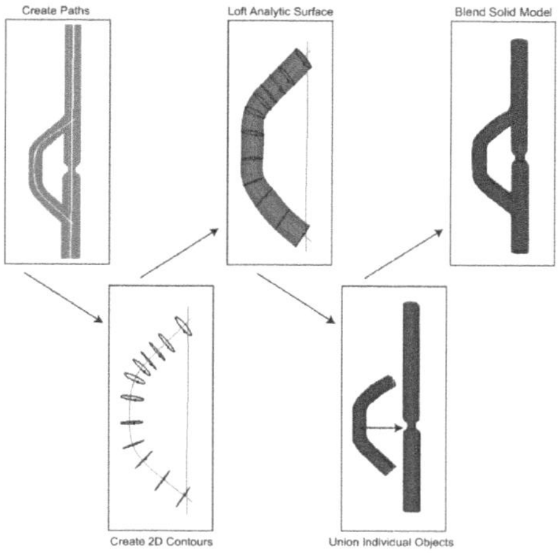

Fig. 2. Illustration of trajectories and segmentation for the creation of solid models. Image obtained from [22].

Once the solid model is created, it can be joined with another existing model, and as a final step, the joining area must be smoothed. For more details on creating these models, it is recommended to visit the GitHub repository [22].

After creating our solid model of interest, the next step in performing a simulation is to generate a discretization, also known as grid or mesh generation. Generally, this process involves dividing a physical domain into smaller subdomains called elements. This is necessary to facilitate the numerical solution of partial differential equations due to the complexity of the geometries of interest [23]. The main challenges of discretization are robustness, quality, and computational efficiency. There are different commercial meshes, some of which use tetrahedral elements (referred to as "Tet") [24] generated automatically. This tetrahedral discretization has the capacity to adapt more robustly to complex geometries and often simplifies the adaptation process during the simulation.

The meshing process is useful for both discrete and continuous solids. To achieve this, it is customary to use open-source libraries such as "TetGen" and a vascular modeling toolkit called "VMTK". For more details, it is recommended to consult the following reference [24]. To perform a simulation as accurately as possible, the algorithm must solve the three-dimensional Navier-Stokes equations [25]. This is a broad and complex topic; therefore, in this work, we will focus only on the practical aspects of the simulation.

There are three main modules in the software: Pre-Solver (svPre), Flow-Solver (svSolver), and Post-Solver (svPost). svPre acts as the preprocessor for svSolver. The input data files used by svPre contain a complete description of the discrete model: nodal coordinates, element connectivity, element adjacency information, and the connectivity of boundary nodes and elements. These input files for svPre are generated from the mesh. To initiate the simulation process, PreSolver (svPre) is executed with a set of instructions that define the problem's boundary conditions, initial conditions, and geometric configuration. svPre's output consists of several files prepared for processing by svSolver to perform a blood flow analysis. Once the analysis is completed, svSolver (the solver) generates files that characterize the finite element solution over a defined period, usually several cardiac cycles. svPost uses these files to generate visualization files, which are employed in post-processing and analyzing the hemodynamic results of interest.

The database was obtained from the "Vascular Model Repository" [26]. The model projects can be downloaded from the repository. The results of these simulations are used for the 3D visualization of flow patterns.

3.2 Visualization

Once models are generated from medical data, meshing and executing hemodynamic simulations, the results must be analyzed and visualized for proper interpretation.

After simulating the models of interest, files are obtained, which are used for visualization [21]. Each file represents a moment in the fluid simulation, from which an image of the flow pattern can be generated. This allows analysis of its behavior. The images are visualized from different angles, such as along the "x" and "y" axes. Subsequently, these images are stored for future training and classification.

Figure 3 presents the proposed methodology. Initially, the flow simulation is performed based on the 3D models. Once the results are obtained, the visualization stage is carried out. The images generated at different time points of the flow are used as input data for the classification neural network.

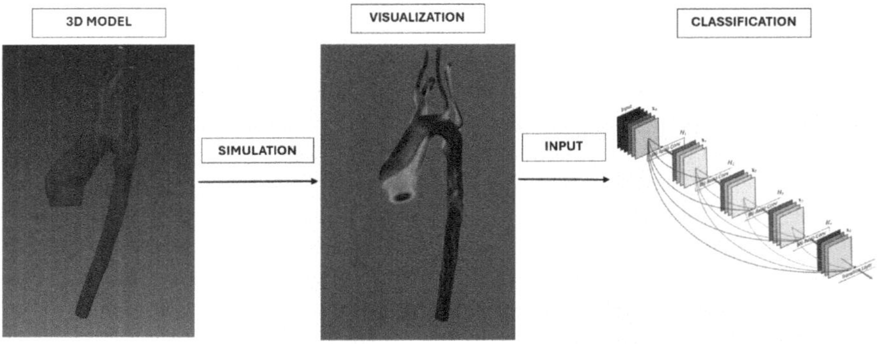

Fig. 3. Illustration of our proposed methodology.

Once the images of flow behavior are collected, they are stored and classified as healthy or with some pathology. In Fig. 4, an example of a healthy aorta is shown viewed from different angles. Similarly, in Fig. 5, the simulation of a coarctation aorta is presented. Finally, in Fig. 6, the flow behavior is observed in an aorta with Marfan syndrome [26].

Fig. 4. Flow behavior in a healthy aorta model, viewed from different angles, at the same moment of simulation.

Fig. 5. Flow behavior in a model with coarctation of the aorta. The increase is represented by shades close to red, right at the aortic arch. (Color figure online)

3.3 Training

During the training process, 452 images were used, of which 388 corresponded to various pathologies, including Marfan syndrome and coarctation, and 64 were from healthy patients. The dataset was divided into 316 images for training (70%), 68 for validation (15%), and 68 for testing (15%), the percentages were selected as a standard in the process of image classification by convolutional neural networks.. All images were sized at 512 × 512 pixels. Pretrained networks used included AlexNet, Compact, Enhanced, MobileNetV2, ResNet-18, and ResNet-50. A total of 100 training epochs were conducted for each network. The batch size parameters were also adjusted for each network, utilizing sizes 8, 16, and 32. The iterations were automatically updated according to these batch sizes, resulting in 4000, 2000, and 1000 totals, respectively. The process was carried out on a computer with an Intel Core i7 13th generation processor and an NVIDIA GeForce RTX 4060 graphics card.

Fig. 6. Flow behavior in a model with Marfan syndrome. A widening is observed at the aortic arch, generating flow turbulence represented by a decrease in speed shown in shades close to blue. (Color figure online)

4 Results

In Table 2, the evaluation results of various pre-trained convolutional neural network architectures are presented, including AlexNet, Compact, Enhanced, MobileNetV2, ResNet-18, and ResNet-50, trained with different batch sizes and number of iterations. It is observed that more complex networks, such as ResNet-50, require significantly longer training times, reaching up to 3 h and 26 min, while lighter models, like AlexNet or Compact, complete their training in under 15 min.

In terms of accuracy, ResNet-18 and MobileNetV2 achieved the best results, suggesting that these architectures are highly effective for this dataset. Networks like Compact and Enhanced also performed well with lower computational costs, making them attractive options for a balance between accuracy and efficiency.

It is also noted that, generally, a smaller batch size tends to provide better validation and evaluation results, although at the expense of longer training times. Conversely, as the batch size increases, the iterations decrease, which can slightly impact the final accuracy in some cases. In this regard, ResNet-50, while powerful, presents a high computational cost, so its use should be evaluated based on resource availability and the need for accuracy. Thus, if the best accuracy is sought without considering training time, MobileNetV2 and ResNet-18 are the standout options, while Compact and Enhanced can be viable alternatives for a balance between time and performance.

Table 2. Results of the evaluation of different networks and configurations. The spaces marked with "-" mean that it was not possible to calculate the value because of the high computational cost required by the network. ***Training Time (TT). **Inference time per image (ITI).**

Red	Batch size	Validation	Evaluation	TT*	ITI**
AlexNet	8	98.50%	89.70%	00:12:26	10.347 ms
	16	98.50%	95.60%	00:11:16	14.046 ms
	32	98.50%	97.10%	00:11:06	12.521 ms
Compact	8	100.00%	98.50%	**0:03:06**	**2.92 ms**
	16	100.00%	97.10%	00:03:08	4.795 ms
	32	98.50%	97.10%	00:12:55	12.784 ms
Enhanced	8	100.00%	97.10%	00:07:32	9.417 ms
	16	100.00%	97.10%	00:28:39	13.446 ms
	32	100.00%	98.50%	01:54:25	122.741 ms
MobileNetV2	8	100.00%	**100.00%**	00:46:13	8.483 ms
	16	100.00%	**100.00%**	02:53:14	62.055 ms
	32	100.00%	95.60%	09:01:52	116.242 ms
ResNet-18	8	100.00%	**100.00%**	00:06:41	10.422 ms
	16	98.50%	98.50%	00:06:24	10.396 ms
	32	98.50%	97.10%	00:58:25	18.286 ms
ResNet-50	8	98.50%	97.10%	03:26:22	98.687 ms
	16	–	–	–	–
	32	–	–	–	–

5 Conclusions

The combination of CFD simulations with deep learning models allows for efficient classification and represents a viable method for the early identification of hemodynamic anomalies in a non-invasive manner. Models like Compact and Enhanced show notably shorter training times and also faster inferences. Larger or classical architectures (AlexNet, ResNet-50) tend to require more training time; in some cases, their inference time per image (ITI) is higher. In some models, moving to larger batch sizes significantly decreases inference time, reflecting better efficiency in the inference phase. In applications where prediction speed per image is a priority (e.g., real-time systems), opting for more compact models or configurations with larger batch sizes can be advantageous. Pre-trained convolutional neural networks have been shown to efficiently classify flow images from CFD simulations, facilitating the identification of alterations in aortic circulation associated with pathologies such as aortic coarctation and Marfan syndrome. In terms of applications, these results open new possibilities in the field of personalized medicine, as they could be integrated into computer-assisted diagnostic systems to improve the detection and evaluation of cardiovascular disorders.

The methodology presented demonstrates the potential of artificial intelligence in optimizing the analysis of complex medical data, establishing a foundation for future research in integrating simulation models and convolutional neural networks for predicting and characterizing flows under various pathological conditions.

Acknowledgments. This work was made possible thanks to the graduate scholarship awarded by SECIHTI, whose support has been fundamental to the development of this research. We also express our gratitude to MVTec for providing the license for the Deep Learning Tool software, which facilitated the processing and analysis of the data.

The data used herein was provided in whole or in part with Federal funds from the National Library of Medicine under Grant No. R01LM013120, and the National Heart, Lung, and Blood Institute, National Institutes of Health, Department of Health and Human Services, under Contract No. HHSN268201100035C.

Disclosure of Interests. The authors declare that there are no conflicts of interest relevant to the content of this article.

References

1. Oliva, N., et al.: Síndrome de Marfán. Revista médica de Chile **134**(11), 1455–1464 (2006). https://doi.org/10.4067/S0034-98872006001100014
2. Bolaños Martínez, I., Mora Membreño, K., Bolaños Umaña, S., Bujan Murillo, S.: Coartación de aorta. Medicina Legal de Costa Rica, **37**(1), 87–92 (2020) http://www.scielo.sa.cr/scielo.php?script=sci_arttext&pid=S1409-00152020000100087&lng=en&tlng=es. Accessed 20 Feb 2025,
3. Zhao, R., Zhang, Y., Zhang, X., Wang, X.: Validation of a Eulerian-Lagrangian numerical algorithm for simulating ultra-coarse particles transported in horizontal and vertical hydraulic pipes. Comput. Fluids **276**, 106263 (2024)
4. Samy, A., Li, S., Yuan, X., Liu, C., Dong, Y.: Vector form of intrinsic finite element method for incompressible fluids. Comput. Fluids **279**, 106319 (2024)
5. Francesco, V., Valentina, M., Roberto, V.: AFSEI approach for the assessment of stenotic aortic valve. Comput. Fluids **265**, 106017 (2023)
6. Xin, L., et al.: Deep learning-based reduced order model for three-dimensional flow fields. Comput. Fluids **285**, 106441 (2024)
7. Nanda, S., Siddharth D.S., Suman, C., Somnath.: A comparative study of Newtonian and non-Newtonian blood flows. Comput. Fluids**279**, 106337 (2024)
8. Ruijie, Z., Yuanhang, Z., Xuzhen, Z., Xikun, W.: Validation of numerical methods for complex fluid simulations. J. Placeholder **276**, 106263 (2024)
9. Guerrero-Hurtado, M., Catalán, J.M., Moriche, M., Gonzalo, A., Flores, O.: A Python-based flow solver for numerical simulations using an immersed boundary method on single GPUs. Comput. Fluids **288**, 106511 (2025)
10. Lan, J., Jie, W., Liming, Y., Qiushuo, Q.: High-order gas kinetic flux solver with TENO-THINC scheme for compressible flows. Comput. Fluids **287**, 106492 (2025)
11. Josip, Z., Alessio, R., Massimiliano, B., Bert, B., Giovanni, S.: Vortex dynamics and radial outflow velocity evolution in downburst-like winds. Comput. Fluids **283**, 106393 (2024)
12. Joel, H., Nick, P., Tim, D.: Probabilistic machine learning to improve generalisation of data-driven turbulence modelling. Comput. Fluids **284**, 106443 (2024)

13. Ludovico, N., et al.: Parallel implementation and performance of super-resolution generative adversarial network turbulence models for large-eddy simulation. Comput. Fluids **288**, 106498 (2025)
14. Bo, S., Rou, C., Weiwei, Y., Huidan, Y.: GPU-accelerated volumetric lattice Boltzmann model for image-based hemodynamics in portal hypertension. Comput. Fluids **266**, 106038 (2023)
15. Filippos, S., Dimitris, D., Ioannis, W.: Comparison of super-resolution deep learning models for flow imaging. Comput. Fluids **283**, 106396 (2024)
16. Mbolahasina, R., et al.: Infectiousness model of expelled droplets exposed to ultraviolet germicidal irradiation coupled with evaporation. Comput. Fluids, 106242 (2024)
17. Xiang, Q., Yuanxiang, M., Bofu, W., Yuxian, X., Yulu, L.: Spatial-temporal prediction models for unsteady near-wall flow around cylinder based on hybrid neural network. Comput. Fluids, **284**, 106420 (2024)
18. Mariotti, A., Antonuccio, M.N., Morello, M., Salvetti, M.V., Celi, S.: Numerical simulation of aortic coarctations of different grades of severity: Flow features and importance of outlet boundary conditions. Comput. Fluids **266**, 106043 (2024)
19. Joel, A.M., Christoph, B.: Heat flux predictions in high-speed fluid flows. Comput. Fluids **269**, 106121 (2024)
20. Updegrove, A., Wilson, N.M., Merkow, J., Lan, H., Marsden, A.L., Shadden, S.C.: SimVascular: an open source pipeline for cardiovascular simulation. Ann. Biomed. Eng. **45**(3), 525–541 (2017)
21. Ahrens, J., Geveci, B., Law, C.: ParaView: An End-User Tool for Large Data Visualization. Elsevier, The Visualization Handbook (2005)
22. SimVascular Trayectoria. https://simvascular.github.io/documentation/modeling.html#modelingImportingExportingPaths
23. SimVascular Malla. https://simvascular.github.io/documentation/meshing.html#tetgenoverview
24. Wias Malla. https://wias-berlin.de/software/tetgen/
25. SimVascular Mat. https://simvascular.github.io/documentation/flowsolver.html#overview
26. Wilson, N.M., Ortiz, A.K., Johnson, A.B.: The vascular model repository: a public resource of medical imaging data and blood flow simulation results. J. Med. Devices **7**(4), 040923 (2013)

Explainable Diagnosis of Bacterial Vaginosis: A Hierarchical Approach Based on XAI

Fidencio Alarcón-López[1], Krissel Ofelia Pesqueira-Ramzahuer[1], Rafael Rivera-López[1(✉)], Noemi del Carmen Tenorio-Prieto[1], Erick De la Cruz Hernández[2], and Juana Canul-Reich[3]

[1] DSC, TecNM, Instituto Tecnológico de Veracruz, Veracruz, Mexico
{120021189,121021182,rafael.rl,noemi.tp}@veracruz.tecnm.mx

[2] DAMC, Universidad Juárez Autónoma de Tabasco, Comalcalco, Mexico
erick.delacruz@ujat.mx

[3] DACyTI, Universidad Juárez Autónoma de Tabasco, Cunduacán, Mexico
juana.canul@ujat.mx

Abstract. This study proposes a hierarchical and explainable diagnostic approach to accurately identify bacterial vaginosis from patient health, pathogen presence, and vaginal microbiota composition. Three explainable models are built from highly accurate black-box models, providing healthcare professionals with technological support to improve decision-making in the follow-up and treatment of patients with suspected bacterial vaginosis. The aim is to reduce diagnostic errors and optimize the use of medical resources in clinical settings. Experimental studies suggest that decision trees as explainers for black-box model predictions outperform the results obtained when directly using a white-box model on the same data. The proposed approach allows for improved diagnostic reliability and helps in the interpretation of results by physicians, increasing the confidence of using artificial intelligence tools in clinical practice.

Keywords: Explainable Artificial Intelligence · Black-box model · Decision trees

1 Introduction

Today, artificial intelligence (AI) is a powerful tool in virtually every field of human knowledge. In particular, AI offers innovative solutions to improve diagnosis, treatment, and patient care. A special case is machine learning (ML) models, whose ability to analyze complex medical data allows them to generate accurate information for disease diagnosis. These models use medical records and genomic data to discover patterns and relationships that are too complex for a physician to identify [15]. One of the most impactful applications of ML includes medical diagnostics assistance. For instance, deep learning algorithms

A. P. López-Monroy et al. (Eds.): MCPR 2025, LNCS 15715, pp. 290–299, 2025.
https://doi.org/10.1007/978-3-031-96255-4_27

have remarkable performance in diagnosing diseases such as cancer, cardiovascular conditions, and infectious diseases, often surpassing traditional methods [31]. ML models also develop predictive diagnostic tools to forecast disease progression and identify at-risk patients before symptoms manifest [21]. This predictive capability impacts by reducing operational costs and improving health services accessibility to more sectors of society [31]. However, the scientific community must address critical issues such as data privacy, algorithmic bias, and the need for explainability in AI systems to ensure equitable and ethical use [23]. For example, highly accurate black-box models such as artificial neural networks (ANNs) often lack transparency, making it difficult for clinicians to trust and interpret their results. To overcome this, explainable AI (XAI) techniques, such as decision trees (DTs) and SHAP (Shapley Additive exPlanations) [17], have been proposed to provide insights into how models arrive at their predictions, thereby improving their utility in clinical settings [17].

On the other hand, bacterial vaginosis (BV) is a common vaginal condition in reproductive-age women, resulting from an imbalance in the vaginal microbiota that favors the growth of anaerobic bacteria [28]. Its early detection is crucial since untreated BV is associated with serious complications, such as premature birth, pelvic inflammatory disease, and an increased risk of contracting sexually transmitted infections [32]. However, one of the most significant challenges in its diagnosis is that about 50% of cases are asymptomatic, complicating prompt identification and treatment [20]. This combination of high prevalence, associated complications, and diagnostic difficulties makes BV a public health problem worldwide, especially in regions with limited access to health services and diagnostic tests [19]. Due to its impact on public health, BV has been widely studied [1,3], and several ML models have been developed to identify relationships between specific biomarkers and BV diagnosis [27,33]. These models use data from established laboratory techniques, such as Amsel Criteria and Gram stain, and other tests, such as pH test strips and Point-of-Care tests [20]. However, to the best of our knowledge, XAI-based techniques have not been extensively applied to improve the performance of predictive BV models. Most existing approaches focus on studying the correlation between the presence of specific bacteria and the BV diagnosis, often relying on traditional statistical methods.

This study proposes a hierarchical and explainable diagnostic approach for accurately identifying BV, using a dataset that includes symptomatic evaluation data, pathogens presence, and polymerase chain reaction (PCR) tests. Three explainable DT models are built from high-accuracy prediction of black-box models. Experimental studies demonstrate that this approach outperforms accuracy of traditional white-box models and contributes to the explainability of BV diagnosis based on black-box models.

The rest of this manuscript is organized as follows: The related studies using ML methods for BV diagnosis are summarized in Sect. 2. The dataset description, the proposed scheme in this study, and the evaluation setup is clarified in Sect. 3, and the results and their discussion is detailed in Sect. 4. Finally, Sect. 5 is related to conclusions and future work.

2 Related Methods

One of the earliest studies applying ML to diagnose BV was conducted by Baker et al. [4]. They use ML techniques to detect BV, conducting experiments to identify the most important features for BV diagnosis. Their work compared different classification algorithms' accuracy, recall, and F-measure, showing that they performed better on a medical dataset after feature selection. In 2020, Drew et al. [10] proposed an interpretation algorithm based on ML for the molecular diagnosis of BV in a maternity hospital. This study shows the feasibility of using ML techniques to improve the accuracy of BV diagnosis in a real clinical setting. Celeste et al. [7] investigated ethnic disparities in the diagnosis of asymptomatic BV using four ML algorithms. Their findings showed that these models do not always perform equally well across different ethnic groups, highlighting the need to improve fairness in predictive models for BV. In 2024, Rodriguez et al. [27] used unsupervised ML algorithms to identify clusters of risk behaviors associated with BV. This study highlighted the utility of unsupervised ML for classifying behavioral risk factors related to BV. Also, in 2024, Wen et al. [33] proposed a rapid method for diagnosing BV using surface-enhanced Raman spectroscopy (SERS) assisted by ML. This approach proved promising for the fast and accurate diagnosis of BV from human vaginal fluids. Bautista Hernández and Canul Reich [5] proposed a Bayesian Network model for qualitative data analysis of BV in pregnant women. Their study aimed to identify coexisting bacteria and their relationship with a positive BV diagnosis. They developed a causal Bayesian Network (CBN) and a conditional probability table detailing the association percentage with positive BV diagnosis. This work highlighted the potential of CBN in understanding the complex relationships between bacterial species and BV diagnosis. Finally, Rivera-López et al. [26] describe an approach where explainable AI techniques, such as DTs, are implemented to interpret ANN and random forest (RF) models used in BV diagnosis based on PCR values.

3 Materials and Methods

This section outlines the methodological framework of the study, structured around three key components: (1) dataset characteristics and preprocessing procedures, (2) the global XAI approach for BV diagnosis, and (3) the experimental design for model evaluation. This comprehensive framework supports the development and assessment of interpretable machine learning models in clinical diagnostics.

3.1 Dataset Description

This study analyzed data from 129 pregnant patients attended at the Laboratory of Research in Metabolic and Infectious Diseases of the Universidad Juárez

Autónoma de Tabasco, Mexico. The study was conducted with the informed consent of the participants and was approved by the Institutional Ethics Committee (protocol UJAT–20160006) [30]. During the clinical examination, two samples were collected: one for cytological evaluation using the liquid-based Papanicolaou test and another for molecular analysis using quantitative PCR (qPCR). In particular, qPCR provides a robust tool for detecting and quantifying genetic material, enabling detailed characterization of the vaginal microbiota and the identification of pathogens relevant to clinical diagnostics [18]. qPCR-BV diagnosis uses the L-index, a ratio of *Lactobacillus crispatus* (normal microbiota) to *Lactobacillus iners* (altered microbiota) [16]. Samples with *BV-associated bacteria* $\geq$ 2 are BV-positive. Those with one *BV-associated bacterium* and an L-index ≥ 1, or none, are BV-negative. Cases with one *BV-associated bacterium* and an L-index < 1 are indeterminate.

Of the 129 patients, 34 were diagnosed as BV-positive, while 95 were diagnosed with normal microbiota. The original dataset contains information on 86 patient features, including general data such as age, sexual hygiene habits, symptoms associated with female reproductive tract diseases, blood test results, and values obtained from qPCR tests. The data were segmented according to three criteria:

- **Disease symptoms:** This includes symptoms such as genital itching, burning, irritation, pain, foul odor, vaginal discharge, and dyspareunia.
- **Pathogens presence:** This includes the detection of pathogens such as *Chlamydia trachomatis*, *Herpes simplex virus*, *Mycoplasma genitalium*, *Ureaplasma parvum*, *Ureaplasma urealyticum*, *Candida*, *Candida krusei*, *Trichomonas vaginalis*, *Streptococcus agalactiae*, *Human papillomavirus*, and *Mycoplasma hominis*.
- **BV-associated bacteria and lactobacilli:** This includes the quantification of bacteria such as *Atopobium vaginae*, *Gardnerella vaginalis*, *Megasphaera type 1*, and *BV-associated bacterium 2*, and *Lactobacillus crispatus*, *Lactobacillus iners*, and *Lactobacillus jensenii*.

This segmentation allowed for a detailed analysis of the dataset, focusing on key aspects of patient health, pathogen presence, and vaginal microbiota composition.

3.2 Goblal XAI-Based Approach

XAI seeks to make ML models more transparent, interpretable, and reliable. XAI helps build confidence in models and allows for identifying biases, errors, and areas for improvement [2]. Local and global explanation techniques are among the most widely used methods in XAI. Local explanations focus on understanding individual predictions of a model, while global explanations seek to provide a general understanding of the behavior of the model as a whole.

The two best-known local explainer approaches are SHAP and LIME (Local Interpretable Model-agnostic Explanations) [25]. On the other hand, global explainers, such as DTs, are essential to understanding a model's overall behavior. They provide a comprehensive view of how the model uses features to make decisions, identifying general patterns, biases, and relationships between variables [29].

This study uses a global explanation approach to support the differential diagnosis of BV using DTs. These models give the physician a complete view of how various factors interact in detecting BV in a patient. The process used to develop XAI-based explainers can be outlined as follows: Firstly, an accurate black-box model is induced using a training set (*learning stage*). Next, a synthetic dataset is generated from the training set using a SMOTE-based technique, but only taking the instances created by the value interpolation [8]. Then, the class labels of the synthetic set are replaced with the model's predictions (*prediction stage*). Finally, a DT is induced using the re-labeled systhetic set (*post hoc stage*). Figure 1 shows the scheme representing this global XAI-based approach.

3.3 Evaluation Setup

Four black-box models (ensembles) are trained to evaluate the proposed approach's performance. Their results are used to create relabeled data, which are then applied to induce four other white-box models (DTs). The ensembles used are RF, Adaptive Boosting (AB), Gradient Boosting (GB), and Extreme Gradient Boosting (XGB). They are implemented in the Python *scikit-learn* and *xgboost* libraries [9,22]. The white-box models are induced by the J48, SimpleCart, JCHAID*, and SPAARC methods implemented in the Weka library and several Java plugins [11].

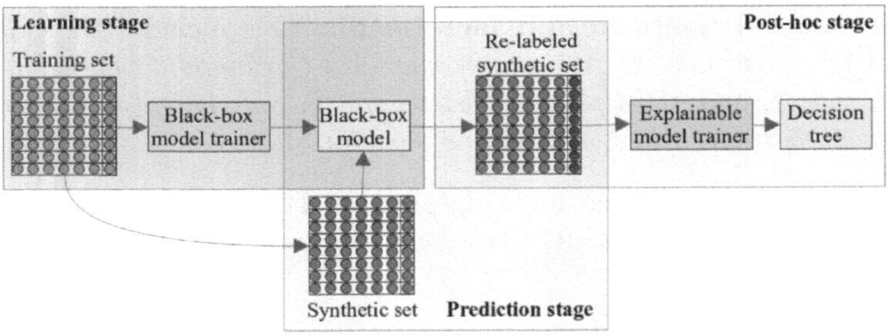

Fig. 1. Global XAI-based approach.

Ensembles are ML methods that combine multiple weak models to produce precise predictions. RF builds multiple DTs randomly and averages their predictions to reduce the risk of overfitting. AB successively fine-tunes simple models (such as small DTs), giving more weight to previous errors to improve their performance. GB optimizes the combination of models by reducing the residual error at each iteration, resulting in more accurate models [13]. XGB, an optimized GB-version, improves mode speed and performance [9].

The white-box models are DT-based algorithms used for classification. J48 is an implementation of the C4.5 algorithm that builds DTs by splitting the data according to the feature that maximizes information gain. J48 also allows for pruning to avoid overfitting [24]. SimpleCart is a simplified version of CART (Classification and Regression Trees) that generates binary DTs and uses criteria such as Gini or entropy to split the data [6]. JCHAID* is a variant of the CHAID (Chi-square Automatic Interaction Detection) algorithm, which creates DTs based on chi-square tests to find significant relationships between variables [14]. SPAARC (Scalable Probabilistic Attribute Reduction and Classification) is a method that optimizes feature selection and classification using probabilistic techniques to improve model accuracy and efficiency [34].

The strategy used in this manuscript to perform the comparison is the following: First, each model is hyperparameter tuned[1]. Then, a five-fold cross-validation (CV) strategy is used to build XAI models and obtain the results. This scheme is repeated ten times. Finally, an average of the training and test accuracies is obtained.

In each experiment, all the models -the DTs and the ensembles- are induced using the same training set. Then, a synthetic dataset is created from the training set. This synthetic set is evaluated with the ensemble models and relabeled with their results. Finally, new DTs are trained with the relabeled synthetic set. All models (DT and ensembles) are evaluated with the same test set, ensuring that the results are independent of the training set manipulation. The CV scheme is implemented in Java, utilizing classes from the Weka library and the *wekaPython* plugin, allowing Integration with CPython on Weka [12].

4 Results and Discussion

Tables 1, 2 and 3 show the average accuracy results for the three data segments (Symptoms, Pathogen Presence, and BV-associated bacteria with lactobacilli), organized with eleven columns: the first identifies the ensemble model used for synthetic data labeling, followed by five column pairs showing training/test accuracies - the first pair presents ensemble results on original data, while the remaining four pairs show DT performance on synthetic data relabeled by the ensemble (corresponding to J48, SimpleCart, JCHAID*, and SPAARC algorithms). The first row shows white-box model results on original data, while subsequent rows display ensemble results on original data and their combination with white-box models, with bold values indicating the best results per interpretable model and underlined values marking cases where interpretable models outperformed their black-box counterparts.

Table 1 shows AB+J48 as the best explainable model for disease symptoms, with explainable models generally outperforming DTs trained directly on the dataset. For pathogen presence (Table 2), AB combined with any DT method performs best, with 10 of 16 explainable models surpassing direct DT performance. Table 3 reveals XGB+J48 as optimal for BV-associated bacteria, though

[1] The models were tuned using grid search with five-fold cross-validation.

only four explainable models exceed direct DT accuracy. While explainable models effectively interpret black-box behavior, ensemble models typically achieve higher training accuracy due to minimal class label changes during synthetic data relabeling. However, it is notable that the DT-based explainers have an accuracy that is not less than that of the ensemble results.

Figure 2 presents two examples of induced DTs: Fig. 2a illustrates a DT created using the original dataset, while Fig. 2b displays an induced DT generated with synthetic data that has been relabeled based on the ensemble results. The key advantage of these models is their ability to explain how a patient is determined to be BV-positive, providing greater detail than traditional models.

Table 1. Average accuracies obtained for disease symptoms.

Model	Black-box		J48		SimpleCART		CHAID*		SPAARC	
	Training	Test	Training	Test	Training	Test	Training	Test	Training	Test
-			78.70	**72.77**	74.68	71.93	76.32	71.85	74.50	72.69
RF	82.33	73.53	98.33	72.27	96.58	72.52	95.86	**72.77**	96.20	72.35
AB	75.74	73.70	100.00	**74.03**	99.78	73.87	99.76	73.61	99.77	73.78
GB	82.44	**74.54**	98.46	72.77	96.36	72.86	95.99	72.35	96.63	**73.19**
XGB	82.33	74.37	98.85	72.94	97.48	**73.61**	97.74	73.45	97.34	**73.61**

Table 2. Average accuracies obtained for presence of pathogens.

Model	Black-box		J48		SimpleCART		CHAID*		SPAARC	
	Training	Test	Training	Test	Training	Test	Training	Test	Training	Test
-			85.82	83.88	85.66	**84.73**	86.13	83.64	85.25	84.03
RF	86.15	83.95	99.88	83.64	99.64	**84.11**	99.51	83.95	99.64	**84.11**
AB	85.60	**85.27**	100.00	**85.27**	100.00	**85.27**	100.00	**85.27**	100.00	**85.27**
GB	83.02	79.69	99.48	**79.38**	99.09	79.15	98.96	79.30	99.01	79.22
XGB	86.96	83.95	99.70	84.19	99.46	**84.73**	99.48	84.19	99.48	**84.73**

Table 3. Average accuracies obtained for BV-associated bacteria and lactobacilli.

Model	Black-box		J48		SimpleCART		CHAID*		SPAARC	
	Training	Test	Training	Test	Training	Test	Training	Test	Training	Test
-			98.13	94.57	96.65	**96.12**	96.67	95.50	96.77	**96.12**
RF	100.00	**97.13**	99.48	**95.89**	99.02	95.50	98.98	95.50	99.05	95.74
AB	96.79	96.12	99.95	96.12	99.93	96.12	99.81	**96.20**	99.92	96.12
GB	100.00	95.27	99.26	95.35	98.78	95.35	98.80	95.04	98.64	**95.50**
XGB	99.22	96.51	99.52	**96.36**	99.10	95.74	98.96	95.27	99.10	95.89

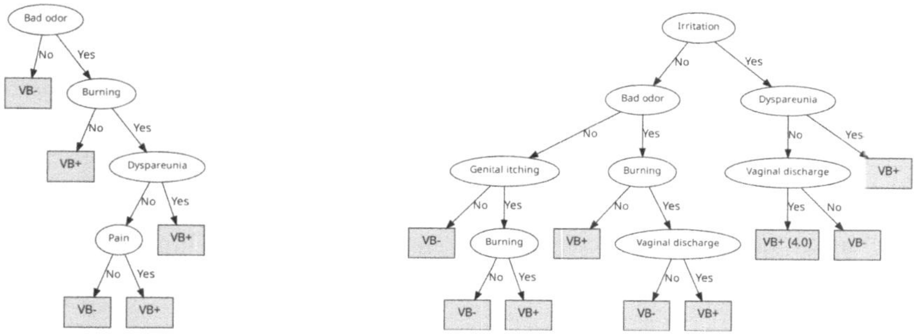

(a) (b)

Fig. 2. Examples of DTs induced with original and synthetic dataset.

The proposed strategy is called *hierarchical*, as it allows physicians to diagnose the patient in three stages. If the first model results are inconclusive, they can request additional studies for the patient. While PCR results are more accurate, the cost of conducting this study is high, and it may not be an alternative for patients in economically disadvantaged areas.

5 Conclusions and Future Work

Results demonstrate that explainable models, especially AB/XGB combinations, consistently surpass traditional white-box approaches. The XAI-derived DTs more accurately capture feature relationships for BV diagnosis, improving both accuracy and interpretability. The proposed hierarchical approach provides clinicians with transparent decision-making insights while maintaining diagnostic reliability.

Current limitations include the synthetic data generation process, which could benefit from improved augmentation techniques and sampling strategies for better generalization. Future research should explore advanced optimization methods like Bayesian optimization or genetic algorithms to enhance hyperparameter tuning beyond current grid search capabilities.

Disclosure of Interests. The authors have no competing interests to declare that are relevant to the content of this article.

References

1. Abou Chacra, L., Fenollar, F., Diop, K.: Bacterial vaginosis: what do we currently know? Front. Cell. Infect. Microbiol. **11**, 672429 (2022). https://doi.org/10.3389/fcimb.2021.672429
2. Arrieta, A.B., Díaz-Rodríguez, N., Del Ser, J., Bennetot, A., Tabik, S., Barbado, A.: Explainable Artificial Intelligence (XAI): Concepts, taxonomies, opportunities and challenges toward responsible AI. Inf. Fusion **58**, 82–115 (2020). https://doi.org/10.1016/j.inffus.2019.12.012

3. Bagnall, P., Rizzolo, D.: Bacterial vaginosis: a practical review. Jaapa **30**(12), 15–21 (2017). https://doi.org/10.1097/01.JAA.0000526770.60197.fa
4. Baker, Y.S., Agrawal, R., Foster, J.A., Beck, D., Dozier, G.: Applying machine learning techniques in detecting bacterial vaginosis. In: 2014 International Conference on Machine Learning and Cybernetics, vol. 1, pp. 241–246 (2014). https://doi.org/10.1109/ICMLC.2014.7009123
5. Bautista Hernández, C., Canul Reich, J.: Un modelo de red bayesiana para datos cualitativos de vaginosis bacteriana en mujeres embarazadas. Ideas en Ciencias de la Ingeniería **2**(2), 62–77 (2024). https://doi.org/10.36677/ideaseningenieria.v2i2.24096
6. Breiman, L., Friedman, J.H., Olshen, R.A., Stone, C.J.: Classification and Regression Trees. Chapman and Hall/CRC, Boca Raton (1984). https://doi.org/10.1201/9781315139470
7. Celeste, C., et al.: Ethnic disparity in diagnosing asymptomatic bacterial vaginosis using machine learning. Digit. Med. **6**(1), 211 (2023). https://doi.org/10.1038/s41746-023-00953-1
8. Chawla, N.V., Bowyer, K.W., Hall, L.O., Kegelmeyer, W.P.: SMOTE: synthetic minority over-sampling technique. J. Artif. Intell. Res. **16**, 321–357 (2002)
9. Chen, T., Guestrin, C.: XGBoost: a scalable tree boosting system. In: Proceedings of the 22nd ACM SIGKDD International Conference on Knowledge Discovery and Data Mining, KDD 2016, pp. 785–794. ACM, New York (2016). https://doi.org/10.1145/2939672.2939785
10. Drew, R.J., Murphy, T., Broderick, D., O'Gorman, J., Eogan, M.: An interpretation algorithm for molecular diagnosis of bacterial vaginosis in a maternity hospital using machine learning: proof-of-concept study. Diagn. Microbiol. Infect. Dis. **96**(2), 114950 (2020). https://doi.org/10.1016/j.diagmicrobio.2019.114950
11. Frank, E., Hall, M., Witten, I.: The WEKA Workbench. Online Appendix (2016). https://www.cs.waikato.ac.nz/ml/weka/Witten_et_al_2016_appendix.pdf
12. Hall, M.: CPython Integration in Weka (2015). http://markahall.blogspot.com/2015/06/cpython-integration-in-weka.html. Accessed 23 Feb 2025
13. Hastie, T., Tibshirani, R., Friedman, J.H., Friedman, J.H.: The Elements of Statistical Learning: Data Mining, Inference, and Prediction., vol. 2 Springer (2009). https://doi.org/10.1007/978-0-387-84858-7
14. Ibarguren, I., Lasarguren, A., Pérez, J.M., Muguerza, J., Gurrutxaga, I., Arbelaitz, O.: BFPART: best-first PART. Inf. Sci. **367–368**, 927–952 (2016). https://doi.org/10.1016/j.ins.2016.07.023
15. Jiang, F., et al.: Artificial intelligence in healthcare: past, present and future. Stroke Vasc. Neurol. **2**(4), 230–243 (2017). https://doi.org/10.1136/svn-2017-000101
16. Kusters, J.G., Reuland, E.A., Bouter, S., Koenig, P., Dorigo-Zetsma, J.W.: A multiplex real-time PCR assay for routine diagnosis of bacterial vaginosis. Eur. J. Clin. Microbiol. Infect. Dis. **34**(9), 1779–1785 (2015). https://doi.org/10.1007/s10096-015-2412-z
17. Lundberg, S.M., Lee, S.I.: A Unified Approach to Interpreting Model Predictions. Adv. Neural. Inf. Process. Syst. **30**, 4765–4774 (2017)
18. Mackay, I.M.: Real-time PCR in the microbiology laboratory. Clin. Microbiol. Infect. **10**(3), 190–212 (2004). https://doi.org/10.1111/j.1198-743X.2004.00722.x
19. Morris, M., Nicoll, A., Simms, I., Wilson, J., Catchpole, M.: Bacterial vaginosis: a public health review. Br. J. Obstet. Gynaecol. **108**(5), 439–450 (2001). https://doi.org/10.1016/S0306-5456(00)00124-8

20. Muzny, C.A., Cerca, N., Elnaggar, J.H., Taylor, C.M., Sobel, J.D., Van Der Pol, B.: State of the art for diagnosis of bacterial vaginosis. J. Clin. Microbiol. **61**(8), e00837-22 (2023). https://doi.org/10.1128/jcm.00837-22
21. Obermeyer, Z., Emanuel, E.J.: Predicting the future-big data, machine learning, and clinical medicine. N. Engl. J. Med. **375**(13), 1216–1219 (2016). https://doi.org/10.1056/NEJMp1606181
22. Pedregosa, F., Varoquaux, G., Gramfort, A., et al.: Scikit-learn: machine learning in python. J. Mach. Learn. Res. **12**, 2825–2830 (2011)
23. Price, W.N., Cohen, I.G.: Privacy in the age of medical big data. Nat. Med. **25**(1), 37–43 (2019). https://doi.org/10.1038/s41591-018-0272-7
24. Quinlan, R.: C4.5: Programs for Machine Learning. Morgan Kaufmann, San Mateo (1993). https://doi.org/10.1016/C2009-0-27846-9
25. Ribeiro, M.T., Singh, S., Guestrin, C.: "Why should I trust you?": Explaining the predictions of any classifier. In: Proc. of the 22nd ACM SIGKDD Int. Conf. on Knowledge Discovery and Data Mining. pp. 1135–1144. KDD'16, ACM, New York, NY (2016). https://doi.org/10.1145/2939672.2939778
26. Rivera-López, R., Canul-Reich, J., De la Cruz Hernández, E., Ceballos-Cancino, H.G., Mezura-Montes, E., Cruz-Chávez, M.A.: Explainable AI through decision trees for black-box models used to support bacterial vaginosis diagnosis. In: Martínez-Villaseñor, L., et al. (eds.) Advances in Computational Intelligence. MICAI 2024. LNCS, vol. 15464. Springer, Cham (2025, to appear)
27. Rodriguez, V.J., et al.: Using unsupervised machine learning to classify behavioral risk markers of bacterial vaginosis. Arch. Gynecol. Obstet. **309**(3), 1053–1063 (2024). https://doi.org/10.1007/s00404-023-07360-7
28. Russo, R., Karadja, E., Seta, F.D.: Evidence-based mixture containing Lactobacillus strains and lactoferrin to prevent recurrent bacterial vaginosis: a double blind, placebo controlled, randomised clinical trial. Beneficial Microbes **10**(1), 19–26 (2019). https://doi.org/10.3920/BM2018.0075
29. Sagi, O., Rokach, L.: Explainable decision forest: transforming a decision forest into an interpretable tree. Inf. Fusion **61**, 124–138 (2020). https://doi.org/10.1016/j.inffus.2020.03.013
30. Sanchez-Garcia, E.K., Contreras-Paredes, A., Martinez-Abundis, E., Garcia-Chan, D., Lizano, M., De la Cruz-Hernandez, E.: Molecular epidemiology of bacterial vaginosis and its association with genital micro-organisms in asymptomatic women. J. Med. Microbiol. **68**(9), 1373–1382 (2019). https://doi.org/10.1099/jmm.0.001044
31. Topol, E.J.: High-performance medicine: the convergence of human and artificial intelligence. Nat. Med. **25**(1), 44–56 (2019). https://doi.org/10.1038/s41591-018-0300-7
32. Watkins, E., et al.: Bacterial vaginosis treatment patterns, associated complications, and health care economic burden of women with Medicaid coverage in the United States. Ann. Pharmacother. **58**(5), 480–493 (2024). https://doi.org/10.1177/10600280231190701
33. Wen, X.R., et al.: Rapid diagnosis of bacterial vaginosis using machine-learning-assisted surface-enhanced Raman spectroscopy of human vaginal fluids. mSystems **10**(1), e01058-24 (2024). https://doi.org/10.1128/msystems.01058-24
34. Yates, D., Islam, M.Z., Gao, J.: SPAARC: a fast decision tree algorithm. In: Islam, R., et al. (eds.) AusDM 2018. CCIS, vol. 996, pp. 43–55. Springer, Singapore (2019). https://doi.org/10.1007/978-981-13-6661-1_4

Reinforcement Learning

Evaluating Deep Reinforcement Learning for Robotic Navigation

Jorge Gutiérrez[1,2](✉), Luis Enrique Sucar[1], Rafael Murrieta-Cid[2], Israel Becerra[2], and Gabriel Omar Flores-Aquino[2]

[1] Instituto Nacional de Astrofísica, Óptica y Electrónica, Luis Enrique Erro #1, Sta María Tonanzintla, 72840 San Andrés Cholula, Puebla, Mexico
{jorge.gutierrez,esucar}@inaoep.mx

[2] Centro de Investigaciones en Matemáticas, De Jalisco s/n, Valenciana, 36023 Guanajuato, Guanajuato, Mexico
{murrieta,israelb,gabriel.flores}@cimat.mx

Abstract. This paper investigates the performance of a deep reinforcement learning (DRL) algorithm in robotic navigation, focusing on how environmental complexity and initial conditions affect learning efficiency. The study aims to identify which environmental factors contribute to faster or slower learning and how intrinsic exploration behavior influences navigation performance. A simulated environment was used to measure success rates, collision rates, time to completion, and the proportion of episodes in which the agent reached the goal or collided. The test scenarios varied the initial positions of the robot and goal (fixed or randomized) and the presence or absence of obstacles. The results indicate that the learning efficiency decreases significantly in obstacle-rich environments with randomized conditions, particularly when the robot and goal positions vary. In contrast, simpler cases with fixed starting conditions or a randomized robot position with a fixed goal led to faster convergence and higher success rates. This study provides a deeper understanding of DRL performance boundaries and highlights key factors influencing the speed and reliability of policy learning in robotic navigation tasks, emphasizing the role of intrinsic exploration driven by a stochastic policy.

Keywords: Reinforcement learning · Robot navigation · Soft Actor-Critic

1 Introduction

Robotic navigation is a core challenge in autonomous systems, requiring agents to navigate complex environments to reach designated goals while avoiding obstacles. Traditional path-planning algorithms have been widely used for this purpose. However, these methods can only be used with robots with few degrees of freedom moving on discrete representations such as meshes or grids.

A. P. López-Monroy et al. (Eds.): MCPR 2025, LNCS 15715, pp. 303–312, 2025.
https://doi.org/10.1007/978-3-031-96255-4_28

More recently, sampling-based planners like PRM, RRT or SST [4,5] or their optimal versions [6,7] have shown to be very efficient to deal with complex robots with many degrees of freedom. There are also some approaches such as MPNet, which have shown advances, integrating trajectory generation with neural networks [1]. Despite these advances, challenges remain. Sampling-based methods require considerable computational time and require a model of the robot. Methods based on learning are faster at inference time and do not require a model of the robot.

Deep reinforcement learning (DRL) offers an alternative paradigm, enabling agents to learn navigation policies directly from environmental interactions without the need for predefined maps or explicit robot models. Model-free methods, including the Soft Actor-Critic (SAC) algorithm, have gained significant attention for their ability to handle continuous action spaces while maintaining sample efficiency and robust exploration [2]. These characteristics make DRL methods suitable for scenarios where accurate models of the robot or environment are unavailable or difficult to construct. However, DRL-based navigation systems face critical limitations, including inefficient learning, poor generalization to unseen environments, and difficulty adapting to diverse initial conditions.

This study systematically evaluates the performance of SAC in robotic navigation under varying environmental conditions. The primary goal is to identify the most challenging scenarios and determine the factors influencing the algorithm's success and convergence rates. By testing SAC across eight experimental cases—varying the presence of obstacles, initial robot positions, and goal placements—we aim to uncover the boundaries of its effectiveness and provide actionable insights into its limitations. The contributions of this paper are twofold.

1. **Comprehensive experimental framework:** We evaluate SAC's navigation performance under diverse cases, exploring how environmental complexity impacts learning efficiency and navigation success.
2. **Performance analysis:** We identify critical factors—such as obstacle density, randomized initial conditions, and goal placements—that affect SAC's learning process and robustness.

2 Background and State of the Art

2.1 Reinforcement Learning and Soft Actor-Critic

Reinforcement learning (RL) provides a framework for agents to learn optimal policies through trial-and-error interactions with an environment. Formally, RL problems are modeled as Markov Decision Processes (MDPs) [3], characterized by the tuple $\langle S, A, P, R, \gamma \rangle$, where:

- **State Space** (S): Represents all possible states of the environment.
- **Action Space** (A): Defines all actions the agent can take.
- **Transition Probability** ($P(s'|s,a)$): The probability of transitioning to state s' after taking action a in state s.

- **Reward Function** ($R(s, a, s')$): Specifies the reward received for transitioning between states via action a.
- **Discount Factor** (γ): Balances immediate and future rewards.

The goal is to learn an optimal policy $\pi^*(a|s)$ that maximizes the expected cumulative reward:

$$G_t = \mathbb{E}\left[\sum_{k=0}^{\infty} \gamma^k R(s_{t+k}, a_{t+k}) \mid S_t = s\right] \tag{1}$$

Soft Actor-Critic (SAC). [2] is a model-free, off-policy RL method tailored for continuous action spaces. Its core innovation lies in its entropy-regularized objective, which balances reward maximization with exploration. The SAC algorithm optimizes the following objective:

$$\mathcal{J}(\pi) = \mathbb{E}_{s \sim D}\left[\sum_{t=0}^{\infty} \gamma^t (R(s_t, a_t) + \alpha \mathcal{H}(\pi(\cdot|s_t)))\right] \tag{2}$$

where $\mathcal{H}(\pi)$ represents the entropy of the policy, encouraging stochastic exploration, and α controls the trade-off between exploration and exploitation. Key components of SAC: (i) **Policy Network (Actor):** Outputs a distribution over continuous actions, (ii) **Q-Value Networks (Critics):** Provide value estimates for state-action pairs, mitigating overestimation bias, and (iii) **Entropy Maximization:** Enhances exploration by encouraging randomness in action selection. SAC is particularly suited for robotic navigation due to its ability to handle:

- **Continuous Action Spaces:** Essential for controlling robots with differential-drive mechanisms or manipulators.
- **Sparse Rewards:** Learns effectively even when rewards are sparse, such as reaching a goal in complex environments.
- **Sample Efficiency:** Utilizes off-policy updates, reducing data requirements.
- **Exploration-Exploitation Balance:** The entropy objective ensures that agents explore effectively while optimizing long-term performance.

2.2 State of the Art in RL-Based Navigation

Robotic navigation has traditionally relied on classical path-planning algorithms. Sampling-based motion planners, such as RRT [4] and PRM [5], excel in high-dimensional planning but are computationally intensive when addressing kinodynamic constraints [6]. Extensions like SST* [7] improve trajectory quality but depend on precise system models, limiting their applicability to real-world scenarios. Hybrid approaches, like MPNet [1], combine learning and planning by using neural networks trained on trajectory data from expert planners.

Recent RL advancements have positioned model-free methods, such as SAC [2], PPO [8], and DDPG [9], as viable alternatives. These methods adapt well to diverse environments without relying on predefined models of system dynamics. SAC, in particular, stands out for its entropy-regularized framework, which stabilizes policy updates and encourages diverse action sampling. Challenges in RL-based navigation include:

- **Exploration in Complex Spaces:** Efficiently navigating environments with sparse rewards remains a challenge.
- **Sample Efficiency:** Prolonged training times limit scalability to real-world systems.
- **Safety and Robustness:** Ensuring collision-free navigation is critical, especially in environments with obstacles.
- **Generalization:** Applying learned policies to unseen environments is an ongoing research focus.

This study adresses these challenges by evaluating SAC in robotic navigation, focusing on its adaptability, robustness, and the impact of environmental complexity. By testing varying conditions of obstacles, goals, and initial positions, we aim to identify critical factors influencing SAC's scalability and generalization. While prior studies have demonstrated the effectiveness of RL algorithms in robotic navigation, many of them evaluate performance in a single or limited set of scenarios [1,10]. In contrast, our work focuses on systematically varying the environment, enabling a deeper analysis of the limitations of SAC.

3 Methodology

3.1 Simulation Environment

The experiments were conducted in a simulated environment developed using MuJoCo [13], a physics-based engine known for its accuracy in simulating robotic dynamics. The environment was specifically designed to evaluate the navigation capabilities of DRL agents under varying conditions, providing a controlled yet challenging testbed for analyzing SAC's performance. The main elements are:

- **Map Dimensions:** Each map consists of a 2D grid with dimensions of 30×30 units, enclosed by impassable boundary walls. This size balances computational efficiency and task complexity.
- **Obstacles:** Both obstacle-free and obstacle-filled scenarios were tested:
  - *No Obstacles:* Only boundary walls, with no internal obstacles.
  - *Configured Obstacles:* Fixed obstacles are strategically placed to increase navigation complexity.

3.2 Robot Model

The differential-drive robot is modeled using the following kinematic equations:

$$\dot{x} = v\cos(\theta), \quad \dot{y} = v\sin(\theta), \quad \dot{\theta} = \omega$$

where $\dot{x}$, $\dot{y}$, and $\dot{\theta}$ denote the derivatives of the robot's position (x, y) and orientation (θ) with respect to time.

The state vector includes:

- **Robot Pose:** The robot's state is encoded as $s_{robot} = [x_{robot}, y_{robot}, \sin\theta_{robot}, \cos\theta_{robot}]$, ensuring smooth representation of orientation.
- **Goal Position:** $g = [x_{goal}, y_{goal}]$.
- **Temporal Context:** The last five positions of the robot pose and goal position are concatenated into the full state vector: $s = [s_{robot}(t-4{:}t),\ g(t-4{:}t)]$

The **reward function** assigns +100 for reaching the goal, −1 for collisions, and 0 otherwise.

3.3 Experimental Setup

The experiments span eight cases to evaluate SAC's adaptability and robustness (Table 1):

Table 1. Experimental configurations.

Environment Type	Initial Robot Configuration	Goal Position	Obstacles
Obstacle-Free	Fixed	Fixed	No
Obstacle-Free	Random	Fixed	No
Obstacle-Free	Fixed	Random	No
Obstacle-Free	Random	Random	No
Obstacle-Present	Fixed	Fixed	Yes
Obstacle-Present	Random	Fixed	Yes
Obstacle-Present	Fixed	Random	Yes
Obstacle-Present	Random	Random	Yes

Initial Robot Configuration refers to the starting state of the robot, including its position and orientation. *Fixed* implies that the robot always starts from the same configuration in every episode. *Random* indicates that the robot's initial position and orientation are sampled uniformly within the environment.

3.4 Training Algorithm

The SAC algorithm was employed for training due to its suitability for continuous action spaces. SAC optimizes a policy $\pi(a|s)$ that maximizes cumulative rewards while encouraging exploration through entropy regularization.

Hyperparameters. The hyperparameters used for the experiments are as follows: a learning rate of 3×10^{-4}, a discount factor (γ) of 0.99, an entropy coefficient (α) of 0.2, a batch size of 256, a replay buffer size of 1,000,000, and a maximum of 300 steps per episode.

3.5 Performance Metrics

- **Success Rate:** Percentage of episodes where the robot reached the goal.
- **Collision Rate:** Percentage of episodes ending in a collision.
- **Neutral Outcomes:** Episodes where the robot neither reached the goal nor collided.
- **Time to Completion:** Average steps taken to reach the goal.

3.6 Hardware Specifications

Experiments were conducted on a high-performance computing setup: **GPU:** NVIDIA RTX 3090, **CPU:** Intel Core i9, **RAM:** 64 GB

4 Results

Table 2 summarizes success rates, collision rates, steps to goal, and training times across all scenarios. In **obstacle-free environments**, the agent consistently reached the goal in 100% of episodes, with no collisions or incomplete runs, converging in under **1.5 h**. In contrast, **obstacle-rich environments** showed reduced performance: the lowest success rate (**68%**), highest collision rate (**31%**), and most incomplete episodes (**13%**) were observed under randomized robot and goal positions. Training times ranged from **45 to 65 h**. The **average steps to goal** showed no clear correlation with task complexity, ranging from **198 to 291** in obstacle-free and **198 to 278** in obstacle-rich settings.

Table 2. Performance metrics and training times for all cases.

Initial Position	Goal Position	Obstacles	Success Rate (%)	Collision Rate (%)	No Result (%)	Avg Steps to Goal	Training Time
Fixed	Fixed	No	100	0	0	291	1 h 21 m
Fixed	Random	No	99	1	0	212	0 h 56 m
Random	Fixed	No	100	0	0	219	0 h 56 m
Random	Random	No	100	0	0	198	1 h 3 m
Fixed	Fixed	Yes	100	0	0	278	64 h 37 m
Fixed	Random	Yes	69	18	13	235	54 h 19 m
Random	Fixed	Yes	98	1	1	226	56 h 14 m
Random	Random	Yes	68	31	1	198	45 h 36 m

4.1 Learning Trends

- **Obstacle-Free Cases:** As shown in Fig. 1, the agent achieved near-perfect success rates across all cases within 10,000 episodes. The training process demonstrated fast and stable convergence.
- **Obstacle-Present Cases:** Figure 2 highlights the increased difficulty introduced by obstacles. Training durations extended to 250,000 episodes, with significantly lower success rates and greater variability in performance. Randomized setups showed the greatest difficulty, underscoring the challenges of navigating in dynamic and obstacle-rich environments.

The significant disparity in training durations between simple and complex cases reflects the computational demands of SAC-based navigation. Obstacle-free environments allowed for rapid learning, while obstacle-rich setups necessitated longer training periods to address the increased difficulty of navigating through constrained spaces and avoiding collisions. These findings emphasize the importance of developing sample-efficient RL methods to mitigate the time and resource requirements for training in complex environments.

Supporting materials in the form of video demonstrations of the experimental results can be accessed at https://jorgeeduardogutierrez.github.io/evaluating-robot-navigation-sac/.

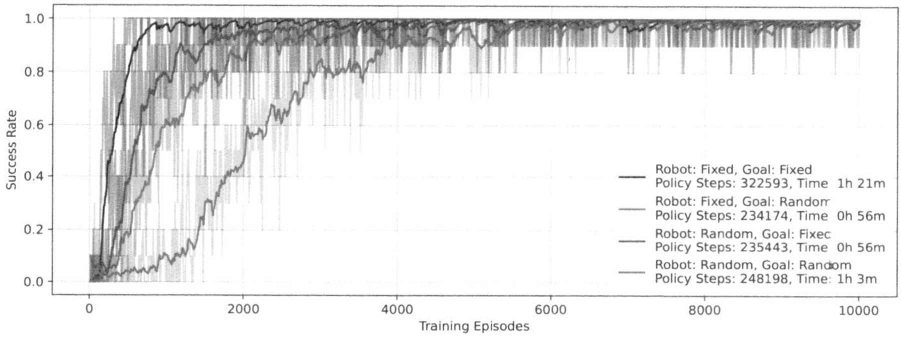

Fig. 1. Learning curves in **obstacle-free environments** over 10,000 training episodes. The Y-axis shows the success rate, and the X-axis indicates training episodes. Legend entries show initial configuration, policy steps, and training time.

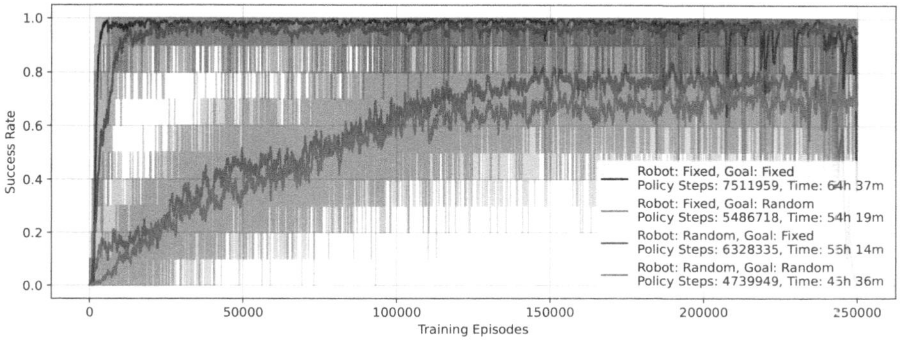

Fig. 2. Learning curves in **obstacle-rich environments** over 250,000 training episodes. The curves reflect longer training durations and more complex dynamics. Policy steps and training time are indicated in the legend.

5 Discussion

The experimental results presented in Sect. 4 provide valuable insights into the capabilities and limitations of reinforcement learning (RL) for robotic navigation, with a specific focus on the Soft Actor-Critic algorithm.

5.1 Impact of Environmental Complexity

The performance of the SAC agent exhibited significant sensitivity to environmental complexity. Success rates in cases with randomized goal positions and obstacles dropped to as low as 68%, while collision rates peaked at 31%. These findings are consistent with previous studies highlighting the challenges posed by dynamic and obstacle-rich environments [12]. The decline in success rates and efficiency in obstacle-rich environments suggests that SAC struggles to effectively generalize to highly variable conditions. They underscore the necessity of robust exploration strategies and adaptive reward mechanisms to improve agent performance in complex scenarios.

Although the Soft Actor-Critic algorithm employs an entropy-regularized objective that encourages exploration, our results suggest that this mechanism may be insufficient in environments with high complexity and sparse rewards. The entropy term promotes action diversity but lacks directional guidance toward promising regions of the state space.

Incorporating complementary strategies, such as progress-based reward shaping, intrinsic motivation [11], or curriculum learning, may improve exploration in sparse-reward settings and enhance the agent's capacity to generalize in complex environments.

5.2 Safety and Collision Avoidance

The results revealed notable safety challenges, with collision rates reaching their highest levels in complex scenarios involving randomized robot and goal positions alongside obstacles. This highlights a critical limitation in the standard reward function, which may not adequately penalize unsafe behaviors in all situations.

5.3 Training Times and Computational Demands

The disparity in training times between simple and complex cases underscores the computational challenges of SAC-based navigation. Obstacle-free setups required less than 1.5 h of training, reflecting the algorithm's rapid convergence in straightforward environments. In contrast, obstacle-present conditions necessitated between 45 and 65 h of training due to the increased complexity of navigating constrained spaces. These findings highlight the importance of developing sample-efficient RL methods to address the time and resource constraints inherent in training RL agents for real-world applications. Leveraging model-based RL methods or transfer learning techniques could significantly reduce training durations and improve scalability to more demanding tasks.

5.4 Limitations of the Study

While the study provides meaningful insights into SAC's capabilities, several limitations must be addressed: **1) Simulation-Only Evaluation:** All experiments were conducted in simulation, which may not fully capture real-world complexities, such as sensor noise, actuator inaccuracies, or environmental unpredictability. **2) Exploration Strategy:** SAC's intrinsic entropy mechanism was the primary exploration strategy employed. This approach may have been insufficient for environments with sparse rewards and high complexity. **3) Safety Mechanisms:** The reliance on the reward function alone for collision avoidance limited the agent's ability to ensure safety in obstacle-rich conditions. Explicit safety constraints were not implemented. **4) Fixed Reward Design:** The static reward structure used in this study might not have been optimal for all cases, particularly in scenarios with significant variation in task difficulty and environmental complexity. These limitations suggest several avenues for future work, including the integration of safety-focused RL techniques, exploration-enhancing mechanisms, and real-world validation to address the gaps identified in this study.

6 Conclusions and Future Work

This study systematically evaluated the performance of the SAC algorithm in robotic navigation across eight distinct cases. These cases varied the initial positions of the robot and goal, as well as the presence of obstacles, providing a comprehensive analysis of SAC's adaptability and robustness under diverse environmental conditions. The results highlight several key findings: **1) Performance in Simple Environments:** SAC demonstrated excellent performance in obstacle-free environments, achieving near-perfect success rates and rapid convergence. These results reflect the algorithm's ability to efficiently learn navigation policies in straightforward scenarios. **2) Challenges in Complex Environments:** In environment with obstacles and randomized initial conditions, SAC faced significant challenges, with success rates dropping to as low as 68% and collision rates peaking at 31%. **3) Stability and Robustness:** Despite these challenges, SAC provided a stable and robust training process, demonstrating its suitability for continuous action spaces and real-time decision-making in robotic navigation. These findings emphasize the importance of balancing environmental complexity, exploration strategies, and reward shaping to achieve stable and reliable robotic navigation using RL techniques. Furthermore, they highlight the limitations of SAC in generalizing to complex and dynamic environments, pointing to the need for algorithmic refinements to enhance scalability and adaptability. By systematically exploring SAC's performance across varying conditions, this study contributes to the understanding of reinforcement learning's capabilities and limitations in robotic navigation. For future work, we plan to investigate how modifications to the reward function affect learning dynamics and generalization. Rather than introducing complex shaping or adaptive rewards, we propose to explore systematic variations of the existing reward signals.

Acknowledgments. This work was supported by the Secretaría de Ciencia, Tecnología e Innovación (SECITI). The authors also thank the Centro de Investigaciones en Matemáticas (CIMAT) for hosting the development of this work.

Disclosure of Interests. The authors have no competing interests to declare that are relevant to the content of this article.

References

1. Qureshi, A.H., Patil, S., Yadav, V.: MPNet: neural motion planning network for autonomous navigation. IEEE Robot. Autom. Lett. **4**(3), 1233–1240 (2019)
2. Haarnoja, T., Zhou, A., Abbeel, P., Levine, S.: Soft actor-critic: off-policy maximum entropy deep reinforcement learning with a stochastic actor. In: Proceedings of the 35th International Conference on Machine Learning (ICML), vol. 80, pp. 1861–1870 (2018)
3. Sutton, R.S., Barto, A.G.: Introduction to Reinforcement Learning. MIT Press (1998)
4. LaValle, S.M., Kuffner, J.J., Jr.: Randomized kinodynamic planning. Int. J. Robot. Res. **20**(5), 378–400 (2001)
5. Kavraki, L.E., Švestka, P., Latombe, J.C., Overmars, M.H.: Probabilistic roadmaps for path planning in high-dimensional configuration spaces. IEEE Trans. Robot. Autom. **12**(4), 566–580 (1996)
6. Karaman, S., Frazzoli, E.: Sampling-based algorithms for optimal motion planning. Int. J. Robot. Res. **30**(7), 846–894 (2011)
7. Li, W., Littlefield, Z., Alterovitz, R.: Efficient motion planning for high-dimensional robots by exploiting local optimality properties of SST*. Proc. Robot. Sci. Syst. (RSS) **2016**, 1–10 (2016)
8. Schulman, J., Wolski, F., Dhariwal, P., Radford, A., Klimov, O.: Proximal Policy Optimization Algorithms. arXiv preprint arXiv:1707.06347 (2017)
9. Lillicrap, T.P., et al.: Continuous Control with Deep Reinforcement Learning. arXiv preprint arXiv:1509.02971 (2015)
10. Faust, A., et al.: PRM-RL: long-range robotic navigation tasks by combining reinforcement learning and sampling-based planning. In: Proceedings of the IEEE International Conference on Robotics and Automation (ICRA), pp. 5113–5120 (2018)
11. Pathak, D., Agrawal, P., Efros, A.A., Darrell, T.: Curiosity-driven exploration by self-supervised prediction. In: Proceedings of the IEEE Conference on Computer Vision and Pattern Recognition (CVPR), pp. 1445–1454 (2017)
12. Zahavy, T., Ben-Zrihem, N., Mannor, S.: Graying the black box: understanding DQNs. In: Proceedings of the 33rd International Conference on Machine Learning (ICML), vol. 48, pp. 1899–1908 (2016)
13. Todorov, E., Erez, T., Tassa, Y.: MuJoCo: a physics engine for model-based control. In: 2012 IEEE/RSJ International Conference on Intelligent Robots and Systems, pp. 5026–5033 (2012)

Determining Optimal Population Management with Reinforcement Learning

Salvador Garcilita-Arguello and Edgar Roman-Rangel(✉)

Department of Computer Science, Instituto Tecnológico Autónomo de México, Rio Hondo 1, 01080 Mexico City, Mexico
salvador.garcilita@bioalgoritmia.com, edgar.roman@itam.mx

Abstract. Reinforcement learning is a promising artificial intelligence area which relies on computational simulations where an agent finds a policy that maximizes a particular reward by mapping states to actions in a non-deterministic environment, with applications in optimization problems. Here, we apply Q-learning, a popular model-free reinforcement learning algorithm to a representative ecological problem: the sustainable harvest of a population which follows a logistic growth rate by modeling it as a valid python gymnasium environment, contributing to the generation of new environments which represent real-world situations and may lead to decision making. We implemented three different scenarios in which the agents determined an optimal policy guided by different reward signals: a greedy agent, which harvests as much as possible; a conscious agent, which seeks to harvest as much as possible while maintaining high population numbers; and a biocentric agent, which harvests only what is needed to avoid the population to exceed the carrying capacity of the environment. By initializing the population size to 100, with a growth rate of 1 and a carrying capacity of 200, the biocentric agent had the largest accumulated harvest, suggesting that a sustainable strategy is more profitable in the long term. Reinforcement learning is a very promising approach for decision making in many ecological real-world situations, where population management is a very straightforward application.

Keywords: Artificial intelligence · Computational ecology · Reinforcement learning · Sustainability · Q-learning

1 Introduction

Distinct sub-fields within natural sciences now have huge data sets which often are difficult to process with traditional statistical techniques or lead to new questions which require innovative methods to be answered, for instance the application of advanced computational techniques in taxonomy, evolution and biogeography [1]. Machine learning, particularly reinforcement learning (RL), has shown promise in biology related areas like omics and brain-body interfaces,

A. P. López-Monroy et al. (Eds.): MCPR 2025, LNCS 15715, pp. 313–323, 2025.
https://doi.org/10.1007/978-3-031-96255-4_29

with many potential applications still emerging, some of them with great interest for other sub-fields such as ecology and conservation [2,3].

In ecology (branch of biology focused on the study of the species with other biotic and abiotic components of the ecosystem [4]), both supervised and unsupervised machine learning algorithms have proven to be valuable for a wide range of applications such as predicting species distribution and ecosystemic interactions [5–8]. However, RL is also a promising approach for ecology and could be useful for decision making under uncertainty in the context of climate change and the biodiversity crisis; unfortunately, until very recently, RL has not been applied extensively to ecology topics [9].

Population ecology usually involves decision making and management decisions, where a population is defined as a set of individuals that belong to the same species and inhabit the same spatial-temporal dimension [4]. Since many populations are exploited by humans, how to sustainably harvest a population is a question with many different approaches, and reinforcement learning could be used as a tool to search for solutions to these kind of problems, as highlighted by Lapeyrolerie and collaborators [9] with an example of harvest quotas in fisheries management, or by Treloar and collaborators [10] who employ model-free deep reinforcement learning for the optimal control of a bacterial multi-species bioreactor, which is a strong challenge in industry.

The challenge in population management lies in balancing over-exploitation, which risks economic insignificance or extinction, and under-exploitation, which fails to maximize sustainable yield. Determining this equilibrium is complex due to biological and socioeconomic factors [4]. Approaches range from simple but risky fixed quotas to more advanced methods like fixed harvesting effort, fixed proportions (requiring preharvest censuses), and sophisticated computational models [4,11].

Reinforcement learning is a computational approach for automating decision-making in nondeterministic contexts. It involves an agent interacting with a dynamic environment and four key elements: a policy (mapping states to actions), a reward signal (guiding the agent's goal), a value function (estimating long-term rewards for each state), and, in model-based methods, a model of the environment for predicting outcomes. Model-free methods rely on trial and error to learn through exploration and applications range from games and robotics to supply chain logistics and operations analysis [5,12–14].

The contribution of this work is the first implementation of a reinforcement learning environment in the gymnasium open-source library to model a sustainable population harvesting, where the environment itself represents a population which follows a logistic growth model and the agent (a model free algorithm) learns through exploration to determine how to harvest flexibly, avoiding fixed quotas and taking into account the population dynamics [15]. To evaluate the use value and the different policies that can be obtained, we experimented with different reward signals, one for each of three different agents that interact independently with its own instance of our environment: a greedy agent, whose reward was as large as the harvest of each iteration; a conscious agent, whose reward balances good harvests with maintaining high population numbers; and a biocentric agent, whose reward is directly proportional to the population size after each harvest so it takes only what is strictly necessary. Our results show that the policies developed by the agents strongly reflect the priority determined by the reward signal, with different resulting distributions for both the actions and the populations; respecting the accumulated harvest at the end of each simulation, the biocentric strategy resulted the more profitable in the long term.

2 Methods

Our implementation represents a situation where an agent harvests a population which follows a logistic growth, and it must do it intelligently so that the population never becomes zero (which means extinction) but also it should harvest as much as possible per season to maximize the economic revenue; also, according to the logistic model, the population must never exceed an upper bound.

The logistic model (presented by Eq. (1) as a discrete population growth) in population ecology is a mathematical representation used to describe the growth of a population within a given environment in a more realistic way than an exponential growth (since no population can grow forever) [16]. It assumes that the population grows exponentially at first when resources are abundant, but as the population size approaches the carrying capacity of the environment (the maximum population size that the environment can sustain, denoted by K), the growth rate (denoted by r) slows down and eventually stabilizes [17]:

$$N_{t+1} = N_t + rN_t \left(1 - \frac{N_t}{K}\right), \tag{1}$$

where N_t represents the population size at time t.

Below, we provide a descriptive explanation of the implementation of both the agents and the environment.

2.1 The Environment

An environment is a mathematical model or computational simulation in which the agent interacts (that is, executes actions while learning). A valid environment must contemplate five components: describe the states that define the environment; enumerate the possible actions available for the agent; update the environment's internal state in response to the action of the agent; provide the agent with an observation of the new state; and provide the agent with a reward based on the environment's state and its action [9].

Gymnasium is an open-source library built by OpenAI. It is designed to standardize and accelerate research in RL [15,18]. The designed environment inherits from the gym.Env() superclass, which is the main gymnasium class for implementing RL environments. Our environment requires the following mandatory arguments when instantiated: K (the habitat's maximum sustainable capacity without degradation), r (growth rate), and the initial population size (N).

A valid gymnasium environment must have the following four main methods: step (which receives the action of an agent and contains almost all the logical interaction between the agent and the environment); reset (which restarts the current value of the population to the initial value for another cycle); render; and close (although the last two are not implemented in this work for being not essential). The module Spaces, which describes mathematical sets that are used in the environments to specify valid actions the agent can choose from, and valid observations (values for the population) as a vector, has two mandatory attributes, action_space and observation_space. In this particular implementation, both of these spaces attributes are instantiated as spaces. Discrete($K+1$), where K is the number of valid discrete values, since a population usually is modeled as a finite possible number of discrete states.

The environment also has three auxiliary methods that are used for the interaction with the agent or to adjust the population value of the environment:

- get_obs(): returns a python dictionary with the current population size.
- get_info(): returns a python dictionary with three keys; number of steps, record of harvest and population dynamics. It is useful for detailed analysis of the interaction of the agent with the environment.
- logistic(): it returns the logistic growth with the current values of r, N and K. Then is added to the population size to update its current value, as presented in Eq. (1).

Finally, the method step(action) contains almost all the logical interaction between the agent and the environment. Essentially, it is called by the agent on each step and stores the current population after executing the action provided by the agent (it's only argument) in the current state of the environment, that is, removing the number of individuals the agent chose, and then applying the logistic growth model (with the method logistic()) in the new population value. Finally, it returns to the agent a tuple with five important elements; observation, reward, terminated, truncated, and info. The reward object contains the numerical value the agent will receive as a consequence of the action it chose.

2.2 The Agent

An agent is a computational entity placed in a given environment with the autonomous capacity of performing actions to reach its design objectives [19]. For this case, we chose the agents to be a Q-learning algorithm, which is a model-free algorithm expensive in computational resources, but that converges to the optimum action-values with probability 1 as long as all actions are repeatedly sampled in all states and the action-values are represented discretely [20,21].

The agents learn by exploring different actions in various states and receiving rewards based on their choices, which are used to update a "Q-table" (state-action table). The Q-table assigns a "Q-value" to each state-action pair, representing the expected future reward for taking a specific action in a given state. By balancing exploration (trying new actions) and exploitation (choosing actions with the highest Q-values currently known), the agents gradually converge toward the best actions for maximizing cumulative rewards over time. We used the pseudocode presented in Algorithm 1 for updating the values in the Q-table.

Algorithm 1. Pseudocode inspired by [12]

```
Initialize Q(s,a), ∀s ∈ A(s), arbitrarily
Initialize Q(terminal-state) = 0
for each episode do
    Initialize S
    for each step in episode do
        Choose A from S using policy derived from Q (e.g., ε-greedy)
        Take action A, observe R, S'
        Q(s,a) ← Q(s,a) + α [R + γ max_a Q(s'a) − Q(s,a)]
        S ← S'
    end for
    until S is terminal
end for
```

Just as the environment, the agents are encapsulated in classes. The agent class has three methods, which contain the interaction with the environment class (env) and implement the two for loops of the Q-learning algorithm.

- train(env): the main method, which receives a valid environment as argument and immediately pass it to the method episodes(env) as argument too. It also keeps track of the time needed to complete training.
- episodes(env): represents the outer loop of the algorithm; it restarts the initial state of the environment (using env.reset()) and also restarts to zero some auxiliary variables that keep track of the learning in the current episode (such as terminated and self.current_reward). It calls the steps() method, and when finished, adjusts the exploration rate and saves in a list (self.rewards_record) the accumulated reward of the entire episode, and loops again until the total number of episodes (self.num_episodes) is reached.
- steps(env, state = int, terminated = bool): it represents the inner loop of the algorithm; it receives from episodes() the environment which the agent is interacting with, the current state of the environment, and a boolean variable which keeps track of changes in the terminated boolean variable provided by the environment after an action.

The method steps() loops until the maximum number of steps is reached, and in each loop, selects an action (based on the exploration-exploitation trade-off) and provides that action to the environment with env.step(action), which returns important information about what happened in the environment with the action of the agent (observation, reward, terminated, truncated and info). If in the current loop, terminated (provided by the environment) results to be true (that is, the population is below 0 or above K), the loop breaks and the algorithm would advance one episode in the outer loop (in episodes()). If terminated is not true, we update the Q value for that state action pair and update to the agent what the current state of the environment is (which was again returned by env.step(action)). Finally, the reward of the current episode is updated with the final reward (provided by env.step(action)) and we increment by one the counter of steps, advancing to the next inner iteration or to the next episode. To analyze different harvesting strategies, we instantiated three different agents with different rewards, which correspond to prioritize different purposes. For all three scenarios, the reward is a penalty of -100 if the population is extinguished (reaches 0) or exceeds K (which turns terminated to 'True' and ends that episode). Otherwise, the reward for each strategy is as listed in Table 1.

Table 1. Objective and reward of each agent while terminated == False.

Agent	Objective	Reward =
Greedy	Maximize revenue by harvesting as much as possible	harvest
Conscious	Balance revenue and long-term sustainability by maintaining the population near K	harvest $-abs$(current_population $-K$)
Biocentric	Prioritize high population numbers by harvesting only what is needed	current_population

2.3 The Training

Finally, the hyperparameters chosen for the agent were:

- Total number of episodes in the outter loop = 10000.
- Total number of steps in the inner loop = 1000.
- Learning rate (α) = 0.1.
- Discount rate (γ) = 0.99.
- Initial exploration rate = 1.
- Max exploration rate = 1.
- Min exploration rate = 0.01.
- Exploration decay rate = 0.001.

These values were chosen for being a standard starting point for the Q-learning algorithm [15]. As for the environment, the initial conditions were fixed as a growing rate r of 1, an initial population of 100 and a maximum number of individuals that can be sustained of 200.

The full implementation (environment and algorithm) was coded using Python 3.10.12, and particularly the environment was coded following the gymnasium library standards [15]. The RL models were trained in a T4 GPU provided by Google Colab. They were evaluated by analyzing the reward increment over time as evidence of the learning process of the agents, as well as with descriptive statistics of the harvest and population records, which represent the action and population dynamics. Also, the final Q-tables were analyzed by visualizing the magnitude of each Q-value respecting its corresponding state-action pair.

3 Results

All three agents showed consistent improvement in their policy in terms of continuous growth across iterations (Fig. 1a). Initially, the negative rewards indicate penalties for overharvesting or exceeding population limits. However, as iterations progress, the rewards increase, demonstrating that the three agents learned appropriate policies. The average reward stabilization suggests convergence to an optimal policy.

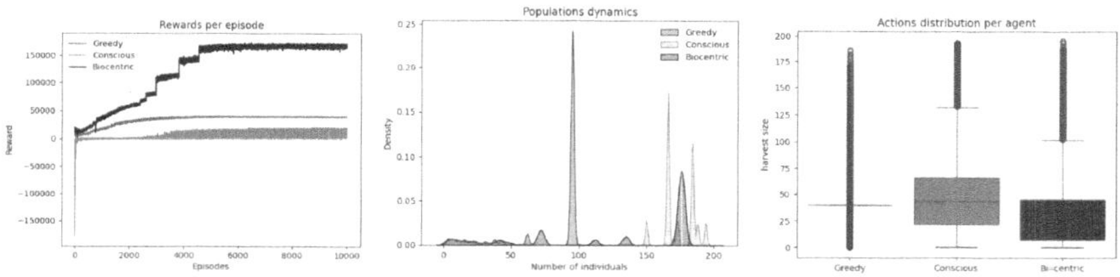

(a) Reward over time. (b) Population density (c) Action distribution

Fig. 1. Agents have different learning patterns. Each agent maintains its population around different values, and each population takes a wide range of values between 0 and $200K$. The space of possible actions, from 0 to $200K$, is almost completely sampled because of the exploratory nature of the algorithm.

As mentioned, actions correspond to the amount of individuals to be harvested at each step (Table 2). On average, the greedy agent harvested 33.69 individuals per iteration, while the conscious and biocentric agents harvested 43.74 and 36.3, respectively. The greedy agent exhibited the least variability in its actions (SD = 17.66), whereas the biocentric agent showed the highest dispersion (SD = 28.2), followed closely by the conscious agent (SD = 24.24). Regarding population levels after each agent's actions and subsequent logistic growth, the greedy agent maintained an average population of 79.32 individuals (SD = 30.29), the conscious agent 171.83 (SD = 19.33), and the biocentric agent 124.45 (SD = 64.03).

Results are consistent with the reward scheme; the greedy agent maintained its population at 95 individuals most of the time (Fig. 1b), with more of the 50% of the population values with this value, as can be seen in the quantile distribution (Table 2), and harvested near half the population (40 individuals) also most of the time (Fig. 1c), representing at least 50% of the total actions. As can be seen in Fig. 1b, the greedy agent's reward quickly stabilizes, showing little

Table 2. Mean and dispersion for the population and actions of each scenario.

Agent		Mean±stdd	Min	Q1	Q2	Q3	Max	Count
Greedy	Action	33.69 ± 17.66	0	40	40	40	186	9'998,842
	Population	79.32 ± 30.29	2	95	95	95	199	9'998,842
Conscious	Action	43.74 ± 24.24	0	22	43	66	193	4'146,660
	Population	171.83 ± 19.33	2	166	166	184	199	4'146,660
Biocentric	Action	36.3 ± 28.20	0	7	45	45	195	9'998,241
	Population	124.45 ± 64.03	2	72	176	176	199	9'998,241

improvement from 5000 episodes onwards. This could suggest the greedy agent found a local optimum, although the actions space was completely sampled.

The conscious agent maintained its population near K (Fig. 1b), with a considerably smaller dispersion than the other two agents. From the quantile distribution we can see that 50% of the time the population values were among 166 and 184 individuals. Actions were centered around 43 individuals (Fig. 1c), with 50% of the actions between 22 and 66 individuals (Table 2), therefore, conscious agent harvests approximately one quarter of the total populations, which is congruent with its programmed purpose; harvest as much as possible while maintaining the population near the maximum individuals possible.

Similarly to the greedy agent, the biocentric agent found a specific value to maintain the population around of, with 25% of the population values at 176 individuals (Table 2), a value very near to the maximum K of 200, and consistent with its purpose of maintaining the population as high as possible as long as it never reaches K (Fig. 1b). To achieve this, also found as optimal to harvest 45 individuals 25% of the time (Table 2), a similar strategy to the greedy agent, but with more dispersion on its actions (Fig. 1c).

Each final agent's Q-table can be visualized in Fig. 2, where each table is presented as a heatmap with rows representing actions and columns representing states, as in the original matrix. The magnitude of each cell represents the Q-value of that action-state pair, which is associated with the quality of taking that action in that specific state. A different pattern can be observed in each Q-table, which matches the relation between the current number of individuals and the harvest, according to the different strategies of each agent.

The final accumulated harvest of each agent is presented in Table 3. Surprisingly, the biocentric was the agent with more final harvest, followed by the greedy and finally the conscious. All three scenarios represent different management strategies with different implications.

Due to its reward scheme, the greedy agent only cares to harvest as much as possible. By maintaining the population at about half the carrying capacity (K), it took advantage of proportionally high harvests (approximately half the current population) with quick population recovery (since in the logistic model the population growth is faster precisely in the first half of the range between zero

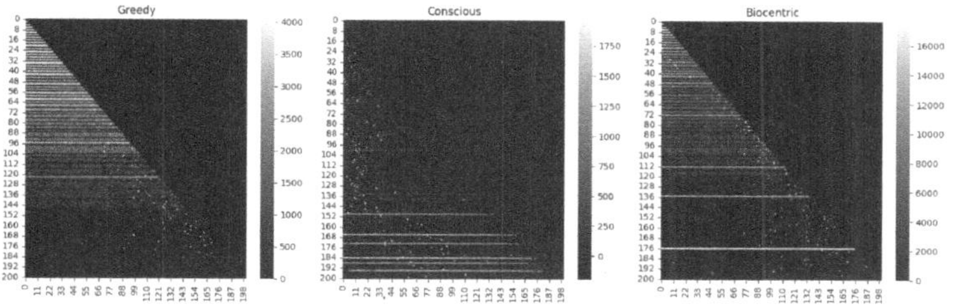

Fig. 2. Final Q-tables. High positive values are optimal action-state pair.

Table 3. Total harvest of each agent.

Agent	Greedy	Conscious	Biocentric
Harvest	336'857,041	181'358,429	362'921,932

and K, following almost an exponential growth, and decreasing when approaches to the upper bound).

Conscious agent reward scheme represents a realistic decision-making problem present in many population exploitation schemes, such as hunting reserves, where an optimum policy would be to have the maximum possible number of individuals (which is important to protect genetic diversity) but also allow to harvest the maximum possible, on which usually depends the economic revenue and viability of a project (manage and protection of the reserve, for example) [22]. Also, modern reserves usually contemplate the maximum number of individuals the ecosystem can sustain (in which case too many individuals are not good either for the financial sustain nor for the ecosystem as a whole). However, to appropriately model such scenarios with populations of vertebrated game species (such as birds and mammals), an extension for this model which contemplates more assumptions, such as age and sex, should be implemented, since the structural composition of these populations strongly affects its dynamics [17]. By contrast, the presented model with just specifying a growth rate and a maximum number of individuals could be applied almost directly to unicellular species industrial exploitation, such as algae, brewer's yeast and bacteria, or even to extensive harvest of duckweed (*Lemna sp.*) and other plants with important applications in the alimentary and biofuel industry [23].

From Fig. 1b, which shows a less concentrated distribution than the other two agents, and both the high dispersion measures and broad quantile values conscious agent reports in Table 2, we can say the optimal policy for the conscious schema was more difficult to find than in the other two scenarios (harvest as much as possible or maintain the population as high as possible). Nevertheless, this highlights the potential use value of reinforcement learning in this context.

Finally, the biocentric scenario, which represents the necessity to only harvest what is needed to avoid the population numbers exceeding the upper bound (an overpopulation problem), although not intended to prioritize profit, ended up with more harvest than the other two scenarios, suggesting that a sustainable and prudent strategy implies more harvest in the long term; this is consistent with the result of Lapeyrolerie and collaborators [9], whose reinforcement learning model applied to harvest quotas in fisheries management prioritized population recovery by even closing the fishery until the stock recovered (contrary to an historical example where, although adjusted, the harvesting never ceased). Probably the greedy agent, with its actions being driven by an avaricious strategy, didn't explore enough of what the long-term implications of having a high population number would be (as can be observed in Fig. 1b), falling to a local optimum which, as biocentric agent shows, could be improvable.

4 Conclusions

Q-learning is effective for finding optimal policies in managing growing populations, requiring only species-specific growth rates, estimated population size, and carrying capacity. The implemented gymnasium environment contributes to increase the use of reinforcement learning algorithms in real-world situations. Although the three agents implemented learned optimal policies, the biocentric agent proved to be the more sustainable, not only in terms of the population integrity but also in the total harvest, suggesting less ambitious strategies, which often are friendlier with the natural resources, can be the more profitable ones in the long term, while ambitious strategies can be potentially counterproductive not only by not harvesting as much as could be done in the long term, but also by maintaining populations in a more vulnerable situation due to relatively low numbers of individuals, which reduces resilience to other external situations such as plagues, diseases, or adverse environmental situations. While the presented model provides useful information, an opportunity for future work would be to implement an even more realistic environment which represents different kinds of individuals, like juveniles and adults, and a distinction between sexes, since for many species in the real world, the proportion of the categories mentioned has important implications on the number of individuals that can be harvested. Probably the real-world use value of reinforcement learning for population management will rely on species-specific environments which accurately represent not only its growth rate, but their interactions and dynamics. Of course, there exist other situations where there is no distinction between the individuals to harvest and the implementation provided here could be enough, such as algae for industrial purposes or unicellular organisms in laboratories.

Acknowledgments. We thank the Asociación Mexicana de Cultura, A. C.

References

1. Pal, S., Mondal, S., Das, G., Khatua, S., Ghosh, Z.: Big data in biology: the hope and present-day challenges in it. Gene Rep. (2020)

2. Mahmud, M., Kaiser, M.S., Hussain, A., Vassanelli, S.: Applications of deep learning and reinforcement learning to biological data. IEEE Trans. Neural Netw. Learn. Syst. (2018)
3. Xu, C., Jackson, S.: Machine learning and complex biological data. Genome Biol. (2019)
4. Begon, M., Townsend, C.R., Harper, J.L.: Ecology: From Individuals to Ecosystems, 4th edn. Blackwell Publishing (2006)
5. Sarker, I.H.: Machine learning: algorithms, real-world applications and research directions. SN Comput. Sci. **2**(3), 1–21 (2021). https://doi.org/10.1007/s42979-021-00592-x
6. Joseph, M.B.: Neural hierarchical models of ecological populations. Ecol. Lett. **23**(4), 734–747 (2020)
7. Llewelyn, J., et al.: Predicting predator–prey interactions in terrestrial endotherms using random forest. Ecography **2023**, e06619 (2023)
8. Garcilita, S., Treviño, D., González, G.: Bat falcon (Falco rufigularis) distribution spatial patterns in Mexico. Int. J. Biol. Nat. Sci. **4**(6) (2024)
9. Lapeyrolerie, M., Chapman, M.S., Norman, K.E.A., Boettiger, C.: Deep reinforcement learning for conservation decisions. Methods Ecol. Evol. **13** (2022)
10. Treloar, N.J., Fedorec, A., Ingalls, B., Barnes, C.P.: Deep reinforcement learning for the control of microbial co-cultures in bioreactors. PLoS Comput. Biol. **16**(4), e1007783 (2020)
11. Stewart, D.J., Amlaner, C.J., Barnett, C.C.: HARVEST: a generalized animal population growth simulation. SIMULATION **59**(1), 57–64 (1992)
12. Sutton, R., Barto, A.: Reinforcement Learning: An Introduction. The MIT Press (1998)
13. Kaelbling, L.P., Littman, M.L., Moore, A.W.: Reinforcement learning: a survey. J. Artif. Intell. Res. **4**, 237–85 (1996)
14. Alcalá Durand, M.F.: Aprendizaje reforzado para el juego de la distribución de cerveza. Instituto Tecnológico Autónomo de México, México (2021)
15. Kwiatkowski, A., et al.: Gymnasium: a standard interface for reinforcement learning environments. arXiv (2024). https://arxiv.org/abs/2407.17032
16. Verhulst, P.F.: Notice sur la loi que la population poursuit dans son accroissement. Correspondance Mathématique et Physique **10**, 113–121 (1838)
17. Gotelli, N.J.: A Primer of Ecology, 4th edn. Sinauer Associates (2008)
18. Brockman, G., et al.: OpenAI gym. arXiv preprint arXiv:1606.01540 (2016)
19. Wooldridge, M.: An Introduction to Multiagent Systems. Wiley, New York (2002)
20. Watkins, C.J.C.H.: Learning from delayed rewards. Ph.D. thesis, University of Cambridge, England (1989)
21. Watkins, C., Dayan, P.: Q-learning. Mach. Learn. **8**, 279–292 (1992)
22. Stokes, M.: Population ecology at work: managing game populations. Nat. Educ. Knowl. **3**(10), 5 (2012)
23. Prada, J., Olga, L.D., Olga, T.R.: Common duckweed (Lemna minor): food and environmental potential. Review. Revista mexicana de ciencias pecuarias **15**(2), 404–424 (2024)

Deep Learning and Neural Networks

Hybrid Deep Learning Architecture for Automatic Detection of Coronary Stenosis in X-Ray Videos

Ulises A. Gonzalez-Valadez[1], Rafa A. García-Ramirez[1], Ivan Cruz-Aceves[2](✉), Arturo Hernández-Aguirre[1], Martha A. Hernandez-González[3], and Sergio E. Solorio-Meza[4]

[1] Centro de Investigación en Matemáticas (CIMAT), Guanajuato, Gto, Mexico
[2] SECIHTI - Centro de Investigación en Matemáticas, Guanajuato, Gto, Mexico
[3] Unidad Médica de Alta Especialidad, Hospital de Especialidades No. 1 IMSS, León, Guanajuato, Mexico
[4] División de Ciencias e Ingenierias, Universidad de Guanajuato, Campus León, León, Guanajuato, Mexico

Abstract. This paper addresses the challenge of automatic detection of coronary stenosis with a new hybrid deep learning architecture. The proposed architecture combines the strengths of Single Shot MultiBox Detector (SSD) for efficient region proposal generation and Faster Region-based Convolutional Neural Network (Faster R-CNN) for accurate classification and bounding box refinement. By integrating these two architectures, SR-CNN optimizes both detection accuracy and computational efficiency, making it suitable for real-time medical applications. SR-CNN introduces a more efficient region proposal generation approach, reducing the number of candidate regions by approximately 75% compared to Faster R-CNN, leading to a significant decrease in computational cost. SR-CNN was compared against state-of-the-art object detection models, including Faster R-CNN, SSD, YOLOv8, YOLOv9, and RetinaNet. Experimental results demonstrate that SR-CNN achieves an F1-score of 0.8232, outperforming all other tested models, while maintaining a competitive inference time of 3.2901 s. In summary, SR-CNN contributes a novel hybrid framework that can enhance real-time clinical decision-making for coronary stenosis detection.

Keywords: CNNs · Coronary Stenosis · Deep Learning · Hybrid Architectures · Object Detection · Video Processing

1 Introduction

Coronary artery disease (CAD) is a prevalent cardiovascular condition characterized by the accumulation of atherosclerotic plaque within the arterial lumen. This buildup leads to impaired blood flow, reducing oxygen delivery to the myocardium [1]. CAD is a leading cause of morbidity worldwide [2], emphasizing

A. P. López-Monroy et al. (Eds.): MCPR 2025, LNCS 15715, pp. 327–336, 2025.
https://doi.org/10.1007/978-3-031-96255-4_30

the importance of early diagnosis and treatment to improve patient outcomes. Coronary angiography is the gold standard for diagnosing CAD. This imaging technique enables direct visualization of the coronary arteries, providing detailed information about their condition [3]. The procedure involves guiding a catheter to the heart through a small incision in the groin or wrist. A contrast medium is then injected through the catheter, allowing the arteries to become visible under specialized X-ray imaging [4]. Sequential X-ray images are captured as the contrast medium flows through the arteries, facilitating the assessment of blood flow and the identification of potential obstructions. In recent years, the automation of coronary stenosis detection has gained attention due to the growing availability of medical imaging data and the increasing demand for fast and accurate diagnostics in clinical practice. In literature, several methods have been developed for automatic detection of coronary stenosis, addressing the problem from different approaches. Some of them are based on classical image processing techniques, such as Cervantes-Sánchez et al. [5] proposed a method in which a Gaussian Matched Filters (GMF) improves the visualization of blood vessels in angiographic images, followed by a genetic algorithm that optimizes the filter parameters. Zijun Gao et al. [6] developed a framework that combines features extracted from traditional filters such as Canny and Sobel. More recently, Tao Han et al. [7] introduced a hybrid approach that integrates CNNs to process temporal sequences of angiographic images. The results of these methods have shown significant improvements in the speed and accuracy of diagnosing stenosis and other cardiovascular diseases with the implementation of deep learning (DL) techniques. This emphasizes the need to automate the analysis and classification of medical images. CNNs are a widely used architecture in deep learning, inspired by the visual perception mechanism of living organisms [8]. These networks are a variant of multilayer perceptrons specifically designed to identify two-dimensional shapes and establish a mapping between the original input and the desired output. In a CNN, each neuron is connected to a local region of the previous layer, allowing hierarchical feature extraction. The structure of a CNN consists of multiple stacked layers, including convolutional, clustering, fully connected, and output layers [9]. Several architectures based on CNNs have been developed for object detection in images and, consequently, in real-time video analysis. These models have evolved to improve both accuracy and computational efficiency in identifying objects within a scene. One of these approaches, R-CNN [10], introduced the concept of region proposals to segment potential objects before classifying them using a deep neural network. Although it achieved high accuracy, its high computational cost made it impractical for real-time applications. Also, SSD [11] eliminated the need for explicit region proposal generation, enabling object detection in a single forward pass through the network, significantly improving inference speed. Another key advancement was YOLO (You Only Look Once) [12], which reformulated object detection as a direct regression problem, dividing the image into grid cells and simultaneously predicting object coordinates and class labels. Finally, RetinaNet [13] introduced Focal Loss, a specialized loss function designed to address the imbalance between foreground and background objects. Each of these architectures has contributed to the development of more efficient and accurate models, laying the foundation for hybrid approaches that seek to leverage their advantages while minimizing their limitations. Despite these advances, there remains a gap between achieving real-time performance and maintaining high diagnostic accuracy in medical contexts. In this paper, a new hybrid architecture based on two CNN-based detection architectures: R-CNN and Single SSD is proposed. This approach is motivated by the need for a model that balances inference time with detection quality in complex angiographic sequences. The architecture is performed on a dataset of angiography images with positive cases of coronary stenosis, enhanced by data augmentation to increase the data from 69 to 552 images. The experimental results compare the proposed architecture with well-known CNNs in terms of precision, recall, F1-score, Average Precision (AP), and average inference times. The rest of the paper is organized as follows. In Sect. 2, the fundamentals of CNNs and the architectures are presented. Section 3 explains the preprocessing step and the architecture proposed. Experimental results are discussed in Sect. 4, and conclusions are given in Sect. 5.

2 Methods

This section describes Faster R-CNN and SSD, the architectures upon which the proposed method is based. Faster R-CNN excels in accurate object localization and classification through refined region proposals, while SSD achieves efficient single-pass detection from feature maps.

2.1 Region-Based Convolutional Neural Network (R-CNN)

R-CNN integrates CNNs with region proposals, significantly improving localization and classification compared to traditional approaches. It employs CNNs on approximately 2000 class-independent region proposals per image, typically generated by methods such as Selective Search [14]. Each region is resized, processed by a pretrained CNN to extract fixed-length feature vectors, and classified using class-specific Support Vector Machines (SVMs). Bounding Box Regression further refines region coordinates [10]. However, the repeated CNN processing for each region is computationally costly, limiting real-time application.

Faster R-CNN enhances computational efficiency by incorporating region proposal generation directly into the CNN through the Region Proposal Network (RPN). The RPN generates predefined anchors at multiple scales and aspect ratios, predicting objectness scores and bounding box coordinates from shared feature maps. This unified approach eliminates external region proposal methods, reduces redundancy, and enables end-to-end training [15].

Regions of Interest (RoIs) from the RPN are passed through an RoI Pooling layer, extracting fixed-size feature maps processed by fully connected layers to output final class probabilities and refined bounding box coordinates.

Figure 1 illustrates Faster R-CNN's architecture.

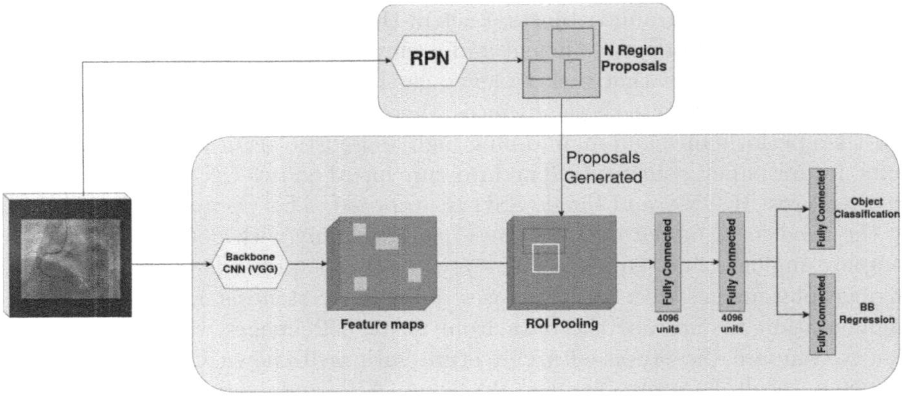

Fig. 1. Architecture of Faster R-CNN. The backbone CNN (e.g., VGG-16) extracts features, the RPN proposes candidate regions resized via RoI Pooling, followed by fully connected layers for classification and bounding box refinement.

2.2 Single Shot Multibox Detector (SSD)

SSD is a single-pass object detection method, eliminating explicit region proposal steps by predicting class scores and bounding box offsets directly from multi-scale feature maps. It assigns predefined anchor boxes at varying scales and aspect ratios across these feature maps, predicting object locations efficiently and accurately.

The standard SSD-300 uses a VGG-16 backbone with additional convolutional layers to generate multi-scale feature maps, enabling detection of objects of different sizes. Higher-resolution feature maps detect smaller objects, while lower-resolution maps capture larger ones, maintaining efficiency and precision.

Localization and classification are performed by small 3×3 convolutional filters applied directly to feature maps, predicting class scores and bounding box offsets. Multiple predictions per object are refined through Non-Maximum Suppression (NMS), retaining only the most confident detections and eliminating redundant bounding boxes [16].

In the context of SR-CNN, SSD-300 serves as a lightweight region proposal generator, leveraging its speed and scale-variant proposal generation to complement Faster R-CNN's subsequent refinement capabilities.

Figure 2 illustrates SSD's architecture.

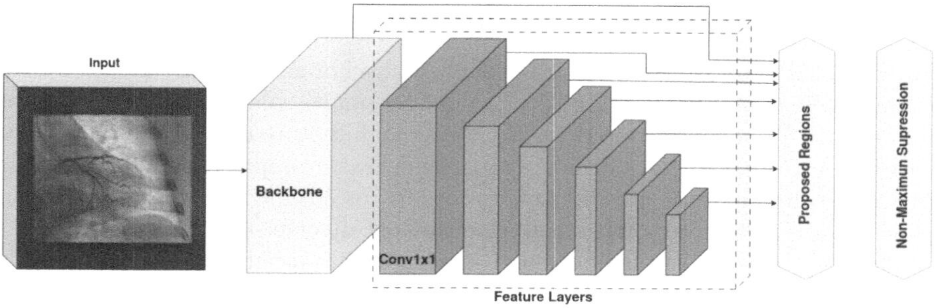

Fig. 2. Architecture of SSD. The backbone network generates multi-scale feature maps predicting class scores and bounding boxes, with NMS filtering redundant detections.

3 Proposed Stenosis Region-CNN Architecture (SR-CNN)

SR-CNN combines the strengths of Faster R-CNN and SSD to enhance real-time object detection in coronary angiography images. It optimizes region proposal generation using SSD's computational efficiency and Faster R-CNN's accuracy for detailed classification and bounding box refinement. This hybrid architecture significantly reduces inference times while maintaining high detection performance. The architecture follows a two-stage detection framework consisting of SSD-based region proposal followed by detailed feature extraction and precise detection.

Stage 1: SSD-Based Region Proposal

In the first stage, an SSD-300 model with a pre-trained VGG-16 backbone generates initial region proposals, replacing the conventional Region Proposal Network (RPN) of Faster R-CNN. SSD directly detects objects at multiple scales from convolutional feature maps, assigning default anchor boxes of varying scales and aspect ratios to each map location. These boxes are subsequently adjusted based on predicted offsets and filtered by confidence thresholds to retain only high-quality candidate regions.

The SSD-300 was separately pre-trained on a coronary angiography dataset and subsequently frozen to exclusively serve as a proposal generator. This specialized SSD stage generates approximately 300âĂŞ500 high-confidence proposals per 512×512 image, significantly fewer than the 2000 proposals typically produced by a traditional RPN, thereby greatly reducing computational demands. The SSD proposal network is implemented in PyTorch as a lightweight custom module dedicated to efficiently identifying plausible object regions without classification.

Stage 2: Feature Extraction and Detection

The second stage employs ResNeXt-101 as the backbone network combined with a Feature Pyramid Network (FPN) to enhance multiscale learning capabilities and improve feature extraction. The ResNeXt architecture uses grouped convolutions for better parameter efficiency and richer feature representation, while the FPN generates semantically informative multi-resolution feature maps, crucial for accurately detecting anatomical structures of diverse sizes.

Proposed regions obtained from the SSD stage are mapped onto suitable FPN levels according to their spatial dimensions and are further processed by RoIAlign, ensuring accurate spatial correspondence. RoIAlign produces fixed-size feature maps, typically 7×7 pixels, which are then fed into fully connected layers to generate a compact 1024-dimensional representation. The final detection consists of a classification head that outputs binary object presence probabilities, and a bounding box regressor that refines region coordinates using Smooth L1 loss. Detections below a certain confidence threshold are discarded, and Non-Maximum Suppression (NMS) with an IoU threshold of 0.9 is applied to eliminate redundant predictions.

Model Assembly and Training

The SR-CNN architecture is implemented using PyTorch's `GeneralizedRCNN` framework, integrating a custom SSD-based proposal module (`SSDProposalNetwork`). Components including the ResNeXt-FPN backbone, RoIAlign, and RoI heads are manually assembled. Images and annotations are loaded via a custom dataset class compatible with the Pascal VOC format.

Training was conducted for 100 epochs with a batch size of 2 using stochastic gradient descent (SGD) with momentum of 0.9, an initial learning rate of 0.005, and weight decay of 0.0005. Input images were normalized using ImageNet statistics and resized to dimensions ranging from 800 to 1333 pixels. Figure 3 presents an overview of the SR-CNN detection process.

4 Experimental Results

This section details the computational experiments conducted to compare the proposed architecture with state-of-the-art approaches. The models selected for comparison were chosen due to their widespread use, established performance, and relevance as benchmark CNN-based detectors in literature. These models represent a diverse range of architectures with varying trade-offs between speed and accuracy, making them suitable references for evaluating the effectiveness of the proposed method. The experiments were performed using a manually labeled dataset provided by the Instituto Mexicano del Seguro Social (IMSS), consisting of 69 images with positive cases of stenosis extracted from continuous DICOM sequences. Each image was labeled by a cardiology specialist using

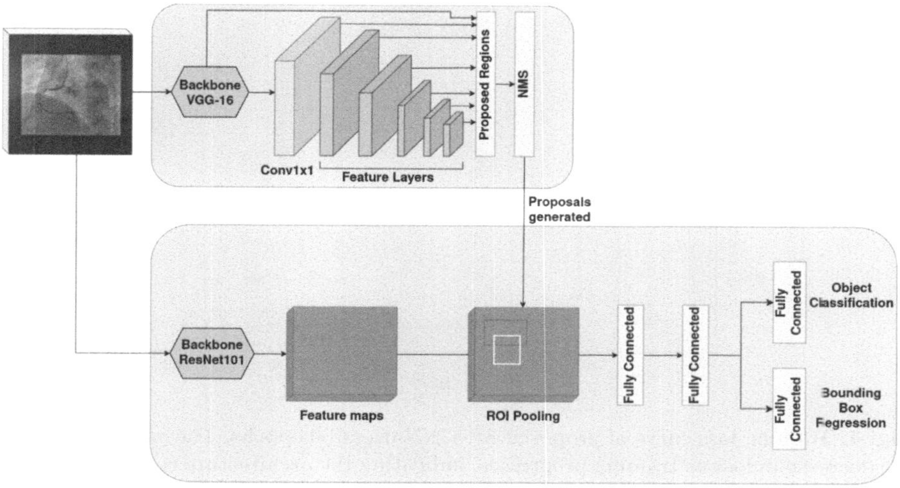

Fig. 3. SR-CNN hybrid architecture. SSD with VGG-16 backbone generates region proposals, which are refined by a ResNeXt-101 backbone with FPN. RoIAlign and fully connected layers facilitate precise classification and bounding box regression, with NMS applied for final detection refinement.

32×32 patches to indicate stenotic regions. To enhance the dataset, data augmentation techniques were applied, performing a series of 7 operations, increasing the number of images with positive cases of stenosis to 552, these operations are: rotation 90°, 280°, 270°, horizontal and vertical reflection and rotation 180° + horizontal and vertical reflection. The dataset was then split into 80% for training and 20% for testing. The experiments were executed on a system with 15.48 GB of RAM and a 238.89 GB storage capacity. The implementation was carried out in Python 3.12.2, using the PyTorch 2.3.1 framework.

To evaluate the performance of the proposed architecture, five deep learning models based on different architectures were compared: SSD with MobileNetV3-Large, Faster R-CNN, YOLOv9m, YOLOv8n, and RetinaNet. All models were trained for 100 epochs, a standard value commonly used in deep learning training. Throughout the training process, the loss function, which quantifies how well the model approximates the expected results, was monitored to assess convergence and optimization efficiency. Figure 4 presents the loss curve for SR-CNN training.

The tests were performed with the test set, which represents 20% of the database not used in training. To evaluate architecture performance, standard metrics for object detection were used, including precision, recall, F1-score, and Average Inference Time (AIT). The AIT was measured using only the CPU, without GPU acceleration, to assess the models efficiency in resource-limited environments. A confidence threshold of 0.65 was applied to reduce false positives and ensure that only high-certainty detections were considered. Additionally, an

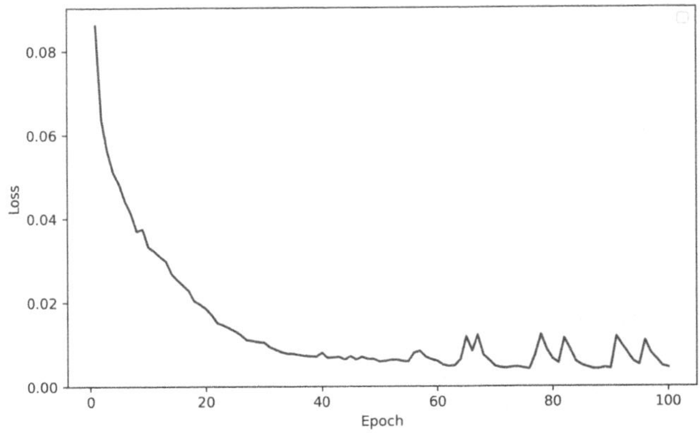

Fig. 4. Training loss curve of proposed SR-CNN over 100 epochs. The graph illustrates the decrease in loss as training progresses, indicating the architecture convergence. The initial rapid decline reflects effective learning, followed by a stabilization phase where the loss oscillates at lower values.

Intersection over Union (IoU) threshold of 0.5 was used to determine whether a predicted bounding box correctly matched a ground truth object, following common evaluation practices in object detection. The results obtained are summarized in Table 1 and Fig. 5 shows some of the predictions made compared to the Ground truth (GT).

Table 1. Performance comparison of different object detection models. The proposed SR-CNN achieves a strong balance between precision, recall, F1-score, and inference time, while also maintaining competitive AP (0.7702). YOLOv9 shows the highest precision (0.9389) but lower F1-score, and SSD is the fastest (0.2869 s) but with significantly reduced accuracy.

Model	Precision	Recall	F1-score	AP	AIT (s)
Faster R-CNN	0.796	**0.8163**	0.806	0.7717	7.2299
SSD	0.875	0.0363	0.0697	0.5420	**0.2869**
Yolov8	0.6989	0.6181	0.656	0.7701	0.4853
Yolov9	**0.9389**	0.6181	0.7455	0.7188	2.536
RetinaNet	0.7617	0.7313	0.7462	0.7717	5.2569
Proposed SR-CNN	0.9342	0.7358	**0.8232**	0.7702	3.2901

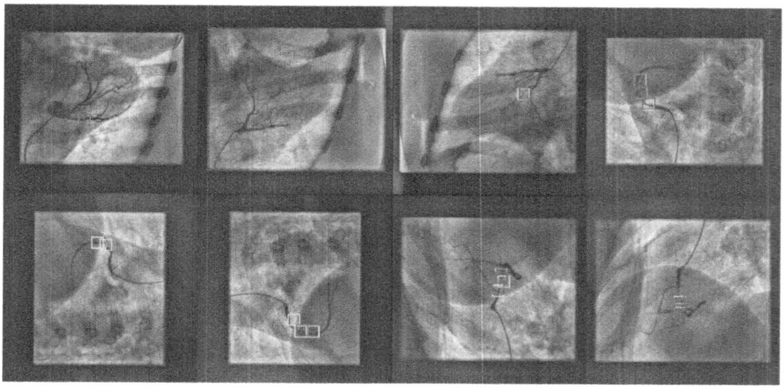

Fig. 5. Predictions of the SR-CNN architecture on coronary angiography images. The top row displays three correctly predicted cases, where the model accurately identifies stenotis cases (red boxes) matching the ground truth (yellow boxes). The bottom row highlights incorrect predictions, including false positives and missed detections. (Color figure online)

5 Conclusions

In this paper, a new hybrid architecture is proposed, SR-CNN combines the efficiency of SSD for proposal generation with the accuracy of Faster R-CNN for detection refinement in angiographic images. Experimental results demonstrated that the model achieves a significant reduction in the number of candidate regions (300âĂŞ500 per image) while maintaining a favorable balance between precision (F1-score of 0.8232) and inference time (3.2901 s). Although the current implementation still requires optimization for deployment in real-time clinical settings, the results suggest that SR-CNN has the potential to be an effective solution to support automated diagnosis of coronary stenosis. Possible future directions include applying techniques such as pruning and quantization to reduce latency and resource usage, as well as integrating both stages of the model into a single shared backbone.

Acknowledgments. This work has been supported by Secretariat for Science, Humanities, Technology and Innovation (SECIHTI), under the national grant for master studies numbers 1308601, 1308597 and IxM-SECIHTI No. 3097-7185.

References

1. Hawaii State Department of Health: Coronary Heart Disease (2013). https://health.hawaii.gov/heart-disease-stroke/files/2013/09/coronaryheartdisease.pdf. Hawaii State Department of Health, Honolulu
2. Dugdale, D., Zieve, D.: Coronary Artery Disease. StatPearls Publishing, Treasure Island (FL) (2023)

3. National University Health Services Group Pte Ltd: Coronary angiography (2022). https://www.ntfgh.com.sg/docs/ntfghlibraries/brochures-document/coronary-angiography.pdf?sfvrsn=bb253c44_1
4. American Heart Association: What is a coronary angiogram? https://www.heart.org/-/media/files/health-topics/answers-by-heart/what-is-a-coronary-angiogram.pdf
5. Cruz-Aceves, I., Cervantes-Sanchez, F., Hernandez-Aguirre, A.: Automatic detection of coronary artery stenosis in X-ray angiograms using gaussian filters and genetic algorithms. In: AIP Conference Proceedings, vol. 1747, p. 020005 (2016)
6. Gao, Z., Yin, L., Zhang, X., Yang, L., Dong, Z.: Vessel segmentation for X-ray coronary angiography using ensemble methods with deep learning and filter-based features. J. Med. Imaging Health Inform. **9**(7), 1451–1458 (2019)
7. Wan, T., Feng, H., Tong, C., Li, D., Qin, Z.: Automated identification and grading of coronary artery stenoses with X-ray angiography. Comput. Methods Programs Biomed. **167**, 13–22 (2018)
8. Gu, J., et al.: Recent advances in convolutional neural networks. Pattern Recogn. **77**, 354–377 (2018)
9. Song, J., Gao, S., Zhu, Y., Ma, C.: A survey of remote sensing image classification based on CNNs. Big Earth Data **3**(3), 232–254 (2019)
10. Girshick, R.: Rich feature hierarchies for accurate object detection and semantic segmentation. In: Proceedings of the IEEE Conference on Computer Vision and Pattern Recognition (CVPR), pp. 580–587 (2014)
11. Liu, W., et al.: SSD: single shot multibox detector. In: Proceedings of the European Conference on Computer Vision (ECCV), pp. 21–37 (2016)
12. Redmon, J., Divvala, S., Girshick, R., Farhadi, A.: You only look once: unified, real-time object detection. In: Proceedings of the IEEE Conference on Computer Vision and Pattern Recognition (CVPR), pp. 779–788 (2016)
13. Lin, T., Goyal, P., Girshick, R., He, K., Dollár, P.: Focal loss for dense object detection. In: Proceedings of the IEEE International Conference on Computer Vision (ICCV), pp. 2980–2988 (2017)
14. Sumit, S., Bisht, S., Joshi, S., Rana, U.: Comprehensive review of R-CNN and its variant architectures. Int. Res. J. Adv. Eng. Hub (IRJAEH) **2**(4), 959–966 (2024)
15. Ren, S., He, K., Girshick, R., Sun, J.: Faster R-CNN: towards real-time object detection with region proposal networks. In: Advances in Neural Information Processing Systems (NeurIPS), pp. 91–99 (2015)
16. Yadav, D., Singh, M., Gupta, A., Raj, A., Pathak, A.: Real-time object detection using SSD mobilenet model of machine learning. Int. J. Eng. Comput. Sci. (IJECS) **12**(05), 25729–25734 (2023)

Predicting Crowd Motion with Diffusion Models

Marcela Morales Quispe and Jean-Bernard Hayet(✉)

Centro de Investigación en Matemáticas, Guanajuato, GTO, Mexico
{marcelamq,jbhayet}@cimat.mx

Abstract. This paper proposes a novel macroscopic approach for forecasting the motion of a crowd in a few seconds time horizon, conditionally to a handful of past visual observations. We leverage a compact, grid-based representation of the crowd through macroscopic properties (local density and velocity) and a conditional diffusion model to generate samples of the predictive distribution for the crowd motion. We propose new evaluation metrics for this problem and compare the performance of several variants of the proposed approach on the ATC dataset.

Keywords: Crowd prediction · Diffusion models · Deep Learning

1 Introduction

There is a world-wide need to understand, model and, if possible, forecast crowd behavior and implement efficient crowd management in places such as urban areas, transport hubs, and large events, with people safety as the primary objective, as crowd behavior has been the source of many tragedies in large human gatherings. To give a very recent example, in January 2025, a stampede caused the death of more than 30 persons in a religious festival in India. These tragic accidents are difficult to prevent, but research in crowd modeling could allow better designs of the public spaces and to the development of early alarms systems.

Crowd modeling has been previously studied with various objectives in mind [10]: *crowd planning, management and evacuation* [14], to limit the possible effects of stampedes; *entertainment*, to reproduce artificial crowds within movies and video games [17]; study of *traffic flow* [21]; planning socially-compliant *robot motions* [11]. It is a complex problem since the crowd behavior may have impact on an individual, and a single individual may be at the origin of a movement of the whole crowd, all of this in a relative short time frame. Our focus in this work is short-term predictive modeling: Given the state of a crowd, what can we say about what may happen in the next seconds? Answering this kind of questions could be useful to trigger alarms, for example, if we can forecast that some dangerous situation may appear with high probability in the near future.

Our approach tackles this problem with two main insights: First, to handle dense crowds, we abandon the path usually followed in human trajectory prediction (HTP) that focuses on individual trajectories and reason instead on the

A. P. López-Monroy et al. (Eds.): MCPR 2025, LNCS 15715, pp. 337–347, 2025.
https://doi.org/10.1007/978-3-031-96255-4_31

crowd *as a whole*, which leads us to a formulation similar to conditional video generation; second, because the associated predictive distributions may be very complex and multimodal in this context, we explore the use of deep generative modeling, in particular diffusion models, to estimate this predictive distribution.

2 Related Work

According to the scale of the study, models operating on crowds can be divided into three categories: *Macroscopic models* describe the crowds overall dynamics; *microscopic models* model the behavior and the interactions of individuals; *hybrid models* combine the two approaches to leverage their respective strengths. In the following, we give a brief summary of existing works in these categories.

2.1 Microscopic Models: Prediction of Individual Trajectories

A number of methods deal with crowds by modeling *individual* agents trajectories. The prediction problem consists in inferring future states $\mathbf{x}_{T_{obs}+1}, ..., \mathbf{x}_{T_{pred}}$ of one agent, given T_{obs} past observations $\mathbf{x}_1, ..., \mathbf{x}_{T_{obs}}$ on this agent and given a context $\mathbf{C}$ (with the map or data from the neighboring agents). States $\mathbf{x}_t$ may include the agent coordinates, velocities or accelerations, with t being a timestep.

For several years, the most successful HTP approaches have been *data-driven* and since predictive distributions may exhibit multiple modes (e.g., at crossroads), most of them rely on *generative models* trained to infer the trajectories predictive distributions with Generative Adversarial Networks (GAN) [7], Variational Auto-Encoders (VAE) [20], or, more recently, diffusion models [6]. These models *encode* the past trajectories and the context, i.e. the "social" interactions of the neighboring agents, or the map of the environment, and decode future trajectories under the aforementioned generative modeling frameworks.

A clear limit of these approaches is that getting the agents individual trajectories through visual tracking may be a problem in very dense situations; also, most existing HTP works do not deal explicitly with *joint* agent distributions.

2.2 Crowd Motion Prediction in High Density Situations

For dense environments, crowds may be considered as a whole, without individualizing the trajectories. This leads to defining *maps* of macroscopic features (e.g., local density and local velocity) [11] and treating the pedestrian flow as a continuous process, as in fluid mechanics [9]. At this macroscopic level, crowd modeling can be cast as a *video generation problem*, since one predicts a sequence of *maps* of future crowd properties conditioned on the past crowd properties sequence. Recurrent Neural Network (RNN) techniques have been early candidates for video prediction and generation, combined with a stochastic latent variable (SV2P) [2]. Stochastic video generation learns both a prior and a stepwise latent variable model, which influences the dynamics of an Long Short

Term Memory network (LSTM) at each step [5]. Convolutional Recurrent Neural Network are used in [11] to encode the past grids and predict the future ones. Subsequently, a constrained Gaussian process reconstructs a smooth representation of the pedestrian crowd's macroscopic features, while adhering to physical constraints [12].

2.3 Diffusion-Based Predictive Models

The seminal diffusion papers of [8,18] have started a broad avenue for possible applications. Diffusion models allow to generate samples through iterative denoising, learned as the reverse of a pre-defined diffusion process. A recent review on crowd modeling [4] confirms that, *up to the writing time of this document*, diffusion models have *not* been applied to crowd modeling at macroscopic level.

In video generation, diffusion models have established a new state of the art. In [19], MCVD is a generative method based on masking past and/or future frames in a blockwise manner, enabling the model to solve multiple video tasks: frame prediction, unconditional generation, and interpolation. Another example is [15], that introduces a method for generating realistic pedestrian trajectories and full-body animations that can be controlled to meet user-defined goals.

3 Crowd Macroscopic Properties

In this work, we focus on *macroscopic* crowd modeling, that considers the entire crowd as a whole and avoids the scalability issues that arise when dealing with high-density crowds. Let a location in space-time be $\mathbf{x} = [t, x, y]^T \in \mathbb{R}^3$. We describe the crowd through two functions, the density $\rho(\mathbf{x}) \in \mathbb{R}$ and local velocity $\mathbf{v}(\mathbf{x}) = [v_x, v_y]^T \in \mathbb{R}^2$, referred to as *macroscopic properties*. The density function $\rho(\mathbf{x})$ is defined as the expected number of pedestrians at position (x, y), per unit area, at time t. The velocity field $\mathbf{v}(\mathbf{x})$ gives the local flow in the crowd.

To get a computationally manageable representation, we *discretize* ρ and $\mathbf{v}$ over a space-time grid, as proposed in [11,12]. At a space-time cell $\mathbf{x}_i$, we associate the average density $\mu_\rho(\mathbf{x}_i) \in \mathbb{R}$ and the average velocity $\boldsymbol{\mu}_\mathbf{v}(\mathbf{x}_i) \in \mathbb{R}^2$ of the pedestrians in $\mathbf{x}_i$, i.e. the predominant flow of the crowd. We depict this *discretized* crowd representation in Fig. 1. We refer to this spatial grid of macroproperties, at timestep t, as $\mathcal{C}_t \in \mathbb{R}^{3\times R\times C}$, with R, C the size of the grid.

Given an input described as a *sequence* of p crowd macroscopic properties $\mathcal{C}_{1-p:0}$, we want a predictive model f_θ that estimates f *future* observations $\hat{\mathcal{C}}_{1:f}$

$$\hat{\mathcal{C}}_{1:f} = f_\theta(\mathcal{C}_{1-p:0}), \tag{1}$$

where the notation $\mathcal{C}_{1-p:0}$ refers to p observations taken at time-steps $-(p-1), ..., 0$. The index 0 refers to the *last* observed frame. Any $\hat{\mathcal{C}}_k$ for $k > 0$ refers to a forecasting for these properties in the future. In this work, we show that it is possible to solve the problem stated above by using *diffusion models*.

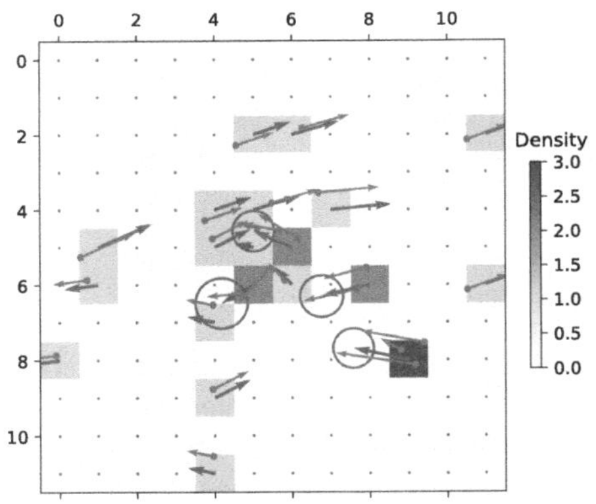

Fig. 1. Macroscopic properties in ATC dataset. Red points and arrows represent individual pedestrians data. The discretised macroscopic representation is shown underneath. Blue levels depict the density μ_ρ; green arrows depict the mean velocities $\boldsymbol{\mu}_{\mathbf{v}}$ (Color figure online).

4 Proposed Approach

In the following, we recall the mathematical setup behind diffusion models, the backbone of our multi-modal predictive system. More details can be found in [8].

4.1 Conditional Diffusion for Sequences of Macroscopic Properties

We follow the steps of approaches such as [19] that directly model the conditional distribution of video frames in the immediate future conditionally to the past frames. Let $\mathcal{C}_{1-p:f}$ a sample data ($f+p$ frames of macroscopic properties, p in the past, f in the future) from our training dataset. We want our conditional diffusion model to produce samples of $\mathcal{C}_{1:f}$ conditionally to $\mathcal{C}_{1-p:0}$. To do so, we start with our original data $\mathcal{C}^{(0)}_{1:f} \triangleq \mathcal{C}_{1:f}$ and corrupt it with noise, from $k=0$ to $k=K$ through the so-called Forward Diffusion Process (FDP) as follows:

$$q(\mathcal{C}^{(k)}_{1:f}|\mathcal{C}^{(k-1)}_{1:f}) = \mathcal{N}(\sqrt{1-\beta_k}\mathcal{C}^{(k-1)}_{1:f}, \beta_k\mathbf{I}), \tag{2}$$

for a *fixed, increasing* sequence $\beta_1, \ldots \beta_K$ of variance parameters $\beta_k \in [0,1]$. Since these distributions are Gaussians, $\mathcal{C}^{(k)}_{1:f}$ can be sampled *directly* from $\mathcal{C}^{(0)}_{1:f}$:

$$\mathcal{C}^{(k)}_{1:f} = \sqrt{\bar{\alpha}_k}\mathcal{C}^{(0)}_{1:f} + \sqrt{1-\bar{\alpha}_k}\boldsymbol{\epsilon}, \tag{3}$$

with $\boldsymbol{\epsilon} \sim \mathcal{N}(\mathbf{0}, I)$ and $\bar{\alpha}_k \triangleq \prod_{i=1}^{k}(1-\beta_i)$. An important property is that if K is large enough, then $\mathcal{C}^{(K)}_{1:f}$ is approximately distributed as a normal distribution.

Generating samples from the non-corrupted, conditional distribution can be seen as *reversing* the FDP and solving the Reverse Diffusion Process (RDP) conditionally to $\mathcal{C}_{1-p:0}$, starting from $\mathcal{C}^{(K)}_{1:f}$. The RDP can be formulated as [8]:

$$p(\mathcal{C}_{1:f}^{(k-1)}|\mathcal{C}_{1:f}^{(k)}, \mathcal{C}_{1:f}^{(0)}) = \mathcal{N}(\boldsymbol{\mu}_k(\mathcal{C}_{1:f}^{(k)}, \mathcal{C}_{1:f}^{(0)}), \tilde{\beta}_k I), \tag{4}$$

where $\boldsymbol{\mu}_k(\mathcal{C}_{1:f}^{(k)}, \mathcal{C}_{1:f}^{(0)}) = \frac{\sqrt{\bar{\alpha}_{k-1}}\beta_k}{1-\bar{\alpha}_k}\mathcal{C}_{1:f}^{(0)} + \frac{\sqrt{\alpha_k}(1-\bar{\alpha}_{k-1})}{1-\bar{\alpha}_k}\mathcal{C}_{1:f}^{(k)}$ and $\tilde{\beta}_k \triangleq \frac{1-\bar{\alpha}_{k-1}}{1-\bar{\alpha}_k}\beta_k$.

Note that $\mathcal{C}_{1:f}^{(0)}$ is unknown but can be estimated using Eq. 3 as $\frac{1}{\sqrt{\bar{\alpha}_k}}(\mathcal{C}_{1:f}^{(k)} - \sqrt{1-\bar{\alpha}_k}\boldsymbol{\epsilon})$, if we have an estimator $\boldsymbol{\epsilon}_\theta(\mathcal{C}_{1:f}^{(k)}|\mathcal{C}_{1-p:0}, k)$ (called *denoising network*, with parameters θ) for $\boldsymbol{\epsilon}$, conditioned on the past frames $\mathcal{C}_{1-p:0}$ and time step k. This allows us to reverse the process from noise to data. The loss function is [8]:

$$\mathcal{L}(\theta) = \mathbb{E}_{\mathcal{C}_{1-p:f}, \boldsymbol{\epsilon}}[||\boldsymbol{\epsilon}_\theta(\sqrt{\bar{\alpha}_k}\mathcal{C}_{1:f}^{(0)} + \sqrt{1-\bar{\alpha}_k}\boldsymbol{\epsilon}|\mathcal{C}_{1-p:0}, k) - \boldsymbol{\epsilon}||^2]. \tag{5}$$

Once $\boldsymbol{\epsilon}_\theta$ is trained, we generate samples from the predictive distribution by sampling $\mathcal{C}_{1:f}^{(K)} \sim \mathcal{N}(0, \mathbf{I})$ and using Eq. 4 recursively (K times) to produce $\mathcal{C}_{1:f}^{(0)}$.

4.2 Model Architecture

Our architecture for $\boldsymbol{\epsilon}_\theta$ is a U-Net [16], depicted in Fig. 2. Because of the space-time nature of the data, it uses 3D convolutions. Also, we use positional encoding of the noise step k with a Fourier-like embedding, which is first adjusted in size and then added to the processed tensor at each level of the U-Net.

The U-Net concatenates the past conditional frames $\mathcal{C}_{1-p:0}$ and the noisy input frames $\mathcal{C}_{1:f}^{(k)}$ in the time dimension. Then, this sequence is processed trough the downsampling, the bottleneck and upsampling stacks. So, the U-Net actually processes input sequences of shape $B\times3\times R\times C\times(p+f)$ and learns to estimate the noise $\boldsymbol{\epsilon}$ of shape $B\times3\times R\times C\times f$, where B is the batch size. Each residual block includes the option to incorporate attention mechanisms. By default, basic attention is applied within the downsampling stack, where the input tensor is reshaped to $[B, H\times W\times L, 3]$ and processed through a multi-head attention layer, where $L = p + f$. This configuration is referred to as our *base model*.

Additionally, experiments have been conducted to analyze the impact of spatial and temporal attention. In the *spa-temp model*, the input tensor is first reshaped to $[B\times L, H\times W, 3]$ and processed through a multi-head attention layer (spatial attention). It is then reshaped again to $[B\times H\times W, L, 3]$ for another multi-head attention layer (temporal attention). Conversely, the *temp-spa model* applies the temporal attention first, followed by spatial attention. A detailed comparison of these models is presented in the experimental results section.

5 Experiments

5.1 Implementation Details

The denoising model[1] is a non-symmetric U-Net, with four levels at the downsampling stack, two ResNet blocks at the bottleneck and five levels at the upsampling stack, with `kernel size=3`, `stride=1` and `padding="same"` for the 3D

[1] Its code is available at https://github.com/marcemq/crowdmod-ddpm-4D..

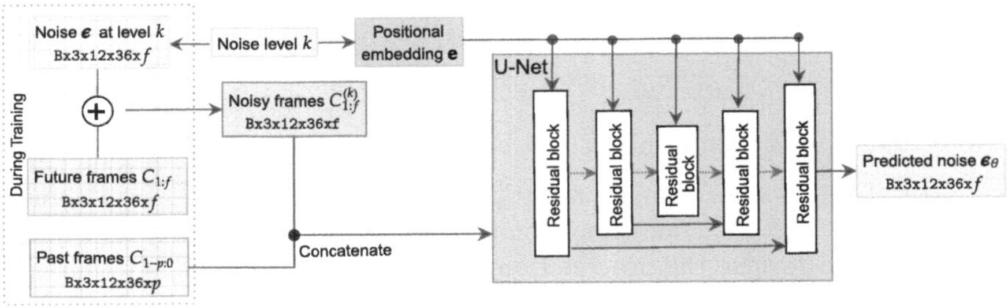

Fig. 2. Model architecture. We feed noisy current frames $\mathcal{C}^{(k)}_{1:f}$ to a U-Net whose residual blocks receive conditional information from past frames and noise-level. The output is the predicted noise in the current frames, which we use to denoise the current frames.

convolutions. The three models uses `Epochs=250`, `batch size=64`, `learning rate=0.00005` and the Adam optimizer with `weight decay=0.003`. Specific hyperparameters used for each model are listed at Table 1.

To produce the samples, we use the direct sampling scheme from Eq. 4, along $K = 1000$ iterations (this is the DDPM sampling scheme in [8]) per sample.

Table 1. Hyperparameters used to train the `base`, `spa-temp` and `temp-spa` variants of our model, altogether with training times and number of parameters.

Model	p	f	Training time	Train params
`base`	**5**	**3**	2 h 9 m 7 s	7200099
`spa-temp`	**5**	**3**	2 h 25 m 22 s	7464291
`temp-spa`	**5**	**3**	2 h 19 m 36 s	7464291

5.2 Datasets

We present experiments held on the ATC dataset [3], as several other works in this field. This dataset captures the motion of pedestrians navigating the *Asia and pacific Trade Center* (ATC), a shopping center in Japan, covering 92 days, on Sundays and Wednesdays. The raw data are processed to track the pedestrians and produce trajectories, with positions specified in a common frame.

As a pre-processing step, we extract the positions and instantaneous velocities from the dataset and compute the macroscopic properties, as explained in Sect. 3. For our experiments, we have selected data from Sundays (because the densities are higher than on weekdays) and from the eastern corridor (see Fig. 3) as it is an especially dense region. This subset still contains a wide variety of densities, as crowd levels fluctuate dramatically according to the time of day. With a total of 46 days, 30 were used for training, 10 for validation, 1 for evaluation (1280 sequences) and 5 were left out because there were anomalies in the tracking process. Figure 3 shows a snapshot of this dataset, with the selected grid and 10000 pedestrian locations depicted as blue points.

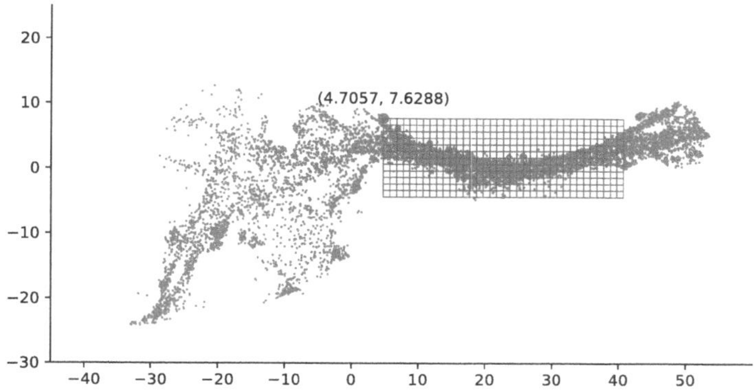

Fig. 3. Visualization of the section of the ATC dataset used for evaluation. The 12×36 grid used for macroscopic properties is shown in green and 10 000 pedestrian locations have been randomly displayed (in blue) for giving context. The original data have been rotated to have the average pedestrian flow appearing as horizontal within the grid. (Color figure online)

5.3 Metrics

Since the trained models generate *samples* from the predictive distribution over the next f frames based on p past frames, following the standards used in HTP [20], for each evaluated data, we sample $S = 20$ future sequences and evaluate if the ground-truth (GT) sequences are "close" to one of these samples.

The predicted sequences are first compared with the GT sequences using traditional metrics from the image and video generation communities, namely Peak Signal-to-Noise Ratio (PSNR) and Structural Similarity Index Measure (SSIM). Because we produce S samples from the predictive distribution, we report the mean of the *maximal* values of these metrics over the S samples, referred to as Max-PSNR and Max-SSIM, across each macroscopic property.

We also introduce two metrics based on *motion features* [13] that map the velocity field of macro-properties $\boldsymbol{\mu}_{\mathbf{v}}$ into spatial and temporal histograms. This involves calculating the magnitude and angle for each bin in the velocity field. Since most vector fields have small magnitudes, a logarithmic transformation is applied to magnitudes, which are then quantized to the nearest integer, resulting in nine discrete bins in range of $[0, 8]$. We also quantize the velocity angles into 8 bins. Then, we employ two methods for calculating histograms of the quantized magnitudes and angles. The first utilizes a quantized *2D histogram*. We divide the f-frame sequence into smaller volumes of size $f \times k \times k$, where f is the number of frames and k the spatial dimensions of each volume. These 2D histograms are then concatenated and flattened into a vector, to represent motion features. The second compiles these 2D histograms into *1D histograms* along the angle dimension by summing magnitudes into the appropriate angle bin, resulting in an 8-point histogram per volume. To evaluate the similarity between the generated and the GT distributions, we compute the Bhattacharyya coefficient. Finally, the median value of each metric is reported for a comprehensive comparison.

5.4 Results

Qualitative Results. In Fig. 4, we give two examples of sequences of macroscopic properties generated by our diffusion model, with similar conventions as in Fig. 1. In each case, we depict three past frames on the left and the three predicted frames on the right. As commented above, generative modeling allows us to explore the full predictive distribution, through the sampling process. To illustrate this important aspect of our approach, we present two samples among the S generated ones. As expected, these samples are diverse, reflecting the multimodal nature of the predictive distributions. Also, we note that the predicted sequences are consistent with the motion trends observed in the past sequences.

Quantitative Results. Using the sampling setup mentioned in Sect. 5.3, we report the mean values for the metrics on the ATC test data in Table 2. The PSNR and SSIM values are given for each of the 3 macroscopic properties. We attribute the differences along the x and y directions to the fact that most y velocity components are near zero and hece are "easier" to predict. Also, from the reported metrics, overall, applying temporal and spatial attention gives better results in most of the metrics.

Table 2. Comparison of models based on Max-$\overline{\text{PSNR}}$, Max-$\overline{\text{SSIM}}$, Bhattacharyya Coefficients in 2D and 1D histograms.

Model	Max-$\overline{\text{PSNR}}$			Max-$\overline{\text{SSIM}}$			Bhatt Coef	
	$\hat{\mu}_\rho$	$\hat{v}_x$	$\hat{v}_y$	$\hat{\mu}_\rho$	$\hat{v}_x$	$\hat{v}_y$	2D	1D
`base`	22.79	28.35	**31.69**	0.51	0.47	**0.60**	0.83	0.25
`spa-temp`	22.45	27.83	30.99	0.51	0.45	0.58	0.83	**0.28**
`temp-spa`	**24.31**	**29.88**	30.54	**0.54**	**0.58**	0.58	**0.95**	0.17

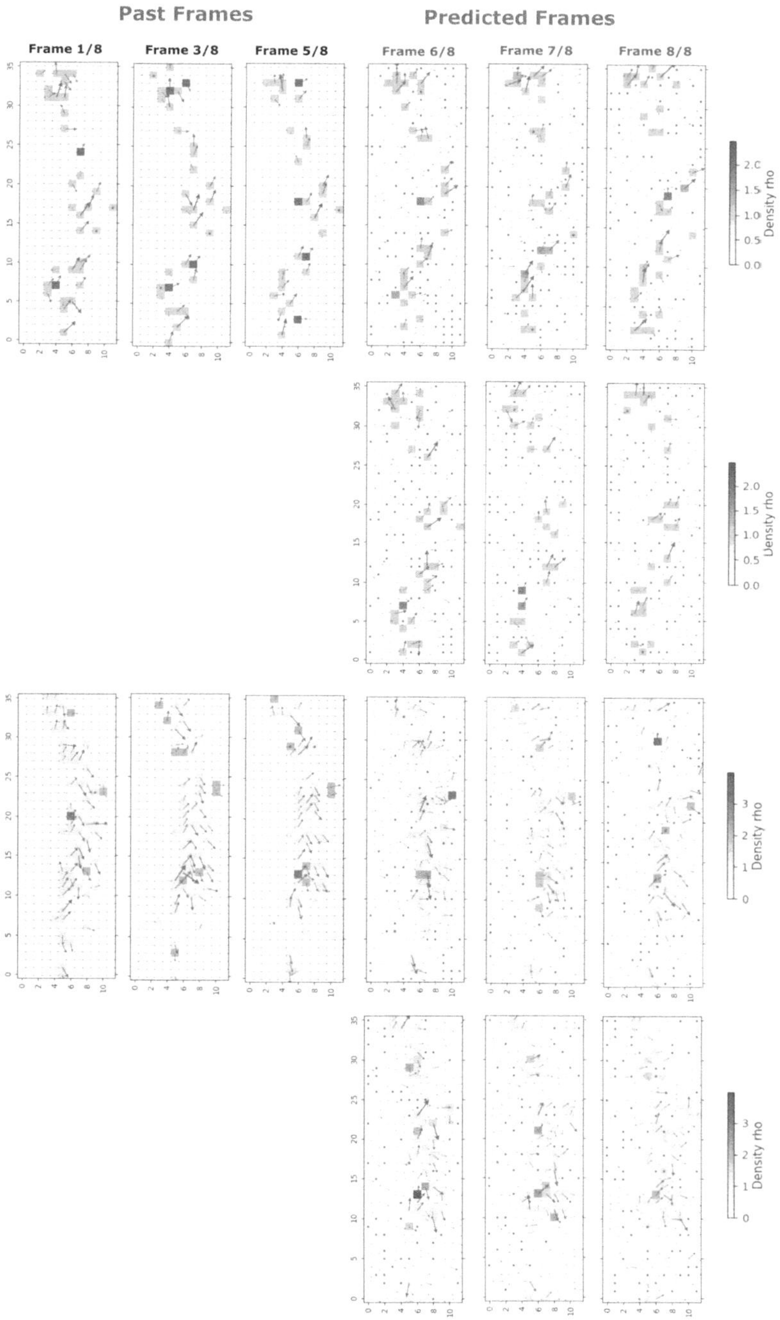

Fig. 4. Two examples of predicted sequences. From a given past sequence (three frames on the left), the model is able to predict diverse and plausible future sequences (three frames on the right; each row is one sample). Best viewed in landscape mode.

6 Discussion

We have proposed a novel macroscopic approach for forecasting crowd motion over a short time horizon using a conditional diffusion model. Our method learns to produce a multi-modal distribution to capture the crowd dynamics. Evaluated on a real life crowd dataset (ATC), it produces very promising results.

As future work, a deeper analysis of the learned model is necessary, along with experiments on denser crowd datasets. Since accessing such datasets can be challenging, we could explore applying density estimation from videos, as this kind of data is more widely available and diverse. Additionally, exploring alternative architectures for the denoiser beyond the U-Net used in our study could further enhance performance. Similarly, given the critical role of past frames in determining future motion, we will investigate alternative encoding strategies beyond data concatenation to integrate more effectively historical information into our model. Finally, we plan to examine energy conservation principles [1].

References

1. Andersson, B., Andersson, R., Håkansson, L., Mortensen, M., Sudiyo, R., Van Wachem, B.: Computational Fluid Dynamics for Engineers. Cambridge University Press, Cambridge (2011)
2. Babaeizadeh, M., Finn, C., Erhan, D., Campbell, R.H., Levine, S.: Stochastic variational video prediction. In: International Conference on Learning Representations (2018)
3. Brscic, D., Kanda, T., Ikeda, T., Miyashita, T.: Person position and body direction tracking in large public spaces using 3d range sensors. IEEE Trans. Hum.-Mach. Syst. **43**(6), 522–534 (2013)
4. Dang, H.T., Gaudou, B., Verstaevel, N.: A literature review of dense crowd simulation. Simul. Model. Pract. Theory **134**, 102955 (2024)
5. Denton, R., Fergus, R.: Stochastic video generation with a learned prior (2018)
6. Gu, T., et al.: Stochastic trajectory prediction via motion indeterminacy diffusion. In: Proceedings of the IEEE/CVF Conference on Computer Vision and Pattern Recognition, pp. 17113–17122 (2022)
7. Gupta, A., Johnson, J., Fei-Fei, L., Savarese, S., Alahi, A.: Social gan: socially acceptable trajectories with generative adversarial networks. In: Proceedings of the International Conference on Computer Vision and Pattern Recognition (CVPR), pp. 2255–2264 (2018)
8. Ho, J., Jain, A., Abbeel, P.: Denoising diffusion probabilistic models. arXiv preprint arxiv:2006.11239 (2020)
9. Hughes, R.L.: A continuum theory for the flow of pedestrians. Transp. Res. Part B: Methodol. **36**(6), 507–535 (2002)
10. Kiran Ijaz, S.S., Hashish, S.: A survey of latest approaches for crowd simulation and modeling using hybrid techniques. In: UKSIM-AMSS International Conference on Modelling and Simulation, pp. 111–116 (2015)
11. Kiss, S.H., Katuwandeniya, K., Alempijevic, A., Vidal-Calleja, T.: Probabilistic dynamic crowd prediction for social navigation. In: 2021 IEEE International Conference on Robotics and Automation (ICRA), pp. 9269–9275 (2021)

12. Kiss, S.H., Katuwandeniya, K., Alempijevic, A., Vidal-Calleja, T.: Constrained gaussian processes with integrated kernels for long-horizon prediction of dense pedestrian crowd flows. IEEE Rob. and Autom. Lett. **7**(3), 7343–7350 (2022)
13. Liu, J., Qu, Y., Yan, Q., Zeng, X., Wang, L., Liao, R.: Fréchet video motion distance: a metric for evaluating motion consistency in videos (2024). https://arxiv.org/abs/2407.16124
14. Pelechano, N., Badler, N.I.: Modeling crowd and trained leader behavior during building evacuation. IEEE Comp. Graph. Appl. **26**(6), 80–86 (2006)
15. Rempe, D., et al.: Trace and pace: controllable pedestrian animation via guided trajectory diffusion (2023)
16. Ronneberger, O., Fischer, P., Brox, T.: U-Net: convolutional networks for biomedical image segmentation. In: Navab, N., Hornegger, J., Wells, W.M., Frangi, A.F. (eds.) MICCAI 2015. LNCS, vol. 9351, pp. 234–241. Springer, Cham (2015). https://doi.org/10.1007/978-3-319-24574-4_28
17. Silverman, B.G., Johns, M., Cornwell, J., O'Brien, K.: Human behavior models for agents in simulators and games: part i: enabling science with pmfserv. Presence **15**(2), 139–162 (2006)
18. Sohl-Dickstein, J., Weiss, E., Maheswaranathan, N., Ganguli, S.: Deep unsupervised learning using nonequilibrium thermodynamics. In: Proceedings of the International Confernce on Machine Learning, vol. 37, pp. 2256–2265 (2015)
19. Voleti, V., Jolicoeur-Martineau, A., Pal, C.: Mcvd: masked conditional video diffusion for prediction, generation, and interpolation. In: (NeurIPS) Advances in Neural Information Processing Systems (2022). https://arxiv.org/abs/2205.09853
20. Xu, P., Hayet, J.B., Karamouzas, I.: Socialvae: human trajectory prediction using timewise latents. In: Proceedings of European Conference on Computer Vision, pp. 511–528 (2022)
21. Zhang, J., Zheng, Y., Qi, D.: Deep spatio-temporal residual networks for citywide crowd flows prediction (2017)

Enhancing Perceptron Learning Through Bayesian Optimisation and Cross-Validation

Maria Fernanda Castro-Colin[1(✉)], Erick G. G. de Paz[2], and Adrian M. Escobar-Ruiz[2]

[1] Universidad Nacional Autónoma de México, Mexico City, Mexico
mafer.colin1105@gmail.com
[2] Universidad Autónoma Metropolitana, Mexico City, Mexico
admau@xanum.uam.mx

Abstract. This study presents a novel approach aimed at enhancing the Perceptron Algorithm by incorporating Bayesian Optimisation based on the cross-validation framework. We bring in Bayesian Optimisation techniques, leveraging the upper bound of a credible interval as an acquisition function to guide the search for optimal parameters. Through extensive simulations on artificial datasets, we demonstrate that this Bayesian-optimised Perceptron consistently outperforms the original algorithm across various dimensions. This work highlights the significance of robust statistical evaluation and Bayesian Optimisation in improving the performance and generalisation ability of even simple machine learning models like the Perceptron. This research could also lay the groundwork for future studies on applying Bayesian Optimisation to enhance the performance of Multilayer Perceptron Networks.

Keywords: Perceptron · Cross-validation · Bayesian Optimisation

1 Introduction

The Perceptron Algorithm (PA) is a foundational and remarkably simple model in the field of machine learning, primarily designed for binary classification tasks involving linearly separable data [13]. However, the Perceptron has notable limitations. It relies on a fixed learning rate and often exhibits slow convergence, particularly in high-dimensional or imbalanced datasets. Other challenges are its tendency to overfit underscores, the need for robust methods to evaluate and enhance its generalisation performance. Given its simplicity, the Perceptron is an excellent candidate for exploring new methodologies that aim to improve error evaluation and adaptability without overcomplicating the underlying model. A key focus of this work is the application of cross-validation as a rigorous statistical tool to evaluate the Perceptron's performance. Cross-validation divides the dataset into multiple folds, systematically alternating between training and testing sets. This approach ensures that the evaluation metrics capture the model's

A. P. López-Monroy et al. (Eds.): MCPR 2025, LNCS 15715, pp. 348–357, 2025.
https://doi.org/10.1007/978-3-031-96255-4_32

true generalisation capabilities, reducing the risk of overfitting and enabling more reliable comparisons across different configurations.

In Bayesian Optimisation (BO) literature, the use of Credible Intervals (CI) in optimisation processes is a prominent concept, particularly through the design of acquisition functions [4]. These functions balance the trade-off between exploration and exploitation, ensuring the search for optimal parameters is both thorough and efficient. Employing the upper bound of a credible interval as an acquisition function fosters exploration in uncertain regions, which not only reduces the risk of overfitting but also increases the likelihood of finding a global optima [1]. The primary contribution of this paper lies in proposing a BO framework grounded in cross-validation. This framework not only improves the evaluation of the Perceptron's performance but also emphasise its adaptability to generelise within unobserved data. By leveraging the model's inherent simplicity, this study demonstrates how thoughtful enhancements can significantly extend the Perceptron's applicability without compromising its simplicity.

This article is divided into six sections. Introduction is located in Sect. 1, the literature review comes afterwards, in Sect. 2. Section 3 is a framework about the PA itself, the overfitting issue addressed with cross-validation and the gradient descent methodology. Then Sect. 4 provides the comparison between the original Perceptron and the BO-based approach through artificial problems. The deep analysis discussion is in Sect. 5. Finally Sect. 6 contains the conclusion and potential future applications.

2 Related Works

Multiple optimisation approaches for training Neural Networks have been explored. For instance, the work of El-Hassani et al. [2] demonstrates parameter optimisation using evolutionary algorithms to configure Multilayer Perceptron Neural Networks. In the context of BO, Zhang et al. [20] advocate for applying BO in an outer loop for tuning neural networks hyper-parameters. Others, such as Solla et al. [17] extends the BO application to train on-line neural networks, i.e. models progressively trained with new observed data. However, what sets our approach apart is integrating BO and cross-validation to improve the generalisation capabilities of a trained model. This BO application based on cross-validation is closely related to the Bayesian estimation of Classification and Regression Trees (CARTs) proposed by de Paz et al. [8]. In this paper and [8], an estimated bound for the model error is used as an acquisition function to search the optimal model. In both cases, the estimation does not depends on defining a likelihood function or Markov Chain Monte Carlo (MCMC) simulations, in contrast to [2,12,20]. In terms of applicability, there are works such as that of Sohi et al. [16], which employ a technique based on the integration of Back Propagation and Genetic Algorithm to address general challenges in weather forecasting. On the other hand, studies like that of Ravi et al. [11] focus on financial time series prediction using two predictive models that combine Chaos Theory and Multi-Layer Perceptron. Their effectiveness was tested on financial datasets, including the exchange rate of the US$ against other currencies.

3 Mathematical Framework

3.1 Perceptron Algorithm

The PA performs a basic form of supervised learning, which consists of classifying any given real vector $X_i \in \mathbb{R}^p$ into a binary label $\{YES, NO\}$ or $\{1, 0\}$. The weight vector w is a set of parameters that represents the internal state of the system. This vector is adjusted during the training process, determining how the features of the input instances X_i influence the model's predictions. Formally, a Perceptron $\mathbb{P}$ is a function $\mathbb{P} : \mathbb{R}^p \to [0, 1]$ defined as:

$$\begin{aligned}
\mathbb{P}(X_i) =& \ell(\sum_{j=1}^{p} x_{i,j} w_j) \\
\text{where} & \\
& X_i = [1, x_{i,2}, \ldots, x_{i,p-1}, x_{i,p}]^T \text{ (1 in every first entry as bias)} \\
& W = [w_1, w_2, \ldots, w_{p-1}, w_p]^T \\
& \ell \text{ is the logistic function}
\end{aligned} \tag{1}$$

Ideally, for a fixed vector W, the function $\mathbb{P}$ must generalise the classification by having as reference a set of labelled observations. Given a training set of n vectors $\mathcal{X}_{\text{train}} = \{X_1, \ldots, X_n\}$, whose expected classification is known $\mathcal{C}_{\text{train}} = \{C_1, \ldots, C_n\}$, the vector W is estimated by minimising the mean squared error:

$$\hat{\mu}(W|\mathcal{X}_{\text{train}}, \mathcal{C}_{\text{train}}) = \frac{1}{n} \sum_{i=1}^{n} (\mathbb{P}(X_i) - C_i)^2 \tag{2}$$

Using $\hat{\mu}(W|\mathcal{X}_{\text{train}}, \mathcal{C}_{\text{train}})$ as the single criterion may cause the so-called over-fitting, which consists of minimising the error measure only for items in the training set. In this regard, to properly generalise the classification, a common practice is stopping the minimisation process before getting a positive trend in a validation error measure $\hat{\mu}(W|\mathcal{X}_{\text{test}}, \mathcal{C}_{\text{test}})$ which is based on additional labelled observations $\mathcal{X}_{\text{test}}, \mathcal{C}_{\text{test}}$ not considered in the training set $\mathcal{X}_{\text{train}}, \mathcal{C}_{\text{train}}$.

In order to illustrate how to prevent the over-fitting, consider the trajectory of an imaginary ball in a landscape (Fig. 1.a) . In this analogy, each error function $\hat{\mu}$ defines a different landscape; and the succession $\{W_1, \ldots, W_t\}$ describes the trajectory of the ball, which is progressively attracted to a valley by gravity. Figure 1a shows the landscapes of $\hat{\mu}(W|\mathcal{X}_{\text{train}}, \mathcal{C}_{\text{train}})$ and $\hat{\mu}(W|\mathcal{X}_{\text{test}}, \mathcal{C}_{\text{test}})$ as two curves in blue and red, respectively. The trajectory of the ball along the training curve (in blue) from an arbitrary point towards the lowest valley is represented by a dotted line. A red cross marks the specific point along this trajectory. Note that if the ball continues from the red cross towards the lowest valley, the validation error (represented by the red curve) shows an upward trend, meaning the validation error increases. Therefore, continuing the trajectory from the red cross will result in improvements only for the training set (overfitting). In this regard, the point marked with the red cross corresponds to the optimal weight vector W for generalising the classification.

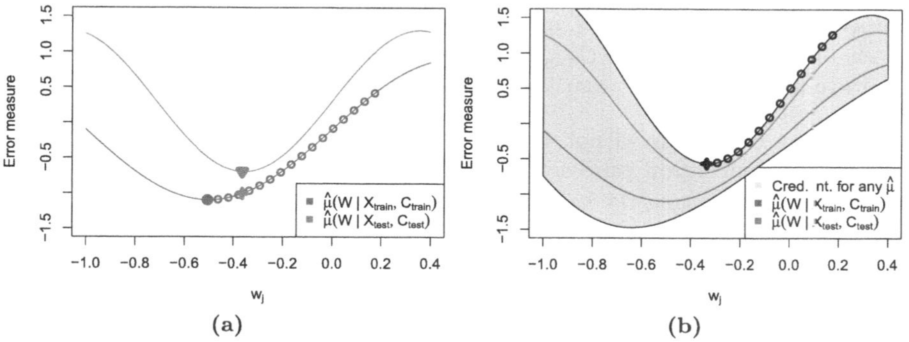

Fig. 1. a) The original Perceptron approach based on a gradient descent over a training curve (in blue) and stopped when it affects negatively a validation error curve (in red); **b) Our approach** based on a gradient descent over the upper bound of a credible interval. In both cases, the stop point is marked with a cross. (Color figure online)

The landscape of any function $\hat{\mu}(W|\mathcal{X}_{\text{sample}}, \mathcal{C}_{\text{sample}})$ is fully defined by the set of n labelled observations $(\mathcal{X}_{\text{sample}}, \mathcal{C}_{\text{sample}})$ which were randomly sampled from a population $(\mathcal{X}, \mathcal{C})$. In this regard, a function $\hat{\mu}$ (Eq. 2) is a sum of random variables with the same distribution, so $\hat{\mu}$ also constitutes a random variable, and by the Central Limit Theorem:

$$\hat{\mu}(W|\mathcal{X}_{\text{sample}}, \mathcal{C}_{\text{sample}}) \sim Normal(\mu(W), \sigma^2(W)/n) \tag{3}$$

where:

$$\mu(W) = \int_{(\mathcal{X},\mathcal{C})} (\mathbb{P}(X_i) - C_i)^2 \Pr(X_i, C_i) d(Xi, C_i)$$

$$\sigma^2(W) = \int_{(\mathcal{X},\mathcal{C})} [(\mathbb{P}(X_i) - C_i)^2 - \mu(W)]^2 \Pr(X_i, C_i) d(X_i, C_i)$$

$\Pr(X_i, C_i)$ is the prob. of sampling $X_i \in \mathcal{X}$ labelled as $C_i \in \mathcal{C}$

In this context, a vector $W^\star$ that minimises $\mu(W^\star)$ is the optimum for generalising the classification, because function $\mu(W)$ is defined over the entire population $(\mathcal{X}, \mathcal{C})$. In practice, it is impossible to know function $\mu(W)$. However, it is feasible to define a credible interval for $\mu(W)$ by means of a n-size sample $\mathcal{X}_{\text{sample}}, \mathcal{C}_{\text{sample}}$. Figure 1b illustrates a 95% credible interval (CI) for $\mu(W)$, which also contains functions $\hat{\mu}(W|\mathcal{X}_{\text{train}}, \mathcal{C}_{\text{train}})$ and $\hat{\mu}(W|\mathcal{X}_{\text{test}}, \mathcal{C}_{\text{test}})$, because both are merely instances of the random function $\hat{\mu}(W|\mathcal{X}_{\text{sample}}, \mathcal{C}_{\text{sample}})$. The upper and lower bounds of the CI can be interpreted as the hardest and the easiest curve for minimising, respectively. The minimum of the lower bound is quite optimistic about $\mu(W)$, i.e. it tends to produce over-fitting. In opposite, the minimum of the upper bound tends to be conservative; and this is a desirable behaviour for preventing overfitting. Hence, we formally enounce:

Conjecture 1. Let $[\mu_{lower}(W), \mu_{upper}(W)]$ be a 95% CI for $\mu(W)$, estimated by means of a training sample $\mathcal{C}_{\text{train}}$. Then, the function $\mu_{upper}(W)$ is more robust for preventing overfitting than $\hat{\mu}(W|\mathcal{X}_{\text{train}}, \mathcal{C}_{\text{train}})$.

The last conjecture is not formally proven. However, the usage of CI for improving optimisation processes is popular in BO literature [4]. The specific approach of conducting the exploration by means of the upper bound of a CI is associated with the BO concept of acquisition function [1]. On the whole, BO is a model-based approach for optimising black-box functions $f : \mathcal{X} \rightarrow \mathbb{R}$, especially those that are expensive to evaluate. It relies on two main components: a probabilistic model, often Gaussian processes [4], which provides a posterior distribution $\mathcal{P}(f \mid \mathcal{D})$ over the function of interest $f(x)$, and an acquisition function that determines the next evaluation point by balancing exploration and exploitation [3,15]. To empirically validate Conjecture 1, $\mu_{upper}(W)$ and $\hat{\mu}(W|\mathcal{X}_{\text{train}}, \mathcal{C}_{\text{train}})$ are statistically compared. For both error functions, the minimisation method used is gradient descent with exactly the same parameters, as described below in Subsect. 3.2.

In machine learning literature, k-fold cross-validation is a widely used technique for evaluating the performance of models [19]. It involves splitting a dataset into k subsets, where k-1 subsets are used as the training set once while the remaining data is used for validation. The training and validating process is repeated for different folds selections, providing a more reliable estimation of the model's accuracy considering the average performance across all iteration. This method helps to reduce the risk of overfitting and offers a better understanding of the model's performance with unobserved data [19]. Within the theoretical framework of the proposal, according to Eq. 3, a different error function $\hat{\mu}$ corresponds to each of the k folds. Therefore, at least 95% of the surfaces of all k functions $\hat{\mu}$ are enclosed by the CI defined by Conjecture 1. A remarkable point to consider is that the selection of parameters as k or the training proportion in Monte Carlo Cross Validation impacts on the evaluation. In contrast, our approach is parameter-free although closely related to the cited techniques for enhancing cross-validation: k-fold and Monte Carlo cross-validation.

3.2 Gradient Descent

Let us consider $f(W)$ as an objective function with p real parameters. The gradient descent algorithm just consists of iterating the following improving step:

$$W_{t+1} = W_t - \eta \nabla f(W_t) \tag{4}$$

where

$\eta > 0$ is a small real, called **learning rate**

$\nabla f(W_t)$ is the gradient of f evaluated in W_t

$W_1 \in \mathbb{R}^p$ is an arbitrarily initial point

In the original Perceptron, the objective function $f(W)$ and its corresponding gradient are given by:

$$f(W) = \hat{\mu}(W|\mathcal{X}_{\text{train}}, \mathcal{C}_{\text{train}}) \tag{5}$$

$$\frac{d}{dw_j}\hat{\mu}(W|\mathcal{X}_{\text{train}}, \mathcal{C}_{\text{train}}) = \frac{2}{n}\sum_{i=1}^{n}(\mathbb{P}(X_i) - C_i)\mathbb{P}(X_i)(1 - \mathbb{P}(X_i))x_{i,j} \tag{6}$$

In our BO-based approach, the objective function $f(W)$ and its corresponding gradient are replaced by:

$$f(W) = \hat{\mu}(W|\mathcal{X}_{\text{train}}, \mathcal{C}_{\text{train}}) + q_{.95}\sqrt{\hat{\sigma}^2(W|\mathcal{X}_{\text{train}}, \mathcal{C}_{\text{train}})/n} \tag{7}$$

$$\frac{d}{dw_j}f(W) = \frac{d}{dw_j}\hat{\mu}(W|\mathcal{X}_{\text{train}}, \mathcal{C}_{\text{train}}) + \frac{q_{.95}}{2}\sqrt{\frac{1}{n\hat{\sigma}^2(W|\mathcal{X}_{\text{train}}, \mathcal{C}_{\text{train}})}}\frac{d}{dw_i}\hat{\sigma}^2(W|\mathcal{X}_{\text{train}}, \mathcal{C}_{\text{train}}) \tag{8}$$

where: $$\hat{\sigma}^2(W|\mathcal{X}_{\text{train}}, \mathcal{C}_{\text{train}}) = \frac{1}{n}\sum_{i=1}^{2}\left[(\mathbb{P}(X_i) - C_i)^2 - \hat{\mu}(W|\mathcal{X}_{\text{train}}, \mathcal{C}_{\text{train}})\right]^2$$

$$\frac{d}{dw_i}\hat{\sigma}^2(W|\mathcal{X}_{\text{train}}, \mathcal{C}_{\text{train}}) = \frac{4}{n}\sum_{i=1}^{n}\left[(\mathbb{P}(X_i) - C_i)^3\mathbb{P}(X_i)(1 - \mathbb{P}(X_i))x_{i,j}\right] - 2\hat{\mu}(W|\mathcal{X}_{\text{train}}, \mathcal{C}_{\text{train}})\frac{d}{dw_j}\hat{\mu}(W|\mathcal{X}_{\text{train}}, \mathcal{C}_{\text{train}})$$

The calculation of the upper credible interval involves an additional step to the original Perceptron algorithm: the estimation of the standard deviation. Despite this difference, the time complexity in Big O notation is the same for both algorithms: $O(n)$. Therefore, both are equally feasible.

4 Experimental Results

To properly compare the original Perceptron vs. our BO-based approach, a collection of non-trivial artificial problems is tested. All problems of this collection consist of splitting up samples from two different Gaussian Mixture Models, which are dimension-scalable. This last property allows to verify if the performance of both approaches is consistent in several dimensions.

4.1 Artificial Problems

Let us consider that, for a dichotomic classification problem in dimension p, any observation $X_i \in \mathbb{R}^p$ comes from one of two random distributions:

$$\Pr(X_i|C_i = 0) = \text{pdf}_{\text{zero}}(x) \quad \text{or} \quad \Pr(X_i|C_i = 1) = \text{pdf}_{\text{one}}(x) \tag{9}$$

Functions pdf_{zero} and pdf_{one} are unknown multivariate density functions. However, according to [14], any density pdf can be approximated by means of a Gaussian Mixture Model (GMM), given k enough kernels. Formally,

$$\text{pdf}(X) \approx \sum_{i=1}^{k} \mathcal{N}(X|\mu_i, \sigma_i I)\pi_i \tag{10}$$

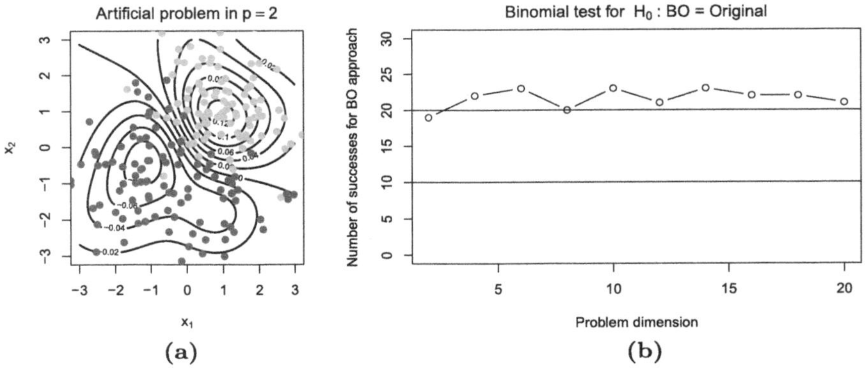

Fig. 2. a) Artificial problem in 2nd dimension. Points represent samples from different Gaussian mixtures, and the contour lines illustrates the corresponding multivariate densities. **b) Series of Binomial tests** for comparing the BO approach vs. the original Perceptron in several dimensions.

In other words, any continuous density function pdf can be fully defined by parameters: $\mu = [\mu_1, \ldots, \mu_k]$, $\sigma = [\sigma_1, \ldots, \sigma_k]$ and $\pi = [\pi_1, \ldots, \pi_k]$. Now, to define a coherent artificial problem, let pdf_{zero} and pdf_{one} be two GMMs defined by the following vectors with $k = 10$:

1. $\pi_{\text{zero}}, \pi_{\text{one}} \sim \text{Uniform}(k - \Delta)$, i.e. π_{zero} and π_{one} are uniformly sampled inside a k simplex $(k - \Delta)$ to ensure that $\sum_{i=1}^{k} \pi_{\text{zero},i} = \sum_{i=1}^{k} \pi_{\text{one},i} = 1$.
2. $\mu_{\text{one},i} \sim \text{Normal}(+\bar{1}, \sigma_i I)$, to ensure that the most of X labelled as 1 belong to the first quadrant.
3. $\mu_{\text{zero},i} \sim \text{Normal}(-\bar{1}, \sigma_i I)$, to ensure that the most of X labelled as 0 belong to the antipodal quadrant.
4. $\sigma_{\text{zero}} = \sigma_{\text{one}} = \frac{1}{2}\bar{1}$

The densities are used to draw 100 samples from pdf_{zero} and 100 from pdf_{one}. Both samples are labelled and then equally separated into two sets: $\mathcal{X}_{\text{train}}$ and $\mathcal{X}_{\text{test}}$. Figure 2a illustrates an artificial problem defined in dimension $p = 2$. The usage of GMMs allows to generate non trivial problems, which can be quite close to real-world problems, due to the possibility of approximating any real-world density by means of GMMs.

4.2 Experimental Design

The original Perceptron and the BO approach are statistically compared by an exhaustive Monte Carlo simulation. For $i = 1, \ldots, 30$ and a given dimension p, let $B_p[i]$ be a Bernoulli random variable computed by the following procedure:

1. Draw two data sets $\mathcal{X}_{\text{train}}$ and $\mathcal{X}_{\text{test}}$ from an artificial problem.
2. Train two Perceptrons $\mathbb{P}_{\text{org}}$ and $\mathbb{P}_{\text{BO}}$ with the same set $\mathcal{X}_{\text{train}}$, but using the gradient descent algorithm to minimise different error measures: the mean squared error ($\mathbb{P}_{\text{org}}$) and the upper bound of a credible interval ($\mathbb{P}_{\text{BO}}$). For both models, the algorithm runs with the same parameters $\eta = 1e-4$ (learning rate), $t = 5e+2$ (epochs) and the same W_0 (initial point).
3. Evaluate the accuracy of $\mathbb{P}_{\text{org}}$ and $\mathbb{P}_{\text{BO}}$, using as reference the test set $\mathcal{X}_{\text{test}}$. According to the accuracy, define $B_p[i]$ as:

$$B_p[i] = \begin{cases} 1 \text{ if } \mathbb{P}_{\text{BO}} \text{ is better} \\ 0 \text{ if } \mathbb{P}_{\text{org}} \text{ is better} \end{cases} \tag{11}$$

For each dimension p, the sum $S_p = \sum_{i=1}^{30} B_p[i]$ counts for how many independent artificial problems the Bayesian approach is better than the original Perceptron. Considering that $S_p \sim Binomial(n = 30, \rho)$, under the null hypothesis $H_0 : \rho = .5$, $\Pr(S_p \notin [10, 20]) < .05$. Therefore, the statistic S_p is useful for applying a Binomial test with error $\alpha < .05$:

- If $S_p \in [10, 20]$, then H_0 is not rejected, i.e. both methods are equivalent
- In the case where $S_p < 10$, the original Perceptron proves to be significantly better
- In the case where $S_p > 20$, the Bayesian approach turns out to be significantly better

Figure 2a illustrates a series of statistics S_p for $p = 2, \ldots, 20$. The selection of this interval of dimensions has theoretical basis on the relevant dimensions to report in terms of the curse of dimensionality [5]. According to the criteria above, if the series is within the area enclosed by the horizontal lines, then there is no significant difference between the methods. However, the most of the series is above the upper bound, so the Bayesian approach is statistically better then the original Perceptron. This behaviour seems consistent along all dimensions.

5 Discussion and Future Work

Figure 2a illustrates a series of statistics for dimensions 2 to 20, which indicates the number of independent artificial problems where the Bayesian approach outperformed the original Perceptron. The visual analysis consistently demonstrates that the Bayesian-optimised Perceptron significantly surpasses the original across all dimensions considered. Despite of having shown that our approach is statistically better than the original, the no-free lunch theorem [18] does not allow us to conclude that our improved version outperforms for any possible classification problem. Another remarkable theoretical nuance is the linearly separability [7], which is a very restrictive prior condition for the data-sets. For the last reason, the experimental design of this work is preliminarily restricted to non-trivial linearly separable artificial problems rather than standard benchmark datasets such as PROBEN1 [10].

In order to be applicable to the modern real-world datasets, it is imperative to extend the proposal to Multilayer Perceptron Networks (MLPs), a neural network that allows to overcome the linear separability. The foundation for using MLPs as universal approximators is supported on algebraic properties arising from the linear partitions of the classification space [6]. The proposed approach only modifies the estimation method, but not the geometry, so these algebraic properties remain. In further work, the idea of exploring credible intervals to improve generalisation may be extended by MCMC-free and dimensionally robust BO methods, such as Convex Partition Optimisation [9].

6 Conclusion

This paper presents a novel version of the Perceptron classifier, whose improvement consists of estimating and minimising the model error by using as reference a credible interval rather than a point estimation. In non-trivial artificial problems, this new version of Perceptron has a statistically better generalisation, i.e. better classification for non-observed data. This work constitutes a preliminary work towards designing an improved Multilayer Perceptron Network, as detailed above. This modification would incorporate the newly discovered insights: utilising the upper credible interval for minimising the model error enhances the generalisation.

References

1. De Ath, G., Everson, R., Rahat, A., Fieldsend, J.: Greed is good: exploration and exploitation trade-offs in Bayesian optimisation. ACM Trans. Evol. Learn. Optim. **1**(1), 1–22 (2021). https://doi.org/10.1145/3425501
2. El-Hassani, F., Amri, M., Joudar, N., Haddouch, K.: A new model for MLP hyperparameter tuning: modeling and resolution by real-coded genetic algorithm. Neural Process. Lett. **56**, 1–31 (2024). https://doi.org/10.1007/s11063-024-11578-0
3. Frazier, P.I.: A tutorial on Bayesian optimization. arXiv preprint arXiv:1807.02811 (2018)
4. Garnett, R.: Bayesian Optimization. Cambridge University Press, Cambridge (2023)
5. Hayes, B.: An adventure in the nth dimension. American Scientist (2008). https://www.americanscientist.org/article/an-adventure-in-the-nth-dimension
6. Hornik, K.: Approximation capabilities of multilayer feedforward networks. Neural Netw. **4**(2), 251–257 (1991). https://doi.org/10.1016/0893-6080(91)90009-T
7. Minsky, M., Papert, S.: An introduction to computational geometry. Cambridge tiass., HIT **479**(480), 104 (1969)

8. de Paz, E.G., Vaquera-Huerta, H., Albores-Velasco, F.J., Bauer-Mengelberg, J.R., Romero-Padilla, J.M.: A splitting criterion for cart models based on Bayesian optimisation. In: National Statistics Forum, pp. 19–35. Springer, Cham (2023). https://doi.org/10.1007/978-3-031-78401-9_2
9. de Paz, E.G., Vaquera-Huerta, H., Albores-Velasco, F.J., Bauer-Mengelberg, J.R., Romero-Padilla, J.M.: Convex partition: a Bayesian regression tree for black-box optimisation. Pattern Recogn. Lett. (2025). https://doi.org/10.1016/j.patrec.2025.03.009
10. Prechelt, L.: Proben1-a set of neural network benchmark problems and benchmarking rules (technical report 21–94). Fakultät für Informatik, Universität Karlsruhe, Karlsruhe, Germany (1994)
11. Ravi, V., Pradeepkumar, D., Deb, K.: Financial time series prediction using hybrids of chaos theory, multi-layer perceptron and multi-objective evolutionary algorithms. ELSEVIER (2017). https://doi.org/10.1016/j.swevo.2017.05.003
12. Rosenblatt, F.: Principles of neurodynamics: perceptrons and the theory of brain mechanisms. Cornell Aeronautical Laboratory. Report no. VG-1196-G-8, Spartan Books (1962). https://books.google.com.mx/books?id=7FhRAAAAMAAJ
13. Rosenblatt, F.: The perceptron: a probabilistic model for information storage and organization in the brain. Psychol. Rev. **65**(6), 386 (1958)
14. Scott, D.: Multivariate Density Estimation: Theory, Practice, and Visualization. Wiley Series in Probability and Mathematical Statistics, Wiley (1992)
15. Shahriari, B., Swersky, K., Wang, Z., Adams, R.P., De Freitas, N.: Taking the human out of the loop: a review of Bayesian optimization. Proc. IEEE **104**(1), 148–175 (2015)
16. Sohi, J., Singh, B., Sohi, S.: Training back propagation neural networks with genetic algorithm for weather forecasting. In: IEEE Xplore, pp. 1–7 (2010). https://doi.org/10.1109/SISY.2010.5647319,
17. Solla, S., Winther, O.: Optimal Perceptron Learning: an On-line Bayesian Approach, p. 379–398. Publications of the Newton Institute, Cambridge University Press (1999)
18. Sterkenburg, T.F., Grünwald, P.D.: The no-free-lunch theorems of supervised learning. Synthese, 9979–10015 (2021). https://doi.org/10.1007/s11229-021-03233-1
19. Tougui, I., Jilbab, A., El Mhamdi, J.: Impact of the choice of cross-validation techniques on the results of machine learning-based diagnostic applications. Healthc. Inform. Res. **27**(3), 189–199 (2021). https://doi.org/10.4258/hir.2021.27.3.189
20. Zhang, B., He, J., Liu, P., Wang, L., Tang, R.: An automated multi-layer perceptron discriminative neural network based on Bayesian optimization achieves high-precision one-source single-snapshot direction-of-arrival estimation. Sci. Rep. **14**(1) (2024). https://doi.org/10.1038/s41598-024-60798-w,

Facial Expression Recognition Using Lightweight CNNs and Soft Voting

Jose Sotelo-Barrales, Mariko Nakano-Miyatake(✉), Hector Perez-Meana, and Giovanny Sanchez-Rivera

ESIME Culhuacan, Instituto Politecnico Nacional, Av. Santa Ana 1000, Coyoacan, Ciudad de Mexico, Mexico
mnakano@ipn.mx

Abstract. This paper proposes an efficient emotion recognition method, achieving classification accuracies of 98.57% on JAFFE, 98.06% on KDEF, 99.3% on CK +, and 99.72% on Oulu-CASIA. The proposed approach utilizes two lightweight convolutional neural networks (CNN), ShuffleNetV2 and MobileNetV2, for feature extraction. The methodology includes four key stages: preprocessing of face images, feature extraction, dimensionality reduction via Neighborhood components analysis (NCA) to produce three distinct feature vectors with different dimensionality, and classification based on support vector machine (SVM). In the training phase, three SVM models are trained using training sets composed of feature vectors with different dimensionalities. In the inference phase, a soft voting mechanism is employed, combining predictions from three individually trained SVM models. The results emphasize the balance between accuracy and computational efficiency, a critical factor for real-world applications requiring real-time processing. This work demonstrates that high performance in emotion recognition can be attained without reliance on overly large architectures, thereby enhancing accessibility and ease of implementation.

Keywords: Facial Expression Recognition · Emotion Detection · Soft Voting · Neighborhood Components Analysis · Support Vector Machine

1 Introduction

Human emotions are essential for interaction contributing to better social engagement and communication [1]. This is particularly important in various settings, both in-person and remote, such as hospital care [2] and the learning process [3], where recognizing emotions can enhance a good relationship between patients and healthcare professionals, as well as between students and teachers. This good relationship maintains a better quality of life in hospital care and higher learning efficiency in educational institutions. Emotions are expressed through body posture, voice, and facial expressions [4]. Among these, facial expressions are especially relevant because they allow emotion recognition in a wider range of individuals, including reserved or non-verbal people.

Due to this importance, several approaches for facial expression recognition (FER) have been proposed to date. In the early stages, hand-crafted features related to human

A. P. López-Monroy et al. (Eds.): MCPR 2025, LNCS 15715, pp. 358–367, 2025.
https://doi.org/10.1007/978-3-031-96255-4_33

emotions were extracted from the face images using several methods, such as Local Binary Patterns (LBP) [5] and Histogram of Oriented Gradients (HOG) [6]. These features are introduced to a classifier to determine an expressed emotion from the face image. However, with the rise of deep learning, feature extraction is performed by Convolutional neural networks (CNNs) [7], which have shown superior performance compared to methods based on hand-crafted features.

In this work, we propose an efficient approach for FER by utilizing two pre-trained CNNs, ShuffleNet V2 [8] and MobileNetV2 [9], for feature extraction. These architectures were selected due to their balance between accuracy and computational efficiency, as they require fewer parameters compared to other deep networks. First, the face image is segmented into four sub-images, and each sub-image and whole image are introduced separately into two CNNs to extract features. All the features extracted from the five input images are concatenated to generate a high-dimensional feature vector. The Neighborhood Component Analysis (NCA) is applied to the feature vectors to reduce dimensionality while keeping relevant feature components.

The degree of dimension reduction by NCA is essential to obtain good recognition performance because high-dimensional feature vectors may contain redundancy, which can negatively influence performance. In contrast, low-dimensional feature vectors may lose relevant emotional information. The optimum dimension cannot be determined in advance as it may depend on the type of emotion and each individual. Considering this, NCAs with three dimensions are applied to the feature vectors to generate three reduced-dimensional feature vectors with three dimensions. Finally, three feature vectors are used to train three Support Vector Machine (SVM) classifiers. In the inference stage, a soft voting technique is implemented, combining the predictions of the three SVMs to produce a more reliable final decision. This approach not only improves accuracy but also reduces computational costs, making it suitable for real-time applications and resource-constrained devices.

The rest of this article is structured as follows: Sect. 2 presents a review of related works in FER. Section 3 describes the proposed methodology, detailing the preprocessing steps, feature extraction using pre-trained CNN models, dimensionality reduction with NCA, and classification. Section 4 presents experimental results, including datasets and evaluation metrics. Section 5 describes the conclusions of this work.

2 Related Works

Some automatic FER methods based on hand-crafted features propose new descriptors for efficient classification. The paper [10] uses Dlib to detect 49 facial landmarks and defines ROIs, introducing the OPD-GQMBP descriptor to integrate shape and texture information. PCA reduces feature dimensionality before SVM classification, evaluated on five databases under person-independent protocols. Similarly, [11] employs Dlib's 68-landmark detector with LBP and ORB descriptors, fusing features via Z-score for SVM-based emotion classification. In deep learning-based FER, [12] preprocesses inputs using Action Units (AUs) to guide an improved cGAN (im-cGAN) for identity-consistent image generation. A Discriminative Deep Fusion (DDF) model combines global/local features, optimized via D-loss for better class separation. Meanwhile, [13] performs face detection, normalization, landmark alignment, and augmentation, then fuses geometric and pixel features in a DNN with Adam/cross-entropy optimization.

Other approaches leverage CNNs: [14] applies Viola-Jones detection and a custom CNN for end-to-end learning. [15] segments faces into 3 × 3 blocks, extracts features via MobileNetV2 and AlexNet, selects optimal features with NCA, and classifies them using SVM. Lastly, [16] uses a custom CNN (CCNN) for deep feature extraction, followed by SVM classification to improve accuracy by filtering non-relevant features. These works demonstrate progress in preprocessing, feature fusion, and classifier design for robust FER.

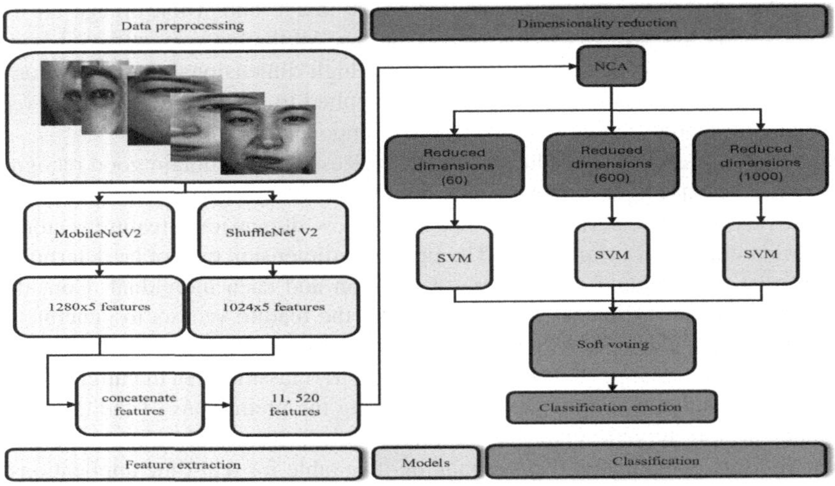

Fig. 1. Proposed methodology block diagram.

3 Proposed Methodology

As shown in Fig. 1, the proposed method starts with the preprocessing stage of the input face image, aiming to enable efficient feature extraction. Subsequently, features are extracted using the two pre-trained ShuffleNetV2 and MobileNetV2, selected for their balance between accuracy and computational efficiency. The extracted features are optimized using NCA, which reduces their dimensionality to 60, 600, and 1000 dimensions. Finally, an SVM classifier is trained on each of the evaluated datasets. In the inference phase, the probabilities of the three trained SVM classifiers are averaged using soft voting to obtain the final classification result.

In the preprocessing stage, face detection is performed using MediaPipe's Face Detector. Once a face is detected, it is segmented and resized to reduce its size to 80% of the original area. This process is repeated; however, instead of using the whole image, it is divided into four equal parts for further analysis. Finally, a total of five images, composed of four segmented images and one whole face image, are resized to 224 × 224 pixels, and introduced sequentially to the feature extraction stage.

Feature extraction from the five images will be conducted using the ShuffleNetV2 and MobileNetV2 architectures, both of which are pre-trained on the ImageNet dataset. For each architecture, a layer preceding the classification stage will be utilized: specifically, a layer comprising 1024 features for ShuffleNetV2 and a layer with 1280 features for MobileNetV2. By concatenating the features extracted from both architectures for each image, a total of 2304 features per image is obtained (1024 from ShuffleNet V2 and 1280 from MobileNetV2). Given that five images are analyzed per individual, this results in a feature vector of 11,520 dimensions per individual (2304 features/image × 5 images). The images are associated with specific labels, which will subsequently be employed for classification tasks.

In the training phase, the extracted features and corresponding labels associated with different emotions are loaded. These features are standardized, ensuring they have a mean zero and unit variance, a critical step to optimize the performance of the dimensionality reduction algorithm. Next, the NCA model, a supervised dimensionality reduction technique, is applied to project the features into a lower-dimensional space. The optimal dimensionality for the feature vector is unknown in advance, and it may vary depending on the facial emotion and/or individual. The higher-dimensional features contain redundancy, while lower-dimensional features lose relevant components to classify facial emotion. Considering it, three different dimensionalities, 60, 600 and 1000, are used.

The proposed methodology employs an SVM with a linear kernel to find the optimal hyperplane for class separation. The linear kernel is selected because it provides the best performance compared with other kernels. For multiclass classification, the 'one-vs-rest' strategy is applied. Model performance is evaluated using k-fold cross-validation, ensuring a robust estimate of the classifier's generalization capability.

In the inference phase, a soft voting strategy was implemented to combine the predictions of three models trained with different dimensionality sets (60, 600, and 1000). Subsequently, the average of these probabilities was calculated, allowing for a weighted and smooth combination of predictions. The final class was determined by selecting the one with the highest average probability. This soft voting approach leverages the individual strengths of each model, enhancing the system's robustness and generalization. To evaluate the performance of the combined model, accuracy was calculated (Fig. 2).

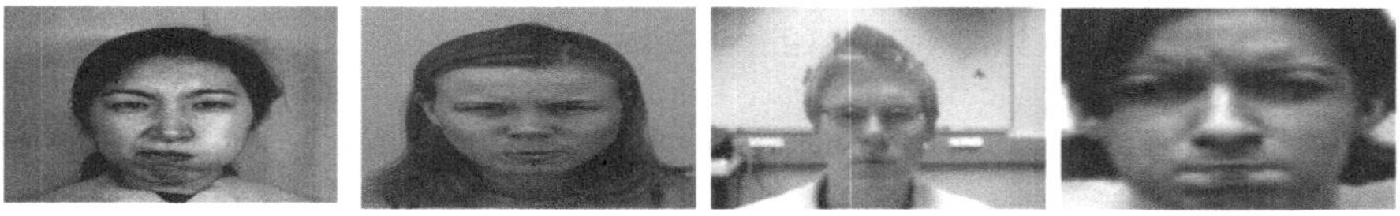

Fig. 2. An example of the used datasets JAFFE, KDEF, CK +, and Oulu-CASIA.

4 Experimental Results

The data sets used in this study are Japanese Female Facial Expression Database (JAFFE) [17], Karolinska Directed Emotional Faces (KDEF) [18], Oulu-CASIA NIR&VIS facial expression database (Oulu-CASIA) [19], and Extended Cohn-Kanade Dataset (CK +) [20]. Table 1 presents the number of expressions in each dataset, which will be used in the analysis of the proposed method.

Table 1. Description of used datasets.

Emotions	JAFFE	KDEF	CK+	Oulu-CASIA
Anger or Angry	30	140	135	1,790
Disgust	29	140	177	1,633
Fear	32	140	75	1,796
Happy or Happiness	31	140	207	1,791
Sad or Sadness	31	140	84	1,668
Surprise	30	140	249	1,701
Neutral	30	140	–	–
Contempt	–	–	54	–
Total images	213	980	981	10,379

The data of each dataset is reduced to 2 dimensions using NCA for visualization purposes (Fig. 3), aiming to observe the emotion distribution in each dataset and whether the classes show any separation patterns that might indicate better class separation in higher dimensions (60, 600, and 1000).

As shown in Fig. 3, the diversity of seven facial emotions in JAFFE is the largest, while the diversity of Oulu-CASIA is the smallest, indicating that JAFFE is the most challenging and Oulu-CASIA is the easiest to classify the seven emotions. However, it is expected to be separated correctly using higher-dimension vectors, such as 60, 600, and 1000 dimensions.

Figure 4 shows an example of the preprocessing using one face image. The first image in the first row is the original image, the second image in the first row is the segmented image using MediaPipe's Face Detector, and the second row is composed of a whole face image and four sub-images created by splitting it into two vertically and two horizontally.

All data are partitioned into an 80% training set and a 20% testing set. The classifier is an SVM with a linear kernel, configured with a regularization parameter $C = 1$ and gamma = 'scale'. The model performance was evaluated using 10-fold cross-validation. Tables 3, 4 and 5 show the performance obtained using three reduced-dimensioned feature vectors (60, 600, and 1000 dimensions) for the four datasets mentioned above. From these tables, higher-dimension feature vectors provide better performance, except for the JAFFE and KDEF datasets. In the case of JAFFE, the lowest dimension feature

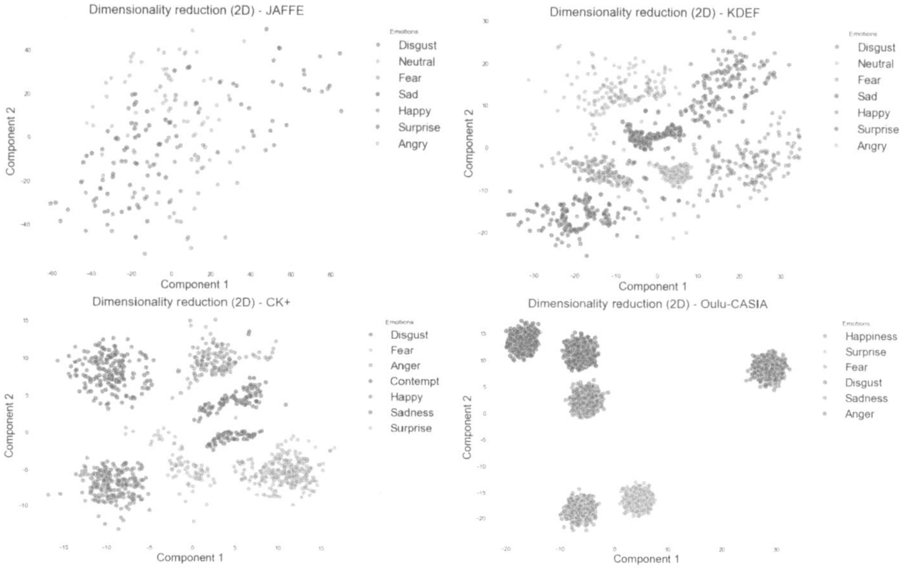

Fig. 3. Dimensionality reduction to 2 dimensions.

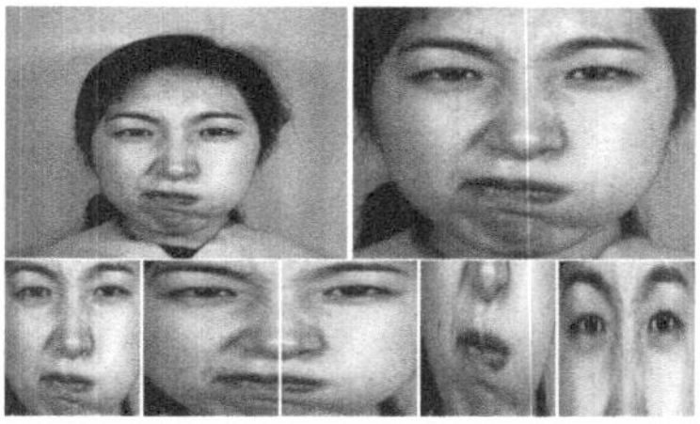

Fig. 4. The figure shows the preprocessing, first row the original image and the segmented image. The second row displays the images from which the features will be extracted: the segmented image and the four divisions of the segmented image.

vectors provide the best performance, while for KDEF, 600-dimensioned feature vectors provide the best performance.

The classification results obtained after applying the soft voting among 60, 600, and 1000 dimensioned feature vectors to make a final decision using four datasets are shown in Table 6.

Table 7 compares the proposed method's classification accuracy with that of the State of Arts (SOTA) methods [10–15], described in the related works section, using four datasets. The feature extraction method (FE) and classifier used are mentioned in the 'Method' column. The number of parameters and validation techniques used in each method are also added to the table. From this table, we can observe the proposed method provides a better performance compared with almost all SOTA methods. The accuracy for datasets JAFFE and Oulu-CASIA, the proposed method provides slightly lower

Table 3. Metrics of the datasets with 60 dimensions.

Metric	JAFFE	KDEF	CK+	Oulu-CASIA
Precision	96%	88%	100%	68%
Recall	95%	87%	100%	68%
F1-score	95%	87%	100%	68%
Accuracy	95.35%	87.24%	100%	67.73%
10-Fold cross validation	87.65%	84.95%	98.47%	67.10%

Table 4. Metrics of the datasets with 600 dimensions.

Metric	JAFFE	KDEF	CK+	Oulu-CASIA
Precision	82%	91%	100%	98%
Recall	77%	90%	100%	98%
F1-score	77%	90%	100%	98%
Accuracy	76.74%	90.31%	100%	97.54%
10-Fold cross validation	79.41%	90.05%	98.60%	97.75%

Table 5. Metrics of the datasets with 1000 dimensions.

Metric	JAFFE	KDEF	CK+	Oulu-CASIA
Precision	89%	87%	100%	99%
Recall	88%	86%	100%	99%
F1-score	88%	86%	100%	99%
Accuracy	88.37%	86.22%	100%	99.04%
10-Fold cross validation	82.35%	83.16%	98.22%	99.02%

Table 6. Metrics applied to soft voting.

Metric	JAFFE	KDEF	CK+	Oulu-CASIA
Precision	99%	98%	100%	100%
Recall	99%	98%	100%	100%
F1-scote	99%	98%	100%	100%
Accuracy	98.59%	98.06%	100%	99.72%
10-Fold cross validation	98.57%	98.06%	100%	99.72%

performance, 0.02% and 0.28%, compared with the method proposed by [15]. However, for the CK+ dataset, the proposed method surpasses more than 3% compared with [15]. It is worth mentioning that the method [15] requires a large number of parameters (trained weights) in the inference phase due to the use of a heavy-weight CNN to extract feature vectors, while the proposed method requires about 20 times smaller parameters, which makes possible for the installation of the proposed method in some mobile devices, expanding the possibility of use.

Table 7. Comparative analysis with the State of the arts methods. FE means feature extraction method, #-f CV means #-fold cross validation, and '---' means no data.

Method FE, Classifier	Params	Validation method	JAFFE (%)	KDEF (%)	CK+ (%)	Oulu CASIA (%)
OPD-GQMBP, SVM [10]	---	LOOCV	77.62	90.20	97.53	77.32
LBP + ORB, SVM [11]	---	10-f CV	88.50	---	93.20	---
im-cGAN + D-loss [12]	---	---	98.37	98.30	98.10	93.34
CNN loss layer [13]	1.41M	10-f CV	91.58	---	92.27	---
2D-CNN + 1D-CNN [14]	---	---	93.07	90.30	98.22	90.13
AlexNet + MobileNet2, SVM [15]	63.4M	10-f CV	**98.59**	94.69	**100**	**100**
CCNN, SVM [16]	0.43M	5-f CV	96.92	87.18	99.3	---
MobileNetV2 + ShuffleNetV2, SVM + Soft Voting Ours	3.47M	10-f CV	98.57	**98.06**	**100**	99.72

5 Conclusions

In this paper, we propose a method for facial expression recognition that achieves an optimal balance between accuracy and computational efficiency. The proposed method combined two lightweight CNNs, ShuffleNetV2 and MobileNetV2, to extract features. The NCA technique is applied to the high-dimensional feature vector to reduce dimensionality. Because the optimal dimension is unknown and can be varied according to the emotion type and individual, we used three target dimensions to reduce the dimensionality of the feature vector. In the inference phase, a soft voting method is utilized, which improves the classification performance and the adaptability of the proposed method.

The proposed method provides a classification accuracy for four public datasets with 98.57% on JAFFE, 98.06% on KDEF, 100% on CK +, and 99.72% on Oulu-CASIA, which outperforms almost all SOTA methods. Although the classification accuracies of the proposed method are slightly lower, –0.02% for the JAFFE dataset and –0.28% for the Oulu-CASIA dataset, compared with the method [15], the proposed method outperforms more than 3% for the KDEF dataset. Additionally, the proposed method requires much smaller parameters, almost 20 times smaller than [15]. This lightweight characteristic of the proposed method opens the possibility of implementing it on mobile devices.

For future work, it is proposed to validate the model on diverse datasets to assess its robustness, implement a real-time monitoring system to optimize its performance, and explore the use of recurrent neural networks, such as Long Short-Term Memory (LSTM) and transformers, to enhance sentiment analysis. Additionally, developing models capable of identifying mixed emotions would enable a more accurate and realistic analysis of complex human expressions. These research directions would expand the current scope and open new opportunities in natural language processing.

Disclosure of Interests. The authors confirm no competing interests exist.

References

1. Alexander, R., et al.: The neuroscience of positive emotions and affect: implications for cultivating happiness and wellbeing. Neurosci. Biobehav. Rev. **121**, 220–249 (2021). https://doi.org/10.1016/j.neubiorev.2020.12.002
2. Alzahrani, N.: The effect of hospitalization on patients' emotional and psychological well-being among adult patients: an integrative review. Appl. Nurs. Res. **61**, 151488 (2021). https://doi.org/10.1016/j.apnr.2021.151488
3. Li, Y., He, K., Xue, C., Li, C., Gu, C.: The impact of self-consistency congruence on non-suicidal self-injury in college students: the mediating role of negative emotion and the moderating role of gender. Int. J. Environ. Res. Public Health **19**(19), 11898 (2022). https://doi.org/10.3390/ijerph191911898
4. van Kleef, G.A., Côté, S.: The social effects of emotions. Annu. Rev. Psychol. **73**, 629–658 (2022). https://doi.org/10.1146/annurev-psych-020821-010855
5. Shan, C., Gong, S., McOwan, P.W.: Facial expression recognition based on local binary patterns: a comprehensive study. Image Vis. Comput. **27**(6), 803–816 (2009). https://doi.org/10.1016/j.imavis.2008.08.005
6. Carcagnì, P., Del Coco, M., Leo, M., Distante, C.: Facial expression recognition and histograms of oriented gradients: a comprehensive study. Springerplus **4**(1), 1–25 (2015). https://doi.org/10.1186/s40064-015-1427-3
7. Tsalera, E., Papadakis, A., Samarakou, M., Voyiatzis, I.: Feature extraction with handcrafted methods and convolutional neural networks for facial emotion recognition. Appl. Sci. **12**(17), 8455 (2022). https://doi.org/10.3390/app12178455
8. Ma, N., Zhang, X., Zheng, H.T., Sun, J.: ShuffleNet V2: practical guidelines for efficient CNN architecture design. arXiv preprint arXiv:1807.11164 (2018). https://arxiv.org/abs/1807.11164

9. Sandler, M., Howard, A., Zhu, M., Zhmoginov, A., Chen, L.C.: MobileNetV2: inverted residuals and linear bottlenecks. arXiv preprint arXiv:1801.04381 (2018). https://arxiv.org/abs/1801.04381
10. Kas, M., El Merabet, Y., Ruichek, Y., Messoussi, R.: New framework for person-independent facial expression recognition combining textural and shape analysis through new feature extraction approach. Inf. Sci. **549**, 200–220 (2021). https://doi.org/10.1016/j.ins.2020.10.065
11. Niu, B., Gao, Z., Guo, B.: Facial expression recognition with LBP and ORB features. Comput. Intell. Neurosci. **2021**, 8828245 (2021). https://doi.org/10.1155/2021/8828245
12. Sun, Z., Zhang, H., Bai, J., Liu, M., Hu, Z.: A discriminatively deep fusión approach with improved conditional GAN (im-cGAN) for facial expression recognition. Pattern Recogn. **135**, 109157 (2023). https://doi.org/10.1016/j.patcog.2022.109157
13. Appasaheb, M.R., Surve, D.S.: Deep learning for facial emotion recognition using custom CNN architecture. J. Phys. Conf. Ser. **2236**(1), 012004 (2012). https://doi.org/10.1088/1742-6596/2236/1/012004
14. Jabbooree, A.I., Khanli, L.M., Salehpour, P., Pourbahrami, S.: Un novedoso algoritmo de reconocimiento de expresiones faciales que utiliza geometría β –esqueleto en fusión basado en CNN profunda. Image Vis. Comput. **134**, 104677 (2023). https://doi.org/10.1016/j.imavis.2023.104677
15. Baygin, M., Tuncer, I., Dogan, S., et al.: Automated facial expression recognition using exemplar hybrid deep feature generation technique. Soft. Comput. **27**, 8721–8737 (2023). https://doi.org/10.1007/s00500-023-08230-9
16. Rashad, M., Alebiary, D.M., Aldawsari, M., El-Sawy, A.A., Abuel-Atta, A.H.: CCNN-SVM: automated model for emotion recognition based on custom convolutional neural networks with SVM. Information **15**(7), 384 (2024). https://doi.org/10.3390/info15070384
17. Lyons, M., Akamatsu, S., Kamachi, M., Gyoba, J.: Coding facial expressions with gabor wavelets. In: 3rd IEEE International Conference on Automatic Face and Gesture Recognition, pp. 200–205, Nara Japan (1998). https://doi.org/10.1109/AFGR.1998.670949
18. Lundqvist, D., Flykt, A., Öhman, A.: The karolinska directed emotional faces - KDEF, CD ROM from department of clinical neuroscience. Psychol. Sect. (1998). ISBN 91-630-7164-9
19. Zhao, G., Huang, X., Taini, M., Li, S.Z., PietikäInen, M.: Facial expression recognition from near-infrared videos. Image Vis. Comput. **29**(9), 607–619 (2011)
20. Lucey, P., Cohn, J.F., Kanade, T., Saragih, J., Ambadar, Z., Matthews, I.: The extended cohn-kanade dataset (CK+): a complete expression dataset for action unit and emotion-specified expression. In: Proceedings of the Third International Workshop on CVPR for Human Communicative Behavior Analysis (CVPR4HB 2010), pp. 94–101, San Francisco (2010)

Automatic Segmentation of the Major Temporal Arcade Using U-Net Attention Architecture

Hiram Efraín Orocio-García[1(✉)], Ivan Cruz-Aceves[2], and Arturo Hernández-Aguirre[1]

[1] Centro de Investigación en Matemáticas (CIMAT), Guanajuato, Gto, Mexico
{hiram.orocio,artha}@cimat.mx
[2] SECIHTI-Centro de Investigación en Matemáticas (CIMAT), Guanajuato, Gto, Mexico
ivan.cruz@cimat.mx

Abstract. This paper introduces a novel approach for the automatic segmentation of the major temporal arcade (MTA) in retinal fundus images, which is based on the U-Net architecture. The segmentation and attention processes make up the approach. The first step involves segmenting vessel-like structures using the well-known VGG-16 deep learning model and transfer learning using the U-Net architecture. In the second stage, an attention module is introduced to capture the MTA form, eliminating all vessel-like structures that are not the MTA. The effectiveness of the proposed approach is assessed in terms of F1-score, sensitivity, specificity, and accuracy, and it is contrasted with various cutting-edge vascular segmentation techniques. Only the training set was subjected to a data augmentation strategy. To identify the blood vessel structure, a specialist classified the MTA ground-truth images from the well-known DRIVE database containing 40 retinal fundus images. To ensure a robust training process, data augmentation was applied, and each training image was divided into 81 patches, resulting in a total of 1,377 patches for training. In the experiments, the numerical results obtained by the proposed method in the automatic MTA segmentation problem outperforms the comparative methods obtaining an accuracy of 0.9923 and F1-score of 0.7700 using the testing set of retinal fundus images. In addition, the average computational time of the proposed deep learning model in testing images is 0.003 s using specialized hardware.

Keywords: Deep Learning · Image segmentation · Major Temporal Arcade · U-Net attention architecture · Retinal fundus images

1 Introduction

Biomedical imaging is a vital tool in medicine, enabling healthcare professionals to examine the internal state of the human body. Various imaging techniques provide detailed insights into different tissue types, such as bones, muscles, and

A. P. López-Monroy et al. (Eds.): MCPR 2025, LNCS 15715, pp. 368–378, 2025.
https://doi.org/10.1007/978-3-031-96255-4_34

nerves. These medical images are indispensable for diagnosis, treatment planning, and disease monitoring. Among these techniques, retinal fundus imaging offers critical information about eye conditions like retinal detachment, as well as systemic diseases such as hypertension, congenital anomalies like vascular malformations, and traumatic injuries. Additionally, fundus imaging allows for general health assessments, as the retina is the only part of the body where blood vessels can be directly observed. This unique feature provides a non-invasive way to evaluate vascular health, offering insights into systemic conditions that may impact a patient's overall health.

One of the main challenges in isolating or segmenting the Major Temporal Arcade (MTA) in retinal fundus images is the low contrast between blood vessels and the image background, the small width of the vessels, and non-uniform illumination. Typically, the automatic segmentation of blood vessels involves two steps: vessel enhancement (detection) and binary classification (segmentation). State-of-the-art methods often use thresholding strategies, with intra-class thresholding [1] being the most common. The key difference among these methods lies in the detection step, where the image is filtered in the spatial or frequency domain to correct non-uniform illumination and enhance vessel-like structures against the background.

In order to segment vessel-like structures, Eiho and Qian [2] suggested a mathematical morphology-based filter that uses a top-hat operator with a disk-shaped structuring element. MTA isolation was aided by the introduction of a multiscale top-hat operator by Qian et al. [3] to detect vessels at multiple scales. In order to calculate a vesselness measure, Frangi et al. [4] created a multiscale filter based on the Hessian matrix eigenvalues, which was subsequently modified in other research [5]. While Chaudhuri et al. [6] introduced the Gaussian Matched Filter, which was later improved for multiscale vessel detection utilizing neural networks [7], Nguyen et al. [8] suggested a multiscale linear filter for retinal vessel detection. Gabor filters, with modifications for multiscale analysis [9], have been extensively used in the frequency domain for automatic vessel detection [10].

Deep learning methods, such as U-Net [11], have advanced automatic vessel segmentation across various medical images, including coronary arteries in X-ray angiograms, retinal fundus images [12], phase-contrast tomography [13], and 3D blood vessel lumen [14]. However, segmenting the MTA remains under-explored. Oloumi et al. [15,16] employed the Hough transform for MTA modeling in diabetic retinopathy, using single-scale and multiscale Gabor filters for segmentation. Alvarado et al. [17] applied U-Net for MTA segmentation using second-order splines. Soto et al. [18] combined multiscale linear filtering with thresholding and length filtering, integrating Jacobi polynomials for numerical modeling. However, these approaches (Gabor filters, U-Net, and multiscale filtering) struggled to robustly separate the MTA from smaller vessels in terms of length and width.

This paper introduces a new method for the automatic segmentation of the Major Temporal Arcade based on the deep learning U-Net architecture ENHANCED with an attention module. The method is evaluated for segmenting the Superior and Inferior Temporal Arcades while removing all non-MTA vessel-like structures. The first step involves transfer learning using the VGG-16 architecture to segment all blood vessel structures, employing a patch-based strategy with 64×64-pixel subimages. The second step uses an attention module to extract the MTA from the segmented image, guided by ground-truth MTA outlines provided by specialists. The method is evaluated using binary metrics such as Sensitivity, Specificity, Accuracy, and F1-score, and compared with state-of-the-art filter-based techniques (spatial and frequency domains) and the U-Net architecture on a retinal fundus image database.

2 Materials and Methods

This section presents the fundamentals of the U-Net architecture, a widely used convolutional neural network for medical image segmentation, as well as the use of VGG16 as a backbone. In addition, the database of manual delineations of the Major Temporal Arcade in retinal fundus images used for this work is described.

2.1 Database of Major Temporal Arcade

For this study, the publicly accessible DRIVE database of retinal fundus images was utilized. Typically, this database serves as a benchmark for comparing algorithms in the context of automatic blood vessel segmentation. The DRIVE images with the specific goal of segmenting the Major Temporal Arcade [19] while eliminating other vessel-like structures that are not part of the MTA. The database comprises 35 RGB images, each with a resolution of 576×576 pixels. The corresponding ground-truth images are in binary format, where low-intensity pixels represent the background and high-intensity pixels indicate the manually outlined MTA.

2.2 U-Net Deep Learning Architecture

Deep learning is a branch of artificial intelligence that utilizes deep neural networks to model and solve complex problems, simulating human decision-making abilities. It has demonstrated remarkable effectiveness in various fields, including image classification. In the domain of biomedical imaging, deep learning has transformed the way these data are analyzed and processed, leading to significant advancements in diagnosis, treatment, and research. The deep learning application in biomedical imaging that is most relevant to our work is segmentation. Through CNNs, it is possible to achieve precise segmentation of organs and tissues in medical images, providing essential support for physicians in clinical decision-making and medical planning.

The capacity of U-Net to process large-scale images while maintaining spatial information–a critical component in segmentation tasks–is one of its main advantages. The encoder and the decoder are the two primary parts of the architecture. After extracting local characteristics like edges and textures using a sequence of convolutional layers, the encoder downsamples the spatial dimensions while keeping the most pertinent features. Furthermore, skip connections ensure that the spatial structure of the original image is maintained and facilitate an efficient reconstruction by connecting the encoder's outputs to the respective layers in the decoder. The U-Net architecture, emphasizing important functions like max pooling, transposed convolutions (also known as up-convolutions), and convolutions.

U-Net has been widely used for a variety of image segmentation tasks, despite being first created for medical imaging purposes. It is especially renowned for having a symmetrical structure and for being able to segment data precisely even with a minimal amount of training data. The encoder, sometimes called the contraction path, and the decoder, also called the expanding path, are the two primary steps around which the architecture is organized. Convolutional layers and downsampling techniques, which lower spatial resolution while capturing high-level information, are used by the encoder to extract key visual features. In the meantime, the decoder uses the features that the encoder extracted to rebuild the segmented image. In order to preserve the form and structure of the objects in the image, it integrates rich spatial information while restoring the original resolution through upsampling and convolutional layers.

VGG16. Today, segmentation networks such as U-Net can use VGG16 as a backbone. The convolutional layers in these applications are initialized using the pretrained weights of VGG16 and subsequently refined or expanded for particular tasks, such medical picture segmentation. This method works very well for identifying structures in biological images. To achieve exact segmentation in medical image analysis, which promotes accurate diagnosis, comprehensive feature extraction is crucial. Convolutional neural networks have proven to be quite effective at capturing complex visual features; VGG16 stands out for its robustness and ease of use. It is highly suited for applications that need to discern fine-grained characteristics like textures, forms, and intensity fluctuations inside images because of its 16-layer deep design, which allows it to learn intricate shapes and patterns. Figure 1 presents the base architecture of VGG16.

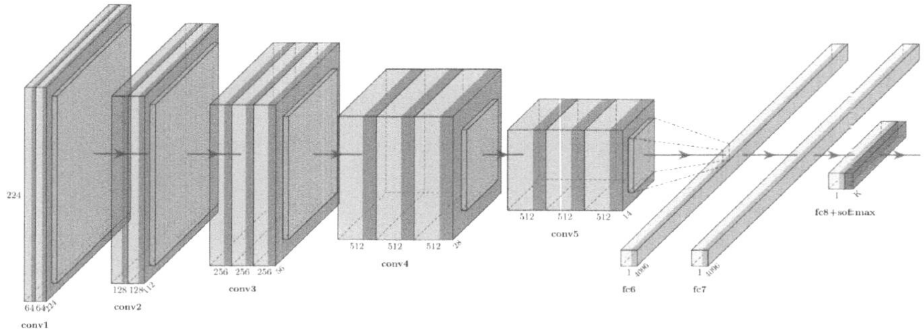

Fig. 1. VGG16 architecture.

The input image is scanned by the 3×3 convolutional filters, which produce feature maps that identify regional patterns. Every filter is made to capture particular characteristics, like textures and edges. Each layer's feature maps are weighted mixtures of the features that were extracted in earlier layers. The network develops a hierarchical representation of pictures by stacking many convolutional layers, collecting both increasingly complex patterns (like forms and objects) and low-level characteristics (like edges and contours).

3 Proposed U-Net Architecture Based Attention Module

To segment the MTA in retinal fundus images (576×576 pixels), we use a U-Net model pre-trained on VGG16 with an attention module. VGG16 extracts features, allowing U-Net to capture both high-level and fine-grained vascular details. The model addresses challenges like noise, overlapping vessels, and variable lighting. By using ground-truth images for training, it separates the Major Temporal Arcade from other veins, improving segmentation accuracy. This approach aids in clinical evaluations, automated measurements, and disease diagnosis by focusing on relevant structures. Figure 2 illustrates the architecture of the U-Net model with integrated attention modules. These modules enhance the network's ability to focus on relevant features, improving segmentation accuracy by filtering out irrelevant information.

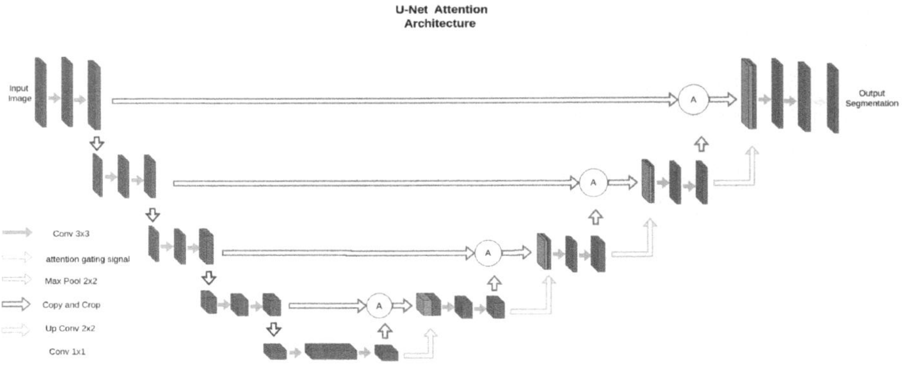

Fig. 2. Proposed U-Net attention architecture.

The attention mechanism, inspired by human cognition, helps neural networks focus on important image areas. It assigns different weights to input features, improving feature selection by highlighting key structures and reducing background noise. This is especially useful in retinal segmentation, where distinguishing vessels of varying sizes and intensities can be challenging. The mechanism calculates importance by comparing queries with keys through a dot product. The softmax function is then used for a normalization step. Attention can be expressed mathematically as follows:

$$\text{Attention}(Q, K, V) = \text{softmax}\left(\frac{QK^T}{\sqrt{d_k}}\right)V \quad (1)$$

where d_k is the dimensionality of the keys, Q is the query matrix, K is the key matrix, and V is the value matrix. By ensuring that the weights assigned to the various input items add up to 1, the softmax operation highlights the most significant features while suppressing those that are less pertinent. By including this method into the segmentation framework, the model can improve segmentation quality by removing interference from nearby vessels and focusing its attention on the Major Temporal Arcade.

In order to manage intricate, overlapping vasculature, a U-Net model uses patch-based segmentation in the first step to segment all visible veins in the retinal fundus image. The MTA and other veins are included in the mask that is created by segmenting the image into patches and then reconstructing it. This method improves accuracy and speed by lowering spatial variability, maintaining details, and enabling parallel processing. The results are then further refined by the attention-enhanced U-Net.

A U-Net with an attention module that has been pre-trained on VGG16 then suppresses noise, irrelevant structures, and changes in lighting in order to concentrate on the MTA. This stage reduces false positives, avoids over-segmentation, and adjusts for vessel thickness and image quality changes using ground-truth pictures that only contain the MTA. More accurate anatomical analysis for medical diagnostics is made possible by the improved segmentation.

4 Experimental Results

This section presents the results obtained from the segmentation of the MTA using the proposed method, along with a comparison against several traditional methods. Two distinct computer hardware configurations were used for the computational studies described in this section. Matlab version R2023b was used to accomplish the set of cutting-edge blood vessel enhancement techniques based on spatial and frequency filtering on a computer with a 12th Gen Intel(R) Core(TM) i7, 2.10 GHz processor, and 32 GB of RAM. The PyTorch 2.4.0 library was used to implement the deep learning architectures, which were run on an Intel(R) Xeon(R) Silver 4214 CPU running at 2.20 GHz with 128 GB of RAM and an Nvidia Titan RTX with 24 GB of RAM.

Five specialized blood vessel enhancement techniques were employed to segment the major temporal arcade and evaluate the effectiveness of the proposed approach. Eiho and Qian [3] introduced a morphology-based filter in the spatial domain using the Top-Hat operator, where the filter size was a key parameter. After testing values within the range [5,15] on the training set, the optimal size was determined to be nine pixels, yielding the highest F1-score. Nguyen et al. [10] proposed a multi-scale spatial filter based on linear structures to enhance blood vessels, tuning the scale parameter within the range [7, 17]. By refining the parameter search, the best-performing range was identified as [15:2:19], achieving the highest F1-score. Frangi et al. [5] developed a Hessian-based vesselness filter that computes a vesselness measure based on the eigenvalues of the Hessian matrix. The method required selecting a sigma range to capture vessels of varying widths, and after evaluating values with a stride of 0.5, the optimal range was found to be [1:0.5:7], maximizing the F1-score. Chaudhuri et al. [11] designed a Gaussian-matrixed filter where the sigma value controls the detected vessel width. By expanding the search space to [1.5,3] and adjusting the stride values, the optimal sigma was determined to be 1.75 based on the highest F1-score. Lastly, the single-scale Gabor filter, operating in the frequency domain, was controlled by width, length, and the number of oriented filters. The width parameter played a crucial role in detecting vessels of varying thicknesses, and after testing values within the range [4.5,7], the highest F1-score was obtained with a width of 7 pixels.

For deep learning architectures, there are two training sessions. In the first, the layers of the VGG16 are frozen to prevent training and allow the model to adjust to the kind of issue at hand. The layers of the VGG16 are unfrozen and all of the data is trained at once after this training is complete and the model starts to be focused on the particular issue. Through this process, the architecture may better adapt to the issue and produce better outcomes. Both models use a retinal fundus picture as input for the MTA segmentation, which includes segmenting the veins in general.

The results of the automatic MTA segmentation comparison between the state-of-the-art, the computational time and the suggested approach are shown in Table 1. Sensitivity, specificity, accuracy, and the F1-score measure are used to compare the methods. The previously calculated parameter tuning step was used in the experiment to carry out the vessel improvement techniques based on spatial or frequency filters. The deep learning architectures and the Hessian-based approach are the best performing methodologies.

Table 1. Comparative and time analysis between the proposed and comparative methods for automatic MTA segmentation.

Method	Sensitivity	Specificity	Accuracy	F1-score	Testing time in seconds (per image)
Mathematical Morphology [3]	0.6715	0.9481	0.9428	0.3097	1.84
Linear Multi-scale [10]	**0.7800**	0.9315	0.9286	0.2946	1.43
Multi-scale Hessian [5]	0.3552	0.9952	0.9829	0.4434	1.63
Gaussian Matched Filter [11]	0.4087	0.9614	0.9508	0.2412	1.46
Single-scale Gabor [16]	0.6991	0.9579	0.9530	0.3624	1.57
U-Net Architecture [17]	0.3457	**0.9994**	0.9869	0.5032	0.0002
Proposed U-Net Attention	0.6730	0.9985	**0.9923**	**0.7700**	0.0003

Figure 3 presents the confusion matrix, which summarizes the classification results of the segmentation model. This matrix provides insights into the model's performance, showing how well it distinguishes between vessel and background pixels. The high number of true negatives suggests that the model effectively identifies non-vessel areas, while the false positive and false negative values indicate the areas where misclassifications occur.

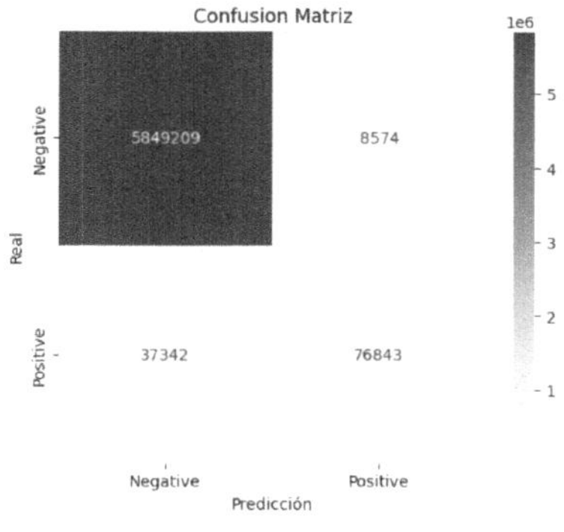

Fig. 3. Confusion matrix of the test images.

In Fig. 4, the results obtained for the initial segmentation of all arterial structures in the DRIVE images are presented. Additionally, the exclusive segmentation of the Major Temporal Arcade is shown, along with a comparison against the ground truth. These visualizations provide a clear assessment of the effectiveness of the proposed method in isolating the MTA while preserving relevant anatomical details.

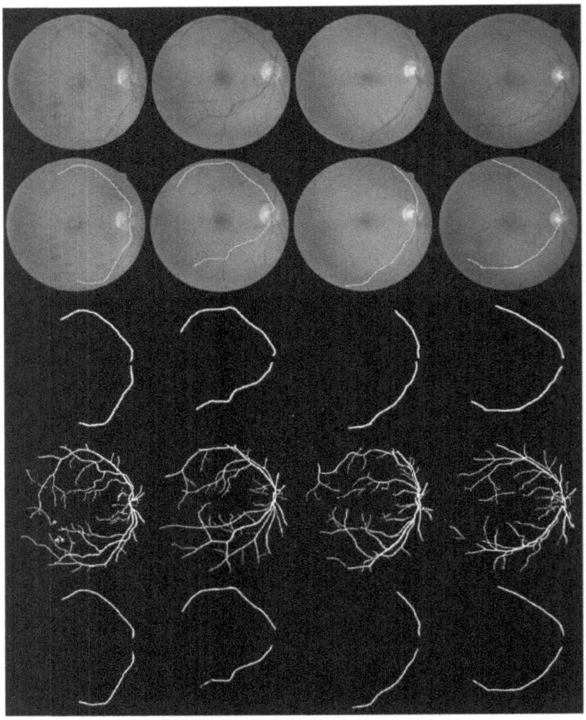

Fig. 4. First row: Retinal fundus images. Second row: Original image with the MTA outline. Third row: Ground truth for MTA segmentation. Fourth row: Results of the initial segmentation of all arterial structures. Fifth row: Exclusive segmentation of the MTA.

5 Conclusions

In this paper a novel deep learning method for the automatic segmentation of the MTA in retinal fundus images using a U-Net-based architecture was introduced. The proposed approach successfully separates the target structure while removing irrelevant vessel-like features by combining a segmentation stage with transfer learning from the VGG-16 model and an attention module for MTA refining. With an accuracy of 0.9923 and an F1-score of 0.7700 on the test set, experimental data show that the method performs better than the most advanced vascular segmentation algorithms. Furthermore, with an average processing time of just 0.003 s per image, the model demonstrates remarkable computational efficiency. These results demonstrate how deep learning-based architectures may be used for precise and effective MTA segmentation, which could lead to better retinal vascular characterization in therapeutic settings.

Acknowledgments. This research has been supported by the project IxM-SECIHTI No. 3097-7185

References

1. Otsu, N.: A threshold selection method from gray-level histograms. IEEE Trans. Syst. Man Cybern. **9**, 62–66 (1979)
2. Eiho, S., Qian, Y.: Detection of coronary artery tree using morphological operator. Comput. Cardiol. **24**, 525–528 (1997)
3. Qian, Y., Eiho, S., Sugimoto, N., Fujita, M.: Automatic extraction of coronary artery tree on coronary angiograms by morphological operators. Comput. Cardiol. **25**, 765–768 (1998)
4. Frangi, A., Niessen, W., Vincken, K., Viergever, M.: Multiscale vessel enhancement filtering. In: Medical Image Computing and Computer-Assisted Intervention (MICCAI 98). LNCS, vol. 1496, pp. 130–137. Springer, Cham (1998)
5. Salem, N.M., Salem, S.A., Nandi, A.K.: Segmentation of retinal blood vessels based on analysis of the hessian matrix and clustering algorithm. In: 15th European Signal Processing Conference (EUSIPCO 2007). Springer Lecture Notes in Computer Science, pp. 428–432 (2007)
6. Chaudhuri, S., Chatterjee, S., Katz, N., Nelson, M., Goldbaum, M.: Detection of blood vessels in retinal images using two-dimensional matched filters. IEEE Trans. Med. Imaging **8**, 263–269 (1989)
7. Cruz-Aceves, I., Cervantes-Sanchez, F., Avila-Garcia, M.S.: A novel multiscale Gaussian-matched filter using neural networks for the segmentation of x-ray coronary angiograms. J. Healthc. Eng. **2018**, 5812059 (2018). https://doi.org/10.1155/2018/5812059
8. Nguyen, U.T., Bhuiyan, A., Park, L.A., Ramamohanarao, K.: An effective retinal blood vessel segmentation method using multi-scale line detection. Pattern Recognit. **46**, 703–715 (2013)
9. Rangayyan, R.M., Ayres, F.J., Oloumi, F., Oloumi, F., Eshghzadeh-Zanjani, P.: Detection of blood vessels in the retina with multiscale Gabor filters, J Electr. Imaging **17**, 023018:1–023018:7 (2008)
10. Ayres, F.J., Rangayyan, R.M.: Design and performance analysis of oriented feature detectors, J. Electr. Imaging **16**, 023007:1–023007:12 (2007)
11. Ronneberger, O., Fischer, P., Brox, T.: U-Net: convolutional networks for biomedical image segmentation. In: Navab, N., Hornegger, J., Wells, W.M., Frangi, A.F. (eds.) MICCAI 2015. LNCS, vol. 9351, pp. 234–241. Springer, Cham (2015). https://doi.org/10.1007/978-3-319-24574-4_28
12. Singh, L.K., Khanna, M., Thawkar, S. et al. Deep-learning based system for effective and automatic blood vessel segmentation from Retinal fundus images. Multimed. Tools Appl. **83**, 6005–6049 (2024). https://doi.org/10.1007/s11042-023-15348-3
13. Yagis, E., et al.: Deep Learning for 3D Vascular Segmentation in Phase Contrast Tomography. Research Square, rs-3 (2024)
14. Materka, A., Jurek, J.: Using deep learning and b-splines to model blood vessel lumen from 3D images. Sensors, **24**(3), 846 (2024). https://doi.org/10.3390/s24030846
15. Oloumi, F., Rangayyan, R.M., Ells, A.L.: Parabolic modeling of the major temporal arcade in retinal fundus images. IEEE Trans. Instrum. Meas. **61**, 1825–1838 (2012)
16. Oloumi, F., Rangayyan, R.M., Ells, A.L.: Computer-aided diagnosis of proliferative diabetic retinopathy via modeling of the major temporal arcade in retinal fundus images. J. Digit. Imaging **26**, 1124–1130 (2013)

17. Alvarado-Carrillo, D.E., Cruz-Aceves, I., Hernández-González, M.A., López-Montero, L.M.: Robust detection and modeling of the major temporal arcade in retinal fundus images. Mathematics **10**, 1334 (2022)
18. Soto-Álvarez, J.A., Cruz-Aceves, I., Hernández-Aguirre, A., Hernández-González, M.A., López-Montero, L.M., Solorio-Meza, S.E.: Numerical modeling of the major temporal arcade using BUMDA and Jacobi polynomials. Axioms, **12**(2), 137 (2023). https://doi.org/10.3390/axioms12020137
19. Soto-Álvarez, J., Cruz-Aceves, I., Hernández-Aguirre, A., Hernández-González, M., López-Montero, L., Solorio-Meza, S.: Numerical modeling of the major temporal arcade using BUMDA and Jacobi polynomials. Axioms, **12**(2), 137 (2023). https://doi.org/10.3390/axioms12020137

A Lightweight Diffusion Model with Modified Sampler

Matias Grynberg Portnoy[1] and Emmanuel Ovalle-Magallanes[2](✉)

[1] Facultad de Ciencias Exactas y Naturales, Universidad de Buenos Aires, Av. Int. Cantilo, C1428, Cdad. Autónoma de Buenos Aires, Argentina

[2] Dirección de Investigación y Doctorado, Facultad de Ingenierías y Tecnologías, Universidad La Salle Bajío, Av. Universidad 602. Col. Lomas del Campestre, 37150 León, Guanajuato, Mexico

eovalle@lasallebajio.edu.mx

Abstract. Generative models hold great potential in various applications, such as anomaly detection, image-to-image translation, super-resolution, and denoising. However, their complexity can make implementation and reproducibility challenging, hindering progress, creating barriers to adoption, and discouraging comparisons with existing methods. In this work, we propose a lightweight diffusion architecture with a simplified sampling procedure. We input the noise multiplier directly into the model rather than the timestep t. This design aims to balance computational cost and performance. We investigate how various parameters and architectural blocks impact generation quality, specifically measured using the Fréchet Inception Distance (FID). The proposed architecture is evaluated on two distinct tasks: face generation and super-resolution using the CelebA dataset. Our results demonstrate that the architecture achieves promising performance across these tasks, making it a viable option for scenarios requiring a compact model. We provide the related architecture and training code at https://github.com/mgp123/diffusion-learning.

Keywords: Diffusion model · Lightweight model · Super-resolution · U-Net · Unconditional face generation

1 Introduction

Current research has rendered modern generative models remarkable in their ability to approximate their target distribution. Diffusion Models (DMs), introduced by Sohl-Dickstein *et al.* [14], are a class of these generative models that have shown impressive results in multiple domains. They have been used in a wide range of applications such as unconditional image generation [2], super-resolution [12], conditional image generation [10], video generation [13], and audio [6].

A. P. López-Monroy et al. (Eds.): MCPR 2025, LNCS 15715, pp. 379–389, 2025.
https://doi.org/10.1007/978-3-031-96255-4_35

DMs aim to generate new data samples by iteratively refining random noise into a structured data point. They involve two main processes: forward diffusion (used during training) and reverse diffusion (used during inference).

In the forward diffusion process, Gaussian noise is progressively added to the data, gradually destroying its structure and transforming it into pure noise. The forward process is a Markov chain, where each step slightly perturbs the data with Gaussian noise and attenuates the input. A variance schedule controls the noise level added at each step. Following the variance-preserving formulation, at each time-step t, the data x_t is generated from the previous time step's data x_{t-1} by scaling the original input tensor and adding Gaussian noise $\epsilon \sim N(0, \boldsymbol{I})$ as follows:

$$x_t = \sqrt{\alpha_t} x_{t-1} + \sqrt{1 - \alpha_t} \epsilon, \tag{1}$$

with α_t being responsible for the variance schedule. This parameter controls the amount of noise added at each step. Thus, we have the conditional distribution of $p(x_t|x_{t-1}) = \mathcal{N}(x_t; \sqrt{\alpha_t} x_{t-1}, (1 - \alpha_t)\mathbf{I})$, with $p(\cdot)$ denoting the true distribution of each diffusion step associated with this technique.

Given that the sum of Gaussian random variables is Gaussian, we can get the distribution of the t step conditioned on the original input x_0 as:

$$x_t = \sqrt{\hat{\alpha_t}} x_0 + \sqrt{1 - \hat{\alpha_t}} \epsilon, \tag{2}$$

with $\hat{\alpha_t} = \prod^t \alpha_k$. The schedule is chosen so that $\hat{\alpha_t}$ decreases monotonically from 1 to 0 as timesteps increase. The associated distribution is $p(x_t|x_0) = \mathcal{N}(x_t; \sqrt{\hat{\alpha_t}} x_0, (1 - \hat{\alpha_t})\mathbf{I})$.

In contrast, the reverse diffusion process aims to reconstruct the original data by reversing the noise addition process. This is achieved by training a neural network to predict the noise ϵ in Eq. 2, allowing the model to iteratively denoise the data step by step until the original distribution is restored. Given that the forward process is a Markov Chain, the reverse process is also a Markov Chain. Thus, the distribution of the previous step x_{t-1} is independent of larger steps when conditioned on x_t.

In this work, we propose a lightweight diffusion architecture with a novel, simplified sampling procedure and explore how different parameters affect generation quality. We also evaluate the model on two tasks: face generation and super-resolution, using the CelebA dataset. Our results show that the proposed architecture performs reasonably well in both tasks, making it a practical, compact model. However, we find that the model is brittle–that is, its final performance is highly sensitive to the training run, which can significantly affect the resulting quality.

2 Related Work

Since DMs were introduced (see Fig. 1 for an illustration of the general pipeline), several modifications have been proposed to improve both the quality and efficiency of these models. One of the main breakthroughs is the Denoising Diffusion

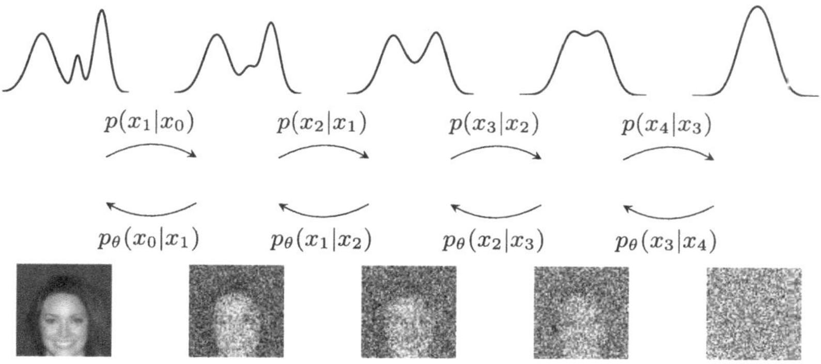

Fig. 1. Diffusion process. The first row depicts the change in the marginal distribution X_i for the different steps. The second row shows the Markov chain and associated learned reverse dynamics. The third row shows the diffusion process for a particular sample.

Probabilistic Model (DDPM), introduced by Ho *et al.* [5], that formulates the reverse diffusion process as follows:

$$x_{t-1} = \frac{1}{\sqrt{\alpha_t}}\left(x_t - \frac{1-\alpha_t}{\sqrt{1-\bar{\alpha}_t}}\epsilon_\theta(x_t, t)\right) + \sigma_t \epsilon, \tag{3}$$

where ϵ_θ is a neural network parameterized by θ, which estimates the noise ϵ described in Eq. 2, and σ_t is a predefined standard deviation for the Gaussian noise added at time step t. Subsequent improvements to DDPMs were made by Nichol et al. [7], who introduced a cosine noise schedule as an alternative to the linear schedule and proposed a learned diagonal Gaussian with a specific parametrization for the reverse process.

Building on these models, Denoising Diffusion Implicit Models (DDIMs), introduced by Song et al. [15], modify DDPMs to allow deterministic and faster sampling. DDIMs improve efficiency without compromising sample quality by altering the reverse process, enabling fewer sampling steps. The sampling process is defined as:

$$\begin{aligned} x_{t-1} = &\sqrt{\hat{\alpha}_{t-1}}\left(\frac{x_t - \sqrt{1-\hat{\alpha}_t}\epsilon_\theta(x_t, t)}{\sqrt{\hat{\alpha}_t}}\right) \\ &+ \sqrt{1-\hat{\alpha}_{t-1}-\sigma_t^2}\epsilon_\theta(x_t, t) + \sigma_t \epsilon, \end{aligned} \tag{4}$$

where ϵ_θ is the predicted noise, ϵ being sampled Gaussian noise, and $\hat{\alpha}_t$ denoting the noise schedule. Here, σ_t acts as a step-dependent multiplier of the new noise added to the previous step. DDIMs are characterized by setting $\sigma_t = 0$, making the reverse process deterministic.

Other architectural modifications for diffusion models have also yielded good results such as using a transformer architecture instead of a U-Net [9] or preprocessing the input using a variational autoencoder [11] to reduce the input size without impacting quality.

Capitalizing on these advances in DMs, several efforts have been made to reduce computational costs, memory footprint, and inference time, making diffusion models more practical for a wider range of applications and resource-constrained environments. The lightweightness of DMs is achieved through a diverse set of techniques targeting various aspects of the model, including network architecture, parameter representation, training and sampling processes, and the integration of complementary methods [16]. In this way, Zhang [19] explores substituting the traditional encoder in the U-Net of DDPM with SqueezeNet and MobileNet, which are designed for efficiency. The results show that these lightweight architectures can achieve comparable performance with reduced computational resources. Similarly, Zhou *et al.* [20] introduces AMamba, which integrates attention mechanisms into the Vision Mamba (Vim) architecture to create a lightweight and efficient backbone. An *et al.* [1] propose an efficient sampling method for remote sensing image super-resolution by using the deterministic nature of DDIM sampling and significantly reducing the number of sampling steps through respacing, leading to faster image generation while maintaining a balance between precision and perceptual quality.

3 Method

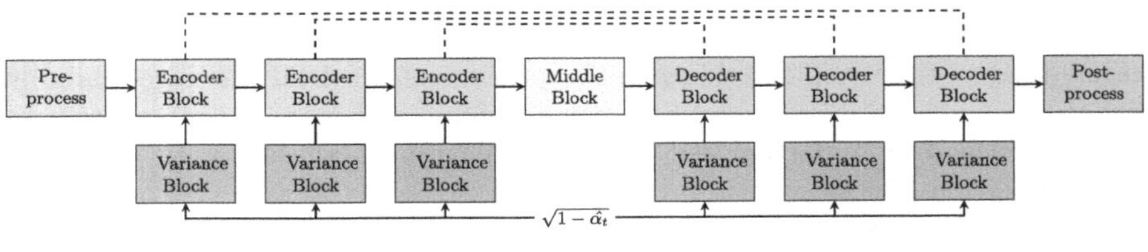

Fig. 2. Diagram of the proposed U-Net architecture. The pre and post-processing are simple blocks that change the channels from and to the original data channels (3 for image generation) to the chosen U-Net internal channels using a hyperparameter. The dashed lines depict residual connections.

We propose a lightweight diffusion architecture with a simplified sampling procedure and explore how different parameters affect generation quality, measured using the Fréchet Inception Distance (FID). We also evaluate the architecture on two tasks: face generation and super-resolution, using the CelebA dataset.

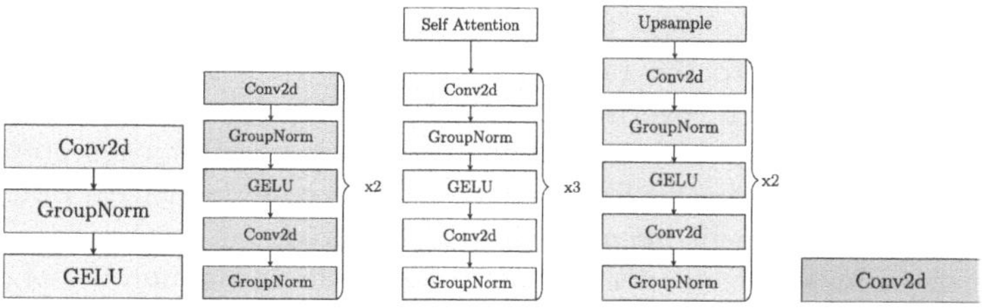

Fig. 3. Architecture of main blocks. From left to right. Pre-processing block, encoder block, middle block, decoder block, and post-processing block.

3.1 Architecture

We employed a U-Net architecture composed of encoder and decoder blocks, each consisting of convolutions, Gaussian Error Linear Units (GELUs), and group normalization layers. The number of channels doubles at each encoder stage. Spatial scaling is performed through strided convolution in the encoder and upsampling in the decoder. The full architecture is illustrated in Fig. 2 and Fig. 3, which shows each model block in detail. In addition, we proposed a specific sampling strategy, implemented a cosine noise schedule with $T = 1000$, and generated samples using 200 steps without learning the reverse variance during the sampling procedure. This unconditional generative model comprises 122,272,515 trainable parameters and requires approximately 2.26×10^{10} FLOPs per diffusion step.

Our approach differs from [3] in several important aspects. First, rather than feeding the model the timestep t, we directly input the noise multiplier $\sqrt{1 - \hat{\alpha}_t}$, aiming to improve training efficiency by removing the need for the model to infer the time-to-noise relationship. The timestep remains recoverable since $\sqrt{1 - \hat{\alpha}_t}$ is a monotonically increasing function of t. The corresponding variance blocks include two linear layers that produce a scale and bias term for input rescaling, followed by group normalization.

Second, instead of interleaving attention blocks with the encoder and decoder stages, we include a single attention block positioned at the beginning of the middle block. This design choice was made in response to computational constraints during training.

Third, our sampling procedure is based on the method proposed by Song *et al.* [15], where the standard deviation is defined as $\sigma_t = \sqrt{c(1 - \hat{\alpha}_{t-1})}$ for a fixed $c \in [0, 1]$. This formulation acts as a variance-preserving interpolation between the model-predicted noise and a newly sampled noise. The sampling update is then expressed as

$$x_{t-1} = \sqrt{\hat{\alpha}_{t-1}}\,\hat{x}_0 + \sqrt{1 - \hat{\alpha}_{t-1}}\left(\sqrt{1-c}\,\epsilon_\theta(x_t, t) + \sqrt{c}\,\epsilon\right), \tag{5}$$

where the predicted image is computed as

$$\hat{x}_0 = \text{clip}\left(\frac{x_t - \sqrt{1 - \hat{\alpha}_t}\,\epsilon_\theta(x_t, t)}{\sqrt{\hat{\alpha}_t}}\right), \tag{6}$$

with $\epsilon \sim \mathcal{N}(0, \boldsymbol{I})$ and $\epsilon_\theta(x_t, t)$ the noise estimated by the model. The reconstruction $\hat{x}_0$ is clipped to the range $[-1, 1]$. Notably, setting $c = 0$ results in deterministic sampling, recovering the vanilla DDIM formulation, while $c = 1$ corresponds to fully stochastic sampling using new noise at each step. To our knowledge, this straightforward adjustment, when combined with our architectural modifications, has not been previously explored.

Lastly, the number of encoder/decoder blocks, the initial number of channels, and the size of the middle block are configurable hyperparameters. In our experiments, we investigate how different values of c influence the quality of generated samples.

3.2 Implementation Details

The diffusion model is implemented in PyTorch. Training is done using a single RTX 4090 GPU and with Adam Optimizer. In Fig. 3, we show the layers that make up the main blocks. The first convolution in the encoder and decoder blocks doubling and halving the channels, respectively. The decoder blocks receive a channel-wise concatenation of the residual connection and the previous block. With the variance blocks simply scaling and shifting the encoder/decoder outputs.

4 Results

To better understand the applicability of our architecture, we test it in different tasks: first, unconditional generation, and then Super-resolution, an example of image-conditioned generation. We use the CelebA dataset for this, where standard partitioning is used: approximately 162,770 images for training.

4.1 Generation

We train on the CelebA dataset, which consists of 218×178 pixels images. We reshape the images to 64×64 by resizing and random cropping to preserve proportions. We also augment the dataset with random horizontal flips. We measure the FID score [4] as a function of the value c for the already trained model. We sample over 1,000 images from the model per multiplier and use a subset of the CelebA dataset for this comparison. Figure 4 shows these results after training. The lowest FID is obtained with $c \approx 0.15$ and a corresponding FID of 26.94. Visually, however, we find results more realistic with $c \approx 0.45$, which can be seen in Fig. 5.

Additionally, in Fig. 6, we show the effect of the different modules on image generation by zeroing out the output connections during sampling. We notice that the first residual connections have the smallest influence on the generated images, mostly contributing to minor changes in the generation but preserving the general structure. This indicates that the most shallow residual connection carries little information. Furthermore, this hints that our network can be pruned

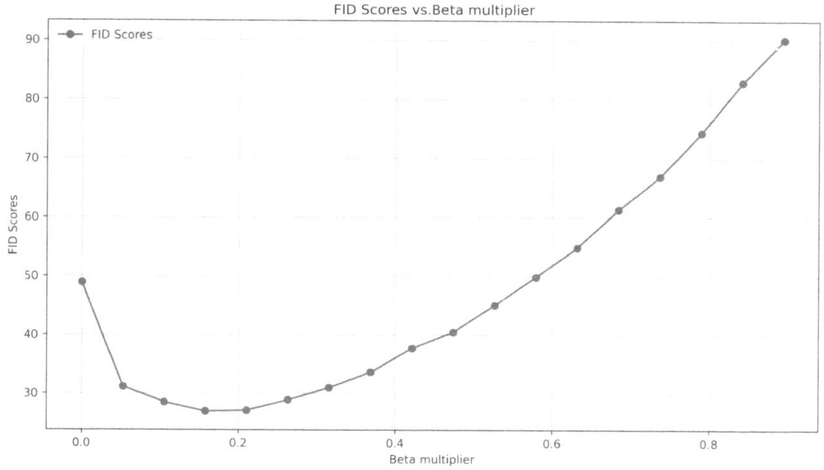

Fig. 4. How the FID score changes as we move c.

Fig. 5. Samples drawn from different noise multipliers while keeping the same seed. From left to right $c = 0.15, 0.25, 0.35, 0.45, 0.5$.

to reduce parameter size while keeping generation quality. One such trick is to remove the related weights and continue training. Furthermore, training a similar, albeit smaller, architecture from scratch may also yield useful results.

Table 1 presents a comparative analysis of various generative models regarding FID, model size, and sampling efficiency on the CelebA-64 × 64 dataset.

Fig. 6. Effect of zeroing outputs from different modules from the network trained with $c = 0.35$. From left to right: Original, First encoder block, first decoder block, first residual connection, second encoder block, second decoder block, second residual connection, third encoder block, third decoder block, third residual connection.

We report the number of model parameters (in millions - M), the number of sampling steps required during inference, and the total number of generated images used to compute the FID.

Diffusion-based models, such as DDPM and DDIM, rely on a reverse denoising process that requires hundreds to thousands of sampling steps, making them computationally intensive but capable of achieving competitive FID scores. In contrast, Patch Diffusion demonstrates improved efficiency by significantly reducing the number of steps to just 25, while also achieving the lowest FID among all methods compared.

While our method achieves a substantially higher FID score, it is included to provide a baseline under a different set of sampling conditions: It uses only 1,000 generated samples (compared to 50,000 in most cases) and employs 200 sampling steps. Additionally, our model is relatively compact at 122.27M parameters. The reduced sample count may partially explain the degraded FID, as this metric is known to be sensitive to the number of images evaluated. This comparison highlights key trade-offs between model complexity, sampling speed, and generation quality across different generative paradigms.

4.2 Super-Resolution

For the super-resolution case, we upsample images from 64×64 resolution to 128×128 resolution. Given the increased memory requirements and the additional information provided to the model to predict the noise, we make the architecture smaller, using two encoder/decoder blocks instead of three. This new architecture has 29,963,907 trainable parameters, approximately four times smaller than our unconditional generative model. We concatenate a lower resolution image upsampled to 128×128 x_{low} via interpolation to the input size. We also incorporate this x_{low} into the sampling procedure to improve results as follows:

Table 1. Comparison of FID scores, model size, and sampling details on CelebA-64×64. N/A: Not Applicable. *Using the same model as DDIM

Method	# Params (M)	Sampling Steps	Sampled images	FID
DiffuseVAE [8]	-	1000	10,000	3.97
DDIM [15]	78.7	1000	50,000	3.51
DDPM* [15]	78.7	1000	50,000	3.26
NVAE [17]	153.3	N/A	50,000	2.03
Patch Diffusion [18]	-	50	50,000	1.77
Ours (Best)	122.27	200	1,000	26.94

$$
\begin{aligned}
x_{t-1} = & \sqrt{\hat{\alpha}_{t-1}}\,(k \cdot x_{low} + (1-k) \cdot \hat{x}_0) \\
& + \sqrt{1-\hat{\alpha}_{t-1}} \cdot \left(\sqrt{1-c} \cdot \epsilon_\theta(x_t, t) + \sqrt{c} \cdot \epsilon\right)
\end{aligned} \tag{7}
$$

Similarly to the previous example, we explore how different metrics are affected by our parameters. First, by keeping $k = 0.95$ and varying c, and then by varying k and keeping c fixed. We measure the Structured Similarity Indexing Method (SSIM), Peak Signal-to-Noise Ratio (PSNR), and Mean Square Error (MSE) with respect to the true high-resolution images normalized to be in the $[0, 1]$ range. Numerical results are shown in Table 2. Naturally, given the high contribution to the resulting image from the upsampled version, the choice of c has little impact on the results. Varying k has a noticeable impact on the results both in terms of the metrics and on the qualitative results. We hypothesize that this is due to the fact that this trick may prevent an undertrained or incorrect model from having a major impact on the generation. Thus, the lower-resolution version serves as an anchor, given that x_{low} lies roughly in the neighborhood of x_{high}, the true high-resolution version. Samples from the model can be seen in Fig. 7.

Fig. 7. Example of applying super-resolution 64×64 to 128×128 using the generated images.

Table 2. Super resolution metrics for different sampling parameters. The best results in each block are highlighted.

Fixed $k = 0.95$, varying c					Fixed $c = 0.50$, varying k				
SSIM	PSNR	MSE	c	k	SSIM	PSNR	MSE	c	k
0.95	**33.92**	**22.38**	0.35	0.95	0.91	29.68	58.71	0.50	0.15
0.95	33.90	22.77	0.15	0.95	0.92	30.26	52.06	0.50	0.50
0.95	33.86	22.60	0.45	0.95	0.94	32.05	35.38	0.50	0.75
0.94	33.33	24.87	0.80	0.95	**0.95**	**33.80**	**22.82**	0.50	0.95

5 Conclusion

In this work, we presented a simple architecture and sampling that yielded promising results in two different tasks: unconditional face generation and super-resolution. Results also seem to hint that our network could be pruned while preserving generation quality. It is well known that the diffusion models require a lot of computational resources. Thus, a weak point of our architecture is that model quality depends on the batch size, leading to image quality diverging. Future work is needed to prevent this phenomenon and run more extensive tests to effectively measure the impact of different hyperparameters on the quality of the results. Moreover, further work could try to study the impact on generation quality using different training methods, such as learning *v-prediction* instead of the noise, comparing the effect of inputting the noise level to the model instead of the timestep, or the progress of the FID during training.

References

1. An, T., Xue, B., Huo, C., Xiang, S., Pan, C.: Efficient remote sensing image super-resolution via lightweight diffusion models. IEEE Geosci. Remote Sens. Lett. **21**, 1–5 (2023). https://doi.org/10.1109/LGRS.2023.3335421
2. Dhariwal, P., Nichol, A.: Diffusion models beat GANs on image synthesis. In: International Conference on Neural Information Processing Systems, pp. 8780–8794. Virtual (2021). https://doi.org/10.5555/3540261.3540933
3. Erdem, K.: Step by step visual introduction to diffusion models (2023). https://erdem.pl, https://erdem.pl/2023/11/step-by-step-visual-introduction-to-diffusion-models
4. Heusel, M., Ramsauer, H., Unterthiner, T., Nessler, B., Hochreiter, S.: Gans trained by a two time-scale update rule converge to a local Nash equilibrium. In: International Conference on Neural Information Processing Systems, vol. 30 (2017). https://doi.org/10.5555/3295222.3295408
5. Ho, J., Jain, A., Abbeel, P.: Denoising diffusion probabilistic models. In: Advances in Neural Information Processing Systems, vol. 33, pp. 6840–6851. Virtual (2020). https://proceedings.neurips.cc/paper/2020/hash/4c5bcfec8584af0d967f1ab10179ca4b-Abstract.html

6. Huang, R., Zhao, Z., Liu, H., Liu, J., Cui, C., Ren, Y.: ProDiff: progressive fast diffusion model for high-quality text-to-speech. In: International Conference on Multimedia, pp. 2595–2605 (2022). https://doi.org/10.1145/3503161.3547855
7. Nichol, A.Q., Dhariwal, P.: Improved denoising diffusion probabilistic models. In: International Conference on Machine Learning, pp. 8162–8171. PMLR (2021). https://proceedings.mlr.press/v139/nichol21a.html
8. Pandey, K., Mukherjee, A., Rai, P., Kumar, A.: DiffuseVAE: efficient, controllable and high-fidelity generation from low-dimensional latents. Trans. Mach. Learn. Res. (2022). https://openreview.net/forum?id=ygoNPRiLxw. accepted at TMLR
9. Peebles, W., Xie, S.: Scalable diffusion models with transformers. In: Proceedings of the IEEE/CVF International Conference on Computer Vision (ICCV), pp. 4172–4182. Paris (2023). https://doi.org/10.1109/ICCV51070.2023.00387
10. Ramesh, A., Dhariwal, P., Nichol, A., Chu, C., Chen, M.: Hierarchical text-conditional image generation with CLIP latents. arXiv preprint arXiv:2204.06125 (2022)
11. Rombach, R., Blattmann, A., Lorenz, D., Esser, P., Ommer, B.: High-resolution image synthesis with latent diffusion models. In: Proceedings of the IEEE/CVF Conference on Computer Vision and Pattern Recognition (CVPR), pp. 10684–10695. New Orleans (2022). https://doi.org/10.1109/CVPR52688.2022.01042
12. Saharia, C., Ho, J., Chan, W., Salimans, T., Fleet, D.J., Norouzi, M.: Image super-resolution via iterative refinement. IEEE Trans. Pattern Anal. Mach. Intell. **45**(4), 4713–4726 (2022). https://doi.org/10.1109/TPAMI.2022.3204461
13. Singer, U., et al.: Make-a-video: text-to-video generation without text-video data. arXiv preprint arXiv:2209.14792 (2022)
14. Sohl-Dickstein, J., Weiss, E., Maheswaranathan, N., Ganguli, S.: Deep unsupervised learning using nonequilibrium thermodynamics. In: International Conference on International Conference on Machine Learning, pp. 2256–2265. PMLR (2015). https://doi.org/10.5555/3045118.3045358
15. Song, J., Meng, C., Ermon, S.: Denoising diffusion implicit models. In: Proceedings of the 9th International Conference on Learning Representations. Virtual (2021). https://openreview.net/forum?id=St1giarCHLP
16. Song, W., Ma, W., Zhang, M., Zhang, Y., Zhao, X.: Lightweight diffusion models: a survey. Artif. Intell. Rev. **57**(6), 161 (2024). https://doi.org/10.1007/s10462-024-10800-8
17. Vahdat, A., Kautz, J.: NVAE: a deep hierarchical variational autoencoder. In: Advances in Neural Information Processing Systems, vol. 33, pp. 19667–19679. Virtual (2020). https://proceedings.neurips.cc/paper/2020/hash/e3b21256183cf7c2c7a66be163579d37-Abstract.html
18. Wang, Z., et al.: Patch diffusion: faster and more data-efficient training of diffusion models. In: Advances in Neural Information Processing Systems, vol. 36, pp. 72137–72154. Curran Associates, Inc., New Orleans, LA, USA (2023). https://openreview.net/forum?id=iv2sTQtbst
19. Zhang, J.: Optimizing denoising diffusion probabilistic models (DDPM) with lightweight architectures: applications of SqueezeNet and MobileNet. In: 2024 IEEE 2nd International Conference on Electrical, Automation and Computer Engineering (ICEACE), pp. 227–232. IEEE (2024). https://doi.org/10.1109/ICEACE63551.2024.10899026
20. Zhou, T., Yu, Y., Gao, Z.: A lightweight mamba backbone for diffusion models. In: 2024 3rd International Conference on Cloud Computing, Big Data Application and Software Engineering (CBASE), pp. 300–304. IEEE (2024). https://doi.org/10.1109/CBASE64041.2024.10824626

Unsupervised Emotion Analysis in Popular Music Lyrics in Mexico Using a BERT-Based Model

Arely Hilda Luis-Tiburcio and Marisol Flores-Garrido(✉)

Escuela Nacional de Estudios Superiores Unidad Morelia, Morelia, Mexico
mflores@enesmorelia.unam.mx

Abstract. This paper presents an unsupervised analysis of emotional patterns in popular lyrics in Mexico across seven decades. We introduce a corpus of 629 number-one hits, compiled from established sources starting in 1950. Our analysis includes lexical diversity, predominant emotion detection, and song characterization based on emotional profiles. For emotion detection, we use RoBERTuito, a BERT-based model trained for emotion classification in Spanish, to compute emotional scores for individual phrases. These scores are aggregated into statistical feature vectors representing each song across six emotions. Applying k-Means clustering, we identify three archetypal song categories and analyze their distribution over time. Additionally, we explore sequences of predominant emotions within songs, uncovering structural patterns in emotional expression. Despite challenges posed by the poetic and ambiguous nature of lyrics, our scalable computational framework advances digital humanities through a unique dataset, replicable emotion-analysis methodology, and the first large-scale data-driven study of popular lyrics in Mexico.

Keywords: Clustering · BERT · Emotional analysis · Song lyrics

1 Introduction

Music, as a cultural expression, is deeply situated within its temporal and spatial context, reflecting the collective ideas and emotions of the society from which it emerges. When music gains widespread adoption within a community, it often encapsulates and articulates shared sentiments, serving as a medium for expressing societal shifts, generational ruptures, and paradigm-breaking ideas. The analysis of song lyrics has proven to be a valuable tool for studying diverse cultural phenomena, ranging from violence and sexuality to themes of love and desire [8,13,14].

Natural Language Processing (NLP), a subfield of artificial intelligence, enables computers to interpret, generate, and manipulate human language [17]. A transformative advancement in NLP was the introduction of Transformers [23], a neural network architecture that leverages deep learning and self-attention mechanisms to process sequential data efficiently. These models have significantly

A. P. López-Monroy et al. (Eds.): MCPR 2025, LNCS 15715, pp. 390–400, 2025.
https://doi.org/10.1007/978-3-031-96255-4_36

enhanced the ability to analyze and understand textual data, making them particularly suitable for emotion analysis in song lyrics.

In this work, we present the first large-scale emotion-based analysis of popular music in Mexico, spanning 71 years and utilizing Spanish-trained transformer-based models. A key contribution of this study is the publicly released corpus of chart-topping songs, which enables both NLP and cultural studies.

Our methodology combines lexical and emotional analysis, employing a BERT-based model, and examines temporal trends and intra-song sequences. Through this approach and clustering techniques, we identify three main song types and trace their evolution over the studied period.

2 Related Work

The analysis of emotions in song lyrics has been explored in various contexts, though few studies have focused on Spanish-language music. Palomeque and Lucio [16] perform sentiment analysis on Billboard Hot 100 lyrics from Spain using VADER. Hernández-Lorenzo et al. [9] conduct a quantitative Digital Humanities analysis of Spanish contemporary song lyrics, examining their thematic and structural properties and comparing them with those found in poetry. In Mexico, studies have examined specific aspects of music lyrics [21, 22], but, to the best of our knowledge, this is the first data-driven and comprehensive exploration of popular lyrics in Mexico.

3 Proposed Methodology

3.1 Data

Since no existing dataset captures the most popular songs in Mexico comprehensively, we constructed one by consulting multiple sources. First, we compiled a list of 165 songs using data from Billboard's Hits of the World chart [1]. However, as this dataset was too limited for the time period we aimed to analyze, averaging only two songs per year, we expanded it by incorporating additional sources including radio charts, music magazines, and industry publications tracking record sales and airplay across different decades [2, 4, 11, 19].

From these sources, we extracted the song title, composer, artist/band, and year of peak popularity. Lyrics were collected using BeautifulSoup4 (bs4), a Python library for HTML parsing, primarily from the *Letras* platform [12]. When lyrics were unavailable on *Letras*, supplementary sources such as Genius [7], Musixmatch [15], and Cancioneros [5] were used. Songs not primarily in Spanish were excluded, though those with occasional phrases in other languages were retained.

The lyrics were segmented into phrases based on punctuation marks or line breaks for systematic analysis. The final corpus comprises 629 songs spanning 71 years, divided into 8 decades. It contains 22,373 phrases and 131,405 words, with each entry structured into five columns: song title, composer, artist/band, release year, and lyrics. The dataset, along with the ranking sources for each song, is available in our project repository[1].

3.2 Text Analysis Framework

For content examination, we employed Term Frequency-Inverse Document Frequency (TF-IDF), chosen for its ability to capture thematic significance while accounting for term distribution across the corpus [24]. The TF-IDF score for a term t in document d from corpus D is: $\text{TF-IDF}(t, d, D) = \text{TF}(t, d) \times \text{IDF}(t, D)$, where $\text{TF}(t, d)$ is term frequency and $\text{IDF}(t, D) = \log \frac{|D|}{|\{d \in D : t \in d\}|}$ is inverse document frequency.

We aggregated the lyrics by decades, treating each decade as a document to capture temporal evolution of themes. After removing stopwords, this analysis yielded the ten most distinctive words per decade (Table 2).

We also evaluated vocabulary richness using the type-token ratio (TTR) [10]:

$$\text{TTR} = \frac{\text{Number of unique words (types)}}{\text{Total number of words (tokens)}}.$$

TTR was calculated both at individual song and decade levels, allowing us to track changes in lexical diversity over time while considering corpus size variations.

3.3 Emotion-Analysis of the Corpus

Emotion detection (ED), a subfield of sentiment analysis, extracts fine-grained emotions from text, speech, or images [3]. Emotions are commonly represented using discrete models, such as Ekman's six basic emotions (happiness, sadness, anger, disgust, surprise, and fear) [6], or dimensional models based on continuous scales [20].

Recent advances in transformer-based language models have significantly enhanced emotion analysis in NLP. For our corpus, we employ RoBERTuito [18], a RoBERTa-based model pre-trained on over 500 million Spanish tweets. While not designed for songs, it detects emotion well in short phrases and remains the closest available Spanish BERT alternative for this task.

The analysis produces a 7-component vector for each phrase, scoring emotions (joy, sadness, disgust, fear, anger, surprise) and an "others" category for ambiguous or neutral phrases. The resulting matrix M $(n_1 \times 7)$ contains non-negative emotional scores for n_1 phrases.

However, song lyrics often include poetic elements, such as invented words, repetitions, and unconventional grammar, which can hinder accurate emotion classification. To address this, we introduce a threshold τ for the "others" category. Phrases with an "others" score below τ are retained, as they likely express identifiable emotions. For these phrases, we normalize the remaining emotion

[1] https://github.com/arelyluis/Emotional-Patterns-in-Mexican-Popular-Music.git.

scores to sum to 1, creating a probability distribution that highlights the relative intensity of each emotion. The predominant emotion (highest score) is then assigned to each phrase, simplifying emotional representation and enabling trend analysis over time.

3.4 Song-Level Analysis

To analyze the corpus at the song level, we represent each song as a vector in $\mathbb{R}^{18}$. This vector consists of six triplets, one for each emotion. Each triplet includes the maximum, average, and variance of the emotional scores across the song's phrases. These measures capture peak emotional intensity, overall emotional tone, and emotional variability, respectively.

We construct a song matrix S of dimensions $n_2 \times 18$, where n_2 is the number of songs. To identify groups of songs with similar emotional profiles, we apply k-Means clustering to S. The number of clusters is determined using the elbow method and silhouette scores. This approach allows us to characterize emotional archetypes within the corpus and explore their prevalence across decades, revealing shifts in emotional expression over time.

Finally, we model each song as a sequence of its phrases' predominant emotions. This representation enables the analysis of emotional transitions and patterns within lyrics. By calculating transition probabilities, we gain insights into the emotional flow and narrative structures of songs. For example, frequent transitions between contrasting emotions (e.g., joy and sadness) may indicate complex emotional narratives, while smoother transitions suggest consistent emotional tones. Phrases classified as "others" are included in this analysis, acknowledging their role in emotional ambiguity and lyrical complexity.

4 Experiments and Results

4.1 Emotion Analysis and Lexical Evolution

We used RoBERTuito (task=*emotion*, language=*es*) on the individual phrases of each song, enabling emotion analysis. Alongside emotion detection, we examined lexical diversity (TTR) to contextualize emotional trends. Table 1 shows that lexical diversity remained relatively stable across decades, peaking in the 1950s (0.2063) and declining to a minimum in the 2010s (0.1194), with an average of 0.16185. The overall corpus diversity, based on 131,405 total words and 11,195 unique words, is 0.08519.

Table 2 shows the top 10 relevant words per decade based on TF-IDF scores, revealing thematic shifts in Mexican popular music.

4.2 Evolution of Dominant Emotions

The dataset spans from 1950 to 2021, with the 2010s being overrepresented (7,265 phrases) and the 2020s already accounting for 1,897 phrases. We set $\tau = 0.75$.

Table 1. Lexical diversity (TTR) across decades

Decade	Total Songs	Total Phrases	Total Words	Different Words	Lexical Diversity
1950	72	1,697	9,051	1,868	0.2063
1960	112	2,612	15,847	2,115	0.1334
1970	77	2,211	12,460	1,969	0.1580
1980	75	2,836	15,839	2,233	0.1409
1990	59	2,252	11,917	2,054	0.1723
2000	43	1,603	9,182	1,561	0.1700
2010	154	7,265	44,439	5,308	0.1194
2020	37	1,897	12,670	2,465	0.1945
All decades	**629**	**22,373**	**131,405**	**11,195**	**0.08519**

Table 2. Top 10 words per decade based on TF-IDF scores

1950	1960	1970	1980	1990	2000	2010	2020
amor	amor	amor	amor	amor	amor	amor	yeah
melón	vida	siempre	acelerar	muévelo	boom	quiero	quiero
vida	vuelve	quiero	noa	quiero	rara	picky	baby
corazón	calienta	señor	tímido	solo	vida	oh	bien
pénjamo	yolanda	vida	quiero	vida	quiero	vida	ahora
ojos	azúcar	corazón	amo	corazón	corazón	solo	amor
ufemia	lupe	solo	perdóname	siempre	siento	yeah	bebe
noche	quiero	nunca	corazón	vuela	siempre	bésame	mami
dios	popotitos	espera	celos	noche	menea	ganas	siempre
feliz	ladronzuelo	perjúmenes	controles	vivo	tiempo	conmigo	odio

Our analysis revealed that only 44.91% of the phrases met the threshold criterion, indicating an emotional predominance. This suggests that more than half of the lyrics were challenging to classify emotionally, which is expected given the metaphorical and abstract nature of song lyrics. Validation on a random sample ($N = 200$) showed accurate identification for direct emotional expressions, although the model struggled with complex or poetic descriptions of emotion (e.g., "te miro y tiemblo" misclassified as fear) and other ambiguous expressions ("ven, ladronzuelo" identified as a provocation denoting anger). Some representative phrases for each dominant identified emotion are shown in Table 3.

Figure 1 shows the evolution of dominant emotions over decades. We can see that *joy* peaked in the 2000s (0.512) and declined in the 2020s (0.399), while *Sadness* was most prominent in the 1950s (0.429) and reached its lowest point in the 2000s (0.308). *Anger* increased over time, doubling from the 1970s (0.036) to the 2020s (0.088). The 1950s and 1960s show a marked contrast in *joy* and *sadness*, while modern music (2010s-2020s) demonstrates a more balanced emotional distribution, with higher levels of *anger* and *surprise*, a decline in the dominance of *joy*, and moderate levels of *sadness*.

4.3 Song-Based Clustering Analysis

We applied k-Means clustering to our proposed song representation, where each song is characterized by the *mean*, *max*, and *variance* of the emotional scores derived from the phrases that compose it. Using the elbow method and Silhouette analysis, we determined $k = 3$ as the appropriate number of groups.

The distribution of songs across the three clusters varies significantly over the decades is shown in Table 4. We can observe that *Cluster* 0 dominates in

Table 3. Sample song lyrics and their predominant emotion as classified by RoBERTuito.

Emotion	Original Phrase	English Translation
Sadness	Paso las noches llorando	I spend the nights crying
	El dolor es fuerte y lo soporto	The pain is strong and I endure it
	Desde hace tiempo ya nada es igual	Nothing has been the same for a while now
	Que no quede huella	Let there be no trace left
	Me niego aceptar que lo nuestro ya se acabó	I refuse to accept that our thing is over
Joy	Ella es la estrella que alumbra mi ser	She is the star that lights up my being
	Yo quiero estar contigo, vivir contigo	I want to be with you, live with you
	Llorando de alegría y no de miedo	Crying from joy and not from fear
	Y yo la paso bailando	And I spend my time dancing
	Me enamoré de ti en un bazar	I fell in love with you in a bazaar
Anger	No soy una tonta pa' dejarme engañar	I'm not a fool to let myself be deceived
	Pero, ven, ven, ven, ven, ven, ladronzuelo ven	But come, come, come, come, come, little thief come
	Era solo un juego cruel de su vanidad	It was just a cruel game of their vanity
	Ya la pagarás	You will pay for it
	Pobre tonto, ingenuo charlatán	Poor fool, naive charlatan
Surprise	Dios bendito cómo se mueve (cómo se mueve)	Good Lord how they move (how they move)
	Qué es lo que paso?, que se desmayó	What happened?, they fainted
	Terremoto (terremoto)	Earthquake (earthquake)
	Si me extrañas o me engañas	If you miss me or deceive me
	Ay yo me quemo, me quemo quemo	Oh I'm burning, burning burning
Disgust	Huele a piel ajena	Smells like someone else's skin
	Hasta a la cárcel, yo iría con él	Even to jail, I would go with him
	Me da vergüenza imaginar que sepa	I'm ashamed to imagine that they know
	Roban y matan a Mario Postigo	They rob and kill Mario Postigo
	Voy a destrozarle el coche	I'm going to destroy their car
Fear	Que cuando me besan tiemblo	That when they kiss me I tremble
	Yo tengo miedo de que me guste	I'm afraid that I'll like it
	Tú me confundes, no sé qué hacer	You confuse me, I don't know what to do
	Yo tengo celos, tengo celos	I'm jealous, I'm jealous
	Pero baila que da pavor	But dances in a frightening way
Others	Y lo hacemo' otro rato	And we'll do it another time
	Deja que te diga cosas al oído	Let me whisper things in your ear
	Y un sombrero grande y feo	And a big ugly hat
	Somo' la candela (Muévelo)	We are fire/heat (Move it)
	El grito de una ciudad	The cry of a city

Table 4. Distribution of clusters across decades (%)

	1950	1960	1970	1980	1990	2000	2010	2020
Cluster 0	63.89	44.44	72.73	47.30	65.52	74.42	40.91	37.84
Cluster 1	25.00	25.00	19.48	33.78	29.31	16.28	40.91	40.54
Cluster 2	11.11	30.56	7.79	18.92	5.17	9.30	18.18	21.62

most decades, particularly in the 1970s and 2000s, while *Cluster* 1 gains prominence in the 2010s and 2020s. On the other hand, *Cluster* 2 remains relatively underrepresented across all decades.

Based on the centroids and emotional profiles (Fig. 2), we propose the following names and descriptions for the clusters:

- **Cluster 0: Bittersweet Songs** (332 songs). Balance between joy ($mean = 0.43$) and sadness ($mean = 0.41$), with very low levels of anger ($mean = 0.02$) and other negative emotions. It is the most common cluster. We could say that it represents songs with a dual emotional tone, blending happiness and melancholy.
- **Cluster 1: Complex Emotional Songs** (187 songs). Moderate levels of sadness ($mean = 0.38$) and joy ($mean = 0.30$), but it also has the highest levels of anger ($mean = 0.15$), as well as elevated disgust and fear. We could say that these songs represent greater emotional complexity, reflecting intense or conflicting feelings.
- **Cluster 2: Happy Songs** (104 songs). Dominated by high joy ($mean = 0.67$) and low sadness ($mean = 0.08$). It also shows moderate levels of surprise ($mean = 0.11$). It is the least common cluster and we could say it represents optimistic and positive songs, with a clear sense of happiness.

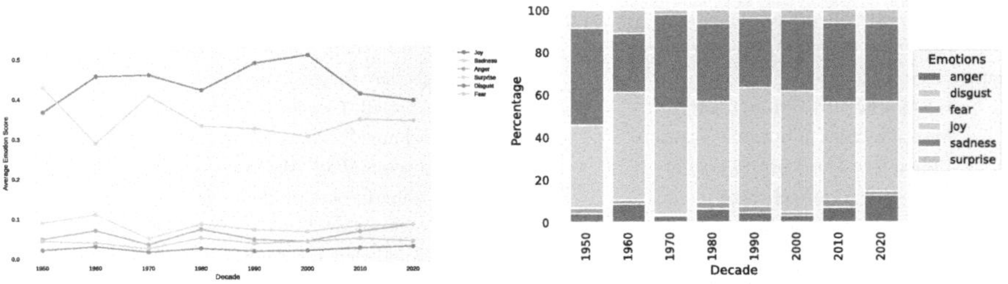

(a) Average emotion scores per decade (b) Emotional composition of each decade as proportions

Fig. 1. Emotional patterns across decades.

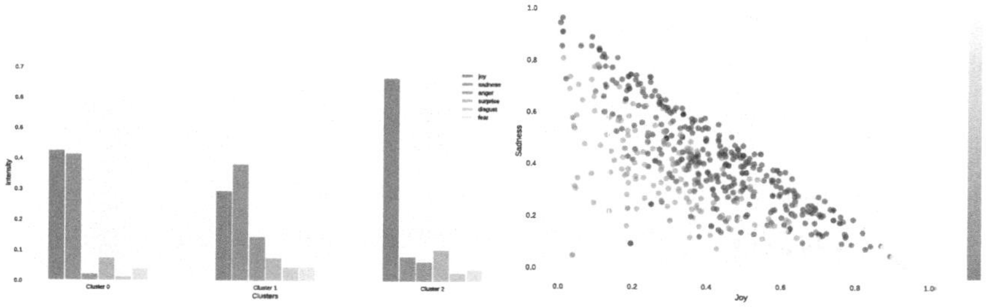

(a) Cluster centroids (b) Songs represented in the Joy-Sadness space

Fig. 2. Clusters identified by k-Means on song vectors, constructed from statistical measures (mean, maximum, variance) of the six emotions detected by RoBERTtuito across song phrases.

Statistical Significance. To investigate the relationship between decades and emotional clusters, we applied a χ^2 test of independence. The results show a significant relationship between song types and decades ($\chi^2 = 59.66$, $df = 14$, $p < 0.001$), confirming the temporal evolution of emotional patterns in Mexican songs. Additionally, we calculated the entropy of each decade to measure emotional diversity (see Table 5). The highest entropy values were observed in the 1960s, 2020s, and 2010s, indicating a more balanced distribution among clusters. In contrast, the lowest entropy values were found in the 2000s, 1970s and 1990s, suggesting a dominance of certain song types.

Table 5. Entropy distribution by decade

1950	1960	1970	1980	1990	2000	2010	2020
1.265	1.543	1.081	1.494	1.140	1.062	1.502	1.536

4.4 Emotional Sequence Analysis

To gain further insight into the emotional dynamics within individual songs, we analyzed the sequences of predominant emotions across the phrases of each song. The average number of phrases per song was 35.57, with a median of 33.00. The most common emotional sequence of length 3 was $(others, others, others)$, occurring 4,743 times, followed by $(others, others, joy)$ with 1,219 occurrences.

The transition probability matrix P was computed as

$$P_{ij} = \frac{C_{ij}}{\sum_k C_{ik}},$$

where C_{ij} is the count of transitions from emotion i to emotion j, and $\sum_k C_{ik}$ is the total number of transitions originating from emotion i. This matrix is given by

$$
\begin{array}{c c l}
 & \begin{array}{ccccccc} \text{joy} & \text{sadness} & \text{fear} & \text{surprise} & \text{anger} & \text{disgust} & \text{others} \end{array} & \\
P = & \begin{pmatrix}
0.339 & 0.135 & 0.012 & 0.027 & 0.018 & 0.000 & 0.468 \\
0.180 & 0.283 & 0.006 & 0.020 & 0.027 & 0.000 & 0.484 \\
0.218 & 0.117 & 0.024 & 0.040 & 0.044 & 0.000 & 0.556 \\
0.232 & 0.144 & 0.007 & 0.138 & 0.041 & 0.002 & 0.437 \\
0.146 & 0.175 & 0.010 & 0.069 & 0.086 & 0.002 & 0.512 \\
0.200 & 0.000 & 0.000 & 0.200 & 0.000 & 0.100 & 0.500 \\
0.180 & 0.143 & 0.013 & 0.023 & 0.026 & 0.000 & 0.615
\end{pmatrix} & \begin{array}{c} \text{joy} \\ \text{sadness} \\ \text{fear} \\ \text{surprise} \\ \text{anger} \\ \text{disgust} \\ \text{others} \end{array} .
\end{array}
$$

The highest probabilities are observed for transitions from $others$ to $others$ (61.5%), $fear$ to $others$ (55.6%), and *anger* to $others$ (51.2%). We observe a tendency for defined emotions to be followed by emotionally ambiguous or neutral phrases.

5 Discussion

The temporal distribution of clusters highlights generational shifts in the emotional landscape of Mexican hit parade songs. The 1950s and 1970s were dominated by *Bittersweet Songs* (Cluster 0), reflecting a preference for emotionally balanced lyrics. In contrast, the 1960s stand out as a unique period, with the highest proportion of *Happy Songs* (Cluster 2) at 30.56%, reflecting a brief but notable trend toward more optimistic and positive lyrics.

The 2010s show a significant turning point, with an equal proportion of *Bittersweet Songs* (Cluster 0) and *Complex Emotional Songs* (Cluster 1). This shift indicates a diversification in emotional expression, with a growing emphasis on more intense and varied emotional themes. The rise of Cluster 1 in the 2010s and 2020s suggests a growing preference for emotionally complex lyrics, accompanied by a decrease in the prevalence of *Bittersweet Songs*.

Both, the χ^2 test and entropy analysis, support a temporal evolution of emotional patterns in the analyzed corpus. The results highlight significant changes in the distribution of song types across decades, with recent years exhibiting greater emotional diversity compared to the dominance of specific clusters in earlier decades.

Finally, regarding emotional sequence analysis, we observe that emotionally ambiguous states ($others$) often serve as "bridges" between defined emotions, with a tendency to return to $others$ after intense emotions (e.g. $fear$ and *anger*). Direct transitions between defined emotions were less common compared to transitions through $others$. This suggests that emotionally ambiguous phrases play a significant role in the emotional structure of songs, providing a link between more intense emotional states.

6 Conclusions

In this work, we analyzed 629 songs spanning seven decades of Mexican popular music. Using a preliminary exploration of significant terms and lexical diversity, alongside RoBERTuito, a BERT-based model for emotion detection in Spanish, we characterized songs based on the dominant emotions in their constituent phrases.

Our analysis identified three broad song categories: bittersweet, emotionally complex, and happy. These categories are not uniformly distributed across decades, revealing significant shifts in emotional composition and thematic elements over time, reflecting changes in cultural and artistic expressions.

Two aspects that could be addressed in future work are improved segmentation of songs into interpretable textual units guided by linguistic criteria, and the adoption of more advanced BERT-based models, especially those designed for Spanish, which could improve emotion detection accuracy.

Computational lyrics analysis is challenging because song lyrics, like poetry, often defy grammatical conventions through wordplay, metaphors, and invented language, relying on evocative phrasing rather than clear textual units, which complicates emotion classification. Nevertheless, our methodology provides a flexible framework for identifying emotional patterns in lyrics and tracking their evolution. The compiled corpus and methodology advance the study of musical heritage, bridging computational methods and humanistic inquiry in digital humanities.

References

1. Hits of the world. Billboard (1960-1970). Accessed 31 Jan 2025
2. Los discos más populares. Notitas Musicales (1980-1990). Accessed 31 Jan 2025
3. Acheampong, F.A., Nunoo-Mensah, H., Chen, W.: Transformer models for text-based emotion detection: a review of BERT-based approaches. Artif. Intell. Rev. **54**(8), 5789–5829 (2021). https://doi.org/10.1007/s10462-021-09958-2
4. Ayala, R.: Musicosas: manual del comentarista de radio y televisión, vol. 1. Editorial Selecciones Musicales (1962)
5. Cancioneros.com: Cancioneros - song lyrics and music database (2025). https://www.cancioneros.com/. Accessed 31 Jan 2025
6. Ekman, P.: Basic Emotions, chap. 3, pp. 45–60. Wiley, Hoboken (1999)
7. Genius: Genius - song lyrics and annotations (2025). https://genius.com/. Accessed 31 Jan 2025
8. Herd, D.: Changing images of violence in rap music lyrics: 1979–1997. J. Public Health Policy **30**, 395–406 (2009)
9. Hernández-Lorenzo, L., Diaz, A., Perez, A., Ros, S., González-Blanco, E.: Exploring spanish contemporary song lyrics through digital humanities methods: some thematic and structural properties. Digital Sch. Humanit. **37**(3), 738–746 (2022)
10. Johansson, V.: Lexical diversity and lexical density in speech and writing: a developmental perspective. Working papers/Lund University. Department of Linguistics and Phonetics, vol. 53, pp. 61–79 (2008)

11. Latino, M.: Monitor latino - rankings y noticias de la industria musical (2010). https://monitorlatino.com/. Accessed 31 Jan 2025
12. Letras.com: Letras.com - lyrics songs (2025). https://www.letras.com/. Aaccessed 31 Jan 2025
13. Madanikia, Y., Bartholomew, K.: Themes of lust and love in popular music lyrics from 1971 to 2011. SAGE Open **4**(3), 2158244014547179 (2014)
14. Mast, J.F., McAndrew, F.T.: Violent lyrics in heavy metal music can increase aggression in males. North Am. J. Psychol. **13**(1) (2011)
15. Musixmatch: Musixmatch - lyrics and translations (2025). https://www.musixmatch.com/. Accessed 31 Jan 2025
16. Palomeque, M., de Lucio, J.: El sentimiento de las letras de las canciones y su relación con las características musicales. Procesamiento del lenguaje Natural **67**, 95–102 (2021)
17. Patwardhan, N., Marrone, S., Sansone, C.: Transformers in the real world: a survey on NLP applications. Information **14**(4), 242 (2023)
18. Pérez, J.M., Furman, D.A., Alemany, L.A., Luque, F.: RoBERTuito: a pre-trained language model for social media text in Spanish. arXiv preprint arXiv:2111.09453 (2021)
19. RadioNotas: Radionotas pop méxico (2000). https://radionotas.com/. Accessed 31 Jan 2025
20. Russell, J.A.: A circumplex model of affect. J. Pers. Soc. Psychol. **39**(6), 1161 (1980)
21. Simonett, H.: Los gallos valientes: examining violence in mexican popular music. Trans. Revista Transcultural de Música (10) (2006)
22. Tickner, A.B.: Aquí en el ghetto: Hip-hop in colombia, cuba, and mexico. Latin Am. Politics Soc. **50**(3), 121–146 (2008)
23. Vaswani, A.: Attention is all you need. In: Advances in Neural Information Processing Systems (2017)
24. Zhang, W., Yoshida, T., Tang, X.: TFIDF, LSI and multi-word in information retrieval and text categorization. In: 2008 IEEE International Conference on Systems, Man and Cybernetics, pp. 108–113. IEEE (2008)

Author Index

A. P. López-Monroy et al. (Eds.): MCPR 2025, LNCS 15715, pp. 401–402, 2025.
https://doi.org/10.1007/978-3-031-96255-4

The manufacturer's authorised representative in the EU is Springer Nature Customer Service Centre GmbH, Europaplatz 3, 69115 Heidelberg, Germany. If you have any concerns regarding our products, please contact ProductSafety@springernature.com

Printed and bound by CPI Group (UK) Ltd, Croydon, CR0 4YY
30/09/2026
02225585-0006